RELIGION AND GREATER IRELAND

MCGILL-QUEEN'S STUDIES IN THE HISTORY OF RELIGION

Volumes in this series have been supported by the Jackman Foundation of Toronto.

SERIES ONE: G.A. RAWLYK, EDITOR

1 Small Differences
Irish Catholics and Irish Protestants, 1815–1922
An International Perspective
Donald Harman Akenson

2 Two Worlds
The Protestant Culture of Nineteenth-Century Ontario
William Westfall

3 An Evangelical Mind
Nathanael Burwash and the Methodist Tradition in Canada, 1839–1918
Marguerite Van Die

4 The Dévotes
Women and Church in Seventeenth-Century France
Elizabeth Rapley

5 The Evangelical Century
College and Creed in English Canada from the Great Revival to the Great Depression
Michael Gauvreau

6 The German Peasants' War and Anabaptist Community of Goods
James M. Stayer

7 A World Mission
Canadian Protestantism and the Quest for a New International Order, 1918–1939
Robert Wright

8 Serving the Present Age
Revivalism, Progressivism, and the Methodist Tradition in Canada
Phyllis D. Airhart

9 A Sensitive Independence
Canadian Methodist Women Missionaries in Canada and the Orient, 1881–1925
Rosemary R. Gagan

10 God's Peoples
Covenant and Land in South Africa, Israel, and Ulster
Donald Harman Akenson

11 Creed and Culture
The Place of English-Speaking Catholics in Canadian Society, 1750–1930
Edited by Terrence Murphy and Gerald Stortz

12 Piety and Nationalism
Lay Voluntary Associations and the Creation of an Irish-Catholic Community in Toronto, 1850–1895
Brian P. Clarke

13 Amazing Grace
Studies in Evangelicalism in Australia, Britain, Canada, and the United States
Edited by George Rawlyk and Mark A. Noll

14 Children of Peace
W. John McIntyre

15 A Solitary Pillar
Montreal's Anglican Church and the Quiet Revolution
Joan Marshall

16 Padres in No Man's Land
Canadian Chaplains and the Great War
Duff Crerar

17 Christian Ethics and Political Economy in North America
A Critical Analysis
P. Travis Kroeker

18 Pilgrims in Lotus Land
Conservative Protestantism in British Columbia, 1917–1981
Robert K. Burkinshaw

19 Through Sunshine and Shadow
The Woman's Christian Temperance Union, Evangelicalism, and Reform in Ontario, 1874–1930
Sharon Cook

20 Church, College, and Clergy
A History of Theological Education at Knox College, Toronto, 1844–1994
Brian J. Fraser

21 The Lord's Dominion
The History of Canadian Methodism
Neil Semple

22 A Full-Orbed Christianity
The Protestant Churches and Social Welfare in Canada, 1900–1940
Nancy Christie and Michael Gauvreau

23 Evangelism and Apostasy
The Evolution and Impact of Evangelicals in Modern Mexico
Kurt Bowen

24 The Chignecto Covenanters
A Regional History of Reformed Presbyterianism in New Brunswick and Nova Scotia, 1827–1905
Eldon Hay

25 Methodists and Women's Education in Ontario, 1836–1925
Johanne Selles

26 Puritanism and Historical Controversy
William Lamont

SERIES TWO: IN MEMORY OF GEORGE RAWLYK
DONALD HARMAN AKENSON, EDITOR

1 Marguerite Bourgeoys and Montreal, 1640–1665
Patricia Simpson

2 Aspects of the Canadian Evangelical Experience
Edited by G.A. Rawlyk

3 Infinity, Faith, and Time
Christian Humanism and Renaissance Literature
John Spencer Hill

4 The Contribution of Presbyterianism to the Maritime Provinces of Canada
Edited by Charles H.H. Scobie and G.A. Rawlyk

5 Labour, Love, and Prayer
Female Piety in Ulster Religious Literature, 1850–1914
Andrea Ebel Brozyna

6 The Waning of the Green
Catholics, the Irish, and Identity in Toronto, 1887–1922
Mark G. McGowan

7 Religion and Nationality in Western Ukraine
The Greek Catholic Church and the Ruthenian National Movement in Galicia, 1867–1900
John-Paul Himka

8 Good Citizens
British Missionaries and Imperial States, 1870–1918
James G. Greenlee and Charles M. Johnston

9 The Theology of the Oral Torah
Revealing the Justice of God
Jacob Neusner

10 Gentle Eminence
A Life of Cardinal Flahiff
P. Wallace Platt

11 Culture, Religion, and Demographic Behaviour Catholics and Lutherans in Alsace, 1750–1870
Kevin McQuillan

12 Between Damnation and Starvation
Priests and Merchants
in Newfoundland Politics,
1745–1855
John P. Greene

13 Martin Luther, German Saviour
German Evangelical Theological Factions
and the Interpretation
of Luther, 1917–1933
James M. Stayer

14 Modernity and the Dilemma
of North American Anglican
Identities, 1880–1950
William H. Katerberg

15 The Methodist Church on
the Prairies, 1896–1914
George Emery

16 Christian Attitudes towards
the State of Israel
Paul Charles Merkley

17 A Social History of the Cloister
Daily Life in the Teaching
Monasteries of the Old Regime
Elizabeth Rapley

18 Households of Faith
Family, Gender, and Community
in Canada, 1760–1969
Edited by Nancy Christie

19 Blood Ground
Colonialism, Missions, and the Contest
for Christianity in the Cape Colony
and Britain, 1799–1853
Elizabeth Elbourne

20 A History of Canadian Catholics
Gallicanism, Romanism, and
Canadianism
Terence J. Fay

21 The View from Rome
Archbishop Stagni's 1915
Reports on the Ontario Bilingual Schools
Question
Edited and translated by
John Zucchi

22 The Founding Moment
Church, Society, and the
Construction of Trinity College
William Westfall

23 The Holocaust, Israel, and
Canadian Protestant Churches
Haim Genizi

24 Governing Charities
Church and State in Toronto's
Catholic Archdiocese, 1850–1950
Paula Maurutto

25 Anglicans and the Atlantic World
High Churchmen, Evangelicals,
and the Quebec Connection
Richard W. Vaudry

26 Evangelicals and the
Continental Divide
The Conservative Protestant Subculture
in Canada and the United States
Sam Reimer

27 Christians in a Secular World
The Canadian Experience
Kurt Bowen

28 Anatomy of a Seance
A History of Spirit Communication
in Central Canada
Stan McMullin

29 With Skilful Hand
The Story of King David
David T. Barnard

30 Faithful Intellect
Samuel S. Nelles and
Victoria University
Neil Semple

31 W. Stanford Reid
An Evangelical Calvinist
in the Academy
Donald MacLeod

32 A Long Eclipse
The Liberal Protestant
Establishment and the Canadian
University, 1920–1970
Catherine Gidney

33 Forkhill Protestants and Forkhill Catholics, 1787–1858
Kyla Madden

34 For Canada's Sake
Public Religion, Centennial Celebrations, and the Re-making of Canada in the 1960s
Gary R. Miedema

35 Revival in the City
The Impact of American Evangelists in Canada, 1884–1914
Eric R. Crouse

36 The Lord for the Body
Religion, Medicine, and Protestant Faith Healing in Canada, 1880–1930
James Opp

37 Six Hundred Years of Reform
Bishops and the French Church, 1190–1789
J. Michael Hayden and Malcolm R. Greenshields

38 The Missionary Oblate Sisters
Vision and Mission
Rosa Bruno-Jofré

39 Religion, Family, and Community in Victorian Canada
The Colbys of Carrollcroft
Marguerite Van Die

40 Michael Power
The Struggle to Build the Catholic Church on the Canadian Frontier
Mark G. McGowan

41 The Catholic Origins of Quebec's Quiet Revolution, 1931–1970
Michael Gauvreau

42 Marguerite Bourgeoys and the Congregation of Notre Dame, 1665–1700
Patricia Simpson

43 To Heal a Fractured World
The Ethics of Responsibility
Jonathan Sacks

44 Revivalists
Marketing the Gospel in English Canada, 1884–1957
Kevin Kee

45 The Churches and Social Order in Nineteenth- and Twentieth-Century Canada
Edited by Michael Gauvreau and Ollivier Hubert

46 Political Ecumenism
Catholics, Jews, and Protestants in De Gaulle's Free France, 1940–1945
Geoffrey Adams

47 From Quaker to Upper Canadian
Faith and Community among Yonge Street Friends, 1801–1850
Robynne Rogers Healey

48 The Congrégation de Notre-Dame, Superiors, and the Paradox of Power, 1693–1796
Colleen Gray

49 Canadian Pentecostalism
Transition and Transformation
Edited by Michael Wilkinson

50 A War with a Silver Lining
Canadian Protestant Churches and the South African War, 1899–1902
Gordon L. Heath

51 In the Aftermath of Catastrophe
Founding Judaism, 70 to 640
Jacob Neusner

52 Imagining Holiness
Classic Hasidic Tales in Modern Times
Justin Jaron Lewis

53 Shouting, Embracing, and Dancing with Ecstasy
The Growth of Methodism in Newfoundland, 1774–1874
Calvin Hollett

54 Into Deep Waters
Evangelical Spirituality and Maritime Calvinist Baptist Ministers, 1790–1855
Daniel C. Goodwin

55 Vanguard of the New Age
The Toronto Theosophical
Society, 1891–1945
Gillian McCann

56 A Commerce of Taste
Church Architecture in
Canada, 1867–1914
Barry Magrill

57 The Big Picture
The Antigonish Movement
of Eastern Nova Scotia
Santo Dodaro and Leonard Pluta

58 My Heart's Best Wishes for You
A Biography of Archbishop
John Walsh
John P. Comiskey

59 The Covenanters in Canada
Reformed Presbyterianism
from 1820 to 2012
Eldon Hay

60 The Guardianship of Best Interests
Institutional Care for the Children
of the Poor in Halifax, 1850–1960
Renée N. Lafferty

61 In Defence of the Faith
Joaquim Marques de Araújo, a Brazilian
Comissário in the
Age of Inquisitional Decline
James E. Wadsworth

62 Contesting the Moral High Ground
Popular Moralists in Mid-Twentieth-
Century Britain
Paul T. Phillips

63 The Catholicisms of Coutances
Varieties of Religion in Early
Modern France, 1350–1789
J. Michael Hayden

64 After Evangelicalism
The Sixties and the United
Church of Canada
Kevin N. Flatt

65 The Return of Ancestral Gods
Modern Ukrainian Paganism
as an Alternative Vision
for a Nation
Mariya Lesiv

66 Transatlantic Methodists
British Wesleyanism and
the Formation of an Evangelical Culture
in Nineteenth-Century Ontario and
Quebec
Todd Webb

67 A Church with the Soul of a Nation
Making and Remaking the United
Church of Canada
Phyllis D. Airhart

68 Fighting over God
A Legal and Political History of Religious
Freedom in Canada
Janet Epp Buckingham

69 From India to Israel
Identity, Immigration, and the Struggle
for Religious Equality
Joseph Hodes

70 Becoming Holy in Early Canada
Timothy G. Pearson

71 The Cistercian Arts
From the 12th to the 21st Century
*Edited by Terryl N. Kinder and Roberto
Cassanelli*

72 The Canny Scot
Archbishop James Morrison
of Antigonish
Peter Ludlow

73 Religion and Greater Ireland
Christianity and Irish Global Networks,
1750–1950
*Edited by Colin Barr and
Hilary M. Carey*

Religion and Greater Ireland

Christianity and Irish Global Networks, 1750–1950

Edited by

COLIN BARR AND HILARY M. CAREY

McGill-Queen's University Press
Montreal & Kingston • London • Chicago

ISBN 978-0-7735-4569-4 (cloth)
ISBN 978-0-7735-4570-0 (paper)
ISBN 978-0-7735-9734-1 (ePDF)
ISBN 978-0-7735-9735-8 (ePUB)

Legal deposit third quarter 2015
Bibliothèque nationale du Québec

Printed in Canada on acid-free paper that is 100% ancient forest free (100% post-consumer recycled), processed chlorine free

McGill-Queen's University Press acknowledges the support of the Canada Council for the Arts for our publishing program. We also acknowledge the financial support of the Government of Canada through the Canada Book Fund for our publishing activities.

Library and Archives Canada Cataloguing in Publication

Religion and greater Ireland: Christianity and Irish global networks, 1750–1950/edited by Colin Barr and Hilary M. Carey.

(McGill-Queen's studies in the history of religion. Series two; 73)
Includes bibliographical references and index.
Issued in print and electronic formats.
ISBN 978-0-7735-4569-4 (bound). – ISBN 978-0-7735-4570-0 (paperback). – ISBN 978-0-7735-9734-1 (ePDF). – ISBN 978-0-7735-9735-8 (ePUB)

1. Ireland – Church history. 2. Irish – Religion. 3. Irish – Ethnic identity. 4. Immigrants – Religious life. I. Barr, Colin, 1974–, author, editor II. Carey, Hilary M. (Hilary Mary), 1957–, editor III. Series: McGill-Queen's studies in the history of religion. Series two; no. 73

BR795.R44 2015 274.15 C2015-903132-X
C2015-903133-8

This book was typeset by Interscript in 10.5/13 Sabon.

Contents

Acknowledgments

The editors would like to express their appreciation to people and funding bodies who have supported us through the long gestation of this project.

A number of the chapters that make up *Religion and Greater Ireland* were presented at a symposium organized and funded by the Humanities Research Institute (HRI) at the University of Newcastle, New South Wales, 3–4 December 2012. The HRI enabled us to bring a number of contributors to Newcastle and later provided Colin Barr with a visiting fellowship at a crucial time for the development of this book.

Funding for archival travel was provided to Hilary Carey by the Australian Research Council as part of an Australian Research Council Discovery Project (DP 1096538) "Liberty, Anti-Transportation and the Moral Empire," and to Colin Barr as part of an Irish Research Council for the Humanities and Social Sciences project, "The Letters of Paul Cullen."

The editors acknowledge the support of the School of Divinity, History and Philosophy and the Centre for the Study of Global Empires, both at the University of Aberdeen, and the School of Humanities at the University of Bristol for additional financial support towards the publication of this book.

Copy-editing was provided by Briony Neilson in Australia and Joanne Richardson in Canada.

We are also grateful to Kyla Madden at McGill-Queen's University Press for sage advice and encouragement and to Mark McGowan for suggesting that we approach MQUP with this proposal.

RELIGION AND GREATER IRELAND

INTRODUCTION

Religion and Greater Ireland

HILARY M. CAREY AND COLIN BARR

When James Joyce's character, the citizen, proclaimed his blustery hope for Irish independence backed up by the nebulous reinforcements of "our greater Ireland beyond the sea," he was referring to those refugees from the darkest days of the Irish famine who had fled in their millions to the United States.[1] In vain, Leopold Bloom hit back with the riposte that Ireland was no more than the sum of its current residents: "A nation," he replied, "is the same people living in the same place." For Bloom, those Irish who had left the land of their birth, or that of their parents and grandparents, had no ties, military or otherwise, with the Ireland of Thursday, 16 June 1904. Bloom was making another point too, one that asserted his own claim to citizenship of a secular Irish nation, regardless of his cultural identity as a Jew. Such an assertion flew in the face of those who assumed, and sometimes loudly proclaimed, that to be Irish was to be Roman Catholic. As Bloom and the citizen were aware, religion had conspired with politics, war, and emigration to fracture the Irish soul into opposing shards. Yet, as the authors of this collection demonstrate, Irish churches retained the cultural power to both bind and loosen. In Ireland, they were emblems of a divided nation; abroad, they generated religious networks of undeniable variety and tenacity that stretched to all corners of the globe. It is this spiritually capacious greater Ireland to which we now turn.

There have been many attempts to define what it meant to be a part of the Irish diaspora,[2] that great outpouring of people who left Ireland for elsewhere – principally the United States, British North America, Australia, and Britain, with smaller populations heading for New Zealand, South Africa, and Argentina – and yet continued to identify with their Irish forbears.[3] In terms of chronology, large-scale Irish emigration is popularly assumed to have begun with the Famine, although there had been considerable migration both well before and long after the demographic crisis of the mid-nineteenth century. These earlier migrations followed complex paths and involved both Protestants (largely, but not only, Presbyterians and Anglicans) and Catholics. Although North America would eventually prove to be the favoured destination, others rose and fell in popularity as times and circumstances changed.

From the Reformation, and indeed before, the Irish overseas were nurtured, literally and figuratively, by a number of religious, political, and commercial institutions. In Counter-Reformation Europe, Irish Catholics built a network of colleges in locations as diverse as Lisbon, Salamanca, Paris, and Leuven, among others. These served not only as bases for training Irish clergy but also as centres around which an Irish Catholic emigrant culture could be nurtured and preserved. Irish Catholics and their descendants could be found in the service, both political and military, of the European Catholic courts, and many enjoyed careers in the European Catholic empires. This could range from relatively humble service in the French East India Company to the career of the Irish-born Ambrosio O'Higgins (1721–1801), who rose to the Spanish title of marquis of Osorno and served as viceroy of Peru. (His illegitimate son, Bernardo O'Higgins, helped lead the revolt against Spain that resulted in the independence of Chile.) In the British Empire, Catholics rarely reached such heights, but, by the 1840s, something like a majority of the East India Company's soldiers were Irish Catholics, and they were the backbone of the British Army throughout the world for much of the period.[4] By the mid-nineteenth century, Irish Catholics such as Sir John Pope Hennessey and Richard More O'Ferrall could enjoy successful colonial careers – Hennessey served as governor of colonies as diverse as Hong Kong, Sierra Leone, and the Bahamas; O'Ferrall's tenure as governor of Malta ended with his resignation in protest against British government policy towards Irish Catholics in Ireland.[5] Many more Irish Catholics enjoyed long careers in one branch or another of the imperial service.

Irish Protestants were also enthusiastic empire and nation builders. They helped establish institutions that ranged from the University of Melbourne, whose first chancellor came from County Cork,[6] to the *Cape Times*, which was founded by a lapsed Church of Ireland priest from Limerick.[7] Irish Protestants served the Empire at every level, from colonial governors such as New South Wales's (and the Eastern Cape's) reforming Richard Bourke (1777–1855) to the disproportionate numbers of largely Protestant Irishmen who staffed the Indian civil and medical services after 1857 or dominated the Cape Mounted Rifles in southern Africa. As Jennifer Ridden and Zoë Laidlaw both point out, Bourke's Irish Protestantism and Irish liberalism shaped his behaviour as a colonial governor, with enduring consequences for Australia.[8] And Bourke was hardly unusual in bringing Ireland to the Empire or the Empire back to Ireland. Despite the modern impression of a largely Catholic Irish diaspora, Protestant migrants were numerically dominant in the American south, Ontario, and southern Africa.

What is often overlooked in considerations of the role of the Irish in the Empire is the fact that many were not looking for a career as a colonial governor or a private soldier or a doctor in the Indian Medical Service. Many, perhaps most, were not looking to do a job and go home but, rather, were looking for a new home entirely. As a consequence, a complete understanding of the role played by Ireland and the Irish in the Empire (and, indeed, in the United States) can only be properly achieved through the framework of "Greater Ireland" and not simply that of the island of Ireland or of the British Empire as such. This holds true for both Catholics and Protestants, and members of both traditions (and all Protestant denominations) quickly assumed positions of real power and influence. In Victoria, for example, consider the Tipperary-born John O'Shannasy (1818–83) who helped found the St Patrick's Society before being elected to Parliament and serving several stints as premier. Or the Monaghan-born nationalist and newspaper editor Charles Gavan Duffy (1816–1903), who was tried multiple times for treason, served as a member of both the British and Victorian parliaments, and briefly as premier of Victoria. Both were Irish nationalists; both were Roman Catholics, one markedly devout; both built their political careers on an avowedly Irish Catholic base; both were knighted by the queen, and O'Shannasy also by the pope. Duffy's son Frank became chief justice of Australia, and his grandson Charles sat on the Supreme Court of Victoria until his death in 1961. They too were knighted. Or consider the career of the Cork-born T.W. Anglin (1822–96). The son of an East India Company employee, Anglin emigrated from Ireland to New Brunswick in 1849 in search of economic opportunity, founded a newspaper for Irish Catholics, entered provincial and then national politics (always as a champion of Irish Catholics), and finished his career as speaker of the Canadian House of Commons.[9] In southern Africa, to take a different example, two Irish Protestants served as premiers of their respective colonies, the Cork-born Anglican Sir Thomas Upington

(1844–98) in the Cape and the Wicklow-born Sir Albert Hime (1842–1919) in Natal. Another, the Ulster Presbyterian William Porter (1805–80), wrote the colour-blind Cape Constitution of 1854 and is remembered as the "Father of Cape Liberalism."[10] Two American presidents – Andrew Jackson and James Buchanan – had Irish-born parents, Protestants from County Antrim and County Donegal, respectively. Irish Catholics and Protestants alike participated in the Empire (and the United States) both as a career and as a home.

As a result of economic stagnation and intermittent starvation, which combined to decimate the population at home and fuel the departure of the ambitious, the unlucky, or simply the survivors, the proportion of the Irish-born who were living outside of Ireland climbed rapidly from 1841 to 1921. D.H. Akenson uses the available statistics to plot a graph of the Irish outside Ireland. This resembles a clawed finger that shoots up from less than 10 percent in 1841 to reach a high of close to 40 percent by 1891 before beginning to decline thereafter.[11] The proportion of Irish-born living abroad continued at high levels for a modern European society well into the twentieth century, and at least a quarter of the Irish-born were living outside Ireland in 1991.[12] Economic prosperity in the 1990s saw this pattern reversed, but the trend for the Irish-born to live abroad has accelerated since the Irish financial crisis began in 2008.[13] An estimate based on current national census returns suggests that in 2012 about 1 million, or 15.6 percent, of the Irish-born live abroad, principally in Britain, the United States, Australia, and Canada.[14] For Ireland, this has had and continues to have profound social, political, and economic implications. Yet for the countries in which the Irish continue to settle, the Irish-born represent only a small (if regularly replenished) segment of the some 70 million people who self-identify as Irish. The Irish diaspora is, then, largely a product of the great emigration event of the nineteenth century and its continuing aftermath in the Anglo world. And the Irishness that distinguishes it is largely that of an Ireland of an earlier age, an age in which religious tensions and cultures were felt more intensely and when religion and national identity were fused.[15]

The mere accident of emigration does not in itself create a diaspora, and there are no rules that determine how a people will reconstitute themselves once they have left their native shores, though place of birth, language, religion, and ethnicity have all been regarded as critical to most national concoctions.[16] As Rogers Brubaker notes, religion is just one of the ways in which identity might be mediated across and beyond national borders.[17] Diasporic people might come to include not just first-generation emigrants but also their children and subsequent descendants in new countries of settlement. Once resettled they might redefine themselves again as a new people with identities that straddle both the homeland and the land of settlement. Some sections of the Irish diaspora became "Irish Americans" or "Irish Canadians" or "Irish Australians," though these identities were stronger in some cases and in some places than in others, not least in the robust survival of Irish Catholic hybrid identities and the relative decline of Irish Protestant ones. Yet their feelings of attachment to Ireland and to their own Irish identity vary from passionate identification with the religion, politics, and supposed cultural mores of their ancestors to an ephemeral nostalgia evoked by the annual arrival of marching season, a flash of the colour green (or, decreasingly, orange), or the smell of burning peat.

RELIGION AND IRISH IDENTITY

Religion has long been seen as both a burden and a blessing of the Irish people. Ireland's fame as a land of saints and scholars reflected not just a tradition of learning and spirituality at home but also the success of medieval Irish monks and missionaries abroad.[18] In modern times, it has become a staple of the heritage publishing market, with books such as Thomas Cahill's *How the Irish Saved Civilization* enjoying runaway popular success despite (or perhaps because of) their green-tinted and largely ahistorical view of the past. In fact, there have been three historical Irish missionary movements, of which the early medieval and early modern are well known. From around the seventh century, the Irish consolidated Christianity at home and spread it to their immediate neighbours. Meanwhile, the Irish abroad under royal patronage made fervent, well-trained, and ascetic foundations in Europe. The creation of a second continental religious diaspora followed in the wake of the Tudor conquest of Ireland and the flight of Catholic aristocratic patronage and clergy to Europe. In the seventeenth and eighteenth centuries, Irish colleges sustained the ambition of the reconversion of Britain and Ireland to the Catholic faith. The Protestant plantation in Ulster, which was mainly seeded by Scottish Presbyterians, added a new and enduring religious dimension to the island. And, in the eighteenth century, Irish Presbyterian emigrants to the United States self-identified as "natural pioneers" whose passion for religious and civil independence made, they said, a natural alliance with the ideals of the new republic.

While religion formed a part of the early, largely Protestant, emigration of Irish settlers in the New World, the third and final missionary movement of the Irish people properly began in the mid-nineteenth century and was dominated numerically by Roman Catholics and marked by the expansion of the Roman Catholic Church to places of Irish settlement abroad. Because the vast majority of the nineteenth-century migrants who left Ireland were driven by poverty even if not literally starving, it is necessarily the case that the vast majority of those migrants were also Catholic: poor Protestants did exist, both Anglican and Presbyterian (and others too), north and south, but not in anything like the same numbers as poor Catholics. As a result it is often assumed that Catholics were the only ones leaving Ireland, or at least leaving in any numbers. But it is important to remember that the era of mass emigration engaged Irish of all denominations, and thus the nineteenth-century missionary movement also involved all Irish denominations. Catholics formed the larger part, but Protestants were everywhere important and in places dominant. It is the religious, social, cultural, and political impacts of this, the third and most numerically significant of the Irish missionary movements, that the chapters in this collection seek to explore.

The outpouring of Irish Catholics occurred at a critical time in the history of church-state relations in the United Kingdom and its growing empire. In 1829, the UK Parliament finally passed Catholic Emancipation, thus freeing itself of the most overt characteristics of a confessional state.[19] The privileges of the (episcopal) established and united Church of England and Ireland and the (presbyterian) established Church of Scotland were slowly abandoned as first dissenters and then Catholics and later Jews and finally atheists entered civil society as equals. The process was never complete as, although the Church of Ireland was disestablished in 1869 and the Church of England met the same fate in Wales in 1914, the Church of England and the Church of Scotland remain today by law established in their respective nations. The gradual change from confessionalism to voluntarism in religion affected all parts of the British polity, but it did not affect all parts equally.

From the early 1830s, it slowly became apparent that the privileges of the Church of England would not extend into the British World. In New South Wales, for example, the Irish Protestant governor Bourke advanced the careers of lay Roman Catholics and extended state aid to their church using monies at least in part previously provided to the Church of England. It amounted to disestablishment.[20] The military authorities in the Cape and India and beyond began to provide Roman Catholic chaplains to their troops and even to encourage Roman Catholic bishops. The bulk of both were Irish. By the mid-1860s, several South

African legal cases (*Long* v. *Bishop of Cape Town* in 1863, *Bishop of Natal* v. *Gladstone* in 1866) finally established that, in the Empire, the Church of England was simply one church like any other, neither specially privileged nor under the control of metropolitan authorities, lay or ecclesiastical. As the chief justice of the British Columbia Supreme Court observed in applying the latter case in an 1872 dispute over Anglican ritualism, "for 'Natal' read 'British Columbia.'"[21] In the United States, the last state-established churches had lost their status and funding by the early 1830s. The consequences were striking in the colonial and former colonial empire, where, instead of a collapse in religious sentiment, attachment, and loyalty, something like the reverse appears to have been the case. Supported by their churches, Anglicans, Catholics, Methodists, Presbyterians, Baptists, and other colonial and emigrant Christians appear to have grown in numbers and, in the British World, in identification with the British cause. In the United States, Irish-born bishops such as John England of South Carolina and John Hughes of New York fused Irish nationality and republican pride into a distinctively Irish American Catholicism; England's diocesan newspaper (the first in the United States) reproduced the text of the First Amendment to the Constitution on its masthead. In this religious free market, Irish emigrants and their denominations could (and did) compete freely.

Two approaches to the religious history of the Irish diaspora hold great potential, particularly if we are to move beyond perennial questions about the relative perseverance of Irish-born religious sectarianism. The first of these focuses on the extent to which religion worked to attenuate old religious antagonisms and to support emerging diasporic nationalisms. For some years now, John Mackenzie has been suggesting that we need to be pursuing a "four nations" approach to the history of the British Empire.[22] By this he means to draw attention to the ways in which the separate ethnic, religious, social, and political characters of the nations that came together to form the United Kingdom of Great Britain and Ireland in 1801 continued to participate and, indeed, to prosper among the British and Irish abroad. Although by no means uncontested, Mackenzie's approach has found many supporters among those keen to draw attention to the multi-layered nature of the imperial experience, the ways in which it allowed for the furtherance and extension of networks and pathways that may have been suppressed or obscured at home, and the ease with which minorities could find the space to continue old attachments and loyalties in new lands, whether in Orange lodges or Catholic parishes or Irish social clubs.

A second useful approach is the presently fashionable "network theory," one consequence of which is a renewed interest in the settler empire and the networks that underpinned it. The most obvious signs of this have been not only the sequence of "British World" conferences but also the success of the journal, now published by Edinburgh University Press, *Britain and the World*. The development of imperial network theory, originally in the work of economic historians and historians of geography, has had a major impact on the ways in which the British Empire is interpreted and imagined today.[23] Network theory was immediately appealing to historians who were seeking to find ways of talking about the connections between Britain and the colonies that recognized the reciprocal nature of these relationships. It emphasized co-operation rather than coercion as the critical feature of the second British Empire and explained its extraordinary cohesiveness in the apparent absence of overt mechanisms of control. Talking about networks also bypassed the uncomfortable hierarchy of values implicit in discussion of periphery and metropole, or the political determinism of postcolonialism, which argues that all aspects of imperial culture are ultimately hegemonic. Network theory opened up tangled relationships that operated at many layers, between different points on the peripheries as well as from periphery to metropole, and that reflected the depth of cultural as well as economic and political ties of empire. It also took into account the way that the existence of an empire – with its chains of command, government, communication, transport, commerce, and culture – worked not just to facilitate the administration of the empire but also the movement of people, ideas, and culture for whom the empire was a path to somewhere else.

Almost immediately there were attempts to extend the idea of imperial networks from its origins in economic history. In a series of influential articles (now gathered together as *Webs of Empire: Locating New Zealand's Colonial Past*), Tony Ballantyne proposes the image of a spider's web to capture the complex interrelations criss-crossing the imperial world, including religious webs.[24] Pioneers such as S.B. Cook and, more recently, Barry Crosbie examine one kind of ethnic network, that of the Irish in the Indian Empire, and migrant networks more generally provide particularly rich pickings for this methodology.[25] Perhaps inevitably, prosopography, the study of individual and collective lives, is another field that has made much use of network theory.[26] The most ambitious development of the idea is probably found in Gary Magee and Andrew Thompson's monumental *Empire and Globalisation*, which focuses largely on networks within the British World.[27] In his important review of Magee and Thompson, Stuart Ward suggests that network theory has, in the last decade, developed in two rather different directions. The first is the transformation of imperial history into a more expansive global history, or world history, one of the purposes of which is to reduce the tendency to Eurocentricity of traditional imperial history. The "new" imperial history, with its focus on discourses of race, gender, and class, has generated a new interest in global history and the history of other world empires.[28] Another factor has been the rise of interest in the British World, something of a transformation from the situation in the 1960s and 1970s, when the settler colonies were quietly forgotten as a field of empire. It was not just British historians who felt this: the same atrophication of attention was evident in national histories that were written in postcolonial states, including Ireland and (to a lesser extent) Scotland as well as in the former settler colonies themselves. As British imperial historians started to become interested in the global, so historians who wrote about Australian, or Canadian, or New Zealand, or (more hesitantly) South African history also began to turn their attention to the imperial aspects of their questions, as, for example, in the work of James Belich, Saul Dubow, Marilyn Lake, Henry Reynolds, and the political historian Duncan Bell.[29]

As fruitful as network theory has been, it is helpful to draw attention to two or three points of critique and possibility. In the first place, we need to consider what constitutes an imperial network and whether we are always talking about the same thing. According to Linton Freeman, network theory originally emerged in the 1930s, came to prominence in the 1940s in two disciplines – sociology and anthropology – and exploded in the 1990s.[30] Economic historians first began working in the field in the 1980s, with historians such as Richard Drayton, Paul Duguid, and others using the theory to explain merchant networking outside formal government structures in the Atlantic World.[31] In 1998, Charles Wetherell published an article that urges historians "to adopt social network theory from sociology," providing a crib for those who want to do so.[32] The charm of network theory was that it could be used to provide predictions about the likely behaviour of individuals in any social system, across national, ethnic, and imperial boundaries, and it worked particularly well for informal systems that lacked overt mechanisms for central control. Sociologists applied network analysis to the study of social relationships in modern cities, ethnographers to kinship networks in traditional societies, social anthropologists to changing family structures, security analysts to organized crime and terrorism.[33] However, it needs to be said that the very success of the methodology has invited overuse, and not all historical research that makes use of the term would be recognized as such within what is now a specialized field.

David Lambert and Alan Lester may have pushed the concept to the limit in their collection of "colonial lives."[34] Can a single individual, however well travelled, constitute a network? Even if he or she is as interesting and distinguished as the missionary Lancelot Threlkeld or the bookish and peripatetic Sir George Grey, who both have chapters in Lambert and Lester's "imperial careering" collection? While fascinating individually, we need to consider the problem of scale – and individual lives need a different methodology than that which emerges from the global movement of people, the rise and fall of imperial dynasties, or the economic and military scaffolding that forged the visible empire. If networks are allowed to include everything that happens in an imperial territory, then this very useful tool will ultimately lose much of its interpretive force. The same problem affects those who choose to work on the periphery of empire, using the language of transnationalism to draw connections between two or more sub-imperial localities: Australia and India, New Zealand and Upper Canada, Scotland and Fiji. The connections are not always powerful or obvious, and perhaps we should admit that some people and places were better connected to each other and to the Empire than others. To provide them all with "imperial network" status is to overdetermine the limited evidence. It also reduces the significance of local and indigenous forces that might provide them with much richer explanatory frameworks.

On the other hand, network theory in some cases has not been extended far enough and marginalizes some things that should remain in the foreground. Showing its roots in economic history, network theory does not invite investigation of the formal apparatus of state power; Magee and Thompson write about "networks of people, goods and capital," and the bonds created by co-operation and mutual self-interest. This leaves out the direct coercive aspects of imperial power, notably the army and navy but also the penal system, which was integrated with the colonial service and the military through the appointment of governors, convict administrators, and other officers (including chaplains) to penal colonies. It is fascinating to track the co-operative strands that knitted the British Empire together as a cultural and commercial entity, but this mode of empire needs to be balanced against the reality of overt agencies that allowed a foreign power to sustain its authority.

Another interpretive field that has scarcely been touched by a consideration of imperial network theory is religion, especially as it relates to the history of the later British Empire. Research on religions and religious migrants in the Atlantic World, particularly in the early modern period, is abundant and arguably central to current understanding of the peopling of the Americas. Summarizing the current situation, Susanne Lachenicht suggests that networks of religious communities "are crucial for transnational, translocal, and circum-Atlantic exchange, including the exchange of goods, knowledge, and peoples. Religious networks were by no means exclusive networks, but were established within and without specific religious communities in order to satisfy these communities' needs."[35] It is the unabashed hope of the editors that this book might precipitate further explorations in the still largely unknown archives of imperial religion.

In contrast to the wealth of studies on religion in the Atlantic World prior to the loss of Britain's American colonies, it would be fair to say that, other than the missionary movement, an imperial religious history hardly exists for the later period. This seems to have been a deliberate choice by the most recent generation of imperial historians. There are, for example, no entries for churches or religious organizations in either Belich or Thompson and Magee. According to the emigration historian Eric Richards, "One is aware, and possibly feels mildly reproved, for such an approach, by Sheridan Gilley's admonition of 'historians who can only understand an institution if it discharges a secular function and who reduce religion to an odd form of collective behaviour, to be understood as an answer to a secular need.'"[36] In fact, network theory provides a new way of looking at religious enterprise in the Empire, one that recognizes the affective power of religious traditions and their extraordinary permeability and flexibility in generating and extending communities of feeling – communities that have proven much more resilient than has the Empire itself. This neglect of religion as an aspect of empire is beginning to change, with new studies of religious diasporas by scholars who include Tony Ballantyne on Sikhism, David Hempton on Methodism in the Atlantic World, Rowan Strong and Joe Hardwick on Anglicans, as well as work by the present editors.[37] Another exception is the study of religious networks and anti-slavery, notably Catherine Hall's study of Baptist missionaries in the West Indies.[38]

IRELAND AND IMPERIAL RELIGIOUS NETWORKS

Within this new body of imperial religious history, specialist studies of Irish religious networks have been slow to emerge. Nor are the Irish dramatically better served by academic treatments of their role in the British Empire more generally. Excepting Cook's and Crosbie's respective treatments of the Irish networks in India (see above), what exists are predominately studies of the Irish in a particular zone of settlement, for example the numerous studies of the Irish in North America or such influential works as Patrick O'Farrell's oft-reprinted *The Irish in Australia*.[39] Over several scholarly generations a rich literature has been built up – one that considers the fate of the overseas Irish in particular places, from the miners of Butte, Montana, to the bandits of the high veldt and almost everywhere in between.[40] We have a clear understanding of both the emigrant experience, most notably via the work of David Fitzpatrick and Angela McCarthy, respectively, and the mechanisms of emigration, including most recently Richard Reid's study of Irish assisted emigration to Australia down to 1870. Our understanding of the context of Ireland's religious diaspora has been enhanced by S. Karly Kehoe's work on Scottish Catholics and their transnational religious associations.[41] What is largely lacking, however, are studies that consider the Irish on an imperial or global scale: what exists is mostly concerned with the Irish in particular places (Australia, the United States, Argentina) or with the movement of the Irish between home and a particular place (Irish migration to New Zealand or New South Wales). There are a handful of exceptions, most notably Malcolm Campbell's *Ireland's New Worlds*, which, uniquely for a single-author monograph, considers Irish immigrants in more than one extra-European jurisdiction, in this case the United States and Australia.[42] Campbell's book is one of the few, in fact, to bridge the gap between the United States and the British World (James Belich's *Replenishing the Earth* is another), reminding the reader that, for the Irish, Greater Ireland was greater than the Empire and that nineteenth-century borders were distinctly permeable.

The two most prominent attempts to survey Ireland's imperial experience, Kevin Kenny's volume in *The Oxford History of the British Empire* and Stephen Howe's *Ireland and Empire*, are useful but limited, not least when it comes to the history of religion. Both are primarily concerned with the impact of the British Empire on Ireland (and Irish complicity in empire) and hardly at all with the Irish in the British Empire, Anglo-world, or Greater Ireland. In his own chapter, Kenny does consider the imperial Irish themselves, but to a great extent his essay (and Howe's book) are overshadowed by the long-standing and increasingly fruitless debate about whether Ireland was or was not an oppressed colony, and was or was not complicit in colonizing and oppressing others. Kenny also discusses the great Irish missionary movement, but he divides his attention almost equally between the settler empire and the much later Irish missionary efforts elsewhere in the imperial world. Astonishingly, he manages not to mention the most important of all Irish missionary organizers, Cardinal Paul Cullen of Dublin. For his part, Stephen Howe's purpose is not so much to examine the Irish experience of empire as the Irish use and misuse of ideas of colonialism, postcolonialism, and the like: it is, he tells us, a "discourse of discourses."[43] It also takes almost no interest in the religious aspects of empire, with Howe confessing to a "secularist's blind-spot" concerning the role of religion.[44] There is also Daniel Murphy's extraordinary and extraordinarily detailed compendium of Irish education abroad, from the Druids to nearly the modern day. The posthumous publication of a life's work, it is by turns fascinating, old-fashioned, indigestible, and indispensible.[45] Nevertheless, religion in general, and Irish religion in particular, remains one of the last variables to be effectively integrated into the understanding of imperial networks and diasporas.

Even Roman Catholic historiography has not been entirely successful in placing the Irish Catholic religious experience in a global context. To its cost traditionally isolated from non-Catholic scholarship and scholars, Catholic historiography has also proven to be surprisingly national in focus. Although relations with Rome are inevitably important – and central to works such as Anne Cunningham's *The Rome Connection: Australia, Ireland and the Empire, 1865–1885* or Christopher Dowd's exhaustive two-volume study *Rome in Australia* – Catholic history is tightly focused within national boundaries.[46] Rome simply replaces London as the imperial metropole. Thus, with a few exceptions, the genuinely rich historiography of settler Catholicism largely fails to link colonial Catholic experience to the Greater Ireland of which it was conspicuously a part.[47]

The historiography of the other Irish denominations is even less developed, in part because the Protestant churches largely lack the historiographical tradition of the Catholics, and in part because the history of Irish Protestantism is badly served in Ireland itself, let alone in Ireland's diaspora. What studies do exist – for example Tom Frame's recent *Anglicans in Australia*, or the multi-author collections separately concerned with Methodists and Presbyterians in Atlantic Canada – do not, or do not usually, ignore the Irish contribution, but nor do they focus on it.[48] All too often, important Irish Protestant networks can only be seen in glimpses in wider studies with secular concerns. The powerful group of Trinity College-educated Irish Anglicans in late Victorian Melbourne is only one example of what must be many such little known or unknown networks.[49] It is frustrating that the only book-length attempt to survey Irish Protestantism on a global basis is focused on one of the smallest Irish denominations, the Methodists.[50] Worse, the scholarship of all the Christian denominations tends not to raise its gaze beyond the particular denomination, seeing other churches, when it sees them at all, as rivals or enemies or simply as other. But the Irish were present in all major colonial and American denominations, and their religious history in Greater Ireland is best served by an attention to religion as such, and not just to denomination or church.

Such an approach can pay dividends in that it can open up the myriad ways in which the Irish participated in the settler worlds of the nineteenth century. This can be seen in the introduction to a special issue of *Britain and the World* concerned entirely with the Irish imperial experience, where Karly Kehoe and Michael Vance suggest that the Irish were adroit participants in the pathways opened up by imperial expansion.[51] They also argue that multiple identities were the norm rather than the exception throughout the British and Irish diasporas. For many the Empire provided abundant scope for a more capacious view of British identity as well as new hybrid identities, such as Anglo-Irish, Irish American, and Scotch Irish, that were facilitated by pre-existing loyalties of faith and confession. They note: "the maintenance and expansion of the empire and the cementing of the idea of greater Britain did not and could not exclude Ireland or the Irish."[52] We would go further and suggest that the identity of the Irish in all the worlds they settled did not and could not exclude religion.

GREATER IRELAND

This collection is built around a phrase that has been used, in different ways, to refer to the Irish beyond Ireland. But what was "the Greater Ireland"? It seems reasonable to suggest that, as a term in general use, "Greater Ireland" gained some of its currency by simple extension of the term "Greater Britain," originally popularized by Charles Wentworth Dilke in the 1860s.[53] As Duncan Bell points out, "Greater Britain" was a flexible term and, while nearly always pro-imperial in sentiment, was also embraced by religious enthusiasts for empire as a way of promoting intangible aspects of the imperial bond. These spiritual aspirations tended to be felt most ardently by British Protestants in the second half of the nineteenth century, for whom Greater Britain was as much a religious as a political ideal.[54] Although all the British churches made use of this idea at different times, the term proved particularly useful for evangelical Anglicans engaged in the work of colonial missions – so much so that the Colonial and Continental Church Society entitled its regular missionary journal the *Greater Britain Messenger*. It is significant that Anglicans should have felt most comfortable with the idea of Greater Britain because, as Bell also points out, the term carried with it the baggage of Anglo – and Anglican – hegemony, which causes many Irish, even today, to reject the term "British Isles" for the islands that make up Great Britain and Ireland.

The idea of Greater Ireland nevertheless long predates Dilke and his project for the British overseas. A small number of medieval sources identify a land found to the west of Ireland as *Hibernia major* (Ireland the Great) in Latin or *Írland hið mikla* (Greater Ireland) in Old Norse. These are sometimes said to support the claims for the Irish St Brendan and his companions to be numbered among the pre-Columban voyagers to North America.[55] The early twelfth-century Icelandic *Landnámabók* (Book of settlements) refers to "'White Men's Land,' which some people call 'Greater Ireland' said to be a six day sail west from Ireland," a place generally identified with Newfoundland.[56] Long before archaeological discoveries gave scientific credence to Viking settlements not just in Newfoundland but also in mainland North America, "Greater Ireland" became a handy way to refer to the Irish emigrant community and to mythic claims for a greater Irish nation beyond the British imperial sway.

Claims for Greater Ireland and for the Irish discovery of North America became more bombastic in the writing of the post-Famine generation. In 1878, Father Hugh Quigley asserted with absolute confidence that not only did the Irish discover North America, led by St Brendan, but that the Scandinavians admitted that when the Vikings arrived there they found the Irish already in situ and that this was why they called it "Great Ireland."[57] References to "the greater Ireland beyond the sea" become more numerous after 1890 and might well have found their way into pub talk in Dublin on 16 June 1904, just as Joyce supposed.[58] It was usually assumed that "the greater Ireland" referred to the Irish in the United States but the Irish elsewhere also made a claim to the title. An Australian newspaper, reporting on a speech given by William Redmond in Wexford in 1884, claimed that Parnell had a million Irishmen in Australia who supported his movement and that the struggle for Irish independence could count on "the moral and material aid of the greater

Ireland in America and Australia."[59] The military muscle of Greater Ireland was also said to be bolstered by spiritual force. In an 1887 lecture on the "Unbroken Catholicity of the Irish Race," delivered at St Kilian's Hall, Bendigo, Victoria, the lecturer asserted: "The beautiful 'Green Isle' of the western seas has become absorbed in a 'Greater Ireland,' the bounds of which embrace the homes of Ireland's children all the world over."[60] Other commentators extended the conceit to include other diasporic peoples of the British Isles. The French wit Max O'Rell (Léon Paul Blouet, 1848–1903) suggested that England should not call its colonies "Greater Britain" since so many were governed by Scots, who were so prevalent in New Zealand that the latter might better be called "Greater Scotland," and the United States "Greater Ireland" for good measure.[61]

Like "Greater Britain" the idea of "Greater Ireland" (usually with capital letters) could be perceived as having a hegemonic political and religious subtext. By 1920, a writer for the *Harvard Crimson* objected to the activities of "Irish propagandists and interfering sympathizers" who suggested that Greater Ireland was co-terminous with the United States.[62] Looking forward in time, some modern Irish unionists regard "Greater Ireland" as a more sinister version of "United Ireland," which attempts to turn an accident of geography – the fact that Ireland is an island – into a political destiny: that Ireland should be one nation rather than two.[63] Overall, the term has proven to be most useful to promoters of Irish identity overseas, especially those who sought to foster diplomatic ties with the countries to which the Irish had moved in such numbers.[64]

The heyday of "Greater Ireland" as a cultural conceit coincided with the most energetic period of Irish emigration. According to Declan Kiberd, references to the overseas diasporic Irish peter out in Ireland itself in the 1960s, though commercial and political considerations have ensured that the concept has not been allowed to fade away entirely. Not long after assuming office in 1990, President Mary Robinson, as a symbolic gesture of inclusion, lit a lamp in Áras an Uachtaráin, her official residence, in memory of Greater Ireland.[65] President Robinson here paid tribute to the expectation, fully enshrined in successive Irish citizenship acts,[66] that Mother Ireland would continue to keep a light burning in loving expectation of the return of those who had fled the country into exile. Even more recently, the Irish government declared 2013 the year of "The Gathering," when an island that "populated the globe with approximately 70 million O'Sullivans, Murphys and Walshes, not to mention the roughly one million Irish-born people who are currently living abroad" invited her sons and daughters "home" to spend their money.[67]

Just as those who thought of "The Gathering" in terms of O'Sullivans, Murphys, and Walshes, and not Carsons, Molyneauxs, and Walkers, those who favoured the term "Greater Ireland" were also inclined to define it in religiously exclusive terms. At the second annual meeting of the American Catholic Historical Association in 1926, Laurence J. Kenny expressed his historical aspirations for a spiritual Greater Ireland, a new apostolic age that would spread Irish Catholicism across the world and turn the United States into a Catholic country. The address is worth quoting at length, as it neatly illustrates the essentially denominational understanding of the Irish diaspora on the part of many Catholics:

> Ireland's destiny is not hidden among the mysteries of the future. It stands out luminous in the records of the past. There was first of all a golden age when all the island rang with child-like praise of God and Mary, when half the people were consecrated to the virgin life, and when every foot of ground entombed a saint. Then came an iron age, when rack and sword and pike sent up to heaven an army of Christian martyrs whose numbers are known to the omniscient God alone. In our day its destiny is clear as the sun and the moon and the stars in the heavens: this is the age of apostles. From Armagh to Baltimore, from Los Angeles to Auckland, from Melbourne to Manila, from Zanzibar to Sierra Leone, from the Cape of Good Hope to Riga, are, from the right hand of the chair of Peter, the sons of Innisfall are the heralds of the pure and true gospel: verily, their sound has gone forth to the ends of the earth. Is America to be *Irland it Mikla*, a Greater Ireland?[68]

A footnote to this passage explains that the bishops of all the dioceses named – from Armagh to Zanzibar – were natives of Ireland, with the exception of the Russian-born bishop of Riga, Edward O'Rourke (1876–1943), whose family claimed Irish as well as Russian and German imperial titles.

Despite Kenny's assumptions, the Irish experience of spiritual empire was not as simple as Catholic triumphalism: as Leigh-Ann Coffey notes in this volume (chap. 2), the magazine of the Church of Ireland found it convenient to refer to the "imperial Irish" when discussing Protestant emigrants not only abroad but also marooned at home, seemingly without feeling the need to explain to readers what this term implied.[69] Yet an exclusively Irish Catholic spiritual empire continued to be promoted well into the twentieth century, as with the 1952 publication of J.J. O'Kelly's book *Ireland's Spiritual Empire: Saint Patrick as a World Figure*. An Irish-language enthusiast and uncompromising nationalist, O'Kelly (1872–1957) edited the *Catholic Bulletin*, was deputy chairman of the first Dáil, and ultimately served as president of both the Gaelic League (1919–22) and Sinn Féin (1926–31). O'Kelly's writings probably represent a high point in Irish nationalist identification with Catholic expansion overseas, especially in the United States and the British settler colonies. He explains his purpose in the Introduction, which states that he intended, echoing Dilke, to "follow [Ireland's] sons and daughters abroad in humble appreciation of the unwavering self-sacrifice through which they have been bringing light into the world's dark places almost since the days of the Apostles."[70] He goes on to enumerate the Irish missionary achievement first in Europe and then in the New World, tracking their global progress in the West Indies, Canada, and the United States in the eighteenth century; Australasia and southern Africa in the nineteenth century; and Africa, India, and the Far East in the twentieth century. Chapter by chapter, century by century, continent by continent, O'Kelly records the expansion of dedications to St Patrick that marked the boundaries of Ireland's spiritual domains.

Regrettably, the Irish in the British World and the United States were no more unified or uniform than were those who remained at home. Just as the Irish in Ireland were divided by politics, religion, class, or region, so too were the Irish abroad. To a degree, this is suggested by the very fragility of umbrella terms such as "Greater Ireland." Nonetheless, the term serves to remind us that the transported allegiances of the Irish overseas underwent multiple transformations in the course of time and travel and that these metamorphoses were reflected in religious institutions and practices, just as they were for the other peoples of the British Isles. Recently, some historians have begun to refer to the idea of Greater Ireland as a way of capturing how this distinctiveness was maintained by the overseas Irish population. The Scottish geographer Adrian Mulligan, for example, adopts the term "Greater Ireland" as a way of referring to the Irish diaspora and the role it played in a transnational dialogue on Irish nationalism, which was as much a global as an insular conversation.[71] Paul Arthur's review of studies by Donald Akenson on the Irish in South Africa and New Zealand is entitled "Our Greater Ireland beyond the Seas."[72] Perhaps there is an irony here, given that Akenson's body of work has so energetically repudiated the nostalgic romanticism of diasporic narratives of Irish identity and the troubled roots of religious nationalism.[73]

In this book, then, we use Greater Ireland not simply as a synonym for the Irish diaspora: it is not merely the collection of places to which the Irish migrated. Rather, Greater Ireland was a shared cultural space in which a sense of home and shared identity jostled with the varying challenges of the host societies and the inherited divisions of the Irish themselves. That identification with Ireland endured longer with some groups than with others, in some places more than others, does not vitiate the observation that the son of Irish migrants in Boston often thought of himself as Irish in much the same way as did the granddaughter of Irish migrants in Ballarat. Greater Ireland was protean, but it was real to the people who would have recognized their residence in it. One of the purposes of gathering the chapters published here is to demonstrate this.

RELIGION AND GREATER IRELAND

This collection brings together scholars with an interest in the global experience of one particular ethnic collectivity within the Union Kingdom – that of the Irish and their religious connections.[74] This is a bold plan because of the people of Ireland's mythic reputation as the origin of, and source for, the relentless religious hostilities in the British Union. As Vincent Comerford notes, the Irish appear to have been one of the few European peoples, certainly one of the few modern nation-states, who have failed to generate an effective collectivity abroad, principally because of the persistence of religious hostilities that have acted to blur and restrict the creation of a pan-Irish diasporic identity. The chapters in this collection address, in different ways, this fundamental paradox of the identity of the Irish overseas. They attempt to assess the extent to which religion both facilitated and prevented the generation of new religious nationalisms in colonies of settlement.

The chapters that follow explore the idea of religion and Greater Ireland by following the Irish to as many of their multiple and varied destinations as possible. In chapter 1, Comerford sets the stage, not only drawing attention to the dangers and temptations of Irish emigration history and concepts such as diaspora but also stressing that, if it is necessary to consider Irish history in light of Greater Ireland, it is equally necessary to consider Greater Ireland in light of events in Ireland. He also usefully reminds us that, whatever their differences, Irish Christians also enjoyed substantial commonalities. Staying in Ireland, Leigh-Ann Coffey, in chapter 2, asks how the Church of Ireland coped with the catastrophe of southern Irish independence and the sudden position of their church as a tiny, threatened, and unpopular minority. Many left, but Coffey tells the fascinating story of how some who stayed adopted the identity of "Imperial Irish" to replace the suddenly anachronistic "unionist." Elements of the Church of Ireland began to see Ireland itself as mission territory; even St Patrick was co-opted as a proto-Protestant imperialist.

The rest of the volume follows the Irish overseas. This policy inevitably orphans the Irish who migrated only across the Irish Sea to England, Scotland, or Wales. England was always the most popular destination for the Irish, while the links between Scotland and Ireland were enduring and reciprocal. Just as Scots Presbyterians had an extraordinary impact on Ireland and, in time, Greater Ireland, so too were both Scotland and Scottish Catholicism profoundly changed by the mass emigration of Irish Catholics from the 1840s. Scotland was in some ways on the frontiers, or borderlands, of Greater Ireland, with flashpoints ranging from the sectarian rivalries of Scottish football to the provocative tour (at the height of the Irish War of Independence) of Daniel Mannix, who was both the Catholic archbishop of Melbourne and a noisy Irish nationalist. English cities such as Liverpool were shaped by migration and sectarianism. That this volume omits Britain's Irish is in no sense a denial of their importance; rather, it is a testament to the complexity of the United Kingdom and, consequently, to the editorial decision that a proper treatment of the Irish in both Greater Ireland and Great Britain would be impossible within the confines of a single volume.

The sheer scale and breadth of Irish migration also made it impossible to provide studies of every aspect or site of their expansion around the globe. Such an approach would in any case duplicate some outstanding scholarship, particularly as it relates to Irish in the North Atlantic world. Nevertheless, there are obvious gaps, where treatment of the Irish religious experience in, say, the Caribbean or Argentina or Western Australia would have proved illuminating. The sheer size of Australia leaves scope for consideration of the Irish in, say, Queensland or the Northern Territory. The emphasis here on South Eastern Australia reflects the dominance of those colonies (and later states) in terms of economy and demography as well as the weight of Irish numbers. Even so, in chapter 12, Eric Richards draws heavily on the experience of South Australia. We also regret not being able to include a consideration of

Irish Jews, such as the Rabbi A.P. Bender, who, in the 1890s, helped found the Cape Town Irish Association with a Catholic bishop and a lapsed Church of Ireland priest.[75] The story of Irish Judaism in the Irish diaspora remains to be told.

Although women are by no means ignored, focused treatment is largely limited to Myrtle Hill's chapter 10, which looks at Presbyterian female missionaries. Another book could be filled with chapters on Irish women of all denominations, both clerical and lay. In particular, Catholicism's Greater Ireland would have been impossible without the thousands of Irish women who served as religious in its schools, orphanages, and hospitals. James Joyce's sister Margaret (the model for "Eveline" in *Dubliners*) was one such woman, training for imperial service at St Brigid's Missionary College in Callan, County Kilkenny, before becoming a Sister of Mercy in New Zealand, where she taught music until her death in Christchurch in 1964. Some two thousand other women hoping to pursue a similar path also attended St Brigid's from the 1880s to the 1950s.[76] Many thousands of others made their way directly from Ireland or were recruited from the emigrant Irish or their descendents. Their comparative absence from this book is in no way a denial of their importance in Greater Ireland.

As a glance at the table of contents will show, *Religion and Greater Ireland* is primarily concerned with Irish Catholics and Irish Protestants in the British World. This is because it was largely in the settler empire that the Irish were forced to negotiate not only the hybrid identities consequent upon emigration but also their ambiguous status as one of the four constituent nations of the imperial power. Nevertheless, it is clearly impossible, and certainly undesirable, entirely to omit the United States of America. Thus, Mimi Cowan's chapter 8 offers a close study of the peculiar challenges faced by the immigrant Irish, mostly Catholic, in nineteenth-century Chicago as they were forced to traverse not only the ethnic complexity of an American metropolis but also the difficulties and opportunities of municipal democracy in the perpetually fraught area of schooling. So too in chapter 6, Rankin Sherling examines how late eighteenth-century Irish Presbyterians created a North Atlantic world that was permeable to both people and theological conflict, with personnel and religious passions passing in both directions.

In chapter 4, Mark McGowan considers the fate of Irish Catholics as a "double minority" in Canada, outnumbered by both Protestants and francophone Catholics. He traces how the Irish came to dominate the Catholic Church outside Quebec, not least by ensuring that new Catholic migrants from outside the British World were educated in English and, thus, inculcated into a distinctively Irish Catholicism. In chapter 5, Carolyn Lambert provides a detailed discussion of the most Irish of all the settler colonies, the island of Newfoundland. A dominion in its own right, Newfoundland's Irish Catholics slowly gained the confidence to develop an Irish Newfoundland consciousness and patriotism that, like its Canadian cousin, would manifest itself in widespread support for the imperial war effort in 1914. In chapter 7, Mike McLaughlin's examination of the temperance movement in Canada demonstrates the enduring power of religion not only in the application of social controls but also in the creation of a distinctively Irish Catholic Canadian identity. He also draws attention not only to similar Irish Catholic efforts in Australia but also to Irish Protestant temperance campaigns such as that of the Reverend Rutherford Waddell in New Zealand, who, in chapter 15, is considered in detail by John Stenhouse. Further afield, in chapter 11 Colin Barr examines Irish Catholicism in the least popular and most Protestant of the settler colonies, the Cape of Good Hope. There, racial complexities and low Catholic numbers have done much to obscure Irish Catholics from historical view, despite the fact that the Roman Catholics of southern Africa were fully integrated into Catholicism's Greater Ireland.

Although the focus of *Religion and Greater Ireland* is the settler empire (and the United States), Asia is not neglected. In chapter 9, Barry Crosbie traces the slow and steady increase of Irish Catholic religious networks as the East India Company, and later the Raj, came to recognize that a reliance on Catholic soldiers implied the necessity of an institutional Catholic church. It did not take the authorities long to decide that they preferred Irish priests to any European alternative. In chapter 10, Myrtle Hill draws our attention to the activities of Irish women in the larger missionary activities of British Presbyterianism in mission fields from India to China. According to Hill, this helped create "an Ulster Presbyterian female imperial identity."

But *Religion and Greater Ireland* has an unapologetic southern bias. As Eric Richards points out in chapter 12, in which he discusses emigration in Australia, the works of Bruce Elliott, Don Akenson, and others provide detailed studies of Irish religious settlement in Canada that cannot be matched in the southern British World. The study of Irish religious networks in Australia and New Zealand is given considerable augmentation not only through Richards's fresh study of the impact of Irish religion on emigration (and of emigration on Irish religion) in Australia, but also by Jeff Kildea's chapter 16, on the extraordinary eruption of sectarianism in Australian politics in 1920; Kevin Molloy's chapter 3, on the networks of religious publishing and book importation from Ireland to the Australian colonies; Dianne Hall's chapter 14, on several Irish Protestant "clusters" in rural New South Wales; and Michael Gladwin's chapter 13, on the crucial Irish contribution to antipodean Anglicanism. New Zealand is represented by John Stenhouse in chapter 15, which offers a case study of the extraordinary Ulster Presbyterian minister Rutherford Waddell, who had to negotiate the religious and social complexities of a Dunedin that also hosted a militant Irish Catholic bishop. As Stenhouse usefully reminds us, New Zealand's history is inseparable from religion in general and, at least in Otago, Irish religion in particular.

A full religious history of the Irish diaspora is beyond the aspirations of this book. But *Religion and Greater Ireland* does hope to shine a light on an important vehicle for the global transformation of the Irish people overseas – a light that will do full justice to the geographical reach, cultural diversity, and perversity of the Irish religious experience in Greater Ireland.

NOTES

1 "We'll put force against force, says the citizen. We have our greater Ireland beyond the sea. They were driven out of house and home in the black 47" (Joyce, *Ulysses*, 316).

2 For reflections on the meaning of "diaspora," see R.V. Comerford (chap. 1, this volume) and Akenson, *Irish Diaspora*. Akenson champions the thesis that the extent of the differences between different Irish religious groups has been exaggerated and that more united the Irish overseas than divided them. See Akenson, *Small Differences*.

3 Fitzpatrick, *Irish Emigration*, 6, fig.2.

4 Bartlett and Jeffery, *Military History of Ireland*, 12.

5 For one aspect of Hennessey's colonial career, see Howell and Lambert, "Sir John Pope Hennessy," 228–56.

6 Redmond Barry (1813–80). See Galbally, *Redmond Barry*.

7 Frederick York St. Leger (1833–1901). See Shaw, *Some Beginnings*.

8 Ridden, "Making Good Citizens"; Laidlaw, "Richard Bourke," 113–44.

9 See Baker, *Timothy Warren Anglin*.

10 J.L. McCracken, *New Light at the Cape of Good Hope.*
11 Akenson, *Small Differences,* 43, fig. 5.
12 Bronwen Walter, Breda Gray, Linda Almeida Dowling, Sarah Morgan, "A study of the existing sources of information and analysis about Irish emigrants and Irish communities abroad," (n.p.: Irish Department of Foreign Affairs, 2002), 26–7, table 2.2, available at http://www.dfa.ie/uploads/documents/taskforcestudy.pdf (viewed 23 May 2015).
13 Population and Migration Estimates, Central Statistics Office of Ireland, statistical release, 29 August 2013.
14 Cory Miller, "How Many Irish People Live Abroad: A Globalirish.Ie Fact Sheet," available at http://www.globalirish.ie/issues/how-many-irish-people-live-abroad-an-ean-factsheet/ (viewed 23 May 2015). The population of the island of Ireland in 2012 was 6.4 million (4.6 million in the Republic of Ireland and 1.8 million in Northern Ireland).
15 For a recent review of nineteenth-century origins of Irish religious nationalism, see Coakley, "Religious Roots."
16 For illuminating approaches to the issue of religion and nationalism, see Van der Veer, "Moral State," 15–43; Van der Veer, *Imperial Encounters*; Van der Veer and Lehmann, *Nation and Religion.*
17 For the suggestion that religion is most likely to be intensified when imbricated or intertwined with nationalism, citing the case of Protestants in Northern Ireland, see Brubaker, "Religion and Nationalism." See also, Brubaker, *Nationalism Reframed.*
18 For cited figures and dates of religions in Ireland, see Dudley Edwards, *Atlas of Irish History*, 104–22 (and 123–49 for the Irish abroad).
19 For an account of the dismantling of the English confessional state that gives extensive consideration to its religious character, see Clark, *English Society*, 501–64.
20 For the perspective of the Church of England on these events, see Shaw, *Patriarch and Patriot*, esp. chaps. 4–5.
21 See Brown, "Judgments of Solomon," 320.
22 Mackenzie, "Irish, Scottish, Welsh."
23 Lester, *Imperial Networks.*
24 Ballantyne, *Webs of Empire.*
25 Cook, *Imperial Affinities*; Crosbie, *Irish Imperial Networks.* Barst, "Pushing the Envelope"; Belchem, "Priests, Publicans and the Irish Poor."
26 Anderson, *Subaltern Lives*; Deacon, Russell, and Woollacott, *Transnational Lives*; Frost and Maxwell-Stewart, *Chain Letters*; Jasanoff, *Edge of Empire*; Lambert and Lester, *Colonial Lives*; Maxwell-Stewart and Hood, *Pack of Thieves*; Townsend, "Reconstructed Lives."

27 Magee and Thompson, *Empire and Globalisation.*
28 Stuart Ward, "Review of Empire and Globalisation: Networks of People, Goods and Capital in the British World, c. 1850–1914 by Gary Magee and Andrew Thompson," *Reviews in History*, available at http://www.history.ac.uk/reviews/review/1000, Review no. 1000 (2010) (viewed 24 May 2015).
29 Belich, *Replenishing the Earth*; Dubow, *Commonwealth of Knowledge*; Lake and Reynolds, *Drawing the Global Colour Line*; Bell, *Idea of Greater Britain.*
30 For a definitive history, see Freeman, *Development of Social Network Analysis*. Freeman dates the beginning of social network analysis to the 1930s.
31 Drayton, "Knowledge and Empire"; Duguid, "Networks and Knowledge."
32 Wetherell, "Historical Social Network Analysis."
33 For examples, see citations in Borgatti et al., "Network Analysis."
34 Lambert and Lester, *Colonial Lives.*
35 Susanne Lachenicht, "Religious Networks," Oxford Bibliographies. Last modified: 28 January 2013, DOI: 10.1093/obo/9780199730414-0151. Available at http://www.oxfordbibliographies.com/.
36 Gilley, "Roman Catholic Church," 206.
37 Hempton, *Methodism*; Ballantyne, *Orientalism and Race*; Ballantyne, *Between Colonialism and Diaspora*; Strong, *Anglicanism and the British Empire*; Hardwick, "Anglican Church Expansion"; Hardwick, *Anglican British World.*
38 Hall, *Civilizing Subjects.*
39 O'Farrell, *Irish in Australia.*
40 Emmons, *Butte Irish*; Van Onselen, *Masked Raiders.*
41 Fitzpatrick, *Oceans of Consolation*; McCarthy, *Irish Migrants in New Zealand*; Reid, *Farewell my Children*; Kehoe, "Catholic Identity in the Diaspora"; Kehoe, "Unionism, Nationalism."
42 Campbell, *Ireland's New Worlds.*
43 Howe, *Ireland and Empire*, 5.
44 Ibid., 9.
45 Murphy, *Irish Emigrant Education.*
46 Cunningham, *Roman Connection*; Dowd, *Rome in Australia.*
47 One conspicuous exception is Gilley's "Roman Catholic Church."
48 Frame, *Anglicans in Australia*; Scobie and Grant, *Contribution of Methodism*; Scobie and Rawlyk, *Contribution of Presbyterianism.*
49 The influence on Melbourne of self-consciously Irish Anglicans trained in Dublin is quite astonishing, and little remarked upon. A glimpse can be caught in Poynter, *Doubts and Certainties.*

50 Taggart, *Irish in World Methodism.*
51 Kehoe and Vance, "Hiberno-British World."
52 Ibid., 151.
53 Dilke, *Greater Britain*; Dilke, *Problems of Greater Britain.*
54 Bell, *Idea of Greater Britain*; Bell, "Unity and Difference."
55 Belief in the Irish claim for the discovery of North America, usually linked to the voyages of St Brendan, was common coin in Irish American writing of the post-famine generation. See, for example, Quigley, *Irish Race in California*. For discussion, see Fanning, *Irish Voice in America*, 141.
56 Pálsson and Edwards, *Book of Settlements*, 61.
57 Quigley, *Irish Race in California*, 91–2.
58 For an extensive collection of references, see Van Mierlo, "Greater Ireland beyond the Sea". The Google Books Ngram viewer shows that "Greater Ireland" first appears in its corpus of printed words in the late 1840s, peaked in popularity in the early 1890s, and faded away, along with "Greater Britain," thereafter.
59 *South Australian Weekly Chronicle*, 26 April 1884.
60 *Bendigo Advertiser*, 23 November 1887.
61 O'Rell, *John Bull & Co*, 53. This was widely reported in the Australian press. See, for example, *Border Watch* (Mount Gambier, South Australia), 9 January 1895.
62 "Greater Ireland," *Harvard Crimson*, 14 December 1920, available at http://www.thecrimson.com/article/1920/12/14/greater-ireland-pirish-propagandists-and-interfering/ (viewed 23 May 2015).
63 Henry C.H. Hill, "One Ireland, One Vote," 22 September 2012, available at http://www.openunionism.com/ (viewed 23 May 2015).
64 Hackett, "Greater Ireland."
65 Kiberd, *Inventing Ireland*, 608. See Eavan Boland's poem, "The Emigrant Irish": "Like oil lamps, we put them out the back – of our houses, of our minds." Boland, *Collected Poems*, 129
66 The 1935 act gave citizenship to any who had been born in Ireland; the 1956 act to any who could claim descent from at least one Irish grandparent. For discussion, see Shanahan, "Scripted Debates," 90.
67 "The Gathering Ireland 2013," http://www.thegatheringireland.com/About/What-it-means-to-be-Irish.aspx#.UovRl6VRw5Q (viewed 19 November 2013).
68 Kenny, "America," 423.
69 Coffey, chap 2, this volume.
70 O'Kelly, *Ireland's Spiritual Empire*, 5.
71 Mulligan, "Forgotten 'Greater Ireland.'"

72 Arthur, "Our Greater Ireland."
73 Akenson, *God's Peoples*; Akenson, *Church of Ireland*; Akenson, *Small Differences*; Akenson, *Irish Diaspora*.
74 Kehoe and Vance, "Hiberno-British World," 149–51.
75 Shaw, *Some Beginnings*, 7.
76 For St Brigid's Missionary College, see Barr and Luminiello, "Leader of the Virgin Choir of Erin."

PART ONE

Irish Global Networks

1

Deference, Accommodation, and Conflict in Irish Confessional Relations[1]

R.V. COMERFORD

When, in 1993, D.H. Akenson devoted a book to exploring the concept of the Irish diaspora, one of his crucial points was that emigration from Ireland should be considered on a global basis rather than in terms of the Irish in just one or two host countries.[2] His use of the metaphor of the Fabergé egg is a telling rhetorical device, not because Irish emigration, even in the round, has a specifically strong aesthetic appeal, but because the invocation of a strikingly integral artefact enabled Akenson to drive home the point about the integral character of his subject. The present volume exemplifies the value of that insight and illustrates the extent to which it has been vindicated. Progress in scholarship will continue to be made largely on the basis of empirical research on individual countries, regions, or urban areas, as most of the chapters in this volume indicate, but the scholarly terms of reference have been globalized, and it will no longer be possible to indulge in generalizations not informed by the wider perspective.

Less easy to remedy than the former want of a global perspective on destinations may be the lack of an inclusive perspective on the people leaving Ireland. For James Joyce's Citizen, invoked by Hilary Carey and Colin Barr in this book's Introduction,[3] as for so many of his real-life counterparts, Greater Ireland constitutes an ethnicity, Catholic and nationalist. By contrast, the core assumption of *Religion and Greater Ireland* is that Greater Ireland is inhabited by those of all denominations and political allegiances who are, or have been, of Ireland. This all-embracing approach, like the awareness of global reach, has been advanced particularly forcefully by Akenson and now has a commanding hold at the academic level.[4]

Nonetheless, the inclusive perspective is in danger of being silently undermined by the now widespread invocation of diaspora in political and academic discourse about the Irish abroad but without any of the precision intended by Akenson and other scholars. The biblical sense of members of a homogenous ethnicity, forcibly exiled and languishing on alien shores, their thoughts ever fixed on the homeland and lamented rituals, lends itself rather readily to being hijacked by the hackneyed self-pitying version of Irish emigration history, in which emigration is a wrong inflicted on the nation.[5] Who *writes* "Irish diaspora" may have a minimalist, literal concept of diaspora, but who *reads* "Irish diaspora" is more likely to connect with a version of the syncretic myth.

In a key article from 2003 interrogating, defining, and eventually validating the concept of diaspora, Kevin Kenny points out that it can tend "to exclude Protestants still further from Irish history by concentrating on British injustice toward the Catholic population."[6] The word "diaspora" can perhaps be shorn of many overtones, including even that of victimhood. What it almost certainly cannot be divorced from is the notion of the ethno-cultural homogeneity of the dispersing group; this notion is quite inimical to an inclusive approach to any aspect of the history of modern Ireland. Those who are of Ireland have long segregated themselves into several distinct collectivities defined in confessional terms.

In recognizing the confessional gulf that renders the concept of diaspora less than fully appropriate, it is important not to assume that the Catholic side had a monopoly on either conscious Irish identity or on a sense of Greater Ireland. Michael Gladwin (chap. 13, this volume) for the nineteenth century and Leigh-Anne Coffey (chap. 2, this volume) for the twentieth discover Protestants identifying themselves as Irish, or relating emigration and mission to the Irish past, or presuming the possession of endearing national character to charm the wider world, just as Catholics did.

Over the centuries many have emigrated from Ireland primarily because they judged that, on account of their confessional allegiance, they would be more at liberty elsewhere. This was the case, for instance, with some adherents of the papacy who moved to continental Europe in the later sixteenth century as well as for some of the Protestants who left the Irish Free State in the 1920s. The specificity of religious affiliation in the mind-sets of categories of nineteenth-century emigrants is probed by Kerby A. Miller in an important book from 2008.[7]

However, it has to be emphasized that the predominant factor in emigration from modern Ireland at all stages and for those of all faiths is to be found in the socio-economic realm. Overwhelmingly, emigrants departed for socio-economic reasons, bringing with them cultural baggage, including their confessional allegiances. Some were committed to their particular faith, others wore it lightly, and many readily dispensed with its practice. A central theme of the study of Greater Ireland, as illustrated particularly by the work of Colin Barr,[8] is the endeavour of the various churches to reassemble the faithful into the fold in their New World settings. Diane Hall (chap. 14, this volume) illustrates how quickly and successfully a migrant community could generate its own ecclesiastical cadres. Discovering the extent to which the confessional cultures, mind-sets, and lived religion of the homeland were accepted or rejected, replicated or replaced, intensified or diluted in Greater Ireland is an interesting and enriching enterprise. Such an exploration can produce, in turn, some useful illumination of the home history of religion, in its various aspects.

For what seems now like several generations there has been exhaustive discussion in the humanities and social sciences about nationalism and ethnicity. This has acquired great prominence because of the extent to which the allegiance of populations within the political order worldwide is seen to be determined by their sense of identity. This debate has flourished since 1989, but it had begun even before the collapse of the Communist bloc, when it was already clear that the thrust of socialism had lost its momentum. We can scarcely say that the struggle for the control of wealth and the means of its production has been resolved, but, rightly or wrongly, it is no longer seen as the great determinant of the political motivations and choices of the democratizing global population, a role now ascribed to identity politics.

The debate associated with the names of Elie Kedourie, Ernest Gellner, Eric Hobsbawm, Anthony D. Smith, and many others has subjected the concept of the nation to a most exhaustive examination and, in many ways, has cut its pretensions down to size. Benedict Anderson's categorization of the nation as an "imagined community" encapsulates the triumph of the realization that individual nations have no claim to be seen as manifestations of essential being.[9] Nonetheless, the status of the nation (albeit now understood as contingent) remains sacrosanct in this debate, if only in the sense that everything is seen as leading to the universal prevalence of the nation-state and the sentiment of nationality.

The conclusions of the debate on nationalism are calculated to explain why the world is divided into nation-states and why most of these states have an official culture of civic nationalism. But that is only part of the story. In fact, most states are not the happy locations of uniform political communities enthusiastically embracing civic nationalism, although there may be some that are. For most countries, happiness consists in successfully accommodating several different constituent collectivities defined by language, religion, presumed common origins, or some other form of "ethnicity." In this respect, Ireland is a normal country that, over the generations, has partaken in the same kind of conflicts as have other lands (albeit with its own unique combination of circumstances). And not only conflicts: for the relationship between contending collectivities within a polity is typically more complex than one of incessant conflict. A collectivity can accept subordination or adopt an attitude of deference over extended periods. While indefinite acceptance of subordination is not to be expected in a modernizing society, self-assertion can take many forms and can be exercised in many modes.

In any case, the history of these collectivities, their relations to one another, and their social implications can provide an understanding of political developments that is frequently as useful as is a focus on nation or empire. A mobilized collectivity can eventually become a nationalist movement, thereby asserting ineluctable claims against its opponents and either challenging the legitimacy of the state or claiming a monopoly over it. Needless to say, the attitudes and actions of the state and its ruling elites are an inseparable part of the story. Ireland is a prime example of a country that has been a theatre of interaction between conflicting collectivities, and obviously these have been defined in the first instance by religion. Mark McGowan (chap. 4, this volume) illustrates how, as is the case in Canada, if there is another criterion present (such as language), a common church can on occasion bring not cohesion but division.

Theobald Wolfe Tone wrote in 1791 of his ambition to see the ending of "the odious distinction of Protestant and Presbyterian and Catholic" and to have "the three great sects blended together under the common and sacred name of Irishman."[10] If that or anything like it had actually happened, no doubt a surplus Irish population would still have been scattered around the globe, but the contents of this chapter, and this volume, would be very different. Tone was advocating a solution to a problem in Irish politics, simmering for decades, which had now come to the boil: how to accommodate the Catholics. The anomaly of the majority of the population being confined to the margins of public and official life had been obvious since at least the middle of the eighteenth century. A series of ameliorations had been enacted, several of them prompted more or less directly by the revolutions in North America and France, meaning that, by 1793, Catholics could obtain the parliamentary franchise on the same basis as others, could acquire and bequeath landed property, and could enter and practise the professions. But there were still significant restrictions: they were excluded from sitting in Parliament and from a series of higher offices in government and judiciary by oaths that incorporated a repudiation of Catholic doctrine. This barrier assumed significance beyond its practical impact, and the project of removing it came to be termed Catholic Emancipation. The respectable, albeit still subordinate, status achieved in 1793 was perfectly acceptable to the body of leading Catholics, especially when, in 1795, the Irish government provided approval and funding for a Catholic college at Maynooth. Only a radical section of Catholic opinion supported Tone and his United Irishmen in the recourse to a French alliance and the subsequent rebellion of 1798.[11]

One consequence of the rebellion was an exacerbation of feelings that rendered Tone's dream for the common name of Irishman even more remote. Another was the Union of Ireland with Great Britain, effective from 1 January 1801. This was welcomed by a large part of the Catholic leadership because it was accompanied by an understanding that, in the new United Kingdom, Catholic Emancipation would be quickly granted. Under the Union the established church remained, privileging Tone's "Protestants." This survival of privilege typified the new situation. The anomalous British approach of conducting reform within the formal structures of the old order worked well for Britain, or at least for England, but not necessarily for anywhere else. The removal of Catholic disabilities – genuinely intended by the authors of the Union – was long delayed. When concessions were made they were framed as such rather than as matters of right.

The Penal Laws, a multifaceted code directed against different aspects of Catholicism and introduced in haphazard fashion from the 1690s, constitute one of the iconic topics of modern Irish history and controversy.[12] The point to be grasped here is that their weight in subsequent discourse is not determined by their objective contents or their contemporary impact (important considerations though these are in themselves) but, rather, by the failure to remove them promptly after their original rationale had disappeared. Already in the 1760s Edmund Burke had denounced them fulsomely as a badge of tyranny. In the early nineteenth century, when new ideas about political rights had taken hold so widely across European society, the failure to treat Catholic political rights as a matter of principle was deeply frustrating and fuelled a highly emotive propaganda campaign in which the Penal Laws became the prime rhetorical exemplum.

In Ireland many Catholics in the early nineteenth century could still contemplate co-existence on the basis of a partial incorporation of their church, inevitably on a subordinate basis, into the establishment. Thus, on a number of occasions attempts were made to offer concessions to Catholics on condition of a Crown veto over nominees for bishoprics (a right long enjoyed by rulers of Catholic countries in Europe). That was a perfectly acceptable proposal in the eyes of the papacy and some of its senior bishops in Ireland. However, it was blocked by opposition fomented by interests further down the hierarchical ladder, including laity.[13] These interests were primarily localist, but the issue attracted the involvement of Daniel O'Connell, a young lawyer with a sense of the potential of things national.

In the event it was lay leadership that, in the 1820s, mobilized the Catholic collectivity into self-assertion. The Catholic Relief Act, 1829, was the outcome of a public campaign in which Daniel O'Connell used the power of popular opinion to force the state into making concessions. The act removed the formal impediment to Catholics entering Parliament and occupying (with a few exceptions) places of influence and profit in political life. This was hailed as "Catholic Emancipation" even though there still remained an established church in the land.

If O'Connell and his lay henchmen had superseded the bishops as leaders of mobilized Catholicism in the 1820s, it was the administrative structures of the church, and especially the parish, that made the mobilization possible. The interconnection of lay and clerical leadership over the following century is a fascinating study. But at all times the predominant unit of political organization was the parish, and this gave the clergy an in-built advantage. If it was occasionally wrong-footed in some parishes or dioceses here or there, or even upstaged nationally by a political leader or a mobilization of the hour, the church still retained the enduring strength of an institution with country-wide structures and perpetually present agents.

Liberal Protestants in Ireland and Britain had supported the objectives of the Catholic campaign of the 1820s. The implications of Catholic emancipation were worked out in the decade following 1829 in the context of Whig/Liberal dominance and, more especially, during the government of Lord Melbourne, which came to power in 1835 with the parliamentary support of O'Connell. Between 1831 and 1841, a series of legislative and administrative changes greatly enhanced the position of Catholics in civil life, and from 1835 individual Catholics were granted the benefit of admission to numerous offices in the gift of Dublin Castle, including senior positions in the legal system and the judiciary. One could be sceptical about the strength of popular attachment to a regime whose direct benefits went preponderantly to lawyers, and the franchise was so limited between 1829 and 1850 that election results offer little or no guide to popular opinion. As chance would have it, a remarkable document has recently come to light in Castle Howard, Yorkshire, that provides striking evidence of popular attitudes – the Morpeth Roll. This is a testimonial presented to Lord Morpeth, the chief secretary from 1835, on the occasion of his leaving office and departing from Ireland in 1841. The address styles the signatories as "the reformers of Ireland." The number of (almost exclusively male) signatures is in the region of 160,000 from all parts of the island. This represents more than 10 percent of the available literate male population and constitutes an astonishing level of participation.[14] The first signatory is the duke of Leinster, followed by a score of Whig notables. But the bulk of the signatures come in batches of a score or two each from towns, villages, and parishes throughout the land. Nothing could exemplify more fully the accommodation between the Catholic collectivity and the liberalizing state that was to make such a large mark on modern Irish society. O'Connell's decision shortly thereafter to agitate for repeal of the union, thus framing the popular Catholic cause in terms of nationality, disrupted the alliance between Whigs and the Catholic democracy. The repeal campaign was launched following the accession of the Conservatives to office; once the Whigs returned to power in 1846, more radical repealers began to notice a weakening of resolve on O'Connell's part. In other words, he was turning back from defiance of the Tories to accommodation with his former allies.

In 1846, normal politics was giving way to the crisis of the Great Famine, for the greater and more calamitous part of which the Whigs, under Lord John Russell, were in power. Many assessments of the political impact of that calamity fail to notice how little it shook Catholic attachment to the old allies. Much more damaging to the relationship was the enactment of the Ecclesiastical Titles Act, 1851, itself a populist response (in the English context) to the "papal aggression" perceived by British opinion in the restoration in 1850 of the Catholic hierarchy in

England and Wales. In reaction, Irish Catholic Liberals rallied to the banner of Independent Opposition at the general election of 1852. However, most of those elected soon dropped their oppositional stance when the Liberals chose the conciliatory Lord Aberdeen as prime minister. As the old Whig/Liberal oligarchy began to evolve into the British Liberal Party in the 1860s, Irish Catholics mobilized in unison with their British counterparts, the Nonconformists and Radicals – a development all too often overlooked because of the understandable fascination with the Fenian movement of the same years. The Liberal Party owed its emergence to the new political self-assertion of the Nonconformists of England, Scotland, and Wales, a development that had obvious parallels with the progress of political Catholicism in Ireland. The Irish constituencies made an impressive contribution to Gladstone's triumph in 1868.

The disestablishment of the state church in Ireland (and the institution of a voluntary Church of Ireland in its place), as happened following upon the passing of the Irish Church Act, 1869, was a certain corollary. But, while vindicating principle was all very well, Gladstone was less forthcoming in conferring benefits on his allies: it was the failure to provide for a state-funded Catholic university that pushed his Irish supporters into voting down his government in 1873 and turning to the Home Rule League for a marketable electoral brand in 1874. When, in his second term (1880–85), Gladstone came to deal again with those commanding the support of the Catholic masses, the terms of discussion, as we shall see, had changed markedly.

The university question that, in the early 1870s, precipitated the demise of the Irish Catholic Liberals as a power in the land typified the complexity of the relationship between the Church of Rome and liberal regimes throughout Europe and elsewhere in the world. The papacy excoriated liberalism and all its works, most notoriously with the publication of the *Syllabus of Errors* by Pius IX in 1864. This reflected the experience of dealing with anti-clerical liberals, especially in Italy. At the same time the Catholic Church took maximum advantage of the opportunities provided by liberal regimes in countries such as the Netherlands and the United Kingdom. Above all, tolerant liberal polities provided the opportunity to create exclusive Catholic social domains, first and foremost in education, and extending (as local circumstances dictated) to the organization of work and pastimes. With numerous local variations, the emergence of a clerically controlled Catholic schooling system is one of the standard themes in the history of religion and of Greater Ireland.

In and out of Ireland or Greater Ireland the collective presence of Catholicism in liberal states is inseparable from issues pertaining to education. These issues arose most frequently from the fact that the Catholic Church sought not only to have an education system of its own but also to have the state pay for it. Liberalism comes in many varieties. Anticlerical liberals intent on keeping the Catholic Church out of schooling posed a serious problem for Rome in many European countries but not in Ireland. More significant in the context of the United Kingdom were those liberals who are quite content to allow faith groups to take their own initiatives in education but who object strenuously to the allocation of public funds in support of these. Another ambiguity within liberalism is also relevant here. In Ireland and the Empire, Catholic ecclesiastics by the second half of the nineteenth century could invoke "our liberties" in making demands for state support for schooling. What they had in mind, of course, was the liberty of the collectivity rather than the rights of individuals. Several questions about the nature of state liberalism in Ireland are illuminated by Colin Barr's authoritative study of the affair of Father Robert O'Keeffe of Callan, County Kilkenny, in the early 1870s. Whatever the instincts of individual politicians might be, there would be no Irish *Kulturkampf*: within his own sphere Cardinal Cullen could triumph to his heart's content; and an individual Roman Catholic who recklessly stood before his car need not expect the state to intervene.[15]

In Ireland the various denominations colonized a state-funded elementary school system first introduced in 1831 and originally intended to be non-denominational.[16] The state thus found itself inveigled against its wishes into funding denominational schooling. Otherwise, the objectors to public funding of denominational institutions in Ireland largely held sway. When concessions were made on this front it was almost invariably by Conservative governments. Thus it was Robert Peel's administration that increased the state grant to Maynooth College in 1845. But the publicly funded Queen's Colleges announced in the same year were to be strictly non-denominational. In reaction, the Catholic Church set out on the course that led to the establishment of the Catholic University over which John Henry Newman presided in the mid-1850s.[17] The lessons from this experiment included a stark reminder of how little could be achieved in the area of higher education without government charters and funding. This was the backdrop to the hopes reposed in Gladstone in 1868 and to the failure to find an accommodation on the issue, resulting in the breakdown of the alliance in 1873 and the definitive switch of the Catholic collectivity towards expressly nationalist politics. At issue in 1873 was the failure of the proposed new scheme to endow the Catholic college that it would have allowed to come into existence, sharing membership of Dublin University with the long-endowed Trinity College. It was clerical pressure, and specifically the determination of Cardinal Cullen, that forced the Catholic Liberal MPs to vote down the university legislation.

The Protestants of Tone's triad, of whom he proclaimed himself to be one, were the members of the established Church of Ireland and accounted for approximately 10 percent of the population. Belonging to an establishment, they by and large feared change and they were generally associated with opposition to the United Irishmen and their rebellion. Despite their relatively small numbers overall, they included the preponderance of the ruling elite in landownership and the professions; a significant proportion of the urban population, especially in Dublin; and farmers scattered thinly over much of the country but in significant numbers in County Armagh and in Mid and West Ulster. In 1795, conflict related to competition among smallholders for land led to the formation of a fraternal association in County Armagh. This was named the Orange Order and, thus, aligned with the revolution of 1688–89, which secured Protestant liberty, and against the more recent revolution in France, the reverberations of which were emboldening Catholics and Presbyterians in Ireland to imagine the overthrow of established power and privilege. By 1800, the Orange Order was well established, with headquarters in Dublin, and many of its members, along with other Protestants, opposed the Act of Union on the basis that it was an attack on the established system that they intended to defend.

One of the more remarkable aspects of Irish politics in the early part of the nineteenth century is the alacrity and thoroughness with which Protestants became ardent supporters of the union that they had initially feared. The alliance of the Whigs/liberals with the Catholics in the 1820s and 1830s propelled members of the established church into the Tory/conservative camp. In particular, most landlords saw the policy embarked upon by the liberals in the 1830s as deeply inimical to the landed interest, even if it did have the support of Whig grandees. The Act of Union had united the established churches in England and Ireland, but by the 1830s the security that that arrangement promised was being undermined. Under the legislation of 1833,[18] the number of bishops was greatly reduced and the management of ecclesiastical property was subjected to statutory intervention. This interference with the ancient establishment was seen as the crossing of a line. The act was a sop to

Irish Catholics and to British utilitarians anxious to see some progress towards the reform of public institutions. Meanwhile, a campaign of resistance to the payment of tithes was under way in various parts of the country, supported in several instances by lay members of the established church. Legislation of 1838 secured the tithes but on a new basis that did little to secure their legitimacy.

The national primary school system established in 1831 was designed to be even-handed as between denominations. This was seen by many Protestants as the state's abandonment of its duty to give preferential support to the catechesis of the church established by law. Having failed to achieve satisfactory changes in the system, churchmen in 1839 set up the Church Education Society. For over two decades this body maintained schools that were independent of the national system and provided scriptural education on its own principles. This created the somewhat anomalous situation of an established church raising funds to conduct a voluntary school system and then demanding state funding to be provided alongside the state aid already being made available to the national system. The national education system posited the neutrality of the state as between the contending confessional entities. This was not merely a loss of advantage for the established church, it amounted to a threat to its raison d'être. Being established implied identification with the state, and it also involved possession of the country's ecclesiastical endowment, including historical church property and substantial holdings in rent-bearing land and tithes. That the church so endowed had the allegiance of only about 10 percent of the population was not a problem in the heyday of privilege, but by the second decade of the nineteenth century there was a utilitarian attitude abroad that made life less comfortable for those sitting on benefices of any kind.

Coincidentally, or perhaps not, the Protestant churches of Europe were experiencing a wave of fervour and renewal in the name of evangelicalism. The confluence of factors induced a significant number of Protestant bishops in Ireland to support a campaign, led by small pressure groups with substantial funding from English evangelicals, to convert the general mass of Irish Catholics to Protestantism. While such missionary efforts would continue through the century, the certain failure of the attempt at mass conversion was already clear by the late 1820s.[19]

So, in the course of that decade, both a Catholic lay leader (O'Connell) and numerous Protestant churchmen had stated a claim to predominance for their respective collectivities. A century later, these attitudes were expressed in the political partition of the country. But that was no ineluctable progression, and the rejection of coexistence was not by any means the dominant attitude on either side for most the nineteenth century. What did endure was an intensive on-the-margins competition for "souls." Protestants initially had advantages when it came to providing nurture, material and spiritual, for the destitute and the orphaned, but these advantages were eventually cancelled out by the resources marshalled on the Catholic side by newly burgeoning religious orders. Under the arrangements made by the Poor Law legislation of 1838 there was some scope for conflict, but by and large the Union and the workhouse served, like the national schools, to place the state as an even-handed agency between the rivals.

Among rich and poor, a prime arena for contention over adherents was that of the children of mixed marriages. Because of the control that the sacrament of Penance gave the priest over the conscience of the individual penitent, something with no parallel in the Reformed churches, the Catholic Church had a unique advantage in this area. Its policy was to discourage mixed marriages, preferably through prior conversion of the partner of the other faith, and, when a mixed marriage did occur, to place an onus on the Catholic partner to ensure that any children were raised as Catholics. A papal document on the canon law of marriage, the decree *Ne Temere* of 1907, came to be seen as the epitome of Catholic intransigence, but, in fact, an intransigent policy had been in place in Ireland for generations, and only a little acquaintance with relevant sources, such as the 1901 census returns for households of religiously mixed parentage, is required in order to realize how effective it was.

Just as supporters of the papacy in the mid-nineteenth century could not envisage how Catholicism might survive the loss of the Papal States, so contemporary Irish Protestants were convinced that the disestablishment of their church would lead to calamity. Under the terms of the Irish Church Act, 1869, the church lost its historic endowments but on the basis of generous compensation for existing benefice holders and grantees. The transition to voluntary status as the reorganized, self-governing Church of Ireland, effective from 1871, was traumatic but orderly. The change had little impact on political loyalties. The axe of disestablishment had been wielded by Gladstone, confirming the decades-old conviction that the Liberals were inimical. In 1870, the government legislated for land tenure changes that alienated the disproportiately Protestant landowning aristocracy. In response to these blows from Westminster, on 1 September 1870 a small number of Protestants organized by the lawyer Isaac Butt formed the Home Government Association. Revamped in 1873 as the Home Rule League it was, ironically, the vehicle to which most of the former Catholic Liberals, disillusioned in their turn with Gladstone, resorted for the purposes of the general election of 1874.

The third of Tone's confessions, the Presbyterians, also about 10 percent of the population but concentrated in the northeast, were sometimes categorized as Dissenters, that description also including smaller groupings besides, especially the Methodists, who played a role out of proportion to their numbers. Presbyterians had been disadvantaged, but not to the same extent as had Catholics, under Ireland's ancien régime. They were granted formal "toleration" in 1719 but were excluded from Parliament for much of the eighteenth century. Their ministers did enjoy state-funded incomes under the provision for the Regium Donum. This annual and ultimately discretionary payment gave the government some leverage. Following the Union the amount was increased, but its application was changed in such a way as to impose more constraint on individual ministers.

Among the professional and commercial cadres of the Presbyterians, particularly in prosperous Belfast, the revolutionary ideas of the United Irishmen had flourished in the 1790s. Their divines were notoriously fractious on theological questions, and these had political as well as religious implications, although liberal religious views did not imply liberal political views. The grim outcome of the 1798 rebellion, into which liberal/radical views had led sizeable numbers of Presbyterians, placed conservatives at an advantage. Like the Established Church, the Presbyterians experienced the strong influence of evangelicalism and were put on the defensive by the Catholic mobilization of the 1820s.

The theologically and politically conservative Reverend Henry Cooke (1788–1868) annoyed many of his fellow Presbyterians by advocating political subordination to the Anglicans for the sake of a united front against the forces of Catholicism.[20] In fact, the relationship between Protestants and Presbyterians is an interesting example of collectivities acting as one against an external enemy without surrendering much at all of their separate ethos and interests. Mutual antagonism would wax and wane with changing circumstances. David Hempton identifies the function of a common evangelicalism in smoothing interaction between nineteenth-century Presbyterians and Anglicans.[21]

However, Irish Protestants and Presbyterians were close to unanimity only on the questions of maintaining the Union and of resisting the threat of Catholicism. There would always be a significant liberal element among the Presbyterians, and, as town dwellers or tenant farmers, where they dominated in parts of East Ulster, Presbyterians would always maximize their socio-economic interests at the expense of the landed classes.[22] Nevertheless, for the purposes of the country's political aspirations, Tone's triad had been reduced not to unity but to two communities of interest, the Roman Catholics and the Reformed (the latter generalized as the "Protestants"). This polarization solidified through the second and third quarters of the century. Both, on occasion, displayed the capacity to claim dominance in the land, but by and large they practised a suspicious, sometimes hostile, mutual toleration. In the final quarter of the century they would be drawn into gargantuan conflict over two great non-religious issues – land ownership and home rule – but without losing much, if anything, of their long-standing confessional shape.

The Irish Land War began at the end of the 1870s in response to the collapse of food prices internationally and poor harvests at home. Irish farmers seeking compensatory rent reductions were encouraged by the Irish National Land League, a body with ulterior political motives, to frame their claims in terms of a rejection of landlord rights on historical grounds. Most Catholic tenants, over a period of a year or so, came to subscribe to the Land League, with its combined program of agrarian and political objectives. That is to say, an anti-landlord plank was incorporated into the existing ideology of the Catholic collectivity. Significantly, Catholics who had no direct material interest in the fortunes of tenant farmers, such as town dwellers and agricultural labourers, were drawn into the campaign of the Land League, which thus succeeded in achieving identification with the wider collectivity as a national project that demanded allegiance. The Land League evolved in the early 1880s, with little change in its constituent parts, into a political party, the National League, under the leadership of Charles Stuart Parnell, the formal objective of which was Home Rule – that is to say, the restoration of the Irish Parliament.

Meanwhile, Presbyterian and Protestant farmers had been obtaining whatever concessions they could from their landlords and generally looking to their financial advantage but conspicuously ignoring the social and political agenda of the Land League. Landlords throughout Ireland lost economic and social clout as a consequence of the agricultural crisis of the period between 1877 and 1882. In the areas where the Land League held sway selected landlords and the society that surrounded them were subjected to a kind of ritual humiliation that extended to the police and many of the agencies of the law and social institutions, even to the pastime of foxhunting. In most of Ulster, in areas of Presbyterian and Protestant dominance, there was no violent rejection of the institutions of landlordism and no comparable antagonism against individual landlords. Accounts from the west and the south of the lawless hostility and social ostracization directed against persons, the most prominent of whom were in most cases Protestant, created a sense of outrage. The perpetrators, for their part, were motivated by the resentment against an entrenched ruling elite typical of a time of social revolution. It would be difficult to exaggerate the extent to which the Land War polarized attitudes and exacerbated animosity.

The Protestant Thomas Davis had, in the 1840s, articulated an inclusive ideology, harking back to Tone, that would put "the common name of Irishman" in place of the Catholic nationalism of O'Connell's movement. As editor of the weekly *Nation*, founded in 1842 by supporters of O'Connell's Repeal campaign, he was operating firmly within one collectivity, and he made little impact on the other one. He was successful, however, to the extent that, in his own day and over the following generations, a small number of Protestants was enabled to adhere to the Catholic collectivity and its projects not as being Catholic but as being national. John Mitchel is a prime example. So, too, is Parnell. But the National League was inseparable from the Catholic interest, as exemplified by the fact that, in 1884, the Catholic bishops entrusted it with the task of defending their educational interests in Parliament. Parnell had prepared the way for this by an opportunistic denunciation of the Queen's Colleges, a touchstone of political Catholicism.[23] Insofar as the National League cultivated grassroots, they were set down on the basis of the Catholic parish framework, and parish priests figured prominently in its parliamentary selection meetings.

A movement as polarizing as that around Parnell was likely to provoke a reaction in like mode. The Orange Order played a role throughout Ireland during the Land War, with volunteers from its Ulster stronghold sallying forth to the assistance of landlords under pressure from the Land League. When Gladstone, now reliant on Home Rule MPs for a majority in the House of Commons, announced in 1886 that he would legislate for Home Rule for Ireland, the Protestant/Presbyterian block saw its greatest fears realized. It now definitively adopted the moniker of Unionism, and, under that banner, there was great mobilization in opposition to Home Rule. Resistance by force was adumbrated, the memory of the Glorious Revolution was invoked, ideas of British nationality were adumbrated, and the menace of subjugation to the power of the pope in a Catholic-dominated Home Rule Ireland was evoked. There was nothing in the attitudes of either side to facilitate accommodation. A political system increasingly responsive to the votes of a democratic electorate had little scope for the promotion of compromise. Home Rule involved the willingness of the Home Rulers to accept a subordinate role for an Irish parliament with respect to Westminster. Such compromise was possible for a nationalist movement in the age of empires. What a nationalist movement could not do was to concede any diminution of majority power within the national territory. Unionism could not contemplate accepting a subordinate role as a minority in a self-governing Ireland because it, too, had taken on the characteristic intransigence of a nationalist movement, except that its nationality was British and its imagined national territory was not confined to one island.

The defeat of the Home Rule bill in June 1886 deferred the crisis until the second Home Rule bill in 1893 prompted another round of mobilization before it, too, was defeated. The two decades that followed witnessed a drastic decline in the formal, economic, and social position of the landed class as ownership of a large proportion of farms was transferred to the occupiers. This meant that Unionism and the Protestant body politic were drastically weakened as a presence outside of the northeast. Over these decades universal state (and thus formally non-denominational) mechanisms were enhanced throughout the land, especially in the arena of local government. At another level the separate systems of Catholic and Protestant existence were thriving. As a matter of course, when they could Catholics and Protestants gave jobs to their own, whether the employment was in private enterprises or in publicly funded institutions or local authorities. An act of 1908, after elaborate negotiations designed to reconcile Irish religious demands with the sensitivities of Liberals, provided the long-sought solution to the universities question. There would be three technically non-denominational universities under implicit denominational control: Trinity College Dublin (not formally dealt with in the act) for Protestants, Queen's University Belfast for Dissenters, the National University of Ireland for Catholics. The Irish language revival movement, initially of interest to many Protestants, became in the new century an emblem of Catholic nationalism. Ostensibly it provided an alternative quintessence for the definition of nationality. In fact, the cohort so thoroughly immersed in it, which seized leadership of Irish nationalism in 1916, was probably the most devoutly and uniformly Catholic grouping in Irish political history. But, by international standards, there was nothing exceptional about all this confessionalization.

Meanwhile open conflict between the two collectivities remained dormant until the conjuncture of forces at Westminster made legislation for Home Rule feasible in 1912. The turmoil that followed demonstrated that the passage of time had not brought any prospect of a resolution and had enhanced the attractions of territorial partition. The outbreak of the Great War provided an opportunity to prevaricate, but nothing that followed made the issue any more tractable, and the Government of Ireland Act, 1920, eventually provided for the creation of two polities.

Patently, the intention was to create two entities in each of which there would be a secure politico-religious majority. This remained the case when, following the negotiation of the Anglo-Irish Treaty in 1921, division of the island into Northern Ireland and Southern Ireland was replaced by division into Northern Ireland and the Irish Free State. In line with the Wilsonian spirit individual rights were formally protected, and privilege on the basis of religious affiliation was outlawed. But, as elsewhere in the new Europe, religious minorities in each part of Ireland (a small Protestant one in the south, a much larger Catholic one in the north) were expected to knuckle under to the ethos of the majority. A prime minister of Northern Ireland could declare frankly that his was a Protestant parliament for a Protestant people. Leaders of various parties in the South, however tolerant of Protestants as individuals, would have no hesitation in asserting that theirs was a Catholic country. For almost half a century the minorities in both polities were, in their different ways, deferential collectivities, however unhappily so.

Irish Jews, numbering fewer than four thousand in the census of 1911, have been too few in number for their community to have become a separate actor in the confessional contests discussed here. Nonetheless, they have a noteworthy place in the story of migration into and out of Ireland. Many of them came to Ireland in the later nineteenth century because they believed it would be better for them as Jews than were the lands they had left, usually located in Eastern Europe. Similarly, over a few generations many of them may have left Ireland because they believed that, as Jews, they could do better somewhere else.[24] However, like the great majority of all creeds emigrating from Ireland, most who left did so on the basis of calculations about individual and family welfare.

By way of balance, one should probably not conclude an exposé of Irish confessional division and its dynamics without considering, if only in passing, the commonalities of religion on the island. It may indeed be the case that, in early modern and modern times, the population of Ireland, behind its various competing confessional identities, participated generally in a common complex of assumptions about the preternatural context of everyday life. The convention of thinking that the Catholic poor, the supposed bearers of subcutaneous pre-Christian, even exotic "Celtic," tradition, had a monopoly on superstition is highly questionable. Raymond Gillespie explores superstition among early modern Irish Protestants.[25] William Butler Yeats did not discover the world of fairy lore as an emerging poet seeking to connect with the folkish past; already, as the child of a middle-class Protestant family in Sligo in the early 1870s, he had been immersed in an ethos of ghosts, banshees, and haunted houses.[26] Belief in magic, curses, cures, and the malevolent attentions of an underworld not known to the Christian churches was part of a common customary culture. Historians of Ireland pay scant attention to this because it carries so little by way of implication for the identities that mark out the socio-political landscape.

If the common superstition of the Irish commands limited interest, the same holds true of their overwhelming adherence to a common Christianity. Discussion of what it meant to be Christian in Ireland at any point from the early sixteenth century onwards is difficult in a landscape marked out for contest between adherents of Rome and the various communities of the Reformed. Nigel Yates makes a valuable intervention with his comparative study of the three ecclesiastical establishments in the period from 1770 to 1850.[27] Much remains to be done to discover to what extent, apart from adherence to early credal formulae, there has been any commonality to the experience of being a Christian in modern times across the Irish denominations, either in Ireland itself or abroad. By comparison with Germans of any denomination, Spanish, Greeks, or Russians, did not all Irish denominations in recent centuries have some things in common with one another – not least in their cultural impact as evangelizers of foreign lands? If so, what might these be? Adroitness in dealing with the state? A focus on schooling? A puritanical sense of religion as restricting rather than fulfilling? Impoverished church music? Ecclesiastical buildings, notably capacious but frequently dull and generally gesturing hopefully to the Gothic revival for inspiration? It may be that study in the global setting will descry some such similarities. But these will be commonalities across a great divide rather than features of a shared confessional or ethnic identity.

NOTES

1 For their comments on an earlier version of this I am grateful to Liam Kennedy and Miriam Moffitt.
2 Akenson, *Irish Diaspora.*
3 Ibid., 3.
4 Especially Akenson, *Small Differences.*
5 This trope is explored in Miller, *Emigrants and Exiles.*
6 Kenny, "Diaspora and Comparison," 145n18.
7 Miller, *Ireland and Irish America.*
8 See Barr, "Imperium in Imperio."
9 Anderson, *Imagined Communities.*
10 Wolfe Tone, *An Argument on behalf of the Catholics of Ireland,* reproduced in Moody, McDowell, and Woods, *Writings of Wolfe Tone,* 1, 124.
11 Keogh, *"French Disease."*
12 Bergin et al., *New Perspectives on the Penal Laws.*
13 Leighton, "Gallicanism and the Veto Controversy."
14 Ridgway, *Morpeth Roll.*
15 Barr, *European Culture Wars in Ireland.*
16 Akenson, *Irish Education Experiment.*
17 Barr, *Paul Cullen.*
18 The Church Temporalities (Ireland) Act, 1833 (*3&4 Will. IV,* c. 37).
19 Whelan, *Bible War in Ireland;* Moffitt, *Society for Irish Church Missions.*
20 Holmes, "Henry Cooke," 2, 813–14.
21 Hempton, *Religion and Political Culture,* 111.
22 The situation is well illustrated in Purdue, "Poverty and Power."
23 Lyons, *Charles Stewart Parnell,* 253–5
24 On the Jews in Ireland, see Ó Gráda, *Jewish Ireland in the Age of Joyce.*
25 Gillespie, *Devoted People.*
26 Foster, *W.B. Yeats: The Apprentice Mage,* 20–1.
27 Yates, *Religious Condition of Ireland.*

2

Drawing Strength from Past Migratory Experiences: The *Church of Ireland Gazette* and Southern Protestant Migration in the Post-Independence Period

LEIGH-ANN COFFEY

"Our regret has often been that emigration takes the cream of our people, and we have often found the answer to our regret in thinking that a Christian Church should give its best."[1] This statement, the conclusion of an editorial entitled "The Church of Ireland Emigrant" published in the *Church of Ireland Gazette* in December 1927, neatly captures the ambivalent response of many Irish Protestants towards the issue of emigration in the early twentieth century. For Irish Protestants, particularly those in southern Ireland, the loss of community members through emigration was a significant source of anxiety, and the concerns of the Church of Ireland community only intensified following the upheavals of the revolutionary period.[2] A minority in the newly created Irish Free State, southern Protestants struggled in the years after 1921 to adapt to the social and economic implications of their dwindling numbers, especially in isolated parishes in the south and west of the island.[3] Yet the Church of Ireland had traditionally expressed great pride in the accomplishments of Irish Protestants abroad, and it continued to admire the efforts of the settlers and missionaries who represented the Irish Church and its members across the globe after the revolution.

In the aftermath of the revolution, southern Irish Protestants in the Free State were forced not only to consider what role the Church of Ireland and its teachings might play in an independent Irish state but also to re-examine their own personal identities and allegiances. Fiercely loyal to the British monarchy and the Empire, southern Protestants worried about the tenuous nature of the ties that bound the Free State to the rest of the British Commonwealth. The issue of emigration assumed a central role in discussions over the future of the Church of Ireland and the fate of minorities in the Free State. Emigration doubtlessly represented a threat to the strength and influence of the Church in Ireland, but the movement of southern Protestants abroad helped to reinforce the Church of Ireland's influence within the wider Anglican community and the British Empire.

This chapter examines the communal narratives that emerged within the Church of Ireland community concerning migration in the immediate post-independence period. Of particular interest are attempts within the official publication of the Church of Ireland, the *Church of Ireland Gazette,* to portray emigration in a more positive and reassuring manner, primarily by considering the experiences of the southern Protestant community within a broader historical context. In the pages of the *Gazette* clergymen and lay observers alike encouraged their fellow church members, especially those who believed that Protestantism was under attack in the Free State, to find comfort in the history of their community and in the accomplishments of earlier generations of Irish Protestant emigrants. The loss of large numbers to emigration was not necessarily a sign of weakness on the part of the Church of Ireland, it was implied, but, rather, was the result of the Church's ongoing mission within the Empire to preserve and to transmit the values and principles that constituted the core of Irish Protestantism. Furthermore, it was argued that past migration had not destabilized the community but, rather, had reinvigorated the Church in the homeland, as the Church had embraced its membership within a wider spiritual empire.[4] While the southern Protestant minority might face considerable challenges in the Free State as a result of its declining numbers, Irish Protestants were encouraged to identify with a broader Church of Ireland community that transcended boundaries of geography and generations, and to celebrate "signs of vitality" in the Church of Ireland wherever they might occur.[5]

Given the difficulties facing southern minorities in the early twentieth century, the uncertainty felt by members of the Church of Ireland regarding their survival in the Free State is hardly surprising. Following the violence of the revolutionary period, southern Protestants found themselves in a state in which they differed from the majority of the population not only in terms of religious beliefs but also in regard to political allegiances. While leading Free State politicians hastened to assure members of the Church of Ireland that they were welcome to remain in the Free State, declaring that sectarian discrimination and criminal harassment would not be tolerated, some Protestants continued to express concerns regarding the vulnerability of their community. Struggling to preserve religious and political identities that were at odds with the values championed by the new state, while simultaneously witnessing the loss of church members due to emigration, many southern Protestants could not envision a future for themselves or their families in Ireland.

It is only recently that the revolutionary experiences of southern minorities have attracted widespread scholarly interest. The resulting arguments regarding the nature of the War of Independence and the Civil War, particularly the question of whether southern Protestants were deliberately targeted during the revolution, have in turn directed the attention of historians to the issue of southern Protestant migration.[6] Writing in 2000, Enda Delaney notes that, in studies of migration in the twentieth century, "the question of the relationship between sectarian violence (and threats of violence) and patterns of migration is a sensitive subject which is often neglected in standard accounts of Irish history."[7] Currently, however, the decline of southern minority populations during and after the revolution is one of the foremost topics in a wider scholarly debate that shows little sign of waning.

For some commentators, the high rate of Protestant emigration appears to confirm their belief that Protestants and other minorities faced considerable discrimination and hostility during the revolution and its aftermath. Desmond Bowen, for example, draws attention to the issue of "forced cultural conformity" in the new state.[8] Others insist, however, that issues unrelated to sectarian discrimination and violence were far more likely to explain the decision of so many Protestants to leave Ireland. Delaney, for instance, acknowledges the significance of Protestant fears and uncertainties in the Free State but warns against exaggerating the impact of revolutionary violence on the decision of individual Protestants to leave Ireland.[9] Kurt Bowen, meanwhile, draws attention to the many economic factors that contributed to Protestant emigration in the years after 1922, writing of the stagnant economy in the post-independence period as well as the displacement of labourers and small farmers as a result of changing farming techniques.[10] In a recent study on Protestant emigration, Andy Bielenberg concludes that, "while it is important to acknowledge the impact of revolutionary violence and terror on minority emigration, it is also important to recognize a wider spectrum of forces at work in this period, which were collectively far more significant in explaining the scale of the exodus."[11]

Scholars seeking to bolster their position regarding the decline of southern minority communities have been obliged to carefully examine the available evidence related to Protestant emigration, and important work has been accomplished in studies that consider the issue from both local and national perspectives. Such studies have helped to build a profile of those who left and their destinations, while providing a more accurate timeline of Protestant emigrant departures. Yet there is a danger that southern Protestants are being considered solely in terms of their conflict with the nationalist majority; the motives and identities of those who perpetrated attacks on minority communities are as often the focus of attention as is the impact of violence and marginalization on the southern Protestant population. In the context of southern Protestant emigration, scholars must be wary of overlooking what the community itself had to say about the issue. Emigration had a significant emotional impact on the southern Protestant community in the Free State, with individual views on the topic determined by personal experiences within families and the wider community. Furthermore, although the early twentieth century undoubtedly witnessed increased challenges and struggles for the southern Protestant community, it is important to remember that emigration was not a new phenomenon within the Church of Ireland population. Even prior to the revolution there existed within the community strategies through which southern Protestants could come to terms with emigration and its effects on the community.

The trials and tribulations facing the Protestant minority in the Free State were readily acknowledged by Church of Ireland clergymen in sermons and written reflections in the years after 1921.[12] However, the Reverend Dudley Fletcher was not alone in observing in the *Church of Ireland Gazette* that "there is a brighter and more hopeful side to the picture."[13] The writings of commentators who insisted that they were not unduly concerned with the survival of either the Church of Ireland or of Protestantism itself in the Free State frequently appeared in editions of the *Gazette* published throughout the 1920s.[14] These letters and editorials urged southern Protestants to draw strength from the history of the Church of Ireland, noting that the church was both an integral part of the Irish nation and that it had "weathered worse storms than the present," emerging from each period of crisis stronger than before.[15] A number of contributors to the *Gazette* emphasized the importance of considering recent population trends within a broader historical context; population decline was not a new challenge for the Church of Ireland community, it was argued in at least one editorial, yet so far the church had successfully continued its work in Ireland.[16] Another editorial in the *Gazette*, published in 1926, states confidently: "We face best what is modern when we feel most what is ancient. The Church of Ireland is no ephemeral shade, destined to give transitory protection to a modern branch of another Christianity ... Rather it abides from age to age to proclaim with prophetic voice, to whosoever will, that a greater than Jonah is here; and for the furtherance of this mission it ought to safeguard its genuine historical credentials."[17] The survival of the Church of Ireland was not an accident, its members agreed. "God has not preserved this Church of Ireland through 15 centuries to let it peter out ignominiously in our times," Reverend Bolton C. Waller asserts in a paper that was republished in the *Gazette* in 1932. He adds that, "if its member have those qualities which this nation and the world needs, courage and steadfastness, truthfulness and righteousness, readiness to spend themselves for the common good, above all, faith and trust in God ... then, in the Providence of God, there will be a better day for the Irish Church and for the Irish nation."[18]

In their efforts to strengthen their own identity as Irish Protestants, while arguing for the continued relevance of the church in the Free State, southern Protestants sought to reaffirm their commitment to the values and principles that they believed constituted the foundations of the Church of Ireland. These principles, particularly freedom of conscience, were not necessarily unique to the Church of Ireland and were acknowledged to be part of the church's Protestant heritage.[19] It was this heritage that was understood to set Protestants apart from the majority in the Free State, however. And, at a time when other episcopal institutions were perceived to be faltering in their devotion to the reformation tradition, members of the Church of Ireland believed that they had an obligation to stand firm in the defence of the values and traditions that they had inherited from earlier generations.[20] While southern Protestants might be divided as to how best to secure the future of the Church of Ireland in the Free State, the community was unanimous in its agreement that the preservation of the values associated with the church was of the utmost importance.

By focusing on the values associated with the Church of Ireland and its historic mission, southern Irish Protestants developed a framework through which they could come to terms with the issue of emigration.

Just as members of the Church of Ireland turned to the past for inspiration while seeking to reaffirm their commitment to the values and traditions of their community, emigration was often viewed in the context of the history of the church, with an emphasis on the accomplishments of past generations of Irish Protestant emigrants. Those who sought to present a more positive account of the Protestant diaspora encouraged the community in Ireland to redirect its attention away from the homeland to the wider Anglican communion and to the British Empire, both of which had greatly benefitted from the efforts of earlier generations of Irish Protestant emigrants. A number of contributors to the *Gazette* insisted that these institutions were not competing with the Church of Ireland for the allegiances of Irish Protestants; they had been established and supported by past generations of church members, it was argued, and were furthermore essential to the church's mission of propagating its teachings to a wider audience.

Although concerns regarding the detrimental impact of emigration on minority communities continued to be voiced by members of the Church of Ireland, others advocated for a more positive understanding of emigration, and their position was clearly stated in the pages of the *Gazette* throughout the 1920s and 1930s. Editorials and published sermons insisted that not all Protestants who had left Ireland in the past had done so unwillingly. Throughout the years many had voluntarily undertaken difficult work in the furthest reaches of the globe, and their contributions to the growth of the Anglican community was testament to their unwavering commitment to the values and traditions associated with their faith. The *Gazette* celebrated these pioneers in a series of articles that were published after the establishment of the Irish Free State. In 1929, for example, the life and work of Charles Inglis from Donegal was brought to the attention of *Gazette* readers. Inglis had been the assistant rector at Trinity Church in New York at the time of the American Revolution, before travelling north to join his fellow loyalists in exile during the war. He was appointed Bishop of Nova Scotia in 1787, making him the first bishop of a British colony. The *Gazette* made much of Inglis's family contributions to the Church of Ireland and praised him for his bravery during the American Revolution, when he refused to abandon his principles. As an exile in Nova Scotia, Inglis had remained dedicated to establishing a strong Anglican presence in Canada, despite the harsh conditions he encountered in his work.[21]

While immensely proud of their community's historic ties to the wider Anglican flock, members of the Church of Ireland were at the same time keen to underscore their Irish heritage and the unique characteristics of the Church of Ireland. Perhaps not surprising in an institution that traced its roots back to Saint Patrick himself, adherents of the Church of Ireland strongly resented suggestions that their church was subordinate to the Church of England, and, likewise, they viewed attempts to minimize Irish contributions to the global Anglican community as a direct attack on the Irish Protestant population. "It is one of the pieces of real service which the Church of Ireland has rendered to the Kingdom of God outside Ireland, that it has for many years produced and equipped numbers of Churchmen who have done, and are doing, excellent service in every quarter of the Anglican Communion," the *Gazette* proudly stated in 1924.[22] In the same edition, the *Gazette* criticized another publication for daring to suggest that Irish Protestants who had chosen to leave Ireland thereby showed little loyalty to the church of their birth; instead, it argued that the values and worldview of past generations of emigrants were firmly rooted in their Irish experiences.[23] Trinity College in particular was commended in a number of editions of the *Gazette* for its role in sending out generations of churchmen educated in Anglo-Irish values and also for its success in cultivating strong ties between its graduates abroad and the homeland.[24] The *Gazette* similarly praised the past contributions made by nameless clergymen, missionaries, and lay settlers to the development of episcopal churches abroad, and it was also careful to acknowledge the efforts of past generations of Protestants in Ireland who had provided invaluable support for missionary efforts overseas.[25]

The work of past generations of Irish Protestant emigrants in establishing a strong Anglican presence overseas also served to reinforce the boundaries of the British Empire. The mutually beneficial relationship that existed between the Empire and the Protestant churches was acknowledged and celebrated in the pages of the *Gazette*. It was suggested in a letter published in the spring of 1931, for example, that Empire Day in the following year should be used to commemorate all that the Empire had done for "the one International in which the world can find peace and salvation, the free Catholic Church of Christ."[26] According to commentators in the *Gazette*, the historic efforts of Irish Protestants to establish and maintain the Empire were entirely consistent with the mission of the Church of Ireland. British rule brought peace, prosperity, and freedom to subject nations, according to members of the Church of Ireland, and many of the values associated with Irish Protestantism, such as justice, tolerance, and individual freedoms, were also linked in the minds of the minority with Britain and its Empire.[27]

So strong was the popular association between Protestantism and the Empire that, in the early twentieth century, southern Irish Protestants did not always explicitly distinguish between "imperial" and "Protestant" identities and allegiances. In the years after 1921 many embraced an "imperial Irish" identity for their community in place of the obsolete "unionist" label.[28] R.B. McDowell describes the southern minority as "exhilarated by the imperial ideal," and the *Church of Ireland Gazette* certainly reflects the minority's desire to firmly position their community at the heart of the imperial tradition.[29] Letters and editorials in the *Gazette* suggested that the Church of Ireland had encouraged a wider worldview from the very beginning of its existence, with Saint Patrick himself described as, "in the highest sense of the word, an Imperialist, a lover of large Order."[30] Turning to more recent contributions made by Irish Protestants to the British Empire, the *Gazette* insisted that the Irish "had taken a conspicuous part in the building and fashioning of the Empire."[31] As soldiers and administrators, settlers and clergymen, Irish Protestants had travelled to every corner of the Empire, where they had "played a leading part in the work of civilization and peace which has been done by that group of peoples who are known as the British Empire."[32] The southern minority was rightfully proud of its contributions to the Empire, stated one editorial, having "furnished their quota towards the foundation and preservation of what are now constellation of great free societies."[33]

For a number of commentators in the *Gazette*, "these great free societies" represented not only an enduring legacy for past generations of Irish Protestant emigrants but also the future of the Church of Ireland. It is important to note that the interest of the southern Protestant population in the history of their church and its community did not necessarily arise out of a desire to avoid acknowledging the difficulties they faced in the post-independence period. Some elements of the southern minority did indeed seek refuge in the past. In his autobiography, Brian Inglis describes how the unionist community in Malahide refused to accept the changing social and political landscape in Ireland, ignoring the treaty settlement and attempting to carry on with their pre-1921 routines in defiance of the new state.[34] However, it appears that, for others within the southern Protestant population, the history of the Church of Ireland and its people provided a useful framework through which they could examine and come to terms with their own experiences. For those leaving the country, affected by the emigration of family members, or concerned about the impact of emigration on the community, references to earlier generations abroad provided comfort as well as valuable knowledge of popular destinations.

Drawing attention to the past held a number of advantages for a community that was struggling to maintain unity and an optimistic outlook in the aftermath of the revolution. As a means of creating some distance between their audience and the contentious topics under consideration, commentators in the *Gazette*, seeking to reassure the Church of Ireland community that it would survive in the new Irish state, frequently began their observations with allusions to the past. By grounding their arguments in the history of the community, they were also seeking to legitimize their positions. Most of the sermons, letters, and editorials in the *Gazette* that referenced earlier generations of emigrants did so in fairly broad terms; it is likely that the authors of such pieces were operating on the underlying assumption that their audience was already aware of the contributions that had been made by previous generations of Irish Protestant emigrants to the worldwide Anglican communion and to the British Empire. However, it seems that these generalized statements were not always intended to be the focus of the letters or editorials in which they appeared, as observations regarding the Protestant diaspora and the history of the church frequently acted as a launching point for discussions regarding the position of the Church of Ireland in the Irish Free State and the issue of emigration in the post-independence period.[35]

Preaching in November 1923, for example, the Reverend G.A. Chamberlain delivered a sermon to his congregation that was later republished in the *Gazette*. He acknowledged the uncertainty facing the community in the Free State and their disappointment in the treaty settlement. The Irish Protestant community had long supported the Anglo-Irish Union and Ireland's place in the Empire, he noted, and it was understandable that they would feel lost and betrayed following the creation of the Free State. However, he urged his listeners to find comfort in the inheritance of imperial Irishmen. Values such as "justice, liberty, order and toleration," which lay at the heart of the Empire, would live on, and there was no reason that southern Protestants could not remain loyal to the values that previous generations of Irish Protestants had embraced in Ireland and nurtured elsewhere. With this sermon Chamberlain vocalized a position promoted by the *Gazette* throughout the 1920s and 1930s: the way forward for the southern Protestant minority was to identify the values of the church that had sustained past generations and to find ways of incorporating these values into daily life, whether one remained in Ireland or emigrated elsewhere.[36]

Above all else, contributors to the *Gazette* emphasized the past in the hope of encouraging their readers to envision the southern Protestant community in a global context. Such an understanding of the community was not only intended to bring hope to the Protestant population remaining in the Free State: it also reflects the church's desire to reinforce ties between Irish Protestant emigrants and their homeland. The "imperial Irish" identity cultivated by the church aided its members in accepting the realities of the post-1922 period; the southern minority was attracted to this label because it was compatible with the terms of the treaty settlement while at the same time it allowed Irish Protestants to emphasize the values they associated with their faith.[37] This imperial identity also permitted the southern minority to lay claim to membership in a larger community that extended beyond the shores of Ireland. In the eyes of the southern minority, the accomplishments of Irish Protestant emigrants over the past few centuries had not only brought honour to their church and homeland but had also laid the foundation for a worldwide imperial community that was united through shared culture and values.[38] This outlook lessened the disheartening impact of emigration on the Church of Ireland community and also allowed emigrants to move outside of Ireland with greater confidence in their identities as Irish Protestants and in their association with the British Empire. Such ideas were hardly original – as Jack White notes, Irish Protestants had long been "taught to regard the whole Empire as their homeland, so it was no great hardship to seek a new future in Canada or Australia" – but there was new-found interest in the imperial heritage of the southern minority in the years after 1921 as well as a greater emphasis on the cultural ties that permanently linked emigrants to the homeland.[39]

Although the primary readership of the *Gazette* consisted of the church population in Ireland itself, the journal took great pride in its role in connecting members of the Church of Ireland community across the globe. It regularly featured in its pages correspondence from Irish Protestants overseas who wished to provide different perspectives on affairs in Ireland and on the challenges facing the southern minority in the post-independence period.[40] Mindful of its international audience and also conscious that some of its readers in the Free State were contemplating a life abroad, the *Gazette* and its contributors occasionally assumed a somewhat moralizing tone when addressing the issue of emigration. The experiences of earlier generations of Irish Protestant emigrants were portrayed in such a manner as to provide inspiration and guidance for their twentieth-century counterparts. Editorials and sermons regarding the service of Irish Protestants to the church abroad or to the British Empire frequently romanticized the sacrifices and achievements of nameless church members, while biographies of prominent clergymen and politicians provided specific examples of the overseas accomplishments of southern Irish Protestants.[41] The articles relating to Charles Inglis, for instance, emphasized his unwillingness to renounce his allegiance to the Crown and Empire, which eventually led to his exile from New York. Despite the difficult conditions in which he laboured, however, Inglis never wavered in his commitment to the church and its community, leading a praiseworthy life built around the values of the church.[42] The message for the current generation of emigrants leaving Ireland was clear: wherever they might journey, whatever challenges they might encounter, they should aspire at all times to abide by the teachings and ideals of the Church of Ireland.

The Church of Ireland has long been credited with playing a key role in reconciling the southern minority to the terms of the treaty settlement in the years after 1921.[43] To counter pessimistic predictions regarding the future of Protestantism in the Free State, clergyman and the church hierarchy repeatedly reassured their congregations that the minority would not encounter discrimination in the new state, and they further insisted that the treaty settlement presented an exciting opportunity for Protestants to become fully engaged in Irish affairs.[44] Similar messages were conveyed in the pages of the *Church of Ireland Gazette,* with commentators arguing that negative or defeatist attitudes would not only fail to advance southern Protestant interests in the new state but would, in fact, result in the community's marginalization in the British Empire as well as in Ireland.[45] The use of the *Gazette* to convey a more positive narrative regarding the issue of the emigration was thus in keeping with wider efforts to raise the morale of the southern Protestant population.

While the church undoubtedly influenced the initial reactions of its members to the creation of the Free State, it had less success in convincing Protestants that they had reasons to be hopeful regarding their prospects in Ireland. Rhetoric rarely translated into action: although members of the minority were encouraged by leading churchmen to assume political and social roles worthy of their education, wealth, and experience in the years after 1921, for example, no Protestant political party emerged in the southern state and many Protestants opted instead to disengage from politics and society in the Free State.[46] In general, Protestants had accepted the treaty settlement, albeit reluctantly, on the advice of their community leaders, but their personal experiences in the aftermath of the revolution led them to become increasingly disillusioned regarding the future of the southern Protestant minority in the Free State.

With regard to the issue of emigration, however, it is important not to entirely dismiss the influence of the communal narratives recorded in the pages of the *Gazette* or to assume that such narratives did not accurately reflect the opinion of at least some individuals in the southern Protestant community. Contributors to the *Gazette* attempting to portray Protestant emigration in a more positive manner by emphasizing the historical context of the Church of Ireland's involvement in the Anglican community and the British Empire were familiar with their intended audience. They appreciated the need to create a persuasive argument that would successfully challenge pessimistic predictions regarding the future of the community in the Free State. The narrative they created in the pages of the *Gazette* identified two themes in particular that strongly resonated with southern Protestants in the post-independence period – the importance of communal ties and enthusiasm for the church's historic mission to propagate its teachings to a wider audience. Although these issues were discussed primarily in the *Gazette* in a historical setting, they also exerted considerable influence over the southern Protestant emigrant experience in the early twentieth century. While contributors to the *Gazette* might have discussed emigration and the Protestant community in somewhat abstract terms, there is evidence to suggest that the narrative they produced accurately reflected southern Protestant views and experiences.

A number of contributors to the *Gazette* who wrote on the issue of emigration agreed that the Church of Ireland drew strength from its members abroad, although there has been little acknowledgment in recent scholarship of the ties that bound southern Protestants emigrants to the community they left behind. Yet sources other than the *Gazette* appear to confirm that, in addition to whatever comfort was provided by the abstract notion of a global community, emigrants did provide practical support for the southern Protestant community in the Free State in the upheavals that followed the revolution. In the late 1920s, for example, Irishmen and women in the Free State who could produce evidence that they had suffered financial losses during the Irish Civil War as a result of their loyalty to the British regime were eligible for compensation from the Irish Grants Committee (IGC). Close to four thousand individuals, many of them members of the Church of Ireland, contacted the London-based committee between October 1926 and February 1928, and in the tens of thousands of documents submitted to the IGC in support of their claims, applicants provided evidence of the existence of a global network of Protestant Irishmen and women. Many applicants from the Free State wrote of their reliance on financial assistance from family members and friends living overseas. In several such cases, the applicants, recognizing the possible advantages of emigration for the wider community, had initially provided the funds for these same relatives and friends to meet the costs associated with relocation.[47]

Southern Protestants living abroad also provided information and advice to their co-religionists who were contemplating leaving Ireland or who had recently departed. A number of applicants to the IGC described how their plans to emigrate were based on information supplied by family members and friends abroad, and it was not uncommon for those who left Ireland to find employment and accommodations through networks of church members already established in other parts of the world.[48] The *Gazette* itself was occasionally a source of such information; while many of those who contributed to the *Gazette* from abroad were concerned primarily with current affairs in Ireland, some also sought to provide practical advice for Protestants emigrating from the Free State. Through letters and articles, overseas contributors described the conditions that existed in regions throughout the Empire, listing the skills that would be required of settlers in rural Australia, for example, or warning of the harsh environment found in the Canadian Prairies.[49]

Such examples of communal co-operation are not in any way unique to the southern Protestant population in the post-revolutionary period; the transmission of information within local communities, the act of emigrants providing financial support to individuals remaining in the homeland, and the phenomenon of chain migration are patterns of behaviour associated with any number of emigrant groups, including Irish Protestants prior to 1921. However, it does appear from available sources that southern Protestants viewed kinship and communal ties with greater respect in the aftermath of the revolution. The events of the early twentieth century had taught them to be wary of depending on support from those outside of the community, while shared experiences during the worst years of the revolution had tested and reinforced bonds between family members, neighbours, and friends. This growing emphasis on communal ties influenced the nature of southern Protestant emigrant experiences: individuals who left Ireland faced expectations that they would continue to support the Church of Ireland and its community in the Free State and abroad, a community they were tied to through kinship ties and a shared Irish Protestant heritage. By reminding readers contemplating a life abroad of their duty to their church and its community, the *Gazette* played a key role in reinforcing these expectations.

As with the growing emphasis on the importance of communal ties, the Church of Ireland community appears to have become more concerned with the preservation and propagation of the values associated with Irish Protestantism in the years after the revolution. "A Church which is not a missionary Church is a dead or dying Church," proclaimed the *Gazette* in 1932, and the growing enthusiasm of the Church of Ireland population for official missionary work undertaken by clergy and laypeople overseas was such that it was remarked upon by contemporary observers.[50] Returning to Ireland in 1927 after years abroad, for example, an unnamed missionary commented in the *Gazette* that he was much struck by the changing attitude of the community. He spoke approvingly of the "more general appreciation of the responsibility of the Home Church for work overseas" demonstrated by Irish Protestants and praised the desire of church members to become more active participants in the global Anglican community.[51] While only a small portion of the church population was directly involved in missionary work overseas, the *Gazette* made considerable efforts to incorporate the missionary ideal into the lives of its readership, reporting on mission work in each of its editions, and encouraging church members to contribute financially to Anglican missionary organizations. Furthermore, as previously acknowledged in this chapter, contributors to the *Gazette* urged emigrants to view themselves as part of the wider historic missionary movement, encouraging them to imitate earlier generations of Irish Protestant migrants who had cultivated the teachings of the church throughout the Empire.

It is not surprising that the official journal of the Church of Ireland would champion missionary work abroad or that it would encourage emigrants to view themselves as representatives of their church and its values. Yet on further reflection the attraction of the church's mission for lay emigrants in the post-independence period is obvious. At a time when many were leaving Ireland due to economic and political circumstances beyond their control, emigrants could reclaim a degree of agency by promising to uphold the values of their church and by contextualizing their departure from Ireland within the wider historical tradition of service to the church overseas.

Testifying to the powerful appeal of the church's historic mission for lay emigrants, individuals alarmed by declining Church of Ireland numbers in the Free State also attempted to incorporate the missionary ideal into their own arguments.[52] While such commentators agreed that the Church of Ireland community had a mission to share its values with the global population, they argued that the southern Protestant community could not lose sight of the need to fulfill its duty in its homeland.[53] As early as 1924 an editorial in the *Gazette* declared, "Her [the Church of Ireland's] mission today is to the Ireland of to-day," while the work undertaken by members of the Church of Ireland community in the Free State was frequently described in terms commonly associated with the experiences of clergymen and settlers abroad.[54] Referring to the "semi-colonial conditions" faced by those undertaking the work of the Church of Ireland in the western counties of the Free State, for example, the Bishop of Kerry likened these scattered church members to "settlers in a new country."[55] It appears, however, that, while the missionary ideal might have provided comfort to individuals leaving the country, it was not as successful in convincing Protestants to remain in the Free State. Throughout the 1920s and 1930s the *Gazette* published letters and editorials written by individuals lamenting the decline of Protestant numbers, particularly among the younger generation, and it was asked how the church could maintain its position and continue "to bear [our] witness to the Truth and Liberty that is in Christ Jesus" if the community could not retain "church members in the country of their birth."[56]

Emigration remained a cause for concern among the southern Protestant population throughout the twentieth century, and efforts within the community to portray it in a more positive light could not disguise the realities of the Church of Ireland's minority status in the new state. As years passed after the treaty settlement, many southern Protestants became more outspoken regarding their opposition to emigration and actively sought to discourage members of the Church of Ireland from leaving the Free State (and later the Republic). At the same time, southern Protestants could not deny the existence of the close relationship between the Church of Ireland and other branches of the Anglican Church in the Empire, nor would they renounce their imperial allegiances. For a community that had long prided itself on its international outlook, and which believed that its wider worldview provided a much needed counterweight to the parochialism of the dominant nationalist culture in the independent Irish state, it was difficult to accept that what its members perceived to be one of its greatest strengths was also a considerable weakness.

Only by turning to the past and regarding their current situation within its wider historical context could southern Protestants attempt to reconcile the contradictions that lay at the heart of their community. The blurring of lines between the church's historic mission to propagate its teachings and the movements of twentieth-century Protestant emigrants, as well as the emphasis on the common cultural background of Protestant Irishmen in the Free State and abroad, demonstrates how southern Protestants were encouraged to envision their community in a way that transcended boundaries of time and geography. At a time of great uncertainty for the southern Protestant population, such an understanding of the Church of Ireland and its community provided both a comforting sense of continuity and a promise of endurance.

NOTES

1 *Church of Ireland Gazette*, 16 December 1927.

2 The term "revolution" is used throughout this chapter to describe the events of the 1919–23 period, namely, the War of Independence and the subsequent Civil War.

3 Unless otherwise stated, the term "Protestant" as used in this chapter refers to members of the Church of Ireland. Although a minority of the overall population of Ireland (approximately 13 percent) prior to partition, the Church of Ireland population constituted the largest non-Roman Catholic religious community in the south of Ireland, and in Ireland as a whole, in the early twentieth century. According to the 1911 census, for example, approximately 50 percent of non-Catholics in Ireland belonged to the Church of Ireland. In the three southern provinces of Ireland, however, this number rises to approximately 82 percent.

After the revolution, the Church of Ireland remained the dominant non-Catholic institution in the south; 74 percent of non-Catholics in the Free State described themselves as belonging to the Church of Ireland in the 1926 census. Following the partition of the island and the creation of the Free State, however, members of the Church of Ireland were increasingly conscious of their minority status. In the 1926 census the Church of Ireland population constituted only 5.5 percent of the total population of the Free State. In addition to coming to terms with its minority status, the Church of Ireland also had to cope with the loss of large numbers of its community. Between 1911 and 1926, the Church of Ireland lost approximately 36 percent of its population, or 93,320 of its members, in the twenty-six southern counties.

This population loss was not distributed evenly throughout the island. The provinces of Munster and Connaught suffered considerable losses compared to Leinster, for example, and urban communities throughout the Free State tended to be more vulnerable to declining Protestant numbers. It is also important to acknowledge that there was considerable internal migration occurring within the Free State throughout this period. The revolution appears to have reinforced an existing trend of Protestant movement towards the suburbs of Dublin, for example: by 1926, 33 percent of the Free State Anglican population lived in the Dublin area, leading R.B. McDowell to dub this region "the new Pale." See McDowell, *Crisis and Decline*, 4.

Census material from Vaughan and Fitzpatrick, *Irish Historical Statistics*. For statistics and analysis of declining Protestant numbers during the revolutionary period, see Bielenberg, "Exodus." See also Bowen, *Protestants in a Catholic State*, 20–31; Delaney, *Demography, State and Society*, 70–3; White, *Minority Report*, 10–13.

4 Alan Megahey has observed that Irish Presbyterians developed a similar approach to the issue of emigration in their own community. See Megahey, *Irish Protestant Churches*.

5 *Church of Ireland Gazette*, 21 December 1928.

6 For an account of the continuing controversy surrounding the works of Peter Hart and other scholars who have addressed the treatment of minorities during the revolution, see Bielenberg, "Exodus", 200–2.

7 Delaney, *Demography, State and Society*, 70.

8 Bowen, *History and the Shaping of Irish Protestantism*, 393.

9 Delaney, *Demography, State and Society*, 73.

10 Bowen, *Protestants in a Catholic State*, 37–40.

11 Bielenberg, "Exodus," 232.

12 For examples, see *Church of Ireland Gazette*, 11 November, 23 December 1921; 29 June, 17 August 1923.

13 *Church of Ireland Gazette*, 17 August 1923.

14 See, for example, *Church of Ireland Gazette*, 23 December 1921; 29 June 1923; 14 June 1929; 24 March 1933.

15 *Church of Ireland Gazette*, 17 August 1923. See also *Church of Ireland Gazette*, 23 October 1925; 18 March 1927; 20 July 1928; 16 August 1929; 22 July, 14 October 1932; 1 February 1935.

16 *Church of Ireland Gazette*, 23 August 1921; 11 April 1924; 27 August 1926. According to the *Gazette*, the Protestant population had begun to decline following the Famine, and the events of the revolutionary period had simply intensified existing trends (*Church of Ireland Gazette*, 17 August 1926). This observation has been confirmed by a number of recent academic studies on long-term Protestant population trends in Ireland. See, for

example, Liam Kennedy's study on the Protestant population in County Longford in his *Colonialism, Religion and Nationalism.* Enda Delaney also warns against viewing Protestant decline solely in the framework of the 1911–26 period. See Delaney, *Demography, State and Society*, 70–95.

17 *Church of Ireland Gazette,* 5 February 1926.

18 Ibid., 20 May 1932.

19 Ibid., 30 December 1921; 7 April, 12 May 1922; 23 October 1925; 28 May, 9 July 1926. Desmond Bowen argues that, "at the heart of the Irish Protestant tradition is an abiding conviction, which has indeed become an integral part of its 'faith' – the 'right of individual freedom in matters of religion is among the dictates of the law of nature." See Bowen, *History and the Shaping of Irish Protestantism*, xi.

20 For examples of how values set the Protestant population apart from their Roman Catholic neighbours, see *Church of Ireland Gazette*, 11 November, 23 December 1921; 18 January 1924; 23 October 1925; 21 January 1927; 2 August 1929.

21 *Church of Ireland Gazette,* 3 May, 27 September 1929.

22 Ibid., 25 April 1924.

23 Ibid.

24 Ibid.; see also 5 November 1926; 11 May 1934.

25 See, for example, *Church of Ireland Gazette,* 23 March 1923; 14 October 1932.

26 *Church of Ireland Gazette,* 22 May 1931.

27 Ibid., 21 September 1922.

28 Ibid., 21 September 1922; 23 November 1923; 9 May 1924. For a consideration of the significance of the "imperial Irish" identity, see also Bowen, *Protestants in a Catholic State,* 34.

29 McDowell, *Crisis and Decline,* 21.

30 *Church of Ireland Gazette,* 18 March 1927.

31 Ibid., 21 September 1922.

32 Ibid., 5 June 1925.

33 Ibid., 9 May 1924.

34 Inglis, *West Briton,* 12.

35 See, for example, *Church of Ireland Gazette,* 13 January 1922; 9 May 1924; 5 June 1925; 5 November 1926; 6 May 1932.

36 *Church of Ireland Gazette,* 23 November 1923.

37 Ibid., 21 September, 23 November 1923; 9 May 1924; 22 May 1925; 29 January 1932.

38 Ibid., 2 October 1936.

39 White, *Minority Report,* 10.

40 *Church of Ireland Gazette,* 21 April 1922; 31 December 1925; 31 May 1929; 11 April 1930; 22 May 1931; 4 March 1932; 28 July 1933.
41 For an example in which it is explicitly stated that Irishmen who served in the army abroad were to serve as an inspiration for future generations, see *Irish Times,* 19 June 1923, for a speech by the Archbishop of Dublin.
42 *Church of Ireland Gazette,* 3 May 1929.
43 Bowen, *Protestants in a Catholic State,* 47, 55; White, *Minority Report,* 96.
44 See, for example, *Church of Ireland Gazette,* 3 August 1923; 18 January, 11 April, 12 December 1924; 21 January 1927; 19 July 1929; 15 January 1932.
45 Ibid., 20 September 1929; 8, 15 January 1932.
46 D'Alton, "Vestigial Population"; White, *Minority Report,* 92–4.
47 See, for example, CO/762/07/49; CO 762/23/300; CO 762/34/506; CO 762/71/1159.
48 See, for example, CO 762/05/27; CO 762/11/90; CO 762/59/903.
49 *Church of Ireland Gazette,* 11 April 1920; 13 February 1921; 28 July 1933.
50 Ibid., 6 May 1932.
51 Ibid., 14 October 1927. See also ibid., 5 June 1925; 5 November 1926.
52 Concerns over declining Protestant numbers became more common following the publication of the census material in 1929. See, for example, *Church of Ireland Gazette,* 22 February, 1 March, 8, 29 November 1929.
53 *Church of Ireland Gazette,* 16 March 1923; 19 December 1924; 11 September 1925; 27 September 1929; 6 May 1932.
54 Ibid., 19 December 1924.
55 Ibid., 12 June 1925. See also ibid., 3, 13 October 1922; 25 September 1925; 25 February 1929; 31 January 1930.
56 Ibid., 19 December 1924; 27 September 1929.

3

Religious Texts for the Catholic Migrant: International Print Networks and the Irish-Australian Book Trade

KEVIN MOLLOY

In studying the development of nineteenth-century print culture and its international networks a number of important factors need to be addressed: first, processes related to the production, dissemination, and reception of printed works – the books, newspapers, and other printed ephemera that constitute the essential components of a complex information or communication circuit; second, the impact of socio-economic forces that impinge upon and ultimately determine the commercial viability of these printed products.[1] In the nineteenth century the various factors that shaped the workings of such information circuits, and the networks that sustained them, varied considerably between communities and across nation-states. Consequently, any posited "production distribution continuum" contains within it a range of complexities that is central to the investigation of developing nineteenth-century colonial societies.[2] For example, for the Irish and Catholic migrants in nineteenth-century Australia and their multi-generational descendants, the ready availability of Catholic and Irish literature relied on a very sophisticated and commercially viable book import trade rather than on the development of local printing and publishing initiatives. This situation differed markedly from other New World societies, such as the United States and Canada, where a considerable Catholic migrant population ensured a ready market for the Boston-, Montreal-, and New York-based Catholic and Irish publishers such as Patrick Donohoe, D. & J. Sadlier & Co., P.J. Kenedy, and Louis Benziger. Such was the strength of local demand for their religious publications that it was only from the 1870s that many of these companies entered the international market in any significant way. The situation is different again in the case of Ireland, where major publishers of Irish national and Catholic devotional works, such as James Duffy and M.H. Gill of Dublin, from the outset engaged with large Irish Catholic populations outside of Ireland to sustain their multiple publishing activities.[3]

It was the economics of international printing and publishing, combined with very efficient distribution systems, that saw the importation into Australia of affordable, commodified, mass-produced texts from Britain, Ireland, and North America. The initial focus of the import trade in Australia was New South Wales and Victoria, colonies with well-defined Irish settlements and a market for a transnational Catholic and Irish literature.[4] While this chapter examines the book-trade practices in both colonies, it should be noted that centralized distribution systems in the Australian colonies enabled Irish Catholic book importers in Sydney and, later, Melbourne to supply the colonies of South Australia, New Zealand, and Queensland over many decades.[5] In assessing the significance of the Catholic religious book trade this chapter examines the international networks that operated between Irish and Catholic publishers in Ireland, Britain, and North America; evaluates what categories of books were being imported into the Australian colonies and in what numbers; and considers why religious works were so important to those Irish working in the book import and retail trades.

The nineteenth-century book trade in Australia saw the rise of multi-skilled individuals working and developing a book import and distribution system; such individuals, described by historian Robert Darnton as effective "cultural agent[s],"[6] multi-tasked in bookselling, printing, publishing, finance, importation, and, often, the newspaper industry, many being at one time newspaper publishers, proprietors, or editors. Through the advertising record and recorded business activities of some of these booksellers, such as Jeremiah Moore and Edward Flanagan in Sydney, and Bernard King and Joseph Winter in Melbourne, we can ascertain their degree of involvment in, and control of, the Australian Catholic book market and can begin to reconstruct their part in fostering a global Irish reading community and its considerable networks – a reading community that lies at the heart of the ethnic cohesion found in many nineteenth-century Irish Catholic settlements.

This study draws upon a select number of newspapers with an Irish and Catholic readership that were published between the years 1839 and 1848: the *Australasian Chronicle* (1839–43), the *Morning Chronicle*

(1843–46), and the *Sydney Chronicle* (1846–48). In addition, it draws upon three of the more enduring newspapers dating from 1850: the *Freeman's Journal* (Sydney) (1850–), the *Advocate* (Melbourne) (1868–), and the *New Zealand Tablet* (1875–), again newspapers with a readership that was primarily Irish and Catholic and that published consistently over the latter half of the nineteenth century and well into the twentieth.

Current evidence suggests that Irish print culture had a global presence, that it was not confined within the boundaries of one nation-state, and that it did not have a single centre of origin. As such, a transnational approach to the study of the Irish Catholic book trade and its reception is vital for a clear understanding of its contours in a nineteenth-century world characterized by mass migration and technical transformations in printing, publishing, and transportation. Coupled with this was the revolution in Irish devotional practice,[7] rising literacy levels for the younger Irish population, and a book production of Catholic and Irish nationalist literature that catered to their perceived needs.[8] While commercial circumstances varied between nation-states and colonies, publishers for the Irish colonial world – especially in Dublin and London – came to rely on an international market for their product, one that was largely sustained by an Irish Catholic migrant community and their descendants.[9] In 1864, the international reach of the Dublin publishing company James Duffy was noted,[10] and certainly surviving correspondence from the 1880s by another Dublin publisher and bookseller, Michael Gill & Sons, testifies to a large and well-patronized export market that included North America, Argentina, Australia, and New Zealand.[11] Similarly with the principal Irish American Catholic publisher D. &. J Sadlier, operating largely out of Montreal and New York but also with outlets in Boston and Toronto. Advertising copy indicates that the export trade from these outlets reached to Ireland, Argentina, and Australia, Sadliers' establishing an agent in Sydney in 1874, an event that coincided with the appearance of Sadlier publications in advertised book lists and, in the colonies, the start of the newspaper serialization of works from the celebrated Irish Canadian-American novelist Mary Anne Sadlier, who was, in effect, managing much of the New York arm of the company from 1860.

The first fully documented initiative discussing the possibility of importing Catholic devotional and other religious works to Australia is recorded in 1810, when Irish political transportee Michael Hayes, in writing to his brother Richard in Dublin, noted the lack of books for

Irish Catholics and their families in Sydney and the surrounding districts: "the Catholics here are destitute of prayer and other religious books. Three thousand or more prayer books would be required as well as catechisms for the children born here."[12] Despite Hayes's knowledge of the Dublin book trade and some of its key personnel,[13] his scheme was never realized. Nevertheless, in the intervening years between 1810 and 1840 the market for Hayes's Catholic literature in New South Wales and Van Diemen's Land did not diminish. Irish Catholics were proportionally a significant cohort in the evolving colonial world, making up 30 percent of the population of New South Wales by 1837, and were, in effect, a market-in-waiting when the Sydney book consignment trade began in the 1840s and books for the "Catholic population of Sydney" began to be advertised with increasing frequency.[14]

What evidence we do have from the end of the Napoleonic War to the mid-1830s, years when the colony lacked direct clerical leadership, confirms the devotional nature of religious practice – the lending of devotional texts, the reading of devotional works at house meetings, and the use of devotional objects. In a climate of financial and legal constraints until the passing of the Catholic Relief Act, 1829, and its extension into New South Wales, the majority Irish of Catholic persuasion had no independent publishing presence in the colony until the appearance of the *Australasian Chronicle* in August 1839, the printing presses of which were used to print and publish the first very limited number of Catholic books in the colony. As early as 1837 Australia's first appointed bishop, the Benedictine Bernard Polding, sympathetic to the position of Ireland and the Irish Catholic population of Sydney, had noted, in the newspaper the *Colonist*, that Catholics had no publishing presence in New South Wales.[15] While his comments refer specifically to the desire for a Catholic newspaper, the need for the dissemination of both newspapers and Catholic books to counter ethnic and denominational prejudice was not lost on figures like Benedictine Bernard Ullathorne and some of those Irish emancipists who organized and funded the *Australasian Chronicle* from 1839.[16] Polding was keenly interested in devotional literature being made available to the Irish Catholic population in the colonies and had personally shipped devotional books to Irish Catholics in the settlement in North Auckland, New Zealand, soon after his arrival in 1835.[17] In 1840, he was also responsible for making devotional books available for use in a small lending library attached to a local Catholic school in central Sydney.[18]

The first recorded advertising of Catholic literature began in Sydney in early 1840 under the direction of William Augustine Duncan and was conducted from the office of the newspaper the *Australasian Chronicle*. After the demise of his bookselling and printing business in Aberdeen, and a brief period spent as a teacher, Duncan, with his wife and family, emigrated from Scotland to New South Wales in 1837 as one of ten teachers recruited by Bernard Ullathorne, who had gained funding from the British Colonial Office to help with Catholic education in the developing colony.[19] On arrival Duncan began teaching in Maitland, publishing the first of a number of important colonial pamphlets on Catholicism and the freedom of religious expression.[20] It was because of his education, his writing abilities, and his knowledge of the printing and publishing business that Duncan was approached in 1839 by Reverend John McEncroe and his Irish compatriots to assume the editorship of the projected newspaper the *Australasian Chronicle*.[21]

A close reading of the first years of the *Australasian Chronicle* reveals a judicious, contemporary, and well-written newspaper, engaging with current social, religious, and political views; literary in outlook; and supportive of a Catholic cause but wary of Irish separatism in the context of the Catholic position in New South Wales (which the publication was ostensibly advocating). Duncan was keenly aware of the need for a Catholic literature and set about ordering large numbers of books from the Catholic publisher Charles Dolman of London.[22] The practice of importing and retailing books from the newspaper premises was continued by Michael D'Arcy from 1843, after he had ousted Duncan from the editorship of the *Australasian Chronicle* and had renamed the newspaper the *Sydney Chronicle*. D'Arcy continued importing from Dolman in London, but he wrote to his brother in Clonmel in 1845 that there was no dedicated Catholic bookseller in Sydney and that he was currently contacting James Duffy and Co. in Dublin to begin importing books. This was the first such contact from Australia.[23]

The Sydney Catholic community of the 1840s contained a number of notable individuals engaged in book importation, bookselling, newspaper copy-editing and printing, small-scale publishing, auctioneering, and the operating of circulating libraries. Figures include Michael D'Arcy, William Duncan, Jeremiah Moore, Peter Joseph Cregin, Church of Ireland engraver William Kellett Baker, and, on the periphery, John Joseph Walsh. With the exception of William Duncan, who moved to Queensland for a period, all these individuals also operated at different times in Victoria and South Australia, the somewhat itinerant lifestyle of those involved in the book and print trades a reflection of the economic uncertainties of the period, as Michael D'Arcy's documentary letters certainly testify. Of the above figures only William Duncan and William Baker had previous printing and publishing experience, Duncan as a bookseller and occasional publisher in Aberdeen and Baker as a lithographer in Dublin. Jeremiah Moore's father was a Dublin grocer, and his profession was listed as cordwainer, or cobbler; Peter Cregin was a Birmingham farm labourer; Michael D'Arcy was a farrier and farm worker from Tipperary, having worked extensively with horses since his arrival in Bathurst in 1835; while J.J. Walsh, noted as a bookseller in Sydney and Melbourne, was brought up on his parents' farm in Galway and was also listed on immigration returns as a farm labourer.[24] However, what characterized all these figures was their literacy and ability to move almost immediately into bookselling and printing within a very few years of their arrival in the colonies. Associationalism is an important marker of acculturation and ethnic homogeneity,[25] and it was the capacity to successfully network through church and ethnic associations, both nationally and internationally, that distinguished these individuals. Their business activities in the fields of bookselling, publishing, and printing can be seen as both the direct result of their interest in Irish and Catholic affairs of the colonial world and the pursuit of its international Irish Catholic dimension. It can also be seen as a by-product of their social status as prominent business figures or ethnic spokespersons in their respective communities. This is something particularly of note with Michael D'Arcy and Jeremiah Moore in Sydney over the decades of the 1840s and 1850s, and with Melbourne newspaper proprietor, bookseller, and political activist Joseph Winter from 1860.[26]

Throughout the 1840s the importation of literature was by consignment, with the Catholic population being catered to by a number of general book importers and import-auctioneers.[27] The *Australasian Chronicle*, the *Morning Chronicle*, and the *Sydney Chronicle* newspapers detail consignment auctions given by a number of entrepreneurs, including the auctioneers J.K. Heydon, William G. Moore, and John Cohen, with many of their advertisements typically addressed to "the Catholics of Sydney." In addition, booksellers William Moffitt, Michael D'Arcy, and W.A. Duncan, along with printer and publisher William Baker, were sporadically importing some Catholic works.[28] These consignments came mostly from the publishers James Duffy in Dublin, Sims and McIntyre in Belfast, and Thomas Richardson in Derby.[29]

In New South Wales evidence suggests that most Irish and Catholic booksellers operating between 1850 and 1900 confined themselves almost exclusively to Catholic and Irish national literatures. Examples include Michael Dalton, who enlisted a clerical friend in Dublin to select his books from the publisher James Duffy; Edward Flanagan, who operated from the "Dublin Book Warehouse," subsequently publishing a number of important Australian religious works;[30] and James Hill, the former British Imperial Regiment staff sergeant from Armagh who ran "Armagh House," specializing largely in Catholic devotional literature but also retailing a general stock of books.[31] In the early 1880s, the partnership of Robert Hannigan and D.R. Mitchell, trading as Hannigan and Mitchell, entered the market as regular importers and retailers, operating from their "Irish National, American and Catholic Literature Depot" in the Royal Arcade.[32] From the 1890s, the Finn Brothers, and their successor, Louis Gille and Co., trading under church patronage as a religious goods warehouse and bookseller, dominated the New South Wales market and continued to do so well into the next century. The situation was largely similar in Melbourne, where Bernard King, Joseph Winter, and Richard Stanley dominated the Irish and Catholic book trade until the mid 1880s, with William Linehan beginning in the 1890s and trading until well into the twentieth century.[33]

The auction consignments and the occasional bookseller's shipment from Ireland and England to Sydney in the 1840s were mostly speculative consignments. It was not until 1850 that an invoicing system transacted through reputable banking establishments enabled entrepreneur bookseller-importers like Jeremiah Moore to put the Catholic Irish-Australian community on a sound footing when he established a regular monthly trade in Catholic literature between the publisher James Duffy & Co. of Dublin and his printing and bookselling firm J.J. Moore of Sydney.[34]

While most Catholic booksellers ran modest operations in the Australian colonies, dealing directly with a select number of publishers in Ireland and Britain, or working through local mercantile houses in Sydney, as did Michael D'Arcy,[35] some of the larger concerns, like J.J. Moore, worked through established London agents. In the late 1850s, Moore expanded his Catholic and Irish operations considerably, catering to all denominations and moving into general and educational literature, his Sydney business dealing with over forty different publishing houses in Britain, Ireland, and Europe. Evidence indicates that Moore, at this stage, utilized the services of the Sydney bookseller George

Robertson, dealing initially with Robertson's brother William, the company's London agent, and, later, Edward Petherick. From the 1870s, Petherick coordinated a complex operation for numerous Australian booksellers, covering purchasing, financial transactions, and shipping.[36] Commercial survival for large-scale but still niche publishing relied on the existence and maintenance of complex and reliable networks for the export of their product, and this became more so as the century progressed.

Nineteenth-century newspaper advertising detailing import and retail data for works directed at an Irish and Catholic readership show that religious publications were the most significant category, estimates indicating that, in New South Wales alone, Irish Catholic booksellers imported four religious books for every imported secular text.[37] Given the nineteenth-century British and North American demand for religious and devotional texts this is not at all unusual, work by English historian Simon Eliot revealing that, until late in the nineteenth century, British readers overwhelmingly consumed more religious works than any other genre. This was a situation that only changed after the 1890s when history and novel reading began to dominate the market in terms of reader preference. Similarly, conclusions suggest that, in terms of the purchasing of religious literatures, Irish and Catholic readers in the colonies had similar reading preferences to their British counterparts.[38]

By the end of the 1840s religious literatures, advertised in multiple subject areas, were more readily available then ever before, something noted by bookseller and newspaper editor Michael D'Arcy. After resigning the editorshop of the *Morning Chronicle* in 1846, D'Arcy had wanted to open a permanent bookshop in Sydney; however, in a letter to his brother in Ireland in October 1847, he lamented the fact that Sydney was "overstocked with Catholic books." Initially he considered sending his stock to Melbourne but ultimately decided on Adelaide, moving £400 worth of books and stationery to South Australia later that year.[39]

Of the books sourced from Irish and Catholic publishers in Ireland, Britain, and North America over the period between 1850 and 1890, texts referred to in advertising as "devotional publications" dominate the import lists. Other imported works, in much smaller numbers, included Irish and Irish American novels, works of history, political criticism, Irish oratory, poetry, and song books. Collectively referred to as the "national literature" of Ireland, the majority of these works also came from the publishing houses of James Duffy, M.H. Gill, or D. & J. Sadlier. Imported works were generally advertised in identifiable categories – devotional,

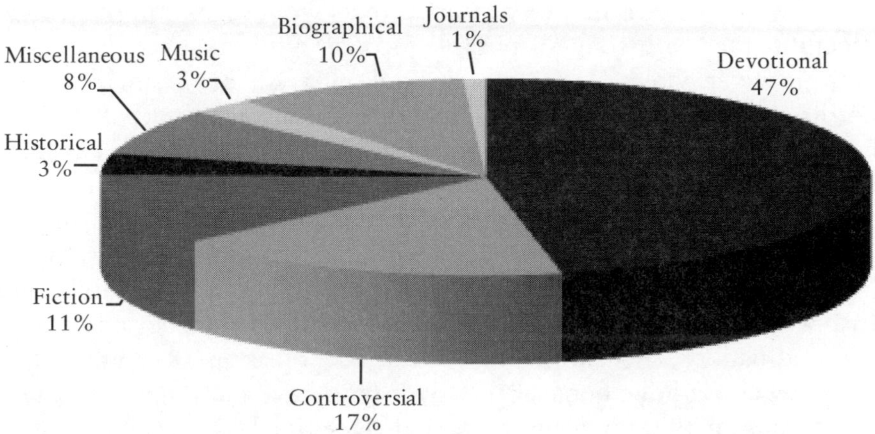

Figure 3.1 *Freeman's Journal* 1850–1900, advertised religious titles, by category number, and overall percentage.

controversial, biographical, historial, and national literature. Journals were listed separately, while religious ephemera, including cards and images, and devotional objects – beads, crucifixes, and other objects – were also noted.[40]

Devotional works included prayer books, breviaries, manuals, sermons, Marian texts, homiletics, testimonies, and liturgies. Controversial literature covered volumes of lectures, philosophy, theology, apologetics, biblical criticism, and religion and science by such well-known writers as Thomas Allies, James Balmes, Jacques-Bénigne Bossuet, Orestes Brownson, Jean-Baptiste Henri Lacordaire, Henry Edward Manning, John Milner, John Henry Newman, John Augustine Zahm, and the best-selling Nicholas Wiseman. Hagiography, memoirs, autobiography, and letters were listed as biographical, while historical works encompassed both religious and church history, with the works of such writers as John Lingard, Johann Dollinger, and Jean-Edmé-Auguste Gosselin listed in advertisements. Later categories include church music and religious fiction by authors like Georgina Fullerton, Clara and Rosa Mulholland, Thomas Potter, Christoph von Schmid, and F.M. Faber. In addition there were juvenile texts, translations, and a broad range of miscellanous works designed for the religiously inclined. While the majority of imported texts were in the English language, some were in French, and a very small number in Irish.[41]

It is clear that readers of the more advanced texts, the "controversial" literature, were more than likely to have been clergy or the educated lay reader, while the vast majority of other texts would have appealed to a general reader with some disposable income. With one exception, that of the insolvency records of Catholic bookseller William Dolman, we do not have the hard data on how much literature was imported. This is because business records have not survived. The Dolman insolvency records are instructive as they reveal both Dolman's local committments and international links. In addition, they give some indication of the imported numbers of religious texts for a medium-sized establishment. Dolman operated as a Sydney wholesaler and importer of Catholic and Irish works from Dublin, London, and New York. He had been previosly declared bankrupt when operating as an auctioneer in 1847 and is the only known Catholic bookseller in Sydney to have succumbed to bankruptcy during this mid-century period. Described as a well-educated Englishman, he was first cousin of English publisher Charles Dolman and was financially connected with the Dolman publishing house. The Dolman Publishing Company succumbed to bankruptcy in 1864 when Charles Dolman died in Paris, where he had moved the business. The firm was subsequently wound up,[42] with William Dolman's Sydney establishment filing for bankruptcy shortly afterwards. In a sworn deposition to the Supreme Court, William Dolman blamed the "dullness of the times," the "falling off in business," and the seizure of the *Freeman's Journal*, of which he was then proprietor,[43] and its disposal by the mortgagee under a bill of sale as the reason for his debts of nearly £1,000 owed to fifty-seven creditors.[44] Over one-third of this amount was due to the Derby booksellers and publishers Thomas Richardson and Sons. Detailed accounts for the years 1857 to 1860, produced at the creditors' meeting by Richardson's representative, plus additional purchases up to 1862, show that Dolman had imported over £800 in books, journals, devotional ephemera, and objects. The complete title list of imported stock, over seven hundred entries listing the importation of seven thousand books and objects from 1858 to 1860, consists overwhelmingly of devotional works – that is, prayer books, missals, sermons, some controversial or disputatious works, ephemera and religious objects, a smaller number of Irish works of fiction, and some miscellaneous titles.

Details from Dolman's accounts concerning the importation of religious texts can be favourably compared to data extracted from advertised newspaper bookseller lists. In analyzing the bookseller advertisements and changes in advertisements, we can estimate the genre percentages based on the persistence of advertised titles over many decades. For example, of approximately eighteen-hundred religious titles identified from bookseller advertisements placed in the *Freeman's Journal* (Sydney) between 1850 and 1900, 838 (46 percent) are devotional works, with controversial literature, that dealing with theology and apologetics, being the next largest category at 16 percent. It is the devotional texts, designed for prayer and reflection, that were the most popular and, over time, appear to be the most persistently advertised. Many of these texts have quite well-known and evocative titles, like *Key of Heaven*, *Garden of the Soul*, *Catholic Piety*, and *Path to Heaven*. More complex and expensive devotional texts included such titles as the *Ursuline Manual*. In Ireland James Duffy is credited with pioneering cheap texts, especially devotional works like the *Key of Heaven*, and a popular chapbook format.[45] Certainly, devotional texts were ubiquitous, being mass-produced in Ireland, as they were in England and North America, in a variety of formats, from the very cheap newsprint paper-wrapper texts to fine morocco- and calf-bound volumes. Exported internationally, such works found their way to English-speaking Catholic communities in Australia, New Zealand, and Argentina. Many of these devotional books were small – compact enough to fit in a breast or coat pocket, to make them easy to hold, often discretely, in the palm of a hand. They were primarily for internal reflection or private recitation during the saying of the Catholic Latin Mass, the words for which many in attendance may not have completely understood. Such books, as devotional objects, can be considered akin to other devotional objects such as the single- and, later, five-decade rosary beads, also often used for reciting devotional prayers during the Latin Mass. However, rosary beads and other devotional objects do not begin to make a major appearance in bookseller advertisements in Australia until the 1860s. The relative scarcity of such objects was noted in an advertisement in 1852, when the French missionary vessel *L'Arche d'Alliance* arrived in Sydney bringing crosses, medals, beads, and prints imported from France by Sydney bookseller Michael Dalton.[46]

Displaying a simplicity of language that, on occasion, heightened into poetry, a devotional prayer book was often the most basic of reading texts for meditation and contemplation or for silent reading during Mass services and other ceremonies.[47] Thus, William Gahan's *Manual of Catholic Piety, containing fervent prayers and pious reflections*, includes prayers for communion, confession, death, Mass; litanies for the sick, the saints, the dearly departed; prayers to St Brigid and prayers to the Holy Virgin. *The Garden of the Soul, a manual of spiritual exercises and instructions*, contains prayers for the morning, for Mass, confession, to prepare oneself for death, and exercises to examine one's conscience. Meanwhile *The Key of Heaven, a manual of prayer*, written by English divine John Milner, contains many of the above, in different forms, but also includes numerous devout prayers – that is, prayers in time of war, in time of famine, a prayer for rain, a prayer for fair weather, a prayer for the living, a prayer for those on a journey, a prayer for friends, and many more.[48] These are uncomplicated elementary texts, almost chapbook in nature, with language that is on occasion both stunning and powerful in its simplicity. They are designed to cover all facets of a person's life – a book that can be easily carried, quickly consulted, and easily concealed.

Religious texts, specifically devotional works, were among the first books to make an appearance in any numbers within the Irish communities of New South Wales, and they were also among the first books printed in Sydney for use by Catholics. Advertising and general notes from the *Australasian Chronicle*, the *Morning Chronicle*, and the *Sydney Chronicle* document both this ongoing importation and the modest efforts at local printing and publishing.[49] Examples of devotional works or instructional religious texts published in Sydney in 1840 on the newspaper presses at the *Australasian Chronicle* office in Pitt Street include such works as *A Short Catechism* (2s per dozen); *Life of Father Mathew*; *An Advice to Masters by a Catholic Priest*; *Wanderings of the Human Mind*, by the then Norfolk Island priest John McEncroe; and an edition of Challoner's *Garden of the Soul, A Manual of Prayers*.[50] Devotional works, both local and imported, were sold at prices that ranged between 2d and 30s,[51] the *Short Catechism* retailing for 2d, and the edition of *Garden of the Soul* retailing at 4s (obviously not a cheap edition). These *Australasian Chronicle* press texts were usually advertised by booksellers as "Colonial Publications."[52]

The Catholic devotional trade played a major role in the funding of secular printing. Surviving copies of nineteenth-century printers' worksheets from the Dublin publisher M.H. Gill show that thousands of volumes were produced in multiple editions for religious works, as compared to the Irish novels, memoirs, and histories also produced by that firm.[53] The devotional publishing phenomenon was the bread-and-butter aspect of the Catholic printing trade in France, England, Ireland, and North America: it ensured the survival of publishing houses like M.H. Gill and James Duffy in Dublin; D. & J. Sadlier and P.J. Kennedy of New York; and, of course, the booksellers in the colonies.[54] In the Australasian colonies the vast market for devotional texts reflected the type of religious practice of the majority of Catholics. Discussions on the Australian Irish in the Jesuit journal the *Irish Ecclesiastical Record* indicate that Irish clergy in Australia took a very dim view of the religious knowledge of Irish Catholics in the colonies,[55] especially noting their inability to articulate what they believed, as compared with their Protestant contemporaries. However, in the Irish Catholic immigrant mind, such things as articulating belief was willingly left to the clergy.[56] With only the occasional exception,[57] there was seemingly very little will on the part of immigrants and their descendents to move beyond a devotional religion. Consequently, Catholic religious practice in New South Wales, Victoria, and New Zealand remained in essence overwhelmingly devotional, something reflected in the advertised book lists and surviving bookseller trade catalogues.

One final point to be noted in the Australian Catholic book trade is the close association between the production and importation of religious and Irish national texts. In post-Famine Irish American fiction a number of writers both dominate the scene and are representatives of a generation of immigrants evolving and adapting in a New World environment. These include John Boyce and Hugh Quigley, both priests; Charles Halpine and David Power Conyngham, both ex-Irish American Civil War soldiers, Halpine a Union Army General; Maurice Francis Egan, a university teacher of English; Finley Peter Dunne, a journalist and newspaper proprietor; and Mary Anne Sadlier, also known as Mrs Sadlier, a translator, publishing proprietor, journalist, and newspaper co-editor.[58] Of the above, Boyce, Conyngham, Halpine, Egan, and Sadlier were readily available in the Irish Catholic bookshops throughout the Australasian colonies.[59]

Irish national texts occupy an important cultural presence in the advertising by Irish booksellers in the colonial world, and nearly all Sydney and Melbourne Irish and Catholic booksellers at one time or another signalled that their trade was in both Catholic and Irish national literatures. This is something noted from the 1840s, although it becomes particularly dominant during the turbulent years of the 1880s and the campaign for Irish Home Rule. In addition, the serialization of national literatures in the Irish Catholic press from the late 1860s became a major selling point for these newspapers, as it was for the mainstream press.[60]

One figure who succinctly brought these two aspects of Irish culture together was Mary Anne Sadlier.[61] Sadlier was a prolific writer and translator of some complexity, with works on fiction, devotion, prayer, and catechetics. In her personal life she was both a very public figure and extremely private, and certainly surviving letters from her son, Francis (Frank) Sadlier, indicate that, despite the fortunes of the Sadlier company, she was a tireless business operator and writer.[62] Sadlier dominated both book lists and the serial-story lists of newspapers like the *Freeman's Journal* (Sydney), the *Sydney Express*, and the *Advocate* (Melbourne). In any Irish Catholic book import lists it is impossible to ignore the presence of this Irish Canadian-American novelist. Emigrating from Ireland to Montreal in 1845, by the 1860s Sadlier had become a major presence in the Irish Catholic publishing world, not only through her novels, numerous religious books, devotional texts, and translations but also through her newspaper, the *New York Tablet*, and her role in running the New York arm of the Sadlier publishing company.

It was Sadlier's strong views on Irish Catholic culture, migration, the process of cultural adjustment, and ethnic formation in the New World that made her fiction so appealing to newspaper editors and to the colonial migrant reader alike. Sadlier was uncompromising with regard to Irish culture and the Catholic religion, Protestant proselytizing in Ireland and North America, and viewed emigration as ultimately detrimental to the survival of Catholic Irish culture. On sale in Sydney from 1854, Sadlier's works, such as her Famine novel *New Lights in Galway*; her emigrant fiction *Bessy Conway, or, the Irish Girl in America*; *The Blakes and the Flanagans*, which deals with the Catholic school issue and the loss of religion and culture; and her historical fiction, such as *The Confederate Chieftains*, documenting the life of Rory O'More, Irish nationalism, and the rebellion of 1641, are examples of works that were continuously in print and that retailed in both Australia and New Zealand until well into the twentieth century. Sadlier was one of a number of Irish American novelists, popular in both Australia and New Zealand, who tackled migration, urbanization, Irish culture in the New World, and the enduring importance of Irish Catholicism. In Sadlier's fiction, the merging of Irish nationalism and devotional Catholicism reach their apotheosis and can be considered seminal Catholic works in the nineteenth-century Australasian colonial world.[63] By the turn of the twentieth century, many of these works were again being recommended on approved reading lists – in the United States, Australia, and New Zealand – but this time in the young adult genre, signalling an interesting shift in texts that were once considered adult reading. The International Catholic Truth Society of New York listed thirty-two of Sadlier's novels and translations on its recommended reading list for young Catholics in 1901, including all her Irish Catholic works set in Ireland, Canada, and the United States.[64]

CONCLUSION

The book trade, as Leslie Howsam notes, is intrinsically commercial, hence bound to all the strictures of nineteenth-century print capitalism.[65] Whether dealing with books or other publications of ethnic, religious, or political import, success in the printing, publishing, and retailing world relied on a cost-effective product, efficient distribution networks, an understanding of reader preference, and, of course, disposable income with which to purchase the preferred product.

What this chapter endeavours to show is that the Catholic Irish in the Australian colonies initiated a regular trade in books through a process of direct contact with publishers in Ireland, England, and the United States, in many cases establishing their own import networks or utilizing existing networks for their own ethnic purposes. In a world in which the newspaper was the great facilitator of advertising and information exchange, and books the vehicles for the transmission of more complex ideas,[66] how the Catholic Irish in Australia accessed, developed, and utilized print helps us to understand the different ways in which these networks operated; how such networks facilitated contact locally and across national boundaries; and how they ultimately fostered a Catholic Irish ethnic cohesion both nationally and globally.[67]

For the Irish in Australia active engagement with the modern world required negotiation with a sometimes complex range of cultural, political, and religious allegiances. In mid-1880, the Irish Catholic newspaper the *Express* (Sydney) serialized the work of political activist, politician, and newspaper proprietor Alexander Sullivan. Echoing ideas similar to those of the Irish and Australian politician Charles Gavan Duffy, Sullivan's memoir, *New Ireland*, acknowledged the fundamental place of Greater Ireland in the new Irish cultural and political world. In travelling to the landscape of his youth in Glengariffe and Beara, and noting not just the linguistic change but also the complete cultural readjustment of the country, he commented: "Old Ireland … can now be seen no more"; "not there, but in Boston, and Milwaukee and San Francisco, c[an] be found the survivors … Yet natural regrets apart, I owned that all the change was not disaster. Much indeed had been lost, but much had been gained."[68]

As Sullivan's comments indicate, "old Ireland" and "new Ireland" are terms that indicate both cultural loss and cultural continuity, that signal an era of great change and new opportunities – one in which an understanding (or at least a collective consensus) of such concepts as emigration, diaspora, and the cultural adjustment to a greater, more expansive Ireland was fundamental for the nineteenth-century Irish experience, whether as a native in Ireland or as a colonial migrant in San Francisco, Toronto, Buenos Aires, Sydney, or Dunedin. Sullivan, whose brother Richard was at one time the editor of the *Freeman's Journal* (Sydney) and, later, the *Monitor* (San Francisco), would have been intimately familiar with the broad contours of a Greater Ireland. And the very international dissemination of Sullivan's text *New Ireland*, through that complex web of publishing and trade networks, was testimony to commercial forces that helped these new Irish communities grow and that shaped and kept immediate the concept of an evolving Irish culture and Greater Ireland.

NOTES

1 For a discussion on several theoretical approaches to book history, see Howsam, *Old Books and New Histories,* 28–45. The two most prominent models for such a trade are those initially mapped by Robert Darnton, along with Thomas Adams and Nicholas Barker. See Darnton, "History of Books," 11, passim; and Adams and Barker, "New Model," 14, 22–7.

2 Howsam, *Old Books and New Histories*, 63. See also Rukavina, "Wonderfully Comprehensive Business," 70.

3 Loeber and Stouthamer-Loeber, "James Duffy and Catholic Nationalism," 121. Duffy was trading with Sydney booksellers from 1847.

4 For a discussion on the nature of transnational religious texts, see Hofmeyr, *Portable Bunyan,* 24, passim.

5 While this chapter focuses on the Irish Catholic experience, this is largely because print sources for this group were more prevalent, prominent, and enduring. For an investigation of the commonality of Irish experience, see the exploratory work by Akenson, *Small Differences*. For an example of the types of Irish national literature imported from Irish, British, and American publishers, see Molloy, "Literature in the Irish Diaspora," app. 1.

6 Darnton, "History of Books," 36.

7 For a discussion of this, see Larkin, "Devotional Revolution in Ireland"; and Larkin, "Economic Growth."

8 [Editorial], *Freeman's Journal* (Sydney), 15 December 1855. The *Freeman's Journal* (hereafter *FJ*). This was sometimes referred to as "the cause of Ireland" in the colonial world, a melding of Irish Catholicism and Irish nationalism in a relationship that was culturally and commercially symbiotic. For a discussion on Irish literacy, see Richards, "Australian Map of British and Irish Literacy." The Irish National School System, providing education to children up to the age of twelve, was established in 1830; from the late 1850s, a dramatic increase in the literacy levels of Irish emigrants is evident. See Akenson, *Irish Education Experiment*, 125.

9 It should be noted that, by 1880, Australia was importing 40 percent of all United Kingdom book exports. See Askew and Hubber, "Colonial Reader Observed," 116. It has been noted that, by 1920, "3.5 million books were sold annually in Australia at a profit to British publishers of over a million pounds." See Nile and Walker, "Paternoster Row Machine," 10.

10 "The Publishing Trade in Ireland," reprinted from the *Freeman's Journal* (Dublin), *Duffy's Hibernian Magazine: A Monthly Journal of Literature, Science and Art* 5, new series (1864): 79–80.

11 See M.H. Gill & Son Ltd., Letterbook, November 1878 – January 1884, microfilm, Trinity College Dublin, Department of Early Printed Books. The Gill letters document trade with North America, Britain, and Australia, while newspaper advertisements in the Buenos Aires *Southern Cross* indicate they were also exporting to Argentina.

12 Michael Hayes to Richard Hayes, 25 November 1812, reproduced in *Footprints: Quarterly Journal of the Melbourne Historical Commission* 2, 11 (1976): 18.

13 Hayes appears to have been familiar with publisher and bookseller Hugh Fitzpatrick, printer to the Catholic Committee of 1792 and printer and bookseller to St Patrick's College Maynooth from 1796 until 1823. For details on Fitzpatrick and his successor Richard Coyne, a publisher whose works also found their way to Australia before 1830, see Pollard, *Dictionary of Members of the Dublin Book Trade*. Both Fitzpatrick and Coyne operated from 44 Capel Street, Dublin.

14 For example, see advertisements by John Sands, "Catholic Books," and W.A. Colman, "Cheap Catholic Prayer Books," *Morning Chronicle* (hereafter *MC*), 11 April 1846; G. Morley, "Catholic Books," *MC*, 6 June 1846; P.J. Cregin, "Catholic Weekly Instructor Published by Richardson & Son, Derby," *MC*, 14 February 1846; J.K. Heydon (auctioneer), "Catholic Books, Ex Sultana," *MC*, 25 February 1846.

15 Letter to the Editor, John Bede Polding (Roman Catholic Bishop) to *Colonist*, 30 March 1837.

16 For examples of the portrayal of the Irish in the Sydney press, see Elizabeth Webby, "Views of the Irish in Australian Newspapers and Magazines, 1803–1850," unpublished conference paper, Society for the History of Authorship, Reading, Printing (SHARP), Halifax, Nova Scotia, 2005, with permission of the author. Most of the criticism levelled was of either a denominational or a theological character. However, under much of it lay some deep-seated, rather complex ethnic anxieties, like the criticism of Ullathorne in the *Colonist* of 19 March 1835 for not addressing, in his latest Sydney-published pamphlet, the issue of the Bible and biblical extracts being translated into Irish, the "vernacular of three or four million of his Majesty's native born Catholic subjects," and presumably the language of many of the newly arrived Sydney Irish. William Bernard Ullathorne, an articulate and competent writer on a range of theological and social issues, had, through the 1830s, used other Sydney newspapers extensively to counteract the ethnic and denominational prejudice in the colony.

17 Letter, John Bede Polding, Bishop (Sydney), to Thomas Poynton (Auckland, New Zealand), 29 October 1835, in Polding, *Letters of John Bede Polding*, 57.

18 Kenny, *Commencement and Progress*, 198.

19 See Suttor, "Ullathorne," 2:544–6.

20 Duncan, *Correspondence*.

21 McEncroe had been a newspaper editor in the United States in the 1820s. See Birch, *John McEncroe*, 9–29.

22 Mention is made by Duncan of Dolman's book catalogues as early as 1841. See *Australasian Chronicle* (hereafter AC), 29 May 1841. See also "Catholic Books," AC, 9 April 1842, indicating books were arriving from London at London prices. For details on Dolman, see "Charles Dolman," *Dictionary of National Biography*, ed. Leslie Stephen and Sidney Lee (London: Smith, Elder and Co., 1908), 5:1104.

23 Letter, Michael D'Arcy (Chronicle Office, Sydney) to David D'Arcy (Clonmel), 12 July 1845, State Library of Victoria (SLV), Australian Manuscripts Collection, MS 9834. By 1847 D'Arcy had established himself as a bookseller of Catholic books in Sydney, importing directly from James Duffy in Dublin. See the advertisement M. D'Arcy, "Catholic Books," SC, 10 July 1847.

24 Index to *Bounty Immigrants Arriving in New South Wales, Australia, 1828–1842* (Sydney: Archives Authority of New South Wales, 1984).

25 For an analysis of colonial Irish associationalism and its effects, see "Irish Associationalism," in Burchall, *San Francisco Irish*, 96–115, especially the concluding comments; and Fraser, *Tara Via Holyhead*, 91–100.

26 For details on Joseph Winter, see Geoffrey Serle, "Winter, Joseph (1844–1915), *ADB*, http://adb.anu.edu.au/biography/winter-joseph-4958/text8153 (viewed 25 August 2013). Further information on Joseph Winter's extensive bookselling activities can be found in Molloy, "Commodification of Texts for the Irish Colonial Reader."

27 For the workings of the Australian consignment trade, see Kirsop, *Books for Colonial Readers*, 11.

28 W. Baker, Engraver, "Catholic Books, Prints," *AC*, 12 August 1841; J.K. Heydon, "Catholic Books," *MC*, 25 February 1846. Heydon's stock is from Richardson of Derby, but includes in a separate section books published by James Duffy & Co.; M. D'Arcy, Printer, Bookseller and Stationer, "Catholic Books," *SC*, 10 July 1847; John Cohen, "Three Cases of Books," *Sydney Morning Herald* (hereafter *SMH*), 5 April 1847.

29 See advertisements, William Baker, King Street, "Catholic Books, Prints," *AC*, 12 August 1841; W.A. Duncan, "Catholic Books. Just Received," *MC*, 22 November 1843; J.K. Heydon, "Catholic Books," *MC*, 25 February 1846; William Moffitt, "Catholic Books … publishers Sims and McIntyre, of Belfast," *SC*, 2 September 1846; M. D'Arcy, "Catholic Books," *SC*, 10 July 1847.

30 For example, Archbishop Vaughan's *Pastorals and Speeches on Education* (1880) and *Occasional Addresses* (1881); and Roderick Flanagan, *The Aborigines of Australia* (1888), co-published with George Robertson. Details on Michael Dalton have been extracted from the *FJ*, 7 January 1854, 15 December 1855, when Dalton moved his premises to Woolloomooloo, and 10 November 1858, when his stock and trade was purchased by Edward Flanagan.

31 For James Hill, see his death notice, *SMH*, 27 September 1874. Hill served in the 99th Imperial Regiment (Foot). He was born in Keady, County Armagh, in 1800, and served in the British Army from 1825 to 1849. It is presumed he took his discharge in Sydney after service in New Zealand and Tasmania. Details from his army record can be found at WO 97/1063/77 and WO 97/323/103, the National Archives of the United Kingdom.

32 Hannigan and Mitchell had ceased advertising by the mid-1890s. *Sands Sydney and Suburban Directory for 1889* (Sydney: J. Sands, 1889), lists a Mitchell (no initial) as operating from the same premises, 30 Royal Arcade, 494 George Street. The *FJ* for 1889 ran frequent advertisements by Mrs D.R. Mitchell. Other booksellers in *Sands* for 1889 include E. Flanagan, the operations of J.J. Moore, and Miss M. Kennedy operating at James Hill's Armagh House. In the 1890s, three firms appear to have dominated

the Irish and Catholic market in Sydney: the Finn Brothers, their successor Louis Gille, and the largest print import and retail book trader in Australia George Robinson and Co., which regularly advertised Catholic and Irish works in the pages of the *FJ*.

33 Dublin-born Bernard King began bookselling in Lonsdale Street, near the church of St Francis, in 1862. He died in 1887, his bookselling business carried on by his son. Little is known of Richard Stanley, who was first listed in the Sands and McDougall *Melbourne Directory* as a Catholic bookseller in 1866. Stanley's establishment operated until his death 1902. William Linehan, Catholic publisher and Irish language enthusiast, first advertised in the *Advocate* (Melbourne) on 2 April 1898, signalling his start in the book retailing trade as an owner-operator. For biographical details on Linehan see "Death of Mr W.P. Linehan, Founder and Principal of well-known Catholic Bookshop," *Advocate*, 5 December 1946.

34 *FJ*, 25 July 1850, 7. Moore noted that he had "formed a direct communication with the celebrated Catholic Publisher, Mr James Duffy, of Dublin, for a constant supply of Catholic Books." For biographical details on Moore, including his Melbourne bookselling partnership with P.J. Cregin, see Molloy, "Cheap Reading for the People."

35 Letter, Michael D'Arcy (Sydney), to David D'Arcy (Clonmel), 20 July 1846, D'Arcy Family Papers, State Library of Victoria (SLV), MS 9834.

36 Rukavina, "Wonderfully Comprehensive Business," 72.

37 Statistical datasets for advertised religious works documented in the Sydney *FJ* 1850–75, and the *New Zealand Tablet* 1873–1914, in the author's possession.

38 Eliot, "Trends in British Book Production."

39 Michael D'Arcy (Sydney) to David D'Arcy (Clonmel, Ireland), 30 October 1847, SLV, MS 9834.

40 Sydney bookseller Edward Flanagan first used such categories to advertise his religious literature in 1858. This practice appears to reflect listings in printed catalogues, such as those produced by James Duffy in Dublin and D. & J. Sadlier of New York. See Flanagan's advertisement, *FJ*, 20 November 1858.

41 Imported prayer books and devotional texts in Irish included O'Gallagher's *Sermons*, *FJ*, 25 July 1850, advertised by J.J. Moore; works by William Gahan, including his *Sermons*; other prayer books imported by Michael Dalton, *FJ*, 19 August 1854; copies of J. Furlong's, *Urnaig*, imported by Flanagan 1 January 1859, and advertised as a prayer book in Irish. Later devotional works include John McHale's *Pentateuch* (Bible), in Irish, *FJ*, 1871 and 1873; and O'Gallagher's sermons in Irish and English,

advertised by Sydney bookseller Hannigan and Mitchell, *FJ*, 27 June 1885. Timothy O'Sullivan's *Pious Miscellany*, a very popular bilingual text of prayers and verses, does not appear on the *FJ* import lists or in surviving catalogues.

42 Walker, *Newspapers in New South Wales*, 152. See also the death notice for Mr Charles Dolman, Catholic Publisher, Paris, *SMH*, 16 March 1864.

43 Dolman had acquired the *FJ* in June 1860 and took on administrative control when Richard O'Sullivan and Richard Blundell joined as partners.

44 "William Dolman, Insolvency File," State Records New South Wales, 2/9121, no. 6743.

45 Loeber and Stouthamber-Loeber, "Duffy and Catholic Nationalism," 117.

46 [Adv.] Michael Dalton, *FJ*, 8 April 1852.

47 For a discussion of aspects of this point, see O'Farrell, "Bible Reading," 17–18.

48 Also included in later church-sanctioned editions, see, for example, Milner, *Key of Heaven*. For other cited editions, see Challoner, *Garden of the Soul*; and Gahan, *Manual of Catholic Piety*.

49 "Catholic Books," *AC*, 25 October 1839; "Catholic Books and Tracts," *AC*, 27 September 1842; "Catholic Books," *SC*, 2 September 1846.

50 "New Publications," *AC*, 22 December 1840.

51 (Adv.) M. D'Arcy, "Catholic Books," *SC*, 10 July 1847.

52 (Adv.) W.A. Duncan, "Catholic Books ... Colonial Publications," *MC*, 22 November 1843.

53 For example, devotional works such as *The Mother of Jesus Christ* (1885, 1/-) and *Consoling Thoughts* (1873–77) each went through multiple editions of between two and three thousand copies each, with Gills producing a further two editions of *Consoling Thoughts* for the American market. *My Little Prayer Book* (1882–88, 4d) went through three editions of three thousand and two of two thousand. This can be compared to the historical work by Denis Murphy, *Cromwell in Ireland. A History of Cromwell's Irish Campaign* (1883–1902, 12/6), produced in three editions of one thousand each over a twenty-year period; and the memoir by John Edward Walsh, *Ireland Ninety Years Ago*, produced in three editions of between one and two thousand (1876–85) and retailed for 1/- per volume. See M.H. Gill & Son Ltd., "Publication Expense Book One, 1872–1883," entries for "Consoling Thoughts," 9, and "Ireland Ninety Years Ago," 81. See also M.H. Gill & Sons Ltd., "Publication Expense Book Two, 1882–1885," 12, 41, 130, 143, both at Trinity College Dublin, Department of Early Printed Books.

54 Brief commercial biographies of the Irish-American publishing firms Sadlier, Collier, and Kenedy can be found in Dzwonkoski, *American Literary*

Publishing Houses; Dublin publishers M.H. Gill began to rely heavily on religious and nationalist publications from the 1870s. See Kinane and Gill, "McGlashan and Gill," 205. For an overview of nineteenth-century North American Irish Catholic publishing in the New York, Boston, Baltimore area, and the role of devotional literature in their publishing success, see Healy, *Catholic Book Chronicle*, 5–28.

55 Long, "Word from Australia," 656. For a similar discussion, see also Hurley, "Reasons Why Catholics Lose the Faith," 206–7. O'Farrell, "In Search of the Hidden Ireland," 328. Added to this were examples of the continuation of traditional Irish cultural forms, O'Farrell noting the persistence of Irish wake practices in New South Wales that were finally banned by the clergy on the Plenary Council of Australasia in 1880 as they were considered an affront to orthodox Catholic practice.

56 Irish religious indifference in Australia, especially on the part of those who had grown up in Ireland before the 1850s, is noted by O'Farrell. See Hayes-McCoy, *Historical Studies X*, 122. An extended discussion on this subject can be found in O'Farrell, "Australia (11) Development."

57 A Melbourne-Sydney difference has been noted by Morgan, especially with the rise of a wealthy Catholic middle class under the guidance of Archbishop Carr. See Morgan, *Melbourne before Mannix*.

58 The definitive work on Irish-American fiction is Fanning, *Irish Voice in America*. Fanning's work is on fiction only; he does not deal with the extensive body of Irish-American poetry or drama. For Irish-American drama, Fanning cites Flynn, "Ethnicity after Sea-Change."

59 For biographical details on the above, see Rolf Loeber and Magda Loeber, with Ann Burnham, *An Electronic Version of* A Guide to Irish Fiction, 1650–1900, An Foras Feasa, National University of Ireland, Maynooth, http://www.lgif.ie (viewed 10 May 2013).

60 Morrison, "Serial Fiction in Australian Colonial Newspapers," 309.

61 A number of key works on aspects of Sadlier's writings include Howes, "Discipline, Sentiment and the Irish-American Public"; Corporaal, "Golden Hills to Sycamore Trees"; McDannell, "Devil Was the First Protestant"; McDannell, "Catholic Women Fiction Writers"; Peters, "Lot's Wife."

62 See the Sadlier-Chadwick correspondence, particularly the extensive F.X. Sadlier letters to Mrs Sadlier, Part 3 1878 – Part 6 1885, Ottawa, Library and Archives Canada, MG 29 C1 22,

63 Sadlier's complete novels serialized in the Sydney *FJ* include *Old House by the Boyne*; *Bessy Conway*; and *Blakes and Flanagans* (1874–77); *Willie Burke, or the Irish Orphan in America* and the *Confederate Chieftains*, were serialized in the *Sydney Express* (1882–84); while *Maureen Dhu*, *Old*

and New, and the *Confederate Chieftains* were serialized in the *Advocate* (Melbourne) in 1879, 1887, and 1890. Sadlier was also serialized in the Auckland-based *New Zealand Freeman's Journal* in the early 1880s.

64 "Works of Fiction for the Young," *New Zealand Tablet*, 24 October 1901.

65 Howsam, *Old Books and New Histories*, 62.

66 William St Clair, "The Political Economy of Reading," School of Advanced Study University of London John Coffin Memorial Lecture in the History of the Book, 2005, 3, http://www.ies.sas.ac.uk/sites/default/files/files/Publications/Coffin%20lectures/StClair_PolEcReading_2012.pdf (viewed 10 May 2013). St Clair notes that, until 1900, "paper imprinted with words or pictures was the only medium by which complex texts, and therefore complex ideas, could be carried in quantity across time and place."

67 Kenny, "Diaspora and Comparison," 138, passim; Gilley, "Roman Catholic Church," 189. Gilley describes this as the creation of an "international consciousness" through the "fusion of religious, national and ethnic identity," and as being "reinforced by newspapers, parochial organisations and political parties."

68 Sullivan, *New Ireland*, 1–2.

PART TWO

Atlantic World

4

The Tales and Trials of a "Double Minority": The Irish and French Catholic Engagement for the Soul of the Canadian Church, 1815–1947

MARK G. McGOWAN

Upon their arrival in every British North American colony, with the exception of Newfoundland, the Irish Catholic migrants of the early nineteenth century discovered that there were Catholics already well-established and exerting their control over the local church. In the colonies of Nova Scotia, Prince Edward Island, and Upper Canada (now Ontario) Irish Catholic sojourners, settlers, and their itinerant priests recognized that Scottish Highlanders were the dominant presence in the church and were willing collaborators with the British colonial establishment. In northern New Brunswick, Quebec, parts of eastern Upper Canada, and the Prairie west, the Irish arrived and became subject to the rule of French Canadian clerics, who had set down deep roots, either through a colonial establishment that dated to the early seventeenth century or by means of *Canadien* or French-born male religious who had established a network of missions among First Nations peoples from the Ottawa River to the Pacific Ocean.

By 1900, the Irish and Scottish coexistence in the Maritime provinces was marked by relative peace and co-operation in the management of the daily life of the Roman Catholic Church, whereas the relations between the French and the Irish were turbulent and at times explosive. As the late John Moir recounted in his landmark essay in 1971, English-speaking Catholics found themselves to be in a "double minority" situation in Canada.[1] On the one hand, they were a religious minority amidst the anglophone Protestant majority in Canada, and, on the other hand, they were a linguistic minority in their own church. This chapter builds on Moir's evaluation and posits that, although the double minority complex was a national phenomenon by the twentieth century, it should be understood that it is difficult to define an Irish Catholic identity that embraces all of Canada's Irish Catholic communities or that assumes a type of Hiberno-Catholic homogeneity. Irish Catholic communities, although bound together by a common faith, built their communities and engaged the social order in ways that varied in intensity depending on their Irish regions of origin, the timing of their emigration and settlement, the region of Canada in which they chose to settle or sojourn, and the other charter and ethnic communities in their midst. By the 1940s, however, the Irish Catholics and their descendants were linked by a principally Canadian-born hierarchy, served by an indigenous clergy, and lived within a Catholic infrastructure that included distinctive social services, schools, and health care founded and operated by members of Catholic religious orders. Using the leverage afforded to them by their fluency in the English language, the tongue of the vast majority of Canadians outside of the Province of Quebec, Irish Catholics were clearly rising in influence and were challenging the French Canadian dominance in the church. When Catholicism in French-speaking Quebec collapsed in the 1960s, Canada's English-speaking Catholics secured even greater prominence in what remained of the Canadian church.

Over the course of this century and a half, between 1815 and the end of the Second World War, Canada's Irish Catholic communities developed an identity that was influenced significantly by their relations with their numerically more powerful francophone co-religionists. As they came to share much in common in terms of political, social, and economic life with anglophone Protestant Canadians, the Irish struggled to be an independent voice within an ecclesiastical world dominated by French Canadians. Without creating impressions of Catholic disunity, which would have delighted the church's detractors and brought public scandal, Irish Catholics in Canada asserted themselves as the natural voice for the church in Canada – outside of Quebec.

In the seventeenth century, travellers to the St Lawrence Valley, in what was then the Royal Colony of New France, would have recognized the names of Irish settlers who had been demobilized from the French army and navy. Although almost thoroughly Frenchified, this Irish presence is likely the earliest appearance of Irish Catholics in Canada, with the possible exception of the villages tied to the fishery surrounding the colony of Newfoundland. Throughout the seventeenth and eighteenth centuries, Catholic sailors and fishers from Waterford, Wexford, Kilkenny, Tipperary, and Cork had frequented the Grand Banks off Newfoundland and eventually established a foothold in the coves of the Avalon Peninsula and St John's, the colony's principal town. The apparatus of the church soon followed with the presence of itinerant clergy and, by 1784, the establishment of a prefecture apostolic, later vicariate apostolic (in 1795), under Franciscan James Louis O'Donel, a native of Tipperary. Although O'Donel was consecrated to his office in 1796 by Bishop Jean-François Hubert of Quebec, the Irish Catholic Church remained isolated geographically and culturally from the sprawling Gallic presence on the continent. Irish Catholic Newfoundlanders tended to look east, back towards their ancestral ports and Episcopal sees in Ireland, which produced the colony's first six bishops, from 1795 to 1893, and thus constitutes a story of its own, which cannot be covered within this framework of this study.[2] Suffice it to say, until Newfoundland's entry into the Canadian Confederation in 1949, the Irish Catholics of Newfoundland and their descendants resisted several attempts to become absorbed into the church on the mainland.[3]

For Irish Catholic settlers elsewhere in British North America the history was written much differently and was punctuated by struggle, both in their engagement with the Protestant majority and in their relations with the French Canadians who dominated the parishes and dioceses west of the Gulf of the St Lawrence. Between 1815 and 1845, nearly 450,000 Irish immigrants landed in British North America.[4] At least two-thirds of these were Protestant, who brought their Church of Ireland and Presbyterian traditions and their desire to recreate the Orange lodges of the homeland. In Canada, the Orange Order offered them fraternity and social benefits and solidarity in the face of a rather imposing Catholic Church, which dominated the interior colony of Lower Canada (now the Province of Quebec) and had a modest presence in all of the other colonies. Irish Catholic settlers were prominent in their settlement of Halifax, the capital of Nova Scotia; St John, New Brunswick (and that province's Miramichi Valley); the tenancies of Prince Edward Island; the cities of Montreal and Quebec; the Ottawa Valley, which divided the colonies of Upper and Lower Canada; and in the towns and recently opened farmlands of the upper colony, now the Province of Ontario.[5] Unlike their cousins in the United States, Irish Catholics in the Canadian colonies were primarily rural, and although many could be found in the cities, they did not tend to form large ethnic enclaves or urban villages akin to the Irish in Boston, New York, Chicago, or Philadelphia.[6]

The numbers of pre-Famine Irish Catholic immigrants was augmented by nearly 100,000 refugees from the Great Irish Famine in 1847 and by another 100,000 in the two decades following "Black '47." In that year alone, nearly thirty-eight thousand migrants, about 80 percent of whom were Catholic, arrived in the port of Toronto, later the capital of Ontario, a fledgling market centre of only about twenty thousand people at that time.[7] The Irish famine migration experience in Canada, although it was the last of mass Irish migrations to Canada, tended to be used by Canadians – both Irish and non-Irish – as a lens through which all Irish migration was viewed. The harrowing images of Irish Catholics being led off the "coffin ships" into quarantine at Grosse-Île, the pestilence and death that stalked the fever shed at Point St Charles in Montreal, or the crowding of sometimes diseased, haggard, and desperate migrants on the wharfs of Toronto tended to become indelible images of the Irish for their Canadian hosts and touchstones of suffering for the Irish themselves.[8] Even the French Canadian church could conjure up memories of how it stepped into the breach to save the Irish, adopt their orphans, and welcome them into its churches.[9]

When they first arrived in the central colonies as early as 1815, Irish Catholics already found themselves in a Catholic world. East of the Ottawa River the French Canadians maintained a strong Catholic infrastructure under the archbishop of Quebec. Catholic churches were prominent in every town and village in Lower Canada, priests walked the streets in full soutanes, sisters from a variety of religious orders operated convent schools, public charities, and the major hospitals in the province. Catholic liberty in these conquered territories had been guaranteed by the passage of the Quebec Act, 1774.[10] Recognizing that their attempts to assimilate the French Catholic population, linguistically, legally, and religiously, had failed in the fifteen years since they conquered New France, and equally aware that the French Canadians might be vulnerable to the political troubles now evident in the American colonies to the south, the British Parliament embarked on a bold and unprecedented move. Inspired by Sir Guy Carleton (Lord Dorchester) the governor of Quebec, the Quebec Act assured the liberty of the Catholic faith, the restitution of the seigneurial system and the tithe, and the preservation of French civil law. When made available by the Constitution Act, 1791, Roman Catholics could vote in elections and sit in the legislatures of both Upper and Lower Canada. In the rest of the British Empire, including the neighbouring Maritime colonies, the Penal Laws and Test Acts were still operative, in varying degrees of effectiveness. In the central

Canadian colonies, however, Irish Catholic immigrants could experience a religious freedom not known in their home country.

The one caveat to this freedom, however, was that the Irish Catholic population would be under the authority of the French Canadian hierarchy and the Scots Catholics who served them in what would become the Diocese of Upper Canada and in the Maritime colonies. In the early nineteenth century, French Canadians secured the erection of new dioceses in Halifax and Charlottetown; in the commercial centre of Montreal, Lower Canada; in the city of Kingston, Upper Canada; and, finally, in 1841, in Toronto, the former capital of Upper Canada.[11] Recent studies indicate that the Irish Catholics of the central colonies, while maintaining certain religious customs of the old country and often served by priests who were born and trained in Ireland, were essentially considered by Ireland's bishops to be under the care of the French Canadian hierarchy and therefore not of immediate concern to the Irish episcopate.[12] In 1844, the interior dioceses all became suffragans to the Archdiocese of Quebec, and its archbishop was officially the primate of Canada. Supported by the opinions of the British government, the dioceses of the Atlantic colonies – St John's, Arichat (later Antigonish), Halifax, Charlottetown, and St John – were excluded from the ecclesiastical province on the grounds that they were not conquered territories and therefore were directly subject to the British government.[13] In Nova Scotia, after severe infighting between the Scots, who dominated the eastern portion of the province, and the Irish, who had been prominent settlers in Halifax since the eighteenth century, the Vatican divided the province into two dioceses, one at Halifax essentially for the Irish and the other at Arichat (later Antigonish) for the Scots, although there were distinctive Irish, Acadian, and Catholic Mi'kmaq minorities in the region.[14]

Living in the shadow of the French Canadian church was not always an easy proposition for Canada's Irish Catholics. Even though he had been trained in Montreal and Quebec City and had served as a pastor in three different western Lower Canadian parishes, Michael Power, the first bishop of Toronto, Upper Canada, made deliberate attempts to differ from his French Canadian mentors in terms of church governance.[15] When he arrived in his new diocese in 1842, Power was disturbed by the lack of priestly discipline and the moral behaviour of the laity,[16] and he was troubled by a system of local parish governance that often placed congregations at odds with their clergy and bishops. Power contemplated a system that would tighten church discipline and make the powers of the bishop indisputable. He knew well the similar system in French Canada, where parishes were run by lay *marguilliers* who reported to the *fabrique*, or parish committee.[17] As a pastor in Lower Canada he had encountered opposition from parishioners, particularly over the use of parish lands and money. He resolved that this was a French Canadian church structure that would not be emulated in his new frontier diocese, where Irish Catholics were dominant.

Looking to the precedents set by the Council of Baltimore in the United States and its eradication of lay trustees, Power set limits on the inspiration of the French Canadian church, fearing that it might ignite lay rebelliousness among the Irish that would be targeted at him. In January 1845, he had a Protestant member of the Legislative Assembly of the United Province of Canada introduce a bill that would create episcopal corporations. The bishop would become, in law, a corporation – one person and all church property would revert to his ownership and control.[18] The bill passed despite the uneasiness of French Canadian members of the house, who anticipated that such legislation might one day be applied to their section of the Province of Canada and not just to Upper Canada, where the legislation was directed. What Power did was to create a distinction in terms of structure between the French Canadian church, focused primarily in what would become Quebec, and the church elsewhere in Canada. The governance of church property by means of corporations would become the model used across English-speaking Canada, with some modifications.[19] While Power imbibed the ultramontane piety of his fellow bishops in Quebec, and would attempt to transform his own diocese devotionally and in discipline by means of norms familiar in Quebec, he proved able to mould his church differently by using examples of church governance found elsewhere, in this case the United States. This was an important moment in the evolution of Irish Catholicism in Canada and a subtle statement that anglophones would not sit by and be the "little brothers" of the faith for very long.

By mid-century, Irish Catholics, reinforced by immigrants in the immediate post-Famine period, by Irish-born clergy, and eventually by Irish-born bishops, consolidated their hold on the infrastructure of the church outside of the Province of Quebec. The two notable exceptions were the Diocese of St John, in the Province of New Brunswick, where the Irish continued to contend with a large francophone Acadian population, and in the Diocese (later Archdiocese) of Ottawa, which straddled the Ottawa River, dividing much of French Catholic Quebec from English Protestant Ontario. West of the Ottawa, sisters and male religious of Irish birth or descent took control of the publicly funded Catholic elementary schools; Irish priests filled the pastoral needs of the hundreds of parishes; Catholic hospitals and charities became integral parts of a Catholic network of services that, with few exceptions, came under the jurisdiction of a "hibernarchy" that was growing outside of Quebec in what essentially was English-speaking Protestant territory.

Religious orders became the vanguard for strengthening the Irish Catholic presence outside of Quebec by advancing the use of the English language in the church's infrastructure. The Institute of the Blessed Virgin Mary (Loreto Sisters), for example, which had been invited by Bishop Power to Canada from Rathfarnam, Ireland, in 1847, quickly established a network of schools for young women across central Canada and witnessed a speedy indigenization of its order with the recruitment of young English-speaking women of Irish descent. Similar patterns of anglophone indigenization could be witnessed among other teaching and service orders, including the Sisters of Charity of New Brunswick and the Congregation of the Sisters of St Joseph, which became dominant in education, health care, and social service across Canada; and the Congregation of St Basil, which became a leading men's religious order in education from Ottawa to Vancouver. Irish Catholics naturally gravitated to anglophone institutions because of language and the comfort derived from living and learning in their own culture.[20]

These cultural concerns were underscored by Archbishop Cornelius O'Brien of Halifax when he made a deliberate attempt to recruit English-speaking Christian brothers from the United States, instead of Canadian brothers, who were primarily French Canadian. In 1884, he explained to Brother Justin (Visitor of the New York District):

> Owing to the language and national characteristics of our people in Halifax, I address myself to you, and not to the Brothers of Montreal. It is not from any … prejudice that I desire to get Brothers dependent directly on the U. States, but from a conviction that since our manners and modes of life are similar to those of Catholics in the U. States, and very different from those of Catholics in the Province of Quebec. Brothers dependent on the U. States would be similar to our special wants, whilst those from Montreal would not understand us, nor us them. Will you, therefore, please lay this request before the proper authorities: you can assure them that I do not mean to insinuate anything against the Province of Canada; but simply that our ways being so different success could not attend the efforts of their

> Brothers here; whereas there is every reason to believe that Brothers dependent on the U. States would do a great work in our midst.[21]

O'Brien understood well that bishops in English Canada were obliged to set limits on the French Canadian Catholic sphere of influence, particularly for the spiritual growth and health of their own flocks largely of Irish birth or descent.

The presence of English-speaking Catholicism, growing, if not thriving, in these regions – often in spite of anti-Catholic rhetoric or sectarian violence – was not unappreciated by some Catholic leaders. Archbishop John Joseph Lynch of Toronto (1860–88), himself a native of Fermanagh, speculated that Providence had bestowed upon the Canadian Irish a special mission to evangelize the English peoples of North America. During the St Patrick's Day festivities in Toronto in March 1875, Lynch prepared a pastoral letter that was frank about the divine mission of the Irish Catholics in Canada:

> Ireland has a divine mission. In the admirable Providence of God, he selects families and nations to be agents of His holy will ... The Jewish people are no longer the people of God. Aaron is no longer His priest ... But through His great mercy God has preserved for a sacred purpose one people inhabiting a little island in the western ocean. Them he has tried with the most bitter earthly afflictions. In His unsearchable providence, He has left them under the rule of an oppressor, scourged them with many stripes of sorrow. Yet He has reserved them for the purest of all gifts, the richest of all treasures, the inheritance of a true faith which promises them eternal life for their perseverance ... In Canada their triumphs are well known ... The Irish in Canada have given magnificent proofs of their love of religion ... My principal aim in this pastoral letter is, to direct the mind of the Irish people and their descendants to their providential destiny, and to exhort them to fulfill it. It is the highest honor God could confer on any people, to make them His co-operators in spreading His Gospel, and saving those who were lost.[22]

These ideas would be perpetuated by others in other provinces and would eventually be considered by the Vatican as representing the most realistic hope of the Church in Canada and North America – to spread Christian truth in the English language for the glory of the Holy Mother Church.[23] Lynch would be easily recalled forty years later when Father

Alfred E. Burke of Prince Edward Island exclaimed of the Catholic mission: "The Catholic Church alone can make it [Canada] what God seems to have intended ... the home of a great race destined to achieve the highest the highest ideals in religion and civicism."[24]

Such ideas of Irish Catholic Providentialism did not translate universally into the lived religion of ordinary members of the faith. Although sharing a common Tridentine practice of the Latin Mass and a certain degree of casuistry on issues of sin and repentance,[25] Irish Catholic devotional practice, architecture, and religious culture did vary from region to region and sometimes with an eye to those things French. As noted in the work of Robert McLaughlin, Irish Catholics also established their own fraternal associations for the purpose of self-betterment. Irish piety was also evident in church structures, such as three named for St Patrick – one in each of Ottawa, Montreal, and Halifax – that were decorated with distinctive Celtic iconography and statuary. Nevertheless, Irish churches elsewhere, in places like the Ottawa Valley, were frequently architecturally indistinguishable from similar churches for French Canadians, whether they were in the Gothic style or (in some cities) more Italian baroque in their appearance.[26] In many Irish churches, however, there was a degree of hybridity: within the Celtic ambiance one might find a German-made way of the cross, Italian marble statuary, or a Cassavant organ (the pride of musical craftsmanship in Montreal). Similar cultural adoptions by the Irish were also evident in devotional life. Although traditional Irish holy wells might be found periodically in the Ottawa Valley in such places as Quyon (Quebec) or Mount St Patrick (Ontario),[27] Irish Catholics quickly adopted French Canadian pilgrimage sites. By the late nineteenth and early twentieth centuries, Irish Catholics could be counted among the thousands of their co-religionists who made the trek by road or rail to French Canadian shrines at Notre-Dame-du-Cap (in Trois-Rivières), Sainte-Anne-de-Beaupré (near Quebec City), and, by the 1930s, to Frère Andre Bissette's oratory honouring St Joseph (in Montreal). Similarly, by 1907, Ontario's Irish Catholics might venture to Midland, Ontario, to the shrine of seven French Jesuits who were martyred for the faith while serving local First Nations peoples in the seventeenth century.[28] Thus, engagement with French Canadians produced not only a firmer sense of self-identification but also a realization that they could learn and borrow from their Catholic neighbours.

By the late nineteenth century, the church outside of the Province of Quebec, with few exceptions, was either dominated by the Irish from the top down or the Irish held a strong minority position. Generally, the intra-church rivalry for territory and episcopal control was kept out of the public eye so as not to "give scandal" to the church and to invite Protestant verbal assaults on its integrity. In fact, Catholic bishops and clergy, regardless of language, stood in solidarity against the assertions of the Orange Order, public criticism of the faith in the Protestant press, or on such occasions as when governments threatened to deprive Catholics of their educational rights, as was the case in Manitoba in the 1890s.[29] By 1900, however, as more French Canadian working-class families migrated from Quebec into the Province of Ontario and points west, tensions arose between francophone Catholics and their co-religionist, whom they often simply referred to as "les Irlandais." Both Irish Catholics and their Protestant neighbours became nervous about the growing presence of the "other" in their midst, and the religious dynamic in Canadian life, between churches and within the Catholic Church itself, became more charged. By 1911, French Catholics made up 8 percent of the population of Ontario, having doubled their numbers from 102,000 in 1881 to over 202,000 in the 1911 census.[30] New French Catholic settlements became dominant in the rural counties of eastern Ontario, where Protestant farmers who had moved to the Prairies had been replaced by land-hungry Quebecois Catholics who were eager to resettle and to recreate their lives in Prescott, Russell, and Glengarry counties. In northern Ontario, French Canadian migrants by the thousands followed the new transcontinental railway lines and left an indelible cultural stamp on the growing mining, forestry, and pulp and paper communities, which, instead of becoming "New Ontario," as the Protestant majority in the province had hoped, was rapidly identified by its settlers as "Nouvel Ontario."

Irish Catholics shared the concern of their Protestant neighbours. The rapid rise of the French Canadian presence, even in Toronto, the industrial centre of the province, alarmed Irish bishops, who were concerned that their recently won control over the church outside of Quebec might be in jeopardy. In the twentieth century, Irish Catholics were adamant that the best defence against the "other" was to bring every episcopal see outside of Quebec firmly under their control. In 1904, the Vatican created the Diocese of Sault Ste Marie, which covered most of northern Ontario, including a large French-speaking and ethnically mixed Catholic population. The Irish faction secured the appointment of David Joseph Scollard, who promptly moved his episcopal headquarters from the linguistically diverse steel town of the Sault to the largely anglophone railway town of North Bay.[31] In 1909, the see of London became vacant, and Irish and French clergy asserted their preferences for a new bishop, with the former wanting to maintain control of the vast southwestern diocese and the latter wanting to defend the French Catholic minority. Both the apostolic delegate to Canada, Donato Sbarretti, and the Vatican's secretary of state, Merry Del Val, took personal interest in the appointment. Each had come to believe that English was the language of the future in North America, and it would be through the vehicle of the English language, and its Irish faithful, that Catholicism would spread throughout the continent. The controversial Oblate priest, Michael Francis Fallon, who had a history of sour relations with francophones, was appointed – much to the horror of French Canadian Catholics.[32]

Much worse was yet to come for French Canadian control in Ontario. In 1910, when the traditionally French-led Archdiocese of Ottawa became vacant, the Vatican selected Charles Hugh Gauthier as the new archbishop. To the unfamiliar eye, the appointment of Gauthier might, on the surface, appear to be a French victory. French Catholics knew that it was only Gauthier's surname that was French: in reality, his ideas and faith had been formed by his Scottish mother. The Irish had no complaint with a bishop whom they felt was a fellow Celt now holding the nation's capital.[33] Michael Joseph Spratt, a Canadian of Irish descent, assumed Gauthier's former see of Kingston. By 1911, the Irish and their allies had consolidated their control over nearly every episcopal see in Ontario, with the aforementioned bishops and with Fergus Patrick McEvay in Toronto, Limerick-born Thomas Joseph Dowling in Hamilton, and Richard O'Connor in Peterborough. Within five years, they would also hold the Diocese of Pembroke, when Irish-born Patrick Ryan succeeded Quebec-born Narcisse-Zepherin Lorraine.

The assertion of Celtic control over the church was not restricted to Ontario. In the Canadian west – including the provinces of Manitoba, Saskatchewan, and Alberta; Canada's Northwest Territories; and British Columbia on the Pacific slopes – French-born and French Canadian priests had long dominated the church and, in particular, its missions among the First Nations peoples. In the late nineteenth century, when the Canadian government aggressively opened up the Prairie west to immigration, and population and cities grew, the requirements of the church changed, and the Irish and French contest over control of the episcopal sees continued. The struggle over the western sees, however, formed part of a much larger contest between the French and the Irish over how the church was to accommodate the new Catholic Canadians who were pouring into the country by the thousands from 1896 to 1914. The presence of new Catholics who spoke neither of the languages of the charter groups in the church posed a new problem: To which side would the "foreign" Catholics ally themselves – the French or the Irish? To complicate matters the Protestant majority outside of Quebec regarded the arrival of tens of thousands of Italian, Polish, Ukrainian, Hungarian, Maltese, Lithuanian, Czech, Slovak, and German Catholics as both a problem and an opportunity. As Methodist minister and future politician James Shaver Woodsworth conjectured, these "Strangers at the Gates" threatened the white Anglo-Saxon Protestant way of life, British culture, and the preservation of British traditions of parliamentary governance and the rule of law. On the other hand, a potential solution might be the mass conversion of these immigrants from popish superstition to true Christianity.[34]

As has been demonstrated by Jeff Kildea in the case of Australia in the same time period, sectarian difficulties were never far from the surface of public life. Facing the threat of highly organized and well-financed Protestant proselytism, and the potential of mass apostasy, Canada's French- and English-speaking Catholics worked feverishly to preserve the Catholicity of immigrant communities.[35] But even in this endeavour the differing Irish and French visions of the church in Canada came into play, and the Irish found themselves once again as a double minority, fending off the Protestant evangelizers while holding their ground within the church against the possibility of the French capturing the hearts of the immigrants and thus tipping the balance of power away from the Irish. Avoiding the problems that had ensued in the United States when Irish bishops consistently blocked the formation of national parishes among immigrants, Irish Catholic bishops did the opposite, as did the French Canadian prelates. In Toronto, Montreal, Ottawa, Hamilton, North Bay, Sault Ste Marie, Sudbury, Fort William, Port Arthur, Winnipeg, and Edmonton bishops created new national parishes for immigrants and incorporated these new Canadians into the existing diocesan structures.[36] The Irish and French bishops co-operated in assisting the development of churches for Ukrainian Catholics of the Byzantine-Greek Rite, and they welcomed the establishment of the Ukrainian Eparchy for Canada in Winnipeg in 1912. For their part, the Irish were strategic in making sure that immigrant children were enrolled in Ontario's English-language separate Catholic schools, that parents were facilitated by English-language classes, and that men and women were welcomed into their own branches of such Catholic voluntary associations as the Holy

Name Society, the Knights of Columbus, and, after 1919, the Catholic Women's League. Irish bishops felt strongly that, if the immigrant was to succeed in Canada, it would have to be through the medium of the English language, although no prohibition was placed upon a Catholic newcomer retaining his or her native tongue to preserve his/her cultural, family, and spiritual traditions.[37]

The founding of the Catholic Church Extension Society by a cast of Catholics of Irish descent provoked significant controversy between the French- and English-speaking Catholics regarding the immigrant question. It was hard for French Canadians not to regard Extension as a vehicle for the "les Irlandais" when its founders were Chief Justice Charles Fitzpatrick, Archbishop Fergus Patrick McEvay, future Bishop Alfred A. Sinnott, and Father Alfred E. Burke (who would hold Extension's presidency from its founding in 1908 until his resignation in 1915).[38] Although the early board of directors contained several French Canadians (including two bishops), and the mandate of Extension was to provide financial support, altar plate and vestments, sacred literature, chapels, and the recruitment of priests for immigrants, within the statements of its Irish supporters, there was always a tone of Hiberno-supremacy and the inevitability of the dominance of the English language within immigrant communities. Archbishop McEvay, chancellor of the society, did little to calm these fears when he addressed the French as follows: "The foreign element ... can in the opinion of us at least be reached in only one of two ways, either through the medium of men who speak their language, or through the offices of those who speak the English language which is that of the majority of the West and which is the language the foreigners must learn of necessity if they are to procure a livelihood."[39] French board members resigned, and, never a supporter of Extension, Archbishop Adélard Langevin of St Boniface, Manitoba, the primate see of the Canadian west, accused *les Irlandais*, among other colourful descriptors, of imperialism over the church in western Canada and of spreading their "anti-French rage and Francophobia" from Ontario to the west.[40] Scarcely masking their contempt of the "grands seigneurs" of the west, Extension leaders explained that they had hoped that French Canadians would have placed the needs of the faith over their national aspirations.[41] Given the nature of the culture wars, the argument could have been turned around on the Irish very easily.

Nevertheless the battle for the Catholic immigrant was a constituent part of a larger struggle for the episcopal sees in western Canada. As had been the case in Ontario, the support of both the apostolic delegate and the Vatican's secretary of state came into play, and it became clear that both the French and the Irish would have to mount a serious lobby effort in Rome to glean the preferred candidates of their "side" as the Vatican deliberated upon each *terna* sent from Canada. In the end, save for a brief French Canadian victory in securing the appointment of Olivier Elzéar Mathieu to Regina in 1911, the Irish and their Scots cousins eventually assumed control of most of the key dioceses west of Ontario. Although Neil McNeil's translation from Vancouver to Toronto, and the subsequent transfer of Timothy Casey to Vancouver in 1912, meant the loss of the see of St John, New Brunswick, to the Acadian French, with the west in Celtic hands by the time of the Great War, it appeared that Lynch's waxing of Irish Providentialism in Canada was taking shape and that the universe was unfolding as many Irish Canadians thought it should.[42]

One of the most contested arenas between Irish and French Catholics, however, was in the area of education. The battle over language and religion in Canadian Catholic schools would fester well into the 1940s. The English-speaking Catholics of the province, primarily Irish, were already experiencing their double minority status in the heated battle over language and religion in Ontario's publicly funded school system. Since the creation of the Canadian Confederation in 1867, Catholics had been constitutionally guaranteed public funds for their denominational, or "separate schools," in Ontario. Section 93 of the British North America Act, however, only guaranteed the rights of religious minorities in the area of education, not linguistic minorities.[43] Thus, when the growing number of French-language schools, or "bilingual schools," two-thirds of which were Catholic separate schools, were challenged by government inspectors in 1911 as being inferior, francophone and anglophone Catholics drew battle lines over whether to retain these schools or not. Bishop Michael Francis Fallon of London, the son of Irish immigrants, was determined to rid his diocese, which had a strong French Catholic minority, of these schools.[44] While Fallon argued that it was entirely a matter of making sure that Catholic children were educated as well as were their non-Catholic neighbours, his francophone detractors suspected something deeper lay behind Fallon's motives. Earlier in the century, while serving as a professor at the bilingual University of Ottawa, Fallon had been the principal advocate of the anglicization of that pontifical institution, much to the anxiety of his francophone colleagues. Although he was removed from the university to keep the peace,

French Catholics never forgot how *the Irish* attempted to seize control of Catholic higher education in the province.[45]

The troubles within the church would deepen. In 1910, while the largely Irish contingent of Catholic bishops negotiated with the provincial government for increased financing for Catholic schools, concessions for special Catholic textbooks in their schools, and the inclusion of Catholic schools in receiving a proportional share of corporate tax revenues, the French Catholics went on the offensive.[46] At a well-attended congress on education in Ottawa, which even attracted the talents of Wilfrid Laurier, Canada's prime minister, the French Catholic faction requested that its educational rights be confirmed and extended in Ontario. Protestant Ontario was aghast at this audacious request, the Orange caucus in Ontario's government demanded an end to bilingual schools, and the province's premier, James Pliny Whitney, broke off his negotiations with the Catholic bishops. Feeling that all of the province's anglophone Catholics had been unfairly treated because of the French actions, the angry contingent of English-speaking bishops distanced itself from the educational claims of its co-religionists. When, in 1912, Whitney's government enacted Regulation 17, which would effectively prohibit French-language education in the province after the second grade, the Irish bishops supported the government action on the grounds that it would improve the quality of education and make Catholic students better suited for the modern society in which they would eventually seek employment. It was also a strategic move in that it asserted that the Irish bishops would be in charge of the Church west of Quebec.[47]

The chasm between Irish Catholics and their French Canadian co-religionists would widen during the imperial wars of the early twentieth century. Bishops of Irish birth and descent were quick to rally to the British cause in both South Africa in 1899 and, later, in August 1914, when Germany invaded Belgium, setting off the Great War. At the turn of the century, Irish-born men and Irish descendants recruited heavily, particularly in Ontario and Nova Scotia, for the Canadian contingents in the South African War. Several Catholic bishops publicly endorsed the war effort; notable among them was Cornelius O'Brien of Halifax, who, in a pastoral letter, claimed the South African engagement to be a "noble and just" cause.[48] Lay politicians, such as federal solicitor-general Charles Fitzpatrick, celebrated the conflict as an opportunity for Canadians to show their imperial colours: "The British Empire is no mere geographical expression for a number of sundered and disunited provinces – the time had come when it was necessary for the whelps of the lion to rally to the defence of the old land. The time had come when every man must be made to understand whether on the European continent or in South Africa, that blow for blow whensoever the blow might come, must be struck back by the British, and would be struck as freely from Australasia and Canada as from the heart of the Empire itself."[49] Other Catholic politicians of Irish descent, such as Chief Justice William Wilfred Sullivan (of Prince Edward Island) and Senator Lawrence Geoffrey Power (of Nova Scotia) would agree and publicly endorse recruitment.[50] Similarly, the lay editors of Catholic newspapers – the *Catholic Record* in London, the *New Freeman* in St John, and eventually the originally neutral the *Casket* in Antigonish and the *Catholic Register* in Toronto – would all demonstrate their support of the Canadian war effort.[51] Upon reflection, a decade after the war, some Catholics would call upon the memory of this first imperial war effort in the veldts of South Africa, seeing it as a precedent for continued Catholic loyalty and duty as Europe descended into the First World War. During the South African campaign, Irish Canadian Catholics battle-tested their first chaplains and their first infantrymen in the imperial cause, which represented the foundation stones upon which they could build in the larger conflagration to come.[52]

As the geopolitical stresses of the spring and summer of 1914 erupted into open war in August, Irish Catholics, like other Canadians, were jolted from the rhythms of their everyday life. Not surprisingly, given the episcopal endorsements by Catholic bishops of the British cause in previous conflicts (such as the American War of Independence and the War of 1812), Canada's Catholic episcopate was uniform in its support of the Canadian and imperial war effort. While the archbishops of the principal francophone Catholic sees in Quebec (Montreal, Quebec City, and Ottawa) issued a joint pastoral letter in support of the British war effort in September 1914,[53] other Catholic bishops outside of Quebec tended to issue endorsements of military action independently and repeated these affirmations of support throughout the duration of the war. Bishops of Irish descent such as Edward McCarthy of Halifax, Louis O'Leary of Chatham, Patrick Ryan of Pembroke, Michael J. Spratt of Kingston, Michael O'Brien of Peterborough, Michael Francis Fallon of London, Neil McNeil of Toronto, James T. McNally of Calgary, Alfred Sinnott of Winnipeg (by 1915), and Timothy Casey of Vancouver were all publicly vocal in their support of the war effort, not only on spiritual grounds as a fight for Christian morality and values but also on imperial grounds as a way of supporting the Empire's defence of small nations under attack from "Prussian Militarism."[54] For the outspoken Bishop Fallon of London, Canadians had no choice in the matter: "It either means victory or the disappearance of the British Empire with its liberty and its tradition. In this peril there is no line of cleavage between us. We are one because we know Britain's cause is just."[55] Never to be outdone by his superiors, Father Alfred E. Burke, the openly conservative and imperialist editor of the *Catholic Register* in Toronto,[56] was second to none in his loyalty when he exclaimed in his paper: "We are as British as we always have been, and we will, praise God, always be."[57]

For their own part, Canadian men and women of Irish descent flocked to infantry units, the modest Canadian Navy, the Canadian Army Medical Corps, and the Royal Canadian Artillery by the thousands.[58] By June 1917, which marked the end of voluntary recruitment, approximately 51,426 Roman Catholics were enlisted in the Canadian Expeditionary Force (CEF), constituting about 14 percent of the total number of recruits.[59] A careful analysis of the recruitment figures suggests, however, that there was a parting of the ways between the Irish and French Canadian Catholics with regard to their eagerness to enlist. English-speaking Catholics, mostly of Irish birth or descent, recruited at levels consistent with their numbers in the Canadian population in general.[60] In 1917, the Reverend Captain John J. O'Gorman of Ottawa reported to his superiors in the Canadian Chaplains Service that 36,512 of the Catholic recruits were English-speaking, making them the single largest Catholic linguistic grouping in the CEF, second only to the Anglicans in terms of the rate of recruitment relative to their numbers in the general population. O'Gorman, who was convalescing from serious wounds received at the front, had plenty of time to crunch numbers and to try to prove the anti-Catholic voices in Canada wrong. He suggested that French Canadian recruitment was about thirteen thousand or only a little over one-third of the entire Catholic total of volunteers, thus making the Irish, Scots, and other Catholic recruits a much more significant proportion of the population than it had appeared at first glance.[61]

During the war, the problems associated with the Irish Catholics' double minority status were exacerbated by the conscription question, on the one hand, and by the Irish Home Rule question, on the other. Vocal Canadian Protestants, particularly from the Orange Order, constantly berated all Catholics for the French Canadian resistance to recruitment and were suspicious of Irish Catholic loyalty after the Easter Rising in 1916.[62] As for the latter, the Irish Catholic press and clergy consistently supported Home Rule in Ireland by constitutional means and denounced all violence, British or Sinn Fein.[63] Father C.J. McLaughlin of New Brunswick vehemently condemned the anti-British positions of the Ancient Order of Hibernians at their annual convention in Boston in July 1916, and J.J. O'Gorman spoke for most of his clerical colleagues when, in 1917, he rallied Catholics to win the war first and then win Home Rule.[64] Father O'Gorman's sense of double duty – to Canada first and then to Ireland – brought no condemnations from his episcopal leaders. The Irish-French division on conscription, however, boiled throughout 1917 and 1918. Despite an initial flurry of enthusiasm in Quebec, the endorsement of the Quebec bishops for the British war effort, and the creation of several distinctive Quebec battalions, recruitment in French Canada was a spectacular failure.[65] Scarred by the bilingual schools crisis in Ontario, and sceptical of the aims of British and Canadian imperialists, Quebec's nationalist politicians did not believe Canadian soil was directly threatened and favoured contributions to the war effort made through agricultural and industrial production. French Canadian Catholics, many of whom lived in rural areas, were disinclined to leave the land,[66] and they had little sentimental attachment to "secular" France. Moreover, the predominantly anglophone and Protestant Department of Militia and Defence had mishandled recruiting in Quebec. Even though the Catholic hierarchy continued to support the war effort, including the national registration of manpower in 1916–17, they begged the prime minister, Sir Robert Borden, not to invoke conscription.[67] When conscription was implemented in late 1917 on the heels of the election of Borden's Union government, which contained no francophone members from Quebec, French Canadian Catholics were isolated and were the objects of scorn not only from many corners of English Canada but also from many of their Irish co-religionists.

Canada's Irish Catholics were caught between a rock and a hard place. In Australia, Home Rule advocate Archbishop Mannix of Melbourne was leading the Catholic charge against conscription, and it seemed that Ireland would be cast into civil chaos if it was introduced there. At home, the Quebec Church did not endorse the Union government's mandate to enact conscription, and by March 1918 there was rioting in Quebec City.[68] While Canada's Irish Catholics were not united on the issue, the majority of its leaders appeared acquiescent to the Military Service Act. Most of the Roman Catholic hierarchy supported conscription in principle as a means of winning the war.[69] No stranger to public controversy, Bishop Fallon openly endorsed the Union government on the eve of the election in December 1917.[70] The *Catholic Register* and one of its leading columnists, Henry Somerville, supported conscription.[71] Both the *Catholic Record* (which had strong Liberal ties and was generally supportive of Wilfrid Laurier (the leader of the opposition) and the *Casket* took a more neutral path, acknowledging Parliament's right to enact the legislation but remaining critical of some of the "fire-breathing" advocates of conscription and their harsh comments about anyone who opposed compulsory military service.[72] Many Catholic organizations and leaders also endorsed conscription.[73] Finally, C.J. Doherty, the minister of justice in the Union government and an Irish Catholic MP from Montreal, actually wrote the legislation.[74]

When the war ended, Irish Catholics took pride in their wartime participation and appeared to have earned a degree of respectability in the eyes of their Anglo-Protestant neighbours. Even in the sectarian-charged environment of Toronto, the Orange mayor, Thomas Church, personally praised the Catholic war effort at a ceremony unveiling a monument to the war dead of St Paul's Parish, a Catholic congregation that had offered more volunteers than any other Christian community in the city.[75] Relations between the Irish and French Canadians were in complete disarray, and attempts were being made by several Irish bishops to heal the wound between the Catholic factions by means of a *bonne entente* movement and a compromise on the separate school issue in Ontario. The competition for episcopal sees, however, did not cease, and, in the mid-twentieth century, "les Irlandais" made continuous inroads, taking control of Canadian dioceses outside of Quebec, including the largely Scottish diocese of Charlottetown, the francophone-dominated diocese of Sault Ste. Marie, and, by 1930, the once highly contested Archdiocese of Regina. In this Prairie see, the late Archbishop Mathieu was succeeded by James Charles McGuigan, a rising star in the Canadian church and a native of Prince Edward Island who spoke Irish as his mother tongue.[76] By 1950, with the exception of the northwest mission territories and parts of New Brunswick and northern Ontario, the French Canadian hierarchy had been completely supplanted by the Irish and their descendants.[77]

There was considerable peaceful coexistence between the French Canadian and Irish factions of the church during the interwar period and during the Second World War. The relaxation of Regulation 17 and its official elimination in 1944 restored peace in the school wars of Ontario,[78] and the shrewd political manoeuvring that facilitated Canada's avoiding a second conscription crisis marked a period of relative peace with the church. In 1946, observers may have sensed a shift in power towards the Irish side when the Vatican appointed James McGuigan, archbishop of Toronto, to the College of Cardinals. He was the first such appointment made in English Canada, giving the Irish a cardinal to complement the presence of a cardinal in Quebec City. A testament to the importance of McGuigan's appointment came within the year, when Pope Pius XII designated him the official papal legate to the International Marian Congress, to be held in Ottawa in late June 1947.[79] The event had been organized by Archbishop Alexandre Vachon of that city and was intended to promote Mary Queen of Peace, an appropriate devotion reflecting the early stages of the Cold War.[80] There was no sitting cardinal in Quebec City, given the untimely death of Cardinal Villeneuve in January of that year while he was vacationing in California. This left McGuigan the most important cleric at a bilingual event that became an international showcase for the Canadian church. McGuigan used the event, as did his fellow American prelates and the Primate of Ireland, John Dalton, archbishop of Armagh, to promote the Catholic Church's firm opposition to atheistic, materialistic communism and to marshal all Catholics behind the liberal democracies of the West to defend against the Soviet Union and its satellites.[81] The irony of the Marian Congress was that even Canada's Protestant churches and politicians, with a few exceptions, became caught up in the enthusiasm generated by the congress, particularly its fierce resistance to the threat posed by Marxism. With McGuigan as papal legate, the Irish constituency had come of age in its own church, which was now being recognized as an ally with all Canadians in the coming battle against international communism.

The movement of Irish Catholics into the Canadian spotlight was epitomized by McGuigan's own performance as papal legate. On the last day of the congress, 22 June 1947, he consecrated the world to the Immaculate Heart of Mary and made another militant call – this time to Canadian Catholics – to "fight valiantly, unafraid, undaunted, unconquered" against the those in the world who "proclaim a false liberty which can only and [*sic*] in the evils of anarchy of [*sic*] despotism."[82] McGuigan's veiled references to communism were lost on few of the 100,000 or so in attendance at Lansdowne Park. What was more interesting for the purposes of examining the double minority character of his church, however, was McGuigan's reinvention of a special mission for Canadian Catholics – a people who had inherited British institutions and liberty, and who must now appeal to Mary "to guard Christian truth as a pearl of great price":

> If the world turns away from Christ it turns away from truth and it delivers itself into bondage. We have seen this in great countries in our own day. If liberty is one of our traditions as Canadians, if British institutions to which we belong and from which we inherited our civic traditions are contrived to safeguard liberty and the sacredness of the human person, if we have been taught by our fathers to abhor political systems which treat the individual merely as a creature and instrument of the State, it is because we belong to a family of nations nourished in infancy on the milk of Christian truth and trained to maturity on the practice of Gospel precepts.[83]

McGuigan's words were loaded. Not only had he concluded with a militant cry for peace and a fight against communism,[84] but he had also placed all Canadian Catholics – not just those of Irish blood – squarely in the context of British traditions, as loyal and faithful citizens of the British "way." In the context of Cold War anti-communism, and in light of the old Canadian chestnut of Catholic loyalty, McGuigan, with great aplomb, had offered doubters of Irish Catholic sincerity – whether they were Protestant or *Canadien* – satisfactory answers to both questions.

By mid-century, in advance of the Second Vatican Council, Canada's Catholics of Irish descent emerged as credible and respected leaders of the church on issues of national importance. Far from taking a back pew to their French Canadian co-religionists, the Irish descendants had been tested by two world wars and were now emerging as allies of Canada's Protestants in the newer and colder war against international communism. The ecumenical bonds would strengthen over the course of Vatican II, and the prominence of the anglophone church in Canada would rise, particularly as both the church and the traditional society it sustained in Quebec would collapse in the wake of the "Quiet Revolution" of the 1960s and 1970s. I do not mean to overstate this emergence of the Irish Catholic presence in Canada. In the United States, Irish Catholics initially encountered French-born bishops and then new American Catholics from Europe and Asia. American Catholic historiography is clear that the Irish, however, engaged these relationships at first from a position of numeric strength and, later, from a position of dominance in Church government. In Britain, too, the Irish ventured into territory held by a small group of recusant Catholics who could be, at times, less than sympathetic to the newcomers from across the Irish Sea. In Canada, however, the Irish faced problems associated with their weakened religious position in British-Canadian Protestant society, where most of them lived, and in a Canadian church that was dominated by francophones – *les Canadiens*. One suspects that the history of Irish Canadian Catholics might have been written as that of a group who merely accepted their double minority status and moved on. They did no such thing. In a period of 150 years, they adapted themselves to many of the social and political norms of their Anglo-Protestant neighbours, while demarcating clear lines of territorial jurisdiction between themselves and francophone Catholics. In the process they entrenched themselves in positions of strength in terms of governance and inter-group relations outside of Quebec, while standing in solidarity with their francophone brothers and sisters when it appeared the Church was threatened. The sense of urgency wrought by the double minority status varied from place to place. In Ottawa, St John, or Montreal, the Irish found their badge of Irishness a mark of distinction from Anglo-Protestants and *Canadiens*, and they promoted this affinity to the old sod proudly, even when such nostalgic loyalties had waned within other Irish communities. In municipalities and provinces outside of these cities, Irish Catholics had built significant ideological bridges with their English-speaking neighbours and had clearly subordinated their francophone co-religionists. However, by 1962, even though new theological and liturgical challenges awaited them, Canada's Catholics of Irish descent were becoming masters of their own house.

NOTES

1 Moir, "Problem of a Double Minority." From this point, "double minority" does not appear within quotes.
2 Chapeau et al., *Evêques Catholiques de Canada*, 80–1. Byrne, *Gentleman Bishops and Faction Fighters*; Lahey, "Catholicism and Colonial Policy."
3 McGowan, "Pregnant with Perils."
4 Figures appear in Wilson, *Irish in Canada*, 5.
5 The best overview of early Irish migration to Canada is Houston and Smyth, *Irish Emigration and Canadian Settlement*.
6 Akenson, *Irish in Ontario*, 3–47.
7 McGowan, *Death or Canada*, 91–2 and 110.
8 McGowan, *Creating Canadian Historical Memory*.
9 The French inscription on the Celtic cross monument at Grosse-Île makes explicit the work of French Canadian priests in their labours with the Famine migrants. See O'Gallagher, *Grosse Île*, 86.
10 Neatby, *Quebec Act*.
11 Rea, *Bishop Alexander Macdonell*.
12 Laura Smith, a PhD candidate at the University of Toronto, has conducted an exhaustive search of ecclesiastical archives in Ireland and found little

correspondence between the Irish and Upper Canadian bishops. One conclusion that might be drawn is that the Irish bishops were either not interested, given the many problems of their own, or were confident that Irish migrants in British North America would be taken care of by the French Canadian hierarchy. Smith begins framing these questions in Corcoran and Smith, "Bishop Macdonell."

13 Library and Archives Canada (hereafter LAC), Lord Stanley Papers, Summary of the Roman Catholic Archbishop for the North American Colonies, app. 4, Extract from the Opinion of the Law Officers, 11 April 1842. For a comprehensive discussion of the issue, see Lemieux, *L'établissement de la premier province écclesiastique en Canada.*

14 Johnston, *History of the Catholic Church*; Murphy, "Trusteeism in Atlantic Canada"; and Bumsted, "Scottish Catholicism in Canada."

15 McGowan, *Michael Power,* 37–56.

16 Ibid., 159–66.

17 Boucher, "La fabrique et les marguilliers," 148–9; Dussureault et Hudon, "Conflits sociaux et élites locales au Bas-Canada," 414 and 438.

18 *Journal of the Legislative Assembly of the Province of Canada*, session 1844–45, 29 November 1844 to 29 March 1845, Petition, 16 December 1844, 52."

19 Archives of the Roman Catholic Archdiocese of Toronto (hereafter ARCAT), Michael Power Papers, letterbook 2, letter 248, Power to Cardinal Fransoni, Rome, 5 August 1845.

20 McGowan, *Waning*, 83–88; Smyth, *Changing Habits*; McGahan, "Sisters of Charity of the Immaculate Conception."

21 Archives of the Generalate (Brothers of the Christian Schools, De la Salle), Rome, no. 242, Halifax, Nouvelle-Écosse, Canada Communautés, 1e Chemise, Halifax, Archbishop O'Brien to Brother Justin, 21 December 1884.

22 Cited in McKeown, *Archbishop John Joseph Lynch*, 226–33. A reprint of the original can be found in *Irish Canadian*, 19 March 1885.

23 Fiorino, "Nomination of Michael Fallon."

24 *Catholic Register*, 18 February 1909.

25 Taves's *Household of Faith* provides an excellent overview of Irish Catholic piety.

26 Bennett, "Early Church Architecture"; Fred McEvoy et al., *Enduring Faith*; Brannen, "Brunswick Street Gothic"; Power et al., *Gather Up the Fragments;* and Riehl et al., *History of the Diocese of Hamilton.*

27 McCuaig, *People of St Patrick's*, 21; and MacKechnie, *What Men They Were*, 102.

28 *Catholic Weekly Review*, 17 September 1887; *Catholic Record*, 17 July 1897; *Catholic Messenger of the Sacred Heart* 11 (August 1901): 363–4;

Catholic Register, 19 August 1909; Shook, "Marian Pilgrimages," 56–9; *Catholic Register*, 22 August 1907, and 19 August 1909.

29 Crunican, *Priests and Politicians;* Perin, *Rome in Canada,* 11–38. Catholic-Protestant relations in Canada are a study worthy of separate treatment and cannot be expanded upon here in any detail. John Moir identifies three phases of engagement between these groups: (1) the colonial period to 1840, which was characterized by peaceful co-existence and toleration; (2) the period of confrontation, which was typical of the next century; and (3) the period of ecumenism. Moir is clear, however, that although the middle period witnessed clashes, both rhetorical and physical, between Christian communities buoyed by either their evangelical fervor or by ultramontanism, the confrontations were not constant and that, in their ordinary lives, anglophone Protestants and anglophone Catholics generally learned to live with one another and intermarried.

30 Choquette, "English-French Relations," 6.

31 Ibid., *La foi gardienne de la langue en Ontario*, 52–9.

32 Fiorino, "Nomination of Michael Fallon," 43–5.

33 Choquette, *La Foi gardienne de la langue en Ontario*, 39–40.

34 Grant, "Reaction of WASP Churches."

35 McGowan, "Toronto's English-speaking Catholics."

36 Ibid., *Waning of the Green,* 219–25.

37 Toronto's Archbishop Neil McNeil was public about the need for Catholic schools to anglicize the newcomers. *Catholic Register*, 22 January 1914.

38 McGowan, *Waning of the Green*, 231–7.

39 LAC, Sir Charles Fitzpatrick Papers, vol. 12, copy of letter from Archbishop Fergus Patrick McEvay to Archbishop Louis-Nazaire Bégin, 27 September 1910, 5816.

40 Archives of the Archdiocese of St Boniface, Adelard Langevin Papers, copy of a letter from Langevin to Archbishop Louis-Nazaire Bégin, Quebec, 21 August 1908; Langevin to Bégin, 20 September 1909; Langevin to Father Thomas Dauson, OMI, 24 October 1912; and Langevin to the Extension Society, 13 January 1913.

41 ARCAT, Archbishop Fergus McEvay Papers, McEvay to Cardinal DeLai, Consistorial Congregation, Rome, 30 April 1911; LAC, Charles Murphy papers, vol. 9, Bishop Michael Francis Fallon to Murphy, 29 April 1909, 3548–51.

42 Huel, "French-Irish Conflict." In 1912, the princely James T. McNally, from Prince Edward Island, was appointed to the newly created Diocese of Calgary; three years later, fellow Islander Alfred Sinnott became archbishop in the newly created see of Winnipeg, carved out of the western

portion of Archbishop Langevin's archdiocese. By 1920, New Brunswick-born Henry O'Leary took over the Archdiocese of Edmonton, Alberta, after the death of French-born Émile-Joseph Légal. In British Columbia, the Scots appeared to have assumed control at the expense of francophone prelates. In 1908, the Vatican had appointed Nova Scotian Alexander MacDonald to the Diocese of Victoria, much to the disappointment of local priests. Two years later, in 1910, the Vatican announced that a second Cape Bretoner, Neil McNeil, was to be transferred from his current see of St George's Newfoundland, on the Atlantic, nearly sixty-five hundred kilometres across Canada to the Archdiocese of Vancouver on the Pacific coast. Despite his highland name, McNeil's mother was a Meagher whose family hailed from County Kilkenny. McNeil's candidacy had been secured after the Vatican rejected a *terna* containing the names of three French-speaking Oblate missionary priests.

43 Walker, *Catholic Education and Politics*, 310–11.

44 Barber, "Ontario Schools Issue"; Prang, "Clerics, Politicians, and the Bilingual Schools Issue."

45 Choquette, *Language and Religion,* 249–58.

46 Archives of Ontario (hereafter AO), James Pliny Whitney Papers, Fergus McEvay to Whitney, 15 February 1910 (and copy, Whitney to McEvay, 9 March 1910).

47 Zucchi, *View from Rome,* xvi–xix.

48 *Le Soleil*, 13 November 1899. O'Brien was in the public eye numerous times in the autumn of 1899, including at the highly successful consecration of the new St Mary's Cathedral in Halifax. *Morning Chronicle* (Halifax), 20 October 1899.

49 *Hansard*, Debates of the House of Commons, 63–4 Victoria, 20 February 1900, 668–9.

50 *Morning Guardian* (Charlottetown), 24 October 1899. See Sullivan's obvious Tory connections in "Hon William Wilfred Sullivan," *The Canadian Men and Women of the Time*, ed. Henry James Morgan (Toronto: William Briggs, 1898), 985. See also *Halifax Herald*, 2 November 1899. Senator Richard Scott was not as impressed, considering the war to be a conspiracy of British "jingos" and their Canadian allies. See W.L. Scott, KC, "Sir Richard Scott, K.C," Canadian Catholic Historical Association, *Report* 4 (1936–37): 59; Clarke, "Sir Richard Scott," 14:915.

51 *Catholic Record*, 9 April and 29 October 1898; 18 November 1899; 25 November 1899; 16 December 1899; 24 March 1900; 29 September 1900; and 9 February 1901. *Register*, 14 and 21 December 1899. The *Casket,* 2 November 1899; 25 January 1900; 15 and 22 February 1900;

24 May 1900; 12 July 1900; 17 May 1901; 24 October 1901. See MacLean, *Casket,* 102. *New Freeman*, 6, 13, and 27 January 1900; 3 February 1900; and 2 June 1900.

52 *New Freeman*, 31 October 1914. *Northwest Review*, 8 August 1914. See also Burke, "Irishman's Place."

53 *Catholic Register*, 22 October 1914.

54 *New Freeman*, 21 August 1915 and 19 February 1916 (Casey); *Casket*, 26 November 1914 (Morrison); Archives of the Diocese of Antigonish, (ADA), James Morrison Papers, Pastoral, 3 March 1915; Archives of the Archdiocese of Halifax (AAH), James T. McNally Papers, vol. 5, documents 761, 771, 790, 791, and 798; AAH, Edward McCarthy Papers, vol. 1, documents 80–81; Archives of the Diocese of Pembroke (ADP), Bishop Ryan Papers, Pastorals and Circulars, 1914–19. *Northwest Review*, 25 December 1915 (Sinnott); *Canadian Freeman*, 9 December 1914 (O'Brien); *Canadian Freeman*, 8 March 1916 (Spratt).

55 *Catholic Record*, 12 September 1914.

56 *Globe*, 14 June 1912.

57 *Catholic Register*, 20 October 1914.

58 McGowan, "Between King, Kaiser, and Canada," table 4.

59 LAC, Department of Militia and Defence, RG 9 III, vol. 4673, Memoranda, Religious Statistics, 1917 (see app. 2).

60 For Catholic population figures, see Choquette, "English-French Relations," 5.

61 LAC, Militia and Defence, RG 9 III, vol. 4636, O'Gorman Memorandum to the Archbishops and Bishops of Ontario, October 1917, 10–11. See also vol. 4673, Religious Statistics and RG 24, vol. 1249, HQ-593-1-77, 22 August 1916. Similar numbers appear in Armstrong, *Crisis of Quebec*, 247. Her evidence is drawn from Sessional Paper 143-B.

62 *Orange Sentinel*, 22 October 1914; 7 January 1915; 18 February 1915; 18 March 1915; 14 October 1915.

63 *Canadian Freeman*, 4 May 1916. See McGowan "Between King, Kaiser, and Canada," 110–14.

64 *New Freeman* 29 July 1916; and *Canadian Freeman* 29 March 1917.

65 Gagnon, *Le 22e Bataillon,* 139–87.

66 Granatstein and Hitsman, *Broken Promises,* 28–31; Dutil, "Against Isolationism," 115–16.

67 LAC, Sir Robert Borden Papers, vol. 219, Archbishop Bruchesi to Borden, 27 May 1917, 123403–6 and 2 June 1917, 123412–3.

68 *New Freeman*, 6 April 1918. This New Brunswick Catholic paper denounced the violence as "monumental folly."

69 Hopkins, *Canada at War*, 263 and 331; *Northwest Review*, 26 May 1917.

70 Archives of the Diocese of London, Fallon Papers, speeches, "Statement of Bishop Fallon in Favour of Union Government," 6 December 1917.

71 *Catholic Register*, 21 and 28 June, 24 July, 2 and 23 August 1917.

72 *Catholic Record*, 30 June, 7 July, and 28 July 1917. *Casket*, 21 June and 19 July 1917.

73 ARCAT, McNeil Papers, AS07.03, J.S. McGinnis to McNeil, 15 April 1918; *Canadian* 26 (June 1918). *Hansard*, House of Commons Debates, 7th Session, 12th Parliament, vol. 3, 29 June 1917, 2847–54. Some of the supporters included the Catholic Mutual Benefit Association, the Catholic Truth Society, individual priests, and Professor A.B. O'Neill, president of St. Joseph's College in New Brunswick.

74 *Ottawa Journal*, 18 December 1917.

75 Kelly, *Story of St Paul's Parish*, 172–75.

76 Reported to the author by Professor Peter Toner, UNB, based on his findings in the Canadian Census of 1901.

77 Farther west, in 1923, the Kerry-born Toronto priest Thomas O'Donnell became bishop of Victoria, British Columbia. In the new dioceses of the interior of British Columbia, Martin Johnson assumed control of Nelson in 1936; Edward Q. Jennings took the mantel in Kamloops in 1946; and Anthony Jordan broke the French Oblate control of Prince George that same year.

78 Oliver, "Resolution of the Ontario Bilingual Schools Crisis," 185–213.

79 *Marian Congress of Ottawa*, trans. Emmett O'Grady (Ottawa: Archdiocese of Ottawa, 1948), 10 and 43.

80 Archives of the Archdiocese of Ottawa, Alexandre Vachon, *Mandements* (1940–53), vol. 3, no. 13, Circular to the Clergy, 31 December 1945.

81 *Marian Congress of Ottawa*, 124.

82 ARCAT, McGuigan Papers, MG SU 22.30, "Text of the address of Cardinal McGuigan at the closing of the Marian Congress," 22 June 1947.

83 Ibid.

84 *Toronto Star*, 23 June 1947.

5

This Sacred Feeling: Patriotism, Nation-Building, and the Catholic Church in Newfoundland, 1850–1914

CAROLYN LAMBERT

In October 1916, in the aftermath of the Newfoundland Regiment's massive losses at Beaumont Hamel in the Somme on 1 July, Catholic bishop Michael Fintan Power exalted those who died as having "offered the supreme sacrifice on the Altar of the Empire."[1] The Catholic hierarchy's belief in devout patriotism originated in the nineteenth century. As an institution, the church played a key role in colonial nation-building under two of the leading nineteenth-century Newfoundland nationalists: Bishops John Thomas Mullock (1850–69) and Michael Francis Howley (1892–1914). Both believed that their duty as spiritual leaders was not only to ensure Catholics' awareness that they were the children of St Patrick but also to instill in the community a sense of patriotism for its native home and loyalty to the Empire. Although their viewpoints were primarily shaped by the prevailing currents of thought, both shared the belief that love for one's country was more than an innate feeling. They taught their flocks that patriotism and loyalty were a matter of duty and conscience that fundamentally sprang from the principles of the Catholic faith, and they imbued both with a transcendental quality. By 1916, the hierarchy proudly boasted that every Catholic child was taught that love of God, of king, and of country were inseparable. It was this "sacrificial spirit of Christian devotion to duty" that impelled young Newfoundland Catholic men to fight in the First World War.[2]

The Catholic community had changed greatly by the time Limerick-born Franciscan bishop John Thomas Mullock succeeded Bishop Michael Anthony Fleming in 1850.[3] Fleming's episcopacy largely occurred at a time of continued Irish immigration. To minister to a majority Irish-born flock Fleming built an Irish church and allowed only Irish-born personnel. When he began building the cathedral in 1839 he intended it to symbolize the permanence of Catholicism in St John's and a specifically Irish Catholic culture and identity.[4] His Irish-centric outlook also applied to the church's political involvement as Fleming maintained power through an immigrant-dominated clique.

By the 1840s, however, a demographic shift caused by lack of immigration meant that the Catholic community was quickly becoming majority native-born. Middle-class leaders altered the parameters of the community's identity with the formal articulation of a Newfoundland identity. Catholics were no longer solely defined by Irish identity and were beginning to see their native home as a distinct place and themselves as a distinct people within the British Empire.[5] Fleming resisted these changes, which ultimately split the community between native and Irish born.[6]

One of Mullock's first tasks as bishop was to heal the rift in the community. Unlike his predecessor, he recognized that the emergence of this nascent Newfoundland consciousness marked a transformation in the purpose of the church in the community. While Fleming assumed an authoritative position as an Irish missionary tending to his flock, Mullock believed himself to be an equal member of the Catholic community. He was a concerned citizen who took a sincere interest in the welfare of the country, which was a place he often referred to as his adopted home.[7] The future of the Catholic Church in Newfoundland, he argued, lay with native-born Catholics and so should include both the Irish and Newfoundland aspects of their identity.[8] He also recognized that the lack of immigration to the colony presented a logistical problem for the church since Irish priests were following their flocks, the majority of which were emigrating to the United States. This would result in a decrease in the number of personnel from Ireland, which meant that the Newfoundland church would be forced to rely on its own Catholic community to supply priests and religious.[9] Mullock reversed Fleming's practice of solely recruiting Irish-born personnel and encouraged local men and women to join its ranks.[10] From the beginning of his episcopacy he actively encouraged native-born men to become priests, stating: "Our most ardent wish is to have an indigenous clergy that the children of the soil may embrace the Ecclesiastical State." His first formal step in this direction was taken in 1856, when he established a seminary in St John's called St Bonaventure's College.[11] Although there was an increase in the number of Newfoundland-born recruits, in the second half of the century the church continued to be dominated by the Irish-born.[12]

In a broader context, Mullock believed that the role of the church was to act as the vanguard of nation-building and to defend the interests of all Newfoundlanders regardless of religion or class.[13] Although an unlikely candidate given his Irish birth, to his contemporaries Mullock was a Newfoundland nationalist.[14] He argued that there was no correlation between birthplace and patriotism.[15] He was one of strongest supporters of "responsible government," which the British government granted in 1855, and he used his position as bishop to drive the colony's social, political, and economic development. He was very outspoken on many political issues, such as steam communication between the colony and Europe, and the construction of an Atlantic cable connecting Newfoundland to Ireland.[16] His mission was to unite the community under an inclusive nationalist banner to advance the progress of the burgeoning country and to ensure that Catholics would be an integral part of the formation of a future nation.[17] To this end he gave two lectures in 1860 to the boys of St Bon's in order to awaken in the future generation of Newfoundlanders "an enlightened love of their native land." In the first lecture, he argued that patriotism and loyalty were one's duty as a good citizen. To illustrate his point he used the example of Catholic bishop James Louis O'Donel's foiling of the United Irishmen rebellion in St John's in 1800. Catholic loyalty, he argued, was "an affair of conscience."[18] In the second lecture he argued that, beyond duty, there was innate feeling. Mullock told the audience that *Dulce et decorum est pro patria mori* was "the universal feeling of all people." He emphasized that love of country was not temporal but a sacred feeling. Patriotism and religion were intertwined, he stated, and love for one's land was a feeling that was second only to religion in people's hearts. Jesus himself, he noted, had patriotic feelings about Jerusalem.[19]

Patriotic sentiment was only one component of Mullock's formula for "forming the character of the future nation." He argued that "religion, education and industry" were essential elements as well. Education, in particular, was the key to nation-building since it was educators who moulded the characters of the future generations of Catholic Newfoundlanders.[20] Mullock decided to make secondary education available by changing the function of St Bon's to provide young men with a classical education so they would be prepared for any situation in life. He even hoped that someday this would lead to the establishment of a Catholic university.[21] He told the community that, while the benefits of the college would not be instantaneous, it would in time allow future generations to become active members of society.[22] Yet his mission was not an easy one, given that the majority of the community were lower-class fishers who did not see the need for education. One of his priests recalled that, given that this was the case, Mullock's zealousness with regard to education could be characterized as an inclination to over-educate.[23] Nevertheless, Mullock stressed that it was future generations that needed the opportunity to advance in their own country: "If the rising Catholic youth be left without the means of a refined education, they must sink in their own land ... [N]ative Catholics will be confined to the humblest occupations, excluded in a great measure, from the learned professions, from every high and honourable position."[24]

Yet the ability to educate the Catholic lower classes was not possible until Mullock's successor, Thomas Joseph Power, secured the Irish Christian Brothers to teach in Newfoundland in January 1876.[25] Like Mullock, Irish-born Power had an appeasing manner, although he was not as outspoken and largely avoided wading into public issues. In fact, Power's tenure is often overlooked for this reason, but he did indeed share an interest in the progress of both the colony and the church.[26] His focus was to finish the projects Mullock had started.

Mullock's mission to have an educated Catholic youth that would take a lead role in nation-building was fulfilled by Power's success in arranging for the Christian Brothers to come to St John's.[27] The Brothers' primary purpose was to provide lower-class boys with a sound religious education. However, their mandate was also to provide Catholic children who had poor economic prospects with the appropriate skills to obtain employment, instil them with self-respect, and make them aware of their potentially useful role in society.[28] The Brothers' task was to mould the future men of the colony to serve the church and the country in Newfoundland.[29] They indeed changed the prospects for many poor Catholic boys whose only option had been to follow their fathers and become fishers. For the first time they had the chance to be placed "on an equality with those of other sections of the country."[30] Many of their students became the leading and commercial men of the city as well as members of the municipal and legislative governments.[31] The Brothers' arrival also meant that Newfoundland-born men were given the opportunity to become members of a religious order. In their very first year, the Brothers saw such an interest among the native born in becoming novices that the Superior Brother requested permission to establish a noviciate in St John's. He argued that this would not only avoid the cost of sending native-born postulants to Ireland but would also secure the foundation for future growth and expansion of the Order in Newfoundland.[32]

Mullock's vision of a native-led church that promoted the welfare of Newfoundland and its people was embodied in the colony's first Newfoundland-born bishop and archbishop, Michael Francis Howley. Howley was a second-generation Catholic born in St John's in 1843 and was one of the first pupils educated at St Bonaventure's. He studied at the Propaganda College in Rome and was ordained in June 1868. While attending the consecration of Power two years later, Power persuaded Howley to return to Newfoundland. Howley did not need much convincing since he wanted to stay in the colony to serve the needs of the people of his homeland.[33] He served for a short time at the cathedral and then moved to the west coast of the island where he served as prefect apostolic and bishop of Amastris. When Power died in 1893, Howley was transferred to the vacant see in St John's, and in 1895 he became the bishop of St John's. He became the colony's first archbishop when Newfoundland was created an ecclesiastical province in 1904.[34]

As a young Catholic growing up in St John's during Mullock's episcopacy, Howley was no doubt greatly influenced by his ideas. Howley greatly admired his devotion to the success of his flock and the progress of the country. He wrote that Mullock "loved the country with a feeling more genuine than many of her home-born sons."[35] An earnest patriotism was something both shared. A historian and prolific writer, Howley's love for his native home shone through his writings and his discourse. He admitted that he had an "absorbing passion to grasp with avidity everything in any way bearing upon the past history of our country."[36] His most important work was the *Ecclesiastical History of Newfoundland* published in 1888, a copy of which found its way to the pope.[37] Through his poetry and other writings, Howley was also instrumental in contributing to Newfoundland national consciousness. He was a frequent contributor to the colony's periodical the *Newfoundland Quarterly*, first published in 1901, and was lauded by the editor as being "possessed of an intensely earnest patriotism."[38] His contributions were quite extensive, most notably a series of articles about the origins of Newfoundland place names. In addition, in 1902 he wrote the patriotic anthem "Flag of Newfoundland," which became very popular, and he also designed the coat of arms for St John's.[39] Howley was also very proud of his Irish heritage. He spoke Gaelic and researched his family tree and coat of arms. He also became a member of the Royal Society of Antiquaries of

Ireland.[40] Like other nineteenth-century Catholic nationalists, his brand of Newfoundland nationalism was based on his interpretation of Irish nationalism, and he often used Ireland's troubled political history to warn his fellow countrypeople of the value of safeguarding their rights and political liberties.[41]

Howley also placed Newfoundland nationalism firmly within an imperial context. At his funeral in 1914, one of his priests stated that he was not only a great Newfoundland patriot but also a "true son of Empire."[42] As in other parts of the Empire, nationalism and imperialism in Newfoundland became intertwined during the era of New Imperialism. This was not an entirely new idea as contemporaries had boasted throughout the nineteenth century that the island was both the oldest colony in the Empire and the most loyal. Similar to Canada, the primary basis for Newfoundland imperial identity was ethnicity and history. Imperialists emphasized that they belonged to a broader British ethnic group as well as to a Britannic nation bound together by ties of race, history, and tradition.[43] They argued that, because it was the place where Sir Humphrey Gilbert planted the first British flag overseas, the island had a special place in the annals of imperial history.[44] The link between nationalism and imperialism was clearly apparent in 1902 when Newfoundland's national anthem, "Ode to Newfoundland," was sung for the first time. Although the purpose of the song was to celebrate national identity, side by side on stage stood the British and Newfoundland flags.[45]

Howley also believed that imperial patriotism came from the bonds of race and nationality, and his rhetoric continually emphasized this link.[46] For example, when speaking at the laying of the foundation stone of Cabot Tower in 1897, his speech mixed nationalist-imperialist themes. The ceremony itself coincided with the marking of the queen's Diamond Jubilee. Howley noted that they were marking both the longest reign of "the noblest Sovereign that ever sat upon the Throne of England" and also the four hundredth anniversary of John Cabot's discovery of their homeland. The laying of the stone, he declared, was a symbol to future generations of "our patriotism and nationality" because of the site's imperial importance in terms of historic battles between the French and the English in the seventeenth and eighteenth centuries as well as because of the island's discovery by Cabot.[47] Howley emphasized the same theme when he spoke at the 1910 commemoration of the three hundredth anniversary of John Guy's first colony at Cupids.[48] The clergy were also active promoters of imperial patriotism. In 1911, for example, Reverend John O'Reilly wrote a piece in the *Newfoundland Quarterly* supporting the idea for a King Edward Memorial on the crest of Castle Hill, Placentia, to coincide with King George's coronation year. He thought it was fitting to pay tribute to a man who promoted international peace but believed that it would also be a way of teaching the younger generation the importance of the colony's place in imperial history. As the centre of France's former presence on the island, he wrote, Placentia was a good example of "ancient but Empire building incidents."[49]

The theological context of patriotism was also something Howley stressed to the Catholic community. He argued that loyalty to the Throne was the duty of all Catholics since it was the "fundamental principal of our faith to serve with truth, honor and respect the sovereign who rules us."[50] The church's expressions of loyalty to the Crown and Empire were consistent and public. For example, to mark annually the queen's birthday the cathedral bells rang out at noon, and members of the clergy sometimes attended the private ball at Government House.[51] The catholic hierarchy also had a prominent role in welcoming members of the royal family to the city. In the fall of 1901, when the Duke and Duchess of Cornwall and York visited St John's, Howley joined other prominent Catholic politicians at a dinner on the royal yacht.[52] The church's actions did not go unnoticed. The Prince of Wales was particularly struck by its expression of loyalty during his visit in July 1914. As his carriage passed by the cathedral the bells rang out, and he reportedly stated that he was "particularly impressed with this beautiful expression of loyalty."[53] To mark the queen's Silver Jubilee in June 1897 not only were the cathedral towers lit but the interior was adorned with lights, bunting, and flags, some of which had been personally designed by Howley.[54] Howley intertwined patriotic celebration with devotional practice by including a song dedicated to the Queen called the "Queen's Song" in the special Mass. The service ended with the singing of "God Save the Queen," which was the first time the national anthem had been played at the cathedral.[55] Howley also illuminated the cathedral and held a Mass in honour of the coronation of Edward VII in 1902.[56]

Devout patriotism spurred the church's attempt to mould young Catholics into loyal and patriotic citizens through the Catholic cadet movement in the last decade of the nineteenth century. Newfoundland became caught up in the new imperialist current of the time, in which military-type cadet movements for boys were emerging all over the Empire. In this era, "British identity ... largely defined itself through martial culture ... [M]artial values became the values of the Victorians."[57] These were now to be inculcated into the Empire's children. In Canada, for example, by the 1890s all Toronto schoolboys participated in an annual military parade, and by 1913 the cadet movement had strong nationwide support, including among Catholic French Canadians.[58] In Newfoundland, drill and military exercises had already been practised at St Bon's and the Christian Brothers' schools for some time before the formal establishment of the Catholic Cadet Corps (CCC) on 26 August 1896. It was organized by members of the political Catholic elite as well as by Howley, the clergy, and members of the Christian Brothers.[59] The involvement of the church was in keeping with the other brigades, which were established along denominational and ethnic lines.[60] The hierarchy had an immediate level of control since Howley was patron and the Christian Brothers and clergy were members of the Committee of Management.[61] In addition, since the Brothers educated almost all the Catholic schoolboys in the city, they had an organizational role to play. The initial three companies were formed from their schools in the city: St Bonaventure's, St Patrick's, and Holy Cross.[62] From its inception the CCC was popular and grew steadily in its initial years.[63] By Spring 1914, the city brigade had grown to five companies with six hundred boys and a band of over forty members.[64] The movement also became popular outside the city in Bell Island and Harbour Grace.[65]

No doubt the existence of a Protestant brigade was one reason that Catholics established their own counterpart. Howley had been very impressed by the Anglican brigade's band when it played at his welcoming reception from Rome.[66] However, the church's aim through the CCC was akin to the aim of other Catholic brigades in Canada, the United States, and the Empire: instilling patriotism and leadership as well as simultaneously imparting Christian virtues such as temperance.[67] The movement would not only produce soldiers to defend the Empire but also create, as Carl Berger says of Canada, "a masterful and upright manhood, order and stability, a necessary aspect of vital national feeling."[68] Military-type activities such as drilling, parading, and war games were designed to enforce discipline, self-reliance, obedience, and restraint.[69] Another benefit was to make Christianity more appealing to boys who may have seen it as effeminate.[70] The movement also reflected the ideas of muscular Christianity, which emphasized that physical activity would build moral character.[71] Cadets were encouraged to participate in so-called "manly sports" such as shooting and football, often with the brigades competing against each other. At an athletic awards ceremony Reverend J. Pippy urged the boys to continue in sports in order to "keep the mind pure and free, thus enabling them to lead a more upright life."[72]

As in Canada, military training in Newfoundland was also designed to infuse sobriety and morality into youth.[73] Just as the church viewed Catholic societies as a means to direct Catholic adults into a sober and productive life, so too did they view the CCC with their children. This goal was fully realized in 1899 when the city's abstinence society took over the management of the corps. The Total Abstinence and Benefit Society (TAB) was one of the oldest, largest, and most financially stable Catholic associations in St John's.[74] The society had a large hall for drilling and a track record of solid, well-organized fundraising that could assist with raising money for the fledgling organization. More important, no society could have provided more moral direction than an abstinence society, of which the Catholic bishop was the partial founder and patron.[75] Howley became a member of the new management committee overseeing the CCC and ensured that cadets took the pledge. Cadets were formally inculcated with the message of abstinence and moral behaviour through monthly lectures given by the joint spiritual director and chaplain that were, not surprisingly, of a spiritual rather than a militaristic nature.[76] Some TAB members believed that the example of the cadets would be an incentive for more youths to take the pledge. New cadets were drawn into the TAB juvenile branch and vice versa, which helped boost their respective rolls.[77] Leading a productive life also meant gainful employment, and so boys could obtain a "Good Conduct Discharge Certificate," which was effectively a reference accepted by employers as evidence of good character.[78]

The Catholic hierarchy believed that the CCC would not only make Catholic boys better citizens and better men but also better Catholics.[79] The centrality of religion to the movement was epitomized in the corps' emblem: a cross between two fixed bayonets. It was also evident on the cover of the corps' magazine, the *Cadet*, which featured a picture of a Union Jack with the caption "The freest flag that courts the breeze of heaven."[80] Howley ensured that the church maintained a guiding hand in all aspects of the CCC. He inspected the cadets, formally presented commissions to candidates, and approved the appointment of new commanding officers.[81] Howley and his priests attended inspections and awards ceremonies, and they distributed the award of promotions, good service stripes, and medals.[82] Cadets often drilled after Mass and were put through manoeuvres outside the cathedral for Howley's approval.[83] Like other Catholic societies, the CCC was present at important social events in the church calendar. For example, it attended service and paraded with the other Catholic societies in the Corpus Christi Procession.[84] In 1911,

Howley proudly let the CCC take a prominent role in welcoming the apostolic delegate to Canada and Newfoundland by firing its guns as a welcome.[85] As their final tribute, the CCC and its officers formed part of Howley's funeral procession in October 1914, and the band played in the procession to Belvedere Cemetery.[86]

The movement was a way for the hierarchy to ensure religious observance.[87] In part this was done through the chaplain, who tended to the devotional needs of the boys and gave moral guidance through monthly lectures.[88] The corps had monthly church parades during Mass priests reiterated the importance of observance of the sacraments.[89] Cadets often acted as acolytes, and the band provided musical support to the choir.[90] The juxtaposition of religion and patriotism was quite overt. For example, to receive their awards each cadet not only saluted as normal but also knelt to receive the episcopal blessing, and on at least one occasion during Mass "a detachment of the corps presented arms at the elevation of the Sacred Host."[91]

Although Howley claimed that loyalty was a duty and sacred obligation, there were two caveats. The first was that he believed loyalty to be conditional. This was a common view in other parts of the Empire, where British subjects argued that it was the duty of the imperial government to protect their interests. Failure to do so was the reason for Ulster Protestant Loyalist resistance to Irish Home Rule, and it was why, in southern Rhodesia, white farmers rose up against the British South Africa Company's control over African labour.[92] In both cases, there was a difference between loyalty to the monarch and loyalty to the state, and none was owed to the latter if subjects believed their rights were being trampled upon. The issue that tested Newfoundland's imperial relationship was French fishing rights on the colony's west coast.[93] The French Shore problem flared up during both Mullock's and Howley's episcopacys in 1857 and 1890, respectively. In both cases Newfoundlanders of all classes and denominations argued that the British government was being indifferent to the rights of its colonists. For the church and all Newfoundlanders, the issue sharpened the blurred line between national and imperial patriotism. The argument was that Newfoundland had continually been a victim of British policy and that it had to stand up for its rights. The press emphasized the broader imperial implications, and other colonies were indeed aware that this was a slippery slope.[94]

Mullock and Howley were both outspoken on the French Shore issue. Mullock's interpretation of the crisis was much like that of his contemporaries, which emphasized the broader rights and freedoms of British subjects. In a formal letter to the press in 1857 he stated: "What the British have given the French [compromises] the very existence of thousands of British subjects, robbing them of their birthright."[95] Howley had the closest connection because at the time he was vicar apostolic in the heart of the affected area on the west coast. His response was much more acute. He used Irish Home Rule, which was at the forefront of Irish politics at the time, as an example with which to illustrate the problem to Catholics at home and abroad. Howley pleaded Newfoundland's case directly to the Irish press and public. In late August 1890, he stopped in Dublin on his way home from Rome to do an interview with the nationalist paper the *Freeman's Journal*, and he also spoke in Kerry the following month.[96] The foundation of his argument was that both Newfoundland and Ireland were trying to run the land of their birth and were now struggling to solve the problems caused by two hundred years of bungled British diplomacy.[97] Howley pointed out that colonies had every right to safeguard their rights against the selfish interests of the British government. He explained that the whole affair would most likely result in "a very indignant expression of disloyalty, and an agitation to throw off allegiance and request admission to the United States." However, he was careful to add that the island would prefer to remain a British dominion. Howley's later comments suggest that he was personally not in favour of annexation but wanted what was best for Newfoundland, whatever that was.[98]

The second caveat was that Howley refused to sanction blind obedience. This was the reason for his muted response to the Boer War. Appearing at a public meeting in November 1899 to establish a patriotic fund to assist widows and orphans of soldiers killed in the conflict, he made clear that his support was based solely on Christian humanity and duty as a citizen. His very brief remarks featured two references to the controversy over the war, though he was careful not to say any more: "our duty [is] not to discuss the justification of the war but to act on the scriptural injunction [to be charitable]."[99] It is unclear how far Howley's personal objections permeated the community since its response seems somewhat ambiguous. Catholics did raise large sums of money for the Patriotic Fund, and fundraising events were filled with jingoistic addresses of loyalty and patriotism.[100] Newfoundland had no local defence force that could be converted to South African use, but some Catholics participated as members of the Canadian contingent.[101] The community joined with its fellow colonists to celebrate major British victories, such as Ladysmith and Pretoria. Some Catholic societies decorated their halls with Union Jacks and sang "Rule Britannia" and "God Save the Queen" while others did not.[102]

In contrast to their Protestant counterparts Catholic societies did not engage the war on an intellectual or political level. Their debates and lectures in late 1899 and early 1900 made no reference to the origins or progression of the conflict, not even at CCC meetings where great interest would be expected. For example, only a week after Protestant Reverend H.P. Cowperthwaite spoke regarding the reason that the British government waged war on Transvaal, the CCC monthly lecture was on physical and moral culture, while the St Bonaventure's College debate centred on whether iron or gold was more useful.[103] Although Protestant clergymen preached about the justification of the conflict and took up collections in aid of the fund, there is no evidence that this was emulated at any of the Catholic churches.[104] No decorations adorned the cathedral, nor did the bells ring out in joy to celebrate military victories.[105]

Given the church's muted response, it was perhaps inevitable that Catholic loyalty would be called into question. In March 1900, Howley admitted this was the case and publicly explained his reasons for not supporting the war to the middle-class leaders of the Catholic community. At his St Patrick's Day address to the Benevolent Irish Society he categorically denied any Catholic disloyalty, arguing that a lack of grandiose display did not mean a lack of proper sentiment. Howley clearly stated his reason for objecting to the war, an opinion he argued was shared by many in Great Britain: the casus belli was "a great deal of exaggeration … [T]he injustices suffered by British subjects in the Transvaal were not of so grievous and unbearable character as to warrant this dreadful war."[106] He pointed out that, while the conflict was raging in South Africa, the British government was depriving subjects in the Empire of their rights. As with the French Shore crisis, Howley used Ireland as an example that he believed would resonate with his audience. Irishmen, he argued, were denied their civil rights at home "for no other reason than their nationality and their religion."[107] Ireland did not enjoy good government and, unlike other imperial subjects such as Scots or French Canadians were being pressured to abandon their heritage. He explained that "all England has any right to claim [is the] silent, inactive loyalty" that comes from the Catholic teaching to "obey even unjust laws," and it was this devout duty that caused Catholic Irishmen to continue to fight for Britain.[108]

The absence of celebration at the war's end showed Howley's continued level of objection. The cathedral bells did not ring out in joy, and although the Protestant churches in the city, like those in Britain and other parts of the Empire, held thanksgiving services for the restoration of peace in South Africa, the Catholic churches did not.[109] Perhaps this was in keeping with the opinion of the Catholic Church in Melbourne, Australia, where the *Catholic Advocate* called the British victory "inglorious."[110]

Howley had no such qualms about the First World War. Although he died shortly after its outbreak, his support for the war effort was immediate. He spoke to the community about the conflict, prayers for peace were said every day in Mass, and he organized special devotions to be offered up in every church in the diocese.[111] It was the first time the colony had the opportunity to offer military support in an imperial conflict, and it was also the first true test of whether the ideals the church had preached to the Catholic community for so long were as firmly rooted as the hierarchy's rhetoric claimed they were. Boys from the CCC, along with the other brigades, were the first volunteers to enlist with the Newfoundland Regiment.[112] In his final sermon before his death in September 1914, Howley emphasized the duty of Catholics to fight for a noble cause. He told the men from the pulpit of the cathedral to be loyal to their god, their king, and their country.[113] He and the hierarchy were confident that they would prove to be loyal sons of the Empire.[114] A few weeks later their regimental chaplain proudly wrote home confirming this, stating that the boys were obeying their officers and maintaining devotional practice. As one newspaper described it, the church was "reaping the fruit of the seeds sown" by Howley.[115] Indeed, the seeds were sown much earlier by Mullock, long before Wilfred Owen was to call *Dulce et decorum est* "the old Lie."[116] The church, however, viewed it as the painful truth of what being a good Catholic really entailed. In his 1916 speech Bishop Power continued to remind Catholics that the loss of so many young Catholic Newfoundland men was justified: "Death here is but the concrete demonstration of the inspiring fact that every man has done his duty, that Faith and love of Fatherland are twin virtues, that Catholicism and Patriotism – love of God and love of Country – cannot be separated ... They did this thing for duty's sake, as they were taught in this College and in every Catholic school, to love their Country, to honour their King, and to die when it was necessary to defend them both."[117]

NOTES

1 Power was Bishop of St Georges on the west coast of Newfoundland. The battle decimated the regiment: of the 801 soldiers who went into battle

that morning, only sixty-eight answered roll call the next day. See *Adelphian* 13, 3 (1916): 126; Nicholson, *Fighting Newfoundlander,* 262, 274.

2 *Adelphian*, 13, 3 (1916): 126.

3 Mullock had already been in St John's for some time, acting as Fleming's coadjutor from 1847 onwards during the latter's ill health. See Jones, "Mullock."

4 FitzGerald, "Conflict and Culture," iv, 402, 459, 447–8.

5 This resulted in the establishment of the Newfoundland Natives' Society in 1840 by middle-class Catholics and Protestants. See Lambert, "Far from the Homes," 255–91; Johnston, "Nativism in Nova Scotia," 24.

6 Fleming's opposition was primarily due to political reasons. This new Newfoundland identity was inclusive and made ethnicity and religion – the two things that the Catholic Church and Irish-born reformers had used to gain and keep their political power in the 1830s – irrelevant. It was a threat to their powerbase. Fleming even denounced Catholic natives from the altar, refusing them last rights and having them forcibly removed from the chapel. See Lambert, "Far from the Homes," 255–91.

7 Biographical Information, Bishop John Thomas Mullock, Archives of the Archdiocese of St. John's (hereafter AASJ), 104/1/1.

8 Biographical Information, Bishop John Thomas Mullock, AASJ, 104/1/1.

9 Richard Howley, "Irish Missionary Types, the Old Priests," *Irish Ecclesiastical Record*, 3rd series, vol. 10, 1889 (Dublin: Browne & Nolan, 1889), 15, AASJ.

10 Lambert, "Far from the Homes," 98–103.

11 Biographical Information, Bishop John Thomas Mullock, AASJ, 104/1/1; *Patriot and Terra Nova Herald*, 26 February 1855; Howley, *Ecclesiastical History of Newfoundland*, 2:87.

12 Lambert, "Far from the Homes," 99–100.

13 *Public Ledger*, 21 February 1854.

14 Cadigan, *Newfoundland and Labrador,* 123.

15 Right Rev. Dr. Mullock, *The Cathedral of St. John's Newfoundland with an Account of Its Consecration* (Dublin: James Duffy, 1856), 47, AASJ, 104/1/3; Biographical Information, Bishop John Thomas Mullock, AASJ, 104/1/1.

16 Howley, *Ecclesiastical History*, 2:96–7, 120–1; *Patriot*, 4 June 1860.

17 *Patriot*, 12 March 1860.

18 Ibid., 20 February 1860.

19 Mullock, *The Cathedral of St. John's*, 47, AASJ, 104/1/3; *Patriot*, 13 February 1860.

20 *Patriot*, 12 March 1860.

21 Ibid., 23 February 1857.

22 "Academy, St. John's (Roman Catholic Branch) for the year ending 31st December, 1859," *Journal of the House of Assembly 1860*, app., 293.
23 Benevolent Irish Society (BIS) Minutes, Provincial Archives of Newfoundland and Labrador, MG 612, 23 May 1869.
24 Mullock's pastoral letter, 1864, AASJ, 104/1/42.
25 Penney, "Study of the Contributions," 148–9; J.G. Higgins, "Right Rev. T.J. Power, D.D., Bishop of St. John's, 1870–1893," *Basilica Centenary Volume 1955*, 126, AASJ.
26 J.G. Higgins, "Right Rev. T.J. Power," 125, AASJ; Hans Rollmann, "POWER, THOMAS JOSEPH," in *Dictionary of Canadian Biography*, vol. 12, University of Toronto/Université Laval, 2003–, http://www.biographi.ca/en/bio/power_thomas_joseph_12E.html (viewed 25 February 2015).
27 *Annals of the Christian Brothers*, Archives of Mount St. Francis, St. John's (hereafter AMSFSJ), Congregation of the Christian Brothers, Newfoundland, 1; Holland to Hoare, Slattery Papers (hereafter SP) no. 18, 27 January 1876, AMSFSJ; Lambert, "Far From the Homes of their Fathers," 126–8.
28 Coldrey, *Faith and Fatherland,* 21, 39–40, 89.
29 *Daily News* (St John's), 23 September 1926.
30 Congregation of the Christian Brothers, *Christian Brothers' Jubilee*, 74.
31 Lambert, "Far from the Homes of Their Fathers," 153–4.
32 Slattery to Maxwell, SP no. 146, 25 November 1889; Crehan to Maxwell, SP NO. 164, 15 October 1890; Slattery to Maxwell, SP no. 168, 22 November 1890.
33 *Evening Telegram* (St John's), 27 June 1892.
34 Biographical Information, Bishop Michael Francis Howley, AASJ, 106/2; *Adelphian*, 11, 3 (1914): 110.
35 Howley, *Ecclesiastical History*, 2:119.
36 Ibid., 1:7.
37 Letter from Tobias Kirby, Archbishop of Ephesus, the Irish College Rome, to Howley, 11 January 1890, AASJ, 106/13/1. A second volume was edited from his papers posthumously and published in 2005.
38 *Newfoundland Quarterly* (hereafter NQ) 14, 2 (1914): 7, 9.
39 Colton, "Imagining Nation," 28–9; Barbara A. Crosbie, "HOWLEY, MICHAEL FRANCIS," in *Dictionary of Canadian Biography*, vol. 14, University of Toronto/Université Laval, 2003–, http://www.biographi.ca/en/bio/howley_michael_francis_14E.html (viewed 25 February 2015).
40 Correspondence, AASJ, 106/2/4; *Evening Telegram*, 9 July 1914; Crosbie, "Howley"; letter from William C. Stubbs, honorary treasurer of the Society, to Howley, 8 March 1901, AASJ, 106/11/3.
41 For example, see Lambert, "Far from the Homes of Their Fathers," 288–9.

42 *Evening Telegram*, 19 October 1914.
43 Cole, "Canada's 'Nationalist' Imperialists," 44–6; Berger, *Sense of Power*, 259; Hiller, "Robert Bond," 120–1, 124.
44 *NQ* 14, 4 (1915): 1; *NQ* 24, 2 (1924): 12.
45 The Newfoundland flag at the time was the Pink, White, and Green. *Daily News*, 15 March 1902; Lambert, "Emblem of Our Country."
46 *Evening Telegram*, 20 March 1900; *NQ* 4, 3 (1904): 9.
47 *Daily News*, 2, 18, 23 and 26 June 1897.
48 *NQ* 10, 2 (1910): 6–7.
49 Ibid., 10, 3 (1910): 26.
50 *Evening Telegram*, 28 January 1901.
51 *Patriot*, 1 June 1883; *Daily News*, 25 May 1897; *Evening Telegram*, 25 May 1896, 16 June 1899.
52 *Daily News*, 25 October 1901.
53 *NQ* 14, 2 (1914): 12.
54 *Daily News*, 8 and 19 June 1897.
55 Ibid., 24 May 1897, 16 June 1897.
56 *Evening Telegram*, 8 August 1902.
57 Miller, *Volunteers on the Veld*, 30–1.
58 Morton, *Military History of Canada*, 122–3.
59 *Evening Telegram*, 11, 16, 23 and 25 January 1896, 26 August 1896.
60 The others were the Anglican Church Lads Brigade (CLB), established first in 1892; the Methodist Guards, established in 1900; and the Newfoundland Highlanders, established in 1907. The latter was geared towards the Scottish population and was smaller due to the fact that that ethnic group was the smallest of the three main ethnic groups in St John's. What it lacked in numbers, however, it made up for in visible appeal. They were the flashiest of all three, wearing tartan plaid and marching with a band of drummers and bagpipes. With the exception of the Methodist Guards, brigades were organized by clergymen and maintained close ties to the church. All had chaplains and regularly attended church services. See *Cadet* 1 (April 1914), 12; *Evening Telegram*, 5 May, 15 June, 6 and 31 July, 10 and 16 November 1896, 2 June 1902; *NQ* 1, 1 (1901): 7–8.
61 *Cadet*, 1 (April 1914), 14.
62 *Evening Telegram*, 29 April 1905; *Cadet*, 1 (April 1914), 12.
63 Between late November and early December 1899, twenty-eight cadets joined, with the number increasing to between seventy-five and eighty by mid-December. See *Daily News*, 2 January 1900; *Evening Telegram*, 28 November, 8 and 12 December 1899.
64 *Cadet*, 1 (April 1914), 12.

65 In 1910 a corps was established at Harbour Grace, and by late September 1911 it consisted of around one hundred cadets. The date the corps was established on Bell Island is not clear. In both places the parish priest was heavily involved in their activities. See *Harbour Grace Standard*, 27 and 29 September 1911; *Evening Telegram*, 20 October and 1 December 1914.
66 *Evening Telegram*, 17 August 1896.
67 The hierarchy established the Catholic Boys Brigade in the United States in 1916 with the aim of making Catholic boys patriotic and faithful. It was also a means to assimilate, or "Americanize," the sons of the foreign-born. The aim of the Cadet Corps formed at De La Salle College in Toronto in 1911 was to teach the Christian virtues of courage, faith, and temperance. Father Kilian, OM Cap., Chief Commissioner, CBB, "The Catholic Boys' Brigade," *America: A Catholic Review of the Week*, 31 December 1921, 262–3; Sheila Dabu Nonato, "De La Salle (Oaklands) Cadet Corps Forms Character," *Catholic Register*, 31 May 2010.
68 Berger, *Sense of Power.*, 254–5; *Cadet*, 1 (April 1914), 12.
69 *Evening Telegram*, 1 December 1914; Cadet, 1 (April 1914), 13.
70 Miller, *Volunteers on the Veld*, 32.
71 Watson, Weir and Friend, "Development of Muscular Christianity," 1.
72 *Evening Telegram*, 30 June 1914.
73 Morton, *Military History of Canada*, 128.
74 *Evening Telegram*, 29 December 1899; *Daily News*, 12 February 1900.
75 *Evening Telegram*, 5, 9, 13, and 16 December 1899.
76 Ibid., 22, 23, and 24 November 1899; *Daily News*, 11 November 1899, 5, 13, and 15 February 1900, 13 and 17 November 1900.
77 *Evening Telegram*, 29 December 1899, 2 January 1901; *Daily News*, 17 November 1900.
78 *Cadet*, 1 (April 1914), 12, 14; *Daily News*, 20 March 1900, 22 October 1901.
79 *Cadet*, 1 (April 1914), 12, 14, 16.
80 *Evening Telegram*, 16 September, 24 October 1914.
81 Ibid., 5 February 1900, 31 July 1914; *Daily News*, 17 January 1900, 5 February 1900.
82 This seems to be in contrast to the CLB, which had the governor and officers present promotions, badges, and good conduct stripes. See *Evening Telegram*, 19 June 1896, 3 January 1902.
83 *Daily News*, 2 January 1900.
84 Ibid., 10 June 1901, 2 June 1902.

85 *NQ* 11, 2 (1911): 4.
86 The Bell Island CCC also attended the funeral. See *Evening Telegram*, 19, 20 October 1914.
87 Kilian, "Catholic Boys' Brigade," 263.
88 *Evening Telegram*, 19 June 1896; *Daily News*, 2 January 1900; *Harbour Grace Standard*, 29 September 1911.
89 *Evening Telegram*, 5 February 1900; *Daily News*, 14 October 1901, 6 March 1902, 9 May 1903, 22 June 1914.
90 *Daily News*, 14 October 1901; *Evening Telegram*, 2 January 1902, 24 and 26 December 1914.
91 *Daily News*, 2 January 1900.
92 Lowry, "Ulster Resistance and Loyalist Rebellion," 193.
93 This refers to the extensive north and west coast area where the French retained fishing rights, including limited land use, granted to them by eighteenth-century treaties. Conflict over this issue lasted until its resolution in the 1904 Entente Cordiale. James K. Hiller has written extensively on this topic. See, for example, his "From 1713 to 3PS: The French Presence in Newfoundland," *NQ* 96, 1 (2003): 40–7.
94 *Western Mail* (Perth), 31 May 1890; *Sydney Morning Herald*, 2 June 1890.
95 *Colonist*, 20 March 1890.
96 *Freeman's Journal*, 5 June, 29 August 1890; *Evening Telegram*, 27 September 1890.
97 *Freeman's Journal*, 5 June 1890.
98 There was very little support in Ireland for the colony's cause. Although a supporter of Home Rule, the editor of the *Freeman's Journal* claimed that the people of the island had "a high idea of their own importance." The editor stated that it was not worth England's going to war and sacrificing a few thousand soldiers for a few thousand lobsters. See *Freeman's Journal*, 5 June, 29 August 1890; *Evening Telegram*, 27 September 1890.
99 *Evening Telegram*, 21 November 1899; *Daily News*, 21 November 1899.
100 *Evening Telegram*, 9, 14, 16, and 17 February 1900.
101 Ibid., 3 February 1900; *Daily News*, 25 October 1901, 13 June 1902; NQ 9, 2 (1909): 8; NQ 18, 1 (1918): 20; NQ 30, 2 (1930): 32; *Cadet*, 4 (March 1915): 19.
102 *Evening Telegram*, 2 March 1900; *Daily News*, 1, 6, and 18 June 1900; *Evening Telegram*, 19 February 1901.
103 *Evening Telegram*, 9, 15, and 23 February 1900; *Daily News*, 8 and 9 February 1900.

104 *Daily News*, 9, 10, and 14 February 1900; *Evening Telegram*, 2, 4, 9, 13, 14, and 24 February 1900.
105 *Evening Telegram*, 2 March 1900, 19 February 1901; *Daily News*, 1, 6, and 18 June 1900.
106 *Evening Telegram*, 20 March 1900; Farwell, *Great Anglo-Boer War*, 144–5, 314–7.
107 *Daily News*, 20 March 1900.
108 *Evening Telegram*, 20 March 1900.
109 Ibid., 9 June 1902.
110 e-Melbourne: the City Past and Present, University of Melbourne, http://www.emelbourne.net.au/biogs/EM01125b.htm.
111 *Evening Telegram*, 31 August, 4, 19, and 28 September, 12 October 1914.
112 Of the first 335 volunteers between 22 and 28 August 1914, 251 were from the city brigades. Both the CCC and the CLB accounted for one-quarter of the total. Of the first 442 men to sign up with the regiment, 39 percent were from the CCC, followed by 29 percent from the CLB, 17 percent from the Methodist Guards, 11 percent from the Highlanders, and 4 percent from the Frontiersmen. See *Daily News*, 3 September 1914.
113 *Evening Telegram*, 12, 14 September, 9 October, 23 November 1914; *Adelphian* 12, 1 (1915): 11.
114 *Adelphian* 13, 3 (1916): 126–7, *Adelphian* 14, 1 (1917): 20; *Adelphian* 17, 2 (1921): 78; *Evening Telegram*, 30 November 1914.
115 *Evening Telegram*, 23 November 1914.
116 The full text is available at http://www.warpoetry.co.uk/owen1.html.
117 *Adelphian* 13, 3 (1916): 126–7.

6

Controversial Immigrants: Theological Conflict in the Transatlantic World of Eighteenth-Century Irish Presbyterianism

RANKIN SHERLING

The so-called "Scotch-Irish" Presbyterians of the early eighteenth century brought with them to America an intra-Presbyterian religious conflict that was already in full swing in Ireland.[1] Once that conflict spread to America, Irish combatants reassembled themselves in their new homeland along very similar lines as had been drawn in Ireland. On the American side of the Atlantic, American ministers were pulled into the fray and, together with Irish immigrant ministers, they succeeded in re-creating an Irish religious crisis in America, one with long-lasting consequences for American Presbyterianism.[2]

This chapter examines a number of important episodes in the religious history of Irish and Irish American Presbyterians through the spectacles of the history of migration and dispersal. Seen through these lenses, episodes familiar to scholars of American religious or Irish Presbyterian history resolve themselves into a larger view of Irish religion and Irish migration.[3] The specific episodes are the crises of orthodoxy and authority in the early-eighteenth-century Irish and American Presbyterian churches, which are usually referred to as the subscription or New Light controversy and the New Side/Old Side schism. Examined from an Irish diasporic perspective, it is evident that, along with the thousands of Irish Presbyterians who arrived in the first half of the eighteenth century, another non-human Irish immigrant arrived, less tangible but just as real. This was a religious, cultural, and theological immigrant, a set of ideas and beliefs and the controversy that surrounded them.

THE SUBSCRIPTION CONTROVERSY IN IRELAND

An understanding of the Irish dimension of the subscription controversy is essential to interpreting the development of the dispute in America. Stripped to its essentials, the controversy proceeded in the following six stages:

First, the Irish Presbyterian community, particularly in Ulster, began to conceive of the Westminster Confession of Faith (1646) as the standard of religious orthodoxy. This, in combination with the fact that Presbyterianism largely survived in Ireland because of the Presbyterian tendency to rally their community around their church in the face of Irish Catholic and Irish Anglican hostility, the Westminster Confession of Faith came to be seen as "the cornerstone of Presbyterian community in Ulster."[4]

Second, after a very public trial and conviction by the Irish government of a Dublin Presbyterian minister for denying the Trinity, Presbyterian bodies all over Ireland worked to ensure the orthodoxy of their clergy and to assure the Irish authorities that such was the case. Heterodoxy was considered a threat to the Irish establishment, and Irish Presbyterians were in no position to anger a government already suspicious of them.[5] The Presbyterian Synod of Ulster attempted this through required subscription to the tenets of the Westminster Confession of Faith. This requirement and reactions to it caused a major divide among Presbyterians in Ireland, and it leads us to the third and fourth points about the subscription controversy in Ireland.

The Dublin Presbytery (some members of which also belonged to the Synod of Ulster) rejected the Synod of Ulster's use of authority in demanding subscription of its clergy. They were essentially congregationalist in government and believed that neither the synod nor the presbyteries of which it was composed had the right to impose subscription upon the ministers of a congregation. Many of the ministers in Ulster also balked at the synod's requirement. So, the third point is that this intra-Presbyterian controversy was about authority – specifically, did the synod have the right to require subscription or not?

Fourth, the fight was also about retaining an orthodox clergy. By law, Presbyterians were not permitted to attend university in Ireland, and for years Presbyterian ministers had been attending university in Scotland, particularly Glasgow University. There, many of them picked up the Enlightenment's less-than-orthodox attitude towards Christian orthodoxy, and while not every non-subscriber was heretical or heterodox in his beliefs, many were and were thus against subscription to an orthodox Calvinist creed. The subscribers knew this, but they had trouble proving it and became suspicious of all non-subscribers. Authority and orthodoxy: these were the axes around which the whole controversy revolved in Ireland (and later in America).

Fifth, the conflict became very nasty as it continued to rage, and eventually a compromise was attempted. It was called the Pacific Act, and it allowed for a not-yet-ordained minister with problems with the Confession of Faith to explain them in his own words. If these problems with the confession were deemed unessential to the faith, then the man was ordained. This practice was called "scrupling." The compromise did not work, however, as several key non-subscribers publicly refused to subscribe even in this compromised form and eventually refused even the most basic authority of the Synod. Schism could not be avoided, and the non-subscribers eventually formed a separate, smaller body called the Non-Subscribing Presbytery of Antrim.

Last, it is important to note just how traumatizing this controversy was to Irish Presbyterians. They had begun to look at the Presbyterian Church as the centre of their community, the mortar that held them all together. Solidarity, they had learned from experience, was their main (non-spiritual) defence against their enemies. Moreover, the teachings of that church, the catechisms that each Presbyterian girl and boy was required to memorize, were based upon the Westminster Confession. In a very real way, then, the subscription controversy – which split the community, weakened the church, questioned presbyterial authority, and publicly defamed the Westminster Confession – robbed Irish Presbyterians of many of their assumptions, much of what they relied upon to give them a sense of security, a sense of direction, and their very foundation.[6]

DUBLIN AND EARLY IRISH AMERICA

The subscription controversy in Ireland was one of the most important events in the Irish Presbyterian community in the eighteenth century.[7] Few remember, however, that the Irish Presbyterian community in the eighteenth century was not confined to Ireland: it was thoroughly transatlantic. By 1717, significant numbers of Presbyterian migrants from Ulster had arrived on American shores; pastors sometimes brought with them whole congregations to start anew in America. Not surprisingly, these transported communities brought their intra-communal conflicts along with them. In this way, Irish Presbyterians were somewhat like the carriers or transmitters of a virulent plague. They carried a highly infectious and fractious religious controversy, one that would eventually affect all Presbyterians in America and shape the future of their denomination. The rest of this chapter examines some prominent aspects of early American Presbyterianism, keeping in mind several key ideas and events: (1) the notion of culture, religion, and ideas as immigrants; (2) the Irish subscription controversy; and (3) eighteenth-century Irish Presbyterian migration to America.

Immigration from Ulster exploded in about 1717, but a relatively steady stream of migration had existed from at least the 1680s.[8] These early Ulster Presbyterians played a crucial role in the founding of Presbyterianism in America. Indeed, early Presbyterianism in America is often associated with Ulster, and there are good reasons for this. Four of the seven original founding members of the first American presbytery were from Ulster. One of these was Francis Makemie. Known as the "father of American Presbyterianism," Makemie was born in County Donegal and emigrated from there to America in 1683. For years, he used his connections with his mother presbytery in County Donegal in order to procure support, especially in the form of ministers.[9] However, despite the fact that the first American presbytery was founded largely by ministers from and mostly peopled by immigrants from Ulster, it is rarely emphasized that the presbytery was originally modelled after the Dublin Presbytery, not the Synod of Ulster.

In the first decade of the eighteenth century, dissenters in America were under attack from the state church. The Act of Uniformity was a sometimes-hostile attempt to bring dissenting colonists back into the Church of England, and Presbyterianism in the colonies was not looked upon kindly.[10] Makemie and Reverend John Hampton, another Donegal man, were even imprisoned by the governor of New York for preaching without a licence.[11] In response to this threat from a greater foe, Makemie needed the co-operation and support from dissenters in America (not just other Presbyterians), and he turned especially to the Puritans of New England.

Here we can see the fortress mindset of a Presbyterian from Ulster.[12] Aid from the New England dissenters would allow for greater strength of numbers and for the continued development of Presbyterianism in America. Together they were stronger in the face of a greater foe. Thankfully for Makemie, the Presbyterianism planted by Irish clerics in America had so far been on good terms with the New England Puritans, who even sent two of their own clergymen to aid in ministering to the Presbyterian population around Chesapeake Bay. These two New England ministers were also among the original members of the American presbytery.[13]

With New England Congregationalist ministers among the founders of the new presbytery, Makemie, like Presbyterian leaders in Dublin, had to incorporate congregationally minded English Calvinists with Scottish Presbyterians and Irish Presbyterians from Ulster into one single presbytery. So the perfect model for this accommodation in America was the Dublin Presbytery, and Makemie made use of it.

By crafting the American presbytery[14] in the likeness of the Dublin Presbytery,[15] Makemie was able to include the English-descended and congregationally minded Puritans from New England in his new presbytery and to ensure future support from his fellow Dissenters in New England. Not only this, but he was also able to increase the possibility of funding and support from the Calvinist ministers of Dublin and London, both of which had created general funds for those interested in spreading the *reformed* faith but not necessarily the more authoritarian form of Presbyterianism that was prevalent in Scotland and in Ulster.[16] It was of vital importance, then, to keep from alienating the ministers of Dublin and London (and their funds) by forming a presbytery that imposed a strict authoritarian superstructure upon its member congregations.

Consequently, Makemie adopted the Dublin model. It was a brilliant manoeuvre, securing future support and funding and also fortifying friendships with strong enough allies for the young presbytery to continue to grow in spite of sometimes-hostile Anglican colonial governments.[17] The Dublin Presbytery even considered the new American presbytery as part of its own missionary effort, sending over three ministers ordained specifically for service in America, arriving in 1709, 1711, and 1713, respectively.[18] The original American presbytery then, was in many ways the daughter of the Dublin Presbytery and not the Synod of Ulster, in spite of the fact that all of its Irish ministers before 1709 were from Ulster.

Even with the steadily increasing numbers of Ulster Presbyterian ministers and people, this arrangement worked well for nearly twenty years (from 1707 to 1727), but the peaceful coexistence of differing parties within the Dublin-model presbytery would not last. The impetus for this change came from Ulster. As more and more immigrants from subscription-controversy-scarred Ulster arrived, they became increasingly insistent upon the insurance of clerical orthodoxy through the Westminster Confession and the authority and rights of the Presbyterian form of church government over those of the individual congregation. In short, they insisted upon an Ulster-style Presbyterianism.

AN ULSTER FIGHT IN AMERICA: THE MIGRATION OF A PRESBYTERIAN CONTROVERSY

Some of the earliest evidence that the "epidemic" of contention over subscription had spread from Ireland to the New World appeared in 1724, in an area overseen by the New Castle Presbytery and heavily populated with Irish Presbyterian immigrants. Like the Irish Presbyterians in America who had arrived before them, they were largely from Ulster. Many in this later group, however, had been through the Irish subscription controversy, and the whole community seems to have been very interested in the Synod of Ulster's tactics in the subscription controversy.

In 1723, the Synod of Ulster had once more attempted to tighten its subscription policy. Frustrated by the non-subscribing tactic of justifying the refusal to subscribe to the Westminster Confession by denouncing human-made creeds, the synod declared that "the condemning of all creeds, confessions, and declarations of faith in human words opens a door to let errors and heresies into the church" and, thus, would no longer be accepted.[19] These proceedings in Ireland are said to have "sent a great wave" through the Irish Presbyterian community across the Atlantic, particularly within the heavily Irish New Castle Presbytery.[20] Very shortly thereafter, as if in chronological tandem, in 1724 the New Castle Presbytery also began to require full subscription from all of its ministers.[21]

Importantly, this tactic was first adopted in an area of America heavily populated by Presbyterian immigrants from Ulster (who were overseen by the New Castle Presbytery and, a short time later, both the New Castle Presbytery and the Donegal Presbytery [which was carved out of the former in 1732]). So many Irish Presbyterian immigrants were to be found there that a clear preference for Irish-born ministers developed. In fact, the Donegal Presbytery at one point would only accept licentiates (or licensed but not-yet ordained ministers) from Ireland.[22]

At least as early as 1727, however, this preference for Irish ministers had begun to cause a problem. Orthodox ministers and laypersons who had themselves emigrated from Ireland feared that the church in America was in danger of being saddled with a ministry, trained or ordained in Ireland, that harboured heterodox principles.[23] Having already adopted a requirement of full subscription from its own ministry in 1724, by 1727 the New Castle Presbytery had begun to call for the adoption of a subscription requirement for the entire ministry of the American synod (formed in 1716).

Those pushing for subscription clearly identified *Ireland* as a source of heterodox, or New Light Presbyterian, ministers in America. To them, Irish New Lights and New Lights in America were identical.

> All our Brethrens' Arguments ... are borrowed from the new-light Men, or Non-subscribers, in the North of Ireland; they are as like them as one Crow's Egg is like another, or rather as an Horse-shoe is like a Mare's, remove the shoe and it changeth its name.[24]

The leaders of those pushing for subscription in America were also Irish, led by the Reverend John Thompson, an immigrant from County Derry. This "Old Light" faction of Irish Presbyterians can be said to have dominated the synod at this time, and the demand for clerical subscription was seen by other Presbyterian ministers in America as an Irish measure. In a 1729 letter, the Reverend Jedediah Andrews complained that Irish ministers in the synod were forcing strict subscription down the throat of all American Presbyterians by the strength of their numbers.

> We are now like to fall into a great difference about subscribing the Westminster Confession of Faith. An overture for it, drawn up by Mr. Thompson of Lewistown was offered to our Synod. Means were then used to stave it off, and I was in hopes we should have heard no more of it. But last Synod it was brought again, recommended by all the Scotch and Irish members present ... The Proposal is, that all ministers and intrants shall sign it or else be disowned as members. Now what shall we do? They will certainly carry it by number. Our countrymen say, they are willing to joyn in vote to make it the Confession of our church, but to agree to the making it the test of orthodoxy and term of ministerial communion, they say they will not. I think all the Scots [and Irish] are on one side, and all the English and Welsh on the other to a man.[25]

Andrews was wrong in asserting that *all* the Scottish and Irish were for strict subscription, for it was the heterodoxy of Irish "New Lights" that was helping to cause the great reaction to push for subscription. But Andrews's point is clear: most of the Irish were calling for strict subscription, and by the strength of their numbers they could force subscription upon the whole synod.

So, Irish Presbyterian immigrants adopted an Irish Presbyterian policy to combat a problem that they perceived as coming from Ireland (even though they were worried about the fact that schism had occurred in Ulster). But there is more. The fight over subscription in America hinged upon the same points. Just as in Ulster, the presbytery or the synod was to do the enforcing of subscription, and therefore this call for American subscription also became a fight over both theological orthodoxy *and* the authority of presbyterial church government. Thompson himself acknowledged this fact, writing that the call for American subscription was made to (1) prevent the "ingression and spreading of dangerous errors among ourselves and our flocks" and (2) to "exert the authority inherent in us for maintaining the purity of gospel truth."[26] So there were two facets to this controversy, and the second concerned the nature of presbyterial government. American Presbyterians would now have to decide whether they would remain more constitutionally congregational, like the Dublin Presbytery upon which they were originally modelled, or whether they would adopt the tiered, authoritarian style of Presbyterianism in Ulster and recommended by the Westminster Confession itself.[27]

But also, just as in Ireland, there were orthodox ministers who were determined neither to adopt the Ulster style of presbyterial government nor to make the Westminster Confession the test of Presbyterian orthodoxy. An impasse was reached, and therefore a compromise was needed. That compromise came in the form of the Adopting Act, 1729. So far, the Irish subscription controversy seems to have been replicated in America almost exactly.

The players in this American act of the larger transatlantic drama were well aware of the similarities in the controversies and even patterned the Adopting Act, 1729, directly after the Synod of Ulster's Pacific Act, 1720.[28] Like the Pacific Act, the Adopting Act required subscription from all of its clergy but allowed for "scrupling" over certain clauses found within the Westminster Confession. The records of the meeting of the American synod that year make it clear, however, that subscription was about theological orthodoxy *and* church government. With the compromise over scrupling agreed upon, all the ministers present at the 1729 meeting (except for one who confessed himself "not prepared") unanimously agreed in "declaring the … [Westminster] Confession and Catechisms to be the Confession of their faith."[29] They also declared the "Directory for worship, *discipline*, and *government*, commonly annexed to the Westminster Confession, to be agreeable in substance to the word of God and founded thereon; and, therefore, do earnestly recommend the same to all their members."[30] Authoritarian presbyterial government and confessional orthodoxy now adopted, the Ulster model had supplanted the Dublin model in America.

Perhaps the Adopting Act was too much like the Pacific Act for the Irish subscribers in America: just like its mother document in Ireland, it failed to keep out either theological heterodoxy or outright heresy. Unlike the subscribers in Ireland, however, Thompson and the Irish subscribing faction (and indeed the entire synod) seemed determined to enforce discipline on those who subscribed in poor faith.

When controversy arose over the heterodox preaching of Samuel Hemphill, an immigrant minister ordained by the Strabane Presbytery in Ireland and who had subscribed to the confession in Ireland and America, the synod demonstrated its willingness to enforce its authority. Despite being vigorously defended in the press by his fellow deist, Benjamin Franklin, Hemphill was deposed from his ministry and faded from sight.[31] However, controversy did not depart the scene as quickly as did Hemphill. Thompson and the Irish faction saw Hemphill as just one more "missionary sent from Ireland to corrupt the Faith once delivered to the Saints," and they moved to shore up that weakness.[32]

The first step was to supersede or to reinterpret the Adopting Act, 1729 – specifically the key portion of it. A largely Irish and conservative majority in the 1736 meeting of the synod rejected the 1729 compromise, which allowed any one who wished to "scruple" a passage or phrase in the Confession. Essentially, there would be subscription in toto.[33]

Moreover, beyond a shadow of a doubt, the American synod and the conservative Irish faction in the American synod regarded *Ireland* as the seedbed of the trouble, and they were resolved to stop that problem, too. The minutes of 1736 reflect this "Irish problem":

> Seeing we are likely to have the most of our Supply [of ministers] to fill our vacancies from the north of Ireland, and seeing it is too evident to be denied and called in Question, [that] we are in great Danger of being imposed upon by [ministers] and Preachers from thence, tho' sufficiently furnished with all Formalities of Presbyterian Credentials, as in the Case of Mr. Hemphill; and seeing also what was done last year may be done this year and the year following, viz. we are still liable to be imposed upon by such Credentials [from Ireland]: upon these and the like Considerations, we humbly overture this [Reverend] Synod to make an order [to halt such impositions].[34]

The American synod did not make only one order to ensure that it was not "imposed upon" by Irish New Lights: it made five.

The first stated that no congregation should allow any minister from Europe to preach to them until he had first been examined by the local presbytery and had subscribed to the Westminster Confession of Faith. The second stated that no preacher or licentiate could be called by a congregation to be their pastor until he had preached for at least six months within the bounds of the synod, enough time for the orthodoxy of his sermons to be judged by ministers in the American synod. Third, a minister could not receive a call from a congregation nor could a congregation make a call to a minister unless that call was moderated and relayed through one of the presbyteries or the synod. Fourth, no student for the ministry could be entered into his "tryals" to become a licentiate until his behaviour had been thoroughly observed by ministers of the presbytery of which he was attempting to become a licentiate.[35]

Each of these rules carries the tell-tale signs of the Ulster Presbyterian model of confessionally imposed orthodoxy enforced by the authority of the synod. Not only had the American synod now explicitly moved from the Dublin model to the Ulster model, but the American synod, mostly at the behest of Irish immigrant ministers from Ulster, was now imposing its authority upon its ministry far more stringently than the Synod of Ulster had ever done.

The fifth and final order deals specifically with Ireland. Not only does it name Irish ministers in America, but it tellingly refers to Ireland as "home." It identifies the problem of heterodox Presbyterian ministers in America as stemming from the Irish practice of ordaining ministers for service in that country (i.e., *sine titulo*) and strongly implies that American ministers would inspect potential ministers far more rigorously for loose dogma than would Irish presbyteries. From that point onward, the practice of ordaining ministers in Ireland *sine titulo* would be seen as a direct insult to the American synod, and the "Irish" synod was asked to cease the practice immediately.[36] To their credit, Irish presbyteries seemed to have stopped ordaining ministers specifically for service in America immediately, and Irish ministers themselves got the message too. As far as can be ascertained, no active ordained minister migrated from Ireland to America from 1734 to 1763.[37]

The Hemphill case concluded and the Irish synod told off, American Presbyterians hoped to live in peaceful coexistence. Yet this was not to be. There was just barely time to catch their collective breath before the greatest religious "disruption" America has ever seen kicked off in their midst, and, like the country itself, American Presbyterians were never the same. Controversy returned, this time, famously, over styles of worship. But, less famously, once again conflict arose over the presbytery's authority to inspect, judge, and choose those who could and could not preach within its bounds during the upheaval of the first Great Awakening.[38]

NEW SIDE / OLD SIDE SCHISM

Just as subscription had failed to fully guard against theological heterodoxy and, indeed, outright heresy within the Presbyterian clergy, so it failed to guard against schism, and American Presbyterians would suffer through their own schism from 1741 to 1758. American religious historians usually describe this schism as the result of whether one chose to embrace or to reject the revivalism that was sweeping through America, but they are often at pains to explain the Old Side, or those who were suspicious of the revivals.[39] The whole episode makes more sense, however, if we view the schism as part of an older, longer-standing debate within the transatlantic Irish Presbyterian community: the subscription controversy.

Keeping in mind that the Great Awakening was the main catalyst for the schism of 1741, there were two main sub-catalysts for that divorce, and in those sub-catalysts, once again, we see that this is a fight that revolves around axes nearly identical to those around which the Irish subscription controversy and the later American subscription controversy revolved. The first of these sub-catalysts was the 1736 reinterpretation of the Adopting Act. It seems that several ministers were absent from the 1736 synodical proceedings, and, partially due to their absence, strict subscription was made the official policy of the synod without their having had a say. This caused resentment among a substantial minority of ministers who felt that the only mandate on subscription as official policy was that found in the compromise of the Adopting Act. In 1736 that compromise was thrown out. So, as early as 1736 there were two opposing camps within American Presbyterianism, both largely created by the "reinterpretation" of the Adopting Act: (1) a majority largely composed of immigrant ministers from Ulster who favoured strict subscription to the Westminster Confession of Faith, to be enforced by the synod as a tool to keep the clergy free of heresy and heterodoxy and (2) a growing minority that resented the authoritarian, heavy-handed tactics of the strict subscriptionists, who had dispensed with the compromise contained in the Adopting Act, 1729, in the wake of the Hemphill trial.[40]

The second sub-catalyst requires more explanation. The Great Awakening was driven, in part, by roving evangelists like George Whitefield, men whose wanderings took them throughout the colonies, often speaking to large outdoor crowds. A typical tactic was to frighten the audience with predictions and promises of eternal torment for their sins. Only when the crowd was sufficiently whipped into a frenzy of panicked terror would the evangelist then offer faith in Christ as a way out of this imminent damnation. Contemporary accounts make it clear that the minister's leading of the crowd through this detailed process from panic and terror to peace and joy was dramatic, emotional, and sometimes bizarre. There are even accounts of people falling and rolling on the ground, screaming, shaking, crying, running into raging rivers, and barking like dogs under the stress and strain of it all.[41]

While these "camp meeting" revivals undoubtedly brought many of the "unchurched" into the church, Presbyterians in America were divided on whether they were a good or a bad thing. Interestingly for us, the two camps divided along the same lines as the two camps that divided over the 1736 reinterpretation of the Adopting Act, 1729. A majority of the Irish-born ministers were in favour of strict subscription, and a majority of the Irish were also on one side of the revival issue. They came down firmly against the revivals in the years leading up to the schism, and this situation makes sense only if one follows the course of the subscription controversy in both Ireland and America.

The subscription controversy in both Ulster and America ultimately revolved around two points of conflict: (1) whether subscription to the Westminster Confession of Faith was seen as a standard of orthodoxy or as tool to root out heresy or heterodoxy from the clergy and (2) whether the presbytery or the synod had the right and the power to enforce uniformity upon its member clergy, congregations, and people. In the fight against heresy and heterodoxy, the subscriptionists had been convinced that the synod *must* ensure the orthodoxy of its ministry.

One way the synod pursued the above goal was through public subscription, while another way was to have each presbytery examine its ministers and ensure their orthodoxy. Each presbytery controlled who could and could not preach to the people within its bounds. With a thorough examination of the messenger, the orthodoxy of the message delivered to the members of each congregation of each presbytery within the synod was ensured. The Hemphill case was a dramatic example of the necessity of controlling who could preach to the people of any given presbytery.

The roving evangelists of the Great Awakening threw a giant wrench into that organized and structured method as the laity flocked to hear whatever dynamic and charismatic speaker was moving through the area. The majority of the Irish-born ministers – caught up (as many of them were) in the fight to ensure presbyterial control of the ministry – largely came down against the revivals. How could they ever hope to ensure the orthodoxy of the doctrine spewed from tree-stump pulpits mounted by itinerants who periodically materialized from the woods to whip their parishioners into frenzied paroxysms?[42] The orthodoxy of the messenger must be ensured, and this was largely impossible when dealing with roving evangelists. Thus, from the Old Side point of view, the controversy over revivals was just a matter of extending an old fight into a different context.

Moreover, once again, the main combatants on both sides of the conflict were Irish immigrants. The Old Side was once again led by John Thompson, but by this point he was periodically working as a missionary to Scottish and Irish Presbyterians settled in the wildernesses of Virginia and North Carolina. So, while Thompson was still probably the leading intellectual of the main Irish faction of Presbyterians in America,[43] others had begun to step in. One of the most visible of these was Thompson's fellow Ulster immigrant, Robert Cross.

Cross presented to the synod a petition calling for a purge of those ministers who fully approved of the revivals and who were openly flaunting the presbytery's authority to deny the right of a roving evangelist to preach within its bounds.[44] Both Cross and the petition came from the Presbytery of Donegal in southeastern Pennsylvania. Not only were both the presbytery and this area of Pennsylvania heavily settled by Presbyterian immigrants from Ulster, but the Donegal Presbytery had at one time been a part of the same presbytery (the New Castle Presbytery) that had first imposed strict subscription upon its own ministry in 1724 and had led the call for a subscription requirement throughout the synod in 1727, 1728, and 1729. So not only does this look to be an extension of an older fight but it also looks as though many of the same people were involved – and, indeed, many of the same people were leading the way.

The argument of the petition itself suggests a strong Ulster influence, particularly regarding the issue of presbyterial authority. In response to the revivals and the lack of presbyterial oversight of those delivering the message at these revivals, the petition delivered by Cross claimed that the Presbyterian Church in America was in danger of quickly "expiring outright ... as to the form, order and constitution of an organized church."[45] Once again, the government of the church was at stake, and once again Irish immigrant Presbyterians were dictating a particularly *Ulster* Presbyterian response to contemporary Presbyterian crises in America.

However, while most Irish ministers in America and the Presbytery of Donegal seem to have been heavily weighted towards the Old Side, the New Side also had its share of Irish Presbyterians. Like the Old Side, the New Side was actually led by Irish ministers. The most conspicuous leaders came from the famous Tennent family. William Tennent, Sr, had arrived in America in 1718 and soon after founded a school that became known as the "Log College." Here, he taught his four Irish-born sons – Gilbert, William Jr, Charles, and John – all of whom became Presbyterian ministers in America. Gilbert, in particular, played a leading role in the New Side faction. Other Irish-born former students of the Log College were conspicuous as leaders of the New Side as well, namely: Samuel Blair and Samuel Finley, the latter of whom wrote the official New Side rebuttal to John Thompson's Old Side treatise "The Government of the Church of Christ." The fact that the Presbytery of Londonderry was one of the three presbyteries that broke away from the (Old Side) Synod of Philadelphia to form the (New Side) Synod of New York suggests that lay Irish Presbyterians were also well represented among New Side laity.

When the two groups and the issues involved in the dispute over the Great Awakening in the late 1730s and early 1740s are viewed in the longer, Irish-diasporic perspective, the dispersal of Irish Presbyterian religio-cultural conflict and a connection with one of the most famous American religious episodes of the colonial period seem clear.

CONCLUSION

Clearly, the subscription controversy in Ireland migrated to America amidst the great migration of Irish Presbyterians from Ulster in the early eighteenth century. By calling attention to this migration, our knowledge of the Irish diaspora has increased to include parts of the religious and theological thought worlds of Irish Presbyterians and the controversies concomitant with them. Indeed, Irish Presbyterians, who have been thought by many historians of the Irish and the "Scotch-Irish" in America to have been removed or cut off from Ireland after their arrival in that county, seem to have been very well connected with their homeland after all. They were aware of the major events in the Irish subscription controversy and tended to follow the Synod of Ulster. Moreover, knowledge of the migration of the subscription controversy from Ireland to America has helped to draw certain important episodes in American religious history into better focus

The two "sides" of the New Side/Old Side schism, for instance, would eventually split and then reunite. This is well known. What is not well known about the Old Side/New Side schism is that it was partially, but substantially and pivotally, a continuation of an older fight, one that was brought to America by Irish Presbyterian immigrants and fought between Irish Presbyterian immigrants, even if it spread to include all Presbyterians in America. The New Side/Old side controversy can, to a certain extent, be seen as a continuation of the desire of the majority of the Irish ministers to use presbyterial authority to control the ministry within the synod's bounds. An excellent example of the misunderstanding of this continuation and, thus, of the Old Side position was clearly demonstrated by the Reverend Richard Webster, perhaps the founding father of American Presbyterian history. Commenting on John Thompson's roll in the New Side/Old Side fight, Webster writes:

> During the distractions following the rending of the synod in 1741, he [Thompson] overtured the presbytery to suffer no person to be inducted into the eldership, or to sit in any judicatory, without having subscribed the Confession of Faith – a vain remedy, when the agitators were as zealous for it as the opposers.[46]

If Webster had viewed the "distractions following the rending" through the lens of dispersal, as we have done here, he would have known that subscription of the Westminster Confession – at least as conceived by Thompson and the Irish faction – was not only a vote for theological orthodoxy (in which, by that point, the entire synod seemed to be in favour) but also a vote for presbyterial authority, which was essentially a vote for the Old Side and for presbyterial control of who could and could not preach within any given presbytery's bounds. Hence, something that was incomprehensible to Webster has become clear to us. Webster simply viewed the conflict from too narrow a perspective.

It is also well known that the factions that developed around the subscription controversy and the Old Side/New Side schism remained in place within the reunited Presbyterian denomination after 1758, existing in an uneasy truce and every so often once again breaking out into open theological warfare. This process of uneasy peace and then virulent conflict would continue at least up until the late nineteenth century (and possibly until today). So much, in fact, were the fault lines in future American Presbyterian controversies set by the early controversies of the eighteenth century that nineteenth-century historian and Presbyterian theologian Charles Augustus Briggs contended that John Thompson – as the person in America who most insisted upon the Ulster methods of church government and confessional assurance of theological orthodoxy – was "the father of all the discord and mischief in the American Presbyterian Church."[47] Clearly, this is an unfair judgment of Thompson on Briggs's part, but it does illustrate the importance of the subscription controversy for American Presbyterianism. And, therefore, in some ways it illustrates the importance of Ireland, of Irish immigration, and of Irish Presbyterian theology to the history of American Presbyterianism.[48]

In conclusion, while I have undoubtedly glossed over – and indeed probably missed – some of the religious and theological complexities involved, sometimes a different, broader perspective can be helpful. By viewing these religious episodes through the lens of Irish diaspora, of the dispersal of people, ideas, and controversies from Ireland, some aspects of the religious history of America have been made clearer, and a new aspect of Irish migration has been elucidated. I hope that both the field of religious studies and the field of theology will find this dimension of Irish dispersal useful.

NOTES

1 The term "Scotch-Irish" is problematic for scholars. This chapter uses the term "Irish Presbyterian" but with the understanding that Irish Presbyterians seem to have made up the majority (but by no means all) of those called "Scotch-Irish."

2 Somewhat similar debates surrounding the Westminster Confession flared up in England, Scotland, and Wales, but it is the contention of this chapter that the subscription controversy migrated to America from Ireland along with the unprecedented numbers of mostly Presbyterian immigrants arriving on American shores from Ulster.

3 Many scholars of American religion have been heavily influenced by the interpretations of Leonard J. Trinterud, who consistently attempted to downplay "Scotch-Irish" influences in Colonial Presbyterianism. This chapter suggests that the dispersal of an Irish Presbyterian religious controversy to America led to significant consequences for Presbyterianism in that country. For other views, see Westerkamp, *Triumph of the Laity,* 155;

Trinterud, *Forming of an American Tradition.* A good counter to Trinterud is Nybaaken, "New Light on the Old Side"; Marsden, *Fundamentalism in American Culture.*

4 See Brooke, *Ulster Presbyterianism*, 74–82; McBride, *Scripture Politics*, 44; and Griffin, *People with No Name*, 47.

5 Indeed, denial of the Trinity remained a civil offence until the nineteenth century. See Holmes, *Our Presbyterian Heritage*, 63; Reid, *Presbyterian Church in Ireland* 2:496–7 and 3:110–214; Emlyn, "Humble Inquiry."

6 For more on the Irish New Light, or First Subscription Controversy, in the eighteenth century, see Reid, *Presbyterian Church in Ireland*, 3:110–214; Haire, *Challenge and Conflict,* 28–45, 96–148; Stewart, *Deeper Silence,* 67–125; Griffin, *People with No Name*, 47–64; McBride, *Scripture Politics*, chap. 2.

7 And, indeed, in all of Presbyterian history in Ireland. In a collection of articles subtitled "Essays in Irish Presbyterian History and Doctrine" written by some of the most esteemed Presbyterian ministers and scholars in Ireland in the early 1980s, five of the eight pieces revolve around either the Westminster Confession or controversies over subscription to it. See Haire, *Challenge and Conflict.*

8 See Miller et al., *Irish Immigrants*; and Kirkham, "Ulster Emigration to North America."

9 Sherling, "Part and Parcel," chap. 4.

10 Schlenther, *Life and Writings of Francis Makemie*, 24n47.

11 Ibid., 187–240.

12 Akenson, *God's Peoples,* 120; McBride, *Siege of Derry;* Hazlett, "Students at Glasgow University," 21; Akenson, *Ireland, Sweden and the Great European Migration*, 120; Holmes, *Shaping of Ulster Presbyterian Belief and Practice*, 306–7.

13 Bolton, *Scotch Irish Pioneers*, 16–17.

14 This first American presbytery was usually referred to at the time of its formation as "the American Presbytery," but it was also called the Presbytery of Philadelphia or the Presbytery of New Castle (Delaware) for the two cities in which it alternately met. However, it came to be known as the Presbytery of Philadelphia.

15 Augustus Briggs writes that, up until 1702, Irish presbyteries "were commissions of Presbytery rather than Presbyteries; and yet they were loosely called Presbyteries even in their official minutes. Their powers were limited, and their acts had only temporary validity until approved by the Presbytery, which was loosely called a Synod ... [T]hese meetings were compelled to act as Presbyteries defectively organized, to license, ordain, and install

ministers ... The first American classical Presbytery was such an Irish *meeting* of ministers, but without subordination to a higher body, resembling in this respect the Presbytery of Dublin. It was very different from a Westminster classical Presbytery, or a Presbytery like the Kirk of Scotland." See Briggs, *American Presbyterianism*, 141–2 (emphasis in original).

16 See Schlenther, *Life and Writings of Francis Makemie*; and Irwin, *Presbyterianism in Dublin*, 41–9.

17 See Irwin, *Presbyterianism in Dublin*, 41–9.

18 Sherling, *The Invisible Irish*, chap. 4

19 Webster, *History of the Presbyterian Church*, 102.

20 Ibid.

21 Hodge, *Constitutional History of the Presbyterian Church*, 74; Webster, *History of the Presbyterian Church*, 102. Not only do the densely Irish Presbyterian population of the New Castle Presbytery and the timing of the two requirements of subscription bear notice but so does the wording of the subscription oaths. Nineteenth-century Presbyterian historian Richard Webster noticed a connection, reporting that the New Castle "formula" of subscription – "I *do own the Westminster Confession as the confession of my faith*" – was very similar to the formula of the Presbytery of Armagh (in Ulster) of the same period: "I do believe the Westminster Confession of Faith to be founded on and agreeable to the word of God, and therefore as such, by this my subscription, *do own it as the confession of my faith*" (emphasis added).

22 Griffin, *People with No Name*, 120.

23 Ibid.

24 Ibid.

25 Fortson, "Adopting Act Compromise," 70–1.

26 Webster, *History of the Presbyterian Church*, 104.

27 *Westminster Confession of Faith*, chap. 31, para. 2, 96.

28 Fortson, "Adopting Act Compromise," 65n6.

29 At least ten of the nineteen ministers present were Irish immigrants. These were Thomas Creaghead (a former moderator of the Synod of Ulster), John Thompson, Samuel Gelston, Joseph Houston, William Tennent, Gilbert Tennent, Adam Boyd, Hugh Conn, and John Wilson. At least four New England ministers and two Irish ministers (Robert Cross and Henry Hook) were not present.

30 Webster, *Presbyterian Church in America*, 108 (emphasis in original).

31 See Christensen, "Franklin on the Hemphill Trial," 422–40.

32 Gillespie, *Treatise against the Deists or Free-Thinkers*, 58, quoted in Griffin, *People with No Name*, 121. George Gillespie was a Presbyterian

minister "at the head of Christiana Creek" (now known as the Christina River) in New Castle County, Delaware, and would have been a member of the heavily Irish and heavily pro-subscriber New Castle Presbytery.

33 There was one small portion that was acceptable to "scruple" over and that had to do with the Westminster Confession's teaching on the civil magistrate. See Hart, "Old Side/New Side," and Fortson, "Adopting Act Compromise."

34 Klett, *Minutes of the Presbyterian Church*, 132.

35 Ibid.

36 Ibid., 132–3 (emphasis added).

37 Ministers ordained in Ireland were viewed with tremendous suspicion in America, and the American synod made this very clear. There can be no wonder at all that clerical migration decreased drastically at this time. See Sherling, *The Invisible Irish*, chap. 6.

38 The formal split occurred in 1745, but in reality it probably existed from 1741. The reunion of the two sides occurred in 1758. The New Side and Old Side are different from New Lights and Old Lights. Most of the members of the American synod were Old Lights. So the American New Side and Old Side factions were necessarily drawn from the orthodox Old Lights. The difference between the two orthodox groups was that the New Side supported the new revivalist measures and practices first seen during the Great Awakening, while the Old Side attempted to use the authority of the presbyteries to limit the ability of unexamined itinerant ministers preaching to the people of their congregations. See Hart, "Old Side/New Side," 174–6.

39 Ibid., 157–79.

40 See Fortson, "Adopting Act Compromise," 63–85; and Hart, "Old Side/New Side," 157–79.

41 For more examples of such bizarre manifestations, see Lambert, *Inventing the "Great Awakening,"* 3, 68, 114, 189, 213, 240.

42 A clear sign that Old Side disapproval of the revivals was based upon this lack of supervision and the authority residing with a presbytery to ensure that the ministry within it was supervised by that presbytery can be seen in the titles of the two most famous New Side/Old Side polemical pamphlets. Whereas the most famous New Side pamphlet, written by Irish immigrant minister Gilbert Tennent and entitled "The Danger of an Unconverted Ministry," attacked and questioned the Christianity of those who disapproved of the revivals, the most famous Old Side pamphlet, written by the now long-embattled John Thompson, was called "The Government of the Church of Christ" and focused on the proper methods of church

organization and government as handed down by the Westminster Confession. See Tennent, "Unconverted Ministry"; and Thompson, "Church of Christ."

43 See previous note.

44 Hart, "Old Side/New Side," 157–8.

45 See Webster, *History of the Presbyterian Church*, 166.

46 Ibid., 356.

47 Briggs, *American Presbyterianism*, 186.

48 Indeed, Fortson contends that "continual tension over subscription in the nineteenth century became so potent that it would be one of the primary factors creating the Old School/New School Presbyterian schism (1838–1869)." See Fortson, "Adopting Act Compromise," 85.

7

Catholicism, Masculinity, and Middle-Class Respectability in the Irish Catholic Temperance Movement in Nineteenth-Century Canada

MIKE McLAUGHLIN

The 1853 St Patrick's Day celebrations in Toronto were marked by future Archbishop John Joseph Lynch's sermon, in which he complimented the Irish Catholics of that city on their numbers and respectability. Lynch emphasized the "orderly and sober conduct of every person engaged in the solemnities of the day" and observed that "it was a proud and consoling sight to witness so many thousands congregated in celebrating the national festival without one solitary instance of intemperance."[1] That same year in Montreal, during his address at the St Patrick's Day dinner, Thomas Ryan, a Montreal lawyer and president of the St Patrick's Society, looked round to the officers of the St Patrick's Total Abstinence Society, who were seated at the head table, and said he felt assured that those officers would act as guarantors that no excess would be indulged in and that he and others would follow their example as closely as possible on this or any other day. He expected that the people there that evening would not forget the evil consequence of intemperance and that every Irishman would unite in discouraging and preventing an offence, no matter how trivial, that was calculated to disgrace their country. If such a sentiment prevailed, Ryan continued, it would ultimately be "beneficial to all and render their prospects and careers in this country bright and successful."[2]

This chapter examines the relationship between alcohol consumption, temperance, and Irish Catholic identity in mid- to late nineteenth-century Canada. Temperance among the Irish Catholic diaspora in Canada has long been an overlooked topic. Studies of temperance and alcohol consumption in Canadian society have explored the wider temperance movement, the working-class movement of the later nineteenth and early twentieth centuries, the role of women in organizations such as the Women's Christian Temperance Union, as well as the regulation of alcohol consumption within both social control and moral regulation frameworks.[3] But alcohol consumption and temperance were also key ethno-religious issues for clerical and lay Irish Catholics.

Two major consequences of the Irish Catholic temperance movement are explored in this chapter. First is the role that temperance played in the evolution of the Roman Catholic Church in Canada through an emphasis on Irish nationality and Catholic values, with the objective of carving out a distinct Irish and Catholic culture. Second, temperance was important in the establishment of an ethno-religious identity that encompassed Catholicism and middle-class respectability and was therefore a contributing factor in the successful integration of Irish Catholics into Canadian society from the 1840s to the 1880s.[4] By examining the issue of temperance, who it appealed to and why, we can better understand how individual alcohol consumption was a significant concern for those involved in the devotional movement in the transnational Roman Catholic Church, contemporaries invested in maintaining patriarchal domesticity, and Irish Catholics in Canada looking to exhibit their national and imperial credentials.

Temperance emerged as part of the Second Great Awakening in the United States in the 1790s, and it became widespread across the Atlantic World and the British Empire in no small part owing to the temperance missionary work undertaken by Protestant evangelical organizations.[5] Temperance thus originated within the evangelical culture of the United States, and, through the work of these evangelical Protestant groups espousing the self-control ethos of temperance on an international scale, it soon became an important issue for English-speaking peoples across the globe, be they American, Canadian, English, South African, or Australian.[6] In New Zealand, for instance, the Ulster Protestant minister Rutherford Waddell was a tireless temperance campaigner. As John Stenhouse notes in chapter 15 (this volume), Waddell's religiosity greatly influenced his anti-alcohol stance, and he believed that Methodism was in the vanguard of progress owing to its support for prohibition, which he saw as a reform effort aimed at helping the mass of the people.[7] Thus, because of the Protestant dimensions of both the Atlantic World and the British Empire, temperance's genesis therein, and the role of evangelical

Protestants in spreading the movement, historians have viewed temperance largely as a Protestant social movement.[8] In *American Catholic Lay Groups and Transatlantic Social Reform in the Progressive Era*, Deirdre Moloney goes so far as to say that, owing to the emphasis that historians have placed on the Protestant attributes of the temperance and prohibition movement, readers of these works "are often left with the impression that Catholics were opposed or indifferent to temperance."[9] But as Moloney and others have shown, this was not the case. Indeed, one of the most successful temperance campaigns originated in Ireland and was led by Capuchin monk Theobold Mathew. Mathew became president of the Cork Total Abstinence Society in 1838.[10] Prior to Mathew's involvement in the movement, Protestant landlords dominated temperance in Ireland.[11] Mathew's temperance crusade was different, however, and would have a major impact both in Ireland and abroad. It is estimated that the Cork society enrolled somewhere between 3 and 5 million Irish men, women, and children into the temperance cause. Mathew's temperance movement was spearheaded by a rising Irish Catholic middle class that had been "emancipated" by Daniel O'Connell's campaign of the 1820s. This group infused temperance with distinct meanings that would be carried across the globe by Irish Catholics who engaged in temperance activities wherever they settled. These meanings presented temperance as a way to achieve spiritual and material self-improvement and regeneration for both the individual and the collective Irish nation. The temperance individual was not the end, argued Mathew's recent biographer Paul Townend, but, rather, "the beginning of a regenerated Ireland and a new social order."[12]

During the early to mid-nineteenth century, Irish Catholics migrated throughout the Atlantic World and the British Empire in record numbers. In their history of diasporic St Patrick's Day celebrations, Mike Cronin and Daryl Adair note that the largest Irish diasporas are found in English-speaking regions such as the United States, Canada, Britain, and Australia.[13] This migration trend accelerated after 1815 until the 1840s. Kerby Miller asserts that, between the end of the Napoleonic Wars and the beginning of the Great Famine, between 800,000 and 1 million Irish emigrants sailed to North America.[14] Though the bulk of Irish migrants from the early part of this thirty-year period were Protestant, by the 1820s the majority of Irish leaving Ireland were Catholic. Irish-born and Irish-trained priests and bishops exported Irish Catholic temperance across the English-speaking world within the context of this massive movement of Irish Catholics, and temperance became an important ethno-religious issue among global diasporic Irish Catholic communities. For instance, in the United States, as Moloney argues, owing to the lack of enthusiasm for temperance activities demonstrated by German Catholics, in the late nineteenth century temperance became a specifically Irish issue among Catholics in that country. This movement was spearheaded by individuals like Bishop John Ireland of St Paul, Minnesota, who had emigrated from Kilkenny to the United States.[15]

In Australia, the first Irish Catholic temperance society was formed under the auspices of Irish priest John T. Lynch. Lynch was born in Dublin and trained at the seminary at Maynooth. He, along with four other Irish-born and -trained priests, arrived in Sydney, Australia, aboard the *Cecilia* on 15 July 1838. They were meant to establish a Catholic infrastructure in colonial New South Wales. One of Lynch's first efforts in this endeavour was the establishment of an Irish Catholic temperance society. Lynch founded the St John's Total Abstinence Society West Maitland on 15 August 1841. His biographer, John O'Brien, notes that Lynch, inspired by Father Mathew's crusade, designed to "take the thing [alcohol] by the throat."[16] Lynch built a meeting hall, which he dubbed "the Temple of Concord," where he gave weekly lectures on the evils of drunkenness. Such evening events included concerts, magic-lantern shows, and various other social gatherings, all organized in the hope of keeping people sober and out of taverns. Lynch founded two other temperance societies in 1842.[17]

Likewise, in Canada, Irish-born priest Patrick Phelan established the first Irish Catholic temperance society in Montreal in 1841. In an article announcing his death in 1857, the organ of Irish Catholics in Montreal, the *True Witness and Catholic Chronicle*, remarked that Phelan exemplified the "good shepherd" who "gave his life for the sheep."[18] Phelan was born in County Kilkenny in 1793. At a young age he immigrated to Canada, where he engaged in ecclesiastical studies at the College of Montreal. He was ordained as a priest on 24 September 1825 and was soon aggregated to the Seminary of St Sulpice. Following this, he was active in administering to the spiritual and temporal needs of the Irish Catholic community of that city and provided medical care during the cholera epidemics of 1832 and 1834.[19] Influenced by the popularity and regenerative potential of Mathew's temperance campaign, Phelan formed the St Patrick's Total Abstinence Society on 24 February 1841. Other Irish Catholic clergy in Canada took Phelan's lead, and Irish Catholic temperance societies were soon established across the British colonies in

North America, where there was a sizable Irish Catholic community, from St John's in Newfoundland to London in Upper Canada.

To understand the transnational community-building work of Irish clerics involved in temperance (such as Ireland, Lynch, and Phelan) across the Atlantic World and the British Empire, it is useful to employ the framework of the Irish spiritual empire. Hilary Carey, Fiona Bateman, Peter Cunich, and others explore the concept of an Irish spiritual empire, which is a concept meant to indicate that the growth of the Catholic Church in the British Empire amounted to a spiritual empire equal to the political and cultural empire established by the British state.[20] The creation of this spiritual empire occurred through the settling of Irish-born and Irish-trained priests and bishops across the empire, and temperance was a major part of the community-building program. Cunich explores this spiritual empire in Australia in the late nineteenth century through the work of Roger Vaughan, who was the archbishop of Sydney between 1877 and 1883. Cunich concludes that, rather than attempting to create an Irish-centric spiritual empire, the development of the Catholic Church in Australia must be considered as a part of the imperial goals of Rome and the Holy See.

This dualism (i.e., an Irish spiritual empire and the British Empire) reflects two dominant trends within the Irish Catholic Church in the mid-nineteenth century. First is the advent of ultramontanism, a philosophy that emphasizes the authority of the pope and that seeks to increase the church's control over Catholics. The other is the devotional revolution, which is tied to ultramontanism but focuses more narrowly on the Irish community. Emmet Larkin points out that, prior to the Great Famine of 1845–49, the Irish, though nominally Catholic, were not practising the rituals of the church to the extent the church deemed appropriate. Adherence to such rituals increased throughout the 1840s and 1850s as the church set new standards of religious behaviour.[21]

In his study of the Irish Catholic community in mid-nineteenth-century Toronto, Brian Clarke argues that the clergy introduced voluntary organizations that emphasized secular pastimes in order to establish an associational environment that would prove more amenable to Irish Catholic men and thus facilitate their incorporation into Catholic culture. "Given the importance of alcohol to male sociability," Clarke argues, "drink was a natural target for a clergy determined to reform the cultural life of Irish Catholic men and to leaven it with the influence of the church."[22] Thus, in Clarke's estimation, a central purpose of Irish Catholic temperance societies was to co-opt otherwise non-practising lay members of the parish into participating in cultural activities within a Catholic world. Irish Catholic temperance fits the outline of ultramontanism, the devotional revolution, and the spiritual empire and must, therefore, be understood within the framework of the clerically led Irish Catholic community building that was so prevalent among the Irish Catholic diaspora in the nineteenth century.

The establishment of parish-level organizations such as temperance societies was an attempt on the part of the Catholic hierarchy in the British colonies in North America to achieve and to exercise a degree of community control and autonomy. Because these organizations were church-directed tools of community formation, Catholic practices and theology were fundamental to the movement. For instance, the rules and by-laws of the Father Mathew Association of St John, New Brunswick, asserted that the chaplain, who was to be a member of the clergy appointed by the bishop of the diocese, would be the head of the society (above the elected officers). In addition, religious duties, such as taking the sacraments of penance and blessed Eucharist at least twice a year, accompanied membership, and most Irish Catholic temperance societies held their regular meetings on Sundays following Vespers.[23]

This emphasis on Catholic theology within the Irish Catholic temperance movement precluded support for legal prohibition of alcohol. Though temperance originated as a moral suasion campaign whose supporters urged individuals to cease their production and consumption of spirits and to reduce their intake of wine, beer, and ciders, by the mid-nineteenth century large swathes of the mainstream Protestant movement jettisoned the moral suasion approach in favour of support for legislated suppression of alcohol production and consumption. Likewise, Irish Catholic temperance advocates supported a measured degree of legislation. For instance, during the debate over North America's first prohibitionary liquor law, the Maine Law of 1851, according to which the State of Maine outlawed the sale of all forms of alcohol, similar laws, though not as far-reaching, were enacted across Canada in the form of the local option, which enabled counties or municipalities to ban the sale of alcohol by popular vote. In 1851 John Gough, secretary of the St Patrick's Temperance Society at Bedford, Quebec, penned a letter that was printed in the Catholic press. In it, he observed that, while temperance supporters ought to feel gratitude towards the government for passing the local option, there was still more to be done. Gough felt that this law was insufficient to battle booze, in part because the low cost of intoxicating drinks meant that people would continue to consume alcohol in large quantities. In order to remedy this, Gough suggested that the friends of temperance "bring the matter before the Legislative body the ensuing session, praying that a heavier duty be imposed upon the distilling of whiskey and that no distiller be allowed to sell any less quantity than five gallons." In addition, Gough recommended that all temperance societies form committees of vigilance in each parish or township for the purpose of "making compliant any person or persons found in a state of intoxication, exposed to public view."[24]

A similar sentiment was expressed in a letter printed in the *Ottawa Tribune*, the Irish Catholic paper in Ottawa, in April 1858. The writer argued that, owing to the harm that is inflicted upon society through alcohol consumption, it was the duty of any government to denounce the production, importation, and sale of alcohol severely and to suppress them by means of needful penalties and punishments. An 1854 pastoral letter signed by the bishops of Quebec, Montreal, Toronto, and Bytown thundered against those who evaded liquor laws and purchased illicit booze. "The flagrant violation of a law framed to protect public order and morality demands the most vigorous repression," the letter read, and it went on to exclaim that people who do evade this law "are unworthy of being admitted to the sacraments of the church."[25]

Such examples notwithstanding, throughout the nineteenth century, anti-alcohol crusade support for complete and legislated prohibition never came from the Irish Catholic temperance movement. Preference for the moral suasion approach was grounded in Catholic theology. It was believed that the law and government could not reform behaviour: this could only be done through the Roman Catholic Church. For instance, according to the *True Witness*, legislative prohibition of alcohol alone was inefficient. To illustrate this, the paper commented on the 1865 annual report of the Montreal chief of police. This report showed that, in 1864, there were 290 licensed establishments in Montreal and 250 unlicensed ones. From 1864 to 1865 unlicensed drinking establishments had decreased by thirty-five, while licensed drinking establishments had increased by thirty-six, with the total number of establishments increasing from 540 to 541.[26] This, according to the *True Witness*, was proof that licensed and unlicensed grog-shops stood in inverse ratio to one another: as one category diminished the other increased by the same number. Having fewer unlicensed grog shops only served to increase the number of licensed liquor sellers.

This happened because the demand for alcohol among the population remained the same. Legislative prohibition, according to this line of thought, did not bring about the moral reformation of the population necessary to ridding society of drunkenness. Moral reformation, not laws, was necessary in order to suppress drunkenness, and this, according to the Irish Catholic clergy, could only come about through the intervention of the Catholic Church. Toronto's archbishop, John Joseph Lynch, expressed this sentiment in an 1884 letter. Lynch discussed the Canada Temperance Act, 1878, which provided municipalities with an option to establish prohibition. He declared his support for the cause of temperance but maintained his belief that changing laws would have little impact if individual behaviour did not change. If the people themselves don't want to stop drinking, he wrote, "prohibition won't do it, they will get it somehow."[27]

Clerical Irish Catholic temperance leaders were adamant that liquor laws and legislative enactments could never replace the sacraments and grace of God. They believed that Christ established His church as the remedy for all the moral evils that have their origin in the corrupt human heart, and drunkenness was certainly one of these. If the church is the remedy for all moral diseases, then it is fully capable of curing society of the disease of drunkenness and intemperance. In denying the state a moral or spiritual jurisdiction, the church opposed "any man made society and organization that gave itself the functions of the Church of Christ and professed to do by its rules and regulations, by its pledges and human devices what the blessed Sacraments are unable to effect and the assertion that in making His Church Christ did His work imperfectly."[28] In the eyes of many Irish Catholics, then, moral reformation had to come through Catholicism, not laws. It was moral reformation that was needed to suppress drunkenness.

Catholic opposition to prohibition was justified through scripture and theology. The *True Witness* argued that, for Catholics, alcohol itself was never something inherently evil that had to be completely banned. In an editorial, it cited the story of Jesus accepting wine on the cross and argued that this was evidence that Christianity sanctioned alcohol. Thus, to denounce the mere use of alcoholic beverages was a most blasphemous and damnable heresy.

In presenting this analysis, Irish Catholic clergy aimed to limit external interference in the Catholic subculture of temperance. They were using Catholic theology to buttress their temperance position and, thus, to preclude Protestant involvement. For instance, the emphasis on the moral suasion approach to temperance, grounded in Catholic teachings, was one of several reasons that co-operation between Catholic and Protestant temperance societies could not occur. Another reason Irish Catholic clerical temperance leaders argued against co-operation between Catholic and Protestant temperance organizations concerns their respective optimal outcomes. Clerical Irish Catholic temperance leaders argued that Protestant temperance was too involved in total prohibition, worldly affairs, and government legislation. In contrast, Irish Catholic temperance advocates insisted that the Catholic movement was more spiritually orientated:

> Catholicity denounces drunkenness because it drags down to hell and excludes forever from Heaven – Protestantism because it entails poverty and is ruinous to thrift and worldly prosperity; Catholicity preaches temperance as a Christian duty – Protestantism as a civic virtue ... [O]ne seeks to reform mankind by spiritual means, spiritual threats, and the hope of spiritual rewards – the other by secular means, by contrasting the poverty, filth and misery of the drunkard with the wealth, thrift, and general comfort of the sober man.[29]

Catholic temperance societies sought to "bring about moral reformation by the use of spiritual means," while Protestant temperance societies were formed outside of the church and attempted to effect a moral reformation without religion.[30] Though Irish Catholic temperance advocates fought against the social problem of excessive consumption of alcohol, both their utilization of temperance as a means for Catholic community building and their fealty to Catholic faith and spirituality led them to establish a Catholic temperance movement that was distinct and separate from the Protestant temperance movement. Temperance thus peaked within the context of the devotional revolution, according to which the Irish Catholic Church undertook measures to carve out a position of community leadership and to create a spiritual empire encompassing a distinct Catholic culture.

Irish clergy also sought to establish a specifically Irish Catholic culture that would be distinct from the French Catholic culture in Canada. As Mark McGowan demonstrates in chapter 4 (this volume), Irish and French Catholics fought for control of the Catholic Church infrastructure in Canada. French Catholics had a longer and more entrenched history in this country and, prior to the influx of Irish Catholics in the nineteenth century, largely controlled the structure of the Catholic Church. Irish

Catholic clergy in Canada saw activities such as temperance as a way to carve out a Catholic culture for the Irish that would separate them from and render them immune to French Catholic influence.

This rivalry for control of the church did not, however, preclude periods of co-operation between Irish and French Catholic temperance activists. For instance, the 6 September 1850 edition of the *True Witness* printed a correspondence between John Hayes, president of the Catholic Total Abstinence Society of Toronto, and noted French Catholic temperance advocate Father Charles Chiniquy on the occasion of the latter's visit to Toronto.[31] Hayes, writing on behalf of the managing committee of the society, welcomed Chiniquy to the city and congratulated him on his success in extending temperance throughout Quebec. Hayes went on to note that Chiniquy was well aware of the obstacles and barriers to the temperance cause in Canada and that, because of this, Hayes and the committee valued Chiniquy's crusade all the more highly. In his response to Hayes's letter, Chiniquy noted the gratitude with which he received the well-wishes of the committee and spoke of the merits of his work of social regeneration.[32]

Yet even during moments of such unity, Irish and French Catholics were well aware of the ethnic and national differences separating them. For instance, though Hayes did note Chiniquy's temperance work, he also specified that his (Chiniquy's) labourers to promote temperance were in aid of achieving "the improved social position of your people," along with "their happiness in the life to come." In other words, Hayes distinguished between Chiniquy's people and himself (and, presumably, the members of the committee for whom he was speaking) as an Irish Catholic. For his part, Chiniquy also distinguished his temperance work from the temperance work of his Irish co-religionists, noting that he was working for Catholics of French origin who inhabit Canada East (Quebec), while lauding Hayes and the Toronto society for continuing and furthering the temperance work done by and for Irish Catholics.[33] Various other factors, such as the linguistic divide, rivalry for control of the Catholic hierarchy in Canada, and increased anxieties among French Canadian leaders regarding the assimilationist policies of British colonists, contributed to the lack of sustained co-operation between Irish and French Catholics with respect to temperance. More germane to this chapter is the emphasis that the Canadian Irish Catholic clerical leaders placed on Catholic values and Irish nationalities in their formulation of temperance and the explicit links made between temperance and Irish Catholic ethno-religious identity. In this way, the Canadian Irish Catholic temperance movement and its advocates aided in the growth of the Catholic culture that was distinct from mainstream Protestantism and an Irish Catholic culture that was distinct from French Catholicism.

In addition to employing the spiritual empire framework to explore the ways in which Irish Catholic temperance was key to the development of an Irish culture and a Catholic culture in Canada, it is also useful to place the temperance work of Ireland, Lynch, Phelan, and other Irish Catholic clergy within the context of an emergent diasporic Irish Catholic middle class. Here, too, Irish Catholics have been left out of the discussion. Like the linkages historians have made between temperance and evangelicalism, the development of a middle class in the English-speaking world has tended to be a Protestant story. Consequently, temperance has been seen as a middle-class Protestant development, with little room for an Irish Catholic angle. But in much the same way as historians have pointed out the global reach of an Irish Catholic temperance movement, there is growing evidence to suggest that, for quite some time, a strong Irish Catholic middle class had been emerging in Ireland.[34] These middle-class Irish Catholics were among the millions who emigrated across the Atlantic World and British Empire in the mid-nineteenth century. Across these vast regions, this social group established itself and evolved within national, regional, and local contexts. In Canada, the development and growth of an Irish Catholic middle class was facilitated by factors such as the advent of responsible government in the 1840s (which made the Irish Catholic vote increasingly important to politicians) and an increasingly commercial economy (which allowed Irish Catholics to make their way as merchants and shopkeepers). However, barriers to Irish Catholic advancement remained in Canada and across what Linda Colley dubs a Protestant Empire.[35] The most potent of these was perhaps the strongly negative view of Irish Catholics. Indeed, scholars such as John Wolffe observe that there is a strong link between imperial rhetoric and anti-Catholic rhetoric.[36] L. Perry Curtis stresses the preponderance of demeaning cultural stereotypes throughout British imperial society that present the Irish as something less than human.[37] Looking specifically at Canada, while it has been famously argued that, during the nineteenth century, Canada was transforming from a British colony into an independent nation-state, it nonetheless remained a part of the British World.[38] As Paula Hastings argues, "English Canadians continuously negotiated their position within the British Empire and their constructions of British identity were often inspired by domestic circumstances."[39] Further, Robert Adamoski,

Dorothy Chunn, and Robert Menzies assert, in their introduction to *Contesting Canadian Citizenship*, that the dominant vision of citizenship in nineteenth-century Canada was one in which the ideal individual was constructed as an imperial male citizen – loyal, autonomous, rational, content, white, and British through and through.[40] Irish Catholics in Canada at this juncture, then, embarked upon the process of ethnic formation within a country that was embedded within an imperial, Protestant, British culture that did not view them on equal terms.

Irish Catholics aimed to overcome such inequalities and to succeed in Canada through various social, cultural, and economic activities. Faced with the type of discriminatory and prejudicial attitudes noted above, however, integrating and advancing meant having to differentiate themselves from crude caricatures of Irish identity. Ambitious Irish Catholics in Canada who joined temperance societies employed tropes of middle-class respectability that would be recognizable to the Protestant majority, and they adapted these norms of respectability to Catholic values and Irish nationality. Emphasis on social uplift and achieving respectability through temperance was not uncommon among marginalized groups in the nineteenth century. In her study of nineteenth-century African Canadian temperance societies, for instance, Lorene Bridgen argues that African Americans who entered Canada in search of freedom found their place in southern Ontario through participation in the temperance movement, which "played a major role in the African Canadian community's struggle for equality and respect." Temperance, Bridgen reasons, "became a path to freedom – moral, social and political freedom. Through it Blacks could show, by example, that they deserved both liberty and citizenship. And by choosing for themselves not to drink they could gain both self-respect and the approval of the Canadian community as a whole."[41] Similarly, Irish Catholic religious and lay temperance advocates sought to employ temperance to gain acceptance for their collective ethno-religious group.

The expansion of a Catholic infrastructure among the Irish in Canada, therefore, occurred in conjunction with the emergence of an Irish Catholic laity seeking to advance and to succeed in its new country. Though membership lists are difficult to track down, the substantial number of members enrolled in these societies suggests a wide range of class positions. For instance, in 1871, Montreal's St Patrick's Total Abstinence and Benefit Society had 12,040 members, an increase of 505 from the previous year.[42] The by-laws of these organizations further reflect a cross-section of class positions among members. For instance, in 1857, the membership fee for entry into the Halifax Catholic Total Abstinence and Benevolent Society was two dollars, with a monthly fee of twenty-five cents. This entitled members to benefits should they require financial assistance – eligible members could receive up to three dollars per week – and also provided funeral coverage for needy members.[43] While the two-dollar initiation fee and subsequent monthly fees indicate that these members likely did not come from the labouring classes, the funeral allowances point to the socio-economic precariousness of members and their families, especially should the male head of the household die. These organizations served a social purpose, often acting as a relief or mutual aid society for incoming immigrants and for Irish Catholics already in Canada. For instance, the Father Mathew Association of St John, New Brunswick, levied a tax of between twenty-five and fifty cents on each regular member in the event of the death of a member, a member's wife, or the widowed mother of an unmarried member. Further, its constitution noted that any member who was six months behind his or her dues would forfeit membership.[44] Members were thus allowed a few months grace should they be unable to afford the twelve-cent monthly fee, but ultimately they had to pay to qualify for membership.

Though the membership of these organizations was diverse with respect to class status, the bulk of the leadership was made up of middle-class individuals as well as those aspiring to middle-class status. Two representative examples of lay individuals active in Irish Catholic temperance societies are John Heney and John O'Rourke. Heney was a long-time officer in the St Patrick's Temperance Society of Ottawa. Heney was a wood merchant who sold firewood, and his main source of income came from government contracts for fuel.[45] In the 1881 census Heney is listed as being married to Ontario-born Mary-Anne, forty-nine, and the couple had five children as well as two boarders, Elizabeth Wade, thirty-two, and Ellen Curley, forty-seven.[46] At the time of the 1891 census four of the children remained in the Heney home, including twenty-one-year-old Thomas, who was employed as a clerk. Elizabeth Wade also remained in the household as a lodger. By this point, the family also employed a domestic servant, Annie McCormack.[47] John O'Rourke was the assistant secretary of St Ann's Total Abstinence and Benevolent Society in Montreal. Listed as a speculator on the 1871 census, he was married to Catherine, who was also born in Ireland. All of their children were born in Quebec. The eldest child, Hugh, was twenty years of age at the time of the 1871 census, meaning that John and Catherine had been in Canada since at least 1850. In all the couple had six children; Hugh was working as a plumber; daughter Mary Ann, seventeen, was listed as a factory worker; while son John, fourteen, was working as a printer.[48] In the 1881 census, John O'Rourke is listed as a "commerçant," French for shopkeeper.[49]

Heney and O'Rourke were representative of Irish Catholic individuals who were most drawn to temperance. Both achieved upward social mobility during their time in Canada, albeit by means of different paths. Heney profited from government contracts for wood, coal, and oil throughout his lifetime. He was involved in patronage networks established by Irish Catholics in government positions. These networks became increasingly important for the Irish Catholic middle class in Canada following the establishment of responsible government in the 1840s as it then behoved politicians to engage Irish Catholics as government employees (e.g., as engineers, surveyors, clerks, or, as in the case of Heney, contractors) owing to their increased numbers and to the importance of the Irish Catholic vote. By succeeding in society as a merchant and shopkeeper, O'Rourke took advantage of a Canadian economy that, in the second half of the nineteenth century, was becoming increasingly urban, commercial, and capitalist. However, the census data suggest that neither the Heneys nor the O'Rourkes were elite clans but, rather, that they were working to achieve and maintain a certain position in society. For instance, Heney's family took in a lodger, an action that scholars have noted was common in the nineteenth century as a strategy to negotiate the precariousness of the nascent wage economy.[50] Both families had working children who remained at home contributing to the family economy. Such strategies of economic survival indicate that these families were cognizant of the precariousness of their socio-economic status. Individuals such as Heney and O'Rourke were leading fairly successful lives in Canada owing to a more liberal economic system and, at least in the case of Heney, the broadening economic reach of the state and the increased population of Irish Catholics. They aimed to integrate into, and advance within, the Canadian economy and society rather than to remain isolated from it. But this desire to integrate and to advance did not mean that the aspiring Irish Catholic middle class, any more than the clergy, would blindly follow the dominant Protestant majority. Strong feelings of ethno-religious sentiment meant that, instead of jettisoning their Irish Catholic identity to further their integrationist objectives, these people intended to enhance their Irish Catholic identity with dominant tropes of respectability.

Clerical and lay leaders in the Irish Catholic temperance movement recognized the key function temperance could perform in the demonstration of respectability with regard to ideal forms of masculinity. Studies have highlighted divergent varieties of masculinities and the ways in which certain forms are seen as superior to others. John Tosh and Michael Roper note that dominant masculinities operate by emphasizing their authority over subordinated masculinities.[51] The idealized masculinity among middle-class Irish Catholics of this period was a respectable, domestically oriented variety. To paraphrase Colleen McDannell in her article on Catholicism and the Irish-American male, promoters of respectable masculinity hoped to curb the disruptive and unsocial tendencies of Irish Catholic men.[52]

Excessive consumption of alcohol was seen as one such disruptive and unsocial tendency. Part of proper manhood and ideal forms of masculine behaviour expressed in Irish Catholic temperance discourse concerns the protection of women. This patriarchal rhetoric and imagery focused on women who were victimized by men who exhibit tendencies associated with rough masculinity, such as the excessive consumption of alcohol, violence, and squandering the family's money on booze. In contrast, respectable men took care of their domestic life, which was one of sobriety and order. In both cases women were presented as dependent upon the type of masculinity evinced by men: being victimized by rough masculinity, while benefitting from respectable masculinity.[53]

Respectable masculinity, critical in Canadian Irish Catholic temperance discourse, was evident in the iconography of the movement, such as in the coat of arms of Montreal's St Patrick's Total Abstinence and Benefit Society.[54] In this illustration, a man in the foreground is shown holding a banner that reads "Sobriety" while a woman stands just behind him holding a banner that reads "Domestic comfort." The man carrying the banner of sobriety allows the woman to achieve domestic comfort within the household. Indeed, the domestic comfort of the woman seems to be dependent upon the man's sobriety and his respectable masculinity in general. However, because this masculinity was domestic in nature and the role of women in the construction of this gender ideal was important, women were not simply dependent. As discussed below, a certain type of femininity was prescribed and was needed in order to round out the domestic, respectable, and middle-class masculinity of Irish Catholic males.

This coat of arms fleshes out the gender identities and responsibilities prescribed to men and women through the middle-class Irish Catholic temperance movement. It is conceivable that, if this woman was not holding the banner of "domestic comfort" and was instead holding the banner of "social drink," then this man could easily be holding the banner of drunkenness and ruin. Irish Catholic men and women each had a part to play in maintaining prosperity and domestic comfort. Men were to be sober, industrious, and protective, while women were to be sober, in charge of domestic comfort, and responsible for regulating the household intake of alcohol. If either men or women failed to live up to these roles, so the thinking went, then drunkenness, violence, and ruin would be sure to follow.

Temperance was also apparent in the exhibition of Irish Catholic respectability on St Patrick's Day, when parades and public processions dominated the landscape of many Canadian cities. Cognizant of the public attention, clerical and lay members of the Irish Catholic community were agreed on the importance of displaying a sober, respectable, and imposing image to the broader community. Thus, public displays on St Patrick's Day, such as the one described below in Ottawa in 1862, were common:

> In the St Patrick procession was the St Patrick's Temperance Society each displaying on the breast of his coat a badge of green and white silk having impressed thereon in gold bronze the Harp of Erin and the title of thc association. At their head was raised the temperance banner showing a life-sized portrait of Father Mathew, the world-renowned temperance advocate. They were led by the St Patrick's band who presented quite an imposing figure being uniformly attired in black cloth pants and coats with scarlet bands round the cuffs and collars ... Their caps were of fine black cloth with bands of gold lace surmounted in front by a silver shamrock.[55]

In order for this project of ethnic formation to be successful it was incumbent upon the clerical and lay leaders of the Irish Catholic temperance movement to police other Irish Catholics. Self-appointed leaders of the Irish Catholic community had a vision of Canadian Irish Catholic ethno-religious identity, and they actively imposed it on other Irish Catholics. At a planning meeting for the 1855 St Patrick's Day parade in Toronto held by the temperance society, a professor in St Michael's College, and member of the organization, Reverend Flannery, spoke of the negativity intemperance had caused for the Irish collectively. He made the following point: "if ever it was becoming expedient for an

Irishman to be enrolled under the banner of temperance it was on St Patrick's Day when drunkenness could no longer be an individual crime, but a stain on the community, an insult to the memory of the Saint we honor and a foul blot on the national and religious character of our people."[56]

In Toronto in 1855, the Irish Catholic temperance society celebrated St Patrick's Day by marching in the parade, and Thomas Fitzhenry led the temperance procession. Later in the evening, Fitzhenry spoke and noted that public opinion had shifted, and that it was currently no credit to be seen drunk. In future, Fitzhenry continued, Irishmen, "instead of foolishly spending their money on St Patrick's Day in taverns," would "celebrate their Patron Saint's day and convert its proceeds to the benefits of the orphans."[57] In 1852, with great enthusiasm the *True Witness* observed the festivities in Bytown. After Mass, the St Patrick's Temperance Society, joined by the other Catholic temperance societies in the vicinity, formed a procession with banners and a band. The *True Witness* glowingly remarked that "good order and regularity prevailed throughout." The paper noted that, while the celebration was "highly enthusiastic," it was nonetheless

> characterized by piety, sobriety, and good will as become Irishmen and Canadians. The demon of dissipation was, to all appearances, banished from our midst ... This was an undoubted triumph of Father Mathew's idea: the day, thank God, is fast passing away when the whiskey bowl enjoyed a prominent place in the arrangements for the festive gathering of Irishmen. Oh! Had that been so a century ago Irishmen might have now occupied another place in the world's history.[58]

Irish Catholics also used St Patrick's Day and temperance discourse to express their loyalty to nation and empire. Noises of national and imperial loyalty demonstrate the complex negotiations of identity undertaken by Irish Catholics in Canada, situated as they were in both the Atlantic World and the British Empire. Indeed, complexity existed because attempts to link Irish Catholic ethno-religious identity to the Empire through temperance activities did not necessarily reflect an Irish Catholic attachment to the British Empire. By and large Irish Catholics saw themselves neither as members of the Empire nor as imperial subjects; rather, they saw themselves as Canadians and as Irish Catholics. Such a perspective reflected their aims of retaining and furthering their Irish Catholic cultural heritage while simultaneously participating and advancing in Canadian society. This negotiation of identity and place was put into practice through issues related to alcohol consumption, and its inconsistencies crystallize the complex position of Irish Catholics in the Empire.

A dominant political culture in Canada was the ideology of loyalism.[59] This way of thinking was established when northern British colonies did not join the southern British colonies in rebelling in 1776. The importance of loyalism was furthered during the War of 1812 between the Americans and the British, which was fought largely in the British North American colonies. A consequence of the colonies' attachment to the Empire was the requirement that individuals in the colony profess their adherence to the loyalist perspective in order to achieve acceptance, belonging, and economic success. This requirement was doubly important for Irish Catholics who came to Canada as they came under suspicion due to both their nationality and their religion. The ambitious Irish Catholics involved in the temperance movement sought to use the issue of alcohol consumption as an opportunity to merge loyalist symbols with Irish Catholic identity. Thus, at St Patrick's Day dinners it was common to have an amalgam of seemingly contradictory toasts, including ones to the queen and royal family, to the pope and the Catholic hierarchy and clergy of Canada, to the governor general of Canada, to the memory of Daniel O'Connell, to Father Mathew, and to the success of the Canadian railways.[60] At the 1871 St Patrick's Day procession in Montreal Toronto's *Globe* – a reform-minded, Protestant newspaper whose editor, George Brown, was known for his sometimes virulent denouncements of Irish Catholics – noted approvingly that "British flags were generally displayed along with the green" and that a "Union Jack alone waved from atop St Patrick's Hall that day."[61]

These expressions of loyalty to the Empire were aimed at achieving a degree of belonging in Canada and did not represent any sense of membership in the British (and Protestant) Empire. Thus, the Irish Catholic press was more than willing to critique symbols of this Empire for encouraging excessive consumption of alcohol and, in so doing, to highlight Irish sobriety and, hence, respectability. For instance, the temperate and respectable Irish Catholic celebrations of St Patrick were contrasted with the celebration of the twelfth of July, when Irish Protestants celebrated King William's victory over the Catholic King James in 1690. The Bytown correspondent for the *True Witness* reported on Orange festivities in that city in 1852. He noted that the Orange parade was "headed by a man named Powell," who was dressed to represent the Dutch King

William and mounted on a white horse. At day's end, observed the Bytown correspondent, "King William is at this moment entering a third-rate grog shop on Rideau Street."[62] And it was with delight in March of 1884 that the *True Witness* reported on the excessive amount of whisky consumed by Queen Victoria, as told in her book, *More Leaves from the Journal of a Life in the Highlands*, which, according to the editorial, was "not much calculated to aid the temperance cause in England." The relation of whisky-infused "incidents as those in the life of the Queen of England," observed the paper, "is far from being exemplary or from producing a salutary effect upon her people who are so strongly inclined towards indulgence in intoxicating liquors."[63]

Gaining acceptance from the wider society through the discourse of temperance thus included looking inward (through encouraging sobriety among the Irish Catholic community) as well as looking outward (through linking their work with loyalist discourse). In this latter endeavour, however, it appears as though they were ambivalent about their place within the imperial sphere, as is suggested by their sarcasm towards imperial symbols. For Irish Catholic temperance activists it was far more important to be seen as members of their new homeland of Canada than to be seen as members of the Empire. In using the temperance movement to project the worth of their people, it was to the nation, not the Empire, that they were speaking. For instance, following the cholera outbreaks of the 1830s and the Irish famine of the 1840s, fears regarding the influx of immigrants were heightened. Recognizing these fears, Irish Catholic temperance supporters aimed to showcase how their work was helping to diminish the negative impact caused by the newcomers. In November 1860, John O'Reilly, a member of the Ottawa Irish Catholic temperance society, penned a letter to the *Ottawa Tribune* in which he noted the increase in drunkenness in the city owing to the "sudden influx of people of all classes." However, he was happy to report that, among Catholics, drunkenness had not increased and that it was, in fact, close to being suppressed altogether. O'Reilly attributed this to the "bold front presented by the Irish Temperance Association" and to the "firm determination of its members" in doing their part to curb drunkenness among newcomers to the city. This association, according to O'Reilly, was aware of its role in the matter and embraced it with enthusiasm. The Irish Temperance Association, O'Reilly asserted, was "alive to the increasing responsibilities devolving upon it" and had not only "checked the evil of intemperance" but also, "by its moral force[,] ha[d] caused a decided reaction to set in."[64] Here O'Reilly positions himself and the Ottawa

Irish Temperance Association as Canadians aiding the incoming immigrants in their adjustment to Ottawa, and, perhaps most important, as Canadians aiding Ottawa in regulating their potentially disruptive behaviour.

By the late 1870s and into the 1880s, the Irish Catholic temperance movement transitioned into a Catholic-orientated phenomenon. Broad Catholic temperance organizations, such as the League of the Cross, replaced Irish-specific organizations. In this, then, temperance seems to have followed the paradigm outlined by Mark McGowan in his study of Irish Catholic identity, becoming less an Irish issue and more a part of a broader Catholic world.[65] In December 1879, for example, a letter was read at the regular monthly meeting of the St Patrick's Total Abstinence and Benefit Society in Montreal, where it was resolved that the society was of the opinion that "a union of a more comprehensive character … should be effected among us." It was further resolved that the society "strongly recommend the formation of a union of the various English-speaking Catholic total abstinence societies of the district of Montreal" and "bring the various English speaking Catholic total abstinence societies into more friendly and social relations with each other."[66] These resolutions passed unanimously, suggesting that the era of temperance as a specifically Irish issue had come to an end.

This happened for two reasons. First, it was the Catholic community-building work of Irish Catholic clergy in areas such as temperance that enabled a distinct English-speaking Catholic temperance movement to continue into the twentieth century without being swallowed up by the wider Protestant majority or the French-speaking Catholic population of Canada. This speaks to the point made by McGowan (chap. 4, this volume) regarding the success of Irish Catholics within Canada's Catholic infrastructure.[67] Second, temperance ceased to be a specifically Irish issue in part because it had succeeded as a strategy of integration. It was instrumental in allowing Irish Catholics to showcase their middle-class respectability while, at the same time, retaining their ethno-religious identity.

Clerical and lay Irish Catholics in Canada involved in the temperance movement were part of the spiritual empire consisting of Irish Catholics who defined and spread a distinct Irish and Catholic culture across the Atlantic World and the British Empire. Moreover, these individuals aided in integrating Irish Catholics into Canadian society by demonstrating to that society their qualifications for ideological citizenship. The wider Canadian society responded favourably. During the 1871 St Patrick's

Day celebrations in Montreal, the mayor of that city, Charles Coursol, spoke in front of a gathering of Irish societies, which included the St Bridget's Temperance Society and the St Patrick's Temperance Society. Coursol remarked that the Irish people of Montreal were a large and important part of the community and a credit to the city. He said that the immense number of them on the streets at one time as well as "the good conduct that was everywhere visible" confirmed this. Not a single instance of intoxication was to be found during that day, the mayor continued, and this was "thanks to the good advice of their noble clergy and the heads of families."[68]

NOTES

1 *True Witness and Catholic Chronicle*, *"St Patrick's Day in Toronto,"* 1 April 1853.

2 Ibid., *"Celebrations of St Patrick's Day,"* 25 March 1853.

3 Noel, *Canada Dry*; Heron, "Boys and Their Booze"; Malleck, "Priorities of Development"; Campbell, "Managing the Marginal."

4 Integration is a major theme in ethnic and immigration studies. Debates have emerged around the meaning of the term "integration" relative to the assimilation model, pioneered by Robert Park in the 1920s and expanded upon by Milton Gordon. In the case of the Irish in Canada, debates have centred on when and how the Irish integrated into Canadian society. This is complicated by the regional particularisms faced by the Irish in the Canadian context. See Gordon, *Assimilation in American Life*; Morawska, "In Defense of the Assimilation Model"; Clarke, *Piety and Nationalism*; McGowan, *Waning of the Green*; and Houston and Smyth, *Irish Emigration and Canadian Settlement.*

5 Tyrell, *Woman's World*. For this point see especially his chapter 1, "Origins of Temperance Internationalism."

6 The literature on American temperance is vast. Among others, see Gusfield, *Symbolic Crusade*; Blocker, *American Temperance Movements*; Fletcher, *Gender and the American Temperance Movement*. For Canada, see Noel, *Canada Dry*; Heron, *Booze*. For England, see Harrison, *Drink and the Victorians*; Nicholls, *Politics of Alcohol*. For South Africa, see Nugent, "Temperance Movement and Wine Farmers." For Australia, see Noyce, "Coffee Palaces in Australia"; Blainey, "Prohibition and Total Abstinence Movement." For the broad international perspective on temperance, see Blocker, Fahey, and Tyrell, *Alcohol and Temperance in Modern History*.

7 Stenhouse (chap. 15, this volume).

8 Fletcher, *Gender and the American Temperance Movement.*
9 Moloney, *American Catholic Lay Groups*, 43.
10 Townend, *Father Mathew*, 3.
11 Bretherton, "Battle between Carnival and Lent."
12 Townend, *Father Mathew*, 85–6. For Mathew and Irish Temperance, see Malcolm, *Ireland Sober.*
13 Cronin and Adair, *Wearing of the Green*, xxv.
14 Miller, *Emigrants and Exiles*, 193.
15 Moloney, *American Catholic Lay Groups*, 50.
16 O'Brien, *Men of '38*, 91.
17 Sternbeck, *Catholic Church in Singleton*, 17.
18 *True Witness and Catholic Chronicle,* 12 June 1857.
19 Ibid.
20 Cunich, "Archbishop Vaughan"; Bateman, "Ireland's Spiritual Empire'; Carey and Barr (Introduction, this volume); Ó hAnnracháin, "Consolidation of Irish Catholicism."
21 Larkin, "Devotional Revolution in Ireland." Larkin's thesis has elicited, and continues to elicit, considerable scholarly debate. See, for example, McGrath, "Tridentine Evolution of Modern Irish Catholicism."
22 Clarke, *Piety and Nationalism.*
23 Constitution and Rules of the Father Mathew Association organized at St John, New Brunswick, 9 March 1871. Toronto Reference Library, CIHM 98690.
24 *True Witness and Catholic Chronicle*, 23 May 1851.
25 *Ottawa Tribune*, 23 July 1854.
26 *True Witness and Catholic Chronicle,* 6 April 1866.
27 Letter from Archbishop John Joseph Lynch, 1884, Archives of the Roman Catholic Archdiocese of Toronto, AH2940.
28 "Maine Liquor Law." *True Witness and Catholic Chronicle*, 17 September 1852, 4.
29 TWCC, 13 February 1852, 5.
30 Ibid.
31 For more on Chiniquy, see Noel, *Canada Dry.*
32 "Temperance," *True Witness and Catholic Chronicle*, 6 September 1850.
33 Ibid.
34 Wall, *Rise of a Catholic Middle Class.*
35 Colley, *Britons.*
36 Wolffe, "Anti-Catholicism and the British Empire."
37 Curtis, *Apes and Angels.*

38 Lower, *Colony to Nation.*
39 Hastings "Our Glorious Anglo-Saxon Race," 92–110, 101.
40 Adamoski, Chunn, and Menzies, *Contesting Canadian Citizenship*, 22.
41 Bridgen, "On Their Own Terms."
42 Proceedings of the Montreal St Patrick's Total Abstinence and Benefit Society, 1868–71, 29 January 1871, Concordia University Archives, HA 219.
43 Constitution and Bylaws of Halifax Catholic Total Abstinence and Benefit Society, 1857, Toronto Reference Library, CIHM 67184.
44 Constitution and Rules of the Father Mathew Association organized at St John, New Brunswick, 9 March 1871, Toronto Reference Library, CIHM 98690
45 Heney, *John Heney & Son.*
46 Census of Canada, 1881.
47 Ibid., 1891.
48 Ibid., 1871.
49 Ibid., 1881.
50 Bradbury, "Pigs, Cows, and Boarders."
51 Tosh and Roper, *Manful Assertions.*
52 McDannell, "True Men as We Need Them."
53 Stenhouse (chap. 15, this volume) makes a similar point about the anti-alcohol crusade presenting itself as protecting women.
54 Coat of Arms of the St Patrick's Total Abstinence Society, McCord Museum, M930 50 1 580
55 *Ottawa Tribune*, 21 March 1862.
56 "The Temperance Society," *Toronto Mirror,* 9 March 1855.
57 "St Patrick's Society," *Toronto Mirror*, 23 March 1855.
58 "St Patrick's Day in Bytown," *True Witness and Catholic Chronicle*, 26 March 1852.
59 Mills, *Idea of Loyalty.*
60 *The True Witness and Catholic Chronicle,* 26 March 1852, 25 March 1853.
61 *Globe,* 18 March 1871.
62 "The Bytown Correspondent," *True Witness and Catholic Chronicle,* 16 July 1852.
63 "Whiskey the Royal Beverage," *True Witness and Catholic Chronicle,* 12 March 1884.
64 *Ottawa Tribune*, 10 November 1860.
65 Mark McGowan argues that the English-speaking Catholic community in Toronto from 1887 to 1922 underwent "changes that transformed it from

an Irish-centric community into a decidedly Canadian Catholic community." See McGowan, *Waning of the Green*, 5.

66 Proceedings of the Montreal St Patrick's Total Abstinence and Benefit Society, 1868–71, 14 December 1879, Concordia University Archives, HA 219.

67 See McGowan (chap. 4, this volume).

68 "St Patrick's Day," *Montreal Gazette*, 18 March 1871.

8

"We Know Neither Catholics, nor Protestants, nor Free-Thinkers Here": Ethnicity, Religion, and the Chicago Public Schools, 1837–94

MIMI COWAN

In 1875, Chicago's Board of Education wrestled with an issue facing many American urban public schools at the time: how to entice Catholics to send their children to public schools.[1] Eventually, most school boards, including Chicago's, decided that the Bible could not be read, studied, or recited in public school classrooms because the King James Bible, which was in use in most schools, was a Protestant version of God's word and was therefore offensive to Catholics.[2] But the apparent conflict between Protestants and Catholics tended to seep into other areas as well. In May 1875, the board discussed whether a particular language lesson book should remain in the school system because the publishers, Harper Brothers, had recently made anti-Catholic comments in the press. One board member said that the book should be evaluated on its own basis, regardless of the beliefs of the publishers. Another commented that "he was a free-thinker" but that the publisher's comments had "embittered the Catholic members of the Board." As the members debated, board president John Richberg interjected: "We know neither Catholics, nor Protestants, nor Free-Thinkers here. We are simply the Chicago Board of Education."[3]

Richberg's dictate was likely more admonition than announcement: certainly issues of ideology crept into the board's discussions and decisions over the years. Nonetheless, the Board of Education was one of the most ethnically and religiously diverse organizations in nineteenth-century Chicago, as were the public schools. In fact, many of the experiences of Irish Catholic students, teachers, and administrators do not conform to the oft-told story of the oppression, both socially and economically, of Irish Americans at the hands of native-born Protestants. While certainly the public schools in Chicago were not completely devoid of instances of anti-Catholicism, the ways in which some Irish Catholics were involved with the public schools demonstrates that not all experiences of religion in the greater Ireland of the nineteenth-century urban United States were defined by antagonism and hostility.

The first major studies on the Irish in the United States were tales of triumph: Irish immigrants fled from the Great Famine, struggled in poverty in the urban centres of the United States, and slowly gained political and economic strength, reaching the American middle class by the end of the nineteenth century.[4] Attaining middle-class respectability was not, however, the goal of all Irish Americans, and for others it was unachievable.[5] Yet many Irish women experienced migration as liberation, not exile and oppression, when they gained economic independence and freedom from familial and cultural expectations.[6]

The history of Irish Catholics in the urban United States of the nineteenth century is rife with stories of their oppression, both socially and economically, at the hands of native-born Protestants. While these stories cannot be ignored, the public school system of Chicago provides a glimpse into an area of urban life that, while it was certainly not entirely free from nativist-inspired hostilities, was relatively welcoming to Irish Catholics. The bulk of Irish immigrants in the United States, from the Great Famine to the end of the century, were Catholic; the majority of them settled in the country's urban centres; and they often lived in poverty.[7] Yet, just as not all nineteenth-century Irish immigrants were Catholic or lived in American cities, the experiences of nineteenth-century Irish Catholic urban immigrants also varied. This chapter examines the students and policy makers of the Chicago public school system to demonstrate this point.[8] Irish Catholic students' choices to attend public schools necessitated their interaction with non-Catholics and, in many instances, gave them financial and social opportunities that a Catholic education may not have supplied. Meanwhile, Irish Catholic leaders of the public school system also worked in a diverse cohort in order to support the public schools. While for some religion may have been their primary loyalty and identity, for others, it was merely one part of their existence in a multi-ethnic and multi-religious greater Ireland.

First, this chapter examines changes in the demographics of the graduates of Chicago's public high schools between 1857 and 1877 to reveal how public education served different segments of the population. Second, it examines how, between 1888 and 1894, the multi-ethnic, multi-religious Board of Education drove educational policy change, which ultimately produced political transformations in the State of Illinois. Together, these examinations of Chicago's public school graduates and policy makers reveal certain things that should be considered when telling the traditional story of how the members of greater Ireland were part of, and helped to build, a multi-ethnic and multi-religious nineteenth-century urban United States.

IRISH STUDENTS IN CHICAGO'S PUBLIC SCHOOLS

The relationship between Irish Catholics and the public school system in the nineteenth-century urban United States was in many ways antagonistic. Catholic leaders in east coast cities began arguing in the 1840s that the public schools' use of the Protestant King James Bible meant that these schools were, in essence, Protestant. They concluded, therefore, that public tax funds should be split proportionally between these ostensibly Protestant schools and Catholic schools.[9] They did not necessarily want the Protestant Bible removed from public school classrooms; a biblically based education was just as important to many Catholics as it was to Protestants.[10] Instead, they wanted to educate Catholic children in Catholic schools. As a result, Catholic leaders instructed their followers to send their children to Catholic parish schools.[11] Yet not all Irish Catholic parents heeded this direction; some sent their children to the city's public schools, which suggests that the relationship between Irish Catholics and advocates of urban public schooling was not as antagonistic as some of the Catholic clergy would have preferred.[12]

Admittedly, the number of Irish-born children who attended public school in Chicago is low. In 1860, about 4 percent of public school children had been born in Ireland. In comparison, about 18 percent of all Chicagoans were Irish by birth in 1860. Although the proportion of Irish-born Chicagoans declined over the next twenty years, dropping to 9 percent in 1880, their representation in the public schools is smaller yet: Irish-born students' proportion of the whole slips to barely above 1 percent by 1870 and stays about the same through 1876.[13] Regardless, the graduates of Chicago's public schools between 1858 and 1877 reveal that the city's schools evolved from a place where mostly native-born and socio-economically elite students took their education to an institution that provided exactly what it was intended to provide: a way for less advantaged immigrants and their children to reach the middle class.

The city started classes at the high school level in 1856, but, rather than a democratic education offered to all, the earliest graduates reveal that high school graduation was reserved for the city's socio-economic elite. In July 1858, Sophia J. Marshall received the city's first high school diploma, followed in December of that same year by six more women, all of whom were graduates of the city's "normal" department, which prepared student to teach in the city's schools. None of the 1858 graduates was born in Ireland; in fact, as far as can be determined, they were all born in the United States and only one of the young women had a foreign-born parent: Elizabeth M. Kennedy's father was born in Scotland in 1815.[14] Aside from her father's foreign birth, Kennedy was very similar to the other first graduates of Chicago's teachers' program. The women tended to be one of the older siblings of their families, and it was not uncommon that one of their younger sisters also graduated from teachers' school. By and large, however, these women were from families who were well-off financially. For instance, Kennedy's father served as a constable in the 1860s and, by the 1880s, was a lumber merchant, which was one of the most profitable businesses in nineteenth-century Chicago. Another graduate, Ann Winchell, was the daughter of a retired farmer who, in 1860, owned about $15,000 worth of land in Chicago. These were not young women seeking teaching posts in order to support struggling families.[15]

Jeremiah Mahoney was one of the first, if not *the* first, Irish-born graduate of the Chicago public schools. Mahoney received his diploma in 1861 in the general high school program and went on to become a teacher and a principal in the city's schools. He married fellow graduate Clara Perkins, the daughter of a wealthy Chicago doctor, and by 1880 the Mahoney family was living in a suburb of the city while Jeremiah worked as a newspaper editor. Unfortunately, there is no record of Mahoney's life prior to his 1861 graduation, except that he was born in Ireland around 1844. But given that he attended school until he was seventeen and married the daughter of a wealthy doctor, it seems likely that Mahoney had financial support from his family. Again, the choice to attend school, even for the city's first immigrant students, does not seem to have been a function of wanting to gain education in order to better one's financial resources; rather, they attended school because they *had* financial resources.[16]

By the late 1870s, however, this had started to change. In June 1876 the last class of normal school graduates received their degrees.[17] Among this group were four women whose parents were Irish born. Three of the graduates had been born in the United States and one in England. These four young women and their families differed both from earlier graduates and from other graduates of their class. The fathers of the four women of Irish heritage were, on the whole, from a lower socio-economic class than were their non-Irish peers. For instance, the fathers of both Mary Walsh and Mary Boughan were day labourers. Lizzie McKeon's father was a stonecutter who, in 1880, left his daughter and her mother, as well as three younger children, in order to find work in Texas. Lizzie's salary as a teacher, along with that of her sister Catherine, who worked in a dry goods store, supported the family. Similarly, in the 1880s Mary Walsh's salary as a teacher likely helped to support her family, which consisted of her parents and six younger siblings, all of whom were at school except for her brother John, who worked as a cooper.[18]

Furthermore, teaching appears to have allowed these women to step up from the socio-economic class into which they were born. By 1900, Lizzie McKeon, still a teacher, owned her own home and shared it with her sister Jennie, who was also a teacher, and a nephew and two nieces, who were in school.[19] Similarly, in 1910, Mary Boughan was a public school principal and lived with her elderly mother and her brother, who was a lawyer. By 1930 Boughan had retired and headed the house of her attorney brother, a widowed sister, and two nephews who were college educated.[20] For the McKeon and Boughan families, the education and teaching positions of these young women who were children of Irish immigrants were part of the story of a broader pattern of Irish families climbing into the middle class by the end of the nineteenth century.

McKeon's and Boughan's stories contrast with that of Eva Moore, who was also born in the United States to immigrant parents. Moore's parents, however, were not Irish. Moore's father, a carpenter by trade, and her mother were both born in England and emigrated to Chicago with their children by 1855. By 1870, Moore's father had amassed property worth over $15,000, which would have easily supported the family for some time. Nonetheless, by 1880, Eva had secured a teaching position, as had her older sister Louisa. In the house with Moore, her sister, and her parents were her two older brothers, both of whom worked white-collar jobs, an infant niece, and a nineteen-year-old black servant girl.[21] Like earlier graduates of the normal school course, Eva Moore likely did not need to work, even though she, like McKeon and Boughan, was the child of immigrants.

Furthermore, unlike McKeon and Boughan, Eva Moore eventually left her parents' home, married an American man of German heritage, and raised a family of her own.[22] The Moores had quickly metamorphosed from an immigrant working-class family into a comfortable middle-class, white-collar American family. While McKeon's and Boughan's families had also become middle class, their elevation appears to have been substantially more dependent upon the working status of their daughters than was the course of the Moore's history.

The stories of McKeon and Boughan do not differ substantially from what we understand about Irish American women who entered the teaching profession in the United States in the late nineteenth century: they were able to support themselves and their families in a way that would not have been otherwise available to them. However, when their stories are juxtaposed with those spanning twenty years of public school graduates in Chicago, the public school system is revealed as an institution that accepted students of both foreign and native birth and a variety of religions and socio-economic classes, and provided an education that, for some, could be transferred into middle-class livelihoods that, for others, signalled that their families had already attained a certain level of financial security. Although it appears that, by the end of the 1870s, more students were using the public school system as a means of improving their fortunes, the system was able to serve all of these students, despite their different reasons for pursuing education. In shirking the dictates of the Catholic clergy, young women like Lizzie McKeon were able to make a different life for themselves and their families.

THE 1888–89 CHICAGO BOARD OF EDUCATION AND THE CREATION OF THE EDWARDS LAW

Irish Catholics did more than simply attend Chicago's public schools: from the very beginning, they were key figures in the organization, maintenance, and administration of the schools and also in the creation of local and state educational policy. In fact, from its inception in the 1830s, the public school system in Chicago was managed by a multi-ethnic group of men and women from a variety of religious backgrounds. Irish Catholics worked alongside German Jews and American Baptists to construct a school system that would serve their growing community's needs. Nearly any year of the Board of Education's existence could be used to demonstrate the diversity of its members' faiths, ethnicities, and politics; but the actions of the 1888–89 board provide an opportunity to examine how Irish Catholic board members, community leaders, and politicians used diversity to their advantage to craft legislation and to create political change.

The ranks of the public schools earliest supporters included Irish Catholics. James Carney and Charles McDonnell, both Irish Catholic immigrants, were leaders in the establishment of Chicago's public schools in the 1840s.[23] James Ward was probably the most prominent Irish Catholic of the Chicago public school administration during the schools' first thirty years.[24] Ward was a member of the Board of Education from 1857 until 1863 and then became its first building and supply agent, a post he held until his death in 1881.[25]

Thomas Brenan, a member of the 1888–89 board, was one of Ward's pall-bearers in 1881, along with a number of other men who had connections with the board, some of whom were Irish Catholics, many of whom were not.[26] Brenan was a member of the Board of Education for twenty-six continuous years, from 1878 until his death in 1904. This Canadian-born Catholic of Irish parentage arrived in Chicago in 1849, where he became a life-long Democrat and leader in Chicago's Irish American community. He formed the Catholic Literary Society with James Mulligan and, later, served as a second lieutenant in Mulligan's Illinois Irish Brigade during the Civil War. After the war, Brenan was an assistant city tax collector, under fellow Irish Catholic politician and 1860s school board member William Onahan. Brenan also served under Irish Democrat Daniel O'Hara as the assistant city treasurer. A biographer writes of Brenen that he was "a Catholic of Catholics," yet when his friends attempted to receive for him a commendation from Pope Leo XIII, he squashed the movement, supposedly claiming "there is no prouder title than that of a plain American citizen."[27]

Any one of Brenan's twenty-six years as a Board of Education member could be used to demonstrate the diversity of people he worked with, but, for example, in the 1888–89 school year, there were Presbyterian, Jewish, and Swedenborgian board members. At least four board members had been born in Germany, and a number, like the first female board member, Ellen Mitchell, were born in the United States. Another Catholic on the board had, like Brenan, been born in Canada; however, David Bremner was as Scottish as Brenan was Irish. Bremner was an officer both of the Chicago Highland Guard military unit and of the Scottish benevolent organization, the St Andrew's Society. He was also a member of more than one Catholic organization, alongside Brenan. For twenty-six years, Brenan was part of this diverse group of men and women who drove educational policy in Chicago.

One frequent topic in the board's meetings was how to ensure that as many children as possible were in school. In October 1888, Charles Kozminski, a Jewish Prussian-born merchant and school board member, brought up the subject of compulsory education at a Board of Education meeting. On Kozminski's suggestion, the board's Committee on Judiciary reviewed the act of 1883 and reported to the board that it found it "inefficient and incapable of enforcement."[28] The board appointed a committee to investigate the situation and to make recommendations regarding what changes should be made. After a public meeting on 19 January 1889, which was attended by members of the Trade and Labor Assembly, women's organizations, and general citizens interested in the subject, the Chicago Board of Education created a committee of board members and citizens to draft bills on compulsory education, child labour, and truancy.[29]

The members of this committee show the variety of Chicagoans who were involved in the city's nineteenth-century educational policy. Judges Richard Prendergast and Richard S. Tuthill were both asked to join the committee by the board. Prendergast, a Catholic and a leader of Chicago's Democratic Party, was born in Ireland in 1854 and immigrated to the United States in 1864. Tuthill, on the other hand, was born in Vermont to Vermont natives, was a life-long Republican and an Episcopalian. Along with Prendergast and Tuthill were Adolf Kraus, a former president of the Board of Education who had emigrated from Germany in the late 1860s and, with Kozminski, was an officer of the Jewish service organization, B'nai B'rith; and Francis W. Parker, who would eventually gain a reputation as an early leader in the progressive education movement and who was, at the time, the principal of the Cook County Normal School.[30] This was a truly diverse committee in terms of ethnicity, politics, and religion.[31]

This committee drafted three bills, which were all sent to the state capital for consideration. The first required children between the ages of seven and fourteen to attend a minimum of twelve weeks of school a year; it declared what subjects must be taught in order for an institution to be considered a school; it set fines for parents who were negligent in sending their children to school; and it afforded for exemptions to the law. The Chicago committee's two other bills restricted child labour and addressed the issue of truancy. The committee argued that compulsory education measures were nothing without the support of bills on the latter two topics.[32]

The committee's efforts met with decidedly mixed success at the state level. The latter two bills were completely dismissed, and, while the state did pass a compulsory education law that closely resembled the bill the Chicago committee had drafted, there were a number of small but ultimately important changes to the state's law. The first adjustment concerned the use of English in the classroom. The Chicago committee's bill instructed that an institution would be considered a school as long as students were instructed in "Reading, Writing, Arithmetic and United States History, in the English language," while the Edwards Law declared that "no school shall be regarded as a school under this Act unless there shall be taught therein the English language reading, writing, arithmetic, history of the United States and geography."[33] Critics of the Edwards Law claimed that it mandated that reading, writing, arithmetic, US history, and geography should *all* be taught in English, while the Chicago version was vague about whether all the subjects, or only US history, should be taught in English.

The second slight, but ultimately important, difference in language between the two bills concerned what kind of school the children could attend in order to fulfill their twelve-week minimum education. The Chicago committee's version of the bill said that children should "attend some public or private day school"; the Edwards Law stated that children must attend "some public day school." Of course, the Edwards Law allowed for private schools, but it required that they be "approved by the Board of Education, or Directors of the city, town or district." This change in wording became the focus of at least half of the battle after the Edwards Law was passed.[34]

German parents and Catholic parents were concerned that the Edwards Law would allow those who for years had railed against parochial and private schools to have them shut down once and for all.[35] German Lutherans and Catholics of all ethnicities argued that the Edwards Law threatened their rights as parents to educate their children as they saw fit. As Chicago's German-language newspaper exclaimed, it was nothing less than a "tyrannical … attack of the Know-Nothings" and a "crime of liberty in education."[36]

Catholics were primarily concerned by the stipulation that private schools had to be approved by the local school board and that, in order to avoid being prosecuted for not sending their children to school, parents had to "prove" that their children had attended private school.

Catholics worried that hostile school board members could easily claim that the parent had not sufficiently proven the child's attendance or, since very few qualifications for approving or disproving private schools were given, could deny approval of the school.[37] A rumour circulated in late 1889 that the state superintendent of education, Richard Edwards, for whom the bill was named, had given local school boards authority to refuse to approve Catholic schools if the aim of the school appeared to be to "draw and keep away children from public schools." The assistant superintendent did not help matters much when he publicly announced that no such ruling had be made and then added the phrase, "as far as I know."[38]

German citizens were concerned about the English-language requirement for curriculum. When pressed, state officials waffled on what exactly the language requirement entailed. By the letter of the law, it seemed to say that all teaching must be conducted in English. But, in interviews with newspapers, some legislators said that, as long as *some* of the school day was in English – or at least half – these schools would be allowed to teach as they chose. The vagueness made leaders in the German community uneasy.[39] One writer to the *Tribune* cited the case of the Lutheran parochial school in Thornton, just south of Chicago. The Cook County School Board had refused to approve the school "unless the English branches were taught from the same text-books as are introduced in the public schools there and unless the school would submit to ... examinations by the board." Similar threats were supposedly being made against private schools throughout the state.[40]

Certainly the German and Catholic members of the Chicago committee, as well as the German and Catholic school board members who approved the committee's actions, did not intend for the bill they drafted to be a means that would infringe the rights of German and Catholic parents. It may be for this reason – the diverse make-up of the Chicago Board of Education – that the board made it a point to note that no one was ever prosecuted for violating the law. The Edwards Law called for each violation to incur a fine, paid by negligent parents, in the sum of no less than three dollars per offence. The 1889–90 annual report noted that over seventeen thousand cases of evading the law had been investigated during the school year. Of that number, almost ten thousand children were placed in public, private, parochial, or evening schools. The rest of the children were granted excuses. Excuses ranged from the child's working wage being necessary to the support of the family to suspension from school to physical or mental handicap to "poverty" to "indifference" or, simply, to "other causes," which constituted 766 cases in itself.[41]

The Edwards Law had allowed for some exceptions, but a number of these categories, notably, "indifference," were exactly the types of violations that were intended to be prosecuted. The school board's annual report in 1890 noted that "no arrests ha[d] been made; the work ha[d] been accomplished by a kind of moral persuasion." Furthermore, they felt it necessary to assure their readers that "not a single instance of interference with parental authority, no prosecution or persecution" had taken place under the name of the compulsory education law. The annual report of 1890–91 used almost identical language in noting that no arrests had been made.[42] By using this language, the board directly addressed the fears expressed by the opponents of the Edwards Law. It seems, therefore, that Chicago's Board of Education was determined to demonstrate that it did not support the controversial sections of the Edwards Law.[43]

POLITICAL OPPORTUNITY: IRISH DEMOCRATS, GERMAN VOTERS, AND THE EDWARDS LAW

The Board of Education may have subtly resisted the unpopular clauses of the Edwards Law, but, as Irish Catholics, German Catholics, and German Lutherans grew increasingly vocal about their dislike of the law, the Irish Democrats of Chicago saw an opportunity to forge an alliance between these groups.[44] This alliance would ultimately change the course of Illinois politics by electing the state's first foreign-born governor and the first Democrat since before the Civil War. And the Edwards Law would be repealed.

In Chicago, some of the most well-known leaders of the Democratic Party were Irish Catholics like Richard Prendergast, who had helped to author the original compulsory education bill promoted by the Chicago Board of Education. These Irish Catholic Democrats began reaching out to German Catholics and German Lutherans who were disgruntled with the passage of the Edwards Law. In fact, the *Tribune* referred to this process as the creation of the "Lutheran-Roman Catholic Committee," and it claimed that Prendergast was the movement's "putative father."[45]

But merely talking about changing or repealing the Edwards Law was not enough to move Chicago's German voters to the Democratic Party. Instead, Irish Catholic Democratic Party leaders began making political deals to nominate Germans to the Democratic ticket for prominent political positions. The state office of superintendent of schools was an obvious first choice to which to apply this theory. Richard Edwards, the man for whom the Edwards Law was named, was up for re-election in 1890 and was running as a Republican. The Democrats nominated a German, Henry Raab, to run against Edwards in a move the *Tribune* referred to as "a bid for the German vote."[46] Raab had announced his unequivocal opposition to the compulsory education law and suggested changes to the Edwards Law rather than a full repeal. His proposed amendment states: "no interference shall be had with the course of study pursued at parochial schools and … the English branches shall not be taught there if not desired."[47]

Raab won the state superintendent position by over thirty thousand votes. In Chicago, he triumphed in twenty-three of the thirty-four wards, beating Edwards by almost sixteen thousand votes.[48] But if Raab's nomination for state superintendent on the Democratic ticket was intended to court German voters in 1890, the 1892 nomination of John Altgeld as the Democratic candidate for governor was a proposal of permanent fidelity. Altgeld, a German-immigrant who had made his fortune in real estate in Chicago and had served as a judge of the county superior court for a number of years, was the choice of the city's Democrats, who believed that he would inspire the loyalty of German voters throughout the state.

Chicago's Irish Democrats were fundamental in securing the nomination for Altgeld. Democrats from outside of Chicago had always controlled the party's gubernatorial nominee. But not in 1892. In fact, the *Tribune* accused Chicago's Irish Catholic Democratic Party leader Mike McDonald of engineering Altgeld's nomination through less than savoury methods. The paper claimed that McDonald kept a stash of letters from pastors of Lutheran churches, supporting Altgeld. When other party leaders questioned the choice of Altgeld, McDonald purportedly showed them these letters in order to prove that Altgeld would bring German Lutheran voters to the Democratic Party. The *Tribune* claimed these letters were all forgeries, intended to dupe the other members of the Democratic Party into nominating Altgeld. Whether or not the paper's claims were accurate, the reporting of the story indicated that both Democrats and their opponents knew that Altgeld was intended to bring German Lutherans, embittered over the Edwards Law, to the Democratic Party.[49]

When the state convention nominated Altgeld as candidate for governor, Democratic Party chairman and Irish-born Catholic Andrew J.

O'Connor confirmed the party's awareness of the challenge of the upcoming election: "without converts to Democracy drawn from the ranks of the Republican party our prospects for electing [a Democratic governor] this year are somewhat problematic." Speaking obliquely about the Edwards Law, O'Connor claimed that Altgeld, unlike the Republican candidate, was "opposed to all sumptuary or unnecessary legislation ... [and believed] that the rights of the people [were] safe with the people." He prophesied that the thirty-thousand-plus majority enjoyed by Raab in 1890 would soon be enjoyed by Altgeld.[50]

O'Connor's prediction was not far off. Illinois elected Altgeld as the first foreign-born Illinois governor, the first Illinois governor from the northern portion of the state, and the first Democratic governor in Illinois since before the Civil War. Altgeld began his inaugural address by making a commitment to repeal the Edwards Law.[51] On 1 February 1893, the Edwards Compulsory Education Law was repealed by unanimous vote of the Illinois Legislature.[52] The state legislature passed a new compulsory education law later that year that was not without its issues but that satisfied religious opponents of the Edwards Law by assuring that private schools could operate without the oversight of the local school boards and that parents, ultimately, could choose their children's education.[53]

The Chicago Board of Education remarked at the end of the 1893 school year that the new law "did not make it necessary to change the organization of the department of compulsory education" because "no enforcement of the penalties for violation of the statute has ever been attempted in Chicago."[54] But the board's annual report also commented on the near impossibility of turning a chronic truant into an obedient student and called once again for the creation of "disciplinary schools," where children who could not be controlled by parents and teachers could be sent in order to "reform their characters and lives." The creation of such an institution had been part of the Chicago committee's original 1889 bill on compulsory education.[55]

CONCLUSION

Chicago Board of Education president Richberg was certainly wrong when he claimed that the board "knew neither Catholics, nor Protestants, nor Free-Thinkers."[56] The Board of Education members did know Catholics, Protestants, and "Free-Thinkers." In fact, they *were* Catholics, Protestants, "Free-Thinkers," and people of other faiths. The experiences of Irish Catholic students and policy makers and Chicago's public schools demonstrate that, for Irish men, women, and children, being a part of greater Ireland necessitated studying, working, and living alongside people of different nationalities and religions. In some cases, Irish Catholics received the brunt of nativist hostilities because of their ethnicity and religion. But, at other times, Irish Catholics were respected and accepted leaders not only among other Irish Catholics but also among groups with diverse memberships, such as the Board of Education.[57] Negotiation, therefore, as much or more than oppression and hostility, may be an important hallmark of the experience of religion and greater Ireland – at least when we consider the examples provided by the nineteenth-century Chicago public school system.

NOTES

1 Public schools in the United States are funded by local and state governments and are obliged to provide free and universal education to all children residing within the set area of the school district. They are intended to be free of sectarian influence, although the degree to which this was true has varied over time.

2 *Twenty-second Annual Report of the Board of Education for the Year Ending July 31, 1876* (Chicago: Geo. J. Titus, 1876), 15–16.

3 *Chicago Tribune*, 26 May 1875.

4 Wittke, *Irish in America*; Shannon, *American Irish*; Greeley, *Irish Americans*.

5 The works of labour historians on the Irish in North America include: Foner, "Class, Ethnicity, and Radicalism"; Kenny, *Making Sense of the Molly Maguires*; Miller, *Emigrants and Exiles*; Roediger, *Wages of Whiteness*.

6 Contributions to our understanding of the experience of Irish women immigrants in North America include: Diner, *Erin's Daughters*; Dublin, *Women at Work*; Harris, "Come All You Courageously"; Nolan, *Ourselves Alone*.

7 Donald Akenson has suggested that emphasis on ghettoized Irish Catholics in urban North America has skewed the vision of the field: "Irish" has become unfairly linked to both "urban" and "Catholic." Akenson points out that there are substantial data to suggest that, given different temporal and geographical bounds, these terms need not be permanently fused to one another. Further, Akenson argues that we cannot assume that Irish immigrants in urban North America were Catholic because the United States has never "collected information on the religious affiliation of

specific individuals." He ignores, however, the variety of primary sources that can be used to establish that the American Irish were primarily urban and overwhelmingly Catholic. For instance, in Chicago, historians have demonstrated this by using city directories, newspapers, and parish records. See Shanabruch, *Chicago's Catholics*; Skerrett, Kantowicz, and Avella, *Catholicism*; Funchion, "Irish Chicago"; Kantowicz, "Ethnic Church"; Akenson, "Agnostic View."

8 Other historians have previously identified the important contribution of Irish women as teachers in the nineteenth-century United States. See, for instance: Barrett and Roediger, "Irish and the 'Americanization' of the 'New Immigrants'"; Barrett, "Americanization from the Bottom Up."

9 In the early 1850s, Bishop Van de Velde of Chicago explained his belief that the King James Bible "contains a very large number of willful perversions and corruptions, having been converted into the spurious work of man." Further, he accused the Protestant Bible of containing "heretical opinions as revealed truths, and thus insidiously propagating error and heresy, under the pretended sanction of the God of Truth." See *Western Tablet* (Chicago), 31 January 1852.

10 Catholic leaders frequently referred to public schools as "godless." See *Western Tablet*, as reprinted in *Chicago Tribune*, 23 March 1853.

11 Many Protestants took issue with the Catholic stance on public education. Educational reformers in the early years of the American republic argued that public schooling was necessary in order to teach children the critical thinking skills required of all citizens in a democracy. Only then, educators reasoned, would the citizens and the nation be immune to the language of demagogues. But to many native-born Protestant Americans, a Catholic education was no better – and in some ways worse – than no education at all. To Protestants, the Roman Catholic Church appeared anti-democratic by its very structure and they therefore feared that children who were educated by it would not understand the responsibilities of democratic citizenship. Charles Shanabruch details the debate over the distribution of public funds between public and private schools in Chicago. While this same battle had reached fever pitch by the mid-1840s in east coast cities, the discussion was not broached in Chicago until almost a full decade later. See Shanabruch, *Chicago's Catholics*, 21–5; Mann, *Life of Horace Mann*, pages 150, 266. See also Mann, "Necessity of Education," 143–88; McGreevy, *Catholicism and American Freedom*, 186–7; Sanders, *Education of an Urban Minority*.

12 Chicago's public school system was established by the charter that created the city itself in 1837. Although some schooling had taken place in

Chicago before then, it was generally temporary in nature. The first Catholic school in Chicago for boys opened in 1844, and one for girls followed three years later. For more details, see "Historical Sketches of the Public School System of the City of Chicago," *Twenty-Fifth Annual Report of the Board of Education for the Year Ending July 31, 1879* (Chicago: Clark and Edwards, 1880), 1–6; Sanders, *Education of an Urban Minority*.

13 The birthplace of public school students was not included in the annual reports past 1877. The disparity between the proportion of Irish-born students in the public schools and the proportion of Irish-born residents of the city is likely partially due to more than one factor. First of all, if it were possible to know the nativity of some of the native-born students' parents, and if those with an Irish-born parent were included in these figures, it would likely be substantially higher. Furthermore, Chicago's parochial schools were, in fact, flourishing, and many, but not all, Irish parents may have opted to send their children to church-run schools.

14 Out of the seven young women, three could be identified in the federal census.

15 *Report of the President of the Board of Education and Fifth Annual Report of the Superintendent of Public Schools, for the Year Ending February 1, 1859* (Chicago: Book and Job Printing Office of Scott & Co. 1859), 76; Seventh Census of the United States, 1850, viewed through www.ancestry.com (July 2013); Eighth Census of the United States, 1860, viewed through www.ancestry.com (July 2013); Ninth Census of the United States, 1870, viewed through www.ancestry.com (July 2013); Tenth Census of the United States, 1880, viewed through www.ancestry.com (July 2013); Twelfth Census of the United States, 1900, viewed through www.ancestry.com (July 2013); Thirteenth Census of the United States, 1910, viewed through www.ancestry.com (July 2013).

16 *Eighth Annual Report of the Board of Education, for the Year Ending December 31, 1861* (Chicago: Chicago Times Book and Job Printing Establishment, 1862), 42; Eighth Census of the United States, 1860, viewed through www.ancestry.com (July 2013); Ninth Census of the United States, 1870, viewed through www.ancestry.com (July 2013); Tenth Census of the United States, 1880, viewed through www.ancestry.com (July 2013).

17 The normal course had become so popular that there were more graduates than available teaching places in the city's schools. Therefore, the course was cancelled for a number of years. See *Twenty-Third Annual Report of the Board of Education for the Year Ending July 31, 1877* (Chicago: Geo. J. Titus, Book and Job Printer, 1877), 23.

18 Tenth Census of the United States, 1880, viewed through www.ancestry.com (July 2013).
19 Twelfth Census of the United States, 1900, viewed through www.ancestry.com (July 2013).
20 Thirteenth Census of the United States, 1910, viewed through www.ancestry.com (July 2013); Fifteenth Census of the United States, 1930, viewed through www.ancestry.com (July 2013).
21 Eighth Census of the United States, 1860, viewed through www.ancestry.com (July 2013); Ninth Census of the United States, 1870, viewed through www.ancestry.com (July 2013); Tenth Census of the United States, 1880, viewed through www.ancestry.com (July 2013).
22 Twelfth Census of the United States, 1900, viewed through www.ancestry.com (July 2013).
23 Andreas, *History of Chicago*, 1:184–85, 249; *Chicago Antiquities, Including Chicago Business Directory for 1839* (Chicago: Eastman and Bartlett, 1875); *General Directory and Business Advertiser of the City of Chicago for the Year 1844 With a Historical Sketch and Statistics Extending from 1837 to 1844* (Chicago: Ellis and Fergus, Printers, 1844); *1855–6 The Chicago City Directory and Business Advertiser, Fourth Edition, with A New Map of the City* (Chicago: Robert Fergus, Book and Job Printer, 1855); John C.W. Bailer's Chicago City Directory, For the Year 1864–5 (Chicago: John C.W. Bailey, Publishers, 1864); *Halpin's Eighth Annual Edition Chicago City Directory 1865–6* (Chicago: T.M. Halpin, Compiler and Publisher, 1865).
24 Carl Sandburg's 1916 poem, "Chicago," opens with the famous line, "Hog Butcher for the World."
25 Andreas, *History of Chicago*, 2:106; *Chicago Tribune*, 9 July 1881, 16 July 1881.
26
27 Ffrench, *Biographical History*, 782–6.
28 *Thirty-Fifth Annual Report of the Board of Education for the Year Ending June 30, 1889* (Chicago: Hack and Anderson, 1890), 23.
29 Ibid., 23–24.
30 "Message of Adolf Kraus, President of the Executive Committee of the Independent Order of B'nai B'rith, to the Constitution Grand Lodge Convention at Washington, DC, April 1910," Washington, DC, Independent Order of B'nai B'rith, 1910.
31 *Thirty-Fifth Annual Report of the Board of Education.*
32 Ibid., 23–5.
33 Ibid., 24–5, 29.

34 Ibid., 24–5, 27, 29.

35 See, for instance, *Chicago Tribune,* 17 November 1889, 29 November 1889.

36 Charles Shanabruch details how Irish Catholics and German Lutherans led the charge to overturn the Edwards Law. Although hostility to the law broke out almost immediately, it was not removed from the state laws until February 1893. The work of educational and child labour reformers then turned towards restricting the ability of employers to hire children rather than attempting to curb child labour by enforcing school attendance. See Shanabruch, *Chicago's Catholics*, 54–77. *Illinois Staats-Zeitung,* 5 March 1893, 3 February 1892; *Chicago Foreign Language Press Survey: German*, vol. 1, Chicago Public Library; *Chicago Tribune*, 26 January 1874.

37 *Chicago Tribune,* 29 November 1889.

38 Ibid.

39 *Chicago Tribune*, 17 November 1889, 29 November 1889, 2 December 1889.

40 *Chicago Tribune,* 29 November 1889.

41 *Thirty-Sixth Annual Report of the Board of Education for the Year Ending June 30, 1890* (Chicago: Hack and Anderson, 1891), 126.

42 *Thirty-Seventh Annual Report of the Board of Education*, 154–5.

43 *Thirty-Sixth Annual Report of the Board of Education*, 125–6.

44 While the Irish of Illinois were not as firmly entrenched in the Democratic Party as they were in places like Massachusetts and New York, the Democrats still generally gained the majority of Irish votes in most political contests. The majority of the city's Germans, on the other hand, had abandoned the Democratic Party in the late 1850s for the newly formed Republican Party. See Levine, *Spirit of 1848*.

45 If Prendergast was the father, his sons were many. The Irish and Irish American Catholic Democrats of the city are too many to list here, but they included aldermen, party delegates, and businesspeople, among others. See *Chicago Tribune*, 4 June 1890, 5 June 1890. Charles Ffrench's *Biographical History of the American Irish in Chicago* details the careers of many of these men.

46 *Chicago Tribune*, 16 June 1890.

47 Ibid., 5 April 1890.

48 Ibid., 7 May 1892.

49 While the paper claimed these letters were a forgery, the outcome of the election suggests that, if the letters existed, they may have been legitimate. See *Chicago Tribune*, 25 September 1891, 28 September 1891, 5 March 1892, 11 April 1892, 20 April 1892, 1 October 1892. For more on Mike McDonald, see Lindberg, *Gambler King of Clark Street*.

50 *Chicago Tribune*, 28 April 1892.

51 Ibid., 11 January 1893.

52 Ibid., 2 February 1893.

53 The main issue with the new bill was that it specified that children had to attend sixteen weeks of school but made no mention of when in the school year those weeks could take place. Therefore, anytime before the last sixteen weeks of the school year, children and their parents could simply reply to charges of truancy by declaring their intent to attend the final sixteen weeks of school. The 1893 compulsory education law was replaced in 1897 by another law that was similar to the earlier law, except that it required attendance to begin at the start of the school year. Meanwhile, Governor Altgeld pursued other methods of limiting child labour, such as the Factory Inspection Act, 1893, which forbade the employment of children under the age of fourteen, the same age at which children were no longer required to be in school. See "An Act to Promote Attendance of Children in Schools and to Prevent Truancy," *Laws of the State of Illinois Enacted by the Fortieth General Assembly* … (Springfield: Phillips Brothers, 1897), 296; *Chicago Tribune*, 14 April 1893, 20 January 1894, 21 January 1894, 24 January 1894; Gordon, "Women and the Anti-Child Labor Movement"; Candela, "Struggle to Limit the Hours."

54 *Thirty-Ninth Annual Report of the Board of Education for the Year Ending June 30, 1893* (Chicago: Geo. K. Hazlitt and Co. 1894), 65.

55 *Thirty-Ninth Annual Report of the Board of Education*, 65–7.

56 *Chicago Tribune*, 26 May 1875.

57 James Barrett has considered this question of how Irish Americans interacted with urbanites of many backgrounds in the late nineteenth and early twentieth centuries. See Barrett, *Irish Way*.

PART THREE

Asia and Africa

9

Irish Religious Networks in Colonial South Asia, ca. 1788–1858

BARRY CROSBIE

Over the past two decades, historians of empire, eager to understand complex historical phenomena, including migration, diaspora, and the formation of identities, have increasingly pointed to the mid-late eighteenth century as a pivotal moment in which both Britain and the worlds with which it came into contact underwent dramatic transformations. Following the loss of its thirteen North American colonies in the aftermath of the American War of Independence, Britain set about consolidating its authority and control on the domestic front (most notably in Ireland after the 1798 rebellion), while it increasingly turned towards Asia and the Pacific in search of new lands, markets, and resources to reignite its faltering economy. Central to British overseas expansion during the late eighteenth and nineteenth centuries was the role of Ireland as an important sub-imperial centre that provided Britain and its empire with a vital repository of workers, knowledge, and skill from which to draw upon when required.[1]

While Ireland's role in the creation of Britain's Atlantic empire is well documented, we know very little about Ireland's significant contribution to the emergence of what Vincent Harlow describes as the "Second British Empire," as British imperial ambitions gradually shifted to the East during the Seven Years' War.[2] This is partly because the study of the British Empire in Ireland has been shaped by varying nationalist and unionist responses to decolonization in the twentieth century, but it is also because of the dominance of older narratives of metropolitan-focused imperial history that have tended to view Britain and its empire almost exclusively from England and London, respectively. In downplaying Ireland's role as an important supplier of goods and commodities, personnel and expertise within the wider imperial system, scholars have failed to sufficiently consider the impact of one component of a supposedly unified "British" people upon the nineteenth-century Empire and vice versa. After all, it was precisely because England, Ireland, Scotland, and Wales were never homogenous economic, political, or religious entities that the Empire was designed to act as a powerful solvent for the different ethnicities and identities of these regions, binding them together and finding a common purpose through a distinctly "British" endeavour. However, recent research has demonstrated that, far from dissolving regional particularisms and unifying the diverse peoples of the United Kingdom and Ireland under a collective British imperial identity, the Empire actually worked in a manner whereby separate relationships between each were formed and national identities reinforced.

Indeed, one of the most significant recent trends in the writing of a "new imperial" historiography has been an attempt by historians to demonstrate how the different peoples and ethnicities of the British Isles – namely, the English, Irish, Scottish, and Welsh – in fact viewed the Empire in different ways and interacted with indigenous people and culture accordingly.[3] At the core of what John M. MacKenzie terms a "four nations approach" to the writing of a new British imperial history is the idea of decentring what has become an increasingly outmoded metrocentric version of imperial history.[4] While not necessarily downplaying the crucial role of the Empire's dominant political and economic metropolitan centres, many historians of the "new imperial history" are now attempting to redress what they argue is a long-standing imbalance in imperial historiography by highlighting the mutually influencing dynamics among colonial societies and the various peoples of Britain and Ireland and, in the process, challenging some of the long-established orthodoxies in late eighteenth- and nineteenth-century British, Irish, and imperial histories.

In its discussion of Irish religious networks and colonial South Asia, this chapter aims to provide one or two examples of the cross-cultural experiences, institutions, and personnel at the centre of imperial networks that were fashioned through Ireland's involvement with the British colonial project in India during the "long" nineteenth century. As such, this chapter argues that, much in the same way that early modern Ireland was central to the construction and maintenance of the "first British Empire" in the Atlantic World, Ireland and Irish people played equally important roles in facilitating the geographical reorientation of the Empire eastward following the loss of Britain's thirteen North

American colonies in the 1780s. From the mid-eighteenth until the late nineteenth century, Ireland and India were joined by an intricate series of networks of military recruitment, intellectual exchange, and political interdependence. These networks were imperial in nature and were borne out of direct Irish involvement in British territorial expansion into South Asia during the Seven Years' War. Here, Irish men and women (both Catholic and Protestant, from the North and the South) served as soldiers, missionaries, educators, doctors, scientists, and administrators within the imperial system, where they played an important part in the formation of the colonial state and in defining the expanding roles and responsibilities of the modern British state in its Indian environment. Through an examination of Irish religious networks (and, specifically, Irish Catholic networks), this chapter addresses the manner in which Ireland – arguably Britain's first colony – functioned as a sort of sub-imperial centre that supplied the Empire with a vital repository of workers, knowledge, and skill that fuelled Britain's drive into South Asia from the 1750s onward.

The principle aim here is not only to demonstrate how Ireland was central to the Empire's second main wave of imperial expansion, or the "swing to the East," but also to examine some of the ways in which Irish involvement in the colonial project in India in turn contributed to the emergence of one of the central themes explored in this volume – namely, the rise of a "Greater Ireland" overseas during this period. This is important as the Irish in the Empire (and especially those in non-settlement colonies such as India) are frequently portrayed as opposing British colonial rule and law, which are seen as agents of despotism. As the history of British rule in India (and, indeed, in Ireland) is often viewed as a continuous narrative of colonial oppression, the Irish (many of whom were employed as government officials in India) have traditionally been viewed as supporters of reform and vociferous opponents of the Raj – the enemy within, so to speak. Yet during the nineteenth century there was a sense that Irish people from a variety of religious persuasions and social backgrounds in India were quite willing and prepared to embrace and share in the work of empire. While many Irish were ambivalent or even ignorant of the ideological underpinnings of Britain's imperial mission in India, the vast majority of them – including those who were there out of economic necessity – supported British colonial rule and policies and stayed for relatively long periods of time. Indeed, the emergence of a pan-Irish diaspora in South Asia during the nineteenth century can be explained partly by the exceptional nature of Irish migration to India at this time. First, India was a very different site of Irish migration during the nineteenth century than was the United States, Australia, or Canada. Migration to India was temporary in nature, typically involving the duration of work contracts, and there was little, if any, evidence of permanent Irish settlement. Unlike the fiercely contested migrant grounds of New England, Newfoundland, or New South Wales, Bombay, Madras, and Calcutta provided relatively structured, organized, and disciplined environments within which Irish migrants were quickly absorbed into the regimental or administrative confines of the Raj. Contentious issues that had the potential to ignite ethnic or class rivalries in the settler colonies, such as religious, political, or cultural practices, were often predetermined (as exemplified by the East India Company's attitude to the presence of all Christian missionaries in India) before the Irish arrived. Moreover, empire-building in the Indian context was not necessarily about recreating Irish communities abroad. As a result, contestations of power, wealth, status, and influence among the different classes and denominations of Irish men and women were far less pronounced in India than in many places in the New World. The temporary nature of Irish involvement in India, coupled with the relative absence of competing settler traditions and rivalries, may have contributed to this phenomenon.

Indeed, in recent times, one of the most successful means of tracing connections between Ireland and India (and, thus, the impact of a Greater Ireland on colonial South Asia) has been the employment of "networks," "webs," and "systems" as methodological tools of analysis. For more than a decade, a whole range of scholars across the humanities and social sciences has been drawing on the study of social network analysis in order to understand more clearly how sets of individuals or organizations were historically interdependent, often tied together by a set of common values, ideas, friendship, conflict, trade, or religion.[5] Resulting social networks borne out of these ties operated on many different levels – ranging from families up to the level of nations – and played critical roles in determining how problems were solved, organizations were run, and the degree to which individuals succeeded in achieving their goals.

According to one recent study by Gary Magee and Andrew Thompson, these supra-national networks – which were "built upon kinship structures, religious institutions, ethnic societies and fraternal organizations" – functioned as a sort of "software of empire."[6] This software enabled the operation of a vast system through which ideas and information, trust and contracts, commodities and people ricocheted from one point of contact to another across the Empire, producing complex circuits of exchange in the process. Through increased migration these networks at once helped bridge the distance between home and migrant/settler communities throughout the Empire while simultaneously constituting a national-, ethnic- or religious-based web of patronage and support for those who participated in them. While Magee and Thompson rightly acknowledge the central role and importance of London in both enabling and sustaining many these imperial networks, they nevertheless point to the multitude of connections and linkages that were established between the colonies themselves, connections that at times by-passed the metropolitan core entirely. Following Catholic emancipation in the late 1820s, for example, newly founded Irish Catholic seminaries and religious institutions played an important role in supplying numerous vicars apostolic and clergy to attend to the spiritual requirements of the Empire's ever-expanding Irish migrant communities. In this way, several Irish religious networks came to dominate numerous Indian Catholic communities and military cantonments throughout the nineteenth century and played a prominent role in shaping Catholic practices in an Indian environment as well as informing official attitudes towards it. This period, in particular, witnessed the beginning of a gradual integration and later steady flow of Irish-born and Irish-educated Catholics (religious figures and university-trained professionals) to complement the large number of Irish Protestants already active within Britain's wider imperial system in the East.

With the renewed confidence that was provided by the psychological boon of emancipation, many early nineteenth-century Irish Catholic clergy on the subcontinent worked to promote the interests of a particular Gaelic Irish dimension within Anglo-Indian society. They ministered to the East India Company's many Gaelic-speaking Irish soldiers; set about introducing a reconstructed parochial system in India that was, in part, modelled on post-emancipation Irish lines through the building of churches and other ecclesiastical infrastructure; and promoted the education of (high- and low-caste) Indian and Eurasian children. Indeed, the varying levels of Irish involvement in issues relating to caste, educational provision, and church administration demonstrate the myriad ways in which Irish Catholic religious networks became gradually embedded not only in Indian society from the 1830s onward but also, more broadly, in the work of empire-building.

The introduction of Irish Roman Catholic clergy in India, generally speaking, coincided with the vigorous recruitment drive undertaken by the East India Company in Ireland to enlist Irish Catholic soldiers into the ranks of its ailing European regiments during the late eighteenth and early nineteenth centuries. Initial recruitment of Irish Catholic soldiers by the regular British Army and East India Company began during the Seven Years' War and reached its highpoint in the early 1800s at a time when the company was engaged in an aggressive campaign to annex Indian territories through military conquest. By the beginning of the nineteenth century full-time company recruiting officers were stationed in Dublin, Belfast, Cork, and Newry, where, between 1825 and 1850, the Bengal Army alone drew an estimated 47.9 percent of its European recruits. In an attempt to cater to the spiritual requirements of the growing number of Irish Catholics overseas as well as at home, six major new seminaries, including ones in Carlow and Maynooth, were founded in Ireland between 1782 and 1837. In addition to these new seminaries and training colleges, a special "foreign missionary seminary," All Hallows College, was established in Dublin in 1842.[7] With over 120 candidates for the priesthood enrolled within the first four years of its inauguration, it was originally anticipated that All Hallows would provide much needed spiritual support for the growing number of emigrant Irish Catholic communities in North America and Australia in the post-Famine years.[8] Perhaps conscious of the growing number of Irish Catholics recruited into the ranks of the imperial armed forces in India at the time, the founder of All Hallows, Father John Hand, was convinced that Ireland, as one of the principal Catholic countries within the Empire, should be the natural centre from which Catholicism should reach out to the non-settler colonies in the East.[9]

From the outset, the East India Company was only too aware of its own status as a secular, foreign institution in India whose primary objective was to engage in profitable commercial activity. From the earliest beginnings, company officials had to petition India's various ruling classes for permission to carry out trade on the subcontinent. As a consequence, official company attitude towards the presence of all foreign missionaries in India (irrespective of religious denomination) was one of caution. They were especially conscious of how religious issues and grievances in a geographical region as large as the Indian subcontinent – already long divided along ethnic, linguistic, religious, and caste lines – had the potential to cause social disharmony and unrest and thus affect the delicate conditions necessary for the company to carry out safe and profitable trade. In order to avoid problems deemed "bad for business," the East India Company generally adopted a policy of religious neutrality when it was called upon to intervene in religious disputes in India and, subsequently, failed to adopt any uniform policy that dealt with the plethora of Christian missionary bodies that emerged there at this time. The company's unofficial policy of religious neutrality was extended even more rigidly after the conquest of Bengal in the 1760s, when it became the de facto ruler of large parts of the Indian subcontinent and its priorities began to shift from those relating to trade to those relating to dominion.[10]

In contrast to its dealings with evangelical Christians, whom the East India Company was initially quite worried about owing to concerns over their attitude towards religious conversion, British concern over the presence of Roman Catholic missionaries was alleviated somewhat by the traditional roots that Catholicism had established in India. Goanese and Portuguese priests had been attending to Indian Catholics along the Malabar Coast long before the company had secured any kind of permanent footing on the subcontinent. During the early years of European imperial expansion, successive popes had granted the Portuguese monarchy rights of *padroado*, or the rights of patronage and protection over dioceses in the East. Official dispatches and instructions from the Vatican were given the royal *bene placitum* before they arrived in Lisbon and thence sent onwards to Goa, the centre of Portuguese missionary life in early colonial India. However, by the beginning of the seventeenth century Portuguese missionary initiatives in India waned, and the Vatican decided that another vehicle to sustain and maintain the Catholic missionary momentum was needed. In 1622, the Sacred Congregation de Propaganda Fide was established.[11] This new missionary institution was responsible for appointing a succession of vicars apostolic, or titular bishops, of various nationalities to India with the express purpose of overseeing Catholic dioceses.

The East India Company hierarchy generally believed that the number of Roman Catholics sent out by Propaganda Fide and those under the *padroado* regime was sufficient to minister to the needs of the relatively small Indian Catholic population. Moreover, company officials became aware early on that Catholic missionaries very rarely attempted to proselytize. If attempts were made to convert individuals on behalf of Roman Catholic missionaries, Protestants rather than Hindus or Muslims were targeted. Given these facts, the company did not initially see Catholic missionaries as being politically dangerous and, in fact, many Catholic prelates earned the patronage and support of the company hierarchy, and it was common for Catholic military chaplains to receive official monthly stipends.[12] Moreover, the company believed that the presence of Roman Catholic missionaries in India would serve to provide spiritual assistance to the large number of European soldiers in its army, of whom a disproportionate number were Irish Roman Catholics.[13]

One such example of numerous Irish Catholic religious networks that were forged in India in the first half of the nineteenth century, and that linked the company's Catholic rank and file to the activities of both the Irish clergy and local Indian Catholic communities, was that established by Father Daniel O'Connor, a former provincial of the Augustinians in Ireland, who was appointed vicar apostolic of the Vicariate of Madras by Propaganda Fide in 1834. Following the appointment of O'Connor, over the next seventy-five years the Vicariate of Madras became something of an Irish Catholic stronghold. In total, there were five successive Irish Catholic bishops appointed to Madras in the nineteenth century: Daniel O'Connor (1834–40), Patrick Carew (1838–40), John Fennelly (1841–68), Stephen Fennelly (1868–80), and Joseph Colgan (1882–1911).[14] Despite initial support from the colonial authorities for their activities in Madras in the 1830s, it is interesting to note that O'Connor and his Irish priests were subjected to much criticism from sections of the Indian Catholic community. Many of O'Connor's Indian detractors, for example, asserted that, while Portuguese priests were lacking in knowledge of Indian languages, they could at least speak Portuguese, which was understood by three-quarters of the congregation of the Capuchin church over which O'Connor presided. Irish priests, they complained, knew neither Tamil nor Portuguese and could only officiate in either English or Latin.[15] Moreover, many of O'Connor's Indian parishioners objected to the particular type of Catholicism that the Irish introduced into Madras in the 1830s.

It was alleged among a group of people who described themselves as "poor Indians," for example, that O'Connor and his Irish priests paid little heed to proper liturgical practices.[16] The "native part of the community" were said to be extremely "displeased and discontented" because of O'Connor's failure to provide High Mass during the week as well as on Sundays. Furthermore, they alleged that O'Connor's Irish priests in Madras did not provide novenas for the lay confraternities, nor did they arrange processions or provide a cross for the pulpit. Other Indian Catholics criticized the Irish clergy's dress code, complaining that the Irish in Madras dressed too informally and that they resembled their Protestant counterparts more than Roman Catholic priests. O'Connor countered such criticism by some of his Indian congregation by stating that he and his fellow Irish priests always wore the soutane while saying

Mass and that only when he went abroad did he, like other "British and Europeans," wear "the same ... dress worn by Priests and Bishops in England, Ireland and Scotland." Furthermore, O'Connor maintained that, by adopting an informal mode of dress, he and his Irish priests were far better placed to gain access to difficult geographical areas outside of Madras City. Although guilty of breaching traditional Catholic ecclesiastical protocol, O'Connor insisted that the adoption of informal dress by his Irish priests would enable them to serve the needs of India's neglected class and would thus "produce the greatest advantage to the religion" of India's poor and distressed.[17]

Many high-caste Indian Catholics belonging to the influential parava caste, however, were far from convinced and interpreted O'Connor's explanations as an affront to high-caste Indian Catholic sensibilities. They complained to the vicar general that the Irish missionary priests in Madras did not speak Tamil and devoted much of their time to the Irish Roman Catholic soldiers in nearby British military cantonments. The Irish, they protested, were trying to treat Indian Catholics as if they were Irish and not Indian at all. They did not adhere to Indian Catholic customs, such as the separation of the sexes during Mass, nor did they take their shoes off before entering the church. For many of O'Connor's Indian detractors, the final straw came when O'Connor decided to rearrange the seating in his new cathedral church in Madras into two distinct sections, an arrangement that some Indian parishioners interpreted as being motivated by caste bias.[18] In the first section, O'Connor assigned seats for Europeans and Indians in European dress only, while in the second he assigned those wearing Indian dress. As a result of O'Connor's actions, many high-caste Tamils, who resented being mixed together with low-caste pariahs, threatened to raise money of their own to build a separate Catholic church in Madras if something were not done to alleviate the problem. What alarmed Indian Catholics most was that it seemed to them as though O'Connor and his Irish priests were somehow trying to blur the lines between high- and low-caste Indian Catholics in Madras. O'Connor, however, was resolute and insisted that his seating arrangement in the cathedral church dissatisfied only a few high-caste Indians, whom, he observed, were small in number. Despite attempts by O'Connor's vicar general, another Irishman, Reverend Moriarty, to subdivide the Indian section of the church into separate high- and low-caste areas, over eighty high-caste families stopped attending O'Connor's services and withdrew to churches under the direct control of the more conservative *padroado*.[19]

However, despite the criticism directed towards O'Connor and his Irish missionaries in Madras in the 1830s, their substantial missionary work and the particular type of Irish Catholicism they introduced to south India did not go unnoticed. In 1838 the Madras vicar general Reverend Moriarty travelled to Rome in an attempt to defend O'Connor's actions in front of Propaganda Fide. Moriarty argued that the Madras mission had already been seriously undermined by the internal feuding and controversies surrounding O'Connor's predecessors, the French and Italian Capuchins. The mission in Madras, Moriarty claimed, contained many different and opposing factions each trying to secure its own particular interest in south India. In addition, Moriarty argued that, before the Irish had arrived in Madras, many Indian Catholics had been paying too much attention to religious pomp and ceremony. Not enough attention, he maintained, had been paid to the practical requirements of the mission itself, such as providing education and welfare for India's poor or the ministering of the sacraments.[20] Though not specifically Irish phenomena, these were all important initiatives undertaken by a reorganized Catholic Church in Ireland in the years following emancipation, whose members largely identified with the marginalized and poorer sections of societies to which they were ministering overseas. In fact, many well-respected and established figures within the Indian Catholic Church, such as the Pondichéry-based Abbé Luquet, praised O'Connor and his Irish priests for their approach to missionary work and their interaction with Indian society in general. Luquet asserted that, in contrast to the social conservatism of the French Jesuits in India, the Irish paid little deference to high-caste Indians, and he applauded their neutral disposition when it came to the issue of caste in general. In Luquet's opinion, the French Jesuits had made a serious error in judgment in their preferential treatment of high-caste Indian Catholics. He maintained that, as O'Connor's guest in Madras in 1835, he had observed schools and churches established by the Irish missionaries open to all castes and that Brahman, Parias, and the Sudras children mixed freely without any complications.[21]

Following O'Connor's retirement in Madras in 1839, John Fennelly, a former Maynooth College bursar, was made the new vicar apostolic. Shortly before Fennelly's arrival, however, another Maynooth College graduate, Dr Patrick Carew, a professor of theology, was briefly appointed as a coadjutor bishop to O'Connor. Upon his arrival in south India in 1839, Carew wrote to Paul Cullen, the rector of the Irish College in Rome, and stated his determination to put things right in the Catholic mission in Madras.[22] Within six months of his arrival on the subcontinent, Carew informed Propaganda Fide that he had succeeded in reconciling some disillusioned high-caste Indians who had left O'Connor's cathedral church because of the offensive seating arrangements.

However, Carew's tenure in Madras was short-lived, and, not long before his departure to take up the vacant vicariate of Calcutta, he too was involved in controversy. During this time, Father Doyle, an Irish military chaplain based at Bellary, had appealed to the Madras government to supply prayer books and other Catholic doctrinal works for the East India Company's Irish Roman Catholic soldiers stationed nearby. Upon referral to the Government of India, it was decided that Doyle's request should be turned down on the ground that, while the supply of the Bible and the Book of Common Prayer to Protestant soldiers was in accordance with the existing Queen's Regulations, there was no such official provision made for Catholics.[23] Carew, however, who had previously been entrenched in promoting the independence of the Irish Catholic Church while based in Maynooth, was incensed by what he believed was an attempt by the British government to exert greater control over Roman Catholic missionaries in India by interfering with their relationship with the company's Irish soldiers. Carew informed the Government of India that, if the spiritual needs of the Roman Catholic soldiers were not met, he would take severe action. Not only would he appeal to all Irish Catholic clergy "to raise their voices from the thousand altars at which they minister, and dissuade their countrymen from engaging in the military service of India," but, if his compatriots' requests were not approved, he would also ensure that, in the future, "all the wealth of the Honourable Company would not succeed in raising a single regiment in Catholic Ireland."[24] In response to Carew's threats, neither Lord Elphinstone (the governor of Madras) nor Lord Auckland (the Governor General of India) accepted responsibility for the controversy over Father Doyle's request and responded by making assurances that, in some special cases, Catholic doctrinal material for the company's Roman Catholic soldiers would be provided.[25] In Ireland, too, there was much public criticism voiced over the East India Company's inability to supply Gaelic-speaking priests for the large native Irish-speaking contingent of soldiers in India both before and after the Indian Mutiny. The southern Catholic press, and, in particular, the *Cork Examiner*, printed numerous scathing editorials denouncing the company's treatment of its Irish Roman Catholic soldiers in the Madras Presidency in the 1850s. As one disgruntled Irish journalist wrote:

> It was the rule of a stranger, alien in creed, language, respect and habit, who has never become a settler in India, nor has he ever fraternalised with its people, but has invariably departed himself towards the natives with the haughty bearing of a conqueror who now in her hour of need calls on Catholic, Celtic Ireland to furnish her quota to her legions – and yet she suffers her Catholic soldiers in the Madras Presidency to be persecuted by bigoted commanding officers in the vain efforts to draw them or their children from their faith.[26]

Another Irish critic complained that, in the wake of the Mutiny,

> while they [the East India Company] are profuse in their assurances of respect for the faithful Hindoo and of the Mussulman, the fiercest enemy of the Cross, they treat with cold indifference the claims of the very boldest and bravest of their Christian chivalry – the very soldiers on whose courage they rely for the restoration of power jeopardised by their own parsimoniousness or incompetency.[27]

Moreover, many observers among the Irish Catholic press resented the deference paid by many of the Christian missionaries in India to the practice of Hinduism and Islam, while Catholicism, in their opinion, was being undermined. One Irish commentator who bitterly criticized the East India Company's policy of non-interference in religious matters in India complained: "the Hindu and the Mussulman are to have their religious alarm allayed, their religious jealousy appeased, their religious scruples respected; but the Irish soldier, who fights and bleeds in their cause, is unworthy of their consideration."[28] In India, newspapers such as the *Bengal Catholic Herald* brought the issue of discontent among Catholic Irish soldiers into the public domain. The *Herald* proclaimed: "Generally speaking Irish Catholics are for a moiety in Queen's regiments in this country [India], and therefore it is the bounded duty of the Bishop in whose Vicariate they may be stationed, to see their religious wants properly provided for."[29] Similarly, the *Bengal Hurkaru*, prompted by the company's military campaigns in the 1840s and 1850s, commented that there were simply not enough chaplains for Irish Roman Catholic soldiers in India. In the wake of such stinging criticism, the company feared that its popular recruiting stations in Ireland would be dramatically hit if something were not done to alleviate the distress of its Roman Catholic Irish soldiers.

Reluctantly, the British authorities agreed to the provision of English/Gaelic-speaking priests for Irish soldiers, and, as a consequence, Irish chaplains and priests succeeded in infiltrating almost every major Indian city and important military cantonment during the nineteenth century. The only major concern of the company's authorities with regard to Irish missionaries bound for India was that they should not be graduates of Maynooth College, Ireland's national Catholic seminary. The British government believed that Maynooth was inextricably linked with Irish nationalism during this period and had "very great objections to Irish clergymen going to the colonies." They alleged that all Irish priests "brought up at Maynooth were particularly obnoxious on account of their extreme political views."[30]

Significantly, then, in addition to their role of maintaining and upholding British colonial rule in South Asia, Irish Catholic religious networks often diverged from the colonial state in India, articulating the grievances of the oppressed, giving a voice to the disenfranchised, and working to reform the Empire from within. In this way, many Catholic prelates played significant roles in the emerging discourse over race and debates centred upon the reconfiguration of imperial authority in India following the ruptures to British colonial rule in the aftermath of the Indian Mutiny in 1857. Indeed, many of these outspoken comments were made public at a time when a developing critique of British responsibility to its imperial subjects was being formulated by nationalist groups throughout the Empire and were receiving much attention among the pages of an expanding imperial press system, both at home and abroad. Although the degree to which open critiques of British colonialism on the part of Irish Catholic religious figures influenced any real measure of policy in India is, of course, open to debate, protests by Carew, along with those that filled the columns of Irish newspapers, gained considerable publicity and drew attention to the perceived failings of the British administration in India in the immediate aftermath of the Indian Mutiny. There can be little doubt that this contributed to the emergence of a new-found language of national sentiment in Ireland, India, and beyond.

While many graduates from both All Hallows and Maynooth College joined Carew and Fennelly in Calcutta and Madras in the 1840s and 1850s, there was in addition a sizeable proportion of young Irish prelates who were posted to the vicariate of Agra in North India during the same period.[31] Unlike Madras and Calcutta, whose Indian Catholic churches were dominated by Irish clerics at this time, Agra during the

1840s was presided over by an Italian Capuchin named Joseph Borghi.[32] In his official duties as bishop of Agra, Borghi developed a close working relationship with the Catholic hierarchy in Dublin and the Irish Roman Catholic community in Agra. A vast expansive terrain, the nineteenth-century vicariate of Agra incorporated much of Punjab, the North-Western Provinces, and the central Indo-Gangetic plain. Here, Borghi and his missionaries were responsible for overseeing and ministering to the large concentration of British military personnel dispersed throughout these regions. In spite of, at times, some opposition from the East India Company, Borghi, along with several of his Irish chaplains, fought tirelessly to maintain the regimental schools that provided education for the orphans and Eurasian children of Catholic Irish soldiers. Many of Borghi's private letters to All Hallows reveal genuine anxiety concerning the level of official suspicion that was being expressed by members of the Government of India towards Irish Catholic priests as well as their alleged mistreatment of Catholic soldiers employed in the imperial armed forces during the 1840s. Writing to Moriarty in Dublin in 1846, Borghi pleaded with the president of All Hallows for additional missionaries to be sent to Agra to tend to the spiritual needs of what he described as his "beloved Irish soldiers." Although he had managed to lay the foundations of a new cathedral church in Agra – St Peter's – Borghi informed Moriarty that "more than 600 Irish Catholics [in India] are obliged to assemble for Divine Service under a kind of shed made of straw."[33] Moreover, Borghi warned Moriarty that, although a military orphan-house had been established in Agra and Sardhana for Irish boys and girls, nothing at all could be expected from the government, which, he alleged, was "supporting Protestants, Hindoos and Mussulmans, but not the Catholics."[34] Despite some official interference, however, Borghi insisted that the Catholic mission in Agra was flourishing. He told Moriarty how he had foiled a government "plan to seize all the poor orphans, and to throw them into a Protestant Asylum," and how he was confident that, in the future, "with the help of some good Irish priests, things [would] go much better."[35]

It was not long before Moriarty responded to Borghi's request. In 1848, two missionaries of All Hallows, Father Joseph Rooney and Father Nicholas Barry, arrived in Agra.[36] Their initial duty was to teach some three hundred pupils in St Peter's College, most of whom were Eurasian but "of Irish parents."[37] However, within days of his arrival Barry wrote to Father Woodlock in Dublin informing him of how "those in high office" were "very much prejudiced against us." He was, however, very impressed by Borghi, whom he referred to as "a real Father" and applauded his skills of diplomacy. According to Barry, not only was the bishop "fully able for them [the Government of India]" but he also succeeded in obtaining salaries for the military chaplains "of about £120 a year each, notwithstanding all their opposition."[38] With the assistance of graduates from All Hallows, Barry informed Woodlock of how Borghi was intent on "lending his entire strength towards the education of the children" in Agra. By April 1848, Bishop Borghi had given Barry charge of a military station at Nomelah just outside Agra whose congregation, according to Barry, was "entirely Irish" and thus "necessitated an Irish priest to go there."[39] With a congregation about five hundred strong, Barry noted that it was composed chiefly of Irish soldiers and their families, with only a few civilians and "about ten Catholic families of native Christians."[40]

During Barry's chaplaincy at Nomelah the military station was in the process of acquiring a new chapel. He noted crucially that the roofing, flooring, and plastering of the church had been achieved through the patronage of the Irish soldiers. In a letter to Woodlock in Dublin he enthused:

> The soldiers have the same warm feelings, the same respect and veneration for their clergy, as at home, the same generosity in contributing to works of charity. These good fellows handed me at the close of the month sometimes 100 rupees, or thirty pounds sterling, given for that purpose. I have known several to give half their monthly pay. The soldiers are indeed the hope of Catholicity in India.[41]

Father Barry also made revealing comments to Woodlock about the social origins and backgrounds of his Irish congregation at Nomelah. Every evening, he observed, Irish soldiers and their families would congregate and talk outside the chapel before entering to say their night prayers. This behaviour, according to Barry, closely resembled what "the people do in the country parishes in Ireland." What surprised him most, however, was the difficulty that he experienced in hearing confessions and in preparing some of his Irish congregation for confirmation, a fact that he attributed to the Irish community in Nomelah consisting of "persons mostly from the west of Ireland, whose education had been neglected." Writing to Woodlock in Dublin, Barry commented that "they [Irish Catholic soldiers] often puzzled" him "as they spoke nothing but Irish" and that, on several occasions, he "had to get a catechist who understood the [Gaelic] language" in order to communicate with them."[42] Nevertheless, in spite of such practical difficulties, it appeared that, once a Gaelic-speaking priest had been found to instruct native Irish-speaking soldiers in the sacraments, Catholic religious practice in and around the British military cantonments in Agra was considered to be quite good.

Moreover, there were indications that, by the early 1850s, Indian Catholics were beginning to respond to the particular type of Irish Catholicism that was being introduced to British India by Irish prelates. Bernard Sheridan, a young Irish Roman Catholic chaplain in Peringhipooram in the 1850s, for example, informed his prefect in Dublin as follows: "[Catholics in India] now appear to be much better informed than persons of the same low rank in Ireland. They follow the priest through the different parts of the Mass most accurately, and this without the aid of a book. There are catechists appointed throughout the several villages, who instruct the Christians in the Christian doctrine." "The children," Sheridan maintained, "are particularly attended to, as they constitute the hope of the mission. They are, almost in every village[,] well instructed in the Catholic doctrine."[43] In addition to active instruction, many Irish priests and bishops in Madras, Calcutta, and Agra took advantage of British reticence in formulating an official policy in dealing with its Irish Catholic missionaries in India and received small stipends in return for keeping records of Catholic activity in Indian towns and villages.

Nathaniel O'Donnell, for example, kept a carefully logged account of all baptisms, holy communions, and confirmations registered at St Mary's Seminary at Cardonagh in Madras between the years 1848 and 1850.[44] Others devoted themselves to the study of Indian languages, thus countermanding the notion that all Irish priests were unwilling to preach in either Tamil or Hindi. John MacIssey, an Irish Roman Catholic chaplain stationed in Hyderabad, wrote to Father James in Dublin in 1855, for example, declaring his intent to master the Indian vernacular languages. He confidently informed James that he often "preached in Hindoostanee as … it is understood by great numbers of the Christians and is the common tongue of the citizens of Hyderabad" and that he was gradually learning "Telegoo … the language of the native Hindoos … studying it every leisure moment of time."[45] The work of chaplains like MacIssey and O'Donnell counter complaints that Irish vicars apostolic, and the priests and nuns who accompanied them to India, worked largely to promote the interests of soldiers and their families in military cantonments and failed to properly minister to the wider Indian Catholic community, often ignoring specific caste sensibilities. Indeed, the involvement of religious networks in debates on caste, education, and the administration of the church demonstrate the myriad ways in which Irish Catholic religious networks became gradually embedded in Indian society from the 1830s onwards. Moreover, co-ethnic Catholic networks, such as those fostered by Bishop Borghi and his Irish priests in Agra, often diverged from the colonial state, articulating grievances that informed the debates over the methods used by the East India Company to establish its authority in India. Yet, surprisingly, despite the enduring commitment and ties to their religion, most Irish Catholic soldiers as well as the Catholic clergy in the employ of the East India Company seemed to strongly identify with British rule. If anything, for many Irish Catholics, identification with the Empire served to expiate feelings of inferiority associated with poor or modest backgrounds, and many of the East India Company's Irish Catholic recruits and religious figures, in fact, recorded pride in the imperial connection. Writing from his cantonment in Indore in 1853, Sergeant William Braithwaite, a gunner in the Bengal Fusiliers, for example, documented how, within the confines of the British Army, he began to learn to play the flute, sang in the Mhow chapel choir, and read daily. According to Braithwaite his experience in the company's army had changed him from a wild, undisciplined youth into a steady young man. Like many other Irishmen from similar social and cultural backgrounds, imperial service in India frequently enabled him to construct a positive identity that was rooted as much in the imperial as it was in the national.

What emerges implicitly from a historical study concerning the interconnections in Catholic religious activity between two very different regions of the Empire, such as Ireland and India, is a conception that neither place was a specific bounded entity within the context of the nineteenth-century British Empire. Rather, both places constituted what Alan Lester describes as an "imperial space" or "sphere of a multiplicity of trajectories," a point that lends credence to the idea that both Ireland and India functioned less as "passive" and "receptive" colonial societies and more as sub-imperial centres in their own right.[46] As an important sub-imperial centre of the British Empire, Ireland possessed the ability to by-pass the traditional "metropolitan" core in the supply of religious personnel to India. Ireland not only supplied the Empire with key personnel who contributed to the spread of Western forms of education in India, promoted charitable activities for India's poor, and aided the development of an Indian Catholic infrastructure, but it also functioned as an important reference point for the colonial authorities in their attempt to understand and make sense of hitherto unknown Indian social norms (such as caste), ultimately laying the path for new legislation and systems of government.

These religious figures were part of emerging nineteenth-century Irish professional networks that viewed the Empire as a legitimate sphere for work and as an arena in which Irish people operating within a "Greater Ireland" could prosper. Moreover, through involvement and deployment of expertise in areas such as education, charity, and missionary work in India, Irish people and Irish institutions, especially religious training colleges and seminaries, played an important role in the development of colonial knowledge – the recognition of which is significant in a field that has been traditionally dominated by Anglo-Indian interactions. Moreover, these networks of Irish religious figures whose experiences in India confound the traditional "colonizer/colonized" binary, effectively functioned as Irish knowledge communities, or networks, of intellectual exchange in their own right, disseminating religious, ethnographic, and scientific knowledge throughout the British Empire. By focusing on the integrative power of various types of networks fashioned through such connections, the relationships mapped out in this chapter centre Irish Catholics within the broader imperial web of connections and global exchange of ideas, information, and practices during the long nineteenth century and challenge us to rethink both how we view imperial relations and how we can accommodate the multiple trajectories and exchanges to which the emergence of a Greater Ireland gave rise during this period.

NOTES

1 Crosbie, *Irish Imperial Networks*.

2 See, for example, Kenny, *Ireland and the British Empire*.

3 See Whelan, *New Imperial History*. This body of work is perhaps best reflected in John M. MacKenzie's ongoing Studies in Imperialism series published by Manchester University Press.

4 MacKenzie, "Irish, Scottish, Welsh and English Worlds?"

5 For a fuller discussion on social network analysis, see, for example, Wasserman, *Social Network Analysis*; Griffin, *New Methods for Social History*; Scott, *Social Network Analysis*. See also Lester, *Imperial Networks*.

6 Magee and Thompson, *Empire and Globalisation*, 13–20.

7 *All Hallows Annual Report* (Dublin: John F. Fowler, 1953), 22.

8 Condon, *All Hallows*, 26.
9 Ibid., 32.
10 See Ballhatchet, *Caste, Class and Catholicism*; Ballhatchet, *Race, Sex and Class*.
11 MacKenzie, "History of Christianity."
12 See Ballhatchet, "East India Company."
13 See Cadet Papers, 1775–1860: Applications for East India Company Cadetships, L/Mil/9/107–269, Oriental and India Office Collection (OIOC) British Library, London.
14 Hogan, *Irish Missionary Movement*, 26–7.
15 See Ballhatchet, "East India Company," 273–88.
16 Memorandum of the Funds and Other Particulars of the Capuchin Church, etc., SC Ind. Or. 5, 605–6v.
17 Memorandum, SC Ind. Or. 5, 605–6v.
18 See Foreign Missionary Correspondence (India) of Dr Russell, President of Maynooth College (1857–80). Russell Papers 13/43 (box 13 – fol. 43), St Patrick's College, Russell Library, Maynooth, County Kildare.
19 G.M. Sinnappa Pillai to Fr Michel d'Onnion, 25 November 1838, SC Ind. Or. 7, 99–100.
20 Moriarty to Propaganda Fide, 8 September 1838, SC Ind. Or. 6, 527–30.
21 Luquet to Propaganda Fide, 9 April 1845, AP, Acta 208, 130ff; de Melo, "Recruitment and Formation," 257ff.
22 Carew to Cullen, n.d., ICRA New Cullen, IV, iv Fi, 9.
23 Government of India to Madras Government, 9 December 1840, Madras Ecclesiastical Proceedings, January 1841, 2–3.
24 Carew to Government of India, 4 January 1841, Madras Ecclesiastical Proceedings, January 1841, 57–65.
25 Government of India to Madras Government, 9 February 1841, Madras Ecclesiastical Proceedings, 10 February 1841, 14.
26 *Cork Examiner*, 7 September 1857.
27 Ibid., 14 October 1857.
28 Ibid.
29 *Bengal Catholic Herald*, quoted in *Cork Examiner*, 14 October 1857.
30 See R. Lythgoe, 16 March 1834, London Jesuit Archives (LJA), Archives of English Province, India 1802–1911, f. 205.
31 Twenty-six out of the twenty-nine Roman Catholic priests in Madras in 1851 were Irish. Nine were graduates of All Hallows College. See Condon, *Missionary College of All Hallows*, 109. The province of Hyderabad also belonged originally to the Madras vicariate. It was committed to the care of Fr Daniel Murphy by Dr Carew in 1841. In 1851 Hyderabad became an

independent vicariate, with Murphy as the vicar apostolic. He had four Irish priests. Two All Hallows missionaries, John McIssey and Joseph Dalton, served in Hyderabad. In 1864 Bishop Murphy left India and later became bishop of Hobart. Calcutta in Bengal and later East Bengal were also heavily influenced by Irish missionaries during the nineteenth century, first under Bishop Carew, then under Carew's vicar general, Thomas Oliffe. Twelve All Hallows missionaries went out to Bengal between 1844 and 1858. See All Hallows College (AHC), *Annual Report*, 1851, 9–11.

32 Borghi (1839–49) was succeeded as vicar apostolic of Agra by Cajetan Carli (1849–54) and then Ignatius Perisco (1854–61). Bishop Perisco, in particular, was associated with many missionaries of All Hallows from the time when he was Capuchin administrator of the Agra Vicariate.

33 Borghi to Moriarty, Agra, 25 May 1846, AHC, *First Annual Report*, 1848, f. 13.

34 Ibid.

35 Ibid.

36 Two other Irishmen from All Hallows also went to Agra in the 1850s. John McGrane was ordained in Agra in 1852 but died two years later. William Gleeson served as a military chaplain in Agra from 1854 to the early 1860s. In 1870 he became the founding pastor of St Anthony's, Oakland, California, and died there in 1903.

37 Fr Nicholas Barry to Woodlock, St Peter's College, Agra, 28 January 1848, AHC, *Annual Report*, 1848, f. 37.

38 Barry to Woodlock, St Peter's College, Agra, 28 January 1848, AHC, *Annual Report*, 1848, f. 38.

39 Barry to Woodlock, Nomelah, Agra, 3 July 1848, AHC, *Annual Report*, 1848, f. 43.

40 Fr Nicholas Barry to Rev. N. O'Donnell, St Peter's College, Agra, 1 February 1848, AHC, *First Annual Report*, 1848, f.3 9.

41 Barry to Woodlock, St Peter's College, Agra, 1 February 1848, AHC, *First Annual Report*, 1848, f.43.

42 Ibid.

43 Rev. Bernard Sheridan to Woodlock, Peringhipooram, Madras, 29 March 1851, AHC, *Fourth Annual Report*, f. 7.

44 O'Donnell to Woodlock, St Mary's Seminary, Madras, Feast of St Gongall, 1 November 1851, AHC, *Fourth Annual Report*, 1851, f. 9.

45 Rev. John MacIssey to Fr James, Hyderabad (Deccan), 27 October 1855, AHC, *Ninth Annual Report* 1855, f. 76.

46 Lambert and Lester, *Colonial Lives*, 14.

10

Saving the Empire? The Role of Irishwomen in Protestant Female Missions, 1870–1914

MYRTLE HILL

Recent missionary historiography points up the diverse and fluid nature of the relationship between empire and religious missions. Challenging more traditional interpretations and cautioning against over-simplistic categorizations, scholars such as Andrew Porter and Jeffrey Cox urge researchers to break through the theoretical boundaries imposed by academia and to acknowledge and explore the complexities, tensions, and contradictions inherent in such encounters.[1]

While influenced by both their sending and receiving cultures, missionaries were, as Hilary Carey and others point out, not just subjects of empire but also players in a larger field.[2] There is evidence of resistance to, as well as complicity with, imperial pressures in their interactions with those whose souls they sought to save. Moreover, the missionary experience varied according to geographical location and, indeed, individual temperament and ambition, while also changing significantly over time. The purpose of this chapter is to add gender to the well-rehearsed debates on these diverse cultural interactions and to consider to what extent gender made a difference to the rhetoric and the reality of life on the mission field.

Given that Ireland's status within the British Empire was under significant threat during the late nineteenth and early twentieth centuries, the north of Ireland makes a particularly interesting case study. The issue of national identity was (and remains) a critical aspect of the historical conflict between those (mainly based in the northeastern six counties of what is now Northern Ireland) who claim constitutional and cultural affiliation with Britain and the wider Irish nationalist community on the island. The terms "British" and "Irish" are thus perhaps in a state of fluidity and the concept of empire particularly significant during the time period under discussion.[3]

Ireland's place in missionary historiography is well documented. Dating back to the fifth century the "land of Saints and Scholars" earned a justifiable reputation for its efforts to convert "the pagan world" to its own version of Christianity. Following the Reformation, Irish Protestant denominations were, generally speaking, slower to follow the example of their Catholic neighbours – indeed, were more interested in converting them to the "true Protestant faith."[4] However, by the mid-nineteenth century the combination of imperial expansion and the pervasion of evangelicalism had resulted in an enthusiastic commitment to spreading the Gospel among the overseas "heathen," and missionary societies were established in Anglican, Methodist, Baptist, and Presbyterian churches.[5] Several more decades would pass, however, before women (other than missionary spouses) were invited to participate in this great endeavour.

As with other areas of mission historiography, the investigation and interpretation of the role of women has evolved in the context of current trends in scholarship. While the earliest writing on female missionaries was, like that of their male counterparts, focused on the heroic and sacrificial nature of their Christian commitment, fresh insights were generated by feminist historians as part of the wider "second wave" project of challenging the marginalization of women in history. In uncovering less conventional sources and applying a feminist analysis to more traditional interpretations, they revealed the possibilities of empowerment and independence offered by an area of work that, on the surface, appeared to be one of "service" and support. Later work, drawing on feminist debates on "difference" as well as postcolonial theory, showed greater awareness of the ways in which such women were themselves part of a racially based power hierarchy, while in recent decades the works of postmodernist and poststructuralist theorists have argued against the tendency of seeing all female missionaries as a hegemonic category. While these shifting theoretical emphases have deeply enriched our understanding of motivations and experiences, an appreciation of the religious/spiritual dimension of individual experience, and, indeed, of the "sending" culture more generally, remains critical to a full appreciation of the contradictions and ambiguities inherent in female missionary work. These various influences and approaches are discussed in the brief study of northern Irish female missionary experience that follows.

From the beginnings of the foreign missionary movement women's role was viewed primarily – as in the domestic arena at home – as that of wives and helpmates, and there is general agreement that the extent of their engagement in the enterprise has been understated by both contemporaries and historians. There is little doubt that, individually and collectively, they were an essential component in sustaining the missionary project, not only supporting their husband's work by replicating the comforts of Western family life, protecting their reputations, and providing role models for indigenous women but also utilizing their own skills and experiences in supervising schools, looking after orphans, helping deliver babies, and tending the sick. Evidence of the difficult, dangerous, and pioneering aspects of their work is patchy and incomplete but sufficient to suggest that high levels of commitment and a great deal of personal sacrifice were characteristics of most missionary wives.[6] This is an area that would reward further research and more focused analysis,[7] but this chapter focuses on the participation of single Protestant women recruited to the mission field in the last quarter of the nineteenth century.

While there are examples of individual women undertaking such work prior to this period, it was in the course of the 1860s and 1870s that the major Protestant denominations accepted the need to facilitate and formalize women's deeper engagement in the missionary project. Rather than a desire to promote the interests of Christian women, this decision was based on more pragmatic reasoning – an acknowledgment that existing missionary organizations were failing to significantly influence or affect foreign customs, traditions, and beliefs. Since "the wives and mothers of one generation are the true moral founders of the whole community of the next,"[8] the importance of reaching the women of indigenous households was clearly recognized. With Eastern cultures denying access to Western men, and missionary wives encumbered by family responsibilities, it was considered necessary – "from the point of view of strategy and policy" – to bring on board appropriately trained women who would be able to devote all their energies both to the wives of Christian converts and to the female "heathen."[9] Thus, in Ireland, as elsewhere, new institutional structures were established with the aim of meeting "the vital demand for the presence of Christian women in the non-Christian world."[10] Anglicans, Baptists, Methodists, and Presbyterians formed female auxiliaries to existing societies, and this chapter focuses on the latter – the Female Association for Promoting Christianity among the Women of the East (hereafter the Female Association), which was founded in Belfast in 1873.[11]

The remit of the new societies was to recruit, train, and support women's roles in the schools, dispensaries, and orphanages that made up the typical missionary compound, and, despite prevailing patriarchal views of "the exceeding delicacy and difficulty of the work of women missionaries,"[12] applications flowed in. By 1939, the Female Association was responsible for sending out around 140 single women missionaries, mostly to India and China. Many commentators have noted the high preponderance of Western women in the foreign mission field in these years and that they frequently outnumbered their male counterparts.[13] However, certainly in terms of the Irish Presbyterian Mission, the significance of this numerical strength is somewhat diluted if we take into consideration length of service. Male missionaries who, as members of the clergy, were entering a long-established and highly regarded profession for which they had been carefully prepared, usually served for much longer periods than did single women.[14] Moreover, while marriage greatly enhanced men's status within the missionary (and, indeed, wider church) community, women who "married in the work" represented "a poor investment" to the organization that had supported them.

Any consideration of the experiences of these women, individually and collectively, and of their influence on the societies they sought to serve, needs to take into account the prevailing discourses and social and cultural fabrics of the missionary home base, which, as Maina Singh convincingly argues, were "crucial in shaping cross-cultural initiatives."[15] As noted above, this point is perhaps particularly pertinent in a society in which questions of identity were prominent in cultural and political discourse. The ethos of late Victorian Irish (increasingly Ulster) Protestantism, rooted in settlement patterns and shaped by its antagonistic relationship with the majority Catholic population, was given urgent intensity in the 1880s with the British government's proposal to introduce a form of Home Rule for Ireland. Already disillusioned by decades of "concessions" to Catholic nationalists, Ulster Protestant opposition to this development reflected economic, cultural, and political vulnerabilities, infused with a vigorous anti-Catholicism that was legitimized by a powerful and all-pervasive evangelical ideology. With a dramatic mid-century religious revival seeming to confirm that God was on their side, the constitutional crisis further facilitated a fusion of religious and political identities that transcended long-standing differences among Ulster Protestants[16] and reinforced the vital importance of the pulpit in Ulster culture and politics.[17]

Moreover, in anti-Home Rule speeches imperial themes were close to the surface: in the light of a growing and increasingly volatile nationalist resistance, the perceived responsibility of stewardship owed to the

"God-given trust" of empire appeared eminently justifiable. Popular enthusiasm for empire waxed and waned, but various commentators note renewed enthusiasm for empire during the 1890s. Mark Doyle, for example, looking at mid-Victorian attitudes, claims that, in Belfast's Sandy Row, people had an imperial dimension to their identities – and that their investment in the vicissitudes of empire helped to frame the rivalries between Catholic and Protestant.[18] In this context, missionary work fostered an even deeper sense of imperial loyalty, while also demonstrating allegiance to a wider community of Christian workers, which set its face against "ignorance and idolatry." In addition, evangelicals had by this stage acknowledged the failure of their campaign to convert the Catholics of Ireland, and the colonies offered a fresh and irresistible challenge to those receiving the call to take Christ's message "into all the World." There was thus a neat logic to the claim that "the Colonial Mission is based on the fact that as long as we are a colonizing people we require to be a colonizing Church."[19] It was evident that, despite Gladstone's "betrayal," the Imperial Crown still mattered in a region whose Protestant politicians demanded to "be allowed to continue [their] triumphant march of Prosperity under the protection of the British flag, a United Parliament and the Imperial Crown."[20] Presbyterians played a central role in the resistance to Home Rule, and the significance of this denomination in the north of Ireland has been thoroughly explored, with its theology, culture, and values critical to Ulster's social and cultural identity. I would suggest that it is this vibrant variety of Irish Protestantism that missionary pioneers sought to transplant to the more exotic surroundings of the East.

Women were clearly not separate from but, rather, an integral part of the religious and political community described above, and several key factors explain the part played by gender in the cultural construction of a female Ulster Protestant imperial identity. Reference has already been made to the Great Revival that shook the religious community in Ulster in 1859, and it is widely agreed that the intensification and diversification of evangelical activity that followed this phenomenon provided a wide range of new opportunities for the laity in general and, more specifically, for women's engagement in the network of voluntary societies and organizations that clustered around the religious denominations. In temperance and Bible societies, Sunday schools, philanthropic societies, and domestic missions, middle-class women enthusiastically engaged in doing "God's work" among the less privileged in their local communities.[21] The 1910 World Missionary Conference noted that such church-based work was a prerequisite for women applying to train as foreign missionaries, and, indeed, this type of background ensured that new recruits were familiar with, and receptive to, the hierarchical and patriarchal structures of religious organizations. Mission boards, after all, had "no desire to send out lay missionaries who would not be prepared to accept male supervision and direction."[22]

Moreover, the dominant social, religious, and cultural "messages" of middle-class Ulster Protestantism were cultivated, shaped, and developed during childhood and adolescence through both direct and indirect influences. At home, at school, and at church (with regular attendance at a range of religious events) a focus on the values of moral behaviour, self-sacrifice, and social justice and participation in a range of religious and philanthropic activities imbued girls and young women with a strong sense of responsibility and encouraged a consciousness of duty towards those less fortunate. Gillian McClelland's social analysis of the Female Association of Fisherwick Presbyterian Church demonstrates how in this period an intricate network of relationships and influences strengthened links between the church, the Zenana Mission, and Victoria College Belfast, forging a social and religious subculture in which the wives and daughters of Belfast industrialists invested heavily.[23]

Moreover, both church and school sent a disproportionate number of missionaries to India and China, and, as McClelland argues, the records suggest that "involvement in this mission encouraged or confirmed women's identification with the Empire."[24] Further such probing of the archives of local congregations is likely to be equally fruitful in furthering our understanding of the creation of an Ulster Presbyterian female imperial identity.

The call to supply women for work on the mission field provided yet another outlet for personal piety and community status both at home and abroad and a further widening of the domestic sphere. For those who made the decision to "serve" in foreign lands, a program of more focused training followed recruitment, and, whether based in Scotland or Ireland, this was designed to further mould character and to ensure individual aspirations matched those of the mission board. Discipline was seen as just as important as experience, and to this end particular emphasis was placed on the subversion of individualism. Despite the innovative nature of the female missionary venture, churchmen stressed that the work to be carried out in India or China was firmly in the tradition of "women's work for women" – teaching, nursing, reaching out to the women in the Zenana, and caring for orphans. The desire for "meek, quiet, self-sacrificing" women reflected the patriarchal hierarchy of both home and church base, and it was designed to safeguard traditional institutional structures on the mission field.[25] So, although the board of the Zenana Mission retained an administration separate from that of the male society,[26] the behaviour and activities of their missionaries, once overseas, came under the authority of either the male head of the station or, indeed, the male head of a mission family.

As products of the Ulster Protestant culture outlined above, it is not surprising that most female missionaries had little difficulty in following the designated agenda. Discord or resistance to these arrangements were rarely recorded, though it is likely that any problems would be kept under wraps. The nature of missionary correspondence and literature, which were largely for public consumption and designed to encourage fundraising, makes it difficult to gain access to the private thoughts of individuals, though a degree of frustration sometimes surfaces. Moreover, particularly strong-minded individuals were unlikely to bind themselves to operating under these constraints, opting instead to work independently of established institutions. And, though several such "missionary heroines" do appear in the historiography, on the whole they were rare indeed. One of the best known from an Irish Presbyterian background is Amy Carmichael, whose Christ-centred devotion and absolute faith that she was a channel for God's word led her to defy convention and to eventually establish her own missionary compound in southern India.[27]

Despite the intentions of the organizers, however, once the practice of sending single women to the mission field was established, it inevitably gathered a momentum of its own and, in its evolution, expanded the opportunities available to the missionaries and affected the nature of cross-cultural relations. Susan Brown, the first Presbyterian female missionary to leave from Belfast in 1873, saw her role as "the continuation and development of the work of the wives of missionaries since the founding of the mission,"[28] and other early recruits found it necessary to exercise flexibility and to employ a range of skills, fitting in where they were needed, with little specialization. Thus, though Miss Forrest and Miss Patterson had been specifically trained for medical work, in fact on reaching the mission station at Surat they spent most of their time assisting in the mission schools.[29] Nonetheless, segregation of the sexes in India and/or China must have facilitated a degree of independence for those working in schools, orphanages, and dispensaries, as did the practice of itinerating around outlying villages, usually in the company of indigenous women. Opportunities to challenge expectations could also depend on local conditions; thus Reverend T. Barker confided that Elsie McMordie, who was establishing a school in China, needed to be "designer, architect and clerk of works."[30]

The key changes affecting women's missionary work were facilitated by advances made in the domestic arena, where legislative reforms in academia enabled women to achieve qualifications in teaching and medicine, fulfilling personal expectations and opening the door to the professions. Traditional patriarchal institutions were reluctant to respond, however, with the Western medical profession, in particular, regarding the female "experiment" in medical training as "a palpable mistake" and placing many obstacles in the path of their advancement. Overseas missionary work, on the other hand, offered a wide scope for newly acquired skills and expertise, with places such as India and China representing "an environment of alternatives."[31] Although their professional status further complicated the profusion of hierarchies in the mission station, the need for properly qualified female medical personnel to treat indigenous women had become a regular issue in missionary and other colonial discourse. It was claimed that existing treatments were "brutish" and "cruel," with an "allegedly compliant colonial clientele," "outside the reach of skilled medical aid … [and subjected to] unalleviated suffering, intolerable misery."[32] Although the difficulty of finding professional positions at home was surely an important factor in attracting women doctors to the mission field, it is difficult to separate out the spiritual and practical motivations behind their decisions. They mostly regarded their own educational achievements as a reflection of the "civilized" society from which they came and which they wished to share with the "imprisoned" women of the East. It was noted that, in the area of women's rights (a bone of contention in the domestic area), "bringing their sisters to Christ [was] the highest right of Christian women,"[33] though it has also been suggested that the male medical hierarchy, fearing there was not sufficient work for everyone at home, was supportive of women's overseas aspirations.[34]

The plight of the women of the East also led to the founding of secular societies to train female nurses and doctors, though Laura Kelly's research indicates that more Irish women doctors in this period chose to work in missionary organizations than in secular ones.[35] Overseas work was certainly challenging, but it was also rewarding. In her first year of practising medicine on the mission station in Manchuria, Dr Isobel Mitchell from Belfast treated a range of exotic diseases and carried out amputations under primitive conditions. In the course of her work as medical missionary in Kuanchengtzu, China – where she served for twenty-six years – Dr Margaret McNeill also advanced her career, using periods of furlough to take several higher degrees – (LRCP, MB, BCH, BAO) – and her experience in the removal of large tumours was written up in the *British Medical Journal*.[36] Such experiences also influenced the perception of women doctors back home; as Antoinette Burton points out, the Zenana system in India provided the new female professions with a necessary outlet and, indeed, "the conviction that Indian women were trapped in the sunless, airless and allegedly unhygienic oriental Zenana motivated the institutionalism of women's medicine and was crucial to the professionalisation of women doctors in Victorian Britain."[37]

However, as was frequently pointed out, "medical work does not mean merely trying to cure the sick in heathen lands; it has a far greater outlook than that. Medical work and Mission work are intimately connected,"[38] with the former regarded chiefly as a means of evangelism – "a smoother of the way and a gainer of confidence."[39] "Missionary zeal was linked to contemporary notions of progress and the individual,"[40] with advances in science and medicine set against the "backwardness" of indigenous practices. Negative outcomes from missionary medical treatment generated suspicion and hostility and were frequently blamed on the non-observation of traditional rites. Dr Mary McGeorge despaired of visits to the homes of her patients: "Here is the battlefield where all the hosts of prejudice are marshalled in full array."[41]

Education was of course seen as a vital tool in the promotion of civilization, particularly when delivered through the medium of Christianity: "where missionaries go education goes, and the extent to which our English language with all its glorious freightage of terms for liberty, purity, honour and humanity, has been spread among the nations, is a cause for profound gratitude to every enlightened and far-seeing mind."[42] The colonial experience had also, however, demonstrated to indigenous peoples the importance of education in terms of their own progress under an alien authority, and it can additionally be seen as a product of modernization more generally. Etherington points out that, in India, there was a "pre-existing appetite for western education" since the early eighteenth century,[43] while at the Qua Iboe Mission, a "wild scramble for education" in southern districts was noted.[44] Nonetheless, such aspirations did not guarantee the success of missionary endeavours, with records, particularly in the early years, indicating fitful progress, stops and starts, problems and confrontations.

It was noted that the use of the Bible in schools was merely tolerated,[45] and teachers such as Miss Stavely acknowledged that, if religious instruction were not given such a prominent place, attendance would greatly improve.[46] Rejection of the more religious aspects of the work carried out in schools was recorded on several occasions. The Girls' High School in Surat, India, for example, became the centre of media attention when a Parsi girl was converted in 1881, resulting in the withdrawal of twenty pupils. On a later occasion local Parsis opened their own school in opposition to the "christianising" of their daughters.[47] Colin Pierson argues that, "in a way not fully understood, their essential differences not yet apparent, religion and education grew up together arm in arm," [48] and a degree of pragmatism was evident in parents' actions, with government grants acting as an inducement. The awarding of prizes for achievement in government exams, for instance, generated good publicity, as when a pupil in the Girls' High School in Surat won the Empire of India Scholarship. Prizes for drawing and needlework were also awarded and indicate that compromise and negotiation were necessary attributes. As one Qua Iboe missionary pointed out, "missionary occupation is not necessarily evangelization,"[49] and missionary workers based their faith on gospel stories that were told when such practical activities were "taking hold."

Nonetheless it is perhaps in the secular field that the greatest influence of these activities was felt; in material terms, the legacy was significant. For example, within fifty years of its founding, the Irish Female Association had established seventeen mission stations in India and ten in China. It also ran five hospitals and twenty-four dispensaries. Two orphanages were fully staffed and operational, while 2,700 pupils attended fifty-seven schools. Local workers trained by the mission comprised a doctor, twenty-four dispensers, 164 teachers, and forty-two Biblewomen.[50] Despite the oft-quoted ignorance and passivity of Indian women, it is already evident that recipients of missionary endeavour were making their own choices; throughout the colonial period Christian women were disproportionately represented in Indian schools and universities, while Maina Singh's research on the Asian experience of mission schools also confirms that the interaction between missionary and "native" could have a positive impact on the latter's construction of identity.[51] Similarly, Eliza Kent's insightful study of the process of conversion in colonial South India stresses that this "was never simply a matter of the imposition of a foreign religion on socially weak, vulnerable elements of the Hindu social body." Rather, by focusing on the perspective of Indian Christians, she argues that "Indians understood Christianity through indigenous categories and selectively appropriated those aspects of it that corresponded to local values and scales of social worth."[52] And Okkenhaug (Anglican Female Mission) claims that "the impact of the missionary enterprise is even today considerable on girls and women in Sub-Saharan Africa, the Middle East and Asia."[53]

Within the colonial context, working for the mission could thus accelerate upward mobility: apart from training in education or medicine, all family members could benefit from their engagement with the association. Sara Paul, daughter of a nineteenth-century Biblewoman, points to the advantages across generations – her older brother teaching in a boys' high school, the younger taking technical school training to be an engineer, she herself employed by the Government of Bombay in educational services.[54] However, in India missionaries were operating within the framework of a caste system that did not facilitate social mobility in the same way as did British class, and this was the cause of significant problems, particularly in the early years. Many examples are given of the hostile reactions of indigenous people outraged by missionary attempts to ignore or minimalize ingrained racial barriers. This seemed to be most difficult in a medical situation, where touching was more likely and attempts to administer treatment were often summarily rejected. In her dispensary in Surat, Miss Forrest responded to the challenge of upper-caste women demanding priority by allocating numbered tickets.[55] Clashes arising from the very different societal structures of India and Ireland were inevitable, however, and go some way to explaining why most converts in the mid-1890s were almost entirely from the same castes that supplied the original Christians. Elizabeth Kent's research provides helpful insight into the issues raised for missionaries by the question of caste.[56] In their attempts to develop cross-cultural relationships, therefore, missionary women were hampered by their "outsider" position: "other" to the women they tried to reach, they continually had to adapt their approaches and alter their aspirations.

Within the framework of significant class divisions, family values were at the core of late Victorian respectability, within which a strict moral code and clearly defined relationships between the sexes were largely unquestioned, and missions utilized the concept of family in their appeals to the community at home. As Miss Shilliday put it, India was "made in God's mysterious providence part of our own empire, its vast population our brothers and sisters in a common citizenship."[57] In practice, however, early female missionaries much more commonly perceived of their role as that of mother, "Amma," reflecting a less equal, more dependent relationship to indigenous women and girls. Biblewoman Sara Paul, on a visit to the north of Ireland in the 1940s, told the Sunday school that had sponsored her that she came "not as a stranger, but as a child of yours ... your adopted daughter."[58] Similarly, Amy Carmichael was described as the "powerful matriarch of a large and dependent family" of women and children,[59] and, even when numbers grew, she structured her mission along family rather than institutional lines. There is, of course, a paradox in the use of "the maternal metaphor" by women who were themselves unmarried. From this "outsider" position, they were lauded by their Western peers for their "maternal gifts," which were regarded as much superior to those of actual Indian mothers. While Eastern women were "slaves of father, husbands, sons," it was claimed that children in India and China "[found] a wealth of love for them in the hearts of the lady missionaries denied them in their homes."[60]

Moreover, missionary activity, when "successful," could significantly disrupt the family life of those who were receptive to the evangelizing message. Conversion frequently resulted in banishment from home and separation from parents and siblings,[61] so that, rather than influencing their own community, early converts were much more likely to be absorbed into the culture of the mission station. Those without existing family ties were easier targets of Christian attention, and missionary communities were heavily dependent on children brought up in mission orphanages. Often outsiders themselves, they came under the direct guidance of female missionaries and, on reaching adulthood, could make their own contribution to the work of the station, frequently as Biblewomen. Following a five-year training program, Biblewomen accompanied female missionaries in their tours of surrounding villages and were vitally important in easing access to the wider community of women in India and/or China for, "while the native women ha[d] great respect for the foreign lady, her teaching may not always have [had] its full effect from the fact that she [was] foreign."[62] The records suggest that these women were often either previous residents of the mission orphanages or widows and so, perhaps, already marginalized figures in the local district. Their activities may well have isolated them further for, in the itinerant work in which they engaged on behalf of the mission station, they were transgressing the social values of their own culture by their "wandering." Local opinion could also be outraged by the insensitivity of missionary women to Eastern social and cultural behaviour. For example, Reverend Shaw, Miss Kennedy, and Miss Couser set out for

China in 1891, but their stay lasted only a few weeks due to "local opposition and affront at Western familiarity between the sexes." The situation was duly investigated by the Mission Board in Belfast, which concluded that the missionaries were not guilty of anything "improper by western standards but acknowledged that Chinese cultural norms which permitted no social exchange between the sexes had been breached."[63]

It should be noted, however, that, by the late nineteenth century, mission authorities were concerned to avoid public confrontations and their negative consequences; the hostility generated by missionaries' burning of idols and/or ridiculing of rituals led to a more sensitive approach, with Churchmen hoping that women could more subtly extend their Christian influence within the Indian and/or Chinese home.[64] The flaunting of their guidelines led to censure and, in the case of the young Presbyterian zealot Amy Carmichael, who was vehemently opposed to compromise or to the display of any kind of tolerance towards "false gods," a degree of alienation that resulted in a "get Carmichael out of India" campaign by the wider missionary body.[65] Reverend John Shilliday noted in 1902 that the Presbyterian Church had "always discouraged every tendency to ape Europeans in dress, mode of life, name etc. we have already had many Ramas and Krishnas who are faithful followers of the Lord Jesus."[66] Moreover, adoption of local dress was seen as a way of proving Presbyterian intentions of creating an indigenous church,[67] and, indeed, the first three Indian elders were ordained in Shahawadi in 1875, the first Indian minister in 1888, and the Presbytery of Gujurat and Kathiawar in 1900. Local control was greatly facilitated by the opening of the first General Assembly of the Presbyterian Church in India in 1904. Power dynamics would, to a large extent, have been determined by individuals; thus, the independent Carmichael was not open to permitting Indian authority in Dhonavur. Though she was also keen to employ local workers, no Indian was given a leadership role in her compound until after her death, while Indian and European members of "the family" ate separately, the latter served by local villagers and surrounded by all the comforts of an English dining room.[68] In 1923, the twenty-seven Dohnavur workers were described as "Indian, English, Scotch and Irish," with Houghton noting that "Ireland supplied an astonishing percentage" of the earlier arrivals and that in later years the cultural mix was enriched by men and women from Switzerland, Australia, and New Zealand.[69] A mix of architectural styles in most mission compounds reflected a wish to assimilate at least some dimensions of foreign life, but it would appear there were many different responses to missionary intervention in the colonial experience.

Careful reading of the available evidence points to a complex and varied set of relations that has been usefully categorized by Barbara Rumasack under three headings: cultural missionary, maternal imperialist, and feminist ally.[70] It is not difficult to see how our Irish examples could slot into the first of the two categories: their language often appears patronizing, reflecting their feelings of cultural and racial superiority, with the "benevolent maternal imperialism" of white women both assuming and constructing the passivity and dependency of those they sought to "serve."[71] However, the categories also frequently overlap, and it is not always easy, perhaps not possible, to distinguish between them. The third category is an interesting one, not least because the term "feminist" is itself contested, with its meaning changing over time. Nonetheless, as already suggested, there is little doubt that many of these young, middle-class women, who had themselves benefited from a sound academic education, equated spiritual advancement with social progress and, indeed, membership in the Empire. As Susan Thorne points out, "the missionary movement was one of the principal sites through which imperialist ideologies infiltrated Victorian feminist consciousness and Christian principles one of the ideological bases that sustained a variety of feminist-imperialist commitments in this period."[72]

Those seeking the betterment of Indian women came from secular as well as religious backgrounds – Lady Dufferin's campaign for the training of nurses, for example, was based on "unsectarian benevolence" and aimed to train British women to train their Indian counterparts.[73] Although drawing attention to the lack of medical experience of female missionary workers, there was little conflict between secular and religious medical women on the mission field, and, indeed, this initiative served to encourage more professional training for missionary women. The practice of such traditions as sati, purdah, and arranged marriages was targeted by indigenous as well as by foreign reformers, with Shirwadka suggesting that Indian women were "influenced by the western progressive outlook which prompted them to look at the miserable conditions of Indian women."[74] Irishwoman Margaret Noble, who, as Sister Nivedita, "gave her all to India," is just one example of whole-hearted female engagement with social reform in India outside of the missionary world.[75] Motivated by religious impulses, missionary women could play their part in this "transnational feminism," which facilitated traditional "rescue work" "far beyond the limits of their home cultures."[76]

Amy Carmichael again serves as an interesting example. Horrified by witnessing the life of "devidas," temple girls whose role was believed to have sunk to the level of child prostitution, she claimed that "the finished product of the temple system of education is something so distorted that it cannot be described."[77] From 1901 until her death in 1951 she dedicated her life to rescuing such children, settling them in a Christian home, and providing them with an education and training. Although agreeing that reform should come from within India, she argued that she could not wait for a resolution.[78] Described by Indians as the "child-catching woman," Carmichael was, on several occasions, brought to court on the charge of kidnapping. But, within the walls of the missionary compound, which have been described as representing "a marked geographical and symbolic boundary" between clashing cultures, she was able to create her "own little empire."[79] Generating international publicity for her cause, she was often required to provide information for the Indian government and, in 1919, was included in the Royal Birthdays Honours list. She was also awarded the Kiser-I-Hind medal for services to India. Though she claimed much sympathy with aspects of Indian culture and openly rejected imperial influences, the contradictions and ambiguities of Carmichael's life provide fascinating evidence that female missionary work in this period cannot easily be classified. Significantly, the fame of this Irishwoman stretches worldwide and across denominational boundaries.

There were, therefore, many paradoxes and tensions in the attempts of white women to influence the lives of their Asian "sisters," and further work is required to tease out these complexities. More straightforward is an evaluation of the impact of the work of Irish missionary women on their home base. With dynamic and efficient home bases, impressive records of fundraising, and well-developed publicity strategies, these missions utilized the enthusiasm and expertise of local women anxious to respond to the call to enlist in "the great battle of the faith."[80] Within their first year of operation the women of Belfast's Female Mission had formed forty-nine congregational and fourteen district branches,[81] and with middle-class women acting as unpaid managers, collectors, editors of the journal, and so forth, financial, business, and marketing arrangements flourished.[82] The "power of the purse" was also evident:[83] within two years it was noted that the female auxiliaries were "contributing two or three times as much as the congregations they represent[ed] used to give to the foreign mission."[84] This enthusiasm at the home base made possible the work in foreign fields and also had the effect of "fostering a special relationship between church and mission."[85]

These transnational networks had solid foundations: the great majority of Irish Protestant missionary women were daughters of either the manse, of missionaries, or of active church members. There is plenty of evidence, too, of generational continuity and sibling engagement – the influential McMordie family established a virtual dynasty in this field – while the tendency of Irish missionary women to "marry in the work" (usually to Irish or Scots colleagues in the field) further reinforced the Ulster-Scots Presbyterian subculture that characterized northern Irish Protestantism. As already noted, family links were enhanced by both secular and Sunday school education and were further reinforced by both missionaries and supporters: students' and children's auxiliaries were established with the aim of "kindling the missionary fire by knowledge."[86] In the Missionary Prayer Union, members' cards were printed with detailed information about individual missionaries in order to make the connection "definite and personal."[87] In addition, popular literature, letters read aloud to home congregations, and personal talks given to packed meeting halls when missionaries were on furlough (illustrated by lantern slides and delivered with passion) all served to strengthen and popularize women's work on the mission field and to create a cohesive and pervasive Irish Protestant evangelical identity, transcending geographical boundaries in its divinely sanctioned mission. While we need to adopt a critical approach and "to interrogate mission and church discourses, published and also archival, in order to expose the complicity of power, knowledge, and representations" inherent in such activities,[88] it is also necessary to acknowledge its power to engage congregations in support of not only the mission but also the Church and its imperial Protestant ideology.

Catherine Hall claims that "missions, established to counter Heathenism both at home and abroad, provided a language through which middle-class and working-class men and women imagined themselves in relation to their nation's Empire."[89] In crisis-ridden early twentieth-century Ulster, where the Empire was increasingly perceived to be under threat, this was particularly pertinent and the battle language and images of missionary discourse fed into the investment of the Presbyterian Church and community in their campaign against Home Rule – perhaps most clearly evidenced in their role in the drawing up of the Ulster Covenant in 1912.[90] As Graham Walker points out, the cultivation of an Ulster identity "could be regarded as another variant on an ethnic form of Britishness which had at its core the concept of a Protestant crown and constitution and an essentially Protestant 'civilising' Empire."[91] In

1912 Andrew Bonar Law told a Unionist demonstration in Belfast: "Once more you hold the pass for the Empire. You are a besieged city."[92]

Neglected until relatively recently is the engagement of women in this campaign to save Protestant Ulster from an "attempt to establish a Roman Catholic ascendancy in Ireland to begin the disintegration of the Empire by securing a second parliament in Dublin."[93] The formation in 1911 of the Ulster Women's Unionist Council (UWUC) saw the consolidation and development of a female campaign to support the continuation of the constitutional union with Britain. Described as "the largest female association in Ireland,"[94] what is most pertinent to this discussion is the involvement in this organization of large numbers of the middle-class philanthropic women of Belfast. We have already noted the significance of familial and congregational networks linking the wives and daughters of influential industrialists, and it would seem that a "significant number" of the office bearers and active numbers of UWUC belonged to Fisherwick Presbyterian Church – which, as noted above, also supplied a considerable number of Presbyterian female missionaries.[95] As many leading Presbyterian families were passionate exponents of Unionism, it is again likely that similar congregational analyses would reveal overlapping missionary/political concerns and connections. The opposition of the UWUC to Home Rule was again understood and articulated in religious language, though with gendered reasoning: "Home Rule was essentially a women's question. It affected their lives, their homes, and their families, and for that reason they affirmed their declaration to assist the men in opposing and defeating home rule. With the sanctity and happiness of home life, faced with peril, and their religious as well as political identity under threat, women's duty to reject a priest-governed Ireland was clear."[96]

A set of cultural and political ideologies thus linked the Irish Presbyterian Mission field with its home base, and there is little doubt of its impact on the home front, both practically and in the reinforcement of Unionist ideologies. As Rakotonirina argues, nineteenth-century missionary societies were "among the most high-profile pressure groups in British life."[97] Their impact on those they sought to save is, however, less clear; a range of motivations, aspirations, experiences, and personalities often meant that pre-planned activities became enmeshed in the web of networks and influences at work in missionary encounters with indigenous peoples. Moreover, each a product of her own culture, their interactions affected both, with missionary portrayals of their material and spiritual superiority contributing significantly to the construction of a white womanhood that was increasingly perceived as modern and professional. Nonetheless, twenty-first-century visitors to the Irish Presbyterian missions in both India and China note that the typical triangle of church, school, and hospital remains in place, with generations of local Christians still "treasuring its links with Ireland."[98] While this may reflect a degree of nostalgia, and indeed propaganda, missionary endeavour was undoubtedly implicated in the process of modernization, which introduced social, scientific, and cultural change to the East and played its part in disrupting traditional norms.

While it is virtually impossible to disentangle feminist, imperialist, and religious impulses behind individual (or even collective) missionary endeavours, it seems likely that many of these women perceived of themselves as belonging to a spiritual rather than to a political empire, agents of God rather than "Man." They were nonetheless aware of, as well as proud and articulate about, the material and spiritual privileges to which membership in the British Empire entitled them. While such membership was hotly disputed in Ireland itself, particularly by the Catholic majority, it would remain an integral aspect of the Irish Protestant tradition, both within and beyond the island. Though an "Ulster" or "Northern Irish" affiliation was increasingly needed to distinguish the northeast from the Catholic Republic, the legacy of this tradition can clearly be traced through the voluminous documents, published and unpublished, recording the contribution of the female missionary movement to the concept of a contested "Greater Ireland."

The nature of foreign missionary work evolved rapidly in the period following the First World War, but placing the spotlight on this early period of experiment and transition facilitates a clearer understanding of how negotiating the intersections of gender, class, race, and national identity presented opportunities for challenges to, or complicity in, the ideologies and expectations of the linked but separate networks of Ireland and the East.

NOTES

1 Porter, *Religion Versus Empire*; Cox, *Imperial Fault Lines*.

2 Carey, *God's Empire*.

3 Walker, *History of the Ulster Unionist Party*; Buckland, *Ulster Unionism*.

4 Hempton and Hill, *Evangelical Protestantism*; Whelan, *Bible War in Ireland*.

5 For a general discussion of the British Protestant response, see Porter, *Religion versus Empire*; for Ireland, denominational and congregational

histories richly detail the progress of missions; for the background to the Irish Presbyterian Mission, see Holmes, "Shaping of Irish Presbyterian Attitudes."

6 The pages of *Woman's Work*, the magazine of the Presbyterian Female Association, and the Annual Reports of all the missionary organizations are full of examples of hardship, illness, and the deaths of infants of missionary families.

7 For a discussion of this in the Australian context, see Carey, "Women's Particular Mission."

8 *World Missionary Conference 1910*, vol. 5 (Edinburgh: Oliphant Anderson and Ferrier 1910), 147.

9 Boyd, *Manchuria*, 79.

10 *World Missionary Conference 1910*, 147.

11 Annual Reports of the Female Association for Promoting Christianity among the Women of the East, held in the offices of the Presbyterian Women's Association, Church House, Belfast.

12 *World Missionary Conference 1910*, 147.

13 The point is frequently made, but see, for example, West, "Role of the Woman Missionary."

14 Boyd, *Prevailing Word*, 148–9. For example, in the period between 1915 and 1939, twice as many women (twenty-six) as men were sent to China on behalf of the Irish Presbyterian Church and thirty-three women (60 percent) compared to twenty-two men to India.

15 Singh, *Gender, Religion and Power*, 9.

16 Hempton and Hill, *Evangelical Protestantism*.

17 Thorne, "Religion and Empire at Home."

18 Doyle, "Sepoys of the Pound and Sandy Row."

19 Quoted in Carey, *God's Empire*, 30.

20 Hempton and Hill, *Evangelical Protestantism*, 183.

21 Hill, "Assessing the Awakening." See also Holmes, "World Turned Upside Down."

22 Rowbotham, "Ministering Angels," 183–4.

23 McClelland, "Evangelical Philanthropy."

24 Ibid., 322. Between 1878 and 1920, all of the eighteen female missionaries who had belonged to this congregation had also been students at Victoria College, representing 22 percent of the total recruitment of the Female Association in these years. See McClelland, "Evangelical Philanthropy," 253.

25 *World Missionary Conference 1910*, 150.

26 The Female Association had an all-female committee, female secretaries, and female treasurer; a committee of ministers was available for consultation.

27 Hill, "From Down to Dohnavur"; Houghton, *Amy Carmichael of Dohnavur*; Elliot, *Chance to Die*. Carmichael's papers are held in the Public Record Office of Northern Ireland (PRONI), D4061.
28 Thompson, *Into All the World*, 174.
29 *Report of the Female Association* (Belfast, 1878).
30 *Missionary Herald*, 2 February 1914, 44.
31 Rumasack, "Cultural Missionaries," 128.
32 *Woman's Work*, January 1914.
33 *Report of the Female Association* (Belfast, 1878).
34 Kelly, "Irish Medical Women c. 1880s–1920s."
35 Ibid, 147.
36 *Fisherwick Messenger*, 1944, 6.
37 Burton, "Contesting the Zenana," 369.
38 *Woman's Work* 84 (1912): 273–4.
39 Boyd, *Prevailing Word*, 58.
40 Burman, *China*, 11.
41 Boyd, *Prevailing Word*, 68.
42 *Christian Advocate*, 1886, quoted in Hempton and Hill, *Evangelical Protestantism*, 175.
43 Etherington, "Education and Medicine," 265.
44 The Qua Iboe Mission Makes History, unpublished typescript in Public Record Office of Northern Ireland, D2308/1, 29.
45 Boyd, *Prevailing Word*, 74.
46 *Report of the Female Association* (1889).
47 Boyd, *Prevailing Word*, 58–95.
48 Parsons, "Literary Study," 32.
49 The Qua Iboe Mission, PRONI, D2308/1, 30.
50 *Hitherto: 1873–1923 – A Record of Fifty Years Work in Connection with the Women's Association for Foreign Missions of the Presbyterian Church in Ireland* (Belfast: Foreign Missions Office, n.d.), 45.
51 Singh, *Gender, Religion and Power*.
52 Kent, *Converting Women*, 239.
53 Okkenhaug, "Women in Christian Mission."
54 Paul, *Land of My Dreams*.
55 Boyd, *Prevailing Word*, 59.
56 Kent, *Converting Women*.
57 In *Woman's Work*, January 1914, no. 89 (new series), 92.
58 Paul, *Land of My Dreams*.
59 Elliot, *Chance to Die*, 303.
60 *Missionary Herald*, 1 May 1890, 120.

61 Boyd, *Prevailing Word*, 54–5.
62 *Report of the Female Association 1875*.
63 Kirkpatrick, *Made in China,* 19.
64 *World Missionary Conference*, 1910.
65 Sharpe, "Legacy of Amy Carmichael," 121–4.
66 Thompson, *Into All the World*, 40.
67 Ibid., 40.
68 Elliot, *Chance to Die*, 268–9.
69 Ibid, 248.
70 Rumasack, "Cultural Missionaries."
71 Lee, "Between Subordination and She-Tiger," 624; Ramusack, "Cultural Missionaries," 133.
72 Quoted in Burton, "Contesting the Zenana," 390.
73 Fealy, *Apprenticeship Nurse Training in Ireland.*
74 Shirwadkar, *Women and Socio-Cultural Changes*, 125.
75 Fraser, "Ireland and India," 84.
76 Ellington, Sklar, and Stemo, *Competing Kingdoms,* 2.
77 Carmichael, *Lotus Buds*, 283.
78 Ibid. 297–8.
79 Hardiman, *Missionaries and Their Medicine*, 147.
80 *Woman's Work*, 1907
81 *Annual Report of the Female Association* (1875).
82 Hill, "Women's Work."
83 Prochaska, *Women and Philanthropy.*
84 *Annual Report of the Female Association* (1877).
85 Addley, "Birth and Development," 247; *Report of the Female Association* (1877).
86 *Woman's Work*, October 1907, 96.
87 *Hitherto: 1873–1923*, 16.
88 Rakotonirina, "Re-reading Missionary Publications," 13, 157–69, 169.
89 See Catherine Hall's review of Susan Thorne's *Congregational Missions and the Making of an Imperial Culture in 19th-Century England* in *Victorian Studies* 43, 4 (2001): 695–7.
90 Leading Presbyterian layman Thomas Sinclair, a strong supporter of both domestic and foreign religious missions, was largely responsible for the wording of the Ulster Covenant of 1912, in which almost half a million men and women declared their refusal to accept an Irish-based constitution.
91 Walker, *History of the Ulster Unionist Party*, 8.
92 Jeffrey, *Irish Empire*, 15.
93 Quoted in Bardon, *History of Ulster*, 437.

94 Urquhart, *Women in Ulster Politics.*
95 McClelland, "Evangelical Philanthropy and Social Control", 308–9.
96 *Belfast Evening Telegraph*, 18 January 1913.
97 Rakotonirina, "Re-reading Missionary Publications," 158.
98 Thompson, *Into All the World*, 51.

11

"Hurrah for Old Ireland!": Irish Catholicism at the Cape of Good Hope

COLIN BARR

The Irish are the lost tribe of southern Africa. Writing in 1991, Donald Akenson claimed that the "Irish in South Africa were not a coherent ethnic group" because they raised no "great memorials to themselves" and lacked the "self-celebration" so notable in the American Irish. Excepting a few "admirable fugitive pieces," Akenson continued, there is "almost no historiographical tradition for the Irish in South Africa."[1] For Donal McCracken, this lacuna was the result both of the country's long academic isolation and the sense within South African academia that the study of a small English-speaking white ethnic group lacked "historical relevancy."[2] This remains the case: modern writing on the Irish in colonial South Africa can fit comfortably on a very small shelf. Other than Akenson's short book, what little there is is, for the most part, concerned with transient nationalists and pro-Boers such as John MacBride and the future Sinn Féin leader Arthur Griffith; exotics like the fenian, police informer, militia commander, doctor, and newspaper editor Alfred Aylward; or the Irish bandits of the Transvaal goldfields.[3] Of the settled Irish there is almost nothing. What exceptions there are are largely associated with the wider McCracken family, including the three volumes of *Southern African-Irish Studies* published in Durban in the 1990s, J.L. McCracken's biography of the Ulster liberal and Cape Colony politician William Porter, Eileen McCracken's essays on Aylward and Arthur Griffith and her unpublished doctoral dissertation on the Cape's demographics, and Donal McCracken's studies of the Irish pro-Boers. But these are the exceptions that prove the rule; and, the Porter biography aside, they tend to confirm Akenson's view that the history of the Irish in southern Africa before 1875 is "*terra incognita.*"[4]

In fact, the Irish seem to be little better represented after 1875. Classic single-volume histories by scholars such as Eric Walker and C.W. de Kiewiet omitted them entirely.[5] They are equally invisible in more recent scholarship, such as Vivian Bickford-Smith's 1995 *Ethnic Pride and Social Prejudice in Victorian Cape Town*. There, the only explicit mentions of Irish people *as Irish* are a quotation from a bigoted letter to the editor signed "Ulster Irishman" and a handful of references to a group of Irish labourers imported into the Cape Town docks in the early 1880s. To Bickford-Smith, the Irish either did not exist in Cape Town or did not exist as a distinct ethnic group; instead, they were subsumed into the larger racial categories of "English" or "White."

In discussing the racially tinged campaigns of the municipal "clean party" in the early 1880s, for example, Bickford-Smith identifies what he calls a "mobilisation of English ethnicity in the city." This "Englishness," he continues, "could potentially assimilate all White English speakers, including the numerous Capetonians from Scotland and even those Dutch speakers who had become sufficiently Anglicised."[6] The Irish are not mentioned, but those who lived in the city must presumably have assimilated along with their Scottish and even Dutch neighbours. Although Noel Ignatiev famously claimed that the American Irish chose to become white, late Victorian Cape Town must be the first modern example of the Irish, or at least of the Catholic Irish, choosing to become English.

The apparent absence of the Irish from the Cape (and from South Africa) is all the more implausible given that evidence of their presence was all around. In Cape Town itself, for example, consider the Cape Town Irish Volunteer Rifles, founded in 1885, or the surprisingly ecumenical Cape Town Irish Association, the first chairman of which was the proprietor of the *Cape Times*, the Limerick-born former Church of Ireland priest Frederick St Leger.[7] The city also had an Irish Town district (centred on a Kildare Street) populated largely by the workers of a nearby brewery. Irish cabbies employed by the Hibernia Omnibus Company dominated the trade in mid-Victorian Cape Town.[8] Cecil Rhodes not only hosted touring Home Rule politicians but also made an extraordinary £10,000 contribution himself;[9] presumably he hoped to be rewarded with Irish votes. Both the Cape and Natal had Irish-born premiers, both Protestant.[10] St Patrick's Day celebrations were widespread and well attended throughout the colony: in 1871, for example, a "standing room" only congregation at the Catholic cathedral in Cape Town (a "large proportion" of whom were Protestant) observed vespers, benediction, and the exposition of the blessed sacrament conducted by priests named O'Haire, McMahon, and O'Reillly. They were edified by a lecture on St Patrick and entertained by the music of the Catholic members of the 86th (Royal County Down) Regiment and the singing of the students of the Catholic St Joseph's Academy.[11] Even the shebeen, the ubiquitous informal bars of the townships, suggests an Irish influence.

This is not to say that the Irish were anything like a large or dominant segment of the population, even of the European population. They were not: for the Irish, southern Africa was by some distance the least congenial of the settler colonies. As one Cape Town newspaper complained in 1876, the Irish "labouring classes" would not come to the colony in any numbers because they "[knew] nothing about it beyond having a dim idea that it [was] associated with Kaffir wars." But they did "know all about America and Australia, or [thought] they [did], having heard them talked about from their infancy by those who had friends there."[12] As late as 1897, a visiting James Bryce noted "hardly any Irish immigration."[13] Still, some Irish did come, although as Donald Akenson points out, precise numbers are hard to establish before 1875. It is clear that the settled population was low, although there was always a large military presence, many of whom would have been accompanied by family. In the 1840s, Harriet Ward recalled the soldiers' wives on a troop ship caught in a storm who "called on the Virgin and their favourite saints to help them in their peril."[14] Some of these individuals or families would have stayed after their service ended or their regiment moved. There was a small group from Ireland among the famous 1820 settlers in the Eastern Cape, and some sixty-five hundred Irish came out as assisted emigrants between 1823 and 1873, with perhaps another eighty-five hundred by 1900.[15] When the Irish priest James O'Haire began his travels into the Western Cape hinterland in the early 1860s, he was surprised by the number of Irish he found who had been living for many years in near-total isolation.[16] By 1891, a rough estimate suggests that there were fourteen thousand Cape residents of Irish birth or extraction, from a total "white" population of 376,000, of which 130,000 identified with one of the constituent parts of the United Kingdom. The Irish were thus 3.7 percent of the European population, but 10.9 percent of those from the British Isles.[17] This proportion seems to have held relatively steady: by 1926, the some fifty-nine thousand Irish represented 3.5 percent of whites.[18] Had this population been evenly scattered across the vast breadth of the Cape Colony, its relative absence in the historiography might be easier to understand. But it was not: the Irish were heavily urbanized, with 85 percent living in towns by 1891.[19] While the Irish were clearly "a minority of a minority,"[20] in places like Cape Town, Port Elizabeth, or Grahamstown they must have been an important and visible minority. In 1856, the newly appointed Bishop Patrick Moran estimated that there were seventeen hundred mostly Irish Catholics in Port Elizabeth and another 450 in Grahamstown.[21] By 1874, a newly arrived priest reported that there were about four thousand Catholics, again mostly Irish, in the Eastern Cape as a whole.[22] When he arrived in 1863, James O'Haire thought that there were about six thousand Irish in Cape Town proper;[23] by 1868, perhaps thirty-five hundred of them were Catholic.[24]

The Irish are not the only white population to have been sent for ethnic reassignment. In his examination of the Scots in South Africa, John Mackenzie takes Bickford-Smith to task for the "rather transparent let-out" of simply defining all British Isles settlers as "English."[25] As Mackenzie correctly observes, the United Kingdom is too often seen as "some kind of undifferentiated whole" and that, consequently, the "metropole needs to be deconstructed as much as the periphery." Only if that were done would it be possible to "understand the complex of forces that were brought to bear upon southern Africa and its peoples."[26] The result is a detailed study that emphasizes the endurance of a distinctly Scottish identity and culture well into the twentieth century. That equal attention has not been paid to the South African Irish is ironic, as Mackenzie himself takes as a model the recent historiography of the global Irish diaspora, which he praises as "subtle, suggestive and sophisticated".[27]

This Irish elusiveness can be attributed to both their relatively small numbers and to the reluctance of South African scholars to consider the history of whites in general and of non-Afrikaners in particular. As Saul Dubow points out: "Important dimensions of South African history risk being occluded or lost if the role of whites is viewed too narrowly in terms of settler colonialism and exploitation, and if resistance to apartheid becomes our only frame of historical reference."[28] In the case of the Irish, this problem seems to be more acute as a result of two peculiarities in the pattern of their migration and settlement in southern Africa: a majority were Protestant, and a high proportion of the total Irish immigrant pool were either prosperous or highly skilled or both.

As so often in Ireland itself, it was the question of religion that was paramount. In the Cape, roughly 44 percent of Irish immigrants were Roman Catholics.[29] Although not entirely unprecedented in the settler empire, this was unusual. It was relatively simple for Irish Anglicans or Presbyterians of a secure social or economic standing to comfortably blend with their English, Scottish, or even Dutch neighbours. As Mackenzie points out, the Calvinist Scots often found more religious and cultural common ground with the Afrikaners than they did with English Anglicans;[30] it is not difficult to imagine Ulster Presbyterians making a similar discovery. And it is equally easy to imagine prosperous Irish Anglicans like Frederick St Leger blending easily with their social and denominational peers; Vivian Bickford-Smith, for example, describes St Leger without mentioning his ethnic origins, despite St Leger's role in founding the Cape Town Irish Association.[31] To take another example, in Port Elizabeth the first Anglican chaplain was an Irishman educated at Trinity College, Dublin, and his successor an Englishman educated at Trinity College, Oxford. Throughout the century ministers from both Ireland and England (and Dublin and Oxford) continued to be appointed to Port Elizabeth, and although there was the usual amount of ecclesiastical infighting it seems never to have taken on an ethnic dimension.[32] It is probably suggestive that Bickford-Smith almost invariably omits the Roman Catholic Church when he considers the behaviour of the various Cape Town denominations (for example, when he gives the number of white and non-white congregants for all churches *except* the Catholic) or his similar failure to discuss Catholic practice when noting the racial segregation of seats, and then services, and finally church buildings on the part of the Dutch Reformed, Methodist, and Anglican communities.[33] As Donal McCracken observes, "assimilation into white society" was easier where "the immigrant Irish population had a high preponderance of Protestants and held a position of status in colonial society." [34] As we see elsewhere in this volume, this was true throughout the settler empire, but it seems to have been especially so in the Cape.

South African Catholics were in a different position: their church obsessively discouraged institutional and matrimonial mixing, either with native Africans or with Protestant Europeans. As elsewhere in the Anglo-world, this tendency became more pronounced as the Catholic Church in the Cape became more established and, subsequently, more Hiberno-Roman.[35] The best way, then, to approach the history of the Irish in southern Africa, at least as a distinct ethnic group with an enduring identity, is through the Roman Catholic Church. And the Cape

Catholics were largely Irish: in the early 1920s, a young Denis Hurley, the future long-serving archbishop of Durban, supposedly answered "Irish" when his teacher asked his religion.[36] John Mackenzie notes that, while there were "of course" some Scottish Catholics, "they [did] not show up well in the record" and probably blended with their Irish co-religionists.[37] The same seems to have been true of English Catholics. There were exceptions, such as an English convert named Goldie who worked in the engineering department of the Cape government, or the Scottish-born historian and politician Alexander Wilmot, who among other things wrote a biography of the Irish Catholic bishop J.D. Ricards and an early history of the Cape Colony itself.[38] But despite individual outliers, isolated communities such as the Catholic soldiers of the British German Legion in Kaffraria, or the colony of Filipino fishers at Kalk Bay, and a smattering of high-profile converts such as F.C. Kolbe and the sister of the campaigning novelist Olive Schreiner, it is nevertheless the case that the great majority of Catholics were Irish, even if the majority of the Irish were not Catholic. As Bishop Grimley of Cape Town boasted to Archbishop Cullen's secretary in 1862: "If you were to remove from this colony the Irish Catholic element, our holy faith would be … utterly unknown."[39] This association was exacerbated by the reluctance or inability of the Irish bishops to engage in missionary activities, choosing instead to concentrate their limited resources on what they called "the children of the household".[40]

This chapter, then, focuses on the Roman Catholic Church and on the Cape of Good Hope. It focuses on the Catholics because it is difficult and perhaps impossible to properly disaggregate Irish Protestants from the wider "white" or "English" population and on the Cape because it was the oldest, largest, wealthiest, and most important of the British possessions in southern Africa, at least until the growth of the Rand and the final absorption of the Transvaal in the wake of the South African War of 1899–1902. By contrast, colonial Natal was tiny, with only some forty-seven thousand white inhabitants in 1891, of whom perhaps one thousand were first-generation resident Irish (there would have been rather more Irish soldiers).[41] As for the future Transvaal and Orange Free State, as late as 1870 the French Oblate bishop Allard of Natal estimated that there were only six hundred to eight hundred Catholics between them, "mostly Irish."[42] It was the Cape of Good Hope that was at the centre of Irish ecclesiastical interest. And, unlike the rest of the Anglo-world excepting Newfoundland, for all practical purposes the Cape was from the beginning an Irish mission: before the 1837 appointment of the Irish Dominican Patrick Griffith as vicar apostolic, Catholicism was at best a marginal presence there. There was for a time a resident Irish priest, Patrick Scully, who secured from the colonial government £75 per annum and land to build a chapel; he left in 1824, his successors a Dutch secular priest and an English Benedictine. Both had departed by 1835. Other than a transient Spanish Dominican, there was no priest in the colony until the arrival of Griffith.[43]

The absence of an institutional Catholic Church did not imply the absence of either Catholics or anti-Catholicism. Cape Town itself had a modest Catholic population, and there were Catholics among the 1820 settlers in the Eastern Cape.[44] And there were without question Catholics among the soldiers of the various regiments assigned to the Cape. Within the British administration, the colonial secretary, Lieutenant Colonel Christopher Bird, was Catholic and had a Jesuit brother: a fact publicly seized upon by William Parker, a disgruntled Irish Protestant settler who blamed Bird for assigning him poor-quality land.[45] In 1821, Bird was dismissed in a power struggle with the authoritarian governor: he blamed religious prejudice; the governor heatedly denied it.[46] Bird remained in Cape Town, a pillar of the small Catholic community.[47] In the 1830s, critics of the lieutenant governor of the Eastern Province, Andries Stockenström, sought to undermine him by falsely claiming he had converted to Rome; some of those who set out on the Great Trek were in part impelled by rumours that the Boers would be forced into Catholicism.[48] Although some sectarianism had an Irish tinge – the first Orange Lodge opened in Cape Town in 1852 – overt anti-Catholicism was largely limited to the Dutch population. In 1843, for example, the newly built village of Burghersdorp refused to permit a Catholic church.[49] But this was not the whole story: the small Catholic (and Irish) population, relative absence of priests, and high social standing of some of the laity minimized tensions, especially in urban areas. In 1828, for example, the committee that founded the South African College included a layman who, in the absence of Catholic clergy, was appointed to speak for Catholic interests.[50] Of all the challenges Bishop Griffith faced when he arrived in Cape Town, anti-Catholic prejudice was far down his list.

Griffith arrived in Cape Town on 14 April 1838 with little more than £60 in passage money and the promise of £200 per annum from the government. He brought with him two priests (one Dominican, one Franciscan – both Irish), a clerical student, several family members, and two servants.[51] The £200 was a chaplain's salary, not a bishop's,[52] and, as Joy Brain points out, this had significant consequences for what would become the Western District: Griffith identified himself primarily as a chaplain, which meant he concentrated his attention on the military and those who presented themselves at his Cape Town church; he did relatively little to seek out existing Catholics and even less to make new ones.[53]

Griffith's situation was certainly challenging. On arrival, he found perhaps five hundred Catholics in Cape Town, no school, no priests, a chapel ruined by floods in 1837, and a nasty conflict over the role of the laity. Griffith was welcomed by the official Cape, both military and civilian.[54] This was no surprise: Cape Town was garrisoned by an Irish unit, the 27th (Inniskilling) Regiment of Foot, comprised, according to Griffith, of "mostly Irish Catholics."[55] By the late 1830s, the British Army was willing, especially in heavily militarized possessions such as the Cape or India, to co-operate in the provision of Catholic religious services to its often very Catholic (and Irish) soldiers, although not to give Catholics or Catholicism equality of status with the Church of England. To the army and the still military-dominated Cape government, Griffith and his colleagues were a positive boon.

It was partly the needs of the military that drove Griffith's early decision to travel to the Eastern Cape. On arriving in Cape Town, he had found a petition from the Catholics of the area – many of them soldiers – begging for a chaplain.[56] He took with him the Irish Franciscan Daniel Burke, intending to leave him in Grahamstown as the sole resident priest. Since 1820, that town had been the centre of British settlement in the turbulent region as well as an important garrison. The Cape government offered £100 for travel expenses and promised to recommend to the Colonial Office that a chaplain's salary be paid to Burke.[57] It was a revealing journey: in Port Elizabeth, Griffith met Irish soldiers stationed at Fort Beaufort who claimed to have been there eight years without a priest, accosted a "red-haired man" on the docks and discovered he was from County Galway (after Burke spoke to him in Irish, the man offered himself to Griffith as a servant), and learned about both the local "degenerate Caffers" and the threatening "Zoolas."[58] Port Elizabeth reminded the bishop of Cobh, and, despite assurances that it contained no Catholics, he soon had a congregation above thirty, largely Irish.[59] Before returning to Cape Town, he continued his tour of the Eastern Province, finding both Catholics and Irish wherever he went, not least among the soldiers.

As Griffith settled in Cape Town, he slowly formed a better picture of his new flock. He upgraded their numbers from his initial estimate of five hundred up to two thousand, military and civilian, and took steps to provide services to the surrounding communities, beginning with Simonstown (not yet a great naval base) and then Stellenbosch, where he noted the presence of "a relative of the Great Dan's" – Daniel O'Connell.[60] His immediate concern was with what he described as "the religious laxity and indifference which ha[d] so long existed."[61] Problems ranged from issues of ecclesiastical governance, such as the dispute over lay control of church property to the many lapsed Catholics he met to the apparent preference for a double hanging above religious services.[62]

Griffith was heavily reliant on this small and imperfectly committed community for support, and money was and would remain an issue, even if matters improved after his first collection brought in a mere £1.13.9d.[63] The cost of living was high, and Griffith lacked everything from suitable vestments to prayer books to a spare chalice.[64] The government did at least pay his own and some of his priests' salaries, a concession that lasted until 1875 in the Cape and 1869 in Natal.[65] Although this brought much needed financial relief, it also imposed obligations. It effectively ruled out any extensive missionary activity, had Griffith been of a mind to attempt any, which he was not: the government would baulk at its chaplains spending months at a time in the bush, let alone at a distant mission station. And at least at first, Griffith himself was under the impression that there were no Catholics living more than forty-eight kilometres beyond Cape Town itself.[66]

Griffith's first act was to open denominational schools: his Mercantile and Classical Academy offered a daunting curriculum and promised prospective Protestant parents that there would be no proselytism; his sister opened what Joy Brain describes as "a more modest school for girls at the same time."[67] The teaching in the boys' school was handled by Griffith himself, George Corcoran (the other Irish Dominican who had travelled with him), and by a small group associated with St Peter's College in Wexford, including its professor of Latin, Aidan Devereux. This party of three – two priests and a deacon who was quickly ordained – had arrived in Cape Town not long after the bishop.[68]

The men did not remain there long: in 1838 the newly ordained Thomas Murphy was sent to Grahamstown, which was just as well as Burke died shortly after his arrival; Corcorcan went to Port Elizabeth in 1841; and Devereux, although he was the driving force at the school, was assigned the following year to George, mid-way between Cape Town and Grahamstown. In each place they ministered to the military and sought to organize the local Catholics into parish life, while imposing as much social and liturgical discipline as possible. They also began to build, for example, Murphy's solid and forbidding St Patrick's church in Grahamstown, erected largely by the free labour of the Inniskillings.

It soon became apparent that the Cape Colony was far too large for one man to oversee, even if he only had responsibility for a handful of priests. In 1847, Griffith sought Roman approval for a division of the vicariate. He was quickly successful: Propaganda created a new Eastern District and appointed Aidan Devereux vicar apostolic. There was little for Devereux to control in his new territory. He had four priests, including himself, and churches at Grahamstown, Fort Beaufort, and Port Elizabeth. There was the embryo of a girls' school in Grahamstown and a more established boys' school in Port Elizabeth, which the Dominican Corcoran had built with assistance from the Lyon-based Society for the Propagation of the Faith.[69] Worse, the region had just endured one of its periodic bouts of warfare.

Devereux was the first of many Irish episcopal appointments in the Cape. Like the rest of the settler empire (excepting francophone Quebec) and the United States, the Cape experienced the concerted attentions of Archbishop Cullen and his allies in Rome. The result was domination by Hiberno-Roman bishops: Devereux was succeeded in 1857 by a young Dublin priest named Patrick Francis Moran (whom we meet again in chapter 15, this volume). When Moran was translated to the newly created diocese of Dunedin in New Zealand in 1870, his successor was J.D. Ricards, who had travelled from Wexford to the Cape with the newly appointed Devereux in the late 1840s. Despite a brief Italian interlude in the 1890s, the Eastern Cape and subsequent diocese of Port Elizabeth remained the most emphatically Irish in South Africa down to very near the present day. In the Western Cape, Griffith was, in 1860, supplanted and then succeeded by another Dublin priest, Thomas Grimley, and Grimley was in turn followed by yet more Dublin priests, first his friend John Leonard, who ruled in Cape Town until 1908, and then John Rooney, who retired in 1924.

Once in place, these Irish bishops began to behave as other Irish bishops did throughout Greater Ireland: they set out to create a distinctively Irish Catholic colonial culture that would ensure the near-total social separation of Catholics and non-Catholics. To do this they built schools, hospitals, and orphanages; founded insurance schemes and social clubs; and worked tirelessly to build a common devotional culture and to impose effective social controls on their flocks, not least through ferocious prohibition of mixed marriages. To a very great extent they succeeded, whether in Grahamstown or Geelong.

As elsewhere, in the Cape the first and primary battleground was education. In Ireland, Cullen had maintained a steady opposition to state encroachments on what he saw as the Catholic community's right to educate its children in its own faith, and to do so at state expense, or at least without state interference. To do so, he advanced a novel argument in the history of Roman Catholicism: that a democratic state should be religiously neutral. By this he did not mean secular but, rather, neutral between the various denominations present within its territory. As all citizens paid tax, Cullen and his protégés argued, all citizens were entitled to state support in proportion to their numbers in the community. That meant that the British state should not only support both Catholic and Protestant (and, in principle, Jewish or other) schools but it should also support them in proportion to the population of Catholics or Protestants or Jews. In Ireland, the consequences of such a policy were obvious, and there was more than a little self-interest in the argument. But it was, in the Catholic Church of Pius IX, extraordinarily liberal, and its premises were accepted and advanced with enthusiasm by Cullen's episcopal and clerical protégés throughout the Anglo-world. In fact, the level of involvement by the Catholic hierarchy in active politics largely corresponded to how closely (or distantly) a jurisdiction approached this ideal. That the Irish of Greater Ireland were perfectly comfortable with democracy and a religiously neutral state was one of its defining characteristics, and this was by no means inevitable, given the illiberal character of the wider Catholic Church in this period.

It was the arrival of Patrick Moran in the autumn of 1856 that changed South African Catholicism. In the Eastern Cape, he oversaw both rapid growth and a new, less compromising and more demanding relationship with the government. He was also unapologetically and unambiguously Irish. What he found was scanty enough: six nuns at Grahamstown teaching eighty-three students and caring for twelve orphans from the most recent frontier war, four free schools without teachers and overseen solely by priests, and twenty-five hundred Catholic civilians and four thousand Catholics "soldiers on [the] Frontier & in lonely graves."[70] He had only eight priests, five of whom told him that they wanted to return home. At least one was a drunkard. Most lived in "hovels," without servants.[71] There were some positives, including the nearly finished church at Port Elizabeth, the "same in size and design as that of Celbridge" in County Kildare.[72]

Moran's immediate task was twofold: providing Catholic schools (and, if possible, government money to support them) and convincing Catholic parents to cease sending their children to non-Catholic schools. As he would in Dunedin with the *New Zealand Tablet*, Moran utilized the columns of his diocesan newspaper to advance his case. In early 1857, for example, the *Colonist* used the occasion of the opening of a secular school in Port Elizabeth to launch a stinging attack on mixed education. In a lengthy leader that was almost certainly written by Moran, the paper denounced undenominational schooling as the source of "all the anarchy, rebellions, revolutions, and many other fearful crimes, for which the 19th century … must be forever memorable." Mixed education was unacceptable, and "infidels" were its most "strenuous advocates." If only, he continued, "statesmen divested themselves of hatred and jealousy" towards the Catholic Church it would be possible to provide government funding to each denomination to manage the education of its own children. In the meantime, the project met with the bishop's "unmitigated" disapproval.[73] In both content and tone, this was identical to the increasingly violent language used by the Irish hierarchy in general and Cullen in particular to denounce an Irish national school system that they claimed had developed in a "narrow-minded, illiberal, and anti-Catholic spirit."[74] It would also have been perfectly familiar to unlucky politicians from Nova Scotia to New South Wales.

Moran was utterly committed to Catholic education: in 1860, he warned his flock they would be "doubly criminal" if they not only failed to patronize Catholic schools but also added "the crime of sending [their] children to non-Catholic schools."[75] By then he had two girls' schools in Grahamstown run by an originally French order of nuns (the Sisters of the Assumption) who had become almost wholly Irish, and two boys' schools in the same town: St Patrick's free school, staffed by two teachers with experience in Ireland's national schools, and a higher school designed to lure the town's "respectable" Catholic children away from Protestant schools and transform them into "thorough and enthusiastic Catholics."[76] In the other major centre, Port Elizabeth, there was the long established boys' school, which by 1860 was run by another former Irish national schoolteacher, and there was also a night school for young men sponsored by the Society of St Vincent de Paul. For girls, there was only a small free school overseen by an apparently untrained laywoman.[77]

Needing above all cheap, trained labour, Moran turned to Ireland for nuns. In 1867, he made a personal appeal to the Dominican community at Sion Hill, Blackrock, County Dublin. How Moran found his way to Blackrock is unclear: probably he was aware that the sisters were open to missionary expansion, and, indeed, they found themselves forced to decide between the Eastern Cape and San Francisco. They chose Africa, and in October 1867 six sisters sailed with Moran on the aptly named *Celt*. The sisters were greeted with enthusiasm: as one wrote home: "the poor Irish Catholics distinguish themselves by crying with joy at seeing us."[78] When Moran was transferred to New Zealand, he took a group of the sisters with him and recruited more from home: in Catholicism's Greater Ireland, such movement was the norm.

Within months, the Dominicans had opened two schools: St Mary's, which was fee-paying and had a small boarding element, and St Joseph's, which was free and aimed at the poor, both white and native. Within a year, it had 269 students.[79] The sisters continued to grow in Port Elizabeth, assuming responsibility for two more Catholic schools in 1895, both focused on the children of Irish immigrants; in 1898, they added a "coloured" school that endured until 1973, when it was destroyed by the Group Areas Act.[80] In 1887, they expanded to Uitenhage, opening both schools and a convent. The sisters maintained their links with Ireland and with Sion Hill, which they relied on for recruitment. There were a few local vocations (the first in 1874), usually but not always of Irish extraction, but for many years they were the exception. [81]

In the Western Cape, Bishop Thomas Grimley followed the same pattern, rapidly building new schools and importing Irish nuns to run them. When he first arrived in Cape Town he had been appalled, telling Moran: "What grieves me most is the state of education."[82] Within weeks, he was "striving to get two Male Schools established."[83] He launched a special collection to "open two schools on a respectable basis," which quickly drew some £300.[84] In four months that sum had risen to £428, and he had purchased land in the city for a new boys' school.[85] By May 1862, Grimley privately boasted of opening "our sixth Catholic school in Cape Town." "That," he wrote, "is not bad."[86] By 1870, both the Eastern and the Western District possessed a full range of schools, overseen by a combination of laity and male and female religious. Given the poverty of the Cape in general and the Catholic community in particular, it was an astonishing achievement. But it was not in itself enough.

It was also necessary to keep the laity institutionally, sexually, and socially apart from Protestants. As elsewhere, this was achieved through compulsion, persuasion, and denominational separatism. The primary threat was withdrawal of sacraments, which had both spiritual and social consequences, and the circumstance in which this threat was most often made and carried out was the education of children. In 1874, for example, John Leonard decreed that Catholic children attending Protestant schools could not receive communion, and their parents could receive no sacraments at all. In 1883, he told a woman who had sent her child to such a school that she was consequently "so cruel a mother" that he had no choice but to "deprive" her of the sacraments. She submitted.[87] In 1859, Moran bluntly refused his blessing to a Catholic woman who had been offered employment as a teacher in Port Elizabeth's undenominational Grey Institute.[88]

Where schools were not directly involved, mixed marriages often were. James O'Haire, for example, refused to administer sacraments to a Catholic widow who had had seven children with her Protestant husband "until she had first tried to snatch her children from heresy."[89] Leonard not only published a pastoral condemning mixed marriages but also refused the sacraments to a Catholic woman who had married in an Anglican church. He ordered her marriage denounced from the altar as "illicit, sinful and sacrilegious." She eventually made a full apology.[90] The fate of orphans was also a perennial concern, and both Cape Town and Grahamstown had Catholic orphanages by 1863 (St Brigid's and St Patrick's, respectively), although, like a number of Irish colonial bishops, Moran preferred to place Catholic orphans with Catholic families, partly to reduce costs but also to eliminate any risk of their being taken into care by the state.[91] As late as 1879, Ricards was forced to fight to secure control over three children whose Catholic father had died at the Battle of Isandlwana: their grandfather had consigned them to Protestants.[92]

This self-segregation required a full range of institutions and not simply schools and orphanages. Cape Town and Port Elizabeth both had a Young Men's Society and Societies of St Vincent de Paul, and both vicariates raised (after Griffith's death) the annual Peter's Pence. Grimley built a Catholic Hall in Cape Town, [93] and the city had two Catholic mutual societies by the mid-1860s;[94] in 1859, Moran opened the inevitably named St Patrick's Mutual Benefit Society in Grahamstown.[95] Grimley established a temperance society in 1862. [96] As well as providing safely Catholic groups and spaces, the Cape bishops sought to shape behaviour. Moran, for example, "often" preached against dances and the "contemptible" people who attended them in an effort to fit in with society. Dancing was, he insisted, a "mortal sin."[97]

But institutions and episcopal threats were not themselves sufficient to maintain order in what was ultimately a voluntary organization: willing conformity was necessary. The Irish bishops in the Cape turned to what they knew in order to achieve it – missions. In describing his famous "devotional revolution" thesis, Emmet Larkin draws particular attention to the growth of parish missions, pointing out that, by 1860, one had been held in almost every Irish parish. These emphasized preaching, lectures, and magnificently staged liturgies that included "music, singing, candles, vestments and incense." The gains were then consolidated by parish and diocesan groups that "included sodalities, confraternities ... the Society of St. Vincent de Paul, and Peter's Pence as well as temperance and altar societies."[98] This was all familiar to Moran, Grimley, and Leonard, who, before coming to the Cape, were not only priests in Cullen's Dublin but also closely linked to the Vincentians, the religious order most closely associated with the Irish missions.[99] It is no surprise that they exported the model to the Cape – other Hiberno-Roman bishops in Greater Ireland were equally enthusiastic. In 1865, for example, Grimley's protegé O'Haire and another priest conducted what seems to have been a fairly typical week-long mission in George. According to a lengthy account in the *George Town Advertiser*, during the day the missioners gave expository lectures on scripture and Catholic doctrine as well as celebrating Mass. Each evening concluded with a rosary, a hymn, "instruction on some point of morality," another hymn, "a dogmatic discourse," and, finally, "the benediction of the Most Holy Sacrament." The mission culminated on the Sunday night with the renewal of baptismal vows. According to the newspaper, the large congregation held lighted candles, which, together with the extravagantly decorated altar, created "a dazzling and splendid effect." The evening ended with communion, including some eighteen first communions, a *Te Deum*, and finally benediction. Again following Irish practice, the missioners instituted a Sodality of the Holy Rosary, "and about forty received the scapular."[100]

Ireland remained the inescapable model for Cape Catholicism. This was represented symbolically, as with the ubiquitous dedication of schools, parishes, mutual societies, and even choirs to St Patrick and other Irish saints. At one point in the twentieth-century, the diocese of Port Elizabeth had no fewer than seven parishes (and seven schools) named for Patrick.[101] As Bishop Grimley wrote when he dedicated the first church in Namaqualand to St Columbanus, "Hurrah for old Ireland!"[102] Irish symbols permeated the church at every level: in 1870, Grimley obtained from the Marquis of Bute money for a new bell for the Cape Town cathedral. It was cast in Dublin and featured a carving of Mary on one side and, on the other "an Irish harp, wolf-dog, and round tower – encircled in a wreath of shamrocks – with the words 'Erin-go-bragh' underneath."[103]

The Catholic Church did not face the racial complexities of the Cape anywhere else in the settler empire, not even in New Zealand. And those complexities informed another difference between the Cape and the rest of the Anglo-world: sectarianism was less of a force there than elsewhere. It is hard, for example, to imagine another late nineteenth-century Irish Catholic colonial bishop participating, as John Rooney of Cape Town did, in an avowedly non-sectarian Irish Association in company with a lapsed Anglican priest and Irish émigré rabbi.[104] The reason, as Donal McCracken points out, is simple: sectarian fervour "was ameliorated by the intimacy of colonial society and by common dangers far more immediate than the threat of Rome or the Orange menace."[105] From the moment of Griffith's arrival, the institutional Catholic Church was welcomed by the state. It was also funded by the state, even if not on grounds of equality. And whatever Moran's complaints, what legal disabilities existed were swept away by 1868, leaving, in Grimley's words, not "a vestige of inferiority, as far as Catholics are concerned."[106]

On a social level there also seems to have been more acceptance of Catholics in the Cape than elsewhere. Even when there was conflict, it was increasingly marginal: when Grimley was humiliated and spat upon by a Dutch lay preacher in Namaqualand, for example, the local Dutch community publicly apologized.[107] As Robert Ross observes, "Anti-Catholic prejudice survived, but decreasingly as the century wore on."[108] In time, the small anglophone society of the Cape, and especially Cape Town, accepted and, to a point, absorbed the Catholic Church: important events such as the opening of a boys' high school were attended by the governor or other officials, as were high-profile lectures on explicitly religious topics. Grimley even accepted an invitation to give a lecture on Father Mathew on behalf of the Methodist temperance campaign, and in the Methodist Hall.[109] On the frontier, the sense of a common threat no doubt made other differences seem less important to the small European population. This is not to say that there were not tensions. Moran's political activism, for example, raised temperatures in Grahamstown. But the Cape Irish can indeed be seen as having become, as discussed above in reference to the work of Niel Ignatiev, "white." But it does not necessarily follow that they also lost their Irish identity and became, as Bickford-Smith would have it, "English" – or at least not immediately. In 1887, for example, Ricards forbade children in the Catholic schools from celebrating Queen Victoria's Golden Jubilee on the grounds of

British cruelty towards Ireland.[110] Touring Home Rule politicians were able to count on a warm welcome at the Cape. Still, when the South African War broke out, the wholly Irish episcopate in the Cape firmly supported the British cause. Whatever their social integration, the Irish retained a firm control of the Catholic Church in the Cape, and the Catholic Church kept firm control of Irish Catholics.

Although South Africa and the Cape of Good Hope both developed in their own fashion, the Cape at least was without doubt a participant in and connected to the global Irish and Cullenite expansion of the nineteenth century – a part of Roman Catholicism's Greater Ireland. As Joy Brain notes: "Irish prelates laid the foundations of the Catholic Church in the Cape and extended them to almost every part of southern Africa."[111] Or as Thomas Grimley more melodramatically wrote not long after he arrived in Cape Town: "When I look around me, and see what Ireland has done for South Africa, I cannot refrain from exclaiming: 'Poor Ireland! God has destined you for the conversion of the world.'"[112]

NOTES

1 Akenson, *Occasional Papers*, 42.
2 McCracken, "Irish Settlement," 134.
3 See, for example, McCracken, *Irish Pro-Boers*; Smith, *Alfred Aylward*; Van Onselen, *Masked Raiders*.
4 Akenson, *Occasional Papers*, 72.
5 Walker, *History of South Africa*; De Kiewiet, *History of South Africa*. Although now outdated, these texts set the tone and agenda for South African history for many decades.
6 Bickford-Smith, *Ethnic Pride*, 39.
7 For St Leger, see Shaw, *Some Beginnings*, 7.
8 McCracken, "Irish Settlement", 142–3.
9 See Rotberg, *Founder*, 230–3.
10 Sir Thomas Upington in the Cape (1884–86), Albert Hime in Natal (1899–1903).
11 *Standard and Mail*, 19 March 1871, quoted in O'Haire, *Recollections*, 544–6.
12 *Capetown Daily News*, 2 February 1876, quoted in O'Haire, *Recollections*, 47.
13 Bryce, *Impressions of South Africa*, 478.
14 Ward, *Five Years in Kaffirland*, 1:16.
15 Akenson, *Occasional Papers*, 53.
16 O'Haire, *Recollections*, 355. There are many other examples in the book.

17 Akenson, *Occasional Papers*, 42; See also McCracken, "Irish Settlement", 135.

18 Akenson, *Occasional Papers*, 68.

19 McCracken, "Irish Settlement", 142.

20 Ibid., "Preface", in *Irish in Southern Africa*, 5.

21 Moran to [Andrew O'Connell], 13 October 1856, Port Elizabeth Diocesan Archives (PEDA), Moran Papers, PM/Doc/162/PM/1.

22 E. Coghlan to Fr Jones, SJ, 8 July 1874, Archivum Britannicum Societatis Iesu, Farm Street, London (ABSI), Zambesi Mission Papers, no. 1.

23 O'Haire, *Recollections*, 37.

24 Boner, "Irish Dominicans," 14–15.

25 Mackenzie, *Scots in South Africa,* 267.

26 Ibid., 268.

27 Ibid., 4.

28 Dubow, *Commonwealth of Knowledge*, 10.

29 Akenson, *Occasional Papers*, 41. This remained relatively constant: in 1926, 43.4 percent of those who self-identified as Irish also indicated that they were Catholics. See Akenson, *Occasional Papers*, 70.

30 Mackenzie, *Scots in South Africa*, 242.

31 Bickford-Smith, *Ethnic Pride*, 46.

32 See Wirgman and Mayo, *Parish of S. Mary Port Elizabeth*.

33 Ibid., 34, 25.

34 McCracken, "Irish Settlement," 145.

35 Hiberno-Romanism is a concept that I use elsewhere to describe the fusion of Irish and Roman churchmanship preferred and propagated by Archbishop Paul Cullen of Dublin and his domestic and imperial protégés. See Barr, "Imperium in Imperio."

36 Kearney, *Guardian of the Light*, 12.

37 Mackenzie, *Scots in South Africa*, 174.

38 Goldie seems to have been converted by Bishop Grant of Southwark: Grimley to Grant, 14 December 1861, Southwark Archdiocesan Archives (SAA), Grant Papers; Wilmot, *James David Ricards*.

39 Thomas Grimley to George Conroy, 20 January 1862, in O'Haire, *Recollections*, 474.

40 See Dischl, *Transkei for Christ*, xii.

41 McCracken, "Irish Settlement," 135.

42 Allard to an unknown correspondent, 30 December 1870, quoted in O'Haire, *Recollections*, 501.

43 Ibid., 9, 23.

44 McCracken, *Irish in Southern Africa*, 2:17.

45 Ross, *Status and Respectability*, 105.
46 Ibid.; and Millar, *Plantagenet in South Africa,* 189.
47 Brain, *Catholic Beginnings in Natal*, 113.
48 Walker, *History of South Africa*, 207.
49 Ross, *Status and Respectability*, 106.
50 Walker, *South African College*, 12.
51 Brown, *Catholic Church in South Africa*, 10.
52 Ibid., 9. The sum offered – or if a sum were to be offered – was at the discretion of the colonial administration. Archbishop Polding of Sydney, for example, was given first £150 per annum and then £500.
53 Brain, "Irish Influence", 122–3.
54 Griffith to Murray, 22 April 1838, in Brain, *Cape Diary*, 101–5.
55 Griffith to an unknown correspondent, 25 May 1838, quoted in Brain, *Cape Diary*, 105.
56 Griffith to Murray, 22 April 1838, in Brain, *Cape Diary*, 104.
57 John Bell to Griffith, 10 May 1838, printed in Brain, *Cape Diary*, 109.
58 7 July 1838, Brain, *Cape Diary*, 122–3. These entries were written up several days later, when Griffith was at Uitenhage.
59 7 July 1838, Brain, *Cape Diary*, 127.
60 28 May 1838, Brain, *Cape Diary*, 106.
61 Griffith to unknown correspondent, Brain, *Cape Diary*, 106.
62 Ibid., 108.
63 Griffith to Murray, 22 April 1838, in Brain, *Cape Diary*, 103.
64 31 May 1838, Brain, *Cape Diary*, 107.
65 Brain, *Catholic Beginnings*, 9.
66 Griffith to Murray, 22 April 1838, in Brain, *Cape Diary*, 104.
67 Brain, "Irish Influence", 124–5.
68 For the school and the Wexford group, see Brown, *Catholic Church in South Africa*, 31–3.
69 Moran to O'Connell, 13 October 1856, PEDA, Moran Papers, PM/DOC/162/PM/1.
70 *Diocesan Chronicle*, PEDA. This handwritten diary, largely in Ricards's hand but with additions and corrections by Moran, is contained in a box labeled "vol. xxv/vol. xxxvi," with no further file numbers. This entry is undated but is probably from the autumn of 1856.
71 Moran to Cullen, 15 May 1860, DDA, Cullen Papers, 333/1/20. In this lengthy letter, Moran recounted for Cullen the history of the vicariate since his own arrival.
72 Moran to [O'Connell], 13 October 1856, PEDA, Moran Papers, PM/Doc/162/PM/1.

73 *Colonist*, 14 February 1857. Given the tone, and its similarity to later articles in the *New Zealand Tablet*, there is no doubt that this was written by Moran.
74 "Letter of the Irish bishops to the right hon. Edward Cardwell MP, chief secretary for Ireland, etc. etc.," in Moran, *Letters of Cardinal Cullen*, 1:119. The editor was the "other" Moran, Cullen's nephew.
75 "Lenten Pastoral, Feast of St Agatha, 1860." There is a copy in Moran's papers in Dunedin.
76 Moran to Cullen, 16 May 1860, DDA, Cullen Papers, 333/1/20.
77 Ibid.
78 Quoted in Boner, *Dominican Women*, 72.
79 Ibid., 78–9.
80 Ibid., 82.
81 Ibid., 77.
82 Grimley to Moran, 30 July 1861, PEDA, Moran Papers, TG/PM/241/PM/1.
83 Grimley to Moran, 23 August 1861, PEDA, Moran Papers, TG/PM/242/PM/1.
84 Grimley to O'Haire, 16 October 1861, in O'Haire, *Recollections*, 10.
85 Grimley to Leonard, 19 December 1861, AACT, Leonard Papers, box 18.
86 Grimley to Leonard, 21 May 1862, AACT, Leonard Papers, box 18.
87 Leonard to Schillinth, 19 July 1883, quoted in Boner, "Irish Dominicans," 17.
88 Moran to Sarah Acton, 1 October 1859, PEDA, Moran Papers, PM/SA/873/PM/3.
89 O'Haire, *Recollections*, 309. No date is given for this encounter.
90 Brown, *Catholic Church in South Africa*, 94.
91 Moran to Grimley, 26 October 1863, AACT, Grimley Papers, box 13.
92 See the series of letters from John Fagan, the parish priest of King William's Town, to Ricards, 19 May, 14 July, 6 August 1879, PEDA, Ricards Papers, JF/JR/278, 279, 280/JR1.
93 Grimley to Leonard, 17 November 1863, AACT, Leonard Papers, box 18.
94 O'Haire, *Recollections*, 45.
95 See "Rules of the Grahamstown St Patrick's Catholic Mutual Benefit Society," Grahamstown, Journal Office, 1890.
96 O'Haire, *Recollections*, 88.
97 Moran to Grimley, 11 December 1865, AACT, Grimley Papers, box 13.
98 Larkin, *Historical Dimensions of Irish Catholicism*, 78.
99 The Redemptorists were the other order most associated with missions in Greater Ireland. Although they enjoyed the support of Archbishop Cullen

and his protégés, they produced nowhere near the same number of bishops, nor were they as distinctively Irish as were the Vincentians.

100 *George Town Advertiser*, 9 November 1865, printed in O'Haire, *Recollections*, 246–8.

101 Bishop Michael Coleman of Port Elizabeth, in conversation with the author, August 2009.

102 Grimley to Leonard, 13 October 1865, AACT, Leonard Papers, box 18.

103 *Standard and Mail*, 15 December 1870, quoted in O'Haire, *Recollections*, 433–4.

104 Shaw, *Some Beginnings*, 7. In addition to St Leger and Rooney, the Cape Town rabbi, A.P. Bender, was a member.

105 McCracken, "Irish Settlement," 140.

106 Grimley to O'Haire, 25 August 1868, in O'Haire, *Recollections*, 368–9.

107 See O'Haire, *Recollections*, 353, quoting from an otherwise undated 1867 number of the *Cape Standard*.

108 Ross, *Status and Respectability*, 105–6.

109 O'Haire, *Recollections*, 102.

110 Brown, *Catholic Church in South Africa*, 320.

111 Brain, "Irish Influence," 121.

112 Grimley to Conroy, 20 January 1862, in O'Haire, *Recollections*, 474.

PART FOUR

Southern World

12

Greater Ireland and the Australian Immigrant: The Religious Dimension

ERIC RICHARDS

The Irish in Australia (and perhaps also in New Zealand) are commonly regarded as founding people in the creation of the new colonial societies in the south. They arrived in large numbers, about a third of a million in the nineteenth century, and were overrepresented compared with their proportions in the home country (and compared with their presence in other destinations of Irish emigrants). The Irish immigrants in Australia were generally more literate, more skilled, and healthier than the average among the populations from which they derived. Many were from the south midland counties of Ireland and a fifth of them were Protestant (more than a quarter in New Zealand). Australia seemed to provide unrestricted opportunities for such immigrants, and together with their sheer numerical strength, the Irish faced few ethnic impediments. The Irish in Australia were generally not blocked by any monopoly of economic or political power at the hands of the English or the Scots.

The Irish in Australia thus experienced a "peculiar lack of disadvantage," and, though there were some temporary "Irishtowns" in the colonies, the immigrants did not generally concentrate in defensive huddles. They may have faced relative deprivation on arrival but they were not frozen into permanent disadvantage. Indeed the establishment of an enduring Irish-Australian community across Australia was undermined by their dispersal into the broader Australian society and by their widespread recourse to inter-marriage with Scots, Welsh, and English. Their social, geographical, and occupational mobility was unhampered, and in Australia the Irish tended not to coagulate into an ethnic community: they were less identified with the homeland, there were fewer returned migrants, and they exhibited lower rates of chain migration and remittances home than did Irish emigrants in other destinations. The dilution of Irish-Australian identities (especially after the subsidence of Irish immigration from the 1890s) was counteracted mainly by the Catholic Church, whose bishops throughout the nineteenth century were mostly Irish-born. The church took upon itself the task of preserving and fostering a sense of "flock identity" and sometimes attempted to buttress a weakening Irish identity in Australia while, of course, ignoring the substantial Protestant element among the immigrant Irish. But the efforts of the church were pitted against the reality that, in Australia, the phenomenon of anti-Irish prejudice was but "a feeble imitation of its American and British originals," and it has been argued that the general character of the Catholic Church in Australia was more Roman than Hibernian.[1]

Nevertheless, Irish emigration and religion, like Siamese twins, are virtually interchangeable and scarcely separable. Ethnic markings among the emigrant Irish are heavily underscored by religious affiliation and loyalties (not to mention antipathies), all relocated in distant places, including Australia. Questions about the impact of emigration on Irish religion quickly lead into familiar, much-mapped territory. The idea of "Greater Ireland" necessarily entails the spread of Irish emigrants across the globe, especially to Australia, which was widely recognized as a distinctively Irish and Catholic place by the end of the nineteenth century.[2] Emigrants were the carriers and the support systems for the outward reach of Irish religious practice, and the history of Irish emigration is often written as though it was coterminous with Irish religion. Indeed, where the data for Irish immigration are sparse or inadequate, religious affiliation has been employed as a proxy for the Irish proportion in the receiving population.[3] Kevin Kenny puts the matter directly when he says that "the expansion of the Catholic Church in Australia, New Zealand and Canada was largely driven by Irish migrants and clergymen."[4]

The flows and directions of emigrants determined the distribution of transposed religions. Religion of all stripes was spread by British and Irish migrants, who carried their faith with the rest of their belongings and characteristics. The transit of religion out of Ireland into the "Angloworld" was deeply affected by the chronology and phasing of Irish emigration.[5] The earliest emigrations in the long history of Greater Ireland were primarily Protestant: this commonly gave them advantages as first-comers in most destinations. The convict colonies of eastern Australia were the curious exception to this rule, and they make Australia a special case in the wider perspective. After 1830 Catholic Ireland joined the torrent of mass emigration, and significant tributaries were channelled to the Australian colonies. The Catholic elements came in alarmingly large numbers, sometimes with hungrier faces, often regarded as threats to the established colonial orders, occasionally generating hostility and communal tension. This simple chronological phasing of Irish emigration set the framework of the Greater Irish world at large and exerted a profound influence on Australia in particular.

Yet the question might well be rotated on its own axis – less conventionally and less easily answered. The question becomes: What effect did religion exert upon emigration, particularly upon Irish emigration to Australia? Religion in the annals of emigration at large is not commonly treated as a special variable, not much counted in the dynamics of mobility and expatriation. Indeed, historians of migration are criticized for failing to give religion sufficient priority. Yet some of the most celebrated collective migrations were associated with conditions of religious turmoil and exodus and, indeed, inspiration, even within the context of British destinations. Religion has been a propellant of international migration, often underpinning the extraordinary act of communal expatriation, investing the process with vital solidarity. The history of migration is full of such stories: from the time of the *Mayflower* there have been recurrent exoduses of dissident elements among Catholics, Presbyterians, Anglicans, and others feeling pressure to seek exile overseas. Spectacular examples of religious solidarity among emigrants would include the Presbyterian Scottish Highlanders who left for Cape Breton in 1810 and re-emigrated as a community to Waipu in New Zealand in the 1850s.[6] In the Outer Hebrides in the 1790s a landlord, outraged by their unco-operative spirit in the local church, implemented blatant policies to oust his Catholic tenants.[7] In the Australian colonies in the 1870s, the marked enthusiasm for German and Scandinavian immigrants was mainly an expression of preference for Lutherans over Catholics.

There are countless examples that immediately warn against any underestimation of the religious factor in the activation of intercontinental migration. Moreover, the churches at large in all denominations operated many agencies supplying the basic infrastructural facilities for international migration, as they still do to this day. It is reasonable to pose the question: What was the impact of religion on Irish emigration to Australia in the nineteenth century?

The place of religion in the hearts and minds of emigrants, Irish or other, is best explored in their correspondence back home and in their shipboard diaries. In her classic commentary on letters written by a selection of English and Scottish immigrants in the United States in the nineteenth century, Charlotte Erickson could find no evidence of direct religious motivation, but she did not fail to notice their "pietist leanings": "To them religion was not primarily a social institution but an intensely personal concern."[8] The common factor in emigrant letters was the heartfelt invocation of religious sentiment that suffused correspondence with home, especially at the start of the nineteenth century. This was so general, so universal, so repeated across regions, religions, destinations, and classes of emigrants, that it became the standard formula for communicating with home.[9] The depth and authenticity of this ubiquitous religious expression cannot be questioned.

Aspirations towards economic betterment were critical features of virtually all emigrant correspondence across all places and periods, and this ambition shaped most of the intercontinental dialogue.[10] The Victorian emigrant transmitted the yearning for economic advancement, often fired by perceptions of narrowing opportunities at home. But another sentiment also communicated, especially in the early nineteenth century, was an unmistakeable sense of religious commitment, a religiosity that undoubtedly moulded the cultural exchange among the millions of emigrants. Religion was expressed in words but also in deeds and actual sacrifices on arrival. One of the most impressive phenomena of so many new communities was the almost immediate dedication of land, energy, and money to the erection of churches and the importation of ministers and the general ornaments of the many denominations conveyed by the migrants – often also urged on by a competitive spirit. Emigrant letters home were pervaded with religious sentiment, which operated as a comforting reciprocation in many of the communications of the time, faith sometimes propelling the very act of emigration itself.

Religion imparted a degree of solidarity and security among groups of emigrants, notably in some of the communal migrations but also at a personal level. The terrors of the emigrant passage in the age of sail intensified religious fervour, which offered consolation and comfort and a greater readiness to invoke the almighty in facing the hazards of the deep.[11] If the Irish were migrating into an essentially alien world (a view associated with Kerby Miller), then the comfort of religion took on an extra significance. Religion was a psychological support in the passage, often institutionalized, with the provision of church services on the journey and on arrival.[12]

Edward Gibbon Wakefield provided an influential theoretical framework for British and Irish emigration in the 1830s, notably to the Australian colonies. But his system was also practical, and he advocated a functional role for religion in the advancement of respectable emigration. As Hilary Carey puts it, Wakefield cynically manipulated religious involvement in colonization because it would attract a better class of migrant: religion was built into his system of recruitment and society-building.[13] Shipping agencies employed church ministers and religious teachers as a means of social control among emigrants, helping to allay the fear of social breakdown. A loss of religious discipline on the voyage could threaten the safety of that voyage.[14]

Migrants flowed out of Britain and Ireland to Australia in myriad ways: at the start most were coerced as convicts; later many were self-financed and self-initiated. Almost half of the free immigrants received assisted passages; some were induced or persuaded by employers, landlords, relatives, and shipping agencies. Religion in its many forms was also a factor in quickening or retarding emigrant flows. Measuring the effect of religion on emigration is not simple, and this is true of the Irish coming to Australia.

In the long history of emigration from Ireland, there were clear biases in the flows. For instance, until the eighteenth century, transatlantic migrations were predominantly undertaken by Protestants (Scots/Irish). Catholic migration was relatively slight and underrepresented until the 1820s. These movements of populations were not directly determined by religious factors: early emigrants poured out of Protestant Ireland for particular economic reasons as well as due to the capacity of the Ulster Irish to fund their own emigrations. They were not emigrating simply because they were Protestants; their departures reflected their economic rather than their religious circumstances (though a larger interpretation might very well connect the two). Similarly, the subsequent emergence of emigration from Catholic Ireland to many destinations, not least to England, was related to changing conditions in Ireland that were not, in this phase, contingent on religion.

The intervention of the churches and their supporters can be traced from several directions. Religious elements made persistent efforts to impede and even to staunch emigration. Sometimes the motives were less than estimable, though more often they were mixed. Thus, in the Scottish Highlands and Islands in the mid-nineteenth century, there was a persistent and recurrent line of argument opposed to emigration on the grounds that it was a landlords' ploy and against the best interests of the people. Such arguments were set against the Malthusian view that it was to everyone's benefit to reduce the population. Opposition to emigration was most robust from the Free Presbyterian Church ministers. By the 1850s, the opposition to emigration hardened and was reinforced by the understanding that ministers would lose not only their flocks as their congregations emigrated but also their stipends and their livelihoods.[15] This particular line of opposition was echoed in many parts of Ireland, and there were diametrically opposed opinions about the utility and wisdom of emigration. In Cork, for instance, there was considerable opposition from priests and anti-Malthusians after the Famine, though emigration nevertheless continued to flow with little pause.[16]

Earlier, in the 1820s and 1830s, Protestant opinion in Ireland was loudly anxious about the disproportionate emigration of Protestant farmers, whose loss was weakening the faith and the future of the Protestant community. This disquiet was not confined to Ulster: Protestants exhibited a higher than average propensity to emigrate from the rest of Ireland. Protestant departures from Wexford, Wicklow, Carlow, and Kilkenny in the years before 1830 were probably prompted by rising sectarian tensions.[17] There was a fear that the Protestant establishment was being fundamentally weakened.

In July 1834, the *Dublin University Magazine* claimed that 175,000 Protestants had left Ireland for America since 1825: "It is a sad disheartening sight to witness whole parishes and districts pouring out their life-blood, and drained so as to become a moral waste." There were "instances where the clergyman has to mourn over the wreck of a once-extensive congregation, now reduced to the merest shadow of its former self."[18] And across the Irish Channel, the *Bristol Mercury* drew a simple conclusion: "so great is the tide of Protestant emigration from Ireland, that it threatens at no very distant day, to leave the 'green island' in exclusive possession of the Pope's subjects." The Protestant anxiety was palpable, "agitated like the leaves of a forest in a wind."[19]

In the Irish context there was a decisive upsurge in emigration from the Catholic regions of the country in the 1830s, a flow that became so immense that church promotion was hardly necessary. Emigration possessed a life and dynamic of its own and was not influenced by institutional intervention except where substantial financial subsidies were incorporated into the ongoing system of emigration.

In the annals of Irish emigration to Australia various blocking mechanisms were employed to counteract the rise of Catholic migration coinciding with the beginnings of mass free emigration to Australia in the mid-1830s. The creation of Australian systems of assisted passages had a dual implication for Ireland: it offered extraordinary opportunities for poor people to emigrate to this expansive but remote destination while, at the same time, giving colonial emigration authorities the tools for controlling the composition of immigration.

At the start there seemed to be little prejudice against the Irish immigrant. It is difficult, for instance, to detect any such antipathy in the writing of Wakefield or in the policies advanced and supervised by the agent-general for emigration, T.F. Elliot, who from 1840 was a member of the Colonial Land and Emigration Commission. But a framework of restriction was soon imposed: the national proportions policy, which rationed assisted passages to the proportions existing within the British Isles (which, of course, changed radically in the late nineteenth century as the Irish population fell while that of the rest of the country continued to rise). This policy, the origins of which are not entirely clear, was in reality a code for preventing Catholic immigration from overwhelming the established balance of religious denominations within the colonial populations.[20] It was repeatedly invoked but did not in fact prevent large numbers of Irish entering the eastern colonies in several periods of the century. The Home government knew of the anxieties of the colonies, and in 1837 Lord John Russell had recognized their protest against "receiving the scum of our population." But he was referring not so much to the Irish elements in the emigrating people as to the poor selection of people from across the entire country.[21] In the outcome, the Irish repeatedly exceeded their proportion as assisted immigrants: in the years from 1839 to 1868 they constituted 47 percent of those entering New South Wales and an only slightly lower percentage of those entering Victoria. In 1850, the Irish made up 80 percent of assisted immigration to New South Wales, and the number remained above 70 percent for most of the 1860s. They also accounted for 70 percent of those arriving in Victoria in 1860, though this proportion fell to between 30 and 50 percent in the rest of that decade.[22]

The two central principles of colonial-assisted immigration were "the equalization of the sexes and the proportion of nationalities."[23] The proportions policy was occasionally used in favour of the Irish component. Thus, in March 1866, there was a complaint in the official correspondence of South Australia that, in recent intakes, the Irish proportion had fallen below the required formula.[24]

In this story the extreme anti-Catholic exponents spoke loudest. Most colonists looked on in bemusement at the excesses of the zealots. One of the most vocal anti-Catholic figures was George Fife Angas, an influential financier and pioneer of the South Australian colony in the late 1830s. He was also a Nonconformist and was alarmed at the very idea of Catholic Irish immigration to the pristine Protestant province.[25] He spent much of his life vituperating against the Catholics. More practically, he promoted his ambitious schemes to introduce a large body of German Lutherans directly to the new colony. This was an expensive enterprise, specifically designed to counter the Catholic threat. It successfully established the German component in the colonial population while, in comparison with the rest of Australia, the Irish element remained modest in number. In the longer run the religious colouring of South Australia was much more influenced by the strictly economic migration of many Cornish and Welsh Methodists, attracted by the booming copper industry. Eventually only about 15 percent of the population of South Australia came from Ireland, partly because the colony had no convict heritage: it is unlikely that Angas was the main influence in the outcome.[26]

Comparable fulminations against Catholic immigration were persistently voiced by John Dunmore Lang, whose career is well known. He imported his hostile anti-Catholic attitudes directly from Lowland Scotland in the 1820s, where the Irish immigrants were regarded as an economic and religious threat and were identified with superstition, poverty, and degradation.[27] Lang's impact on the pattern of immigration in Australia was not insignificant. Like Angas, he aroused opposition to Catholic immigration, but he also recruited countervailing Protestant immigration – first by attracting skilled Lowland Scottish mechanics as early as the 1820s, then by attracting a body of Highlanders anxious to escape the destitution of the 1830s, and, finally, by implementing a scheme to introduce non-Catholics into Queensland in the 1850s. All this was blatantly and transparently sectarian and, indeed, boosted Protestant numbers, but even these numbers were no more than a drop in the ocean in terms of the larger story of Australian immigration. Clearly, this was an attempt to manipulate the migrant flows on religious grounds, which were radical not in outcome but only in conception.

There were also parallel efforts to achieve the opposite outcome: that is, to enhance the flow of Catholics to Australia. The best known was that of James Quinn, bishop of Brisbane (1859–81), in Queensland, who initiated a specific and practical effort on the part of the Catholic Church to extend its reach in Australia. Here indeed was the "Irish Empire" at work, and it enjoyed some local success, as is seen in the numbers Quinn actually recruited for Queensland in the early 1860s.[28] The Queensland Immigration Society sought to alleviate suffering in Ireland while simultaneously solving labour shortages in the colony.[29] Queensland offered assistance to people with farming skills and capital who would contribute to the development of the colony. The Catholic Church and the Queensland Immigration Society were especially keen to reduce suffering in King's County. For instance, on the Digby Estate near Tullamore, landlord agents were engaged in rationalizng leases, which provoked local turmoil among the tenantry and was followed by evictions that appear to have induced some of the victims to take up offers of assisted migration to Queensland. Such clearing landlords were often middle-class Catholics, keen to rid themselves of "unviable tenants." The local priesthood was placed in an invidious position. As Gerard Moran says, the emigrants were "accompanied by their priests," and this made them feel more secure. More particularly, the schemes had "the support of the one institution in which the people had confidence, the Catholic Church." As Moran remarks, the "people were more likely to listen to their priests than their landlords or Government officials".[30]

Ministers were frequently torn regarding whether to encourage or to deter emigration. They might be losing their flocks and their livings, yet emigration might be best for the people. Nevertheless it was scarcely a conundrum exclusive to Ireland or to the Catholic Church: the dilemma was perfectly mirrored among the Presbyterian clergy in the Scottish Highlands.[31] There were also opponents of emigration in England, such as William Ashton, who, in 1838, had denounced the emigrant trade to Australia, singling out the shipping agent, William Marshall, as "that dealer in human flesh and misery."[32]

But in Ireland there was sometimes a disjunction between the views of the local clergy and the centre. The Famine certainly divided the Catholic Church. While many local priests supported rapid expatriation as the only short-term solution to the crisis, in 1847 the bishop of Killala, for one, emphasized the problem of emigrants leaving behind "a huge inert mass of wretched paupers, incapable of cultivating the soil."[33] And within Ireland, paralleling similar currents in Scotland and even in England, there was always a background chorus of opposition to emigration. In Cork in 1855 there was vocal resistance, and by the 1860s there were even some landlords opposing further emigration, perhaps sensing labour difficulties.[34] The churches in Ireland were ambivalent about emigration, and the clergy were conflicted – a story much echoed in Scotland and even in England.[35]

After the Famine the bishops remained adamantly opposed to emigration, not only because of the loss of souls in the colonies or North America but also because "they feared that the exodus could have financial repercussions for dioceses and parishes."[36] By the 1880s, Catholic clergy had received nine hundred requests for assistance to emigrate: the local priesthood generally seemed to support such emigration. But the bishops continued to oppose the outflow, even though they "had no major influence or control of the flood of people leaving the county, especially during years of harvest failure."[37]

In Ireland after the Famine pressures to emigrate were increasingly found within the Catholic community. Kevin Kenny points out that "strong commercial farmers" in post-Famine Ireland benefited from the "massive financial remittances [they] received from their families abroad," and they themselves pushed emigration "by evicting their subtenants, consolidating their land-holdings, and converting their farms from tillage to pasture." Sometimes the clergy reinforced this highly rationalizing process, and sometimes they resisted it.[38]

The strength of the efforts to impede or to enhance the flow of Irish emigration to Australia is not easily measured. But the numbers affected were minor in comparison with the total Irish migration to the colonies – which became a flood by the 1850s and constituted a very large proportion of total assisted migration throughout the remainder of the century. It enabled the Australian colonies to become more Irish and, indeed, more Catholic than most other destinations of Anglo-Irish emigration in the nineteenth century. In effect, the processes of selection and religious affiliation were overtaken by the wider influences that determined emigration.

Emigration was propelled by forces that could only be marginally channelled, enhanced, restricted, or modified. It was a gravitational phenomenon operating across the globe. At issue here is the degree to which religion skewed the "normal" recruitment patterns to Australia and how much interference there was in the process.

Emigration was selective and subject to phasing, especially out of Ireland. The initial dominance of the Protestant intakes was followed after 1830 by overwhelming numbers of Catholics. At the start of this phase of free immigration (in the 1830s), we can detect that better-off families in Ireland were siphoning younger sons to Australia, forming the Irish components of the "Pastoral Pioneers" (Protestants being disproportionately well represented in these early migrations to Australia).[39]

There was also an uneven migration of Irish professionals to Australia: mostly, this consisted of clergy. As Emmett Larkin demonstrates, Ireland continued to train increasing numbers of clerics even while the Irish population was rapidly falling.[40] Ireland experienced a degree of "disguised unemployment" among clerics, which was eased by its massive export of priests and missionaries. The colonies, especially in Australia, offered "outdoor relief" for a redundant priesthood that became an instrument of Greater Ireland. This was part of the general exodus of Irish clergy of all stripes throughout the nineteenth century,[41] many of whom went to destinations such as Australia. Irish-trained doctors and lawyers also reached Australia in surprisingly large numbers.[42]

This sort of procurement was not confined to the Catholic Church. The Church of Ireland accounted for only a minority of Ireland's population, but it also "produced more clergy than it could accommodate." Frederic Barker, Anglican bishop of Sydney (1855–80), "used his extensive Irish contacts to encourage the immigration of clergy from Ireland." He "licensed 18 clergymen who had been ordained in Ireland or were of Irish origin but ordained in England." Judd and Cable remark that "there was a steady emigration of these men to England and the Empire. Having little hope of preferment at home, they were more likely to remain in colonial dioceses than were emigrant English clergy."[43]

The swelling numbers of Catholic Irish reaching Australia were recruited not because of their Irishness or their Catholicism but because they were ideal under the terms of the emigration schemes – sometimes, of course, in spite of their nationality and their religion. The Irish came because they were, in each of the most important immigrant categories, the most recruitable and the most available. In simple terms, the colonies needed agricultural labourers and domestic servants in particular age groups, in large numbers, and in equal proportions in terms of gender and marital status. In England, and even in Scotland, it was increasingly difficult to obtain these people. Not enough English women were emigrating under the assistance schemes, and the shortfall was balanced out of Ireland – which meant that many of these women ultimately married non-Catholic English and Scots in the colonies, a source of sectarian tensions.[44] The Australian schemes also encouraged family kinship migration and a sort of family reconstitution – effectively promoted under the terms of the nomination schemes, which required considerable contributions from the nominators in the colonies and at home.[45] It institutionalized a form of communality that Ian Levitt and Christopher Smout usefully describe as "coagulated" migration.[46]

In Ireland these potential emigrants were richly available: they matched, in a strictly reciprocal and complementary fashion, the essential requirements of the colonies. It was, at base, a fundamentally rational exchange as specified by those most rational advocates, Malthus and Wakefield. None of the fulminations of Lang and Angas had much influence on the deeper forces driving the complementarity of Ireland and colonial Australia.[47]

The Australian assistance schemes extended the range of possible emigration among the Irish population to the poorest and more remote parts of the west and south, the most Catholic zones, building special links with Tipperary, Clare, and Cork, and helping residents to escape the constraints of isolation and poverty. It inevitably led to increasing proportions of Catholic migrants. Practical realities therefore transcended religious and ideological hurdles that had been placed in the way of Catholic migration. The Australian assistance schemes successfully siphoned emigration from Ireland but were skewed towards certain well-defined districts.[48]

The fact that Irish migrants as a whole fitted colonial needs like a glove did not, of course, remove the sense of disappointment, reluctance, or outright hostility with which many Irish were greeted in the colonies. Yet in some respects the Irishness and the Catholicity of the target population was a curtain obscuring a more fundamental and more generic reaction to certain categories of immigrants at large.

Indeed, the condemnation of immigrant inadequacies has a long pedigree. Lined up over the decades of free colonization, these less desirable migrants included large swathes of people from across the British Isles – from unsatisfactory Cockney urbanites to every sort of pauper "shovelled out" to Australia. Particularly striking was the reputation of Scottish Highlanders who were assisted to the colonies in the 1830s and 1850s: they were disparaged on arrival on account of their poverty, their ignorance, their failure to know English, their diseases, and their general incompetence. These criticisms easily assumed a racial tinge: they were unsatisfactory "Celts." Yet similar condemnation was also directed at many English immigrants whose unsuitability made them reluctant to leave the towns for the country, for which their assisted passage had been paid by their erstwhile employers.

Distaste for the Irish was transposed directly from England, where, as David Fitzpatrick points out, the Irish were concentrated in certain categories that made them liable for such treatment – namely, in the "most menial, casual and impermanent sectors of manual employment," at the bottom of the heap.[49] At other times the Irish were equally able to arouse their own disdain for other immigrants: they were scornful of their fellow Catholics in New York and Boston in the late nineteenth and early twentieth centuries, specifically Italians, whom they regarded as peasants, a view that clearly transcended sectarian matters.[50]

There is a view that the Celtic regions existed as a "very large reservoir of unskilled labour not only for industrialization, but also for colonization," drawing upon the "painfully uprooted peasants of Ireland and Scotland."[51] Sir John Trevelyan captured this perception of Celtic emigrants in a speech of 1851: "Ethnologically the Celtic Race is an inferior one ... destined to give way to the higher capabilities of the Anglo-Saxons." North America and Australia were the only available remedies for the "miseries of the race, whether squatting listlessly in filth and rags in Ireland, or dreaming in idleness and poverty in the Highlands and Islands of Scotland."[52] The sense of racial disadvantage was heightened for the Irish by the sense that they were joining the empire of a country that many of them considered to be their oppressor.[53]

The most likely site of religious tension was aboard the congested emigrant ships upon which sectarian differences were concentrated. Sometimes frissons of anti-Irish sentiment crept into shipboard diaries. Andrew Hassam draws attention to the division of migrants into national groupings aboard ship, and he quotes one observer reporting the "Irish talking over everybody's business but their own and vowing eternal hatred to the English."[54] But the experience of the emigrant voyage also acted as "a means of overcoming the social and national diversity of the emigrants – a common Australian experience."[55]

The Irish attracted disproportionate hostility not only because of their concentrated numbers but also because they fit Australian needs so well. They were rural people, mostly less urbanized and less literate, on average, than the rest of the immigrants. They confronted the common reception that peasants faced across the entire immigrant world (and, indeed, within the countries from which they themselves came). Many of the Irish immigrants in Australia were derived from strata above the lowest in Ireland, and their numbers also included many displaced tenantry and rural labourers. They were probably above the average of the home population in terms of literacy and assets, and they possessed good economic and demographic characteristics to assist with induction into the colonial workforce.[56] Stressing such attributes redirects the interpretation away from Irish and Catholic essentialism.

Bruce Elliott, in his study of nineteenth-century Ontario, shows that chain migration was not exclusive to the Catholic migrants from Ireland.[57] In Australia chain migration was virtually institutionalized by the nomination system, which encouraged families to negotiate with and to assist kinsfolk into the assistance arrangements. Here the Irish – mostly Catholic – were exceedingly effective and adept. Engineering the intimate chains of migration required trust, savings, determination, and the most dependable of kinship ties. It was a sophisticated use of immigrants' savings and dedication; it spoke loudly of their application and loyalty and, more obviously, of the colonial success of the Irish.[58]

Irish emigration to the Australian colonies was far from homogeneous. Irish professionals, Irish Protestants, landowners, and urbanites – all tend to be subsumed beneath the larger numbers of the rural Catholic inflows. These subsidiary elements also had special structural relationships with their colonial hosts and the donor societies whence they came.

The arrival of immigrants, sometimes in concentrated numbers, imposed pressures on churches and exposed the priorities within the migrating communities. Typically, the local churches took up the challenge, as captured in the words of Christopher Reynolds, the Catholic bishop of Adelaide, in 1876: "The influx of Catholic immigrants and the opening up of new areas or agricultural districts cause a greater demand for priests, and I have them not."[59] Impressive was the urgency that, immediately upon arrival, groups of immigrants brought to establishing the structures of their transposed faith in the colonies. It was a universal story across the Anglo-Irish world. It was typified, in one minor example, in the story of the extremely poor Highlanders who arrived in South Australia in the early 1850s. Despite their severe penury, during and after their immigration, on their arrival they were immediately scraping together money (and muscular effort) to build a Free Presbyterian church, often with their bare hands and even before they had settled into the colony.[60]

The question of how emigrants from Ireland "used religious sensibility to construct new cultural communities" was answered first by the construction of the fabric of their churches, the physical infrastructure, and then its embellishment (which was sometimes extravagant). One universal reality of such immigrant communities was the channelling of their colonial labour into the establishment and aggrandizement of the imported churches. In the 1870s Dr Reynolds in Adelaide praised the generosity of his flock – "their contributions to pay debts, establish schools, build churches, and educate priests." They also supported an orphanage. He added, perhaps irritably, that "the Protestants … do very little."[61] The churches in Australia widely absorbed immigrants' funds into the fabric of their faith, and this was manifested in the construction of a thousand church buildings, schools, and convents as well as in the importation of the clergy themselves. And it is not hard to find evidence of the vitality and priority of this investment: it was competitive and glorious in its conspicuous display of commitment and piety as well as of colonial advancement. Some of it was distantly reminiscent of aristocratic building excesses in early eighteenth-century England, which Nikolaus Pevsner memorably describes as a display of "almost megalomaniac magnificence."[62]

These "Church structures," to use Colin Barr's expression, were ubiquitous across the Anglo-Irish world and were imposing and expensive in every way.[63] The Australian account is less well-documented, but Peter Murphy has recently celebrated the "building of gothic piles in Australia," the mountainous edifices of Victorian religion in all the cities and towns of the colonies.[64] As for the building of Catholic churches in Victoria, "for the most part, the money came from the hands of the labouring poor."[65] In North America the evidence of parallel immigrant communities is denser – for instance in Newburyport, Massachusetts, in 1880 where the new Catholic church was built out of the slender earnings of working-class Irish immigrants.[66] Stephan Thernstrom remarks that it was all orchestrated by the clergy who were "dedicated to accumulating property as well as saving souls, and they saw clearly that a thrifty, hard-working, well-educated congregation would contribute to that end."[67] In Thernstrom's view the church was "a heavy drain on resources which, from the point of view of worldly success, might have been put to more productive uses."[68]

Church-building diverted energy and capital away from higher education as well as from the needs of apprenticeship: the communal sacrifice entailed in the building of churches probably delayed the upward social mobility of the working class.[69] Sustaining and building faith and its infrastructures was not cheap, and the burden was carried by the poorest of the community in Australia, as elsewhere in the immigrant world.[70]

The most spectacular use of emigrant remittances was directed towards the vast edifice of St Colman's Cathedral at Cobh, built between 1867 and 1915. At £235,000 (ten times the original estimate), this was the most costly ecclesiastical building in nineteenth-century Ireland. About 12 percent of the funding was raised overseas from Irish emigrant communities, some of whom were decidedly frosty in their response to requests for donations. In Kadina, South Australia, it was reported that the bishop was loathe to grant permission to collect funds from parishioners, "as they are very much in debt themselves and are badly circumstanced in regard to churches and schools." In 1876, Bishop Reynolds of Adelaide was unenthusiastic: "Every pound I got, after I had made £300, was, I have been told, as much regretted by him ... as if I were drawing away their hearts' blood."[71]

There were evidently several dimensions to the immigrant mentality, which certainly embraced spiritual values. Dirk Hoerder and Horst Rossler argue that emigrants typically experienced a psychological transition: at home, before their migration, they knew only the timeless "dichotomy between drudgery and misery on earth," which was to be compensated ultimately by a "better life in heaven." But emigrants, Hoerder argues, adopted a quite different mentality: "they felt now that life could be bettered on earth by moving to better parts of the world." The new world of the immigrants allowed for a secularization of hope.[72] Similarly, and more recently, James Belich hypothesizes about the notion of "Settler Utopianism," which gripped and inspired so many new immigrants across the Anglo-world.[73] Such speculations connect with competing ideas – for example, that immigrant communities were prone to an intensification of religious fervour and, as Kerby Miller argues, that the sense of exile was disproportionate among the emigrating Irish.

Greater Ireland in Australia is probably most comparable with the Canadian experience. But Irish Protestants in Canada outnumbered their Catholic counterparts by two to one. In Australia these proportions were reversed – mainly because there was not as much self-funded immigration to Australia as there was to Canada. Canadian research has yielded some enviably precise results. In particular, there has emerged an interesting degree of critical scepticism about the effect of religion on Irish immigrant life in Ontario. Donald Akenson, always provocative, argues that, on most social indices, Irish Catholic immigrants were not significantly different from Protestants from Ireland, most notably in their relative propensities towards urban and rural life. He quotes David Fitzpatrick to the effect that the Irish possessed a special advantage in the colonies: "their predominantly rural background ... gave most Irish settlers knowledge of how to work the land not shown by their urban counterparts from England."[74] Such claims reaffirm the effective adaptability of the Irish emigrant and apply no less to colonial Australia. The idea that Catholics were less likely to accept the imperial mantle or the entrepreneurial vest seems also to be seriously subverted by Akenson's evidence of their success as socially upward mobile settlers in many places across the sites of Greater Ireland.

No less striking in the Canadian account is the record of Protestant emigrants from North Tipperary who migrated in the years between 1818 and 1855. Bruce Elliott offers the most detailed analysis and documentation of such migrants in eastern Canada. In his study of 775 Protestant immigrant families he finds that they employed chain migration just as much as did their Catholic counterparts and that there was no real difference between their respective values and aspirations: family strategies were equally vital among both Protestants and Catholics. Elliott shows that the Protestants in Ontario shared many of the characteristics of the Catholic tenant farmers coming to Australia: they were mostly "middling farmers and tradesmen who faced declining status and property in the over-populated agricultural regions." And they were motivated primarily by concerns about their children and their futures. Moreover, they possessed no more and no less a sense of exile than did their Catholic counterparts.

Australia mirrored these Canadian experiences. The Irish in Australia were heterogeneous in religion and they encompassed sizeable minorities, including about 15 percent who were Protestant, many of whom were from the south of Ireland. Akenson demonstrates that the Catholic Irish in Victoria did not display any strong proclivity towards town life and that they were as likely to grasp economic opportunities as was anyone else. He demonstrates the close demographic profiles of the two sides in terms of social class and patterns of settlement, and he argues that Catholics and Protestants in Australia, New Zealand, and Canada were more similar than different in social attitudes and basic aspirations.

In the Australian context the argument for the special characteristics of Catholic Irish immigrants – for example, their being tied to inherited communal values and anti-capitalistic sentiments – are counterbalanced by several primary features. Their pronounced recourse to the nomination system required special reserves of trust, savings, determination, and confidence in kinship, not to mention the ability to make canny use of official regulations. Their contributions to church infrastructure also testified to their dependability. And given that, on average, they started at a lower social rung in colonial society, their record of upward mobility is impressive and effectively debunks received stereotypes.

The Australian case has not yet been subjected to as finely detailed an analysis as has the Canadian one, partly because the Australian archival and statistical sources are less amenable than are the Canadian. This represents a challenge to the next generation of social historians. The work that comes closest to displaying such precise detail in Irish Australian immigration history is Richard Reid's study of forty-four thousand assisted migrants to New South Wales in the mid-nineteenth century.[75] This is not comparative history since virtually all Reid's migrants were Catholic; but the direction of his findings points towards a convergence with those found for Canada, shrinking the sense of difference amid the migrant populations. Parallels with other immigrants and other religions in Australia and beyond – among, for instance, Scottish Presbyterians, Cockneys, and Cornish Methodists – expose similarities and differences that give perspective and a reasonable scepticism to our understanding of "Greater Ireland."

NOTES

1 These two paragraphs draw on Fitzpatrick, "Settlers"; and Richards, "Irish Life and Progress." See also Molony, *Roman Mould*.
2 See, for instance, Reid, *Farewell My Children*, 9.
3 See McDonagh, "Irish in Victoria." See, however, Akenson, *Small Differences*, 66.
4 Kenny, "Irish in the Empire," 114.
5 See Miller et al., *Irish Immigrants*, 4–5.
6 See Richards, "Highland Emigration."
7 See Bumsted, "Scottish Diaspora," 138; and MacDonell, *Emigrant Experience*, 10.
8 Erickson, *Invisible Immigrants*, 30.
9 See Richards, "Human Traffic." Angela McCarthy dwells on the special importance of faith among Irish emigrants of different religions to New Zealand. See McCarthy, *Irish Migrants,* 260. See also Fitzpatrick, *Oceans of Consolation*, 602, in which he suggests that the "injunction to piety" was equal between Protestants and Catholics.
10 But see Akenson, *Small Differences*, 71. See also McCarthy, *Irish Migrants*, 238ff; and Akenson, "Reading the Texts."
11 Note the warning about approaching religion in a secular spirit in Gilley, "Roman Catholic Church," 206.
12 Cf. Fitzpatrick, *Oceans of Consolation,* 603; see also Northey, *Living the Truth*, 78–81.
13 Carey, *God's Empire*, 329.
14 A good example of this exact anxiety was witnessed on the voyage of the *Planter*, as recounted in the diary of James Bell, from Dumfries to Port

Adelaide. State Library of South Australia, D8274(L), James Bell, Journal of a Voyage to Australia, 1838–39.

15 On Highland attitudes to emigration, see MacColl, *Land, Faith and the Crofting Community*.

16 See Donnelly, *Land and People*, 232–3.

17 See Elliott, "Emigration from South Leinster," 7:279.

18 "Emigration of the Protestants of Ireland," *Dublin University Magazine*, vol. 4, July 1834, 2.

19 *Bristol Mercury*, 26 July 1834.

20 It sustained a fiction of fairness not unlike that of the United States Quota Acts of 1921 and 1924.

21 Quoted in the *Belfast News Letter*, 8 December 1837.

22 Figures quoted in the appendices of Hamilton, "No Irish Need Apply." Charles Gavan Duffy claimed, eccentrically, that the selection system for Victoria was entrusted to "parsons and squires whose vote could be counted on, or persons to be got rid of – 'rotten seed' for the colony." The requisite numbers could not be found in England and, hence, overwhelming numbers of Irish Catholic female servants were admitted, partly because they would not get the vote. See Duffy, *My Life*, 2:303–4.

23 *South Australian Government Gazette*, 26 February 1863.

24 Ibid.

25 From the start South Australia proclaimed a special promise to intending migrants: it would be so much more "preferable to rambling over the back settlements of America, mixing with Catholics in the bleak unhealthy wilds of Canada or to enduring the depraved society of the penal colonies." See Pike, *Paradise of Dissent*, 146.

26 Richards, "Importance of Being Irish."

27 See Baker, *Preacher, Politician, Patriot*, 4.

28 See Macginley, "Irish in Queensland," 106.

29 See Moran, *Sending Out*, 149–51. See also Harrison, "From King's County."

30 Moran, *Sending Out*, 159–60. More generally, see MacDonagh, "Irish Catholic Clergy"; and Fitzpatrick, "Irish Emigration," 132.

31 See Richards, "Highland Emigration."

32 William Ashton, *A Lecture on the Evils of Emigration and Transportation, delivered at the Town-hall, Sheffield, 23 July 1838*, pamphlet, second edition.

33 Quoted in Moran, *Sending Out*, 75.

34 See Donnelly, *Land and People*, 232.

35 Carey, *God's Empire*, 307.
36 Moran, *Sending Out*, 75–7.
37 Ibid., 183. There was also increasing resistance among Catholic bishops in the New World to further "Wholesale and Improvident Emigration from Ireland." See Moran, "Faith, Famine and Fenianism," 171.
38 Kenny, "Irish in the Empire," 100.
39 See Ó Grada and Mokyr, "Poor and Getting Poorer?"
40 Larkin, "Economic Growth."
41 For more on this, see Larkin, "Economic Growth."
42 Geary, "Australia Felix."
43 Judd and Cable, *Sydney Anglicans*, 21, 76, 80.
44 See Lang, *Visit to Geelong*, 50. For broader treatments of the inter-denominational marrying patterns in the Victorian era, see McConville, "Victorian Irish"; Herraman and Richards, "Irish Women."
45 See Reid, *Farewell My Children*, 220.
46 Levitt and Smout, *State of the Scottish Working Class*, 243.
47 This argument is elaborated in Eric Richards, *Sorting Out the Irish Emigrant in Colonial Australia,* Australasian Irish Studies Conference, July 2011, National Museum of Australia, Canberra, transcript available online at http:/www.nma.gov.au/audio/transcripts/irish studies/NMA Irish Richards 20110701.html.
48 See Reid, *Farewell My Children*, 108.
49 Fitzpatrick, "Curious Middle Place," 10. See also Fitzpatrick, "Irish Emigration," 134–5.
50 See Stack, *International Conflict*, 29, 33–5; Bayor, *Neighbors in Conflict*, 4.
51 Kiernan, "Britons Old and New," 43ff. Regarding the reluctance of English employers to employ Irish domestic servants, see Kiernan, "Britons Old and New," 185.
52 Quoted by Bennett, "Quebec Hebridean to les Ecossais-Quebecois," 123. See also Devine, *Ends of the Earth*, 110, 116–7, 122; Morton and Morris, "Civil Society," 376. See also Watson, *Caledonia Australis*, 52 et seq., 66, 134–5. See also Fenyo, *Contempt, Sympathy and Romance*, 100.
53 See Barr, "'Imperium in Imperio'," 613.
54 Hassam, "Our Floating Home," 17.
55 See Hassam, quoting Cochrane and Gordon, "Great Australian Fairness." The idea that "the common experience" of the journey transcended "religious and racial elements" is supported by Reid, *Farewell My Children*, 219.
56 See Richards, "Australian Map"; Richards, "First Mass Migration."
57 See Elliott, *Irish Migrants in the Canadas*.

58 Reid points out that remittance regulations in New South Wales eventually required a contribution of up to half of the fare, though more usually a third. See Reid, *Farewell My Children*, 197–9. This was a valuable method of supporting the immigration fund. Reid points out that, from 1848 to 1870, 59 percent of Irish assisted immigrants were nominated as against 6 percent of the English. A surprising amount of the aid derived from Ireland itself: "Home" money, which, in effect, had to be sent to Australia to secure the passage (209). Moreover, the nomination system reinforced the regional characteristic of Irish emigration to Australia. David Fitzpatrick describes the system as a "self-perpetuating chain" though also influenced by parish priests. See Fitzpatrick, "Irish Emigration," 132.
59 Quoted in Moran, *History of the Catholic Church*, 533.
60 Richards, "Highland Scots of South Australia," 33–64.
61 Moran, *History of the Catholic Church*, 535.
62 Quoted by Nunn, "Aristocratic Estates," 37. One is reminded of Virginia Woolf's reflections on the building of Oxbridge colleges: "Teams of horses and oxen must have hauled the stone in wagons from far … and then the painters brought their glass for the windows, and the masons were busy … up on the roof with putty, spade and trowel … An unending stream of gold and silver … must have flowed into this court perpetually to keep the stones coming and the masons working" (Woolf, *Room of One's Own*, 15).
63 Barr, "Imperium in Imperio", 622–3.
64 Murphy, "Sacredism," 289.
65 Bourke, *Catholic Church in Victoria*, 60–6.
66 Thernstrom, *Poverty and Progress*, 172, 176.
67 Ibid., 175.
68 Ibid., 176.
69 Ibid., 177. The competitive spirit of church building was best exemplified in Chicago in the 1850s, where the Church of the Holy Family was erected expressly to outdo the rival Protestant edifices – at a time of great deprivation, misery, and poverty among the contributing congregations. As its historian asks: "Considering the material circumstances of Holy Family parishioners, did it make sense to invest so much money in a permanent church capable of accommodating six thousand people?" But the project created jobs for immigrant labourers and also created a sense of community spirit. See Skerrett, "Irish of Chicago's Hull House Neighbourhood," 194–5.
70 Larkin remarks that the Catholic Church expanded its expenditure and wealth as though it had become imbued with the "Protestant ethic." During the decades each side of the Famine it built "cathedrals, churches,

chapels, convent, monasteries, seminaries, parochial houses, episcopal palaces, schools, colleges, orphanages, hospitals, and asylums" – "all mushroomed in every part of Ireland." It was "a building revolution." See Larkin, "Economic Growth," 869. In the process, the church had appropriated a large share of Irish and migrant resources (264).

71 Quoted in Wilson, "Gothic Revival in Ireland," 20.

72 Hoerder and Roessler, *Distant Magnets*, 2.

73 Belich, *Replenishing the Earth*.

74 Cited in Akenson, *Small Differences*, 67. This might be contrasted with Lang's jibe that they only knew about pigs. The urban propensities of Irish emigrants is repeated in Dudley Baines, *Emigration from Europe*, 24.

75 Reid, *Farewell My Children*, esp. 220. Another important example is Proudfoot and Hall, "Points of Departure."

13

"Mindful of Her St Columbas and Gaels": Ireland, Empire, and Australian Anglicanism, 1788–1850

MICHAEL GLADWIN

In December 1846, Francis Russell, a talented and well-connected young graduate from Trinity College Dublin, wrote to the Society of the Propagation of the Gospel (SPG), the main agency for sending Anglican clergymen to the colonies of the British World. "Indeed I have no doubt," he wrote on the eve of his voyage from Dublin to Sydney, "that the Antient Church of Ireland, mindful of her St Columbas and Gaels – will as of old send forth many zealous labourers to the abundant harvest."[1] Originally destined by his family to follow a distinguished career as a Dublin barrister, Russell had instead discerned a vocation as an Anglican clergyman for the Australian colonies. Along with his best friend and fellow ordination candidate, Peter Beamish, Russell went on to a highly successful and influential thirty-year ministry on the colonial frontier of western Victoria. Nineteenth-century Australian historian James Bonwick described him as "a learned, witty man, vastly popular with all men in his district." The astute colonial writer and commentator, Ada Cambridge, noted Russell's parish on the Wannon as "the most important country parish in the diocese."[2] Russell's own allusion to the overseas missionary efforts of the sixth-century Irish monk, St Columba, and his decision to serve as an Anglican clergymen in colonial Australia, gesture towards some of the key themes of this chapter – namely, the background and influence of Irish clergy in colonial Australian Anglicanism and the wider British World before 1850.

Historians have only recently begun to reassess the place of religion in the nineteenth-century British World. In a growing body of scholarship it is possible to discern a new and definite shift in scholarly emphasis away from "missionaries and empire" towards what Hilary Carey labels the "colonial missionary movement." An important debate within this burgeoning field concerns the national character and mission of Anglicanism, by far the largest contributor to the colonial missionary movement. Anglican clergy, in particular, have been seen as key agents of colonial expansion and English national identity, a High Church-Tory intellectual elite, charged with the responsibility of transmitting both English and Anglican culture to the colonies. Scholars such as C.A. Bayly have also characterized Anglican Church and clergy as tools of empire, or part of what he calls an imperial "Anglican design." In the Australian context there has likewise been a long-standing popular and scholarly view that Australian Anglicanism was "quintessentially English," particularly during its formative phase up to 1850. In terms of churchmanship, recent scholarship also foregrounds the "High Church" character of Anglicanism over a predominantly "evangelical" character. These views have been questioned more recently, however, by recognition of the significant numbers of Irish Anglican clergy who were recruited for the English-speaking settler colonies. Many of these Anglican clergymen were actually Irish – or worse (in the opinion of some contemporaries), Irish evangelicals.

A key contention of this volume is that there existed during the period of the Second British Empire a "Greater Ireland," akin to the old concept of a "Greater Britain," in which the Irish transformed into a global people, actively participating in British imperial expansion and colonial nation-building in Australia, Canada, India, South Africa, South America, New Zealand, and the United States. A lacuna in the existing literature, however, is a detailed study of Irish clergy in the Australian colonies. The purpose of this chapter, therefore, is to examine the backgrounds and influence of Irish clergy within colonial Australian Anglicanism before 1850. Irish clergymen, as we shall see, made up nearly a quarter of Australian Anglican clergymen during this period. Moreover, they adapted well to colonial conditions and exerted influence out of all proportion to their numbers on the Anglican Church and on colonial Australia's fledgling cultural, intellectual, and political life. Contemporary observers identified their Irishness in their confident reformism, national pride, combativeness, and their enhanced Protestant identity. In turn, this green hue in the complexion of Australian Anglicanism casts doubt on monolithic ideas of Anglican clergy as agents of Englishness. Additionally, the Irish clergy's complex and sometimes adversarial relationship with colonial and imperial projects challenges notions of clergy as tools of an imperial "Anglican design."

ANGLO-IRISH CLERGY IN AUSTRALIA: SOCIAL BACKGROUNDS AND MOTIVATION

The Anglo-Irish factor has been neglected in Australian history, in part because of the much larger numbers of Irish Roman Catholics in the Australian colonies.[3] This is particularly surprising in the case of Anglican clergymen, given that Irish clergy made up nearly a quarter (23 percent) of the 235 Anglican clergymen who served in the Australian colonies before 1850.[4] A quarter of Tasmanian clergy and nearly a third of Western Australian clergy were Irish. This is close to the figure given in the 1846 census of New South Wales (NSW), the first to provide information on national origins, which shows that 25.4 per cent of the population were born in Ireland. In terms of the educational backgrounds of Australian Anglican clergymen, it is striking that, between 1788 and 1850, as many studied at Trinity College Dublin as at Oxford, two of the three main vicar factories of that period.

Nevertheless, the importance of Anglo-Irish and Australian influence should not obscure the fact that the majority (68 percent) of clergymen were English-born and, as such, usually regarded England as "Home" or "the mother country." In terms of national background (i.e., English parentage and citizenship), the figure is 71.6 percent. By comparison, 33.3 percent of the whole population in NSW in 1846 were English-born, making Anglican clergy roughly double the national average.[5] James Jupp reminds us that Australia is the "second most English country in the world" and that her "largest overseas-born 'ethnic group'" has always been the English.[6] Clergy birthplaces in Britain, illustrated in figure 13.1, fit with Jupp's observation that most Australian elites hail from the Greater London area and provincial centres, especially in Yorkshire. Most English-born clergymen who wrote or spoke of England and empire did so in patriotic terms, but not uncritically. National and imperial imperatives were consistently subordinated to the universal aims of the church and the gospel of Christ. On the other hand, Irish and Australian-bred (and born) clergy were generally more ambivalent.[7]

What motivated Irish clergy to migrate to Australia? In the historiography of the metropolitan Anglican Church, the Irish clergy have been characterized as "mountain" clergy, typically migrating from Ireland to the northwest of England in the wake of the Irish Temporalities Act,

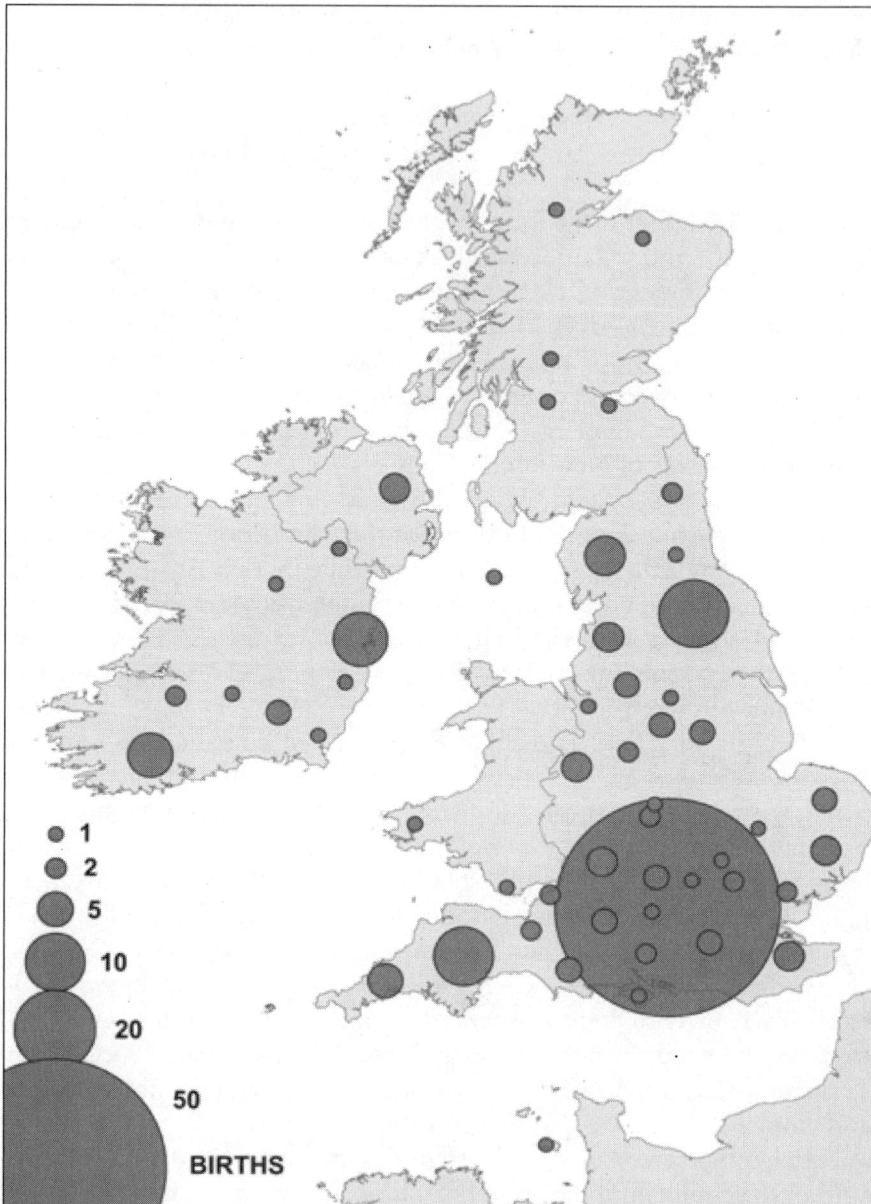

Figure 13.1 Birthplaces of British-born Anglican clergymen who served in Australia, 1788–1850

Source: Michael Gladwin, *Anglican Clergy in Australia, 1788–1850: Building a British World*, Royal Historical Society/Boydell Press, Woodbridge, UK, 2015, p. 54. Circle size indicates relative numbers. Largest circle represents clergy born in London.

1833 – or, after 1845, due to the Famine.[8] The Reverend George Wilkins of Nottingham, for example, was one among many who lamented the arrival of "raw, fresh caught Irish curates imported by shoals from Liverpool."[9] There is support for this profile among some of the Irish clergy who served in Australia. Only seven Irish-born clergymen migrated to Australia before the passing of the Irish Temporalities Act, 1833; forty-one clergymen (85 percent of all Irish Australian clergymen) migrated between 1833 and 1850. The Irish Famine was a big factor: twenty-four clergymen (half of all Irish clergymen) arrived during the height of the Famine between 1845 and 1850.

It is clear, however, that the majority (88 percent) of the Irish clergyman in Australia can be located firmly in the substantial middle-class, gentry, or upper ranks of the Anglo-Irish elite – the "Ascendancy."[10] This can be demonstrated in terms of education. Ninety percent of Irish clergy coming to Australia were university educated, with 81 percent of these studying at Trinity College Dublin, 6 percent at Oxford, and 2 percent at Cambridge.[11] The high percentage of Anglo-Irish clergy contrasts with Jarlath Ronayne's reckoning that the Anglo-Irish were never more than about 5 percent of Australia's nineteenth-century non-indigenous population and about 10 percent of the Irish-born in nineteenth-century Australia. In terms of motivation for migration to Australia, economic push factors were clearly important. Yet this does not exclude a distinct sense of spiritual vocation. Indeed, the clergy's ego-documents and careers demonstrate a high sense of vocation among the majority of Irish clergy.[12]

THE INFLUENCE OF IRISH ANGLICAN CLERGY IN THE AUSTRALIAN COLONIES

Irish clergy punched above their weight in terms of their influence on colonial Australia's fledgling cultural, intellectual, and political life. Several Irishmen held key posts as archdeacons and rural deans in Port Phillip (Victoria) and Van Diemen's Land (Tasmania). In South Australia, founded in 1836 as the first Australian free colony, the first two clergymen were Irish evangelicals, dominating the church as the senior clergy until the arrival of a bishop in 1847. In Ireland the Famine pushed up into the middle classes during the 1840s, encouraging the migration of Trinity-educated lawyers and doctors to Melbourne and Port Phillip. One result of this was that an elite circle of blood relations called the "Irish cousinage" dominated the bar, bench, and early public life in

Victoria. This circle included Attorney-General William Stawell and the later dean of Melbourne, the Reverend Hussey Macartney, son of an Irish MP with baronets in both family lines. The families of Macartney and other Irish clergymen were at the centre of Melbourne's religious, cultural, and public life until the late nineteenth century, a social milieu evocatively reconstructed by Australian historian Penny Russell.[13]

A striking feature of the Irish clergy's influence is their advocacy of convicts, a fact that belies facile caricatures of colonial Anglican clergy as "flogging parsons" and pantomime villains who uncritically aligned themselves with the free landed classes – the so-called exclusives. I examine the relationship between Anglican clergymen and convicts elsewhere in detail, but it is worth highlighting the Irish dimensions of this interaction.[14] In the first place, it is remarkable that the first Irish clergyman to come to Australia did so at His Majesty's pleasure. The scholarly Reverend Henry Fulton arrived in Sydney in 1800, having been implicated in the Irish Rebellion of 1798. Due to his good behaviour and a shortage of clergy, Fulton was quickly pressed into service as an Anglican chaplain and magistrate. While still a magistrate, Fulton publicly aligned himself with convicts and emancipists when his name headed a petition of fifty-five leading men and thirteen hundred emancipists who sought to secure the legal status of the pardons they had received from governors of New South Wales.[15] On another occasion Fulton annoyed Governor Brisbane by petitioning the government against the Commissariat's paying for supplies in Spanish dollars, on the grounds that this had a deleterious effect on the price of labour and agricultural produce. Complaining to Lord Bathurst, Brisbane expressed his displeasure at the liberty such "public officers of the Colony" arrogated to themselves in "opposing public measures."[16] Brisbane was further irritated by the magisterial signature of Fulton on a petition that deprecated government wool duties as a hindrance to landholders and livestock proprietors' ability to compete with European woolgrowers.[17]

The local and personal interaction of clergymen with convicts was accompanied by aspirations for structural change of the convict system itself. In Tasmania during the 1840s a coterie of Anglican clergymen, acting as magistrates and journalists, was at the forefront of campaigns both to reform and to abolish convict transportation. Three of the most influential were Irish: the Reverends Thomas Rogers, Henry Phibbs Fry, and William Henry Browne. Their editorials, letters to the editor, pamphlets, and monographs constituted strident attacks on both government policy and the convict system's inherent failure.[18]

The tenor of this activism is encapsulated in the writing and activities of Thomas Rogers. In many ways he represents the antithesis of the "flogging parson" caricature of Anglican clergymen: revered and loved by the convicts to whom he ministered, an able scholar, and a real-life Irish counterpart of Australia's first fictional muscular parson, the Reverend Frank Maberly of *Geoffrey Hamlyn*.[19] The bespectacled Rogers stood at over 1.83 metres and, on one occasion, responded to an assault by a drunk military officer with a crashing fist to the officer's jaw (to the approval of the officers and ladies present, who commended his "manly" response).[20]

On Norfolk Island, the most brutal of all Australian penal stations, Rogers was one of several Anglican clergymen who advocated the cause of a number of convicts, including Henry Barber, a solicitor wrongly convicted of forgery whose freedom they secured after several years of lobbying government. Rogers also helped to provide for Barber's welfare when he was left destitute and penniless after his discharge.[21] As a magistrate, Rogers helped illiterate convicts to both understand and write depositions, and he gave convicts his opinions on how far the evidence was either for or against them.[22]

Rogers published a book and a long pamphlet in 1849, against the orders of both his bishop and the governor, a decision that forced his resignation and departure to England in 1850. These publications constituted a devastating exposé: of government authorities' brutal mistreatment and torture of convicts, of the obstruction of clergy in their duties, and of the unfounded dismissal of both Rogers and a fellow Anglican chaplain.[23] Rogers, like his clerical colleagues, spared no detail in his graphic accounts of men "bad with anal disease" due to rape, the infliction of 20,624 lashes in sixteen months, and a flogging ground that, on "flogging mornings," was "saturated with human gore, as if a bucket of blood had been spilled on it … running out in little streams of two or three feet long."[24] Rogers's *Review* condemned the convict system's administration of justice as "an iniquitous and demoralizing farce."[25]

In 1850, Rogers and fellow Anglican clergyman and Irishman, the evangelical William Henry Browne, aided by his daughters Isabella and Fanny, helped to co-found the Anti-Transportation League in Launceston. Launceston remained the locus of the league, which by 1851 had lobbyists in London and a flag, emblazoned with Union Jack and Southern Cross, that flew as far away as Adelaide and New Zealand. Rogers's writings were also quoted extensively in the most influential of all anti-transportation polemics, John West's *History of Tasmania* (1852). Two decades later Marcus Clarke's gothic masterpiece, *His Natural Life* (1874–75), incorporated lengthy verbatim extracts from Rogers's writings and modelled a main character, the Reverend James North, on Rogers.

Also important was the clergy's direct influence on the shift in colonial and imperial policy towards ending convict transportation to the eastern colonies by 1853. One of the many pamphlets of Irish clergymen and journalist Henry Phibbs Fry was singled out by government as an important catalyst for Earl Grey's decision to adopt a "modified probation" scheme and to dismantle the Norfolk Island penal settlement. Fry's later book on Tasmanian convictism damned the system and became a classic study in Victorian penology.[26] In Fry's opinion, the colonies' filial affection for the mother country depended on Britain's abolition of transportation and its provision of Tasmanian self-government.[27] The Irish clergy's social concern extended to their wide-ranging welfare work among all classes. Henry Fry, the fiery John Keane, the genteel William Dry, the kangaroo-steak-eating William Stack, and the extempore-preaching George Wilkinson were all noted for their creative efforts on behalf of the poor and working classes. William Horatio Walsh was a co-founder of the Australian Mutual Providence Society (AMP) to provide insurance for working men; Rowland Davies founded savings banks for the same reason in Tasmania; and George King championed the cause of Swan River Aborigines.

These clergymen were hardly uncritical supporters of the status quo. They supported both church and empire, but not without qualification. They presented discussions of convict transportation in the context of a distinctly providential Christian understanding of humanity and the social order. There is support here for Hilary Carey's contention that the church's interaction with the Empire in the Australian colonies encompassed a range of liberal and humanitarian interventions to "mitigate the perceived evils of empire" while at the same time providing ideological support for the imperial ideal.[28]

The majority of Irish clergymen were influential and successful, although there were a few instances of clergy behaving badly: Matthew Meares, for example, did penance for adultery; Robert Drought's servant turned out to be his illegitimate daughter; and John Andrewartha went into debt as co-owner of a sawmill and tramway in Huon, Tasmania.

THE IRISH INFLUENCE IN AUSTRALIAN CLERGY RECRUITMENT

The influence of Irish Anglican clergymen was also felt in relation to clergy recruitment. A significant challenge to scholarly characterizations of colonial Australian Anglicanism as High Church, English, and imperialist is the simple fact that evangelicalism was probably the dominant force in the Australian Church. This was the case even during 1836–50, when all bishops but one (Charles Perry of Melbourne) were of a High Church or moderate Tractarian stamp. Furthermore, many of those recruited through the SPG were both evangelical and Irish.

The first generation of South Australian clergymen illustrates the personal and Irish nature of evangelical recruitment. Most South Australian clergymen came under the auspices of the SPG, but the majority were evangelicals – five of the first six up to 1847. The second senior chaplain, James Farrell, was a product of an evangelical coterie known as the Dublin Rotunda School, an Irish equivalent of London's Exeter Hall, so named for its meetings in a rotunda of the Dublin Lying-In Hospital.

In 1835, prominent London evangelical the Reverend Baptist Noel and Western Australian military commander Colonel Frederick Irwin, aided by the Reverend Edward Bickersteth, were the driving forces behind the creation of the first evangelical society for colonial clergy, the Western Australian Missionary Society, later renamed the Colonial Church Society (CCS).[29] The society's minute books reveal how Irwin utilized his Irish connections, aided by Bickersteth's preaching tours and Noel's well-connected London base.[30] Australian clergymen such as Phillip Palmer in Hobart provided important links as secretaries of correspondence committees. Palmer secured Edward Henry Bryan for Tasmania (and Bryan promptly secured Palmer's daughter, Ursula). Upon his return from Hobart to London in 1840, the Reverend Michael Mayers urged upon the CCS the provision of two unmarried itinerant clergymen for Tasmania.[31] By 1851, the society had provided six clergymen, two of whom were in Western Australia and two in Port Phillip, as well as four catechists and schoolmasters.[32] These were modest beginnings before 1850, but they laid the foundation for the later Bush Church Aid Society and an influx of evangelical clergymen, including the first Bishop of Goulburn, Thomas Mesac.[33]

The efforts of the Reverend Dr Elrington, regius professor of divinity at Trinity College Dublin, suggest the importance of High Church networks in Ireland. Elrington was a close friend of Hackney Phalanx leader Joshua Watson. In 1840, Elrington asked Watson to press the SPG Committee for clergy in Western Australia, after he was alerted to the need by the sister of a former pupil.[34] Elrington knew personally of eight or nine expatriate Irishmen of high character, and at least one of considerable fortune, who would warmly support the church in Western Australia. Archbishop Whately, outspoken critic of penal transportation to Australia, also suggested landed estates for clergy endowments in Western Australia, but his proposal was politely declined by Governor Hutt.[35] The efforts of the Reverend Michael Disney, evince the speed at which recruitment could move. William Singleton came to his notice for his excellent work in four private asylums in Finglas, with which Disney's brother was intimately acquainted. Keen to do something for Singleton on account of his "useful" work, his discreet zeal, and his support of a family of ten children on £60 p.a., Disney immediately dashed off two letters to the SPG. Within five days Singleton passed a successful interview with Bishop Perry's commissaries; within seven weeks he and his family were on a ship to Port Phillip.[36]

Samuel Wilberforce's missionary preaching tours are well known, but the preaching of the Reverend Dr Samuel Hinds, a former West Indian missionary himself, electrified several Trinity College Dublin undergraduates. In his audience was Francis Russell, the young student we met at the beginning of this chapter. Russell's missionary zeal issued in cultivating three fellow students for Australian service, in addition to his own thirty years of service in the Australian colonies.[37] Such networks might also help to explain why, in 1850, a third of Western Australian clergymen and a large contingent in Port Phillip were Irish.[38] Russell's Irishness embodies a key influence that provides a further challenge to an imperial High Church ideal.

"HIS MOTHER WAS AN IRISHWOMAN": IRISH IDENTITY AND AUSTRALIAN ANGLICANISM

To what extent did the Irishness of the clergy matter to them? There is substantial evidence that it did matter, which fits with Ronayne's findings about the majority of the Anglo-Irish immigrants of this period.[39] Contemporary observers identified the clergy's Irishness in their confident reformism, combativeness, strong-mindedness, and sense of superiority. Roy Foster labels this the "ascendancy mind": a use of "wit, satire, rhetoric and verbal dexterity that even now characterises an Irish style" and that has its antecedents in Swift, Burke, Congreve, and Sheridan.[40] This was probably what Lady Jane Franklin had in mind when she described the outspoken Reverend John Keane as a "mercurial Irishman."[41] Another shrewd contemporary English observer, Anthony Trollope, commented that the Irish clergyman was "of course, the son of an Irish Protestant gentleman," who sucked high Protestant principles in with his mother's milk. "Find him asleep," Trollope suggested, "and you will find him preaching with a long-protracted, indignant, low-church, Protestant snore, very eloquent as to the scarlet woman [the Church of Rome]." For Australian evangelical clergy an Irish background tended to enhance their Protestant identity, colouring their anti-Catholicism and suspicions of Anglo-Catholicism, though most lacked the extreme sectarian outlook of later Irish migrants, partly because their experience of Ireland predated the Ulster revival of 1859 and Gladstone's inflammatory Home Rule proposals of 1886.[42] Several Irish clergymen, the majority of whom were evangelicals, were nevertheless involved in controversies with Tractarians, Roman Catholics, and even Methodists: Beamish, Russell, Keane, and Fulton conducted sermon and pamphlet wars with opponents in NSW; Macartney did the same in Port Phillip; as did Browne and Fry in Tasmania; and King in Western Australia. Several of these men also did battle with their own bishops over issues ranging from fears of Catholic inroads into Anglicanism to dissatisfaction with their parish post. The Reverend Thomas Wigmore took Bishop Nixon of Hobart to court after Nixon sacked him on apparently inadequate grounds. This notorious case helped to precipitate a parliamentary inquiry into clergy discipline in the colonies. It is instructive to compare historian Malcolm Prentis's finding for Presbyterian clergymen that the greater "evangelical warmth" of Queensland Presbyterianism was "a clear inheritance from the Irish."[43] At the other end of the spectrum, however, Rowland Davies and William Walsh were leading Anglo-Catholic exponents in Tasmania and NSW, respectively (as was Henry Fry in Tasmania before his evangelical "conversion" in 1850). At the extreme end Thomas Rogers converted to Roman Catholicism after quitting the Anglican ministry.[44]

There is little doubt that the Irish clergy's experience of being a minority church in Ireland equipped them to minister effectively in a voluntary church in the Australian colonies.[45] It is also likely that a strong professional ethos was produced by having worked in the Irish system where, unlike in the English Church, most benefices were in the gift of bishops. Trollope suggests that clergy tended therefore to be rewarded on the basis of merit over private patronage.[46]

After seventy years of ministry the Reverend Hussey Macartney observed that "there is something in Irish Christian love and family affection which you do not meet anywhere else. The Irish not only feel, but show feelings."[47] An emphasis on distinctively Celtic traits was likewise evident in Scotsman John Gregor's remark that his visit with John Balfour included "a real Scotch welcome of gentlemanly kindness."[48] Elsewhere Macartney referred to an acquaintance as "a truly excellent man, of sense and intelligence, in short his mother was an Irishwoman."[49] One of Macartney's lectures to the Melbourne YMCA captures something of the stylistic flourish and anti-Catholic bite of his Irish Protestantism:

> Undisguised infidelity is the plain, undiluted poison which man sickens at and rejects. Popery is the drugged wine-cup, sweet, sparkling, refreshing, which we madly quaff, and return to with aggravated thirst; less able to resist the more it intoxicates; and needing its refreshing coolness to our lips the more, because its poison has inflamed the brain, and withered all the vital functions. For ages after ages have nations been made drunk with the wine of her deceiving … [W]e forget, that if Rome has her absurdities, human nature has hers, and that the one suits itself to the other; so that, like a garment, it only fits the more closely, and is worn the more easily.[50]

IRISHNESS AND THE IDEAL COLONIAL CLERGYMAN

The Irish also figure prominently in contemporary Australian discussions of the ideal colonial clergyman. Qualities of manliness, a robust constitution, and a muscular brand of Christianity were all valued for colonial work, although these notions were not grounded in martial or imperial aims. Such qualities also commended clergy to the military officers and elite with whom clergy often worked closely, as we saw in the case of Thomas Rogers, who on one occasion returned the blow of a drunk military officer. Another Irish clergyman, Thomas O'Reilly, was remembered for his bold preaching and the "splendid physique" he had honed while rowing kilometres to visit far-flung parishioners.[51]

Numerous accounts exist of clergymen preaching to bushrangers at gunpoint. One Australian clergyman recounted the story of Henry

Fulton, whom he described as "a characteristic specimen of the fearless Irishman":

> Once three bushrangers sprang out from a stone-quarry on the Western Road, between Parramatta and Penrith, and called him to stop. He was driving his gig and had a young man with him. Instead of stopping he thrashed his horse into a gallop and when the bushrangers fired at him he called out, "Fire away, boys! Fire away!" The gig was riddled, and for many years after the bullet-holes might be seen in the back of the old trap. Luckily he and his companion escaped unhurt.[52]

Perhaps the complete package of a boys' own parson was the Reverend David Boyd, who influenced a generation of young colonial men as a teacher at the prestigious Sydney College. One of Boyd's most famous students, Rolf Boldrewood, author of *Robbery under Arms*, recalled Boyd fondly:

> He was an accomplished person … [a] first-rate classical scholar, with a fair knowledge of French, German and Italian – possibly Hebrew for he knew pretty well everything, from astronomy to single-stick fencing to comparative philology. He rode, drove, shot, fished, painted, was musical, mathematical – a mesmerist, doubtless … We boys looked upon him as a successor of the Admirable Crichton, and revered him accordingly.[53]

Boldrewood's reflections hint at the significant contribution of Irish clergymen to educational and literary life, which I discuss in detail elsewhere.[54]

The few literary representations of Australian clergy before 1850 generally emphasize their ability to be all things to all men – and women. Thus the Reverend Chargreaves, the protagonist in the serial fiction of the Anglican *Sydney Guardian* (1848–50), defied bushrangers, an inadequate stipend, and the rigours of bush life to pioneer a rural church. Chargreaves was, in the anonymous author's words,

> ardent, and affectionate … [and] few persons ever exercised more watchfulness, or discharged more faithfully the duties which adorn a Christian man's life. Few men were ever blessed with a more

> generous disposition, or a higher order of intellect; it was impossible not to love him.[55]

Tellingly, he was also of Irish descent, having migrated to England and then Australia to work as a clergyman. He stands in contrast with another stock clerical character in the colonial fiction of the day: the scholarly Jesuit, straight from central casting, the "black-clad, sinister, sacerdotal enemy, who never walks but always glides."[56]

Some recruiters of clergy were nevertheless hesitant about Irish clergy.[57] The Reverend Henry Wolfenden, a metropolitan recruiter for the SPG, wrote of one applicant that, although he was a "good quiet useful clergyman," this was "not sufficient to counter balance his Irishism & six children."[58] Englishmen generally considered Trinity College Dublin inferior to Oxbridge, while Bishops Charles Perry and William Broughton occasionally complained about their Irish clergy.[59] "Although they possess many valuable qualities," Perry admitted to Broughton,

> there is in almost all of them more or less of wrongheadedness … which is continually bringing them into difficulties, and putting them into a false position. I … feel very thankful when I can secure the services of a sound, sensible, sober minded Englishman.[60]

Francis Nixon, bishop of Hobart, thanked the SPG for "an excellent and zealous clergymen in the person of Mr Fry. He is the most dutiful son of the Church in the Island: not, at all times, discreet – but then he is an Irishman."[61] Such concerns were not entirely unfounded, as we have seen. "Celtic warmth" could sometimes denote a loose cannon, as John Keane's bishop found out when he heard that Keane was facing the courts for slashing the arm of a trespassing convict with a sabre.[62]

Prentis notes the same reticence about Irish clergy among Presbyterians. One Scottish minister complained that they represented a "coarser development of Christianity than our countrymen do. Our people do not like them."[63] Nevertheless, Perry's most valuable clergyman and choice for archdeacon was Macartney, while his clerical roster included long-serving Irish clergymen such as Francis Russell, Peter Beamish, John Cheyne, Francis Hales, and William Singleton. Both Perry and other bishops, especially Nixon in Tasmania, continued to accept significant numbers of Irish clergymen, the latter bishop to a diocese in which a quarter of the clergymen were Irish-born.

IRELAND, EMPIRE, AND AUSTRALIAN ANGLICANISM, 1788–1850

In conclusion, it is fair to say that Francis Russell's plea – for the Antient Church of Ireland to be mindful of her St Columbas and Gaels – was heard with regard to the Australian colonies. Russell himself followed in St Columba's itinerant footsteps, earning a reputation as "the Apostle of the Western District." The national backgrounds and careers of Australian Irish clergy like Russell challenge recent scholarly accounts of imperial Anglican designs, or a Coleridgean clerisy of an English gentlemanly elite, charged with a mission to promote Englishness and empire. Few Australian clergymen, Irish or otherwise, were bred on the cricket grounds of the Clarendon schools; and few flexed a muscular Christianity or a clerical vocation that was grounded in English or imperial loyalty. Many Australian Anglican clergymen, as we have seen, were a different kind of Irish and evangelical gentleman. Their Irishness mattered to them and to their contemporaries. It was expressed in predominantly Protestant identities; in a self-understanding that foregrounded Irish over British identities; in their critical and liberal posture towards both church and state; and in their significant influence on the Australian colonies' formative cultural and intellectual life.

This chapter's use of prosopography, or "collective biography," also suggests its potency as a methodological tool for exploring social history, not least aspects of the Irish diaspora such as its social, educational and national backgrounds; migration networks; professional cohorts; friendship groups; and coteries. Scholars such as John Tosh highlight the value of prosopography for increasing the precision of factual statements about the past. "Impressionistic estimates," he argues, are replaced by "vigorously controlled calculation" to reveal overall trends as well as the variations and discrepancies within them.[64] This is another reason for the importance of the Church of Ireland as an influential subgroup of the Irish diaspora. Using clerical indices such as *Crockfords Clerical Directory*, for example, provides one of the few techniques that allows for the disaggregation of Irish Anglicans from other British Protestants. Further promising avenues of future research lie in determining the continued expression of Irish as political Liberals in relation to issues such as penal reform and other humanitarian issues.

John Mackenzie once remarked that Scots missionaries painted the nineteenth-century British World a tartan colour. I want to suggest that

Irish Anglican clergymen added a prominent tinge of green – and perhaps a dash of orange.[65]

NOTES

1 F.T.C. Russell to SPG, 16 December 1846, Canberra, NLA, USPG, Australian Papers, Candidates' Papers, 1821–98, AJCP Mfm M1223.

2 James Bonwick and Ada Cambridge, quoted in http://www.swvic.org/coleraine/holy_trinity_coleraine.htm (viewed 29 June 2012).

3 Prentis, "Presbyterian Ministry in Australia," 57, has, however, demonstrated the importance of Irish clergymen in filling "the breach of a depleted establishment" in the 1850s.

4 That is to say, forty-nine clergymen out of a total of 235.

5 Jupp and York, *Birthplaces of the Australian People*, 2, 11–27.

6 Jupp, *English in Australia,* 1, 7. Jupp adds that, because Australia was colonized and developed after 1788 by more settlers from England than from anywhere else, "their distinctive characters and experiences have often been overlooked or taken as the norm to which all others must conform."

7 This is suggested in the number of Australian-bred clergy who returned to serve in Australia after studying overseas. For an immigrant clergyman who thought Australia far superior to the old country, see Strickland, *Australian Pastor*, 62–3.

8 Jupp and York, *Birthplaces of the Australian People*, 2, 11–27; Jupp, *English in Australia*, 1, 7; Haig, *Victorian Clergy*, 123–6. For a useful introduction to the background and context of the metropolitan Irish Church, see Acheson, *History of the Church of Ireland*, especially for Church of Ireland Evangelicals and low churchmen and their writings during the 1830s-40s; Bowen, "A.R.C. Dallas"; Hempton, *Religion and Political Culture*; and Yates, *Religious Condition of Ireland* (Yates is less sympathetic to Irish Evangelicals). For Irish clergy generally, see Barnard and Neely, *Clergy of the Church of Ireland*.

9 Knight, *Church and English Society*, 125.

10 Analysis of fathers' occupations and university education suggests that forty-two out of forty-eight clergymen had middle- to upper-class social backgrounds. Fathers' occupations are not known for nine out of forty-eight clergymen, but their social location can be pieced together from university attendance and other assorted sources of evidence. Some were sizars, suggesting a humbler background than those of the substantial middle class. See Gladwin, "Australian Anglican Clergymen," chap. 1, sec. 6, for methodology and categories of social background. For the Anglo-Irish

"Ascendancy" in Australia during our period, see Ronayne, *First Fleet to Federation,* 3–7. For the Anglo-Irish in Ireland, see Foster, *Modern Ireland.*

11 Some forty-three clergymen were educated at a university: thirty-nine at Trinity College, Dublin, three at Oxford, and one at Cambridge. Anthony Trollope's observation in, "The Irish Beneficed Clergyman," *Pall Mall Gazette* (1866), 110, that the Irish clergyman was "of course, the son of an Irish Protestant gentleman," would appear to fit the colonies as well as the metropole. Trollope adds that the Irish clergyman was almost always "educated at Trinity, Dublin" and there "indoctrinated with those high Protestant principles" that they take in with their mother's milk.

12 Ronayne, *First Fleet to Federation*, 12–13. For the motivation of Anglican clergy's service in Australian prior to 1850, see Gladwin, "Australian Anglican Clergymen," 127–50.

13 Russell, *Wish of Distinction.*

14 Gladwin, "Flogging Parsons?" The substance of the following few paragraphs on Irish clergy and convicts is adapted from this journal article.

15 Macquarie to Bathurst, 22 October 1821, *Historical Records of Australia* (hereafter HRA), Canberra, Commonwealth of Australia, ser. 1, vol. 10 (1971), 556.

16 Brisbane to Bathurst, 2 September 1822, HRA, ser. 1, vol. 10 (1971), 730, 738.

17 Wilmot Horton to Brisbane, 7 September 1822, HRA, ser. 1, vol. 10, (1971), 782–3. The Rev. Thomas Hassall also signed the document.

18 Thomas Rogers, *Correspondence*; Rogers, *Review*; Naylor, "Tale of Norfolk Island," 1:16 ; "Extract of a Paper by the Rev. T.B. Naylor, addressed to Lord Stanley," n.d. [1846], in UK Parl. Papers, Commons, 785 (1847): 68–73, 76; Ison, *Appeal to the Secretary of State*; Henry Fry to W.E. Gladstone, 17 August 1846, and Earl Grey to Lt Gov Sir W. Denison, 5 February 1847, in UK Parl. Papers, *Convict Discipline and Transportation: Correspondence on the subject of Convict Discipline and Transportation*, 785 (1847): 188–91, 193; [Henry Fry], *Herald of Tasmania*, 1 August 1845; *Hobart Town Herald*, 25 March 1846; Fry, *System of Penal Discipline*, 160–97; W.H. Browne to Rowland Davies, 18 October 1849, NS419/1/2, SLTAS, Hobart; Marriott, *Is a Penal Colony Reconcilable*. Most Van Diemen's Land and New South Wales clergymen signed the anti-transportation petitions of the bishops of Sydney and Tasmania.

19 Kingsley, *Recollections of Geoffrey Hamlyn*; Barry, *Life and Death of John Price*, 31–6.

20 Rogers, *Correspondence*, 201–2.

21 W. Foster Rogers, "Man's Inhumanity, Being a Chaplain's Chronicles of Norfolk Island in the Forties," typescript MSS C214, f. 3, Mitchell Library, Sydney; *Courier* (Hobart), 14 March 1856.

22 The martinet commandant, John Price, on hearing of this practice, abused Rogers in front of some convicts, declaring it "a bad custom." In reply, Rogers asked Price "if he did not think it a human and friendly thing … to explain the depositions of some of the men who could hardly read or write; and was not humanity a part of religion?" See Rogers, *Correspondence*, 27–8.

23 Rogers, *Correspondence*; Rogers, *Review*. Nixon's opposition to Rogers originated in Rogers's criticisms of episcopal inaction in the face of government persecution.

24 Rogers, *Correspondence*, 25–6, 58.

25 Ibid., *Review*, 5.

26 As was the pamphlet of Englishmen Thomas Naylor. See Earl Grey to Lt Gov. Sir W. Denison, Downing Street, 30 September 1846, 5 February 1847, in UK Parl. Papers, Commons, 785, 1847: 66–7.

27 Fry, *System of Penal Discipline*, 205–7.

28 Carey, "Religion and Society," 187. Similarly, Ronayne avers that gentlemen "by training and inclination, their loyalty was to the idea of a civilised liberal empire and to the notion of progress." See Ronayne, *Irish Supremacy*, 8.

29 See *The Annual Report of the Colonial Church and School Society* (London: the Colonial Church and School Society, 1851). For a recent scholarly account of the Colonial Church Society, see Carey, *God's Empire*, 148–69.

30 For the activities of Irwin, Noel, and Bickersteth, see the society's annual reports, the Committee Minute Book 1839–42, London, Guildhall Library, Colonial Church Society, CCS/MS/15673; and the General Committee Minute Book 1850–55, London, Guildhall Library, Colonial Church Society, CCS/MS/15674. The minute books cover the periods from 1839 to 1842 and 1850 to 1855 onwards, with gaps apparently due to bomb damage during the Second World War. For the society's early history, see the *Record*, 12 October 1835 (for an early advertisement outlining the society's intentions); and Mullins, *Our Beginnings*, 3–20. Important figures in the early formation of the society in June 1823 include several Evangelical grandees: John Wells MP, Josiah Pratt, Edward Bickersteth, Daniel Wilson, Samuel Crowther, Lord Liverpool, Henry Bathurst, Lord Gambier, William Wilberforce MP, and John Gladstone MP. According to Mullins, *Our*

Beginnings, 13, Irwin secured crucial early assistance from the patronage of Lord Teignmouth, later Lord Barham.

31 *The Annual Report of the Colonial Church and School Society* (London: Colonial Church and School Society 1851), 32–3. For Mayers, see the Committee Minute Book 1839–42, 14 July, 18 August 1840, London, Guildhall Library, Colonial Church Society, CCS/MS/15673, fols. 118, 125. In 1840 Mayers returned from a Tasmanian chaplaincy to propose the recruitment of two itinerary missionaries to Tasmania. Fluent in several European languages, Mayers also offered to take a tour in Spain on behalf of the CCS, although his offer was declined.

32 "List of Missionaries and Agents," *Colonial Church and School Society Annual Report* (London: Colonial Church and School Society 1851), x. Altogether the society had eighteen clergymen, sixty-three catechists, and twenty female teachers serving in thirteen colonies by 1851. The Rev. E.H. Bryan had served in Tasmania before being transferred, while the first clergyman, Rev. Giustiniani, had been asked to resign in 1837 over his advocacy of Aborigines in Swan River colony (Western Australia).

33 The Bush Church Aid Society, which grew directly out of the work of the CCS, was founded in 1919.

34 C.R. Elrington to Joshua Watson, 26 June 1840, Canberra, NLA USPG, Unbound Australian Papers, Dio. Sydney, Western Australia, Letters Various 1837–42, AJCP Mfm ML1222.

35 John Hutt to Mr Phillips, 19 May 1842, Canberra, NLA USPG, Unbound Australian Papers, Spiritual needs of WA 1837–41, box 16, AJCP Mfm ML1222. Hutt was constrained by the Ripon Regulations. For their application to Western Australia, see Strong, "Church and State," 526–9.

36 Disney to Ernest Hawkins, 15 and 17 March 1849; Chaplain Archbishop of Dublin to Ernest Hawkins, 17 March 1849; Mr Cooper to Ernest Hawkins, 22 March 1849; William Singleton to Ernest Hawkins, 3 and 28 May, 5 June 1849. All of the preceding to be found in Canberra, NLA, USPG, Home, Australian Papers, including Candidates Papers 1821–98, AJCP Mfm M1222.

37 F.T.C. Russell to SPG, 16 December 1848; Charles Strong to SPG, 27 August 1846. Both of the preceding to be found in F.T.C. Russell Candidate Papers, Canberra, NLA, USPG, Australian Papers, Candidates' Papers, 1821–98, AJCP Mfm M1223.

38 J.W. Schoales to Ernest Hawkins, 11 and 15 February, 25 March 1841, Canberra, NLA, USPG, Unbound Australian Papers, Spiritual needs of WA 1837–41, box 16, AJCP Mfm ML1222.

39 Ronayne, *Irish Supremacy*, 6–15.
40 Roy Foster quoted in Ronayne, *Irish Supremacy*, 5–6.
41 For Lady Franklin's diary comment on the Rev. John Keane, see Franklin, *This Errant Lady*, 25. Contemporaries routinely singled out a clergyman's Irishness in terms of wit, loquacity, or an adversarial bent.
42 Grant, *Victoria's Debt*, 23. See also Trollope's comments in, Trollope, "Irish Beneficed Clergyman," 106, 110.
43 Prentis, "Presbyterian Ministry," 63. Anthony Trollope observed that the Irish clergyman was "of course, the son of an Irish Protestant gentleman." He added that the Irish clergyman was almost always "educated at Trinity, Dublin," and there "indoctrinated with those high Protestant principles." His observations would appear to fit the colonies as well as the metropole. Trollope, "Irish Beneficed Clergyman," 110.
44 It should be noted that, although William Dry's father was Irish, Dry was born in Tasmania and was the first Tasmanian-born man to receive holy orders.
45 Grant, *Victoria's Debt*, 23; Grant, *Episcopally Led*, 24–5, 28.
46 See Anthony Trollope's observations to this effect in "Irish Beneficed Clergyman," 111–12. Roberts, "Private Patronage," 204–5, notes the number of English livings in the gift of bishops doubling in the middle forty years of the nineteenth century. More clergy were also buying up livings and advowsons. Samuel Wilberforce's efforts in this regard are the most well known.
47 Curry, "Macartney," 9.
48 Gregor, "Extracts from Journals, 29.
49 Grant, *Victoria's Debt*, 9.
50 Macartney, *Antichrist*, 15–16.
51 Neil O'Reilly, "O'Reilly, Thomas (1819–1881)," *Australian Dictionary of Biography*, National Centre of Biography, Australian National University, http://adb.anu.edu.au/biography/oreilly-thomas-4339/text6985 (viewed 13 November 2011).
52 Hassall, *In Old Australia*, 28. Few early clergy memoirs did not contain at least one such episode. The colonial press likewise praised clergy who took such stands against bushrangers. See, for example, the *Cornwall Chronicle*, 28 October 1837.
53 Thomas Alexander Browne (also known as Rolf Boldrewood), quoted by his daughter in the *Argus*, 18 April 1925. For Boyd, see *Newcastle Morning Herald* (NSW), 9 April 1892 (obituary).
54 See Gladwin, "Journalist in the Rectory," especially in relation to the published writings of Henry Fulton, John Schoales, and Henry Fry (Fry even edited a number of Hobart newspapers).

55 "Tale of a Township, Chapter II," *Sydney Guardian*, 1 June 1848.

56 Robert Lee Wolff, quoted by McKiernan, "Introduction," 15–16, 43.

57 A. Hamilton to T.H. Scott, 7 October 1826, Oxford, Rhodes House Library, USPG, X Series Miscellaneous, X/154, fols. 286–9. For the various applications to the SPG during these years, see their correspondence in the Candidates' Book, Oxford, RHL, USPG, miscellaneous, X ser., X/106. In 1826 the secretary of the SPG and Chaplain-General Archdeacon Hamilton complained that, amid applications to Australia was an "abundance of a different description" from the sort of men required (the sort required consisting of those with a university education, unmarried, and with experience in teaching both the lower and upper classes). "Among these applications, moreover, were: several Irish clergymen, who have renounced the errors of Popery, whose pretensions are backed by the Parliamentary influence of the opponents of emancipation – but I am not disposed to encourage such tenders of service, as it is difficult to ascertain the true character of such convict[ion]s."

58 Henry Wolfenden to USPG, 8 May 1850, Canberra, NLA, USPG, Home, Candidates Papers 1849–50, AJCP Mfm M1317.

59 Haig, *Victorian Clergy*, 119; Hardwick, "Anglican Church Expansion," 374; W.G. Broughton to Edward Coleridge, 8 May 1850, Sydney, Moore Theological College Library, Broughton MSS Papers. Broughton hoped that the SPG would not be "induced to accept too a large proportion of *Irish* graduates" (emphasis in original).

60 Charles Perry to W.G. Broughton, 7 June 1850, quoted in Hardwick, "Anglican Church Expansion," 374.

61 F.R. Nixon to Ernest Hawkins, 9 January 1844, Canberra, NLA, USPG, SPG/C/MSS, Unbound Australian Papers, Diocese of Tasmania, 1842–49, box 17, AJCP Mfm M1470. Some of Nixon's most outspoken clerical opponents were Irishmen: Fry, Wigmore, Rogers, and Browne. See also Bishop Short's comment, quoted in Hilliard, *Godliness and Good Order*, 15, that he was looking for "a few more able good men" to command "the Colony in which Churchmen predominate and which is thoroughly English in notions & habits."

62 For Keane, see Colonial Secretary to John Keane, 21 March, 11 April 1831, Sydney, State Records of NSW (SRNSW), Colonial Secretary Outward Letters (CSOL), 4/3616, Mfm 2982. For Wilton, see Colonial Secretary to Charles Wilton, 17 March 1840, Sydney, SRNSW, CSOL, 4/3619, Mfm 2983.

63 The Rev. George Mackie, c. 1863, quoted in Prentis, "Presbyterian Ministry," 63.

64 John Tosh, quoted in Jones, "Researching Groups," 331. See also Tosh, *Pursuit of History*, 77, 165, 168, on the value of prosopography for analyzing defined groups of elites.

65 For John Mackenzie's work on Scots missions and empire, see his "Making Black Scotsmen."

14

"God Sent Me Here to Raise a Society": Irishness, Protestantism, and Colonial Identity in New South Wales[1]

DIANNE HALL

In 1840, James Robinson, a Methodist preacher from Fintona, County Tyrone, sent a long open letter to the Monaghan-based *Northern Standard*. His letter was designed to encourage emigration to the colony of New South Wales and was enthusiastic about the weather and business opportunities. He also commented on the number of fellow religious from Fermanagh and Tyrone he had met since arriving in Wollongong two years before.

> I found that 2/3 of the people here were from Ireland. I took advantage of this and spoke to any who appeared moral. I made out 5 who were members of the society in Ireland. I reasoned with them and got them all to consent to come to my cottage next Sunday morning, they all came and surely it was a weeping melting time. I formed a class, got their names, I then proposed preaching every Sunday evening if I got a place to preach in ... [Mr B] lives one mile out of town on the Government road among a number of Tyrone and Fermanagh Protestants, we expect to raise a society amongst them shortly.[2]

While most of those who left Ireland in the nineteenth century came from the rural south and west of the country and were largely Catholic, a significant group originated in Ulster, which was the most populous and prosperous Irish province throughout the nineteenth century – and many of these emigrants were, like James Robinson, Protestant.[3] The nine counties of Ulster, which were home to about one-third of the total

Irish population in the late nineteenth-century, supplied 29 percent of all Irish emigrants in the period from 1851 to 1920, so that in total some 1.25 million people left Ulster during the seventy years between 1850 and 1920.[4] The numbers choosing to come to the Australian colonies, one of the furthest and most expensive destinations, were always less than those choosing nearby ports in England or the lure of North America.[5] It was in recognition of this that the colonial authorities instituted various assistance schemes designed to augment the slow stream of those wealthy enough to pay their own fares. Assisted migration to the Australian colonies was enthusiastically taken up by Irish-born migrants, both Catholic and Protestant, with over a quarter of a million arriving through one of these schemes between 1836 and 1919.[6]

Analysis of the denominational differentiation of this migrant stream is not as straightforward as it is in other destinations, such as the United Kingdom and North America, as Australian census data were only kept in aggregate form, and enumerators' forms were routinely destroyed. In its published format, the categories of place of birth and religion were not cross-tabulated until the 1911 census, meaning that, for the nineteenth century, it is not possible to extract data on the number of overseas-born of any particular religious denomination. In the 1911 census, 71 percent of Irish-born Australians were Catholic, with 14 percent Anglican, 9 percent Presbyterian, and 3 percent Methodist. The data, however, are only broken down to the broad level of the six states and two territories, so while these aggregate figures are useful, they cannot explain small- or medium-scale settlement patterns based on place of birth and religion.[7] On the basis of these figures, however, it is usually generalized that between 25 and 30 percent of Irish-born migrants to the Australian colonies were Protestant.[8]

The census data on place of birth and religion were given separately at the level of regions and townships after 1856, so settlement patterns of Irish-born, Catholics, and Protestants, for example, can be analyzed separately. These data are not, however, differentiated to the level of county of birth and, of course, are not cross-tabulated, so it is not possible to correlate the origins of migrants and their place of settlement within Australia. Some generalizations can be made, in that probably a number of the Presbyterians were from northeast Ulster, where Presbyterianism was strongest. However, apart from that, more nuanced analysis needs additional data.[9]

Largely because of these inherent difficulties with available population figures, research into Irish Protestant identity in Australia has to date been relatively muted compared with analysis of Irish Catholic settlers and identities. One of the most productive methods of inquiry to date is found in histories of individuals through analysis of collections of letters. Both David Fitzpatrick and Patrick O'Farrell include letters from Protestant Ulster settlers in their analyses of Irish migration and letter writing.[10] There has also been some work on histories of Anglo-Irish professional migrants and, more recently, analysis of the Loyal Orange Order has begun with Fitzpatrick's fine study of the records of the South Australian Institution.[11]

Identifying Irish Protestants within colonial settlements is thus not easy on a macro level; however, using datasets such as the records of Irish-born migrants generated by the various assisted migrations schemes, together with careful analysis of census data that can be cross-tabulated, it is possible to identify clusters of Irish-born Protestants in the Australian colonies. Analysis of the available data on counties of origins of migrants indicate that there were several distinct clusters, with the most numerous emigrants to the Australian colonies coming from the south-central midlands of Clare, Limerick, and Tipperary. There was also a secondary cluster in the south Ulster borderlands of Fermanagh/Tyrone, Cavan, and Armagh.[12] Further investigation of this secondary cluster reveals that a disproportionate percentage of the Anglican/Church of Ireland population from this area of Ulster chose to migrate to New South Wales.[13] In the colonies, analysis of the available census data for 1856 and 1861 shows that there was a substantial Protestant element to the Irish-born population of several areas in Victoria, and, during the nineteenth century, this was consistent in the area around Kiama, south of Sydney.[14]

There were two main ways that migrants from the United Kingdom, including Ireland, could obtain assistance with the fares to the Australian colonies – either through direct application to the Emigration Commission in London or through nomination from a friend or relative who paid a deposit in the colonies to assist with their passage.[15] One reason that the various assistance schemes are so important to the study of Irish migration to the Australian colonies concerns the remarkably efficient bureaucracy that collected identifying information pertaining to all the arrivals. The remittance, or deposit, scheme included information not only on emigrants' names but also on their home addresses, parents' names, religion, and literacy standards as well as the names and addresses of those who had paid the deposit for their voyage.[16]

Efforts to combine this data with settlement studies within the colonies have been hampered by the difficulties in identifying large numbers of individuals from the cluster of sending counties and then tracing them through different areas of the colonies. This is especially acute when the analysis is extended beyond the arriving generation. Surname searches have proved very unreliable as so many of these Irish Protestant migrants had surnames in common with Scots and English.[17] However, using methodologies based on demographic-, family-, and locality-based studies, it is possible to locate and trace groups of families from their point of migration through to the second and sometimes third generation. Linked methodologies of family reconstruction and individual biographies of groups of migrants allow for analysis of specific localities and circumstances that cannot be reached through broad or aggregate data approaches. Elliott, in his pioneering study of Protestant migrants, uses these methods to follow his group from its townlands in Tipperary to Canada, including further internal migration after its initial settlement.[18] The wealth of detail that can be gleaned from individual biographical data in the Australian context has also been demonstrated by David Fitzpatrick's painstaking research into letter-writers and their families.[19] Family reconstruction and collective biographies of Ulster Protestant migrants and their families allows for identification and analysis of threads of ethnic, religious, and social identities over time and place. As, with archival digitalization and a broadening of public interest in family history, more data become available, there will be more opportunities to use these methodologies. In this study, data on Protestant migrants from the identified Ulster cluster of origin is used in conjunction with extensive data on the Kiama destination cluster to extend our understanding of Irish Protestant familial, communal, and religious links.

ULSTER IN KIAMA

It has long been recognized that the area south of Sydney around Kiama and Wollongong, where James Robinson and his family settled, had a high concentration of Irish Protestants from the 1830s onwards.[20] Throughout the nineteenth century, the Kiama area became the place of first settlement for significant numbers of Ulster Protestant migrants. This was where they could find friends and relatives from neighbouring parishes in Ireland.[21] In Kiama, according to the 1861 census, 21 percent were born in Ireland, with an overall Catholic population of 9.5 percent, meaning there were a large number of Irish Protestants living in the township.[22] Many of these farming families then moved again in the next generation, resettling in the Northern Rivers area, north of Sydney, close to the New South Wales/Queensland border. These groups of families formed a coherent, self-consciously Protestant group with multilayered narratives of social, ethnic, and religious identities. As such, this group provides an opportunity to analyze how Irish Protestantism was lived in a colonial setting, its intense localism infused with knowledge of global networks and events.

The majority of the Protestants who settled in the Kiama area were migrants from northwest Ulster, many of them members of the Church of Ireland and Methodist circuits from a triangle of parishes in Donegal, Tyrone, and Fermanagh. Some of these parishes had a particularly high Anglican population, many of whom migrated. For example, between 1858 and 1884 the parish of Derryvullan, County Fermanagh, had an Anglican population of 49.4 percent. When the religion of all the migrants who arrived through the deposit scheme is calculated, 73 percent of those from Derryvullan were Anglican, indicating that there was a significant and sustained drain of Anglicans from parishes such as Derryvullan and its neighbouring parishes of Drumkeeran and Magheracross to New South Wales.[23] Methodism also found fertile ground in Fermanagh after its initial introduction in 1780, with a healthy revivalist campaign in the 1850s and continuing open-air preaching.[24] The chain migration of many of these families had started in the 1830s, with targeted recruiting of migrants by Protestant Ulster-born estate owners such as the Tyrone-born Osborne brothers and James Mackey Gray from Armagh, who were looking for tenant farmers to clear the thick rainforest that covered the rugged landscape in the Kiama and Wollongong districts.[25] On lecture tours during the 1830s, Alick Osborne recruited migrants from his home parish and its surrounds, eventually arranging for the passage of three shiploads.[26] He had a preference for Protestant workers, and, once settled in and around the Kiama area, many of these people then set in motion a strong chain migration. People from these clusters of parishes in Fermanagh, Cavan, and Tyrone used information and patronage networks to gain access to the bureaucratic systems of remittance and other assisted migration schemes. Under the remittance systems, operating between 1858 and 1884, friends or family lodged money in New South Wales to contribute to the passage and support of intending migrants. Intending migrants then needed references and support from "persons of note." These were often based around local religious networks, usually parish clergy, and the vast majority of the migrants using this system from Fermanagh and Cavan were Protestants.[27] In an analysis of six parishes in County Fermanagh, from which most emigrants departed using the deposit-assisted migration system, 14 percent initially settled in and around Kiama. Given that this is, of necessity, an underestimation since it only accounts for six parishes and only examines one particular series of assistance schemes, it clearly indicates that a significant stream of migrants from one area in Ulster who settled in one area of New South Wales.[28] It also means that many of the Anglican, Presbyterian, and Methodist congregations of Kiama and the hinterland villages of Jamberoo, Gerringong, Kangaroo Valley, and Kangaloon were from Ulster.[29]

These families cleared the subtropical cedar and eventually helped set up a thriving dairy industry. The younger members of these Kiama-region families then looked for their own land and headed north to the newly opened area known initially as the Big Scrub. Here, in the 1840s, two Ulster-born landowners opened up pastoral runs and the cedar trade. These and other landowners employed many of the younger generation from the Kiama region.[30] When these men had the means to select their own land they brought up members of their extended families from the Kiama and Wollongong districts.[31] The way these networks operated can be seen through the narratives related by the Hetherington and Crawford families, explaining their movement from the South Coast to the Big Scrub.

Christopher Hetherington was the Kiama-born son of Jane Hetherington, who had emigrated with her husband, four brothers, and their families. One of her brothers, George, had organized purchases of clearing leases in the heavily timbered region of Kiama. George Grey then organized for a group of his family and friends from neighbouring parishes in Fermanagh to settle on these clearing leases.[32] In a familiar pattern, young Christopher in turn married Jane Johnston, the daughter of other Fermanagh migrants who had settled in the Kiama region. He went to the Big Scrub, as the Northern Rivers area was known, in 1878, and when he returned he told anyone who would listen about the great opportunities he had seen. His obituary recorded that many people from the Kiama area stayed with his family at his home near Coraki, while they surveyed the land on offer in the Northern Rivers area.[33] Other families followed similar paths. William Crawford arrived in Kiama from Derryneve, Fermanagh, in 1863; his cousin John Johnston, almost certainly from the same family that Christopher Hetherington married into, had paid the deposit for him to travel under the remittance system. A few years earlier, John and his family had themselves migrated under the deposit scheme, with support from another family member. A year later, William used the same scheme to bring out two of his siblings, Robert and Sarah Jane. After working as a labourer on farms around Kiama, William got work in the Northern Rivers area with Samuel Grey just after the Selection Act was proclaimed. And then, liking what he saw, he selected land at Alstonville, where the Freeborn brothers, also from Fermanagh via Kiama, had selected the first blocks. A little later his brother Robert saved the money to select a property not far from William's. Their cousins, the Johnstons, then followed them to the Big Scrub. Then, in 1878, after the brothers had selected and cleared their farms in Alstonville, Robert paid the deposits for two more siblings, James and Caroline. Finally, in 1882, James in turn paid the deposits for their parents and the remaining siblings; however, they stayed in Ireland, probably due to the ill health of their elderly parents.[34]

William and his family maintained imaginative and symbolic connections with Fermanagh, with William telling his children stories of his own childhood, which his son remembered into old age. William signalled his connections with both his birthplace and the process of migration by naming his farm in Alstonville "Brookida" – "Ida" after the ship on which he had come to Australia and "Brook" almost certainly after Brook Hill, his home in Fermanagh. William's son Foreman later named his own farm near Alstonville "Fermanagh" to honour his father's birthplace. There is thus evidence of strong networks operating, keeping two and sometimes three generations of these farming families in close contact through information on availability of employment, land, and social groups.

PROTESTANT NETWORKS

These familial networks were underpinned by Protestant religious and political networks such as those mentioned by James Robinson in his open letter to the *Northern Standard*. The importance of the churches, with their regular rounds of social and religious activities, in nourishing and fostering communal migrant ethnic identities has long been recognized.[35] The social, religious, and political activities of these Irish Protestants often slip beneath the historical gaze because they are subsumed within the predominantly English character of mainstream Protestantism. An 1869 description of the Jamberoo Anglican Church, dominated by parishioners originally from Fermanagh parishes, gives an indication of the importance of the physical place of the church and the social space of church-going.

> Though the village is small there are farms all around, for miles, no lack of inhabitants. The farms are generally small with some exceptions but it is quite astonishing what numbers of people come from these rural abodes, situated here and there amongst the hills. On a Sunday the young men and young women come trooping down on horseback to attend the services of the Church you see horses every where round the fencing of the ground. They don't dream of leaving their horses at the Inn but ride direct into the church yard tie their horses or rather throw their bridles over the fence and at the end mount and away home.[36]

The English visitor was charmed by this rural idyll, and his description underlines the fact that church-going was a major social event for these families. The bonds of family and community were set within the plain stone walls of small churches like the Church of the Resurrection in Jamberoo, and when these young people were looking for marriage partners, many of them chosen from within this small, tight-knit community. The Noble family was only one of many families that engaged in significant inter-marriage with other Ulster Protestant families originally from neighbouring townlands in Fermanagh. When they first arrived, John Noble and his wife Anne Fletcher rented a property in Kiama, then they bought a farm in Jamberoo in the 1840s and, finally, a larger property in Kangaloon in the 1860s. All of their twelve children married spouses from other Fermanagh families before many moved on to Bexhill in the Northern Rivers.[37]

While the every-day importance of religious and ethnic affiliations of the Ulster Protestants can be lost within mainstream society, in moments of sectarian crises they move more fully into the spotlight. For this reason analysis of these crises is useful for illuminating more about these groups. In Kiama one such series of crises occurred in the aftermath of a self-confessed Fenian's assassination attempt on Prince Alfred in Sydney in March 1868. Fights between Irish Catholics and Orangemen were not uncommon in and around the streets of Kiama, particularly around the Beehive Hotel owned by Laurence O'Toole, an Irish-born Catholic. Throughout 1868 there were meetings and discussions about religion that ended with threats and counter-threats, with Protestants attending prayer meetings complaining that they felt under pressure from the Catholic community.[38] There were also anonymous letters sent to men who were known to be Orangemen, and these were reported in full detail in the local newspaper and even further afield in Sydney, increasing the sense of dread and threat. An article reprinted from a Kiama newspaper in the *Sydney Morning Herald* gives the characteristic tone: "Hints with other threats already published on the persons of loyal subjects surely affirm that there is evil lurking in our midst and that no trust or confidence can be reposed in our fellow men."[39]

All this tension then exploded when John Grey, one of the Fermanagh-born Anglican migrants and also the grand master of Loyal Orange Lodge (LOL) no. 5 at Jamberoo, reported that shots had been fired at him on the road between Jamberoo and Kiama. There was also a further incident when Grey reported that a fire that destroyed some of his home was the work of Fenians. Local Catholics were suspicious, and one of them, Frank McCaffery, reported that a mutual neighbour rushed down to assist the Grey family and found them all sitting calmly outside the burning building with their best furniture safely around them, including the big wooden screens used to divide the parlour during Orange Lodge meetings. He concluded that the fire had been deliberately lit.[40] This was not the end of the reported attacks on John Grey for his Orange beliefs. In November 1868, the *Kiama Pilot* reported that he had been shot at on the night of 5 November while an Orange Lodge celebration of Guy Fawkes Night was being held at his home.[41] The subsequent investigation cleared the three Catholic labourers initially charged with the shooting. Locally, there were suspicions that the attack had been staged by John Grey and his cousin Christopher Hetherington. John Grey, however, remained convinced of the threat posed by Irish Catholics in the area and reported the incidents to the Grand Lodge in Sydney.[42]

When members of these families moved to the Northern Rivers area, they also formed communities centred around farming, church-going, and membership in Protestant organizations such as the Orange Order. Again an episode of sectarianism brought their numbers as well as their concerns to wider attention. In 1886, the Lismore Loyal Orange Lodge no. 99 sponsored a visit by the self-styled "Escaped Nun," Edith O'Gorman, an Irish-American woman who had left an order of nuns in the 1860s and spent the rest of her life touring the world lecturing about the evils of convents and Catholicism.[43] In the aftermath of her second lecture, a group of irate Irish Catholics clashed with the Protestant audience, and the fracas descended into a riot that resulted in numerous arrests and a tense few days. On the day of her third lecture, about two thousand armed Protestants, mostly members of regional Orange lodges, marched in formation into Lismore from surrounding districts. The Sydney *Protestant Standard* reported that many of these men had come "filled with the spirit of Martyrs ... ready to fight and die. Some had made and signed wills before leaving and had said farewell to home and family."[44] The town was in lockdown. All the pubs were shut, the theatre cordoned off, and police were drafted from all over the district, along with perhaps as many as 125 specially sworn-in special constables (mostly members of the Orange Order).[45] In the event, Catholic Dean Doyle had calmed his congregation and the lecture went off smoothly with no reaction. Charges were laid over the riots, including against some of the Catholics, who were eventually convicted for assault.[46] Members of the Kiama Ulster Protestant families were also involved in the melee surrounding the O'Gorman lectures, including John Grey's cousin Christopher Hetherington and his father-in-law John Johnston, and Charles Staff, the brother-in-law of William Crawford.[47] While sectarianism was not the only defining feature of Ulster Protestants who settled in colonial New South Wales, the involvement of the same group of families in these two incidents suggests that their interpretation of their Protestant faith was imbued with a particular willingness to physically fight against what they perceived as the dangers of Catholicism.[48]

Aside from explosive episodes such as these, for the majority of Protestants from Ulster and their families, daily life in the farming districts around Kiama and Lismore comprised a round of church attendance alongside the social events of the Protestant calendar (e.g., 12 July and various events in November such as Empire Day and Guy Fawkes Night). Underpinning these events were the monthly meetings of the various Orange lodges, the Protestant Alliance Friendly Society, and the Australian Protestant Defence Association.

In February 1883, the Protestant Alliance celebrated its anniversary at no. 52 Mount Joy Lodge at Broughton Creek near Kiama with a march and picnic attended by about eight hundred people. The crowning glory of the march was the unfurling of the new Alliance Banner depicting a portrait of Queen Victoria on a background of blue and orange and, on the other side, a Londonderry Cathedral during the 1689 siege, with a section of the city walls. In the foreground, before the famous walls of Derry, was painted two ships sailing up the River Foyle to relieve the besieged city. As the newspaper report carefully outlined, this showed the ship, the *Mount Joy*, after which the Lodge was named. The justification for using this symbol of Protestantism was that the siege was the most important event connected with the Great Revolution of 1688, "which really laid the foundation of the power of the British Empire as the *head* of the Protestant world."[49] The present and past masters of the

Lodge, Hugh Boyd and John Grey, presided over proceedings. Both men were from Ulster Protestant families, and many of the families who attended the event would have been as well.

A particularly large number of Ulster Protestant settlers and their families who had originally settled in the Kiama region moved to the district around Clunes, near Lismore. In the 1891 census there were about 246 people living in the Clunes area.[50] There were as many as five Protestant churches in the township and no Catholic church, which underlined Clunes's reputation as a Protestant town. Clunes had many well-attended 12 July parades in the early decades of the twentieth century, when newspapers frequently recorded attendance of nearly a thousand.[51] In 1904, the parade along the main road in Clunes was accompanied by bands and members of the Orange Lodges from Clunes, Federal, Lismore, Dunoon, Rous, Byron Bay, and Murwillumbah, followed by speeches outlining the events of the Battle of the Boyne and the arguments for Protestant liberty as opposed to living under Catholicism.[52] There was a significant overlap in membership with the Protestant institutions in the town. The first worshipful master of the Clunes Orange Lodge was John Armstrong, who was also involved in building the Methodist church in Clunes, while another stalwart of the Lodge was David Weir, who took an active part in the formation of the Clunes Anglican church and parish.[53]

Previous research into Orange lodges in Australia has suggested that, by the second half of the nineteenth century, the majority of members were born in England, Wales, Scotland, and, increasingly, Australia rather than in Ireland.[54] While this is certainly true on the broad scale, there are significant regional variations, especially when the Australian-born sons and grandsons of Irish members are included. Analysis of the Orange lodges and Protestant organizations in the villages of Broughton Creek, Gerringong, and Jamberoo in the Kiama region; and in Clunes and Alstonville in the Northern Rivers area; reveals that there were a large number of members from Ulster families.[55] Some moved between the two areas at different times in their lives. John Weir was not untypical. The son of Ulster migrants, as a young man Weir spent time on the North Coast, before returning to Gerringong to marry another member of the old-time Fermanagh families. At his death, he was described as being a staunch member of the Church of England as well as a hard worker for both the Orange Lodge and the Good Templars.[56] His life story is similar to those of many of these Ulster families who moved between the south and north coasts, finding connections and networks in familiar faith and political organizations, such as the Protestant churches and the Orange Order.

The Clunes Loyal Orange Lodge had seventy-eight members in 1904 and forty-nine in 1910. Membership included sons and grandsons of Ulster migrants, so that nearly 50 percent of the members came from identified Ulster families, including four of the six 1910 office bearers.[57] This reflects the settlement patterns of the area, with many farms in the Clunes and Eureka areas worked by connected families of Ulster Protestant descent. Large families originally from Ulster and with strong links to the Kiama region, such as the Armstrong, Johnstons, Beacoms, and Walkers, lived on these farms, and some of their men were active members of the Loyal Orange Lodge.[58] In the Clunes Lodge minutes for August 1911 a clearance certificate for Robert Strong of Gerringong was discussed, so that he, a member of an Ulster Protestant family, could join the Clunes Lodge when he moved from the South. There was also a further motion about membership proposed and carried by R.E. Walker and A. Weir. All these men were sons of Ulster Protestant migrants, who had initially settled in the Kiama region before moving to the Northern Rivers area. This indicates that there was a strong, although by no means exclusive, Ulster Protestant inflection in the congregations and lodges of Clunes.

In 1897 Gerringong no. 115 Lodge had thirty-two members, of whom only five were not of Ulster background.[59] At social functions these men were joined by women of their families who sang and played the piano. The Ulster connections of the Gerringong Lodge were particularly noted in the speech at its annual anniversary celebration in 1907, when Reverend Waddell remarked: "Nowhere in the world could a sturdier race of Protestants be found than in Gerringong, which he [Waddell] was proud to say he believed could be traced to the North of Ireland ancestry and no element could be relied on for a more sturdy maintenance of our grand liberty."[60] The lodge included two of the six Chittick brothers, who had emigrated as young adults in 1880 with their widowed mother from Rotten Mountain, County Fermanagh, under the deposit scheme.[61] The Chittick brothers and their sons were also members of Loyal Orange lodges, initially in Gerringong and then in other lodges as some of them moved away when they were able to purchase properties further afield.[62] James moved from Gerringong to the Kangaroo Valley in the same district, while William John, John, and Robert Chittick continued as members of no. 115 Lodge and were joined by the next generation – William and Henry by 1916 and Nelson Chittick by 1922. Another Chittick brother, Andrew, was a Methodist preacher for many years in the Jamberoo area and, along with the eldest brother, Thomas, was a member of the Saddleback Kiama no. 5 Lodge, which had been established by the Gray family. Andrew moved to the Northern Rivers area in 1910, and he joined the Orange Lodge no. 278 in Rosebank, along with younger family members Thomas and Augustus.[63]

While the Chittick brothers and their sons were perhaps unusual in the longevity of their LOL membership, which spanned many years, membership of those from other Fermanagh/Donegal/Tyrone families also continued until at least 1922. Alongside these members there were also increasing numbers of Orangemen with other connections to these Ulster families, usually through marriage. In Gerringong, George Lee was not from an Ulster family; however, his daughter Susan married George Grey, who was the Kiama-born son of one of the Fermanagh Grey families.[64] The first wife of James Miller, one of the members in 1903, was the granddaughter on both sides of Fermanagh migrants, and Miller's second wife was from the extended Grey family.[65] In Lismore the grand master at the time of the O'Gorman riot was Charles Staff, who, though not from an Ulster family himself, married into the family of William Crawford, who had maintained strong symbolic connections with Fermanagh and then became a much loved member of the Crawford family in Alstonville.[66] William Crawford and his sons William, Henry, and Norman were all members of the Alstonville Lodge. While intermarriage does not necessarily mean a shared worldview, it does indicate shared social and usually religious interactions. These connections indicate the need to examine wider networks than those comprised of people born in Ireland in order to analyze the reach of an Ulster-inflected Irish Protestant empire.

POLITICAL NETWORKS

The Ulster Protestant families and their wider connections, through membership in the Orange lodges, Protestant churches, and other Protestant organizations, were certainly involved in local affairs; however, they were also part of a national and international information network that linked them to a global world of Protestant ideas and politics, usually with an emphasis on events in Ireland. In the surviving minutes of the Gerringong and Clunes Orange lodges it is possible to assess some of the level of interest in international Protestant and Irish events and campaigns.[67] Not all international matters were taken up by local

Orange lodges, although they were aware of them. In March 1886, the Gerringong no. 115 Lodge voted against taking any action on a petition to oppose France's annexation of the New Hebrides.[68] However, Irish events were usually acted upon in some form at these lodge meetings and events. During the height of the debates over the Second Home Rule bill in 1886, speeches at Orange events throughout both the Kiama and Northern Rivers regions showed that members and speakers were familiar with the campaigns. The Jamberoo celebration of 12 July 1886 included speeches by clergymen who argued that, if the inhabitants of Ireland were Protestant, there would be no talk of Home Rule, and how happy a place Ireland would be in that case.[69] While in Gerringong, the lodge raised money throughout 1886 and 1887 in aid of Ulster Orange lodges and later, in 1889, voted to join the Kiama Lodge in its demonstrations and meetings protesting against visiting Irish National League delegates.[70] In 1892, the Gerringong Lodge, although suffering declining numbers, was confident enough to order fifty copies of a pamphlet entitled *Battle of Glenow*, published in 1861 by Harry Henderson and subtitled "Scenes from an Ulster Orangeman."[71] In Lismore in 1887, Brother Irving argued that the recent riots around Edith O'Gorman's visit were linked to the wider historical context of the Siege of Derry and the need for Orangemen to stand firm against the empire of Catholicism.[72] In 1912, the Clunes Lodge read out a letter from the Grand Lodge of New South Wales regarding the campaign against the third Home Rule bill, and, in 1914, it was subscribing to anti-Home Rule campaigns.[73]

Colonial politics were closely watched by local Orangemen, and they attempted to intervene whenever they could on issues that they felt were of concern to them. The issues with which Orangemen in New South Wales generally became involved concerned restricting Catholic education by ensuring that it was not supported by state money; inspecting and restricting Catholic convents for women; temperance; and Sunday observance of the day of rest from work.[74] David Weir, one of the Ulster families who settled in Gerringong, supported a motion at the regular Gerringong Lodge meeting in March 1886 that a letter be written to an Orange member of the New South Wales Parliament opposing financial assistance for students to travel to various schools. Presumably this was aimed at restricting aid to Catholic students who did not go to the nearby state schools.[75] In Wyrallah, one of the small villages near Lismore, matters of wider colonial politics were debated at meetings in 1891, with a motion to ask the New South Wales Parliament to inspect convents.[76] Meanwhile, in June of that year Brother Nixon, a member of one of the

Ulster families, supported a motion to urge the creation of a by-law to require municipalities to prohibit burials on private land.[77] This was all part of wider Orange Order moves to restrict the operation of Catholic convents throughout the colonies. These small Orange lodges took their political responsibilities seriously, and, at a Clunes meeting in 1911, three members – A.A. King, R.E. Walker, and W. Weir – all members of Ulster families, read and discussed a paper on their responsibilities at the ballot box.[78]

CONCLUSION

As the Protestant sons and daughters raised on small Ulster farms scattered to new homes throughout the diaspora, they took their religion and traditions with them. While many settled within dominant Protestant communities in the destination countries and so fade from historical view, significant groups of Ulster Protestant migrants remain visible, demonstrating strong intellectual, political, and communal links with each other and with a broad idea of Protestantism and accompanying anti-Catholicism formed in the farmlands of Ulster. Sectarian disputes over Fenianism or women's convents are the most visible arenas in which these Irish Protestant ideologies emerge. However, for most of these members of the Irish Protestant religious empire, their twin engagement with politics and religion was performed through meetings, church services, and social events that are much harder for historians to discover. A strong Protestant ideology with enduring Ulster accents can clearly be seen in colonial- and early Federation-era New South Wales in the two broadly coherent and related communities of Ulster Protestant families that originated in neighbouring parishes in Fermanagh, Tyrone, and Donegal and that included their children and the families into which they married. Contrary to expectations of Ulster Protestant denominational membership, they belonged almost exclusively to Anglican (and less often Methodist) congregations rather than to Presbyterianism. This cluster of Ulster Protestant families showed a strong sense of familial and communal coherence over several generations. This coherence was sustained by church and Orange lodges and other Protestant organizations and activities. The global networks of Irish Protestant faith and politics constituted many small local lodges and parishes, such as Gerringong and Clunes, with their regular monthly meetings and all the accompanying minutiae as well as public festivals and events attended by broader Protestant communities. Family members expressed a deep sense of their importance as bulwarks in the spread of British Protestant freedoms and liberties won on the battlefields of Ireland. Their own struggles against Catholicism and what they saw as the forces of tyranny were performed through Orange marches and festivals, with music, songs, and speeches riddled with references to their own history and sense of place and identity. Their expressions of loyalty to the British Empire as well as to their historical identities thus included a wider British and Australian dimension while remaining linked to Ulster-inflected Protestant religious and political practices. The "society" – both religious and secular – that James Robinson so confidently envisioned building in 1840 had grown and developed on the South Coast and in the Northern Rivers in ways that he would have recognized, with its distinctive Ulster accents, customs, and histories. While its character had shifted with the passing generations, there remained, into the early years of the twentieth century, discernable elements of a distinctive Ulster Protestantism.

NOTES

1 Initial research for this chapter was funded by the Leverhulme Trust, London, through a project headed by Lindsay Proudfoot, Queen's University, Belfast. I am very grateful to Dr Proudfoot for his ongoing support for this continuation of that research. I have also benefitted from discussions with Elizabeth Malcolm and Val Noone from the University of Melbourne. My thanks also to Mr Hilton Wickham of the Loyal Orange Institution of New South Wales for access to the records in his care and for informative discussions of the history of the Loyal Orange Institution of New South Wales.

2 McMahon, "Fintona to Wollongong, 1838".

3 Fitzpatrick, *Irish Emigration*, 3–4.

4 "Population by Counties and Provinces, 1821–1911," table 6 in Vaughan and Fitzpatrick, *Irish Historical Statistics*, 5–16.

5 See the tables in Fitzpatrick, *Oceans of Consolation*, 11.

6 Ibid. See also Reid, *Farewell My Children*, 14.

7 Population according to birthplace and religion, part 2, Census of the Commonwealth of Australia, 1911, 232–91. http://www.abs.gov.au/AUSSTATS/abs@.nsf/DetailsPage/2112.01911?OpenDocument (viewed 27 August 2013).

8 McClaughlin, "Protestant Irish in Australia."

9 On the generalization about Presbyterians, see Fitzpatrick, *Oceans of Consolation*, 14.

10 Fitzpatrick, *Oceans of Consolation*, 361–466; and O'Farrell and Trainor, *Letters from Irish-Australia*.

11 Forth, "Anglo-Irish in Australia." And on Trinity College Dublin graduates see Ronayne, *Irish in Australia*. For the Orange Order in South Australia, see Fitzpatrick, "Exporting Brotherhood."

12 Fitzpatrick, *Oceans of Consolation,* 15–16. For similar findings from 1841, see McDonald and Richards, "Great Emigration of 1841."

13 Proudfoot and Hall, "Points of Departure."

14 McClaughlin, "Protestant Irish in Australia," 89; O'Farrell, *Irish in Australia*, 101–2.

15 Variations on these schemes with differing criteria and rules operated between 1836 and the 1890s. For discussion of the various rules, see Reid, *Farewell My Children*, 17; and Proudfoot and Hall, "Points of Departure," 248–9. For the wider context of such assisted migration schemes, see Moran, "Shovelling out the Poor."

16 Not every record included the full range of possibilities. See Proudfoot and Hall, "Points of Departure," 251–5; and Reid, *Farewell My Children,* 91–116.

17 O'Farrell, *Irish in Australia*, 3rd ed. 101.

18 For methodology, see Elliott, *Irish Migrants in the Canadas*, 4–6.

19 Fitzpatrick, *Oceans of Consolation.*

20 McClaughlin, "Protestant Irish in Australia", 88–98; Fitzpatrick, "Irish Emigration"; McConville, *Croppies, Celts and Catholics*; O'Farrell, *Irish in Australia,* 3rd ed.

21 The New South Wales government's Remittance Deposit Journals and Emigrant Arrival Journals were sampled. There were 1,904 migrants from a sample of twelve parishes in Fermanagh and Cavan between 1858 and 1884; of these, 660 addresses of friends and relatives in the colony were recorded. Half, 333, gave addresses in Sydney. Sixty-nine, or 10 percent, of those giving addresses gave Kiama as the address of their friends. All of these were Protestants. State Records Authority of New South Wales (hereafter SRNSW): Immigration Department, Assisted immigrants inwards to Sydney, 4/4974, 4976, 4978–4981, 4984, 4986–4988, 4990–4991, 5000–5026, 5028; SRNSW, Immigration Department, persons on bounty ships (Agent's Immigrant Lists), 4/4789, 4795–4798, 4808, 4812, 5031; SRNSW, Immigration Department, Immigration deposits journals, 1853–1900, 4/4576–4598.

22 O'Farrell, *Irish in Australia,* 3rd ed. 101–2. The population of the Kiama township in 1861 was 741, of which 21 percent were born in Ireland and 43 percent born in NSW. Of these, only 9.5 percent were Catholic, with 38 percent Church of England, 26 percent Presbyterian, and 15 percent Methodist. See *Census of the Colony of New South Wales, 1861* (Sydney, 1862), 110 and 130, http://hccda.anu.edu.au/pages/NSW-1861-census-05_110 (viewed 18 September 2012).

23 Data are analyzed and tabulated in Proudfoot and Hall, "Points of Departure," 266.

24 Livingstone, *Fermanagh Story*, 233.

25 Alick Osborne went on a speaking and recruiting tour across Ulster and especially around his home parish of Dromore in Tyrone. Alick Osborne, "Journal of Occurrences connected with emigration, 8 July 1839–17 July 1837," State Library of New South Wales, MS D248; Frank Osbourne, "Alick Osborne and the Adam Lodge," 1997 typescript, Kiama Family History Centre. James Armstrong, for example, a key anchor in chain migration from Pettigo in Fermanagh, was said to have known the Osborne family prior to his migration in 1839. See Young, "Armstrong Story," 3–7.

26 Osborne, *Notes*; Osborne, *Immigration.* And see Proudfoot and Hall, "Points of Departure", 341–78.

27 Proudfoot and Hall, "Points of Departure."

28 Analysis is based on databases of all migrants from the thirteen sample parishes in Cavan and Fermanagh correlated with demographic and biographical data from newspapers, family histories, and the Registry of Births, Deaths and Marriages. These data are the basis for the analysis in Proudfoot and Hall, "Points of Departure." There were 1,167 emigrants from the six parishes in County Fermanagh recorded in this data. Of these, 564 are listed as Protestant and 239 as Catholic. The remaining 364 are without religion noted on the forms. A rough calculation of religion based on surname, which though not completely reliable in this context is a reasonable substitute, adds another 125 Catholics, meaning that there are 803 Protestants in the sample.

29 Elaine Dunn analyzed the parish registers of the Church of England, Kiama, and found that 50 percent of spouses marrying between 1856 and 1875 were from Ulster. See Dunn, "Kiama Region," 24.

30 Keats, *Wollumbin*, 381.

31 Hall, "Defending the Faith."

32 Then, in 1854, he manipulated the remittance system designed to bring out labourers for specific farms. See Reid, *Farewell My Children,* 202–3, 15.

33 *Richmond River Herald*, 18 July 1919.

34 SRNSW: Immigration Department, Immigrant Deposit Journals, 4/4592; 4594; 4591; 4586; 4584. See also Crawford, *Duck Creek Mountain*, 133–6, for letters sent from William Snr and Margaret Crawford to their son William.

35 Hoerder, "Migrants to Ethnics."

36 State Library of New South Wales, MS A1502, "Papers of Rev. Thomas Sharpe, 1826–1869: Journal for 1869," 210.

37 *Illawarra Pioneers pre-1900*, Wollongong, Illawarra Family History Group, 1988, 63; and Johnston, *Rich Heritage*, 173.

38 See, for example, *Kiama Independent*, 9 July 1868.

39 *Sydney Morning Herald*, 2 May 1868.

40 University of Wollongong Archives, McCaffery Papers, MS D92. McCaffery, whose father knew the Gray family in Fermanagh, clearly disliked John Gray.

41 Reported in the *Sydney Morning Herald*, 10 November 1868.

42 Minutes, Grand Lodge Orange Institution of New South Wales, 12 May 1868, held by Loyal Orange Institution of New South Wales, Sydney. These records remain in the custody of the Loyal Orange Institution, and I am very grateful to Grand Secretary, Mr Hilton Wickham, for facilitating my access to these and other records of the Loyal Orange Institution in New South Wales.

43 Hall, "Defending the Faith." For a full account of the content of her usual lectures, see *Bathurst Free Press and Mining Journal*, 15 July 1886. See also Ruth Seddon, *Edith O'Gorman: Escaped Nun* (The author: 2010), http://www.lulu.com/shop/ruth-seddon/edith-ogorman-the-escaped-nun/paperback/product-6521792.html (viewed 27 August 2013); Kollar, "American 'Escaped Nun.'"

44 *Protestant Standard*, 6 November 1886.

45 *Protestant Standard*, 6 November 1886; and *Clarence and Richmond Examiner*, 6 November 1886.

46 *Clarence and Richmond River Examiner*, 30 April 1887; *New England Advertiser*, 30 April 1887.

47 *Northern Star*, 7 May 1887; *Freeman's Journal*, 30 April 1887; *Protestant Standard*, 7 and 14 May 1887.

48 Hall, "Defending the Faith".

49 *Kiama Independent and Shoalhaven Advertiser*, 2 February 1883 (emphasis in original).

50 Clunes was not a township that was reported separately in the 1891 census. The figure is derived from counting the numbers in the Householder

lists for Clunes, Eureka, Rose Bank, and Coopers Creek. See Householder returns, County of Rous, District of Lismore, Parish of Bexhill, SRNSW, NRS 683, book 7, 2/8401, roll 2510.

51 Christine Alexander, "ABC Open 'Now and Then' Exposes a Holy History," ABC North Coast NSW, 10 January 2011, http://www.abc.net.au/local/stories/2011/01/10/3109642.htm?site=northcoast (viewed 2 August 2013).

52 *Northern Star*, 30 July 1904; and see Hall, "Defending the Faith," for more detail on the performance of Orange identity.

53 Johnston, *Rich Heritage,* 191.

54 Fitzpatrick, "Exporting Brotherhood," 277–310; Laffan, *How Orange Was My Valley*; Davis, *Orangeism in Tasmania*; and Eric Turner, "Not Narrow Minded Bigots – Proceedings of the Loyal Orange Institution of New South Wales, 1845–1895," University of New England, Dixon Library, New South Wales, 2002.

55 Loyal Orange Institution of New South Wales: Membership Records New South Wales Lodges from 1897 onwards and the minutes for Clunes Lodge no. 230 (1902–25). I have also used University of Wollongong Archives, "Minutes of Gerringong LOL no. 151 (1886–1892)," MS D45. LOI Membership records were sampled for the years 1897, 1903/4, 1910, 1916 and 1922. The records were then correlated with biographical information from a range of sources, including Registry of Births, Deaths and Marriages; census collectors books for the 1891 and 1901 NSW census; and family histories collected through www.northtothebigscrub.org. See also Rawson, *Illawarra Grays*; *Illawarra Pioneers: Pre-1900* (Wollongong: The Group, 1988); *Illawarra Pioneers: Post-1900* (Wollongong: Illawarra Family History Group, 1988); and through the Kiama Family History Centre and the Richmond-Tweed Regional Library family history service.

56 *Kiama Independent and Shoalhaven Advertiser*, 12 December 1942.

57 Membership returns, Clunes LOL no. 234, 1910.

58 For the Eureka area families see Johnston, *Rich Heritage*.

59 Membership returns, Gerringong LOL no. 115, 1897.

60 *Kiama Independent and Shoalhaven Advertiser*, 20 November 1907.

61 Chittick and Chittick, *Chittick Family History*.

62 Gerringong Lodge minutes do not include full membership lists, but they do mention office holders and those who moved and seconded motions. James Chittick is mentioned in the minutes. The other Chittick men are named in the full membership lists from 1897. Membership returns, Gerringong LOL no. 115.

63 Chittick and Chittick, *Chittick Family History*.

64 *Illawarra Pioneers: Pre-1900*.

65 Ibid., 7.
66 Crawford, *Duck Creek Mountain.*
67 The surviving minutes are not comprehensive. For Gerringong Lodge no. 115, there are minutes from 1886 to 1892. Clunes Lodge no. 230 minute books survive from 1902 to 1925, while there is also a minute book from Wyrallah Lodge no. 142 from 1889. As always with minutes, the level of detail varies and is dependent on the enthusiasm and energy of the secretary. See MacRaild, *Faith, Fraternity and Fighting*, for discussion of the range of activities and interests recorded in English Orange Lodge minutes.
68 Minutes of Gerringong LOL no. 115, 17 May 1886.
69 *Kiama Independent and Shoalhaven Advertiser*, 16 July 1886.
70 Minutes of Gerringong LOL no. 115, 2 May 1887 and 5 August 1889. For the loyalist meeting opposing Home Rule in Kiama, attended by Rev. Dill Macky, see *Evening News*, 9 September 1889.
71 Minutes of Gerringong LOL no. 115, 4 July 1892. Henderson, *Battle of Glenow.*
72 *Northern Star*, 16 July 1887.
73 Minutes of the Clunes LOL no. 234, 27 June 1912, 1 July 1914.
74 All these were regularly discussed by the Grand Lodge. See Turner, "Not Narrow Minded Bigots," 319, for discussion of Orange interest in convents.
75 Minutes of the Gerringong LOL no. 115, March 1886.
76 Minutes of the Wyrallah LOL no. 142, 24 January 1891.
77 Minutes of the Wyrallah LOL no. 142, June 1891.
78 Minutes of the Clunes LOL no. 234, 7 September 1911.

15

Building "God's Own Country": The Reverend Rutherford Waddell, the Global Irish, and New Zealand History

JOHN STENHOUSE

This chapter focuses on an Ulster Presbyterian minister, Rutherford Waddell, who migrated to New Zealand with his wife, Kathleen, in 1877. Settling in the colony's largest city, Dunedin, in 1879, Waddell became perhaps the most well known and influential Protestant minister in the country until his death in 1932. Shortly after arriving, he launched a campaign against sweated labour that helped the Liberal government of the 1890s, led by fellow Ulsterman John Ballance, a freethinker, win power. Leading Liberal politician William Pember Reeves, another freethinker, capitalized on the popular demand for reform galvanized by Waddell in order to push through worker-friendly labour and industrial laws. Waddell also provided important support for the female suffrage campaign, which, in 1893, made New Zealand the first country in the world to grant women the right to vote. Impressed by all this progressive legislation, liberal-minded overseas visitors hailed New Zealand as the social laboratory of the world. Waddell also campaigned for prohibition, Bibles in schools, and strict Sabbath observance. A tireless preacher and public speaker, he reached an even larger audience with the pen, serving as founding editor of the *Christian Outlook* weekly in 1894 and for twenty-seven years writing a much-loved column in Dunedin's *Evening Star* newspaper. It is hard to exaggerate Waddell's significance in the literary, educational, cultural, political, and religious life of New Zealand – the southernmost reaches of Greater Ireland. Testimony to the breadth of his popularity came from *New Zealand Truth*, the country's most popular weekly newspaper, when, in 1927, it praised Waddell as a "scholarly, broad-minded man … idolized by all" who had dedicated his life "to elevat[ing], to liv[ing] justly and to help[ing] the fallen."[1] Coming from a paper that normally ridiculed prohibitionists and suffragists – and Waddell championed both causes – this was high praise indeed.

After exploring Waddell's Ulster upbringing and education, I focus on his involvement in the great reform movements transforming New Zealand between the 1880s and the 1930s. Here I raise a series of questions similar to those that other contributors to this volume explore in different contexts. What kind of Irish consciousness, if any, did Waddell carry to and make use of in New Zealand? Did he find common ground with Irish Catholics, forging a pan-Irish diasporic identity that transcended the old sectarian divide? Some transplanted Ulster Presbyterians, such as Waddell's ministerial colleague at Temuka, the Reverend John Dickson from Ballycarry, earned a reputation as anti-Catholic.[2] Where should Waddell be situated on the sectarian spectrum, if at all? Did he clash with Catholics, and, if so, when, where, how, and why?

A second set of questions concerns Waddell's relationships with the many non-Irish and non-Presbyterians with whom he rubbed shoulders. How did he get along with the English Anglicans, Dissenters, Jews, and freethinkers who played prominent roles in Dunedin and New Zealand politics during this period? Did he privatize his faith for the sake of social harmony and political consensus, systematically separating religion and politics and the sacred from the secular? Was he the kind of liberal Protestant minister who, carefully confining religion to the heart, home, and house of worship, helped to lay the foundations for the more secular society that, according to some New Zealand historians, emerged after the First World War?

A third set of questions zooms out to place this case study in a broader perspective. Though surely one of the most remarkable ministers in the global Irish diaspora, Waddell may also illuminate larger historical dynamics transforming New Zealand during this period. Were other transplanted Ulster Protestants playing important roles in New Zealand politics and culture during this formative half-century? If, instead of assuming a great gap between politics and religion, we draw these realms into a single interconnected analytic framework, is it possible to detect a certain family resemblance in the ways successful and influential clergy and politicians operated? Might Waddell illustrate historical dynamics that may also be discerned, more subtly perhaps, in the lives of other colonial Irish, Catholic as well as Protestant? With these questions in mind, I turn now to Waddell's Ulster background.

ULSTER

Rutherford Waddell was born at Ballyroney, County Down, around 1850 and grew up in Antrim and Down, the heartland of rural Irish Presbyterianism. Descended from a long line of Presbyterian ministers on both sides, he was named after the Scottish theologian Samuel Rutherford, one of the architects of the Westminster Confession of 1646. Accused of treason in 1660 for rejecting the Divine Right of Kings, Rutherford, on his deathbed, refused to answer the summons: "Tell them I have got a summons already before a superior Judge … and ere your day come I will be where few kings and great folks come."[3]

Literary interests and talent flourished in Waddell's family of origin. His mother's brother, Captain Thomas Mayne Reid, settled in the United States, where he wrote best-selling adventure stories such as *The Rifle Rangers* (1850), *The Scalp Hunters* (1851), and *The Headless Horseman* (1866). Translated into several European languages, Reid's novels delighted American president Theodore Roosevelt and writers such as Arthur Conan Doyle, Vladimir Nabokov, and Czeslaw Milosz.[4]

Rutherford Waddell grew up a boy of sorrows, much acquainted with grief. He had no memory of his mother, who died when he was little. His father, a minister busy with parish affairs, rarely appears in Waddell's autobiographical reminiscences. Raised by an aunt, whose strict but loving piety he credited with saving him from ruin, he attended a one-room country school run by a one-armed Roman Catholic teacher. This "all-supreme dominie," displaying a "hot, hasty, ungovernable temper," often beat pupils with a large wooden ruler and then tried to comfort them, especially those from well-to-do families. A shy, sensitive boy, Waddell grew "so afraid of doing anything wrong" that he "hesitated about doing anything even right." Crushed by "cruelty," he lost "all originality and initiative" and often tried to avoid going to school by falling sick or playing truant. He spent the rest of his life "battling" this "nightmare," finding solace in his "love of reading, especially poetry."[5]

Leaving school at fourteen, Waddell worked long and hard for little for four years in the mid-1860s as a draper's apprentice in the town of Banbridge, a centre of the Irish linen industry. Waddell's high-profile role in industrial and labour politics soon after arriving in New Zealand suggests that he probably brought such concerns with him. During the eighteenth century, a flourishing linen industry made Ulster an important player in Europe's first industrial revolution. After 1800, however, steam-powered mills in Belfast, Manchester, and Leeds steadily drove smaller firms to the wall. Only the largest and most efficient survived. Workers supplanted by machines flocked to northern Irish towns and cities in search of work. When the potato blight destroyed the staple food of the poor in 1845 and 1846, thousands died. Led by Quakers, church people took the lead in providing relief, which brought them into close contact with mass suffering. Ulster Presbyterian ministers, always keen to challenge the power of Anglican landlords, played leading roles in the Ulster Tenant Right Association founded in 1847 to defend the rights of small tenant farmers. The Great Famine sent thousands of Ulster Irish to the New World.[6]

Waddell's youthful experiences of loss, suffering, exploitation, and cruelty instilled a life-long capacity to identify and empathize with the lowly, the victims, the suffering, and the poor. "I can never see wrecked lives today," he reflected late in life, "without a profound sense of humiliation" that "had my [boyhood] environment been different, I might have been such as they."[7] He never lost the sense that environments profoundly shaped human lives, for good and for ill. These experiences also developed in him a deep and abiding dislike of domineering people and exploitative systems.

Sitting in hard wooden pews during long and dreary services explained why "the Church had not much attraction for us boys," Waddell recalled of his youth. Bored by church, he focused as a teenager on "self-pleasing and enjoyment." The great Ulster evangelical revival that erupted from 1859 passed him by. At the age of eighteen, however, he visited a country church, where a sharp sermon by a preacher "quivering with passion to his fingertips" sparked a spiritual crisis. Waddell's subsequent decision to study for the ministry also drew inspiration from his older brother, Hugh, who pioneered the Irish Presbyterian mission to China and Japan. Combining strong evangelical faith with "love of fun and mischief," Hugh impressed his younger brother as the "bravest ... blythest [*sic*], and ... best man I have ever known." Dedicating his life to spreading the gospel in Asia, Hugh's unselfconscious "devotion" and "sacrifice" impressed his younger brother, whose own "easy-going, devil-may-care life" seemed "ignoble and unworthy" by comparison.[8] Rutherford studied literature at Queen's College and theology at the Presbyterian Theological College at Belfast between 1873 and 1876.

Science and critical study of the Bible sparked lively debates among educated Protestants during the second half of the century. Belfast hosted one of the most explosive confrontations of all. In a presidential address to the British Association for the Advancement of Science in 1874 the

Irish physicist John Tyndall exalted evolution, depicted Christianity as the perennial enemy of science, and claimed to discern in "matter" the "promise and potency of every form and quality of life." Tyndall's immediate target was the Irish Catholic hierarchy, which had just rejected a proposal to include physics in the curriculum of the proposed new Catholic university. Presbyterian theologians, led by J.L. Porter and Robert Watts, also attacked Tyndall's aggressive scientism. According to historian David Livingstone, Tyndall's militancy soured Belfast Presbyterians on evolution. In Edinburgh and Princeton, by contrast, Presbyterians gave evolution a fairer hearing.[9] "I do not think that the faith has ever had so great a fight for its existence as when I was a student," recalled Waddell. Tyndall, T.H. Huxley, Herbert Spencer, Darwin, and rationalistic German biblical critics blew "sceptical blizzards" from the "icy fields of science" that struck fear into "raw and half-educated students."[10]

Wrestling with God, Waddell, an omnivorous reader, was drawn for a time to Unitarianism (which rejected Christ's divinity) by his "profound admiration" for the sermons and essays of James Martineau and other Unitarian leaders. But long and careful study of the gospel accounts of Jesus's life, death, and resurrection eventually convinced him to "give over to Christ the passion of my heart and the utmost labor of my hands." Waddell came to centre his faith on Christ, understood as fully human and fully divine. Growing alongside biblical and rational evidence Waddell identified "an entirely new kind of evidence" of "personal experience gained through obedience to Him." Too many "thinking men and women" identified religion primarily with "doctrines … creeds" or "theologies," whereas faith is really "the knowing of a Person." Someone committed "to Christ in trust, obedience and communion gets to know Him in a way that no hostile criticism can ever stagger and shatter."[11]

At Theological College Waddell came to dislike Robert Watts, professor of systematic theology, who "rammed down the throats" of students the conservative Calvinism he learned from Charles Hodge at Princeton. Watts probably reminded Waddell too much of his cruel schoolteacher. Waddell responded warmly, by contrast, to a kindly, open-minded, young-at-heart Presbyterian minister who "talked with him, not at him or over him," and lent him books. English novelist George Eliot's *Adam Bede*, with its deep empathy for and understanding of the religious lives of ordinary people, moved Waddell deeply, opening "another world" of "mental and moral insight," marking a "turning point." Though well aware that Eliot had translated D.F. Strauss's rationalistic *Life of Jesus* into English in 1846, Waddell considered Eliot his favourite novelist, on whom he often lectured in New Zealand.[12]

Waddell's interest in and empathy for those at or beyond the margins of Christianity, one of the secrets of his success in New Zealand, developed first in Ireland. It may be illustrated by his admiring respect not only for Eliot but also for the Scottish poet Robert Burns. Well aware of Burns's fondness for whisky and women, Waddell defended the poet when a pious fellow student called him a "drunken sot." Rejecting this "inconsiderate description," Waddell insisted that Burns drank from a "deeper source of inspiration" than liquor, and he hung a picture of the poet above the couch in his college room. Elected president of the Presbyterian students' Theological Society in 1875, Waddell, who graduated with an MA in English literature at Queen's the same year, urged theologians to take seriously the insights and visions of poets and novelists.[13]

Grappling with faith and doubt during his student days in Belfast equipped Waddell well for ministry in Dunedin, home of New Zealand's first university. Debates about science and Scripture erupted at the University of Otago, in scientific societies and in churches and para-church organizations from the mid-1870s, just before he arrived.[14] Having wrestled his way to Christian convictions in Belfast, Waddell, at ease with questions and doubt, was well equipped to handle such issues in New Zealand. Regularly addressing scientific, literary, and philosophical questions in sermons, lectures, and newspaper columns, he developed a reputation as a kindly, well-read and broad-minded minister with whom it was safe to discuss hard questions.[15]

After licensing in Belfast in 1876, Waddell, following his brother's example, applied to become a missionary to Syria. He was turned down. Then he preached a trial sermon at Six Road Ends in Bangor, hoping for a call. The congregation thought the sermon so good that he must have borrowed one from Charles Spurgeon, the famous English Baptist preacher. After a second rejection, Waddell sailed with his new wife, Kathleen, to New Zealand in 1877.[16]

DUNEDIN

After two years' ministry in and around Christchurch for the Canterbury Presbyterian Association, Waddell travelled south to fill in at St Andrew's in Dunedin. Scottish Free Churchmen had founded the Otago settlement in 1848. Unlike the Presbyterian Church north of the Waitaki river, the

Synod of Otago and Southland remained heavily Scottish and Free Church, calling only two Irish Presbyterians before Waddell.[17]

His new parish, St Andrew's, had begun as a mission church to the gold miners flooding into Otago, often from Victoria, after 1861. This "New Iniquity," as the Free Church "Old Identities" called them, included thousands of Irish Catholics, many Irish Protestants, and, after 1865, hundreds of Chinese miners. In 1871, Bishop Patrick Moran arrived from the Cape Colony in South Africa to head the new diocese of Dunedin. Extending Cardinal Paul Cullen's spiritual empire to the ends of the earth, Moran came via Rome and the First Vatican Council. In a proudly Protestant province, Moran's Irish Catholic nationalism soon raised tensions.[18]

By the time Waddell arrived in 1879, no single denomination had the numbers to dominate Dunedin on its own. Presbyterians, almost two-fifths of the population, faced a large English Anglican minority of around 30 percent. Methodists and Baptists, mostly English in origin, led a lively assortment of evangelical churches that collectively comprised about a sixth of the population. Catholics, mostly Irish, were almost as numerous, peaking at about one-fifth of the working-class borough of South Dunedin. Freethinkers, mostly male, enjoyed a high public profile, despite their small numbers (almost 2 percent of the total). Even in the colony's Presbyterian-dominated south, then, ethno-religious pluralism favoured clergy, politicians, and community leaders who could build connections beyond their own denomination or political constituency.[19]

Waddell's preaching impressed the St Andrew's congregation, which immediately issued a call. The parish included wealthy and influential community leaders living in handsome houses in and around upper High Street as well as many poor people living in cottages and slums. Immediately below St Andrew's stretched a triangle bounded by Maitland, MacLaggan, and Princes streets, which locals called the Devil's Half Acre, the city's red light district. Its inhabitants, mostly poor, included Irish Catholics, Lebanese Catholics, and Orthodox as well as most of the city's Chinese population, mainly single men who had come to New Gold Mountain from southern China.

THE "SIN OF CHEAPNESS" AND THE ANTI-SWEATING CAMPAIGN

Waddell arrived in the country's most industrialized city as a global economic downturn began to bite. In September of 1883, he told a meeting of 150 people at Dunedin's Trinity Methodist Church Literary Society that exploiting child and female labour was "only too common here as elsewhere."[20] Public concern that New Zealand had not left such Old World evils behind began to bubble.

After publishing reports on poverty and crime in London and Glasgow early in 1884, the *Otago Daily Times* carried a two-part report on "Outcast Dunedin" in February 1884, probably penned by reporter Silas Spragg. Although New Zealand faced fewer problems than overseas, Dunedin, too, had its "plague-spots." In a "small nest of misery" off Stafford Street the reporters found a "young Irishwoman," poor, dishevelled, drunk, and sarcastic. Nearby, the Devil's Half Acre contained "the most criminal and degraded members" of the city's population, crowded into "small and squalid huts" for which landlords charged "preposterously high rents."[21] "Outcast Dunedin" aimed to spark moral concern and practical action. Most of the problem areas that the report identified lay within St Andrew's parish boundaries.

In 1887, wages fell suddenly in the clothing industry, which employed hundreds of Dunedin women. Early in 1888, Waddell delivered a series of lectures on "Social Problems" at St Andrews in which he argued that "the present system" of industrial capitalism was "founded on systematic injustice" to "the working classes."[22] Irish Catholics were overrepresented among skilled and unskilled occupational groups, especially in Dunedin's industrial southern suburbs, while most Protestant churches contained many people from skilled working-class families.[23]

In early October Waddell preached the sermon that made him famous, "The Sin of Cheapness." Although no copies have survived, we can reconstruct its main thrust, if not the actual words, from press reports. Some Dunedin women were working from 8:00 AM to 11:00 PM finishing moleskin trousers at two-and-a-half pence a pair, and earning only two shillings per day. The community's enormous rage to get cheap things, spurring excessive competition between manufacturers to cut prices and costs, drove wages down to subsistence level or below. Everyone, especially Christians, had to take responsibility for the sin of cheapness. Newspapers around the country erupted with articles and letters for and against Waddell's views over the following weeks.[24]

Seeking to mobilize Presbyterian support, early in November Waddell urged the Synod of Otago and Southland to oppose "social injustice" by condemning the "sin of covetousness" driving the sweating system. The "laws of Christ," he said, applied to "commercial and social as well as religious life." They would remain remote, "ideal and dreamy" until "people were prepared to undergo great sacrifice" to make them "real" in this world. Ministers must "bring their people up to the laws of Christ," said Waddell, not "bring the laws down to the people." Determined to keep the church in vital touch with the whole of society, not just respectable churchgoers, Waddell intended to prevent a rift opening up between working people and the churches. After long debate, during which a couple of senior Scottish clergy criticized Waddell's views, the synod passed by twenty votes to six a motion deploring "the existence of the 'sweating' system in the colony" and instructing "ministers and office-bearers to discourage it by every means in their power." [25] Far from confining Christianity to the private sphere of heart, home, and house of worship, Waddell and his supporters, like John Calvin in sixteenth-century Geneva, gave it potent public and this-worldly meaning. He refused to conceptualize "commercial and social life" as autonomous secular domains off-limits to religion. Christ's command to love one's neighbour had concrete practical implications for economic and political affairs.

Thanks to his energy, conviction, and ability to work with a wide range of people, Waddell's anti-sweating campaign soon won support from across the social and religious spectrum. Middling and working-class Presbyterians played leading roles. So did community leaders, businesspeople, and unionists from other churches, especially those with large working-class constituencies. Condemning sweating as a "great injustice" to "many in the working classes," the national Wesleyan Conference called for some "well-considered measure" to protect working women from "totally unremunerative" wages.[26] Writing in the *Tablet*, Bishop Moran condemned the "sin" of "defrauding the labourer of his hire" and described the "sweating system" as "deplorable beyond description."[27] Church of England clergy and laity, by contrast, spoke out seldom.

The Presbyterian-dominated anti-sweating committee that Waddell led included lawyer-politician William Downie Stewart from Knox Church and two St Andrew's women, Rachel Reynolds and Miss Bathgate. It secured individual agreements from major Dunedin firms to pay minimum wages. Soon, however, four leading warehouse firms got together. Disclaiming any desire to "screw down" the workers, they declared that, unless the new minimum wage rates operated throughout the country, they would not require their contractors to pay them. Waddell's committee should mediate between contractors and workers.[28]

On the platform of a packed Choral Hall on the night of 7 June, beside Waddell's committee sat George Fenwick, editor of the *Otago Daily Times*; Sir Robert Stout, a freethinking liberal politician; populist mayor Henry Smith Fish, nominally Anglican; and a dozen other Dunedin politicians, unionists, business leaders, and clergy. Waddell began politely, acknowledging that the four warehousemen had "very courteously received" his committee, had promised to "aid [it] as far as possible," and had agreed to pay minimum wages. But once these "estimable gentlemen" got "their heads together" as a group, "they refused collectively to do" what each had promised individually, without giving any reason for this sudden change. To those who dismissed minimum wages as "unworkable" Waddell replied that they were already working perfectly well in Melbourne.[29] By speaking politely, and appealing to reason and evidence, Waddell was making it hard for critics to dismiss him as a fanatic.

But he refused to muzzle his moral and religious convictions. Waddell charged the warehousemen with being "indirectly involved in the iniquities of a system which we all deplore, and which they themselves profess to abhor." The crowd applauded. The warehousemen had set "an example of selfishness and narrowness unworthy their position." He then named the four firms responsible: Ross and Glendining; Bing, Harris and Co.; Sargood, Son, and Ewen; and Butterworth Brothers. At least two of these, Ross and Glendining, were prominent Presbyterians. If they sustain this "iniquitous system of sweating," said Waddell, "I say these warehousemen will morally occupy a position almost, if not altogether, analagous [*sic*] to the receiver of stolen goods ... I charge these warehousemen with caring more for money than for men." The audience repeatedly applauded. That a prominent Presbyterian minister was willing publicly to rebuke wealthy pillars of his own church probably enhanced his standing in a community quick to denounce religious hypocrisy.[30]

Treating his audience as a Christian congregation, Waddell then asked if, after eighteen centuries "of professed worship and service" of "the greatest master of the human heart," they were willing to "permit in our midst a system that in this young fair land threatens to reproduce here ... those very evils that are eating the heart and soul out of the older countries?" Shall we "sit down here and allow it to suck the souls out of the lives of our women and girls?" He concluded by urging the meeting to "take this system" of sweating, "with all its aiders and abettors, [and] place them high up on the pillory of public opinion for all men's scorn – yea, till the very geese take courage and hiss derision at them!"[31]

The crowd responded with "loud and continuous applause." Robert Stout, a leading freethinker and powerful left-liberal politician, observed that Waddell had spoken so effectively that the crowd would have passed any resolution he cared to propose. Critics responded hotly. Frederick Fitchett, a lawyer who represented Dunedin Central in Parliament, condemned the "feverish enthusiasm" with which Waddell had "preached a crusade." Impractical idealists who "run their heads into the clouds ... must inevitably come to grief" with "vain" proposals to regulate wages "by act of Parliament." Several in the audience agreed, shouting: "Hear, hear."[32]

Most subsequent speakers defended Waddell. Henry Shacklock, a Congregationalist businessman, won laughter and applause by dismissing Fitchett's views as "simply the defence of the warehousemen." George Fenwick identified the firm and manager leading the "offending." Jewish businessman Bendix Hallenstein, a clothing manufacturer, thanked Waddell for stirring up "public indignation" and said: "we would prefer to abandon our business rather than carry it on, if it can only be made remunerative by starvation wages. I, for one, would not feel happy to live on the misery of others." Expressing "no sympathy" with Fitchett's views, Henry Smith Fish said that the four offenders fully deserved "the censure of the community." Several seconded Waddell's calls for the establishment of a government commission of inquiry and female trades unions.[33] Writing in the *Tablet*, Bishop Moran concluded that "the public must co-operate" with the campaign because "the welfare of the State and of the whole population" depended on "the overthrow of the sweating system."[34]

Hundreds, including many Catholics, joined the country's first female union, the Tailoresses Union, over the following days. From July 1889, Waddell served as its first president, working closely with Harriet Morison, an Irish Methodist, the country's leading female unionist. In 1890, the Atkinson government appointed Waddell to its Sweating Commission, whose report found that sweating as it existed in London and elsewhere did not exist in New Zealand. Unconvinced, Waddell penned a minority report insisting that "abundant evidence" of sweating existed here.[35] Bishop Moran agreed.[36] Once again, Waddell and Moran saw eye to eye.

Anti-sweating illustrated Waddell's ability to launch and lead a reform campaign that brought together people of all churches and creeds (and none) in a remarkably ecumenical and cross-class coalition that packed a powerful political punch. Rippling outward from Dunedin across the country, the anti-sweating campaign made Waddell a household name. Stimulating popular enthusiasm for reform, it helped John Ballance's Liberal Party win power in the national election of 1890. Throughout the campaign, Bishop Moran supported the strong stands taken by Waddell. Neither idolized the free play of market forces. Both believed that church leaders ought to defend the rights and welfare of the working classes and the poor. On this issue, Dunedin's Irish Catholic bishop and its leading Irish Presbyterian minister found considerable common ground.

IRISH CONNECTIONS

Anti-sweating was not the only cause that brought the Irish diaspora together across sectarian lines. So too, sometimes, did Ireland. In January 1880, as famine threatened the homeland, Waddell joined a committee to raise funds for relief. At a public meeting called to organize the relief campaign, the Reverend Dr D.M. Stuart, the popular and widely respected minister of Knox Presbyterian Church, urged citizens to give generously to the suffering Irish as "fellow subjects and fellow Christians." Judge Joshua Williams, an English Anglican, encouraged "all nationalities" to do "their duty as fellow citizens, as Christians, as human beings" and "respond liberally." Discerning no "sectarian" feeling dividing the community, Williams won applause when he identified "clergy of every denomination" attending the meeting. William Downie Stewart, a lawyer, politician, and elder of Knox Presbyterian Church, identified the "unfair and oppressive land laws" under which Ireland had suffered as an enduring cause of distress. He urged the audience not to allow "a few wealthy men" to monopolize land in New Zealand and to give generously to alleviate Ireland's "great distress." Endorsing these views, Robert Stout rejected as unfounded the claim that the Irish relief movement in the colonies was "sectarian." Bishop Moran applauded the generosity with which the people of Dunedin always "came forward to relieve distress." John Callan, a Dublin-born Catholic lawyer, praised the "kindly" generosity of Otago's "Englishmen and Scotchmen" as well as Irish. Irish Catholics such as John Carroll, Callan, Thomas Bracken, Father O'Leary, and Bishop Moran joined Scottish and Irish Presbyterians, English Anglicans, Jews, and freethinkers on an impressively ecumenical relief committee. Several members – Waddell, Moran, W.D. Stewart, Stout, Henry Fish, and Bendix Hallenstein – would play prominent roles in the anti-sweating campaign a few years later.[37]

In 1887, the "Irishmen of Dunedin" met in the Christian Brothers schoolroom to formulate plans for a civic reception for the Earl and Countess of Aberdeen, soon to visit the city. On a committee convened by John Callan, Waddell joined Irish Catholics such as John Carroll and

Francis Meenan, a stalwart of the Dunedin Jockey Club who, with Moran, founded the *Tablet*.[38]

In 1894, writing as editor of the *Christian Outlook*, the national Presbyterian weekly, Waddell addressed a sectarian controversy attracting national attention. The Moa Flat School Committee in rural Central Otago, dominated by Protestants, refused to appoint a female Roman Catholic, Miss White, to a teaching position. Urging Protestants to abandon "religious intolerance of this sort," Waddell urged every "right-hearted" reader to defend "the principle of civil and religious liberty."[39]

Waddell forged a lasting friendship with Thomas Bracken, who had strong Catholic as well as Protestant connections. Born at Clonee, County Meath, to a Catholic mother who died in childbirth, Bracken left after his Protestant father died in 1852 to live near Melbourne with his maternal uncle, a devout Catholic. Sailing to Dunedin in 1869, he raised funds for the *New Zealand Tablet* from 1873 but failed to win the post of editor, possibly because Bishop Moran disliked his Masonic and Protestant connections. Bracken's anguish found expression in his poem "Not Understood," which, lamenting "poisoned shafts of falsehood and derision," became hugely popular after 1879. Another poem, "God Defend New Zealand," celebrated a country in which "Men of every creed and race gather here before Thy face." Much later it became the country's national anthem, today sung in Maori and English before All Black rugby internationals. Waddell wrote a preface to a volume of Bracken's poetry, chaired his public lectures, and, after Bracken's marriage broke down, visited him when he was living sick and alone behind the Mornington tram sheds.[40]

In a city numerically dominated by Scots and English, Waddell made the most of his Irishness. In May of 1900 a record audience packed St Andrew's Church Hall to listen to Waddell lecture on "Irish Humourists [*sic*]." In lilting tones he told stories about ordinary Irish people – beggars, soldiers, servants, and peasants – highlighting their fondness for fighting, whisky, and witty repartee. The *Otago Daily Times* reported that Waddell kept the crowd in "a state of great merriment," repeatedly "convulsed with laughter," for "almost two hours."[41]

PROHIBITION, SABBATH OBSERVANCE, AND BIBLES IN SCHOOLS

If anti-sweating, famine relief, and Irish humour could bring the Irish diaspora together, other causes dear to Waddell sparked greater division.

The pan-Irish consciousness explored above could fracture as quickly as it formed. The following section explores Waddell's involvement in the prohibition, Sabbath observance, and women's suffrage campaigns. Though strong in New Zealand, these movements also flourished among the Protestant diaspora elsewhere, as other contributors to this volume show. I pay particular attention to temperance and suffrage, campaigns boosted by the arrival from the United States in 1885 of the Women's Christian Temperance Union (WCTU). WCTU branches mushroomed in and around Dunedin, which became the chief national centre of both temperance and women's suffrage agitation.

Early issues of Moran's *Tablet* advertised around forty Otago hotels and public houses, often with Irish names and Catholic proprietors. Waddell, by contrast, established a branch of the Blue Ribbon Army at St Andrew's in 1883; dozens signed a petition supporting the Local Option Extension Bill introduced into parliament by M.W. Green, MHR for Dunedin East and a Church of Christ evangelist.[42] In February of 1889, as anti-sweating heated up, Waddell praised Methodism as a "people's church" in the "vanguard of progress" because it supported a humane reform – prohibition – that would help "the mass of the people," especially women and children.[43] Waddell's support for prohibition was inspired by similar concerns over anti-sweating: he believed that poorer people, especially women and children, suffered most from alcohol abuse.

As founding editor of the *Christian Outlook*, the national Presbyterian weekly, Waddell supported Sabbath observance for similar reasons. Criticizing North Island mining companies that forced employees to work on Sundays in order "to swell the dividends of shareholders," Waddell argued that God intended the Fourth Commandment to "preserve the liberties of the working man." Parliament must safeguard the Sabbath by law, he urged in 1897.[44] Earlier, Waddell warned *Outlook* readers that Liberal premier Richard Seddon, an Anglican and ex-publican, and his cabinet minister James Carroll had travelled by train to visit the Waitomo Caves, a popular tourist attraction, on a Sunday. Waddell urged readers to call the premier to account "in Parliament for this outrage upon the religious convictions of the people, and gross misuse of public funds."[45] Waddell did not hesitate to criticize the nation's leaders when they flouted the Fourth Commandment.

In July 1892, at a raucous meeting in the Dunedin Town Hall that repeatedly spiralled out of control, Waddell led the "temperance party," dominated by prohibitionists from the evangelical churches, against the "moderate party," led by Anglicans, Catholics, and Jews connected to the Licensed Victualler's Association, a wealthy and powerful lobby group. Waddell's friend John Wesley Jago, Congregationalist editor of the *Prohibitionist* newspaper, moved that the meeting urge Parliament to reject the Compensation to Licensed Victuallers Bill. If liquor sellers lost their licences, government should not compensate them. Dismissing Jago's "claptrap," Irish ex-publican John Carroll, who became Dunedin's first Catholic mayor, called compensation "fair and just." He might "sympathize" with his opponents, said Carroll, if they were not "so aggressive and dishonest." After the "hisses and uproar" died down, Jewish brewer Maurice Joel, supporting Carroll, praised the "British nation" for its "liberal ideas" on "justice to all." He had gone into brewing, said Joel, because it was "just" and "profitable," but, thanks to the prohibitionists, he had already lost ten to fifteen thousand pounds of income.[46]

The Reverend William Ready, a Bible Christian minister from an Irish Catholic background, replied. His fiery preaching regularly attracted over fifteen hundred people to Sunday night services in the Garrison Hall – probably the largest congregation in the country. Ready urged "the people" to "throw off the shackles of the divine right of brewers" and refuse "to allow a few men who are interested in their trade to rule the thousands of people in this colony": the "British people are not to be oppressed – by publicans." Echoing Waddell's anti-sweating rhetoric, Ready thundered: "[We] have been fighting for the protection of property too much, and not enough for men and women. All who believe in the grand old Book should compensate the publicans for all the empty coffins, pawnbrokers' tickets, and drafts on the bank of hell." Ready founded the Methodist Central Mission on Stafford Street, next door to St Andrew's. He worked with Waddell not only against drink but also in the areas of social work and evangelism in the Devil's Half Acre.

Stirred by Ready's rhetoric, the crowd called for Waddell. This caused such a commotion that it took some time for the mayor to restore order. He felt "a good deal of pain," said Waddell, in opposing "gentlemen whom he respected," including several "intimate friends." Although it seemed "a little hard" that licensees should be dispossessed "without getting some compensation," the "interests of a large number of citizens" harmed by drink outweighed this consideration. Since the law had already reduced the hours during which liquor could be sold, how could temperance advocates "be such terrible confiscators," asked Waddell, "if they said that publicans should not sell" liquor not just on Sunday but also "on Monday, Tuesday, Wednesday and Thursday." Pandemonium erupted. Drowned out, Waddell stopped trying to speak after several minutes and sat down. The meeting voted to reject compensation.

As ever, Waddell sought to mobilize public opinion to promote the common good, as he saw it, without demonizing those with whom he disagreed. The respect he expressed for non-prohibitionists went beyond mere rhetoric: his St Andrew's congregation probably included those who liked a wee dram.

Although initially a supporter of the secular state primary school system established by the Education Act, 1877, Waddell joined the evangelical-dominated Bible-in-Schools movement in 1893, advocating "a scheme of lessons from the Bible" over "mere general reading."[47] By "excluding the Bible from our national schools," he told readers of the *Christian Outlook* the following year, we dismiss "the noblest element from our national life" and encourage moral "degeneration" and "selfishness."[48] Extolling the Bible as "an instrument of salvation" with "saving, transforming power" he told his St Andrew's congregation in 1908 they that should not expect it "to teach science, or philosophy, or history, or literature." But keeping "the Word of God" out of the people's "hands in their homes and in their schools" was "the direst blunder."[49]

WOMEN'S SUFFRAGE

Campaigning for prohibition, Sabbath observance, and Bibles in schools, Waddell found some of his strongest supporters among the evangelical Protestant women who dominated first wave feminism in Dunedin. Waddell was one of four ministers present at the founding meeting of the Dunedin Women's Christian Temperance Union in 1885. Led and numerically dominated by Presbyterian, Baptist, and Methodist women such as Rachel Reynolds, Catherine Fulton, Mary Downie Stewart, and Harriet Morison, the WCTU campaigned for prohibition, Sabbath observance, Bibles in schools, votes for women, and the raising of the age of consent. Reynolds and Morison played prominent roles in Waddell's anti-sweating campaign and in the formation of the Tailoresses Union.[50]

Morison, born in Ireland to a master tailor and his wife, served as a lay preacher for the Bible Christians, a working-class offshoot of Wesleyan Methodism, and probably attended the Reverend Ready's services in the Garrison Hall. Preaching prepared her well for the suffrage campaign. Addressing a crowded public meeting in Dunedin's Choral Hall in July 1891, Morison spoke for "a very large number of working women ... who earnestly desired the franchise extended to them, because they felt the need of it." Applause greeted Morison's claim that working women wanted "many reforms" and "would like to have a voice in the return of members to Parliament, who would look faithfully after their interests." Far from inevitably preferring "the Tory candidate," as critics alleged, Morison insisted that women, "broad and liberal in their views," would "only vote for those candidates who were pure in their lives and conduct."[51]

After four more Protestant pillars of the community supported suffrage, Rachel Reynolds took the floor. She had worked closely with Waddell in anti-sweating, unionism, and, with Jewish journalist Mark Cohen, to establish free kindergartens. Determined to refute anti-suffragists who quoted Scripture, Reynolds set out to show that "woman had a right to equality with man in the very nature of things" by showing that Genesis, "the first and oldest constitution about which anything was known," supported female equality. Women had long suffered "injustice" through "a misunderstanding and misinterpretation of the fall of man" in Genesis, Chapter Three. After Adam and Eve ate the "forbidden fruit," God cursed "the man," not the woman, and turned "the man alone ... out of the garden." A "great many" people, Reynolds concluded, "would be sufficiently noble to admit that woman had a right not only to be regarded as man's equal but even as his superior." The audience exploded with laughter and applause.[52]

Far from disagreeing, Waddell, speaking next, dismissed all the arguments against suffrage as "wanting singularly in lucidity, in logic, and in sense of justice." The claim that women were incompetent to vote he dismissed as "a relic of the old barbaric theory that woman was lesser than a man, and was not to be counted as a unit in citizenship." Women possessed "as much intelligence and common sense," and as many "of the qualities which were essential in politics" as men. New Zealand would "never have fair and true laws for women and children until they got women in the House of Representatives" because on issues affecting women, children, and families "the judgment of women ranked far higher than the judgment of men." Waddell hoped for the day when "men should have the privilege of voting for women as their representatives."[53] Dunedin's most high-profile Presbyterian minister strongly endorsed female suffrage. Critics noticed.

MALE CRITICS

By 1892–93, Waddell's support for prohibition, female suffrage, and Bibles in schools – causes also championed by the WCTU – sparked criticism from some of the men who had supported anti-sweating. In July 1892, Samuel Lister, speaking for the white working man, warned readers of the *Otago Workman* newspaper that the "tabbies" leading the franchise campaign had joined forces with their "favourite parson" to lobby for prohibition, Bibles in schools, and votes for women. This unholy alliance between "male women" and "female men" threatened a man's right to drink and the country's free secular primary school system, "the dearest privilege the children enjoy."[54]

Alarmed, Lister forged an alliance with populist politician Henry Smith Fish and William Dawson, manager of Speights brewery. Dawson's colleague at Speights, Charles Greenslade, joined them.[55] Fish, Dawson, and Greenslade were all English-born, nominally Anglican, and profited handsomely, politically as well as financially, from the liquor trade. Dawson became mayor of Dunedin in 1887 and entered Parliament in 1890, representing Dunedin Suburbs, mainly to stop the prohibitionists. According to his biographer, he built a palatial villa in Duncan Street, filled it with treasures from around the world (including a pet monkey), banished his wife from the family home, and introduced a succession of mistresses.[56]

During the first of his six terms as mayor of Dunedin, Fish won popular support by halving the price of gas. Representing Dunedin electorates in Parliament for eleven years between 1881 and 1897, he served as the leading Dunedin and parliamentary lobbyist for the liquor trade. Although he had supported anti-sweating, by 1892, alarmed at the strong links between prohibition and suffrage, Fish, speaking in Parliament, described giving women the vote as worse than giving children "razors and revolvers" to play with. He cemented his reputation as chief enemy of the women's movement in 1892 by organizing anti-suffrage petitions that, he claimed, obtained five thousand signatures. But his paid canvassers often presented the first petition as pro-suffrage. In July, Sir John Hall and Helen Nicol of the WCTU exposed Fish's dubious tactics in Parliament and the press.[57]

WCTU leaders, furious, urged "every member of our unions" and "every member of our sex, by all that is womanly, to make an indignant protest against the actions of Mr Fish and his allies."[58] The WCTU and the Women's Franchise League, led by Harriet Morison and Nicol, a Presbyterian, took a pro-suffrage petition to the streets. By the time it reached Parliament in 1893, a remarkable 57 percent of southern Dunedin women had signed it, more than twice as many as the 25 percent of adult New Zealand women who signed.[59] Women affiliated with the area's evangelical churches, which had many working-class members, dominated the signatories, far outnumbering Catholic and, especially, Anglican signatories.[60] Unwittingly, Fish turned out to be the feminists' best friend. When he plummeted to defeat in the 1893 general election, a vast crowd of women, delighted, "indulged in a war dance, fast and furious, reaching from Garrison Hall to the Octagon."[61]

Before the election, Robert Slater, secretary of the Trades and Labour Council and a staunch Methodist, announced that Dunedin's Workers' Political Committee had chosen five Labour candidates. All accepted women's suffrage and the political demands of the New Zealand Alliance for the Abolition of the Liquor Traffic. Lister and Fish, furious at how many working-class men were supporting the parson-feminist coalition, turned on each other.[62] To them, Dunedin had far too much political religion of the wrong kind.[63] Bishop Moran, who had supported Waddell on anti-sweating and famine relief, disliked prohibition and suffrage. Dismissing prohibition as tyrannical "fanaticism," he wrote in the *Tablet* that only an "unlovely loud-voiced woman" would want the vote.[64]

Yet neither Lister nor Moran determined the behaviour of their womenfolk. At least eighteen Dunedin Catholic women signed the 1892 suffrage petition, ignoring their bishop's advice. Lister's wife, Jane, a strong Presbyterian, also signed.[65]

Moran clashed sharply with Waddell at least once. The bishop had launched the *New Zealand Tablet* in 1873 partly to campaign for state aid to Catholic schools as a matter of justice. In 1891, Moran criticized Waddell's support for secular primary schools as inconsistent with "his character as a Christian minister." Lurking behind Waddell, however, Moran spied a more sinister figure. Jewish journalist Mark Cohen had urged Waddell and Rachel Reynolds not to base their free kindergarten movement at St Andrew's but to keep it secular and open to all. Upholding "our duty" to "tell the truth," Moran warned *Tablet* readers that "no more persistent enemy of the Christian religion" could be found among "the whole world of unbelieving Jews, now engaged in an attempt to destroy Christianity." That Waddell, a "Christian minister," heeded Cohen's advice to keep kindergartens secular showed that Christianity must now be "defended from its friends."[66]

CONCLUSION

In a province founded by Scottish Free Church Presbyterians, and numerically dominated by Scots and English, two remarkable Irishmen,

Waddell and Moran, became probably the most high-profile and controversial religious leaders of their day. Both men launched and led campaigns that, controversial then and since, enduringly shaped New Zealand politics, culture, and religion. A shared pan-Irish consciousness sometimes brought them together, most easily when it came to relieving the suffering of the Irish at home. The anti-sweating campaign that Waddell launched and led also won strong support from Moran. Although neither explicitly invoked a pan-Irish identity during this campaign, it seems likely that both men battled sweating in order to build a fairer and more inclusive society in which everyone, not least the Irish, could enjoy a better life.

Although settlers of Irish birth or descent constituted just over a fifth of the total population, quite a few played prominent roles in politics, society, and the churches during this formative half-century of New Zealand history. Transplanted Ulster Protestants included John Ballance, born in County Antrim to a Protestant father and Quaker mother, who capitalized on the popular reform energies mobilized by Waddell, Moran, and others to lead the Liberal Party to victory in the 1890 general election. Horrified by sectarian riots in Belfast during his youth, Ballance became, with his friend Robert Stout, one of New Zealand's leading freethinkers. His Liberal government passed land, labour, and industrial legislation designed to enhance opportunities for small and middling people, thereby ensuring that the poverty and misery that fuelled sectarian conflict in the Old World would decline in the New.

The long reign of the Liberals lasted until 1912 when another Ulsterman, William Massey, a staunch Presbyterian born at Limavady near Londonderry, led the country. Traditionally depicted as a bigoted Orangeman, whose heavily Protestant Reform government sparked virulent sectarianism during and after the First World War, "Farmer Bill" Massey has recently received less condescending and judgmental treatment. Historian Erik Olssen argues that Massey championed widespread private property ownership in a manner that, like Ballance's Liberals, appealed to Catholic and Protestant voters alike. Rory Sweetman shows that Massey, a loyal Protestant supporter of Empire, worked to defuse the extremism of the Protestant Political Association, founded in 1917. "If there is anything I hate more than sectarianism I cannot think what it is," Massey wrote after narrowly winning the 1922 election. "I do not care what a man's religion is, or what church he attends, so long as he is a loyal citizen ... I have many Roman Catholic friends in the Tauranga Electorate, and I am glad to say that many of them voted for the Government candidate."[67]

If Waddell, Ballance, and Massey are any indication, then, it seems that transplanted Ulster Protestants who won influence in church, state, and society in New Zealand did so by widening the circle of the "we." Despite their differences, all three worked to build a fairer, more inclusive society in which socio-economic and religious differences would not reinforce one another in potentially explosive ways.

Similar dynamics may be discerned in the lives and relationships of Catholic politicians such as the Southland businessman Joseph Ward, Liberal prime minister between 1906 and 1912, regularly elected to Parliament in the predominantly Protestant electorate of Awarua. Moran's successor as editor of the *Tablet*, Henry Cleary, born in County Wexford, defended Irish and Catholic causes less abrasively than did Moran, winning respect and goodwill from Protestants for so doing. Consecrated bishop of Auckland in 1910, Cleary banned the use of provocative Irish flags and emblems in his diocese, and, disliking the fierce Irish nationalism of the *Tablet* under the editorship of Father James Kelley, he launched a rival paper, the *Month*, in 1918. Cleary corresponded with politicians in all parties and, in 1922, described Massey's Reform Government as "the very best friends that New Zealand Catholics ever had in the matter of education."[68]

NOTES

1 *New Zealand Truth*, 2 June 1927, 6.

2 *New Zealand Tablet*, 18 September 1896, 4.

3 Coffey, *Politics*.

4 *Oxford Dictionary of National Biography Online*, s.v. "Reid, (Thomas) Mayne (1818–1883)," by Dennis Butts, http://www.oxforddnb.com/view/article/23335 (viewed 4 April 2013).

5 Waddell, *My Pathway*, 5–7; J. Collie, *Waddell*, 22–3.

6 Bardon, *History of Ulster*, 240–316.

7 Waddell, *My Pathway*, 6.

8 Collie, *Rutherford Waddell*, 22–4; Waddell, *My Pathway*, 8–9.

9 Livingstone, "Science."

10 Waddell, *My Pathway*, 9–11.

11 Ibid., 13–22.

12 Collie, *Memoir*, 32–4, 39–41.

13 *Belfast Witness*, 26 August 1932, n.p. This appears in a miscellaneous collection of newspaper clippings on Waddell contained in St Andrew's,

Dunedin, Historical Papers, miscellaneous, c. 1880s–1950s, Presbyterian Archives, Knox College, Dunedin.

14 Stenhouse, "Darwinism in New Zealand."

15 Collie, *Memoir*, 76.

16 *Dictionary of New Zealand Biography. Te Ara – The Encyclopedia of New Zealand*, s.v. "Waddell, Rutherford," by Ian Breward, last modified 30 October 2012, http://www.TeAra.govt.nz/en/biographies/2w1/waddell-rutherford.

17 Brosnahan, "Rutherford Waddell."

18 Laracy, "Life and Context"; Laracy, "Bishop Moran"; Davis, *Irish Issues*.

19 Stenhouse, "God, the Devil and Gender."

20 *Otago Daily Times*, 8 September 1883.

21 This account is based on the reports appearing in *Otago Daily Times*, 4 February 1884, 25 February 1884.

22 *Otago Daily Times*, 27 July 1888.

23 Stenhouse, "Christianity."

24 *Otago Witness*, 26 October 1888; *Otago Daily Times*, 20 October 1888; *Southland Times*, 22 October 1888; *Tuapeka Times*, 24 October 1888; *Star*, 22 October 1888; *Wanganui Chronicle*, 26 October 1888; *Poverty Bay Herald*, 29 October 1888.

25 *Otago Daily Times*, 8 November 1888.

26 Ibid., 6 February 1889.

27 *New Zealand Tablet*, 9 November 1888, 1.

28 Ibid.

29 *Otago Daily Times*, 8 June 1889. The following account is based on this report of the meeting, which may be regarded as a general reference.

30 On popular antagonism to religious hypocrisy, see Stenhouse, "Christianity," 38–43.

31 *Otago Daily Times*, 8 June 1889.

32 Ibid., 15 February 1889.

33 Ibid., 8 June 1889.

34 *New Zealand Tablet*, 14 June 1889, 17.

35 Appendices to the Journals of the House of Representatives 1890, H-5.

36 *New Zealand Tablet*, 23 May 1890, 16.

37 Ibid., 23 January 1880, 17.

38 Ibid., 6 May 1887, 15.

39 *Christian Outlook* 27 October (1894): 48.

40 *Dictionary of New Zealand Biography. Te Ara – the Encyclopedia of New Zealand*, s.v. "Bracken, Thomas – Bracken, Thomas," by W.S. Broughton,

last modified 30 October 2012, http://www.TeAra.govt.nz/en/biographies/2b35/bracken-thomas; Olssen, *Accidental Utopia*, 237–8.

41 *Otago Daily Times*, 8 May 1890.

42 Ibid., 30 June 1883.

43 Ibid., 1 February 1889.

44 *Christian Outlook* 24, 4 (1897): 277.

45 Ibid., 8, 1 (1893): 86.

46 The following account of this meeting is based on the report in *Otago Daily Times*, 6 July 1892, which may be regarded as a general reference for this and the following two paragraphs.

47 *Otago Witness*, 29 June 1893.

48 *Christian Outlook* 7, 1 (1894): 80–2.

49 *Otago Witness*, 20 May 1908, 33.

50 *Otago Daily Times*, 8 May 1889; Page, "Introduction," 7.

51 *Otago Daily Times*, 11 July 1891; see also *Evening Star*, 11 July 1891, suppl., 1.

52 *Otago Daily Times*, 11 July 1891.

53 Ibid.

54 *Otago Workman*, 9 July 1892.

55 Olssen, *Building the New World*, 180–3.

56 Gordon, "Dawson, 122–3.

57 *Otago Daily Times*, 26 July 1892. On Fish, see Turner, "Henry Smith Fish."

58 *Prohibitionist* 1892 (the Hocken microfiche copy lacks issue and page numbers). For a fuller discussion, see Turner, "Henry Smith Fish," 52–9.

59 Thomlinson, "We the Undersigned."

60 Stenhouse, "God, the Devil and Gender."

61 *Otago Workman*, 2 December 1893, 4.

62 Olssen, *Building the New World*, 185–6.

63 *Otago Workman*, 23 April 1892, 4.

64 *New Zealand Tablet*, 8 September 1893, 17, 27–8; 15 September 1893, 17.

65 Stenhouse, "God, the Devil and Gender," 328–9.

66 *New Zealand Tablet*, 25 December 1891, 1.

67 Olssen, "Towards a Reassessment"; Sweetman, "Beery Bill"; Watson and Paterson, "Introduction," 10.

68 Rory Sweetman. "Cleary, Henry William," from the Dictionary of New Zealand Biography. Te Ara – the Encyclopedia of New Zealand, updated 30 October 2012, http://www.TeAra.govt.nz/en/biographies/3c22/cleary-henry-william; Sweetman, "Beery Bill," quotation on 79.

16

"A Veritable Hurricane of Sectarianism": The Year 1920 and Ethno-Religious Conflict in Australia

JEFF KILDEA

Throughout the nineteenth century the Irish formed a substantial minority of immigrants to Australia, justifying its claim to be an outpost of "Greater Ireland." Up to the 1880s, the Irish who went to Australia were mainly from the south, particularly the Province of Munster, with the result that Irish immigrants were mostly Catholics. Thereafter the emigration map changed, with Leinster and Ulster, provinces that were more Protestant than Munster, accounting for an increasing proportion of immigrants, with Ulster taking the lead in the early 1900s. Nevertheless, despite particular geographical concentrations of Protestant Irish in Australia as identified by Dianne Hall (chap. 14, this volume), there was overall a close identification of Catholicism and Irishness. As noted by Eric Richards (chap. 12, this volume): "Irish emigration and religion, like Siamese twins, are virtually interchangeable and scarcely separable." The presence of this Irish Catholic minority in the British Protestant-dominated Australian colonies led to friction and episodes of sectarianism.

While this chapter examines four such episodes that occurred in Australia in 1920, similar events occurred in other parts of the British Empire during the nineteenth and early twentieth centuries. As John Wolffe explains, the "early nineteenth-century expansion of settlement in British North America and Australia – and eventually New Zealand and southern Africa – coincided with a revival in anti-Catholic activity in Britain."[1] Events such as the Act of Union, 1800, and Catholic Emancipation in 1829 provided the impetus for a reassertion of a national Protestant identity, particularly in Ireland.

According to Wolffe, the concept of empire took hold as the outflow into the settler colonies increased and there emerged an identification between Protestantism and empire. Consequently, the Empire's unity was seen as essential to the maintenance of Protestantism, which was under challenge from a resurgent Catholicism. Ireland was central to this struggle, particularly with the agitation for Irish Home Rule, which, in the opinion of empire loyalists, would inevitably lead to the Empire's disintegration. Protestant societies were formed within the settler societies, where itinerant preachers (such as the Canadian ex-priest Charles Chiniquy) and organizations (such as the Orange Order) promoted the cause. From the 1890s, Protestant organization assumed an imperial dimension with the establishment of the Imperial Protestant Federation. Whenever the Irish were a sizeable proportion in these settler societies ethno-religious discord occurred. Sometimes it was a local interest only, but often there was an imperial dimension, such as with regard to the debates in 1901 and 1910 over the anti-Catholic language in the coronation oath and the continuing arguments over Home Rule. The four episodes examined here are a manifestation of the sectarian conflict that occurred with the expansion of Greater Ireland.

SECTARIANISM IN AUSTRALIA

Sectarianism, in the sense of religious conflict and division, has a long history in Australia.[2] While its essence is religious difference, sectarianism is much more than theological disputation. It has been described as "a complex socio-cultural phenomenon: a synthesis of religious, socio-cultural and ethno-political relationships that use religion as a symbolic and expedient means of forming identities, asserting ideologies and articulating rivalries and grievances."[3] In the Australian context sectarianism principally manifested itself in terms of the ethno-religious rivalry between the Protestant majority, mostly of British heritage, and the Catholic minority, almost totally of Irish heritage.[4]

Generally, sectarianism in Australia has simmered just below the surface, breaking out every now and again into open displays of hostility. A striking example is the rioting between Orangemen and Irish Catholics in Melbourne in 1846, at which time shots were exchanged.[5] Thankfully, such violent outbursts have been the exception, with the most frequent manifestation of the phenomenon being angry rhetoric published in newspapers or delivered from public platforms by overexcited orators.

In the history of sectarianism in Australia, 1920 stands out as a particularly busy year, when month after month newspaper headlines announced stories with a sectarian theme. So much so that, in December 1920, New South Wales (NSW) attorney general E.A. McTiernan used the term "a veritable hurricane of sectarianism" to describe to Archbishop Kelly, who had just returned from overseas, what had occurred during his absence that year.[6] This chapter examines a number of incidents that grabbed the headlines in 1920 in an endeavour to illustrate what McTiernan might have had in mind when he used that phrase.

The events of 1920 covered in this chapter need to be seen within the context of the issues that had divided Catholics and Protestants for decades in Australia – namely, state aid for Catholic schools and the Irish struggle for self-government. In addition, memories of the First World War, and of how the Catholics were often accused of disloyalty and shirking (particularly following the conscription campaigns), were still fresh.

STATE AID

The most significant local issue that had the ability to arouse sectarian feeling in early twentieth-century Australia was the campaign for the restoration of state financing of Catholic schools. During the 1870s and 1880s, the various Australian colonies had abolished denominational education funding and had established systems of free, secular, and state-run education. The Catholic Church had responded to this change by continuing to run and to fund its own schools. At first the Catholic bishops expected the colonial governments to realize that the new system was inadequate and to restore denominational funding. For their part, the governments expected the Catholics to abandon their endeavour to maintain their own schools. However, as the years passed the predictions of both sides proved to be wrong. A separate Catholic school system grew and flourished.[7]

In the early part of the twentieth century Catholics began to agitate more vigorously for a restoration of denominational funding, eventually institutionalizing that agitation through the Catholic Federation. In New South Wales, Victoria, South Australia, and Tasmania the Catholic Federation acted as the main political lobby group in pursuit of state aid for Catholic schools, putting pressure, in particular, on the Labor Party, which was seen by Catholics as the most likely to be sympathetic to their claims. However, given that 75 percent of the electorate was Protestant and largely hostile to the state's providing assistance to Catholics, whom they regarded as deliberately separating their children from the rest of the community, Labor politicians, including Catholics, rejected these approaches, though Labor governments did provide concessions, such as bursaries. The Catholic Federation's aggressive tactics during state elections strained relations between the Catholic Church and the Labor Party, particularly in NSW in 1913 and in Victoria in 1914.[8]

The Catholic Federation's campaign was largely suspended during the First World War, but it resumed soon thereafter, particularly in NSW, which, in December 1918, adopted proportional representation for the upcoming 1920 elections. The Catholic Federation saw its opportunity to win seats in Parliament. In October 1919, the federation resolved to establish the Democratic Party to contest the state elections. Many Protestants regarded the decision with alarm, predicting "the approach in time of a tremendous trouble" that foreshadowed the need to form a Protestant party "to defend the country against Papal aggression."[9] The response was not a political party but the establishment of the Protestant Federation.[10] Its purpose was to "conserve and preserve the rights and liberties possessed by us under the British flag," and its principal objective was "to maintain loyalty to the Throne, the unity of the Empire, and to promote the national development of Australia."[11]

As it turned out, none of the Democratic Party's candidates was successful at the elections held on 20 March 1920, and Labor, which had won forty-three of the ninety seats, formed a minority government. The Catholic community would pay a price for the Democratic Party's intrusion into electoral politics.

Apart from angering the Labor Party, which in government had provided concessions to Catholic schools that the non-Labor parties had refused to provide, the Democratic Party signalled to the Protestant community that Catholic militancy had entered a new phase.[12] The concerns that this generated strengthened the hand of those Protestants most opposed to the Catholic Church, and it provided the Protestant Federation with an opportunity to promote its own brand of militancy. In NSW this would ultimately lead to the 1922 election of a Nationalist government pledged to the restoration of Protestant values and to curbing the influence of the Catholic Church.[13]

However, it was not only the Catholic Church's intrusion into electoral politics that accounted for the rise of Protestant militancy following the elections: the presence of a large number of Catholics in the

Labor government also caused alarm among Protestants.[14] Ironically, the same elections at which the Catholic Federation had considered it necessary to stand its own candidates for Parliament resulted in Catholics under the Labor banner entering Parliament and the cabinet in record numbers. Of the forty-three members of the new caucus, twenty-five were Catholics, and in the cabinet, five of the thirteen ministers were Catholics.[15] Although Catholics accounted for less than 25 percent of the population of NSW, they constituted almost 60 percent of the Labor Caucus and held almost 40 percent of the cabinet positions in the state government.

To many Protestants, this was a potentially menacing situation, coming as it did just a few months after T.J. Ryan, former Queensland premier and aspiring federal Labor leader, had chaired the Irish Race Convention in Melbourne, at which a resolution, moved by Archbishop Mannix, had called for self-determination for Ireland. Protestant commentators declared this to be evidence of a dangerous alliance between the Catholic Church and the Labor Party.[16]

In the past, Protestant spokespeople who raised the spectre of "Rome rule" in Australia could be dismissed as alarmist and irrational – after all, Catholics were a minority. The NSW elections demonstrated the dangers of such complacency. When Labor was last in government, before the split over conscription, Protestants controlled the party and were able to keep Catholic militants in check. Now that Labor was back in government, with Catholics in control, many Protestants feared that it would only be a matter of time before the party and the government would dance to the tune called by Archbishop Kelly and the Catholic Federation.[17]

IRISH WAR OF INDEPENDENCE

Meanwhile, as the votes were still being counted in the NSW elections, in Ireland a special force of reinforcements for the Royal Irish Constabulary (RIC) was being deployed. They were British ex-servicemen who would soon become known as the "Black and Tans." Their deployment, together with the increased use of the military and the deployment in July of another RIC force known as the Auxiliaries, signalled a new phase in the British government's response to the deteriorating security position in Ireland. The escalation of the war and the use of terrorist tactics by the ill-disciplined and brutal Black and Tans and Auxiliaries would soon cause hardship in Ireland and consternation throughout the British Empire.

Australians, both Catholic and Protestant, were generally well informed about events in Ireland and had been for a long time, though the nuances of the situation were not always well understood. What they did not learn from the metropolitan dailies was made up for by the religious press, which, in the early twentieth century, was prolific and carried detailed reports and commentary on the Irish troubles.

Interest in Irish affairs had increased from 1912 onwards with the introduction of the third Home Rule bill, the Easter Rising, and the War of Independence. Generally, Catholic newspapers took the side of the Irish Nationalists, while Protestant newspapers, as well as the metropolitan dailies, supported the Crown forces. During 1920, as the fighting in Ireland escalated and the atrocities increased, there was no shortage of lurid facts that editors on either side could report in order to justify their newspaper's editorial line.

Catholics were encouraged to see in the suffering of the Irish people a reflection of their own position as second-class citizens forced to bear the burden of funding their children's education without government assistance.[18] To many Protestants the situation in Ireland demonstrated the fate that would befall them if the Romanists succeeded in gaining control in Australia – epithets such as Romanism, Mannixism, Sinn Feinism, disloyalty, revolutionism, enemies of the Empire, and so on littered the pages of Protestant newspapers. This is the context within which the events described below took place.

DEPORTATION OF FATHER CHARLES JERGER[19]

At the end of the First World War the federal government had established procedures to determine the fate of thousands of persons who had been interned during hostilities. As a result, nearly five thousand persons of German origin were deported, one of them being Father Charles Jerger, a German-born Catholic priest who had emigrated from Germany to England and then to Australia when he was five years old.

Following a series of inquiries and reviews and an unsuccessful appeal to the High Court on 21 May 1920, Jerger's deportation was imminent.[20] The Catholic Federation organized a meeting in Sydney to protest the priest's deportation. In his address to the meeting, the federation's president, P.S. Cleary, linked Father Jerger's case with the troubles in Ireland by charging that the same tactics practised with respect to Father Jerger were being practised in Ireland. The epithet "Brit-Hun" was frequently used during the evening to describe those against whom the anger of the meeting was then being directed.[21] This was an instance in which the situation in Ireland was informing the nature of the response of Irish Australian Catholics to a purely local affair, and in which the federal government's ham-fisted treatment of an otherwise obscure individual was being translated into an attack on the Catholic Church and community.

That meeting was the precursor of many more across the country. In Melbourne, John Wren, with the support of Archbishop Mannix, organized a protest meeting at the Cathedral Hall,[22] but the biggest demonstration by far was held in Sydney's Moore Park on Sunday, 30 May 1920. The *Daily Telegraph* estimated the crowd to be 150,000.[23] This monster meeting, which was organized by the Catholic Federation, almost turned into a riot when a group of ex-servicemen, flying the Union Jack, took over one of the speaking platforms and ejected the speakers.

The case continued to attract wide public attention, with the government moving Jerger from Sydney to Melbourne and then to Adelaide, but public protests followed him to each city. Catholics were supported in their protests by trade unionists who used their industrial power to delay his deportation. However, this was to no avail, and once Jerger was safely out of the country the controversy subsided.[24]

Gerard Henderson argues that Prime Minister Hughes and Defence Minister George Foster Pearce conducted their case against the priest with "a ruthless and vindictive intensity." He refers to an address by Hughes to the Bendigo branch of the Protestant Federation in which the prime minister launched a frontal attack on those disloyal elements within Australia – of whom he specifically named Jerger and Archbishop Mannix – who would plunge a dagger into the heart of the Empire.[25] Henderson concludes that "Jerger's deportation was the loyalists' revenge on those Catholics who had spoken out against the Government of Hughes and Pearce during and immediately after the war."[26] Henderson's assessment reflects the view held by many Catholics at the time. The Catholic Federation's column in the *Catholic Press* records: "[Jerger] is being sent away at the irresponsible whim of a dictator, who is acting under the pressure of organised anti-Catholic bigots."[27]

Those hoping that the priest's deportation would extinguish the sectarian firestorm that had blazed around him were soon to be disappointed. Two days before Father Jerger's ship slipped out of Freemantle an event occurred thousands of kilometres away in outback NSW – an event that would reignite the flames and once more set Irish Catholics and British Protestants against each other.

SISTER LIGUORI AFFAIR[28]

On Saturday night, 24 July 1920, Sister Liguori (Bridget Partridge), clad only in her nightdress, walked barefoot out of the convent of the Presentation Sisters at Mount Erin, Wagga Wagga. After crossing a paddock, wet with recent rain, the nun sought refuge in a house in Coleman Street. Soon afterwards she found herself under the protection of R.E. Barton, the grand master of the Loyal Orange Institution.

Bridget Partridge had emigrated to Australia from County Kildare in 1908 at the age of eighteen years, shortly after being received into the Order of the Sisters of the Presentation of the Blessed Virgin Mary. On her arrival in Australia she entered the Mount Erin convent at Wagga Wagga where she was professed in 1911. At first she worked as a teacher. However, after an adverse report in 1918, she was relegated to domestic duties. Resentful of her demotion and suffering poor health, she came to the view that she no longer had a vocation; however, preferring to avoid the moral pressure that she feared would be brought to bear on her should she apply to be released from her vows, Sister Liguori brooded, allowing her resentment to grow.

Eventually, a paranoid fear that she was about to be murdered by her Mother Superior triggered the nun's sudden departure from the convent. When the Mother Superior realized that Sister Liguori was missing, she alerted the police, who organized a search. However, the search was in vain as the family with whom Bridget had taken refuge had made contact with the Loyal Orange Institution, and within twenty-four hours the nun was on her way to Sydney. After a few days, the bishop of Wagga Wagga, Joseph Wilfrid Dwyer, who was responsible for the nun's welfare and was acting on the advice of her doctor, who indicated that she was "mentally unhinged," instituted proceedings under the Lunacy Act for her apprehension. Within a short time the police ascertained her whereabouts, and at midnight on Saturday, 7 August 1920, Bridget Partridge was taken into custody and lodged at the Darlinghurst Reception House.

On the following Monday Bridget appeared at the Reception Court, where T.J. Ryan KC (the former Queensland premier and, at that time, a member of the House of Representatives) announced to the magistrate that he appeared for Miss Partridge. Ryan had been retained by the prominent Catholic layman, P.J. Minahan MLA, who claimed to be a friend of Miss Partridge. However, Mr F.B. Boyce of counsel, who had been briefed by solicitors retained by the Orange Order, also claimed to appear for Miss Partridge. When Boyce challenged Ryan's right to appear for the nun, the magistrate remanded her in custody pending receipt of a psychiatric report.

On the following Friday, the chief medical officer reported to the court that, in his opinion, Bridget was sane, and the magistrate thereupon ordered her release, allowing her to leave the court in the company of Reverend Touchell and his wife. Outside the courtroom a large crowd had assembled, and when news of the magistrate's decision was conveyed to them it was greeted by cheers and boos from different sections of the gathering, with much heckling and pushing and shoving. This was only the beginning of what would build up to be a major public controversy, lapped up by an enthusiastic press eager to inform a scandalized public of the salacious details.

Lurid accounts of convent cruelty and runaway nuns had spawned a genre of anti-Catholic literature across the British Empire and in the United States. Names such as Maria Monk (Canada), Rebecca Reed (United States), Susanna Saurin (England), Edith O'Gorman (United States), and Mary Basil (Canada) were familiar to Protestants through their racy and popular exposés of convent life. In the 1870s and 1880s O'Gorman had lectured on her experiences in the United States, Canada, Britain, Australia, and New Zealand.[29] Australia now had its own runaway nun to excite public interest.

Both the Orange Lodge and the Catholic Federation made public appeals to defray the costs of the case,[30] and Catholics who believed that Sister Liguori was being held against her will wrote to newspapers offering her accommodation in Catholic homes.[31] In the meantime, Protestant congregations, Orange lodges, and branches of the Protestant Federation passed resolutions endorsing the action taken by Barton and calling for government inspection of convents.[32] Similar resolutions were also passed at meetings in other states.[33]

At a rally at Bexley on 26 August 1920, speakers included W.R.C. Bagnall MLA who, according to the *Sydney Morning Herald*,

> emphasised the need for organisation among the Protestant Churches to combat the evil forces of the Roman Catholic Church. He was opposed to sectarianism, but this struggle was one of patriotism. The Church of Rome had done its best to destroy the Empire by bringing about disintegration within the countries that formed it. All through the war the Vatican had been hand-in-glove with the enemy.[34]

That month the Address in Reply debate gave parliamentarians an opportunity to air their views on the Sr Liguori affair, with Protestant members speaking in support of Bridget's right to liberty, railing against Catholic institutions, and demanding government inspection of convents to prevent young women being held against their will. Catholic members, in an equally strident manner, refuted the allegations made against the convents.[35] In September, Thomas Henley MLA called on the government to appoint a Royal Commission to inquire into women in convents,[36] and in November he sought leave to introduce a private member's bill "to provide security against detention of persons against their will, in any institutions, or by any persons." Catholic members responded with derision to Henley's thinly disguised attack on the convent system, and, at times, the debates became very heated, with P.J. Minahan declaring, "If you in any way interfere with these Catholic institutions there will be a 'mess-up' here worse than that which occurred on the plains of Flanders." At the close of one of the debates, members had to intervene to prevent physical violence between Henley and C.C. Lazzarini.[37]

While the politicians made what they could out of the affair, Bridget's private life was in turmoil. Her younger brother Joseph lived in Hong Kong. In response to a cable sent to him by the Mount Erin convent, Joseph arrived in Sydney on 7 September 1920. His arrival in Australia was accompanied by the sort of intrigue that might be expected in a John Le Carré novel. To avoid his falling into the hands of the Orange Order, Joseph was taken off the ship at Townsville and transported by train to Brisbane, where Charles Lawlor, secretary of the Catholic Federation, met him and accompanied him to Sydney. All the while, Archbishop Duhig kept Bishop Dwyer informed of Joseph's movements using coded telegrams.[38]

The Catholic Federation, which was acting in the affair on behalf of Bishop Dwyer, took charge of Joseph and made use of him to gain publicity in its campaign against Barton and Touchell, whom it accused of detaining Bridget against her will. The federation also launched a public appeal for funds to assist Joseph to recover his sister.[39] Joseph, who was an accomplished musician, performed at many of these functions. There were some in the federation who opposed these tactics, believing that, because Joseph had come to Australia to return his sister to Ireland, he should not be paraded like a "show puppy" at publicity stunts. It was also being suggested that the Catholic Federation had in fact prevented Joseph from taking his sister home.[40]

Although by the close of 1920 publicity surrounding the affair had died down, it was reignited in the following year when, on 30 June 1921, Justice David Ferguson of the Supreme Court commenced hearing an action for damages brought by Bridget Partridge against Bishop Dwyer in which the former nun alleged that the bishop had procured her arrest and imprisonment without just cause. However, the jury found against her.[41] On the following Monday night, Sydney's Catholics, numbering upwards of ten thousand, filled the Town Hall for a meeting to celebrate the victory.[42]

Bridget Partridge's lawsuit had commenced not long after the Protestant press had carried a report of the Canadian ex-nun, Sister Mary Basil, receiving an award of $24,000 damages against her bishop for attempted abduction. It is not known whether the Canadian case prompted Bridget Partridge's action, but it would add another chapter to the annals of "runaway nuns," reinforcing anti-Catholic attitudes that were already widespread across Greater Ireland.[43]

Wagga Wagga was deeply divided over the affair. In July 1921 division turned to violence when Reverend Touchell visited the area to establish branches of the Protestant Federation, a counterweight to the Catholic Federation. At meetings held at Marrar and Coolamon, Touchell was assaulted and had to be rescued by police. A number of men were later convicted of riotous behaviour and assault.[44]

ARREST OF ARCHBISHOP MANNIX ON THE HIGH SEAS[45]

In the midst of the Sister Liguori affair and within days of Father Jerger's deportation, a new controversy was about to erupt that would reverberate across Greater Ireland. Early in 1920, Archbishop Mannix announced that, for his forthcoming *ad limina* visit to Rome to report to the pope on his diocese, he would travel via the United States and Ireland, where he would visit his mother, aged ninety years, whom he had not seen since 1913. British intelligence, however, feared the archbishop had another agenda and advised the British government that Mannix intended to excite disaffection in Ireland over Britain's handling of affairs there.[46] As the archbishop's six-week tour of the United States progressed, British concern increased, especially after Mannix met up with Eamon De Valera in Omaha and then, later, at a Catholic Summer School at Cliff Haven, outside New York.[47] At Cliff Haven Mannix delivered a fiery speech in which, according to the report in the *Times* (London) he "denounced England as the perpetual enemy of the United States, and demanded American recognition of Sinn Féin."[48] After telling his American audience that Ireland was ruled by an alien government, he continued:

> England never was a friend of the United States. When your fathers fought it was against England. Ireland has the same grievance against the same enemy, only ten times greater. I hope Ireland will make a fight equally successful. England was your enemy; England is your enemy today; England will be your enemy for all time.[49]

On 23 July 1920, the British government instructed its consul general in New York to inform Archbishop Mannix that he would not be permitted to land in Ireland.[50]

On 31 July, Mannix left the United States on board the SS *Baltic* bound for Queenstown (Cobh), County Cork. Just before midnight on Sunday, 8 August 1920, with the Irish coast in sight and bonfires ablaze to welcome Mannix home, a British destroyer, HMS *Wivern*, pulled alongside the *Baltic*. After being served with orders banning him from landing in Ireland and from visiting a number of British cities with large Irish populations, Mannix was taken from the *Baltic* and transferred to the *Wivern*, which landed him at Penzance in England.

News of Archbishop Mannix's arrest on the *Baltic* led to a wave of protest meetings in England, the United States, and Australia. In Australia, meetings were held in Melbourne, Sydney, and other cities and towns around the country. The Sydney meeting, which was organized by the Catholic Federation and attracted about fifty thousand people to the Domain, was chaired by P.S. Cleary, who told the gathering that "they would not be justified in keeping quiet under the insults which had been heaped upon the Catholic community and the great democratic leader, Archbishop Mannix."[51] Father Maurice O'Reilly, whose fiery rhetoric was legendary, did not disappoint the crowd, managing to link the incident not only with anti-Catholic and anti-Irish sentiment but also with a plot by Hughes and "the reptile press" to oppress the workers.[52]

Despite the international protests, the British government maintained the ban on Mannix's visiting Ireland. For the next few months, while he remained in Britain, the archbishop of Melbourne was happy to exploit for the Irish cause the notoriety that his arrest on the high seas had generated. He made a number of speeches in support of Ireland and administered the last rites to Terence MacSwiney, the lord mayor of Cork, who was on hunger strike in Brixton Prison. MacSwiney had become a symbol of Irish resistance around the world, particularly in Australia. A month later, on 25 October 1920, MacSwiney died. His death led to more protest rallies in Australia, which would have further repercussions in connection with the next event, the expulsion of Hugh Mahon from the Australian Parliament.

In August 1921 Mannix returned to Australia. Protestant and loyalist groups demanded that the federal government prevent Mannix's landing unless he agreed to take the oath of allegiance to the Crown. Hughes resisted, arguing that to do so would endanger the truce recently agreed in Ireland.[53] Across the Tasman the New Zealand government was not so accommodating to its pro-republican prelate, Bishop James Liston of Auckland. In 1922, he was prosecuted for making seditious utterances during a St Patrick's Day address. To the government's chagrin an all-Protestant jury acquitted him.[54]

EXPULSION OF HUGH MAHON MHR[55]

On 11 November 1920, Prime Minister W.M. Hughes moved in the House of Representatives that Hugh Mahon, the member for Kalgoorlie, be expelled from the House because of "conduct unfitting him to remain a member" by reason of "seditious and disloyal utterances" that he was alleged to have made four days before at a public meeting that had been called to protest the death of Terence MacSwiney. The motion was carried, with only the Labor Party dissenting.[56]

Mahon, a prominent Catholic, had been born in Ireland and had impeccable credentials as an Irish patriot, having served two months in Dublin's Kilmainham Gaol in 1881 with Charles Stewart Parnell. The following year he emigrated to Australia where he helped organize the Redmond brothers' Australian tour in 1883 and then worked as a journalist before being elected in 1901 to the first federal Parliament. Mahon served in the ministry under Watson and Fisher, and in 1914 he became minister for external affairs. In 1917 he lost his seat but regained it in 1919.

When Terence MacSwiney died Mahon was president of the Irish Ireland League and, in the absence of Archbishop Mannix (who was overseas), was a prominent leader of the protests in Melbourne. On 5 November Mahon tried to have MacSwiney's death discussed in the House of Representatives by raising it during the adjournment debate. However, he was frustrated in his attempt by interjections and points of order and, ultimately, the gagging of the debate.[57]

On 7 November, the opportunity arose to express his pent-up anger at MacSwiney's death when he was listed to speak at a protest rally at the Richmond Reserve in Melbourne. The meeting attracted a crowd of three to five thousand, including Mr F.J. Kelly, a freelance journalist who wrote for the *Argus* newspaper as well as for the Catholic paper the *Advocate*. It was Kelly's report of the meeting in the *Argus* which alerted the prime minister, Billy Hughes, to Mahon's "seditious and disloyal utterances," resulting in Hughes's moving the motion for Mahon's expulsion. According to Kelly's report, Mahon gave full vent to his anger, castigating British rule in Ireland and telling his audience:

> Never in Russia under the worst rule of the Czars had there been such an infamous murder as that of the late Alderman McSwiney. They were told in the papers that Alderman McSwiney's poor widow sobbed over his coffin. If there was a just God in heaven that sob would reach round the world, and one day would shake the foundations of this bloody and accursed Empire.[58]

To many Australians, especially empire loyalists of British Protestant stock, this was too much. The speech was made just four days before the second anniversary of the Armistice that ended the war in which sixty thousand Australians had died fighting for that "bloody and accursed Empire" that Mahon had denounced. Within a short time of the *Argus* appearing on the streets of Melbourne, Protestant, loyalist, Orange, and ex-service organizations began a campaign of "righteous indignation" over Mahon's speech, denouncing the member for Kalgoorlie as a danger to the Empire and to the peace and harmony of the community. Public meetings were called to protest Mahon's sedition and to affirm the loyalty of the Australian people to the Crown and the Empire.[59]

On 9 November the matter was discussed in cabinet. The next day Hughes wrote to Mahon advising him of his intention to move for his expulsion. On 11 November at 2:43 PM Hughes moved his motion to expel Mahon from the Parliament. After a debate lasting through the night the motion was put at 4:00 AM and carried thirty-four to seventeen along party lines. Thereafter Orange lodges, Protestant congregations, and Protestant organizations passed resolutions expressing their warm approval of Hughes's action. But Mahon's expulsion provoked protests from the Catholic community, with the *Freeman's Journal* complaining:

> It is not Mr Hughes' fault if any Catholics remain in public life, after his unceasing assaults on both the clergy and the laity, and his attempts to persuade the electors that Catholics are vile and deadly menaces to the well-being of Australia. Indeed, so virulent has been the Nationalist heresy hunt against Catholics, and so heartily have the daily papers supported their mean and despicable propaganda, that only Catholic politicians with strong faith care to remind the community that they owe spiritual allegiance to the Pope.[60]

L.F. Fitzhardinge, Hughes's biographer, also attributes sectarian motives to Hughes's decision to have Mahon expelled: "It seems ... that he hoped to conciliate the right-wing and ultra-Protestant sections of the public."[61] However, he also acknowledges the possibility that brute politics may have played a part, with Hughes's wishing to pick up Mahon's seat in a by-election.

Mahon had not attended Parliament to defend himself. Faced with a motion for his expulsion from a house, a majority of whose members were embittered against him, he could see only futility in resistance: better to seek vindication from his constituents. Unfortunately for Mahon, following a campaign in which the Nationalists made loyalty to the British Empire a major issue,[62] Kalgoorlie proved less than loyal to its former member. Mahon lost the by-election by 443 votes: 8,382 to 7,939.

CONCLUSION

These are but four of a number of events that occurred during 1920 in which issues combining religion, ethnicity, loyalty, and class became the subject of newspaper headlines for days on end, often overlapping with each other. There were other incidents that were widely reported, such as Melbourne's St Patrick's Day parade in which empire loyalists were scandalized when the Union Jack was not carried at the head of the march,[63] and the Ballarat by-election in July in which the Nationalist candidate was accused of sectarianism for referring to "Sinn Féin priests" as disloyal.[64]

The frequency and intensity of such incidents produced or confirmed in the minds of many Catholics a sense of their being a persecuted minority.[65] At the same time, they left many Protestants feeling more than a little insecure. To these troubled Protestants, militant Catholicism was on the march. This had been demonstrated by the entry of the Catholic Federation into electoral politics and the Federation's ability to organize at short notice mass rallies attended by tens of thousands of near riotous and disloyal Irish. But worse still, through the Labor government, Catholics had placed their hands on the levers of power in NSW, posing a real threat to Protestants and the Protestant faith.

Reading through the secular and religious newspapers of 1920 one gets an eerie sense that organized Catholicism and organized Protestantism were lining up for a showdown. In fact, some commentators predicted a violent conflict. According to a correspondent to the *Australian Christian World*: "Australia will be embroiled in a war such as that now being waged in Russia; in other words Australia will have a bloody time with Bolshevism and Sinn Feinism arrayed on one side and constitutionalism and Protestantism on the other."[66] The *Australian Christian World* published an account of an organized plot to have Roman Catholics take over Australia by having priests form federations in the parishes so as to train Catholics and to infiltrate trade unions and the Labor Party. It alleged that twenty priests were sent out from Ireland for this purpose.[67] Mr W. Copeland Trimble, a prominent newspaper owner of Enniskillen and a member of the Ulster Unionist Council, told a Protestant Federation luncheon that the Irish rebels were being financed by Bolshevik and German money and that large numbers of priests were coming to Australia to organize the disintegration of the Empire.[68]

In the end, despite the high-blown rhetoric, Australia did not descend into sectarian warfare, and heightened tensions eventually subsided, particularly after the signing of the Anglo-Irish Treaty in December 1921. Australians on both sides of the religious divide could support the treaty as it gave to Ireland (or that part constituted by the twenty-six counties) the same status within the British Empire that Australia enjoyed. Although Mannix opposed the treaty, his was a minority position among Australian Catholics. Consequently, in Australia, the Irish Question soon ceased to be either the litmus test of one's loyalty or a source of disputation. In addition, after a decade of confrontation, the Catholic Church accepted that its aggressive approach to the education funding issue was both futile and counterproductive, and the Catholic federations were either dissolved or allowed to languish. Sectarianism did not disappear – some say it continues to this day – but it ceased to dominate the headlines as it did in 1920.

NOTES

1 Wolffe, "Anti-Catholicism and the British Empire," 44.

2 Michael Hogan locates its roots in the earliest years of the colony. See Hogan, *Sectarian Strand*, 28.

3 Edwards, "Proddy-Dogs," 5.

4 While this chapter concentrates on this ethno-religious rivalry, it must be acknowledged that much harmony existed between Australians of different ethno-religious backgrounds as well as there being differences within Protestantism and within religious denominations that at times became as intense as the Catholic/Protestant rivalry. An example of the latter is the opposition of a number of leading Catholics, such as Charles Heydon and Herbert Moran, to Archbishop Mannix's role in the conscription debates. See, for example, Moran, *Viewless Winds*, 158–9.

5 Hogan, *Sectarian Strand*, 65.

6 *Australian Christian World* (hereafter ACW), 4 February 1921, 11.

7 For accounts of the evolution of state aid see Wilkinson et al., *History of State Aid*; and Burke, "Funding Schools."

8 In Victoria the Federation was proscribed after the elections and many Catholics who were Federation members were expelled from the party. For a history of the Catholic Federation, particularly in New South Wales, see Kildea, *Tearing the Fabric*.

9 ACW, 24 October 1919, 5.

10 Hogan and Clune, *People's Choice*, 1:207.

11 *Freeman's Journal*, 18 October 1917, 27.

12 For an account of the 1920 NSW elections and the role of the Democratic Party, see Kildea, *Tearing the Fabric*, 201–13; Hogan and Clune, *People's Choice*, 1:181–234.

13 An example of this was the so-called Ne Temere bill, which was directed at Catholic marriage laws. See Moore, "Sectarianism in NSW."

14 See, for example, the *Methodist*, 27 March 1920, 7; 10 April 1920, 7; 17 April 1920, 7.

15 *Catholic Press*, 8 April 1920, 27; *Freeman's Journal*, 15 April 1920, 18. Many of them were not practising Catholics or were not proponents of Catholic claims.

16 ACW, 2 January 1920, 12. The ACW frequently made the point in articles published between November 1920 and January 1921.

17 ACW, 2 July 1920, 12; 29 April 1921, 9.

18 Editorials sometimes referred to the Penal Laws, as if they applied in Australia, and bore emotive headlines such as "Catholics Attacked" and "Are we to remain the hewers of wood and the drawers of water?"

19 Henderson, "Deportation of Charles Jerger," provides a detailed account of the internment and deportation of Father Jerger.

20 *Jerger v. Pearce* (1920) 27 C.L.R. 526.
21 *Freeman's Journal*, 27 May 1920, 17.
22 Ibid., 10 June 1920, 18.
23 *Daily Telegraph*, 31 May 1920.
24 After his deportation Jerger lived in Holland, the United States, Ireland, and England, where he died in 1927 after an operation (see P. L'Estrange's entry on Charles Jerger in *The Australian Dictionary of Biography*, 9:484).
25 Henderson, "Deportation of Charles Jerger," 76.
26 Ibid., 77.
27 *Catholic Press*, 15 July 1920, 11.
28 The events described here are derived largely from contemporary reports appearing in Catholic, Protestant, and secular newspapers and from the papers of Bishop Joseph Dwyer in the Wagga Wagga Diocesan Archives. An account of the Sister Liguori affair is in Kildea, *Tearing the Fabric*, 218–26.
29 Blacklow and West, "Sectarianism and sisterhood"; Arnstein, *Protestant vs Catholic.*
30 *Sydney Morning Herald*, 9 August 1920; 11 August 1920; *Freeman's Journal*, 16 September 1920, 25; 4 November 1920, 30.
31 The allegations were denied at first by Miss Partridge's solicitor (*Sydney Morning Herald*, 17 August 1920) and then by Bridget herself in a letter published in the newspapers (*Sydney Morning Herald*, 25 August 1920). Charles Heydon was one of the Catholics who made an offer of accommodation (*Sydney Morning Herald*, 16 August 1920; *Freeman's Journal*, 26 August 1920, 15).
32 See, for example, *Sydney Morning Herald*, 9 August 1920; 11 August 1920; 12 August 1920; 16 August 1920; 26 August 1920; 27 August 1920.
33 *Sydney Morning Herald*, 18 September 1920.
34 Ibid., 27 August 1920.
35 See, for example, *NSW Parliamentary Debates* (NSWPD) 79 (25 August 1920), 420–5, 452–5; (31 August 1920), 534–41. Father J.M. Cusack wrote a lengthy article for the *Freeman's Journal* in which he defended the convents against such attacks (*Freeman's Journal*, 19 August 1920, 16–17).
36 *Sydney Morning Herald*, 2 September 1920; 4 September 1920.
37 NSWPD, 81 (30 November 1920), 2902–13; 82, (7 December 1920), 3215–22; (21 December 1920), 3971–74; *Daily Telegraph*, 1 December 1920; 8 December 1920; 22 December 1920; *Sydney Morning Herald*, 8 December 1920.
38 For example, a telegram dated 6 September 1920 to Bishop Dwyer states, "Bringing Perdriau tyre train arriving Sydney Tuesday splendid condition" (Wagga Wagga Diocesan Archives).

39 *Catholic Press*, 16 September 1920, 11, 20.

40 Letter 2, December 1920, from Charles Lawlor to Bishop Dwyer (Wagga Wagga Diocesan Archives). The Diocesan Archives contain a number of letters from Lawlor reporting to the bishop on the latest developments.

41 Eventually the affair faded from public sight. Bridget Partridge remained with the Touchells for the next forty years before she was admitted to Rydalmere Hospital where she died on 4 December 1966. See Tearle, "I Remember Sister Ligouri."

42 *Freeman's Journal*, 21 July 1921, 14.

43 ACW, 8 October 1920, 6; 5 November 1920, 6, 10. The story of Sr Basil's "escape" and attempted abduction were told in ACW, 30 August 1918, 7–8; 6 September 1918, 7–8. Fifty years earlier Susanna Saurin had received damages of £500 (including return of her dowry of £300). A verbatim account of the *Times*'s report of the Saurin's case is in Saurin, *Trial of Saurin v. Star*.

44 *Wagga Wagga Daily Express*, 14 July 1921; 29 July 1921; ACW, 5 August 1921, 9. Logan, "Sectarianism in Ganmain."

45 The story of Archbishop Mannix's hijacking is told in varying degrees of detail by his various biographers. For more specific treatment, see Hachey, "Quarantine of Archbishop Mannix"; Kiernan, *Mannix and Ireland*, 145–70.

46 Extract from Draft Conclusions, Cabinet meeting 24 June 1920, the National Archives (TNA), CO 537/1144.

47 Cliff Haven in Plattsburgh, New York State, on the shore of Lake Champlain, was the site of the nationally known Catholic Summer School of America, which was held between the 1890s and the 1940s and which covered the attitude of the Roman Catholic Church on current matters as well as educational, cultural, and political issues. It attracted many participants and visitors, including two American presidents. Colm Kiernan argues that Mannix's meeting with de Valera in Omaha, where they both spoke from the same platform, is what fanned Mannix's radicalism. See Kiernan, *Mannix and Ireland*, 148–9.

48 *Times* (London), 16 July 1920; 20 July 1920; *New York Times*, 19 July 1920; 20 July 1920.

49 *Times* (London), 16 July 1920.

50 *New York Times*, 27 July 1920; 28 July 1920.

51 Reports of the meeting are contained in *Freeman's Journal*, 19 August 1920, 21; and *Catholic Press*, 19 August 1920, 19.

52 *Freeman's Journal*, 19 August 1920, 21.

53 ACW, 5 August 1921, 9

54 Sweetman, *Bishop in the Dock*.

55 This incident is discussed, inter alia, in Fitzhardinge, *Little Digger*, 452–6; Sawer, *Australian Federal Politics and Law*, 207.

56 *Commonwealth Parliamentary Debates* (hereafter CPD), House of Representatives, 11 November 1920, 6382–475.

57 Ibid., 5 November 1920, 6257–65.

58 *Argus*, 8 November 1920.

59 National Archives of Australia A457 514/1/4 Disloyalty, Utterances by M. Mahon; A11804 1921/11 Loyalty (in Australia) to British Empire (Including Irish Question & Expulsion of Hon Hugh Mahon from Commonwealth Parliament); A457 547/1/17 Resolutions. Protestant Federation Vic. Re. Mr Mahon.

60 *Freeman's Journal*, 18 November 1920, 22.

61 Fitzhardinge, *Little Digger*, 456.

62 *Kalgoorlie Miner*, 3 December 1920, 4; *West Australian*, 6 December 1920.

63 Kwan, "St Patrick's Day Procession."

64 *Tribune*, 17 June 1920; *Argus*, 20 July 1920; 21 July 1920; 23 July 1920.

65 This was expressly stated in an editorial in the *Freeman's Journal* in the early stages of the Sister Liguori affair. See *Freeman's Journal*, 19 August 1920, 22. See also *Freeman's Journal*, 10 November 1921, 20.

66 Letter from "A Justice" published in ACW, 12 November 1920, 10. In the same edition of that newspaper there is an account of an organized plot to have Roman Catholics take over Australia by having priests form federations in the parishes so as to train Catholics and to infiltrate trade unions and the Labor Party. It alleged that twenty priests had been sent out from Ireland for this purpose.

67 ACW, 12 November 1920, 10.

68 Ibid., 24 June 1921, 11.

Conclusion

COLIN BARR AND HILARY M. CAREY

In early February 1853, Archbishop John Hughes of New York sat down to answer a letter from Manuel José Mosquera y Arboleda, the archbishop of Nueva Granada (modern Bogotá) in Colombia. Mosquera had wanted to know how the Roman Catholic Church coped in the secular, republican United States. Was it persecuted? Could it support itself? These were pressing questions: Mosquera had recently been exiled by a liberal government that had expelled the Jesuits, embraced secular education, legalized divorce, and introduced compulsory civil marriage and the popular election of parish priests.[1] In reply, Hughes was enthusiastic about American religious freedom. There was, he wrote, "no impediment thrown in our way by the civil authority of the State." Bishops were appointed freely and without interference, while "the people never look to the government for any support, and would be exceedingly indignant at any interference on the part of the government with their religious and ecclesiastical immunities." Even the financial burden was manageable, Hughes wrote, because "most" American Catholics were Irish – "the descendants of a persecuted ancestry" – and therefore "accustomed to support their clergy and their Church from their own free and voluntary contributions."[2]

Born in County Tyrone in 1797, John Hughes arrived in the United States as an impoverished teenager, working as a gardener at Mount St Mary's Seminary in Emmitsburg, Maryland, before convincing its French president to admit him as a student. Some twenty years later, he succeeded that same Frenchman as bishop of America's largest city, New York. In 1850, he became its first archbishop. His legacy was as a builder of schools, churches, and political power. As Hasia Diner notes, Hughes and the institutions he established blended "Catholic piety, love of the

Irish homeland, and American patriotism."[3] Hughes's career, his success in the United States, and his answer to Mosquera encapsulate the constant that makes "Greater Ireland" a useful category for historians: from the late 1820s, in the United States and British World – and only in the United States and British World – the Irish found themselves in a religious free market with a mostly level playing field.

It was this level playing field that allowed Irish religion to flourish. In the dominions and the United States, religious difference was given free reign, the result being not that religious feeling became attenuated, or religious institutions weakened, but the opposite. And, just as with Archbishop Hughes in the United States, the freedom of religion available in the British World tended to draw the emigrant Irish towards a loyalty to the state (and the Empire) that many would never have felt at home. As the Irish-born cardinal archbishop of Sydney boasted in 1894, "our colonial administration, linked as it is to the Crown of Great Britain" is "the most perfect form of republican government," enjoying the "freedom which a republican government imparts" without "unpleasant influences" that act upon an elected head of state.[4] In this book, Carolyn Lambert's chapter demonstrates how such an enthusiasm manifested itself in Newfoundland, where Catholicism and Irishness underpinned a national and imperial identity that embraced the Empire's wars. A similar process occurred in Canada, Australia, and New Zealand. Emigrant Irish Protestants, and especially Irish Anglicans, were already conditioned, and most remained minded to look to the link with Britain as a bulwark of their own identity. Even in India and China, as Barry Crosbie's and Myrtle Hill's respective chapters point out, the British state sought, albeit sometimes grudgingly and not always successfully, to guarantee the freedom of operation of all Irish denominations, whether it was a Catholic chaplain in Hyderabad or a female Presbyterian missionary in northern China.

But as we have seen in the chapters in this book, Greater Ireland did not mean simply the Irish in the British World, nor the British World plus the United States (and Argentina). Nor do we intend it solely as a synonym for the global Irish diaspora. Rather, we suggest that, like Sir Charles Dilke's "Greater Britain," "Greater Ireland" had a real (if protean) shape and meaning to many of the Irish and their descendants scattered around the globe. And, while it lacked the constitutional and military links that bound the British Empire, it possessed bonds of culture, emotion, and symbol that were more than accidental or tangential and that have proved durable. Very often, and for a surprisingly long time, the emigrant Irish (and particularly the Catholic Irish) had as much or more in common with their brethren thousands of kilometres and continents away – with whom they shared a common culture and institutions – than they did with their fellow Americans, Australians, or Argentines.

The intellectual and cultural boundaries of Greater Ireland were as permeable as its political ones. This could take the form of the Presbyterian theological debates passing backwards and forwards across the Atlantic described in Rankin Sherling's chapter, or the influence of Francis Patrick Kenrick, a Dublin-born, Roman-educated Irish priest who immigrated to Kentucky and rose to become a leading intellectual influence on both the American and Irish Catholics churches.[5] As Kevin Molloy points out in chapter 3, Irish American novelists such as Mary Anne Sadlier became Irish Australian favourites; Catholic newspapers from Boston to Ballarat reported on Irish news as home news and reproduced stories about the doings of Irish Catholics from other similar newspapers around the world; Belleek porcelain decorated with small green shamrocks could be found in nineteenth-century Australian convents and can still be purchased from twenty-first-century American gift shops; Irish Catholic priests and nuns moved freely between the United States and one or more of the settler colonies (Archbishop Thomas Croke of Cashel, for example, began his episcopal career in New Zealand, while his brother was a priest in San Francisco and one of his sisters the Mother Superior of a convent in Bathurst, New South Wales); activists such as John Boyle O'Reilly could, in turn, rebel in Ireland, escape from Australia, and edit an Irish Catholic newspaper in the United States.[6]

Consider as an exemplar the career of Thomas D'Arcy McGee, who emigrated from Ireland as a young man, edited the Irish Catholic Boston *Pilot*, returned to write for the Dublin *Freeman's Journal*, and then for the *Nation*, and rebelled in 1848. He fled, founded the *American Celt and Adopted Citizen* in Boston, and published, among other things, a biography of an Irish Catholic bishop, *A History of the Irish Settlers in North America*, and *A Catholic History of North America*.[7] In 1857, he moved to Montreal at the invitation of the city's Irish community and founded a short-lived newspaper primarily concerned with attacking the Orange Order. He was elected to the legislature as the candidate of the St Patrick's Society and the champion of Irish Catholics. A high profile political career ended with his 1868 assassination at the hands of an Irish immigrant.[8] Although an active politician with more than religious and ethnic concerns, McGee's career was never independent of either his faith or his origins. Does he belong to the history of Ireland, the United States, or Canada? Do the nuns who sailed in 1856 from Dublin to Buenos Aires before moving on to Adelaide in 1880 properly belong to Argentina or Australia?[9] Richard Bourke's liberal Protestantism to the history of Ireland, the British Empire, the Eastern Cape, or New South Wales? As the chapters in this book make clear, events in, say, Ontario, very often had their nearest analogue in Otago.

This is not to say that the Irish experience was not different between the British and non-British worlds, or within the British World. The Irish condition in New Jersey was different from that in New South Wales, just as the New Zealand and New Brunswick Irish faced different challenges and responded in different ways. The Irish-speaking Anglicans of New Brunswick unearthed by Peter Toner, for example, seem to have had no equivalents elsewhere. So, too, Irish-inflected or inspired sectarianism took on very different forms and followed different paths, as Carolyn Lambert and Jeff Kildea made clear in their chapters on Newfoundland and the Great War and postwar Australian politics, respectively. But this diversity should not obscure either the migrants' common identification as Irish or the great overlaps in that identity's meanings, institutions, and symbolism – or its astonishing resilience. And just as with the island of Ireland itself, so it was religion and religious difference more than any other force that shaped Greater Ireland.

But the editors are acutely aware that the contributions to *Religion and Greater Ireland* do not come close to a full treatment of the Irish religious experience abroad. Indeed, we hope that this book sparks others to consider the history of Ireland's religions in both its particular regions as well as in a global, Greater Ireland context. Several avenues for further research immediately suggest themselves. In geographic terms, Argentina would be a useful site to examine how the Irish fared when they migrated to a non-English speaking republic with a religious culture in the Spanish tradition. Building on Helen Kelly's work, did their Catholicism help them integrate into Argentine society? Or did its institutions facilitate the retention of an Irish identity even as the English language was abandoned?[10] How did Irish Protestant migrants cope with a society that was overwhelmingly Roman Catholic? Did they become "English" (or "British") or simply "European"? Further work is needed on Irish settlement or presence (including military) outwith the settler empire. Were there among the administrators of tropical Africa traces of the Ulster Presbyterian-inflected liberalism so influential at the

Cape of Good Hope? How were Irish missionaries received in the Islamic world, and did that vary between, say, Borneo and coastal Kenya? How did Irish American chaplains engage with Filipino Catholics in the US Pacific empire? Did the missionary strategies of Irish Catholics change over time? And did they take a different approach from Irish Protestants? And did Irish Protestants differ from one another? Was Irishness a relevant category when the only Irish were missionaries, administrators, or soldiers? Was there a peculiarly Irish Catholic or Irish Protestant way of dealing with indigenous peoples? Graeme Morton and David Wilson recently edited an important collection of chapters considering Irish and Scottish encounters with indigenous groups, and several of their contributors touch upon or directly consider the role of missionaries.[11] It would be useful to follow up these insights and test them across the full range of Irish settlement and religious activity.

This is particularly true of Britain, direct consideration of which we omit from this book. This decision was not a statement on the absence or unimportance of Irish migration within the United Kingdom: the Irish were of course an often overwhelming reality in urban Britain. Limitations of space led the editors to focus *Religion and Greater Ireland* on the Greater Ireland beyond the polity that encompassed, however uncomfortably, Ireland itself. However, our understanding of the Irish religious experience in England, Scotland, and Wales would surely repay a transnational, Greater Ireland, perspective. The Irish in Wales, for example, have been dealt with at book length by Paul O'Leary, who also brought together a number of contributors in the volume *Irish Migrants in Modern Wales*.[12] Beyond that, however, little has been done, despite the dominance of a Methodism that straddled both the Irish Sea and the Atlantic, or the centrality of the Catholic clergy in shaping Irish community life in Cardiff.[13] The Irish in Scotland have received more sustained attention, particularly in the work of Karly Kehoe, Martin J. Mitchell, Geraldine Vaughan, and in the pages of the *Innes Review*.[14] But much of this has naturally focused on the Catholic Church and the consequences of the massive Irish migration of the mid-nineteenth century. There is more to be done in unpicking the relationship between Irish and Scottish Presbyterianism in a Scottish context. Ian Meredith draws attention to the impact of Irish Anglicans in a Scottish episcopal diocese, and such interactions were unlikely to be limited to greater Glasgow.[15] In modern Scotland, the occasionally violent rivalry between Celtic and Rangers football clubs has tended to conflate Irish nationalist symbolism with Roman Catholic faith: in 2014, ScotRail trains displayed posters threatening prison time for the use of sectarian language. But that is surely not the whole story of Irish religious experience in Scotland.

As for England, there is a long-established and impressive historiography concerned with Irish migration. The edited volumes of Roger Swift and Sheridan Gilley, and the work of Graham Davies and Enda Delaney, among others, trace the course of the Irish experience in Britain down to very near the present day.[16] Nevertheless, relatively little attention has been devoted to the religious lives of the migrants and their international contexts. An exception is Liverpool, which has itself generated an important body of work attentive to the religion and religious institutions of immigrant Irish Catholics, from James Murphy's pioneering study of the city's schools through to P.J. Waller and, more recently, John Belchem's studies of Irish identity and sectarianism.[17] One of the many topics that would likely repay further attention would be the success of the English Catholic Church in resisting Irish domination and the consequences for the Irish themselves. Also interesting would be a detailed study of the interactions within the Church of England and Ireland (notionally united between 1801 and 1869) and the presence and impact of Irish Anglican clergy in England.

Research by D.H. Akenson, Bruce Elliott, Donal McCracken, and Brad Patterson, among others, stresses the significant and, in places, dominant character of Irish Protestant immigration to places such as Ontario, New Zealand, and/or South Africa.[18] In this volume, the contributions of Leigh-Ann Coffey, Michael Gladwin, Dianne Hall, Myrtle Hill, Ranking Sherling, and John Stenhouse demonstrate and emphasize the robust transmission of both Irish Protestants and Irish Protestant concerns to the various worlds of Irish settlement. But where have the Protestants gone? Unlike Irish Catholics who, as Akenson remarks of New Zealand, "simply refused to go away," Irish Protestant had largely vanished as a category of self-identification by the mid-twentieth century, if not before.[19] Not only did Irish Protestants "not stand out," they "blended so quickly with the dominant culture in New Zealand that they are hard to trace."[20] This seems to have been the fate of Ireland's Protestants throughout Greater Ireland, whether they became simply "British" (or even "English") in Australia, New Zealand, or Canada; or, as Vivian Bickford-Smith implies, "white" in South Africa.[21] But did Anglicans and Presbyterians assimilate in the same way, at the same speed, and for the same reasons? (The history of the "Scotch-Irish" in America suggests not.) Did the accelerating triumphalism of Irish

Catholicism encourage the concomitant abandonment of Irish Protestant identities, with or without the apparent "indecent haste" of New Zealand?[22] Traces of Irish influence can still be found – in New South Wales Anglicanism, for example – but outside of the American south they seem to be fleeting. The Orange Order has effectively vanished outwith Northern Ireland and parts of Scotland. And what of the smaller Protestant denominations? In New Zealand, a number of scholars have heeded Akenson's call to consider that country's Irish Protestants – for example, in the work of Gerard Horn and the chapters published in Brad Patterson's *Ulster-New Zealand Migration and Cultural Transfers*.[23] John Stenhouse's chapter in this volume is an important contribution to that literature. But much more work needs to be done across Greater Ireland into the Irish Protestants of the era of mass migration and their descendants. Leigh-Ann Coffey's chapter in this book should be followed up to further examine not only how post-independence southern Protestants felt about empire but also their experience as migrants. These are just a few suggestions: readers will have their own.

In pursuing the Irish to their many destinations, *Religion in Greater Ireland* seeks to point to the interconnections, influences, and commonalities of the Irish migrant experience. The Irish of Greater Ireland were indeed bound by a "web of empire," but the orb lines of Irish religion reached beyond the British World to the United States and even further afield. The contributors to this book have, in their varied ways, insisted on the centrality of religion to the Irish experience and on the fact that that religion was more complex than simply the Catholic Irish and the Protestant other. Like in Ireland itself, religion in Greater Ireland was important, complex, changing, and varied. It is also fascinating.

NOTES

1 See Londoño-Vega, *Religion, Culture, and Society*, 33.

2 John Hughes to Manuel José Mosquera y Arboleda, 7 February 1853, Columbia University, Henry Joseph Browne Papers, MS 1296, ser. 1, subser. 1, box 5.

3 Diner, "Most Irish City," 103.

4 Ryan, *Attitude of the Catholic Church*, 48.

5 For Kenrick, see Barr, *Ireland's Empire*.

6 See Evans, *Romantic Heart*.

7 McGee, *Life of the Rt. Rev. Edward Maginn*; McGee, *History of the Irish settlers*; McGee, *Catholic history of North America*.

8 For McGee, see David A. Wilson's magisterial *Thomas D'Arcy McGee*, 2 vols.
9 See McLay, *Women on the Move*.
10 Kelly, *Irish "Ingleses,"* esp. chap. 4.
11 Morton and Wilson, *Irish and Scottish Encounters*.
12 O'Leary, *Immigration and Integration*; O'Leary, *Irish Migrants*.
13 For the latter, see Hickey, "Irish Settlement," 49–50.
14 For example, Kehoe, *Creating a Scottish Church*; Mitchell, *New Perspectives*; and Mitchell, *Irish in the West of Scotland*; Vaughan, *"Local" Irish*.
15 Meredith, "Irish Episcopalians."
16 Swift and Gilley, *Irish in the Victorian City*; Swift and Gilley, *Irish in Victorian Britain*; Swift and Gilley, *Irish Identities*; Davies, *Irish in Britain*; Delaney, *Demography, State and Society*; Delaney, *Irish in Post-War Britain*.
17 Murphy, *Religious Problem*; Waller, *Democracy and Sectarianism*; Belchem, *Irish, Catholic, and Scouse*.
18 See, for example, Akenson, *Irish in Ontario*; and Akenson, *Irish in South Africa*; Elliott, *Irish Migrants*; McCracken, "Irish settlement and identity."
19 Akenson, *Half the World from Home*, 196.
20 Ibid., 198.
21 Bickford-Smith, *Ethnic Pride and Racial Prejudice*, 39. Bickford-Smith rarely mentions the Irish but, rather, assumes that all British migrants adopted first an "English" and then a "white" identity.
22 Horn, "Loyal United and Happy People," 14.
23 Horn, "Ulster Protestants in New Zealand"; Patterson, *Ulster-New Zealand Migration*.

Bibliography

Acheson, Alan R. *A History of the Church of Ireland, 1691–1996*. Dublin: Columba Press/APCK, 1997.

Adamoski, Robert, Dorothy Chunn, and Robert Menzies, eds. *Contesting Canadian Citizenship*. Peterborough, ON: Broadview Press, 2002.

Adams, Thomas, and Nicholas Barker. "A New Model for the Study of the Book." In *A Potencie of Life: Books in Society*, ed. Nicholas Barker, 5–43. London: British Library, 1993.

Addley, William Palmer. "A Study of the Birth and Development of the Overseas Mission of the Presbyterian Church in Ireland up to 1910." PhD diss., Queen's University of Belfast, 1994.

Akenson, Donald Harman. "An Agnostic View of the Historiography of the Irish Americans." *Labour/Le Travail* 14 (1984): 123–59.

– *The Church of Ireland: Ecclesiastical Reform and Revolution, 1800–1885*. New Haven, NY: Yale University Press, 1971).

– *God's Peoples: Covenant and Land in South Africa, Israel, and Ulster*. Ithaca, NY: Cornell University Press, 1992.

– *Half the World from Home: Perspectives on the Irish in New Zealand, 1860–1950*. Wellington: Victoria University Press, 1990.

– *Ireland, Sweden and the Great European Migration, 1815–1914*. Montreal and Kingston: McGill-Queen's University Press, 2011.

– *The Irish Diaspora: A Primer*. Toronto: P.D. Meany, 1993.

– *The Irish Education Experiment: The National System of Education in the Nineteenth Century*. London: Routledge and Kegan Paul, 1970.

– *The Irish in Ontario: A Study in Rural History*. Montreal and Kingston: McGill-Queen's University Press, 1984.

– *Small Differences: Irish Catholics and Irish Protestants, 1815–1922: An International Perspective* Kingston, ON: McGill-Queen's University Press, 1988.

– *Occasional Papers on the Irish in South Africa*. Grahamstown: Institute of Social and Economic Research, Rhodes University 1991.
– "Reading the Texts of Rural Immigrants: Letters from the Irish in Australia, New Zealand and North America." *Canadian Papers in Rural History*, vol. 7, 387–406. Gananoque, ON: Langdale Press, 1990.
Anderson, Benedict. *Imagined Communities: Reflections on the Origins and Spread of Nationalism*. London: Verso, 1983.
Anderson, Clare. *Subaltern Lives: Biographies of Colonialism in the Indian Ocean World, 1790–1920*. Cambridge: Cambridge University Press, 2012.
Andreas, A.T. *History of Chicago from the Earliest Period to the Present Time*, 2 vols Chicago: R.R. Donnelly and Sons, 1884.
Armstrong, Elizabeth. *The Crisis of Quebec*. Toronto: McClelland and Stewart, Carleton Library Series, 1974.
Arnstein, Walter L. *Protestant v. Catholic in Mid-Victorian Britain: Mr Newdegate and the Nuns*. Columbia: University of Missouri Press, 1982.
Arthur, Paul. "Our Greater Ireland beyond the Seas." *Diaspora: A Journal of Transnational Studies* 1, 3 (1991): 365–71.
Askew, Marc, and Brian Hubber. "The Colonial Reader Observed: Reading in Its Cultural Context." In *The Book in Australia: Essays Towards a Cultural and Social History*, ed. D.H. Borchardt and Wallace Kirsop, 110–37. Melbourne: Centre for Bibliographical and Textual Studies, Monash University, 1988.
Baines, Dudley. *Emigration from Europe, 1815–1930*. Basingstoke: Macmillan, 1991.
Baker, D.W.A. *Preacher, Politician, Patriot: A Life of John Dunmore Lang*. Melbourne: Melbourne University Press, 1998.
Baker, William M. *Timothy Warren Anglin, 1822–90: Irish Catholic Canadian*. Toronto: University of Toronto Press, 1977.
Ballantyne, Tony. *Between Colonialism and Diaspora: Sikh Cultural Formations in an Imperial World*. Durham, NC: Duke University Press, 2006.
– *Orientalism and Race: Aryanism in the British Empire*. Basingstoke: Palgrave, 2001.
– *Webs of Empire: Locating New Zealand's Colonial Past*. Wellington: Bridget Williams Books, 2012.
Ballhatchet, Kenneth. *Caste, Class and Catholicism in India 1789–1914*. London: Curzon, 1998.
– "The East India Company and Roman Catholic Missionaries." *Journal of Ecclesiastical History* 44, 2 (1993): 273–88.

– *Race, Sex and Class under the Raj: Imperial Attitudes Policies and Their Critics, 1793–1905*. London: Weidenfeld and Nicolson, 1980.

Barber, Marilyn. "The Ontario Schools Issue: Sources of Conflict." *Canadian Historical Review* 47 (1966): 227–48.

Bardon, Jonathan. *A History of Ulster*. Belfast: Blackstaff Press, 1992.

Barnard, T.C., and W.G. Neely. *The Clergy of the Church of Ireland, 1000–2000: Messengers, Watchmen and Stewards*. Dublin: Four Courts Press, 2006.

Barr, Colin. *The European Culture Wars in Ireland: The Callan Schools Affair, 1868–81*. Dublin: University College Dublin Press, 2010.

– "'Imperium in Imperio': Irish Episcopal Imperialism in the Nineteenth Century." *English Historical Review* 123, 502 (2008): 611–50.

– *Paul Cullen, John Henry Newman, and the Catholic University of Ireland, 1845–65*. Notre Dame, IN: Notre Dame University Press, 2003.

Barr, Colin, and Rose Luminiello. "'The Leader of the Virgin Choir of Erin': St Brigid's Missionary College, 1883–1914." In *Ireland's Imperial Cultures*, ed. Michael DeNie, Timothy McMahon, and Paul Townend, forthcoming.

– *Ireland's Empire: The Roman Catholic Church in the Anglo-World, 1830–1914*. Cambridge: Cambridge University Press, forthcoming.

Barrett, James R. "Americanization from the Bottom Up: Immigration and the Remaking of the Working Class in the United States, 1880–1930." *Journal of American History* 79, 3 (1992): 996–1020.

– *The Irish Way: Becoming American in the Multi-Ethnic City*. New York: Penguin, 2012.

Barrett, James R., and David Roediger. "The Irish and the 'Americanization' of the 'New Immigrants' in the Streets and in the Churches of the Urban United States, 1900–1930." *Journal of American Ethnic History* 24, 4 (2005): 3–33.

Barry, John Vincent. *Life and Death of John Price: A Study of the Exercise of Naked Power*. Melbourne: Melbourne University Press, 1964.

Barst, Julie M. "Pushing the Envelope: Caroline Chisholm, Colonial Australia, and the Transformative Power of Postal Networks." *Prose Studies: History, Theory, Criticism* 33, 3 (2011): 200–16.

Bartlett, Thomas, and Jeffery, Keith, eds. *A Military History of Ireland*. Cambridge: Cambridge University Press, 1996.

Bateman, Fiona. "Ireland's Spiritual Empire: Territory and Landscape in Irish Catholic Missionary Discourse." In *Empires of Religion*, ed. Hilary M. Carey, 267–87. London: Palgrave Macmillan, 2008.

Bayor, Ronald H. *Neighbors in Conflict*. Baltimore: Johns Hopkins University Press, 1978.

Belchem, John. *Irish, Catholic, and Scouse: The History of the Liverpool Irish, 1800–1939*. Liverpool: Liverpool University Press, 2007.

– "Priests, Publicans and the Irish Poor: Ethnic Enterprise and Migrant Networks in Mid-Nineteenth Century Liverpool." *Immigrants and Minorities* 23, 2/3 (2005): 207–31.

Belich, James. *Replenishing the Earth: The Settler Revolution and the Rise of the Anglo-World, 1783–1939*. Oxford: Oxford University Press, 2009.

Bell, Duncan. *The Idea of Greater Britain: Empire and the Future of World Order, 1860–1900*. Princeton: Princeton University Press, 2007.

– "Unity and Difference: John Robert Seeley and the Political Theology of International Relations." *Review of International Studies* 31 (2005): 559–79.

Bennett, Margaret. "From the Quebec Hebridean to les Écossais-Québécois." In *Transatlantic Scots*, ed. Celeste Ray, 120–55. Tuscaloosa: University of Alabama Press, 2005.

Bennett, Victoria. "Early Church Architecture in the Ottawa Valley: An Initial Investigation of the Nineteenth-Century Parish Church." Canadian Catholic Historical Association, *Historical Studies* 60 (1993–94): 17–42.

Berger, Carl. *The Sense of Power: Studies in the Ideas of Canadian Imperialism, 1867–1914*. Toronto: University of Toronto Press, 1970.

Bergin, John, Eoin Magennis, Lesa Ní Mhunghaile and Patrick Walsh, eds. *New Perspectives on the Penal Laws*. Dublin: Eighteenth-Century Ireland Society, 2011.

Bickford-Smith, Vivian. *Ethnic Pride and Racial Prejudice in Victorian Cape Town*. Cambridge: Cambridge University Press, 1995.

Bielenberg, Andy. "Exodus: The Emigration of Southern Irish Protestants during the Irish War of Independence and the Civil War." *Past and Present* 218 (2013): 199–233.

Birch, Delia. *John McEncroe Colonial Democrat*. Victoria: Collins Dove, 1986.

Blacklow, Nancy, and Elizabeth West. "Sectarianism and Sisterhood: Research in Progress." *Rural Society* 10 (2000): 243–8.

Blainey, Anna. "The Prohibition and Total Abstinence Movement in Australia, 1880–1910." In *Food, Power and Communities: Essays in the History of Food and Drink*, ed. Robert Dare, 142–52. Adelaide: Wakefield Press, 1999.

Blocker, Jack S. *American Temperance Movements: Cycles of Reform*. Boston: Twayne Publishers, 1989.

Blocker, Jack S., David M. Fahey, and Ian R. Tyrell. *Alcohol and Temperance in Modern History: An International Encyclopedia*. Santa Barbara: ABC-CLIO, 2003.

Boland, Eavon. *Collected Poems*. Manchester: Carcanet, 1995.

Bolton, Charles Knowles. *Scotch Irish Pioneers in Ulster and America*. Boston: Bacon and Brown, 1910.

Boner, Kathleen. *Dominican Women: A Time to Speak*. Pietermaritzburg: Cluster Publications, 2000.

– "The Irish Dominicans and Education in the Western Cape, 1863–1892." MA thesis, University of South Africa, 1976.

Borgatti, Stephan P., Martin G. Everett and Jeffrey C. Johnson. "Network Analysis in the Social Sciences." *Science* 323 (2009): 892–5.

Boucher, André. "La fabrique et les marguilliers." In *Le laic dans l'église canadien-français de 1830 à nos jours*, ed. Pierre Hurtubise and Germain Lesage. Montreal: Fides, 1972.

Bourke, D.F. *A History of the Catholic Church in Victoria*. Melbourne: Catholic Education Office, 1988.

Bowen, Desmond. "A.R.C. Dallas: The Warrior Saint." In *The View from the Pulpit: Victorian Ministers and Society*, ed. P.T. Phillips, 17–37. Toronto: Macmillan of Canada, 1978.

– *History and the Shaping of Irish Protestantism*. New York: Peter Lang, 1995.

Bowen, Kurt. *Protestants in a Catholic State: Ireland's Privileged Minority*. Montreal-Kingston: McGill-Queen's Press, 1983.

Boyd, R.H. *Manchuria and Our Mission There*. Belfast: Foreign Missions Office, 1908.

– *The Prevailing Word*. Belfast: Foreign Mission Office, 1953.

Bradbury, Bettina. "Pigs, Cows, and Boarders: Non-Wage Forms of Survival among Montreal Families, 1861–1891." *Labour/Le Travail* 14 (1984): 9–46.

Brain, J.B., ed., *The Cape Diary of Patrick Raymond Griffith for the years 1837 to 1839*. Cape Town: South African Catholic Bishops Conference, 1988.

– *Catholic Beginnings in Natal and Beyond*. Durban: T.W. Griggs, 1975.

– "The Irish influence on the Catholic Church in South Africa." In *Southern African-Irish Studies*. Vol. 2: *The Irish in Southern Africa, 1795–1910*, ed. Donal P. McCraken, 242–60. Durban: Ireland and Southern Africa Project, 1992.

Brannen, Wallace, "Brunswick Street Gothic: St Patrick's Catholic Church," *The Griffin* 32 (June 2007): 1–4.

Bretherton, George. "The Battle Between Carnival and Lent: Temperance and Repeal in Ireland, 1829–1845." *Histoire Sociale/Social History* 27, 54 (1994): 295–320.

Bridgen, Lorene. "On Their Own Terms: Temperance in Southern Ontario's Black Community, 1830–1860." *Ontario History* 101, 1 (2009): 64–82.

Briggs, Charles Augustus. *American Presbyterianism: Its Origin and Early History*. New York: Scribner's and Sons, 1885.

Brooke, Peter. *Ulster Presbyterianism: The Historical Perspective, 1610–1970*. New York: St Martin's Press, 1987.

Brosnahan, Sean. "Rutherford Waddell: An Ulster Radical in Otago's Scottish Kirk." In *Ulster-New Zealand Migration and Cultural Transfers*, ed. Brad Patterson, 131–41. Dublin: Four Courts Press, 2006.

Brown, Russ. "Judgments of Solomon: Law, Doctrine, and the Cridge Controversy of 1872–1874." In *Essays in the History of Canadian Law: The Legal History of British Columbia and the Yukon*, ed. Hamar Foster and John McLaren, 313–51. Toronto: Osgoode Society for Canadian Legal History, 1995.

Brown, W.E. *The Catholic Church in South Africa,* ed. Michael Derrick. London: Burns and Oates, 1960.

Brubaker, Rogers. *Nationalism Reframed: Nationhood and the National Question in the New Europe*. Cambridge: Cambridge University Press, 1996.

– "Religion and Nationalism: Four Approaches." *Nations and Nationalism* 18, 1 (2012): 2–20.

Bryce, James. *Impressions of South Africa*. London: Macmillan & Co., 1897.

Buckland, Patrick. *Ulster Unionism and the Origins of Northern Ireland, 1886–1920*. Dublin: Gill and Macmillan, 1973.

Bumsted, J. M. "Scottish Catholicism in Canada, 1770–1830." In *Creed and Culture: The Place of English-speaking Catholics in Canadian Society, 1750–1930*, ed. Terrence Murphy and Gerald J. Stortz, 79–99. Montreal and Kingston: McGill-Queen's University Press, 1993.

– "The Scottish Diaspora: Emigration to British North America 1763–1815." In *Nation and Province in the First British Empire: Scotland and the Americas, 1600–1800*, ed. Ned Landsman, 127–42. Lewisburg, PA: Bucknell University Press, 2001.

Burchall, R.A. *The San Francisco Irish, 1848–1880*. Manchester: University Press, 1979.

Burke, Alfred E. "The Irishman's Place in the Empire." In *Empire Club Speeches, 1909–1910*, ed. J. Castell Hopkins, 225–32. Toronto: Warwick and Bros and Rutter Ltd, 1910.

Burke, Gerald. "Funding Schools." *Educare News*, April 2002, 42–7.

Burman, Edward. *China: The Stealth Empire – Why the World Is Not Chinese Yet*. Gloucestershire: History Press, 2008.

Burton, Antoinette. "Contesting the Zenana: The Mission to Make 'Lady Doctors for India,' 1874–1885." *Journal of British Studies* 35 (1996): 368–97.

Byrne, Cyril, ed. *Gentleman Bishops and Faction Fighter: The Letters of Bishops O'Donel, Lambert, Scallan and Others*. St. John's: Jesperson Press, 1984.

Cadigan, Sean. *Newfoundland and Labrador: A History*. Toronto: University of Toronto Press, 2009.

Campbell, Malcolm. *Ireland's New Worlds: Immigrants, Politics, and Society in the United States and Australia, 1815–1922*. Madison: University of Wisconsin Press, 2008.

Campbell, Robert. "Managing the Marginal: Regulating and Negotiating Decency in Vancouver's Beer Parlours, 1925–1954." *Labour/Le Travail* 44 (1999): 172–92.

Candela, Jr., Joseph. "The Struggle to Limit the Hours and Raise the Wages of Working Women in Illinois, 1893–1917." *Social Service Review* 53, 1 (March): 15–34.

Carey, Hilary M. *God's Empire: Religion and Colonialism in the British World, c. 1801–1908*. Cambridge: Cambridge University Press, 2011.

– "Religion and Society." in *The Oxford History of the British Empire*. Companion vol.: *Australia's Empire*, ed. Deryck Schreuder and Stuart Ward, 186–210. Oxford: Oxford University Press, 2008.

– "Women's Particular Mission to the Heathen: Protestant Missionary Wives in Australia, 1788–1900." In *Long Patient Struggle: Studies in the Role of Women in Australian Charity*, ed. M. Hutchinson and E. Campion, vol. 2, 25–44. Sydney: Centre for the Study of Australian Christianity, 1994.

Carmichael, Amy. *Lotus Buds*. London: Morgan and Scott, 1912.

Challoner, Richard. *The Garden of the Soul: A Manual of Spiritual Exercises and Reflections*. Dublin: James Duffy, 1764.

Chapeau, André, Louis-Philippe Normand, Lucienne Plante. *Evêques Catholiques de Canada – Canadian R.C. Bishops 1658–1979*. Ottawa: Research Centre in the Religious History of Canada, St Paul University, 1980.

Chittick, J.H., and B. Chittick. *The Chittick Family History*. Jamberoo: Chittick Family Reunion, 1988.

Choquette, Robert. *La Foi gardienne de la langue en Ontario, 1900–1950*. Montreal: Bellarmin, 1987.

– "English-French Relations in the Canadian Catholic Community." In *Creed and Culture: The Place of English-speaking Catholics in Canadian Society, 1750–1930*, ed. Terrence Murphy and Gerald J. Stortz,3–25. Montreal and Kingston: McGill-Queen's University Press, 1993.

– *Language and Religion: A History of English-French Conflict in Ontario*. Ottawa: University of Ottawa Press, 1975.

Christensen, Merton A. "Franklin on the Hemphill Trial: Deism versus Presbyterian Orthodoxy." *William and Mary Quarterly* 3rd ser., 10, 3 (1953): 422–40.

Clark, J.C.D. *English Society, 1660–1832: Religion, Ideology and Politics During the during the Ancien Régime*, 2nd ed. Cambridge: Cambridge University Press, 2000.

Clarke, Brian. *Piety and Nationalism: Lay Voluntary Associations and the Creation of an Irish-Catholic Community in Toronto, 1850–1895*. Montreal and Kingston: McGill-Queen's University Press, 1993.

– "Sir Richard Scott." In *Dictionary of Canadian Biography*. Vol. 14, 915. Toronto: University of Toronto Press, 1998.

Coakley, J.F. "The Religious Roots of Irish Nationalism." *Social Compass* 59 (2012): 3–20.

Cochrane, Peter, and David Goodman. "The Great Australian Journey: Cultural Logic and Nationalism in the Postmodern Era." *Australian Historical Studies* 23, 91 (1988): 21–44.

Coffey, John. *Politics, Religion and the British Revolutions: The Mind of Samuel Rutherford*. New York: Cambridge University Press, 1997.

Coldrey, Barry M. *Faith and Fatherland: The Christian Brothers and the Development of Irish Nationalism, 1838–1921*. Goldenbridge, Dublin: Gill and Macmillan, 1988.

Cole, Douglas L. "Canada's 'Nationalist' Imperialists." *Journal of Canadian Studies* 5, 3 (1970): 44–9.

Colley, Linda. *Britons: Forging the Nation, 1707–1837*. New Haven: Yale University Press, 1992.

Collie, J. *Rutherford Waddell: Memoir and Addresses*. Dunedin: A.H. Reed, 1932.

Colton, Glen. "Imagining Nation: Music and Identity in Pre-Confederation Newfoundland." *Newfoundland and Labrador Studies* 22, 1 (2007): 9–49.

Condon, Kevin. *The Missionary College of All Hallows, 1842–91*. Dublin: All Hallows College, 1986.

Congregation of the Christian Brothers. *Christian Brothers' Jubilee [in Newfoundland], 1876–1926*. St John's: Robinson and Co., 1926.

Cook, S.B. *Imperial Affinities: Nineteenth-Century Analogies and Exchanges between India and Ireland*. Delhi: Sage, 1993.

Corcoran, Brandon S., and Laura J. Smith, "Bishop Macdonell and the Friends of Ireland: Mixing Politics and Religion in Upper Canada," Canadian Catholic Historical Association, *Historical Studies* 79 (2013), 7–23.

Corporaal, Marguérite. "From Golden Hills to Sycamore Trees: Pastoral Homelands and Ethnic Identity in Irish Immigrant Fiction, 1860–75." *Irish Studies Review* 18, 3 (2010): 331–46.

Cox, Jeffrey. *Imperial Fault Lines: Christianity and Colonial Power in India, 1818–1940*. Stanford: Stanford University Press, 2002.

Crawford, Foreman. *Duck Creek Mountain now Alstonville: A Story of Early Settlement and Progress Told by a Son of One of the Earliest Selectors*. Alstonville: Foreman Crawford, 1983.

Cronin, Mike, and Daryl Adair. *The Wearing of the Green: A History of St Patrick's Day*. London: Routledge, 2002.

Crosbie, Barbara A. "Howley, Michael Francis," *Dictionary of Canadian Biography*, vol. 14, Toronto: University of Toronto/Université Laval, 1998. http://www.biographi.ca/en/bio/howley_michael_francis_14E.html (viewed 3 March 2015).

Crosbie, Barry. *Irish Imperial Networks: Migration, Social Communication and Exchange in Nineteenth-Century India*. Cambridge: Cambridge University Press, 2012.

Crunican, Paul. *Priests and Politicians: Manitoba Schools and the Election of 1896*. Toronto: University of Toronto Press, 1972.

Cunich, Peter. "Archbishop Vaughan and the Empires of Religion in Colonial New South Wales." In *Empires of Religion*, ed. Hilary M. Carey, 137–60. London: Palgrave Macmillan, 2008.

Cunningham, Anne. *The Roman Connection: Australia, Ireland and the Empire, 1865–1885*. Darlinghurst: Crossing Press, 2002.

Curry, Norman. "Macartney – The Man and His Ministry." In *Victoria's Debt to the Irish Church: Sermon and Papers Delivered at the Hussey Burgh Macartney Commemoration*, ed. James Grant. Melbourne: St Paul's Cathedral, 1995.

Curtis, L.P. *Apes and Angels: The Irishman in Victorian Caricature*. Washington: Smithsonian Institution Press, 1971.

D'Alton, Ian. "'A Vestigial Population?': Perspectives on Southern Irish Protestants in the Twentieth Century." *Eire-Ireland* 44, 3 and 4, 2009: 9–42.

Darnton, Robert. "What Is the History of Books?" In *Books and Society in History*, ed. Kenneth E. Carpenter, 65–83. New York: R.R. Bowker, 1983.

Davies, Graham. *The Irish in Britain, 1815–1914*. Dublin: Gill and Macmillan, 1991.

Davis, Richard P. *Irish Issues in New Zealand Politics, 1868–1922*. Dunedin: University of Otago Press, 1974.

– *Orangeism in Tasmania, 1832–1967*. Newtownabbey: University of Ulster, 2010.

de Kiewiet, C.W. *A History of South Africa: Social and Economic*. Oxford: Oxford University Press, 1975 [1941].

de Melo, Carlo Merces. "The Recruitment and Formation of the Native Clergy in India (16th-19th Century): An Historical-Canonical Study." PhD diss., Pontificia Università gregoriana, 1955.

Deacon, Desley, Penny Russell, and Angela Woollacott. *Transnational Lives: Biographies of Global Modernity, 1700-Present*. The Palgrave Macmillan Transnational History Series. Basingstoke: Palgrave Macmillan, 2010.

Delaney, Enda. *Demography, State and Society: Irish Migration to Britain, 1921–1971*. Liverpool: Liverpool University Press, 2000.

– *The Irish in Post-War Britain*. Oxford: Oxford University Press, 2007.

Devine, T.M. *To the Ends of the Earth: Scotland's Global Diaspora*. London: Allen Lane, 2011.

Dilke, Charles Wentworth. *Greater Britain: A Record of Travel in English-Speaking Countries during 1866 and 1867*, 2 vols. London: Macmillan, 1868.

– *Problems of Greater Britain*, 4th ed. London: Macmillan, 1890.

Diner, Hasia. *Erin's Daughters in America: Irish Immigrant Women in the Nineteenth Century*. Baltimore: Johns Hopkins University Press, 1983.

– "'The Most Irish City in the Union': The Era of the Great Migration, 1844–1877." In *The New York Irish*, ed. Ronald H. Bayor and Timothy J. Meagher, 87–106. Baltimore: Johns Hopkins University Press, 1996.

Dischl, Marcel. *Transkei for Christ: A History of the Catholic Church in the Transkeian Territories*. N.p.: The Author, 1982.

Donnelly Jr, James S. *Land and People of Nineteenth-Century Cork: The Rural Economy and the Land Question*. London: Routledge, 1975.

Dowd, Christopher. *Rome in Australia: The Papacy and Conflict in the Australian Catholic Missions, 1834–1884*, 2 vols. Leiden: Brill, 2008.

Doyle, Mark. "The Sepoys of the Pound and Sandy Row: Empire and Identity in Mid-Victorian Belfast." *Journal of Urban History* 36 (2010): 849–67.

Drayton, Richard. "Knowledge and Empire." In *The Oxford History of the British Empire*. Vol. 2: *The Eighteenth Century*, ed. P.J. Marshall, 231–52. Oxford: Oxford University Press, 1998.

Dublin, Thomas. *Women at Work: The Transformation of Work and Community in Lowell Massachusetts, 1826–1860*. New York: Columbia University Press, 1979.

Dubow, Saul. *A Commonwealth of Knowledge: Science, Sensibility, and White South Africa, 1820–2000*. Oxford: Oxford University Press, 2006.

Dudley Edwards, Ruth. *An Atlas of Irish History*, 3rd. ed. London: Methuen, 2005.

Duffy, Charles Gavan. *My Life in Two Hemispheres*. London: Fisher Unwin, 1898.

Duguid, Paul. "Networks and Knowledge: The Beginning and End of the Port Commodity Chain, 1703–1860." *Business History Review* 79 (2005): 493–526.

Duncan, William. *Correspondence between the Rev. Mr. Stack, Protestant minister, and W.A. Duncan, Catholic schoolmaster, Maitland: with remarks on Mr. Stack's lecture upon the Man of Sin, delivered in the English Church*, Maitland, March 6, 1839. Sydney: Abraham Cohen, 1839.

Dunn, Elaine. "The Kiama Region and Its Social and Industrial Evolution in the Nineteenth Century." BA honours thesis, University of Wollongong, 2003.

Dessureault, Christian, and Christine Hudon. "Conflits sociaux et élites locales au Bas-Canada: Le clergé, les notables, les paysannerie et la contrôle de la fabrique." *Canadian Historical Review* 80 (1990): 413–39.

Dutil, Patrice A. "Against Isolationism: Napoleon Belcourt, French Canada, and 'La grande guerre.'" In *Canada and the First World War*, ed. David Mackenzie, 96–137. Toronto: University of Toronto Press, 2008.

Dzwonkoski, Peter, ed. *American Literary Publishing Houses, 1638–1899*. Part 2: *N-Z*. Detroit: Bruccoli Clark, 1986.

Edwards, Benjamin. "Proddy-Dogs, Cattleticks and Ecumaniacs: Aspects of Sectarianism in New South Wales, 1945–1981." PhD diss., University of New South Wales 2007.

Eliot, Simon. "Some Trends in British Book Production, 1800–1919." In *Literature in the Marketplace: Nineteenth-Century British Publishing and Reading Practices*, ed. John O. Jordan and Robert L. Patten, 36–41. Cambridge: Cambridge University Press, 1995.

Ellington, Barbara Reeves, Kathryn Kish Sklar, and Connie Anne Stemo, eds. *Competing Kingdoms: Women, Mission, Nation and the American Protestant Empire, 1812–1960*. Durham, NC: Duke University Press, 2010.

Elliot, Elisabeth. *A Chance to Die: The Life and Legacy of Amy Carmichael*. Carlisle: OM Publishing, 1987.

Elliott, Bruce. "Emigration from South Leinster to Eastern Upper Canada." In *Canadian Papers in Rural History*, vol. 87, ed. Donald Harman Akenson, 277–305. Ganonoque, ON: Langdale Press, 1992.

– *Irish Migrants in the Canadas*, 2nd ed. Montreal and Kingston: McGill-Queen's University Press, 2004.

Emlyn, Thomas. "An Humble Inquiry into the Scripture Account of Jesus Christ: Mr. Emlyn's Account of the Scripture Account of Jesus Christ." Boston: Edes & Gill, 1756.

Emmons, David M. *The Butte Irish: Class and Ethnicity in an American Mining Town, 1875–1925*. Champaign: University of Illinois Press, 1990.

Erickson, Charlotte. *Invisible Immigrants*. London: Weidenfeld and Nicolson, 1972.

Etherington, Norman. "Education and Medicine." In *Missions and Empire*, ed. Norman Etherington, 261–84. Oxford: Oxford University Press, 2005.

Evans, A.G. *Romantic Heart: A Life of John Boyle O'Reilly, 1844–1890*. Perth: University of Western Australia Press, 1997.

Fanning, Charles. *The Irish Voice in America: Irish-American Fiction from the Eighteenth Century to the Present*, 2nd ed. Lexington: University Press of Kentucky, 1999.

Farwell, Byron. *The Great Anglo-Boer War*. New York: Harper and Row, 1976.

Fealy, Gerard M. *A History of Apprenticeship Nurse Training in Ireland*. New York: Routledge, 2006.

Fenyo, Krisztina. *Contempt, Sympathy and Romance: Lowland Perceptions of the Highlands and the Clearances during the Famine Years, 1845–1855*. East Lothian: Tuckwell, 2000.

Ffrench, Charles. *Biographical History of the American Irish in Chicago*. Chicago: American Biographical Publishing Company, 1897.

Fiorino, Pasquale. "The Nomination of Michael Fallon as Bishop of London." Canadian Catholic Historical Association, *Historical Studies* 62 (1996): 33–46.

FitzGerald, John. "Conflict and Culture in Irish Newfoundland Roman Catholicism, 1829–1850." PhD diss., University of Ottawa, 1997.

Fitzhardinge, L.F. *The Little Digger, 1914–1952*. Sydney: Angus and Robertson, 1979.

Fitzpatrick, David. "A Curious Middle Place: The Irish in Britain 1871–1921." In *The Irish in Britain, 1815–1939*, ed. Roger Swift and Sheridan Gilley, 10–59. London: Pinter Publishers, 1989.

– "Exporting Brotherhood: Orangeism in South Australia." *Immigrants and Minorities* 23, 2–3 (2005): 277–310.

– "Irish Emigration in the Later Nineteenth Century." *Irish Historical Studies* 22, 86 (1980): 126–43.

– *Irish Emigration, 1801–1921: Studies in Irish Economic and Social History*. Dublin: Economic and Social History Society of Ireland, 1984.

– *Oceans of Consolation: Personal Accounts of Irish Migration to Australia*. Melbourne: Melbourne University Press, 1995.

– "The Settlers: Immigration from Ireland in the Nineteenth Century." In *Ireland and Australia*, ed. Colm Kiernan. North Ryde: Angus and Robertson, 1984.

Fletcher, Holly Berkley. *Gender and the American Temperance Movement*. London: Routledge, 2008.

Flynn, Joyce. "Ethnicity after Sea-Change: The Irish Tradition in Nineteenth-Century American Drama." PhD diss., Harvard University, 1985

Foner, Eric. "Class, Ethnicity, and Radicalism in the Gilded Age: The Land League and Irish America." In *Politics and Ideology in the Age of the Civil War*, ed. Eric Foner, 150–200. New York: Oxford University Press, 1980.

Forth, Gordon. "The Anglo-Irish in Australia: Old World Origins and Colonial Experiences." In *Irish-Australian Studies: Papers Delivered at the Sixth Irish-Australian Conference*, ed. Noel McLachlan, 51–62. Melbourne: La Trobe University, 1991.

Fortson III, S. Donald. "The Adopting Act Compromise." In *Colonial Presbyterianism: Old Faith in a New Land*, ed. S. Donald Fortson III, Princeton Theological Monograph Series 71, 63–85. Eugene, OR: Pickwick Publications, 2007.

Foster R.F. *Modern Ireland, 1600–1972*. New York: Oxford University Press 1989.

– *W.B. Yeats: A Life*. Part 1: *The Apprentice Mage, 1865–1914*. Oxford: Oxford University Press, 1997.

Frame, Tom. *Anglicans in Australia*. Sydney: University of New South Wales Press, 2007.

Franklin, Jane. *This Errant Lady: Jane Franklin's Overland Journey to Port Phillip and Sydney, 1839*. Ed. Penny Russell. Canberra: National Library of Australia, 2002.

Fraser, Lyndon. *To Tara Via Holyhead: Irish Catholic Immigrants in Nineteenth-Century Christchurch*. Auckland: Auckland University Press, 1997.

Fraser, T.G. "Ireland and India." In *An Irish Empire?: Aspects of Ireland and the British Empire*, ed. Keith Jeffrey, 77–93. Manchester: Manchester University Press, 1996.

Freeman, Linton C. *The Development of Social Network Analysis: A Study in the Sociology of Science*. Vancouver: Empirical Press, 2004.

Frost, Lucy, and Hamish Maxwell-Stewart. *Chain Letters: Narrating Convict Lives*. Melbourne: Melbourne University Press, 2001.

Fry, Henry. *A System of Penal Discipline*. London: Longman, 1850.

Funchion, Michael F. "Irish Chicago: Church, Homeland, Politics, and Class – The Shaping of an Ethnic Group, 1870–1900." In *Ethnic Chicago: A Multicultural Portrait*, ed. Melvin G. Holli and Peter d'A. Jones, 4th ed., 57–92 Grand Rapids, MI: William B. Eerdmans, 1995.

Gagnon, Jean-Pierre. *Le 22e Bataillon (canadien-français) 1914–1919: Étude socio-militaire*. Québec: Les Presses de l'Université Laval, 1986.

Gahan, W.M. *The Manual of Catholic Piety*. Dublin: Charles Eason, c. 1900.

Galbally, Ann. *Redmond Barry: An Anglo-Irish Australian*. Melbourne: Melbourne University Press, 1995.

Geary, L.M. "Australia Felix: Irish Doctors in Nineteenth-Century Victoria." In *The Irish World Wide*, ed. P. O'Sullivan, 162–79. Leicester: Leicester University Press, 1992.

Gillespie, George. *A Treatise against the Deists or Free-Thinkers*. Philadelphia: Printed for the Author by A. Bradford, 1735.

Gillespie, Raymond. *Devoted People: Belief and Religion in Early Modern Ireland*. Manchester: Manchester University Press, 1997.

Gilley, Sheridan. "The Roman Catholic Church and the Nineteenth-Century Irish Diaspora." *Journal of Ecclesiastical History* 35 (1984): 188–207.

Gladwin, Michael. *Anglican Clergy in Australia, 1788–1850: Building a British World*, Woodbridge, UK: Royal Historical Society/Boydell Press, 2015

– "Flogging Parsons?: Australian Anglican Clergymen, the Magistracy and Convicts, 1788–1850." *Journal of Religious History* 36, 3 (2012): 1–18.

– "The Journalist in the Rectory: Anglican Clergymen and Australian Intellectual Life, 1788–1850." *History Australia* 7, 4 (2010): 56.1–56.28.

Gordon, Donald. "Dawson, William, 1852–1923." In *Southern People: A Dictionary of Otago Southland Biography*, ed. Jane Thomson. Dunedin: Longacre Press, 1998.

Gordon, Lynn. "Women and the Anti-Child Labor Movement in Illinois, 1890–1920." *Social Service Review* 51, 2 (1977): 228–48.

Gordon, Milton. *Assimilation in American Life*. New York: Oxford University Press, 1964.

Granatstein, J.L., and J.M. Hitsman. *Broken Promises: A History of Conscription in Canada*. Toronto: Oxford University Press, 1977.

Grant, James. *Episcopally Led and Synodically Governed: Anglicans in Victoria, 1803–1997*. Melbourne: Australian Scholarly Publishing, 2010.

– ed. *Victoria's Debt to the Irish Church: Sermon and Papers Delivered at the Hussey Burgh Macartney Commemoration*. Melbourne: St Paul's Cathedral, 1995.

Grant, John Webster. "The Reaction of WASP Churches to Non-WASP Immigration." *Canadian Society of Church History Papers* 3, 75 (1968): 1–15.

Greeley, Andrew M., *The Irish Americans: The Rise to Money and Power*. New York: Harper and Row 1981.

Gregor, John. "Extracts from Journals of Missionary Tours in the Moreton Bay District." In United Society for the Propagation of the Gospel, *Two Journals of Missionary Tours in the Districts of Maneroo and Moreton Bay, NSW, in 1843*. London: USPG, 1846.

Griffin, Larry J. *New Methods for Social History*. Cambridge: Cambridge University Press, 1999.

Griffin, Patrick. *The People with No Name: Ireland's Ulster Scots, America's Scots Irish, and the Creation of a British Atlantic World, 1689–1764*. Princeton: Princeton University Press, 2001.

Gusfield, Joseph R. *Symbolic Crusade: Status Politics and the American Temperance Movement*. Urbana: University of Illinois Press, 1963.

Hachey, Thomas E. "The Quarantine of Archbishop Mannix: A British Preventive Policy During the Anglo-Irish Troubles." *Irish University Review* 1 (1970): 111–30.

Hackett, Francis. "The Great Ireland (Describing the Irish at Home and Especially in the USA)." *Ireland Today* 1, 1 (1936).

Haig, Alan. *The Victorian Clergy*. London: Croom Helm, 1980.

Haire, J.L.M., ed. *Challenge and Conflict: Essays in Irish Presbyterian History and Doctrine*. Antrim: W. and G. Baird, 1981.

Hall, Catherine. *Civilizing Subjects: Metropole and Colony in the English Imagination*. Oxford: Polity Press, 2002.

Hall, Dianne. "Defending the Faith: Orangeism and Ulster Protestant Identities in Colonial New South Wales." *Journal of Religious History*, forthcoming.

Hamilton, Paula. "'No Irish Need Apply': Prejudice as a Factor in the Development of Immigration Policy in New South Wales." PhD diss., University of New South Wales, 1980.

Hardiman, David. *Missionaries and Their Medicine: A Christian Modernity for India*. Manchester: Manchester University Press, 2008.

Hardwick, Joe. *An Anglican British World: The Church of England and the Settler Empire, c. 1790–1860*. Manchester: Manchester University Press, 2014.

– "Anglican Church Expansion and the Recruitment of Colonial Clergy for New South Wales and the Cape Colony, c. 1790–1850." *Journal of Imperial and Commonwealth History* 37, 3 (2009): 361–81.

Harris, Ruth-Ann. "'Come All You Courageously': Irish Women in America Write Home." In *New Directions in Irish-American History*, ed. Kevin Kenny, 209–26. Madison: University of Wisconsin Press, 2003.

Harrison, Brian Howard. *Drink and the Victorians: The Temperance Question in England, 1815–1872*. London: Faber, 1971.

Harrison, Jennifer. "From King's County to 'Qinnsland.'" In *Offaly: History and Society*, ed. William Nolan and Timothy P. O'Neill. Dublin: Geography Publications, 1998.

Hart, D.G. "Old Side/New Side Schism and Reunion." In *Colonial Presbyterianism: Old Faith in a New Land*, ed. S. Donald Fortson III, Princeton Theological Monograph Series 71, 157–79. Eugene, OR: Pickwick Publications, 2007.

Hassall, James S. *In Old Australia: Records and Reminiscences from 1794*. Brisbane: Hews, 1902.

Hassam, Andrew. *Our Floating Home*. London: Sir Robert Menzies Centre for Australian Studies, 1992.

Hastings, Paula. "Our Glorious Anglo-Saxon Race Shall Ever Fill Earth's Highest Place: The Anglo-Saxon and the Construction of Identity in Late Nineteenth-Century Canada." In *Canada and the British World: Culture, Migration, and Identity*, ed. Phillip Buckner and R. Douglas Francis, 92–110. Vancouver: UBC Press, 2006.

Hayes-McCoy, G.A., ed. *Historical Studies X*. Dublin: Cló Chois Fharraige, 1976. 122.

Hazlett, Ian, "Students at Glasgow University from 1747 to 1768 connected with Ireland: an analytical probe," in *Ebb and Flow: Essays in Church History in Honour of R. Finlay Holmes*, ed. Donald Patton. Belfast: Presbyterian Historical Society of Ireland 2002.

Healy, Robert C. *A Catholic Book Chronicle: The Story of P. J. Kenedy and Sons, 1826–1951*. New York: P.J. Kennedy and Sons, 1951.

Hempton, David. *Religion and Political Culture in Britain and Ireland: From the Glorious Revolution to the Decline of Empire*. Cambridge: Cambridge University Press, 1996.

Hempton, David. *Methodism: Empire of the Spirit*. New Haven: Yale University Press, 2005.

Hempton, David, and Myrtle Hill. *Evangelical Protestantism in Ulster Society, 1740–1890*. London: Routledge, 1992.

Henderson, Gerard. "The Deportation of Charles Jerger." *Labour History* 31 (1976): 61–78.

Henderson, H. *Battle of Glenow: Scenes from an Ulster Orangeman*. Lurgan: *Lurgan Gazette*, 1861.

Heney, John J. *John Heney & Son: The Saga of an Ottawa Irish Family*. Renfrew, ON: General Store Publishing House, 2010.

Heron, Craig. *Booze: A Distilled History*. Toronto: Between the Lines, 2003.

– "The Boys and Their Booze: Masculinities and Public Drinking in Working-Class Hamilton, 1890–1946." *Canadian Historical Review* 86, 3 (2005): 411–52.

Herraman, Ann and Richards, Eric. "'If she was to be hard up she would sooner be hard up in a strange land than where she would be known': Irish Women in Colonial South Australia," in *Irish Women in Colonial Australia*, ed. Trevor McClaughlin, 82–115. Sydney: Allen & Unwin 1998.

Hickey, John. "Irish Settlement in Nineteenth-Century Cardiff." In *Irish Migrants in Modern Wales*, ed. Paul O'Leary, 34–53. Liverpool: Liverpool University Press, 2004.

Hill, Myrtle. "Assessing the Awakening: The 1859 Revival in Ulster." In *Church and People in Britain and Scandinavia*, ed. Ingmar Brohed, 197–213. Lund and Bromley: Lund University Press, 1996.

– "From Down to Dohnavur: Amy Carmichael and 'The Higher Christian Life.'" In *Ireland: Looking East*, ed. Christopher Gillisen, 23–36. Brussels: Peter Lang, 2010.

– "Women's Work: The Presbyterian Zenana Mission, 1873–1914." in *Religious Women and Their History: Breaking the Silence*, ed. Rosemary Raughter, 82–97. Dublin: Irish Academic Press, 2005.

Hiller, James K. "Robert Bond and the Pink, White and Green: Newfoundland Nationalism in Perspective." *Acadiensis* 36, 2 (2007): 113–33.

Hilliard, David. *Godliness and Good Order: A History of the Anglican Church in South Australia*. Adelaide: Wakefield Press, 1986.

Hodge, Charles. *The Constitutional History of the Presbyterian Church in the United States of America*. Philadelphia: Presbyterian Board of Publication, 1851.

Hoerder, Dirk. "From Migrants to Ethnics: Acculturation in a Societal Framework." In *European Migrants: Global and Local Perspectives*, ed. Dirk Hoerder and Leslie Page Moch, 211–62. Boston: Northeastern University Press, 1996.

Hoerder, Dirk, and Horst Roessler, eds. *Distant Magnets: Expectations and Realities in the Immigrant Experience, 1840–1930*. New York: Holmes and Meier, 1993.

Hofmeyr, Isabel. *The Portable Bunyan: A Transnational History of* The Pilgrim's Progress. Princeton: Princeton University Press, 2004.

Hogan, Edmund M. *The Irish Missionary Movement: A Historical Survey, 1830–1980*. Dublin: Gill and Macmillan, 1990.

Hogan, Michael. *The Sectarian Strand: Religion in Australian History*. Ringwood: Penguin, 1987.

Hogan, Michael, and David Clune. *The People's Choice: Electoral Politics in Twentieth-Century New South Wales*. Sydney: Parliament of NSW, 2001.

Holmes, Andrew R. *The Shaping of Ulster Presbyterian Belief and Practice, 1770–1840*. Oxford: Oxford University Press, 2006.

– "The Shaping of Irish Presbyterian Attitudes to Mission, 1790–1840." *Journal of Ecclesiastical History* 4 (2006): 711–37.

Holmes, Janice, "The World Turned Upside Down: Women in the Ulster Revival of 1859," in *Coming into the Light: The Work, Politics and Religion of Women in Ulster, 1840–1940*, edited by Janice Holmes and Diane Urquhart. Belfast: Institute of Irish Studies, 1995: 125–53.

Holmes, R.F. "Henry Cooke." In *Dictionary of Irish Biography*, ed. James McGuire and James Quinn. Cambridge: Cambridge University Press, 2009.

Holmes, R.F.G. *Our Presbyterian Heritage*. Belfast: Publications Committee, Presbyterian Church in Ireland, 1985.

Hopkins, J. Castell. *Canada at War: A Record of Heroism and Achievement, 1914–1918*. Toronto: Canadian Annual Review Ltd, 1919.

Horn, Gerard. "'A Loyal United and Happy People': Irish Protestant Migrants to Wellington Province, 1840–1930: Aspects of Migration, Settlement, and Community." Phd diss., Victoria University of Wellington, 2010.

– "Ulster Protestants in New Zealand: A Bibliographic Essay." *Immigrants and Minorities: Historical Studies in Ethnicity, Migration and Diaspora*, 32, 3 (2014): 315–42.

Houghton, Frank. *Amy Carmichael of Dohnavur*. London: Christian Literature Crusade, 1993.

Houston, Cecil, and William B. Smyth. *Irish Emigration and Canadian Settlement: Patterns, Links, and Letters*. Toronto: University of Toronto Press, 1990.

Howe, Stephen. *Ireland and Empire: Colonial Legacies in Irish History and Culture*, 2nd ed. Oxford: Oxford University Press, 2000.

Howell, Philip, and David Lambert. "Sir John Pope Hennessy and Colonial Government: Humanitarianism and the Translation of Slavery in the Imperial Network." In *Colonial Lives across the British Empire: Imperial Careering in the Long Nineteenth Century*, ed. David Lambert and Alan Lester, 228–56. Cambridge: Cambridge University Press, 2006.

Howes, Marjorie. "Discipline, Sentiment and the Irish-American Public: Mary Ann Sadlier's Popular Fiction." *Éire-Ireland* 40, 1 and 2 (2005): 140–69.

Howley, Michael. F., *Ecclesiastical History of Newfoundland*, vol. 1. Boston: Doyle and Whittle, 1888.

– *Ecclesiastical History of Newfoundland*, vol. 2, ed. Brother Joseph B. Darcy, C.F.C. and John F. O'Mara. St John's: Terra Nova Publishing, 2005.

Howsam, Leslie. *Old Books and New Histories: An Orientation to Studies in Book and Print Culture*. Toronto: University of Toronto Press, 2006.

Huel, Raymond. "The French-Irish Conflict in Catholic Episcopal Nominations: The Western Sees and Domination within the Church." Canadian Catholic Historical Association, *Study Sessions* 42 (1975): 51–70.

Hurley, P.E. "Some Reasons Why Catholics Lose the Faith in New Zealand." *Irish Ecclesiastical Record*, 3rd series, 8 (1887): 206–7.

Inglis, Brian. *West Briton*. London: Faber and Faber, 1962.

Irwin, Clarke H. *A History of Presbyterianism in Dublin and the South and West of Ireland*. London: Hodder & Stoughton, 1890.

Ison, John. *Appeal to the Secretary of State relative to the dismissal of the Rev. John L. Ison from his Chaplaincy at Norfolk Island*. Oatlands, Van Diemen's Land: s.n., 1850.

Jasanoff, Maya. *Edge of Empire: Lives, Culture, and Conquest in the East, 1750–1850*. New York: Vintage, 2006.

Jeffrey, Keith, ed. *An Irish Empire?: Aspects of Ireland and the British Empire*. Manchester: Manchester University Press, 1996.

Johnston, A.A. *A History of the Catholic Church in Eastern Nova Scotia*. 2 vols. Antigonish: St Francis Xavier University, 1960.

Johnston, A.J.B. "Nativism in Nova Scotia: Anti-Irish Ideology in a Mid-Nineteenth-Century British Colony." In *The Irish in Atlantic Canada, 1780–1900*, ed. T. Power, 23–9. Fredericton, NB: New Ireland Press, 1991.

Johnston, Douglas. *Rich Heritage: The Story of Eureka and Its People*. Kyogle: Douglas Johnston, 1987.

Jones, Diana K. "Researching Groups of Lives: A Collective Biographical Perspective on the Protestant Ethic Debate.' *Qualitative Research* 1 (2001): 325–46.

Jones, Frederick. "Mullock, John Thomas." *Dictionary of Canadian Biography*, vol. 9. Toronto: University of Toronto/Université Laval, 2003–, accessed March 3, 2015. http://www.biographi.ca/en/bio/mullock_john_thomas_9E.html (viewed 2 March 2015).

Joyce, James. *Ulysses*. Oxford World's Classics. Oxford: Oxford University Press, 1998.

Judd, Stephen, and Ken Cable. *Sydney Anglicans: A History of the Diocese*. Sydney: Anglican Information Office, 1987.

Jupp, James. *The English in Australia*. Melbourne: Cambridge University Press, 2004.

Jupp, James, and Barry York. *Birthplaces of the Australian People: Colonial and Commonwealth Censuses, 1828–1991*. Canberra: Australian National University, 1995.

Kantowicz, Edward R. "The Ethnic Church." In *Ethnic Chicago: A Multicultural Portrait,* ed. Melvin G. Holli and Peter d'A. Jones, 4th ed., 574–603. Grand Rapids, MI: William B. Eerdmans, 1995.

Kearney, Paddy. *Guardian of the Light: Denis Hurley – Renewing the Church, Opposing Apartheid*. New York: Continuum, 2009.

Keats, N.C. *Wollumbin: The Creation and Early Habitation of the Tweed Brunswick and Richmond Rivers*. Point Clare: The Author, 1988.

Kehoe, S. Karly. "Catholic Identity in the Diaspora: Nineteenth-Century Ontario." In *Bluid, Kin and Countrie: Scottish Associational Culture in the Diaspora*, ed. Andrew Hinson and Graeme Morton Tanja Bueltmann, 83–100. Toronto: Stewart Publishing, 2009.

– *Creating a Scottish Church: Catholicism, Gender and Ethnicity in Nineteenth-Century Scotland*. Manchester: Manchester University Press, 2010.

– "Unionism, Nationalism and the Scottish Catholic Periphery." *Britain and the World* 4, 1 (2011): 65–83.

Kehoe, S. Karly, and Michael Vance. "A Hiberno-British World." *Britain and the World* 6, 2 (2013): 149–51.

Kelly, Edward. *The Story of St Paul's Parish, Toronto*. Toronto: n.p., 1922.

Kelly, Helen. *Irish "Ingleses": The Irish Immigrant Experience in Argentina, 1840–1920*. Dublin: Irish Academic Press, 2009.

Kelly, Laura. "Irish Medical Women c. 1880s–1920s: The Origins, Education and Careers of Early Women Medical Graduates from Irish Institutions." PhD diss., National University of Ireland, 2010.

Kennedy, Liam. *Colonialism, Religion and Nationalism in Ireland*. Belfast: Institute of Irish Studies, Queen's University of Belfast, 1996.

Kenny, Dean. *A History of the Commencement and Progress of Catholicity in Australia up to the Year 1840*. Sydney: Cunningham & Co. 1886.

Kenny, Kevin. "Diaspora and Comparison: the Global Irish as a Case Study." *Journal of American History* 90, 1 (2003): 134–62.

– "The Irish in the Empire." In *Ireland and the British Empire*, ed. Kevin Kenny, 90–122. Oxford: Oxford University Press, 2004.

– *Making Sense of the Molly Maguires*. New York: Oxford University Press, 1998.

Kenny, Kevin, ed. *Ireland and the British Empire*. Oxford History of the British Empire Companion Series. Oxford: Oxford University Press, 2004.

Kenny, Laurence J. "America – A Land of Destiny." *Catholic Historical Review* new series 6, 3 (1926): 423–47.

Kent, Elizabeth. *Converting Women: Gender and Protestant Christianity in Colonial South India*. Oxford: Oxford University Press, 2004.

Keogh, Dáire. *"The French Disease": The Catholic Church and Radicalism in Ireland, 1790–1800*. Dublin: Four Courts Press, 1993.

Kiberd, Declan. *Inventing Ireland: The Literature of the Modern Nation*. London: Jonathon Cape, 1995.

Kiernan, Colm, *Daniel Mannix and Ireland*. Morwell: Alella Books, 1984.

Kiernan, V.G. "Britons Old and New." In *Immigrants and Minorities in British Society*, ed. Colin Holmes, 23–43. London: Allen and Unwin, 1978.

Kildea, Jeff. *Tearing the Fabric: Sectarianism in Australia, 1910–1925*. Sydney: Citadel Books, 2002.

Kilian, O.M. "The Catholic Boys' Brigade," *America* 26, 11 (1921): 262–3.

Kinane, Vincent, and Michael Gill. "McGlashan and Gill." In *British Literary Publishing Houses, 1820–1880*, ed. Patrick Anderson and Jonathan Rose. London: Bruccoli Clark Layman, 1991.

Kingsley, Henry. *The Recollections of Geoffrey Hamlyn*. Melbourne: Currey O'Neill, 1981 [1859].

Kirkham, Graeme. "Ulster Emigration to North America, 1680–1720." In *Ulster and North America: Transatlantic Perspectives on the Scotch-Irish*, ed. H. Tyler Blethen and Curtis W. Wood. Tuscaloosa: University of Alabama Press, 1997.

Kirkpatrick, Laurence. *Made in China: The Story of Irish Presbyterianism in China*. Belfast: Manley, 2008.

Kirsop, Wallace. *Books for Colonial Readers: The Nineteenth-Century Australian Experience*. Melbourne: Bibliographical Society of Australia and New Zealand in association with the Centre for Bibliographical and Textual Studies, Monash University, 1994.

Klett, Guy S., ed. *Minutes of the Presbyterian Church in America, 1706–1788*. Philadelphia, PA: Presbyterian Historical Society, 1976.

Knight, Frances. *The Nineteenth-Century Church and English Society*. Cambridge: Cambridge University Press, 1995.

Kollar, Rene,. "An American 'Escaped Nun' on Tour in England: Edith O'Gorman's Critique of Convent Life." *Feminist Theology* 14, 2 (2006): 205–20.

Kwan, Elizabeth. "St Patrick's Day Procession, Melbourne, 1920: An Australian or Irish Event?" In *Echoes of Irish Australia: Rebellion to Republic*, ed. Jeff Brownrigg, Cheryl Morgan, and Richard Reid, 145–54. Galong, NSW: St Clement's Retreat and Conference Centre, 2007.

Laffan, Tony. *How Orange Was My Valley*. Singleton: Toiler Editions, 2009.

Lahey, Raymond J. "Catholicism and Colonial Policy in Newfoundland, 1779–1830." In *Creed and Culture: The Place of English-Speaking Catholics in Canadian Society, 1750–1930*, ed. Terrence Murphy and Gerald J. Stortz, 49–78. Montreal and Kingston: McGill-Queen's University Press, 1993.

Laidlaw, Zoë. "Richard Bourke: Irish Liberalism Tempered by Empire." In *Colonial Lives across the British Empire: Imperial Careering in the Long Nineteenth Century*, ed. David Lambert and Alan Lester, 113–44. Cambridge: Cambridge University Press, 2006.

Lake, Marilyn, and Henry Reynolds. *Drawing the Global Colour Line: White Men's Countries and the International Challenge of Racial Equality*. Cambridge: Cambridge University Press, 2008.

Lambert, Carolyn. "Emblem of Our Country: The Red, White, and Green Tricolour." *Newfoundland and Labrador Studies* 23, 1 (2008): 21–43.

– "Far from the Homes of their Fathers: Irish Catholics in St John's, Newfoundland, 1840–86." PhD. diss., Memorial University of Newfoundland, 2010.

Lambert, Frank. *Inventing the "Great Awakening."* Princeton: Princeton University Press, 1999.

Lambert, David, and Alan Lester. *Colonial Lives across the British Empire: Imperial Careering in the Long Nineteenth Century*. Cambridge: Cambridge University Press, 2006.

Lang, J. Dunmore. *Visit to Geelong and the Western Districts of Victoria in 1846*. Parkville: University of Melbourne Library, 1987.

Laracy, Hugh. "Bishop Moran: Irish Politics and Catholicism in New Zealand." *Journal of Religious History* 6, 1 (1970): 62–76.

– "The Life and Context of Bishop Patrick Moran." MA thesis, Victoria University of Wellington, 1964.

Larkin, Emmet. "The Devotional Revolution in Ireland 1850–75." *American Historical Review* 77, 3 (1972): 625–52.

– "Economic Growth, Capital Investment, and the Roman Catholic Church in Nineteenth Century Ireland." *American Historical Review* 72, 3 (1967): 852–84.

– *The Historical Dimensions of Irish Catholicism*. Washington, DC: Catholic University of America Press, 1997.

Lee, Janet. "Between Subordination and She-Tiger: Social Constructions of White Femininity in the Lives of Single, Protestant Missionaries in China, 1905–1930." *Women's Studies International Forum* 19, 6 (1996): 621–32.

Leighton, C.D.A. "Gallicanism and the Veto Controversy: Church, State and Catholic Community in Early Nineteenth-Century Ireland." In *Religion, Conflict and Coexistence in Ireland: Essays Presented to Monsignor Patrick Corish*, ed. R.V. Comerford, Mary Cullen, Jacqueline R. Hill, and Colm Lennon, 135–55. Dublin: Gill and Macmillan, 1990.

Lemieux, Lucien. *L'établissement de la premier province écclesiastique en Canada, 1783–1844*. Montreal: Fides, 1968.

Lester, Alan. *Imperial Networks: Creating Identities in Nineteenth-Century South Africa and Britain*. London: Routledge, 2001.

Levine, Bruce C. *The Spirit of 1848: German Immigrants, Labor Conflict, and the Coming of the Civil War*. Urbana: University of Illinois Press, 1992.

Levitt, Ian, and Christopher Smout. *The State of the Scottish Working Class in 1843*. Edinburgh: Scottish Academic Press, 1979.

Lindberg, Richard C. *The Gambler King of Clark Street: Michael C. McDonald and the Rise of Chicago's Democratic Machine*. Carbondale: Southern Illinois University, 2009.

Livingstone, David N. "Science, Region and Religion: The Reception of Darwinism in Princeton, Belfast and Edinburgh." In *Disseminating Darwinism: The Role of Place, Race, Religion and Gender*, ed. Ronald L. Numbers and John Stenhouse, 7–38. New York: Cambridge University Press, 1999.

Livingstone, Peadar. *The Fermanagh Story: A Documented History of the County Fermanagh from the Earliest Times to the Present Day*. Enniskillen: Cumann Seanchais Chlochair, 1969.

Loeber, Rolf, and Magda Stouthamer-Loeber. "James Duffy and Catholic Nationalism." In *History of the Irish Book, 1800–1899*, ed. James H. Murphy, 115–21. Oxford: Oxford University Press, 2011.

Logan, James. "Sectarianism in Ganmain: A Local Study, 1912–21." *Rural Society* 10 (2000): 121–38.

Londoño-Vega, Patricia. *Religion, Culture, and Society in Colombia: Medellín and Antioquia, 1850–1930*. Oxford: Oxford University Press, 2002.

Long, M. "A Word from Australia." *Irish Ecclesiastical Record* 3rd series 4 (1883): 653–59.

Lower, Arthur R.M. *Colony to Nation: A History of Canada*. Don Mills, ON: Longmans, 1946).

Lowry, Donal. "Ulster Resistance and Loyalist Rebellion in the Empire." In *An Irish Empire? Aspects of Ireland and the British Empire*, ed. Keith Jeffrey, 191–216. Manchester: Manchester University Press, 1996.

Lyons, F.S.L. *Charles Stewart Parnell*. Fontana: London, 1978.

MacColl, Allan W. *Land, Faith and the Crofting Community: Christianity and Social Criticism in the Highlands of Scotland*. Edinburgh: Edinburgh University Press, 2006.

MacDonagh, Oliver. "The Irish Catholic Clergy and Emigration during the Great Famine." *Irish Historical Studies* 5 (1946–47): 287–301.

MacDonell, Margaret. *The Emigrant Experience: Songs of Highland Emigrants in North America*. Toronto: University of Toronto Press 1982.

MacGinley, M.E.R. "The Irish in Queensland: An Overview." In *The Irish Emigrant Experience in Australia,* ed. J. O'Brien and P. Travers, 103–19. Dublin: Poolbeg Press, 1991.

MacKechnie, S. Wyman. *What Men They Were!* Shawville, QC: Dickson Enterprises, 1974.

MacKenzie, G.T. "History of Christianity of Travancore." In *The Travancore State Manual*, vol. 1, ed. V. Nagum Aiya, 191–5. Trivandrum: Travancore Government Press, 1906).

MacKenzie, John M. "Irish, Scottish, Welsh and English Worlds? A Four Nations Approach to the History of the British Empire." *History Compass* 6, 5 (2008): 1244–63.

Mackenzie, John. "'Making Black Scotsmen and Scotswomen?': Scottish Missionaries and Eastern Cape Colony in the Nineteenth Century." In *Empires of Religion*, ed. Hilary M. Carey, 113–36. London: Palgrave Macmillan, 2008.

Mackenzie, John M., with Nigel R. Dalziel. *The Scots in South Africa: Ethnicity, Identity, Gender and Race, 1772–1914*. Manchester: Manchester University Press, 2007.

MacLean, Ray A. *The* Casket, *1852–1992: From Gutenberg to Internet – The Story of a Small-Town Weekly*. Antigonish: *The Casket*, 1995.

MacRaild, Donald M. *Faith, Fraternity and Fighting: The Orange Order and Irish Migrants in Northern England, c. 1850–1920*. Liverpool: Liverpool University Press, 2005.

Malcolm, Elizabeth. *Ireland Sober, Ireland Free: Drink and Temperance in Nineteenth-Century Ireland*. Syracuse: Syracuse University Press, 1986.

Malleck, Daniel J. "Priorities of Development in Four Local Women's Christian Temperance Unions in Ontario, 1877–1895." in *The Changing Face of Drink: Substance, Imagery, and Behaviour*, ed. Jack S. Blocker and Cheryl Krasnick-Warsh, 189–208. Ottawa: Histoire sociale, 1997.

Mann, Horace. "The Necessity of Education in a Republican Government (1838)." In *Lectures and Annual Reports on Education*, ed. with introduction by Mary Mann, 143–90. Cambridge: Published for the editor, 1867.

Mann, Mary. *The Life of Horace Mann*. Boston: Lee and Shepard 1891.

Marsden, George. *Fundamentalism in American Culture: The Shaping of Twentieth-Century Evangelicalism, 1870–1925*. New York: Oxford University Press, 1980.

Maxwell-Stewart, Hamish, and Susan Hood. *Pack of Thieves? 52 Port Arthur Lives*. Port Arthur, Tas.: Port Arthur Historic Site Management Authority, 2001.

McBride, Ian R. *Scripture Politics: Ulster Presbyterians and Irish Radicalism in the Late Eighteenth Century*. Oxford: Clarendon Press, 1998.

– *The Siege of Derry in Ulster Protestant Mythology*. Dublin: Four Courts Press, 1997.

McCarthy, Angela. *Irish Migrants in New Zealand, 1840–1937: "The Desired Haven."* Woodbridge: Boydell Press, 2005.

McClaughlin, Trevor. "Protestant Irish in Australia." In *Echoes of Irish Australia: Rebellion to Republic – A Collection of Essays*, ed. Jeff Brownrigg, Cheryl Mongan, and Richard Reid, 88–98. Galong, NSW: St Clements Retreat and Conference Centre, 2007.

McClelland, Gillian. "Evangelical Philanthropy and Social Control or Emancipatory Feminism?: A Case Study of Fisherwick Presbyterian Working Women's Association, 1870–1918." PhD diss., Queen's University of Belfast, 2000.

McConville, Chris. *Croppies, Celts and Catholics: The Irish in Australia*. Melbourne: Edward Arnold, 1987.

– "The Victorian Irish: Emigrants and Families, 1851–1891," in *Families in Colonial Australia*, ed. Patricia Grimshaw, Chris McConville and Ellen McEwen. Sydney: Allen & Unwin 1985.

McCracken, Donal P. *The Irish Pro-Boers, 1877–1902*. Johannesburg: Perskor, 1989.

– "Irish settlement and identity in South Africa before 1910," *Irish Historical Studies*, vol. 28, no. 110 (Nov. 1992): 134–49.

– "Preface," in *The Irish in Southern Africa, 1795–1910*, Volume 2 of Southern African-Irish Studies, edited by Donal P. McCraken (Durban: Ireland and Southern Africa Project 1992).

McCracken, J.L. *New Light at the Cape of Good Hope: William Porter, the Father of Cape Liberalism*. Belfast: Ulster Historical Foundation Publications, 1993.

McCuaig, Carol Bennett. *People of St Patrick's*. Renfrew: Juniper Books, 1993.

McDannell, Colleen. "Catholic Women Fiction Writers, 1840–1920." *Women's Studies* 19 (1991): 385–405.

– "'The Devil was the First Protestant': Gender and Intolerance in Irish Catholic Fiction." *US Catholic Historian* 8, 1 and 2 (1989): 51–65.

– "'True Men as We Need Them:' Catholicism and the Irish-American Male." *American Studies* 27, 2 (1986): 19–36.

McDonagh, Oliver. "The Irish in Victoria, 1851–91: A Demographic Essay." *Historical Studies* 7 (1971): 67–92.

McDonald, John, and Eric Richards. "The Great Emigration of 1841: Recruitment for New South Wales in British Emigration Fields." *Population Studies* 15 (1997): 337–55.

McDowell, R.B. *Crisis and Decline: The Fate of Southern Unionists*. Dublin: Lilliput Press, 1997.

McEvoy, Fred, et al. *Enduring Faith: A History of St Patrick's Basilica, Ottawa, 1855–2005*. Ottawa: St Patrick's Basilica 2006.

McGahan, Elizabeth W. "The Sisters of Charity of the Immaculate Conception: A Canadian Case Study," Canadian Catholic Historical Association *Historical Studies* 61 (1995): 99–134.

McGee, Thomas D'Arcy. *The Catholic history of North America: five discourses, to which are added two discourses on the relations of Ireland and America*. Boston: P. Donahoe, 1855.

– *A history of the Irish settlers in North America: From the earliest period to the census of 1850*. Boston: Boston Celt, 1851.

– *A Life of the Rt. Rev. Edward Maginn, Coadjutor Bishop of Derry, with selections from his* correspondence. New York: P. O'Shea, 1857.

McGowan, Mark G. "Between King, Kaiser, and Canada: Irish Catholics in Canada and the Great War, 1914–1918." In *Irish Nationalism in Canada*, ed. David A. Wilson, 97–120. Montreal and Kingston: McGill-Queen's University Press, 2009.

– *Creating Canadian Historical Memory: The Case of the Famine Migration of 1847*. Ottawa: Canadian Historical Association, Canada's Ethnic Groups, Booklet 30, 2006.

– *Death or Canada: The Irish Famine Migration to Toronto, 1847*. Toronto: Novalis, 2009.

– *Michael Power: The Struggle to Build the Catholic Church on the Canadian Frontier*. Montreal and Kingston: McGill-Queen's University Press, 2005.

– '"Pregnant with Perils": Canadian Catholicism and Its Relation to the Catholic Churches of Newfoundland, 1840–1949." *Newfoundland and Labrador Studies* 28, 2 (2013): 193–218.

– "Toronto's English-Speaking Catholics, Immigrants, and the Making of a Canadian Catholic Identity." In *Creed and Culture: The Place of English-Speaking Catholics in Canadian Society, 1750–1930*, ed. Terrence Murphy and Gerald Stortz, 204–45. Montreal and Kingston: McGill-Queen's University Press, 1993.

– *The Waning of the Green: Catholics, the Irish, and Identity in Toronto, 1887–1922*. Montreal and Kingston: McGill-Queen's University Press, 1999.

McGrath, Thomas G. "The Tridentine Evolution of Modern Irish Catholicism, 1563–1962: A Re-examination of the 'Devotional Revolution' Thesis." *Recusant History* 20, 4 (1991): 512–23.

McGreevy, John C. *Catholicism and American Freedom: A History*. New York: W.W. Norton, 2003.

McKiernan, Susan. "Introduction." In Mary Theresa Vidal, *Bengala, or, Some Time Ago*, ed. Susan McKiernan. Sydney: University of Sydney Library, 2000 [1860].

McKeown, H.C. *The Life and Labors of Archbishop John Joseph Lynch*. Montreal: James A Sadlier, 1886.

McLay, Anne. *Women on the Move: Mercy's Triple Spiral*. Adelaide: Sisters of Mercy, 1996.

McMahon, Theo. "From Fintona to Wollongong, 1838." *Clogher Record* 13, 1 (1988): 116–25.

Macarney, Hussey Burgh. *The Antichrist: A Lecture Delivered in the Hall of the Mechanics' Institute before the John Knox Young Men's Association on Wednesday, May 31st, 1854*. Melbourne: Hugh M'Coll, 1854.

Magee, Gary B., and Andrew S. Thompson. *Empire and Globalisation: Networks of People, Goods and Capital in the British World, c. 1850–1914*. Cambridge: Cambridge University Press, 2010.

Marriott, Fitzherbert Adams. *Is a Penal Colony Reconcilable with God's Constitution of Human Society and the Laws of Christ's Kingdom?* Hobart: William Gore Elliston, 1847.

Megahey, Alan. *The Irish Protestant Churches in the Twentieth Century*. London: Macmillan, 2000.

Meredith, Ian. "Irish Episcopalians in the Scottish Episcopal Diocese of Glasgow and Galloway during the Nineteenth Century." In *Irish Identities in Victorian Britain*, ed. Roger Swift and Sheridan Gilley, 121–50. Abingdon: Routledge, 2009.

Millar, Anthony Kendal. *Plantagenet in South Africa: Lord Charles Somerset*. Cape Town: Oxford University Press, 1965.

Miller, Kerby A. *Emigrants and Exiles: Ireland and the Irish Exodus to North America*. New York: Oxford University Press, 1985.

– *Ireland and Irish America: Culture, Class, and Transatlantic Migration*. Dublin: Field Day 2008.

– Arnold Schrier, Bruce D. Boling, and David N. Doyle, eds., *Irish Immigrants in the Land of Canaan: Letters and Memoirs from Colonial and Revolutionary America*. Oxford: Oxford University Press, 2002.

Miller, Stephen M. *Volunteers on the Veld: Britain's Citizen-Soldiers and the South African War, 1899–1902*. Norman: University of Oklahoma Press, 2007.

Mills, David. *The Idea of Loyalty in Upper Canada, 1784–1850*. Montreal and Kingston: McGill-Queen's University Press, 1988.

Milner, John. *Key of Heaven: A Manual of Prayer*. Dublin: Charles Eason, c. 1900.

Mitchell, Martin J. *The Irish in the West of Scotland*. Edinburgh: John Donald, 1998.

Mitchell, Martin J., ed. *New Perspectives on the Irish in Scotland*. Edinburgh: John Donald, 2008.

Moffitt, Miriam. *The Society for Irish Church Missions to the Roman Catholics, 1849–1950*. Manchester: Manchester University Press, 2010.

Moir, John S. "The Problem of a Double Minority: Some Reflections on the Development of the English-Speaking Catholic Church in Canada in the Nineteenth Century." *Histoire sociale-Social History* 7 (1971): 53–67.

Molloy, Kevin. "Cheap Reading for the People: Jeremiah Moore and the Development of the New South Wales Book Trade, 1840–1883." *Script and Print: Bulletin of the Bibliographical Society of Australia and New Zealand* 34, 4 (2010): 216–39.

– "The Commodification of Texts for the Irish Colonial Reader: A Survey of Market Practice, 1840–1900." *Australasian Journal of Irish Studies* 9 (2009): 73–94.

– "Literature in the Irish Diaspora: The New Zealand Case, 1873–1918." *Journal of New Zealand Studies* 2/3 (2004): 87–128.

Moloney, Deirdre. *American Catholic Lay Groups and Transatlantic Social Reform in the Progressive Era*. Chapel Hill: University of North Carolina Press, 2002.

Molony, John N. *The Roman Mould of the Australian Catholic Church*. Melbourne: Melbourne University Press, 1969.

Moody, T.W., R.B. McDowell, and C.J. Woods, eds. *The Writings of Wolfe Tone, 1763–98*, 3 vols. Oxford: Oxford University Press, 1998–2001.

Moore, Brigid. "Sectarianism in NSW: The Ne Temere Legislation 1924–1925." *Journal of the Australian Catholic Historical Society* 9 (1987): 3–15.

Moran, Gerard. "Faith, Famine and Fenianism: Paul Cullen and the Irish Emigrant World." In *Cardinal Paul Cullen and His World*, ed. D. Keogh and A. McDonnell. Dublin: Four Courts Press, 2011.

– *Sending Out Ireland's Poor: Assisted Emigration to North America in the Nineteenth Century*. Dublin: Four Courts Press, 2004.

– "'Shovelling out the Poor': Assisted Emigration from Ireland from the Great Famine to the Fall of Parnell." In *To and From Ireland: Planned Migration Schemes, c. 1600–2000*, ed. P.J. Duffy, 137–54. Dublin: Geography Publications, 2004.

Moran, Herbert M. *Viewless Winds: Being the Recollections and Digressions of an Australian Surgeon*. London: Peter Davies, 1939.

Moran, Patrick Francis, ed., *The Pastoral Letters and Other Writings of Cardinal Cullen, Archbishop of Dublin*, 3 vols. Dublin: Browne & Nolan, 1882.

– *The History of the Catholic Church in Australasia*. Sydney: Oceanic Publishing, 1895.

Morawska, Ewa, "In Defense of the Assimilation Model," *Journal of American Ethnic History,* 13 no. 2 (1994): 76–86.

Morgan, Patrick. *Melbourne before Mannix: Catholics in Public Life, 1880–1920*. Melbourne: Conor Publishing, 2012.

Morrison, Elizabeth. "Serial Fiction in Australian Colonial Newspapers." In *Literature in the Marketplace: Nineteenth-Century British Publishing and Reading Practices*, ed. John O. Jordan and Robert L. Patten, 306–24. Cambridge: Cambridge University Press, 1995.

Morton, Desmond. *A Military History of Canada*, 5th ed. Toronto: McClelland and Stewart, 2007.

Morton, Graeme, and R.J. Morris. "Civil Society, Governance and Nation, 1832–1914." In *The New Penguin History of Scotland*, ed. R.A. Houston and W.W.J. Knox, 355–416. London: Penguin, 2002.

Morton, Graeme, and David A. Wilson. *Irish and Scottish Encounters with Indigenous Peoples*. Montreal and Kingston: McGill-Queen's University Press, 2013.

Mulligan, Adrian N. "A Forgotten 'Greater Ireland': The Transatlantic Development of Irish Nationalism." *Scottish Geographical Journal* 118, 3 (2002): 219–34.

Mullins, J.D. *Our Beginnings: Being a Short Sketch of the History of the Colonial and Continental Church Society*. London: Colonial and Continental Church Society, 1923.

Murphy, Daniel. *A History of Irish Emigrant Education and Missionary Education*. Dublin: Four Courts Press, 2000.

Murphy, James. *The Religious Problem in English Education: The Crucial Experiment*. Liverpool: Liverpool University Press, 1959.

Murphy, Peter. "Sacred Icon: Jorn Utzon's Sydney Opera House." In *Sacred Australia*, ed. Makarand Paranjape, 286–305. Melbourne: Clouds of Magellan, 2009.

Murphy, Terrence. "Trusteeism in Atlantic Canada: The Struggle for Leadership among the Irish Catholics of Halifax, St John's, and Saint John, 1780–1850." in *Creed and Culture: The Place of English-Speaking Catholics in Canadian Society, 1750–1930*, ed. Terrence Murphy and Gerald Stortz, 126–51. Montreal and Kingston: McGill-Queen's University Press, 1993.

Naylor, T.B. "A Tale of Norfolk Island." In William and Robert Chambers, *Chambers's Miscellany of Useful and Entertaining Tracts*, vol. 1. Edinburgh: Chambers, 1844.

Neatby, Hilda. *The Quebec Act: Protest and Policy*. Scarborough: Prentice-Hall, 1972.

Nicholls, James. *The Politics of Alcohol: A History of the Drink Question in England*. Manchester: Manchester University Press, 2009.

Nicholson, Gerald W.L. *The Fighting Newfoundlander: A History of the Royal Newfoundland Regiment*. St John's: Government of Newfoundland, 1964.

Nile, Richard, and David Walker. "The Paternoster Row Machine and the Australian Book Trade, 1890–1945." In *A History of the Book in Australia, 1891–1945*, ed. Martyn Lyons and John Arnold, 3–18. St Lucia: University of Queensland Press, 2001.

Noel, Jan. *Canada Dry: Temperance Crusades before Confederation*. Toronto: University of Toronto Press, 1995.

Nolan, Janet. *Ourselves Alone: Women's Emigration from Ireland, 1885–1920*. Lexington: University Press of Kentucky, 1989.

Northey, Helen. *Living the Truth*. Adelaide: Holy Cross Congregation of the Dominican Sisters, 1999.

Noyce, Diana Christine. "Coffee Palaces in Australia: A Pub with No Beer." *M/C Journal* 15, 2 (2012). http://journal.media-culture.org.au/index.php/mcjournal/article/view/464 (viewed 4 March 2015).

Nugent, Paul. "The Temperance Movement and Wine Farmers at the Cape: Collective Action, Racial Discourse, and Legislative Reform, 1890–1965." *Journal of African History* 52 (2011): 341–63.

Nunn, Paul. "Aristocratic Estates and Employment in South Yorkshire, 1700–1800." In *Essays in the Economic and Social History of South Yorkshire*, ed. Sidney Pollard and Colin Holmes, 28–45. Barnsley: South Yorkshire County Council, 1976.

Nybaaken, Elizabeth I. "New Light on the Old Side: Irish Influences on Colonial Presbyterianism." *Journal of American History* 68, 4 (1982): 813–32.

Ó Gráda, Cormac. *Jewish Ireland in the Age of Joyce: A Socioeconomic History*. Princeton: Princeton University Press, 2006.

Ó Gráda, Cormac, and Joel Mokyr. "Poor and Getting Poorer? Living Standards in Ireland before the Famine." In *Ireland's Great Famine: Interdisciplinary Perspectives*, ed. Cormac Ó Gráda, 209–35. Dublin: University College Dublin Press, 2006.

Ó hAnnracháin, Tadhg. "The Consolidation of Irish Catholicism within a Hostile Imperial Framework: A Comparative Study of Early Modern Ireland and Hungary." In *Empires of Religion*, ed. Hilary M. Carey, 25–42. London: Palgrave Macmillan, 2008.

O'Brien, John. *The Men of '38 and Other Pioneer Priests*. Kilmore: Lowden, 1975.

O'Farrell, Patrick. "Australia (11) Development." In *A History of Irish Catholicism*, ed. Patrick Corish, 15–75. Dublin: Gill and MacMillan, 1971.

– "Bible Reading and Related Mental Furniture." *Australian Cultural History* 11 (1992): 16–27.

– *The Irish in Australia*. Kensington: University of New South Wales Press, 1987.

– *The Irish in Australia*, 3rd ed. Sydney: University of New South Wales Press, 2000.
– "In Search of the Hidden Ireland." *Journal of Religious History* 12, 3 (1983): 322–30.
O'Farrell, Patrick, and Brian Trainor. *Letters from Irish-Australia, 1825–1929*. Sydney: University of New South Wales Press, 1984.
O'Gallagher, Marianna. *Grosse Ile: Gateway to Canada, 1832–1937*. Ste-Foy, QC: Carraig Books, 1984.
O'Haire, James. *Recollections of Twelve Years' Residence (as a Missionary Priest) Viz: From July 1863 to June 1875 in the Western District of the Cape of Good Hope, South Africa, Selected Chiefly from his Diary*. Dublin: Cooke, Keating & Co., 1876.
O'Kelly, J.J. *Ireland's Spiritual Empire: Saint Patrick as a World Figure*. Dublin: M.H. Gill, 1952.
O'Leary, Paul. *Immigration and Integration: The Irish in Wales, 1798–1922*. Cardiff: University of Wales Press, 2000.
O'Leary, Paul, ed. *Irish Migrants in Modern Wales*. Liverpool: Liverpool University Press, 2004.
O'Rell, Max. *John Bull & Co: The Great Colonial Branches of the Firm, Canada, Australia, New Zealand and South Africa*. New York: C. Webster, 1894.
Okkenhaug, Inger Marie. "Women in Christian Mission: Protestant Encounters from the 19th and 20th Century." In *World Christianity*, ed. Anthony O'Mahony and Michael Kirwan, 120–39. London: Melisende, 2004.
Oliver, Peter. "The Resolution of the Ontario Bilingual Schools Crisis, 1919–1929." In T*he History of Ontario: Selected Readings*, ed. Michael J. Piva, 185–213. Toronto: Copp Clark Pitman Ltd, 1988.
Olssen, Erik. *An Accidental Utopia?: Social Mobility and the Foundations of an Egalitarian Society, 1880–1940*. Dunedin: University of Otago Press, 2011.
– *Building the New World: Work, Politics and Society in Caversham, 1880s-1920s*. Auckland: Auckland University Press, 1995.
– "Towards a Reassessment of W.F. Massey: One of New Zealand's Greatest Prime Ministers (Arguably)." In *A Great New Zealand Prime Minister?: Reappraising William Ferguson Massey*, ed. James Watson and Lachy Paterson, 15–30. Dunedin: Otago University Press, 2011.
Osborne, Alick. *Immigration: Despatches on the subject of immigration into New South Wales*. Sydney: Legislative Council, 1837.
– *Notes on the present state and prospects of society in New South Wales: with an historical, statistical, and topographical account of Manilla and Singapore*. London: J. Cross, 1833.

Page, Dorothy. "Introduction." In *The Suffragists: Women Who Worked for the Vote – Essays from the Dictionary of New Zealand Biography*, 1–23. Wellington: Bridget Williams Books, 1993.

Pálsson, Hermann, and Paul Edwards, eds. *The Book of Settlements: Landnámabók*. Winnipeg: University of Manitoba Press, 1972.

Parsons, Cóilín. "Literary Study and Elementary Education in the Nineteenth Century." In *Ireland and India: Colonies, Culture and Empire*, ed. Tadgh Foley and Maureen O'Connor, 26–36. Dublin: Irish Academic Press, 2006.

Patterson, Brad, (ed.), *Ulster-New Zealand Migration and Cultural Transfers* Dublin: Four Courts 2006.

Paul, Sara. *In the Land of My Dreams*. Belfast: Foreign Mission Office, 1954.

Penney, Mary Paula. "A Study of the Contributions of Three Religious Congregations to the Growth of Education in the Province of Newfoundland." PhD diss., Boston College, 1980.

Perin, Roberto. *Rome in Canada: The Vatican and Canadian Affairs in the Late Victorian Age*. Toronto: University of Toronto Press, 1990.

Peters, Janelle. "Lot's Wife in the Novels of Mary Anne Sadlier." *Postscripts* 5, 2 (2009): 185–204.

Pike, Douglas. *Paradise of Dissent*, 2nd ed. Melbourne: Melbourne University Press, 1967.

Polding, J.B. *The Letters of John Bede Polding* OSB *1819–1843*. Vol. 1. New South Wales: Sisters of the Good Samaritan, 1994.

Pollard, Mary. *A Dictionary of Members of the Dublin Book Trade, 1550–1800*. London: Bibliographical Society, 2000.

Porter, Andrew. *Religion Versus Empire?: British Protestant Missionaries and Overseas Expansion, 1700–1914*. Manchester: Manchester University Press, 2004.

Power, Michael, et al., *Gather Up the Fragments: A History of the Diocese of London*. London: Diocese of London 2008.

Poynter, John. *Doubts and Certainties: A Life of Alexander Leeper*. Melbourne: Melbourne University Press, 1997.

Prang, Margaret. "Clerics, Politicians, and the Bilingual Schools Issue in Ontario, 1910–1917." *Canadian Historical Review* 41 (1960): 281–307.

Prentis, Malcolm D. "The Presbyterian Ministry in Australia, 1822–1900: Recruitment and Composition." *Journal of Religious History* 13, 1 (1984): 46–65.

Prochaska, Frank. *Women and Philanthropy in Nineteenth-Century England*. Oxford: Oxford University Press, 1980.

Proudfoot, Lindsay, and Dianne Hall. "Points of Departure: Remittance Emigration from South-West Ulster to New South Wales in the Later

Nineteenth Century." *International Review of Social History* 50, 2 (2005): 341–78.

Purdue, Olwen. "Poverty and Power: The Irish Poor Laws in a North Antrim Town, 1861–1921." *Irish Historical Studies* 37, 148 (2011): 567–83.

Quigley, Hugh. *The Irish Race in California and on the Pacific Coast: With an Introductory Historical Dissertation on the Principal Races of Mankind, and a Vocabulary of Ancient and Modern Irish Family Names.* San Francisco: A. Roman & Co., 1878.

Rakotonirina, Rachel A. "Re-reading Missionary Publications." In *Missions and Missionaries: Studies in Church History*, ed. Pieter N. Holtrop and Hugh McLeod, 157–69. Martlesham: Boydell Press, 2000.

Rawson, Lynn. *Illawarra Grays.* Melbourne: Lynn Rawson, 1990.

Rea, J.E. *Bishop Alexander Macdonell and the Politics of Upper Canada.* Toronto: Ontario Historical Society, 1974.

Reid, J.S. *History of the Presbyterian Church in Ireland*, ed. William Dool Killen, 3 vols. Belfast: William Mullan, 1867.

Reid, Richard E. *Farewell My Children: Irish Assisted Emigration to Australia, 1848–1870.* Spit Junction, NSW: Anchor Books, 2011.

Richards, Eric. "An Australian Map of British and Irish Literacy in 1841." *Population Studies* 53 (1999): 345–59.

– "The First Mass Migration from Ireland to Australia." *Australian Journal of Irish Studies* 2 (2002): 166–87.

– "Highland Emigration in the Age of Malthus: Scourie, 1841–55," *Northern Scotland* 2:1 (2011): 60–82.

– "The Highland Scots of South Australia." *Journal of the Historical Society of South Australia* 4 (1978): 33–64.

– "Human Traffic." In *The Victorian World*, ed. Martin Hewitt, 141–59. London: Routledge, 2012.

– "The Importance of Being Irish in Colonial South Australia." In *The Irish Emigrant Experience in Australia*, ed. J. O'Brien and P. Travers, 62–103. Dublin: Poolbeg Press, 1991.

– "Irish Life and Progress in Colonial South Australia," *Irish Historical Studies* 27, No. 107 (May 1991).

– "Leaving the Highlands: Colonial Destinations in Canada and Australia." In *Myth, Migration, and the Making of Memory: Scotia and Nova Scotia, c. 1700–1990*, ed. Marjory Harper and Michael E. Vance, 105–26. Edinburgh: John Donald, 1999.

Ridden, Jennifer. "'Making Good Citizens': National Identity, Religion, and Liberalism among the Irish Elite, c. 1800–1850." PhD diss., King's College, London, 1998.

Ridgway, Christopher, ed. *The Morpeth Roll: Ireland Identified, 1841*. Dublin: Four Courts Press, 2013.

Riehl, Christian, et al., *A History of the Diocese of Hamilton* (Strasbourg: Editions du Signe 2007).

Roberts, M.J.D. "Private Patronage and the Church of England, 1800–1900." *Journal of Ecclesiastical History* 32, 2 (1981): 191–223.

Roediger, David. *The Wages of Whiteness: Race and the Making of the American Working Class*. New York: Verso, 1991.

Rogers, Thomas. *Correspondence relating to the Dismissal of the Rev. T. Rogers from his Chaplaincy at Norfolk Island*. Launceston, 1849.

– *Review of Dr Hampton's First Report on Norfolk Island*. Hobart: Henry Dowling, 1849.

Ronayne, Jarlath. *First Fleet to Federation: Irish Supremacy in Colonial Australia*. Dublin: Trinity College Dublin Press, 2002.

– *The Irish in Australia: Rogues and Reformers – First Fleet to Federation*. Camberwell, Victoria: Viking/Penguin, 2002.

Ross, Robert. *Status and Respectability in the Cape Colony, 1750–1870: A Tragedy of Manners*. Cambridge: Cambridge University Press, 1999.

Rotberg, Robert I. *The Founder: Cecil Rhodes and the Pursuit of Power*. New York: Oxford University Press, 1988.

Rowbotham, Sheila. "Ministering Angels, Not Ministers: Women's Involvement in the Foreign Missionary Movement, c. 1860–1910." In *Women, Religion and Feminism in Britain, 1750–1900*, ed. Sue Morgan, 179–96. New York: Palgrave Macmillan, 2002.

Rukavina, Alison. "'This Is a Wonderfully Comprehensive Business': The Development of the British-Australian and International Book Trades, 1870–1887." *Script and Print* 32, 2 (2008): 69–79.

Rumasack, Barbara. "Cultural Missionaries, Maternal Imperialists, Feminist Allies: British Women Activists in India, 1865–1945." In *Western Women and Imperialism: Complicity and Resistance*, ed. N. Chauduri and M. Strobel, 119–36. Bloomington: Indiana University Press, 1992.

Russell, Penelope Ann. *A Wish of Distinction: Colonial Gentility and Femininity*. Melbourne: Melbourne University Press, 1994.

Ryan, J. Tighe. *The Attitude of the Catholic Church: A Special Interview with his Eminence Cardinal Moran*. Sydney: George Robertson & Co., 1894.

Sanders, James. *The Education of an Urban Minority: Catholics in Chicago, 1833–1965*. New York: Oxford University Press, 1977.

Saurin, Susanna Mary. *The Trial of Saurin v. Star and Another, in the Court of Queen's Bench*. London: Diprose and Bateman, 1869.

Sawer, Geoffrey. *Australian Federal Politics and Law, 190–1929*. Clayton: Melbourne University Press, 1956.

Schlenther, Boyd Stanley. *The Life and Writings of Francis Makemie, Father of American Presbyterianism, c. 1658–1708*. Lewiston, NY: Edwin Mellen Press, 1999.

Scobie, Charles H.H., and John Webster Grant, eds. *The Contribution of Methodism to Atlantic Canada*. Montreal and Kingston: McGill-Queen's University Press, 1992.

Scobie, Charles H.H., and G.A. Rawlyk, eds. *The Contribution of Presbyterianism to the Maritime Provinces of Canada*. Montreal and Kingston: McGill-Queen's University Press, 1997.

Scott, John. *Social Network Analysis: A Handbook*. London: Sage, 2000.

Shanabruch, Charles. *Chicago's Catholics: The Evolution of an American Identity*. Notre Dame, IN: University of Notre Dame Press, 1981.

Shanahan, Suzanne. "Scripted Debates: Twentieth-Century Immigration and Citizenship Policy in Great Britain, Ireland, and the United States." In *Extending Citizenship, Reconfiguring States*, ed. Michael P. Hanagan and Charles Tilly, 67–96. Lanham, MD: Rowman and Littlefield, 1999.

Shannon, William. *The American Irish*. New York: Collier Books, 1974.

Sharpe, Eric J. "The Legacy of Amy Carmichael." *International Bulletin of Missionary Research* 20, 3 (1996): 121–4.

Shaw, G.P. *Patriarch and Patriot: William Grant Broughton, 1788–1853: Colonial Statesman and Ecclesiastic*. Melbourne: Melbourne University Press, 1978.

Shaw, Gerald. *Some Beginnings: The* Cape Times, *1876–1910*. Cape Town: Oxford University Press, 1975.

Sherling, Rankin. *The Invisible Irish: Finding Protestants in the Nineteenth-Century Migrations to America*. Montreal and Kingston: McGill-Queen's University Press, 2015.

Shirwadkar, Swati. *Women and Socio-Cultural Changes*. New Delhi: Gyan Publishing House, 1999.

Shook, Laurence. "Marian Pilgrimages in the Archdiocese of Toronto." *Canadian Catholic Historical Association Report* 20 (1953): 56–9.

Singh, Maina Chawla. *Gender, Religion and Power in Heathen Lands: North American Women in South Asia, 1860s–1940s*. New York: Garland, 2000.

Skerrett, Ellen. "The Irish of Chicago's Hull House Neighbourhood." In *New Perspectives on the Irish Diaspora*, ed. Charles Fanning, 189–222. Carbondale: Southern Illinois University Press, 2000.

Skerrett, Ellen, Edward R. Kantowicz, and Steven M. Avella, eds. *Catholicism, Chicago Style*. Chicago: Loyola University Press, 1993.

Smith, Ken. *Alfred Aylward: The Tireless Agitator*. Johannesburg: A.D. Donker, 1983.

Smyth, Elizabeth M., ed. *Changing Habits: Women's Religious Orders in Canada*. Toronto: Novalis, 2007.

Stack, John F. *International Conflict in an American City*. Westport, CT: Greenwood Press, 1979.

Stenhouse, John. "Christianity, Gender and the Working Class in Southern Dunedin, 1880–1940." *Journal of Religious History* 30, 1 (2006): 18–44.

– "Darwinism in New Zealand, 1859–1900." In *Disseminating Darwinism: The Role of Place, Race, Religion and Gender*, ed. Ronald L. Numbers and John Stenhouse, 61–90. New York: Cambridge University Press, 1999.

– "God, the Devil and Gender." In *Sites of Gender: Women, Men and Modernity in Southern Dunedin, 1890–1939*, ed. Barbara Brookes, Annabel Cooper, and Robin Law, 313–47. Auckland: Auckland University Press, 2003.

Sternbeck, Michael. *The Catholic Church in Singleton: An Historical Look at Its People and Progress*. Broadmeadow: Newey and Beath Printers, 1981.

Stewart, A.T.Q. *A Deeper Silence: The Hidden Origins of the United Irishmen*. London: Faber and Faber, 1993.

Strickland, E. 1862. *The Australian Pastor: A Record of the Remarkable Changes in Mind and Outward State of Henry Elliott*. London: Wertheim, Macintosh and Hunt.

Strong, Rowan. *Anglicanism and the British Empire, c. 1700–1850*. Oxford: Oxford University Press, 2007.

– "Church and State in Western Australia: Implementing New Imperial Paradigms in the Swan River Colony, 1827–1857." *Journal of Ecclesiastical History* 61, 3 (2010): 517–40.

Sullivan, A.M. *New Ireland: Political Sketches and Personal Reminiscences of Thirty Years of Irish Public Life*. Glasgow: Cameron and Ferguson, n.d.

Suttor, T.L. "Ullathorne, William Bernard (1806–1889)." In *Australian Dictionary of Biography*. Vol. 2. Melbourne: Melbourne University Press, 1967.

Sweetman, Rory. "'Beery Bill the Orangeman': Another Look at William Ferguson Massey." In *A Great New Zealand Prime Minister?: Reappraising William Ferguson Massey*, ed. James Watson and Lachy Paterson, 77–86. Dunedin: Otago University Press, 2011.

– *Bishop in the Dock: The Sedition Trial of James Liston*. Auckland: Auckland University Press, 1997.

Swift, Roger, and Sheridan Gilley, eds. *The Irish in Britain, 1815–1939*. London: Rowan and Littlefield, 1989.

– *Irish Identities in Victorian Britain*. Previously published as a special issue of *Immigrants and Minorities*, 27, 2–3 (2009). Abingdon: Routledge, 2011.
– *The Irish in Victorian Britain: The Local Dimension*. Dublin: Four Courts Press, 1999.
– *The Irish in the Victorian City*. London: Croom Helm, 1985.

Taggart, Norman W. *The Irish in World Methodism, 1760–1900*. London: Epworth Press, 1986.

Taves, Anne. *The Household of Faith: Roman Catholic Devotions in Mid-Nineteenth Century America*. Notre Dame, IN: University of Notre Dame Press, 1986.

Tearle, Sheila. "I Remember Sister Ligouri." *Footprints* 2, 12 (1977): 9–10.

Tennent, Gilbert. "The Danger of an Unconverted Ministry: Considered in a Sermon on Mark IV,34." Philadelphia, 1741 (2nd ed.); reprinted Boston, 1742.

Thernstrom, Stephen. *Poverty and Progress: Social Mobility in a Nineteenth-Century City*. Cambridge: Harvard University Press, 1964.

Thomlinson, Kirsten. "We the Undersigned: An Analysis of Signatories to the 1893 Suffrage Petition from Southern Dunedin." MA thesis, University of Otago, 2001.

Thompson, Jack. *Into All the World: A History of 150 Years of the Overseas Work of the Presbyterian Church in Ireland*. Belfast: Overseas Board of the Presbyterian Church, 1990.

Thompson, John. "The Government of the Church of Christ: The Matter of Difference between the Synod of Philadelphia and the Protesting Brethren Justly and Fairly Stated." Philadelphia, PA: A. Bradford, 1741.

Thompson, Scott and Genosko, Gary, *Punched Drunk: Alcohol, Surveillance, and the LCBO, 1927–1975*. Halifax: Fernwood, 2009.

Thorne, Susan. "Religion and Empire at Home." In *Missions and Empire*, ed. Norman Etherington, 143–297. Oxford: Oxford University Press, 2005.

Tosh, John. *The Pursuit of History: Aims, Methods and New Directions of Modern History*, 3rd ed. New York: Longman, 2000.

Tosh, John, and Michael Roper, eds. *Manful Assertions: Masculinities in Britain Since 1800*. London: Routledge, 1991.

Townend, Paul. *Father Mathew, Temperance and Irish Identity*. Dublin: Irish Academic Press, 2002.

Townsend, Norma. "Reconstructed Lives: The Swing Transportees in New South Wales." *Australian Studies* 16, 2 (2001): 19–40.

Trinterud, Leonard J. *The Forming of an American Tradition: A Re-Examination of Colonial Presbyterianism*. Philadelphia: Westminster Press, 1949.

Turner, Eric. "Not Narrow Minded Bigots – Proceedings of the Loyal Orange Institution of New South Wales, 1845–1895." PhD diss., University of New England, New South Wales, 2002.

Turner, Kenneth W. "Henry Smith Fish and the Opposition to the Female Franchise in Dunedin, 1890–93." BA Honours, University of Otago, 1985.

Tyrell, Ian. *Woman's World, Woman's Empire: The Woman's Christian Temperance Union in International Perspective, 1880–1930*. Chapel Hill: University of North Carolina Press, 1991.

Urquhart, Diane. *Women in Ulster Politics, 1890–1940*. Dublin: Irish Academic Press, 2000.

Van der Veer, Peter. *Imperial Encounters: Religion and Modernity in India and Britain*. Princeton, NJ: Princeton University Press, 2001.

– "The Moral State: Religion, Nation, and Empire in Victorian Britain and British India." In *Religion and Nationalism in Europe and Asia*, ed. P. Van der Veer, 15–44. Princeton: Princeton University Press, 1999.

Van der Veer, Peter, and Hartmut Lehmann. *Nation and Religion: Perspectives on Europe and Asia*. Princeton, NJ: Princeton University Press, 1999.

Van Mierlo, Wim. "The Greater Ireland beyond the Sea: Joyce, Exile and Irish Emigration." In *Joyce, Ireland and Britain*, ed. Len Platt and Andrew Gibson, 178–97. Gainesville: University Press of Florida, 2007.

Van Onselen, Charles. *Masked Raiders: Irish Banditry in Southern Africa, 1880–1899*. Cape Town: Zebra Press, 2010.

Vaughan, Geraldine. *The "Local" Irish in the West of Scotland*. Basingstoke: Palgrave Pivot, 2013.

Vaughan, W.E., and A.J. Fitzpatrick, eds. *Irish Historical Statistics: Population 1821–1971*. Dublin: Royal Irish Academy, 1978.

Waddell, Rutherford. *My Pathway to Christ: A Confession of Faith*. Dunedin: New Zealand Bible, Tract and Book Society, 1920.

Walker, Eric A. *A History of South Africa*. London: Longmans, Green and Co. 1935 [1928]).

– *The South African College and the University of Cape Town*. Cape Town: Cape Times, 1929.

Walker, Franklin. *Catholic Education and Politics in Upper Canada*. Toronto: Catholic Educational Foundation of Ontario, 1955.

Walker, Graham. *A History of the Ulster Unionist Party: Protest, Pragmatism and Pessimism*. Manchester: Manchester University Press, 2004.

Walker, R.B. *The Newspaper Press in New South Wales, 1803–1920*. Sydney: Sydney University Press, 1976.

Wall, Maureen. *The Rise of a Catholic Middle-Class in Eighteenth Century Ireland*. Chicago: University of Chicago Press 1971.

Waller, P. J. *Democracy and Sectarianism: A Political and Social History of Liverpool, 1868–1939*. Liverpool: Liverpool University Press, 1981.

Ward, Harriet. *Five Years in Kaffirland; With Sketches of the Late War in that Country, to the Conclusion of the Peace. Written on the Spot*, 2nd ed., 2 vols. London: Henry Colburn, 1848.

Wasserman, Stanley. *Social Network Analysis: Methods and Applications*. Cambridge: Cambridge University Press, 1997.

Watson, Don. *Caledonia Australis*. Sydney: Collins, 1984.

Watson, James, and Lachy Paterson. "Introduction." In *A Great New Zealand Prime Minister?: Reappraising William Ferguson Massey*, ed. James Watson and Lachy Paterson, 7–14. Dunedin: Otago University Press, 2011.

Watson, Nick J., Stuart Weir, and Stephen Friend. "The Development of Muscular Christianity in Victorian Britain and Beyond." *Journal of Religion and Society* 7 (2005): 1–21.

Webster, Richard. *A History of the Presbyterian Church in America, From its Origin Until the Year 1760*. Philadelphia: Joseph M. Wilson, 1857.

West, Janet. "The Role of the Woman Missionary, 1880–1914." *Lucas* 21 and 22 (1996): 31–60.

Westerkamp, Marilyn J. *Triumph of the Laity: Scots-Irish Piety and the Great Awakening, 1625–1760*. Oxford: Oxford University Press, 1988.

Wetherell, Charles. "Historical Social Network Analysis." *International Review of Social History* 43 (1998): 125–44.

Whelan, Irene. *The Bible War in Ireland: The "Second Reformation" and the Polarisation of Protestant-Catholic Relations, 1800–1840*. Dublin: Lilliput Press, 2005.

Whelan, Kathleen, ed. *A New Imperial History: Culture, Identity and Modernity in Britain and the Empire, 1660–1840*. Cambridge: Cambridge University Press, 2004.

White, Jack. *Minority Report: The Protestant Community in the Irish Republic*. Dublin: Gill and Macmillan, 1975.

Wilkinson, Ian R., Brian J. Caldwell, R.J.W. Selleck, Jessica Harris, and Pam Dettman. *A History of State Aid to Non-Government Schools in Australia*. Canberra: Department of Education, Science and Training, 2007.

Wilmot, Alexander. *The Life and Times of the Right Rev. James David Ricards, Bishop of Retimo, in partibus infidelium, and Vicar-Apostolic of the Eastern Districts of the Cape Colony*. Cape Town: The Salesian Institute 1908.

Wilson, Ann. "The Gothic Revival in Ireland: St Colman's Cathedral, Cobh, 1868–1916." *Antiphon* 11 (2007): 14–42.

Wilson, David A. *The Irish in Canada*. Ottawa: Canadian Historical Association, Canada's Ethnic Groups, Booklet 12, 1989.

– *Thomas D'Arcy McGee*. Vol. 1: *Passion, Reason, and Politics, 1825–1857*. Montreal and Kingston: McGill-Queen's University Press, 2008.

– *Thomas D'Arcy McGee*. Vol. 2: *The Extreme Moderate, 1857–1868*. Montreal and Kingston: McGill-Queen's University Press, 2011.

Wirgman, A., and Cuthbert Edward Mayo. *The Collegiate Church and Parish of S. Mary Port Elizabeth, A Record of Parochial History*. London: Longmans, Green & Co., 1935.

Wittke, Carl. *The Irish in America*. New York: Russell and Russell, 1970.

Wolfe Tone, Theobald. *An Argument on behalf of the Catholics of Ireland*. Dublin: P. Byrne, 1791. Reproduced in *The Writings of Wolfe Tone, 1763–98*, ed. T.W. Moody, R.B. McDowell, and C.J. Woods, 3 vols. Oxford: Oxford University Press, 1998–2001.

Wolffe, John. "Anti-Catholicism and the British Empire, 1815–1914." In *Empires of Religion*, ed. Hilary M. Carey, 43–63. London: Palgrave Macmillan, 2008.

Woolf, Virginia. *A Room of One's Own*. London: Hogarth Press, 1929.

Yates, Nigel. *The Religious Condition of Ireland, 1770–1850*. Oxford: Oxford University Press, 2006.

Young Ian C. "Armstrong Story." *Khanterintee* 32 (1998): 3–7.

Zucchi, John. *The View From Rome: Archbishop Stagni's 1915 Reports on the Ontario Bilingual Schools Question*. Montreal and Kingston: McGill-Queen's University Press, 2002.

Contributors

COLIN BARR is senior lecturer in history at the University of Aberdeen. His books include *Nation-Nazione: Irish Nationalism and the Italian Risorgimento* (edited with Michele Finelli and Anne O'Connor 2014); *The European Culture Wars in Ireland: The Callan Schools Affair, 1868-1881* (2010); and *Paul Cullen, John Henry Newman, and the Catholic University of Ireland, 1845–65* (2003). He is presently writing a history of Irish Catholicism in the English-speaking world. Dr Barr is also the co-editor of *The Correspondence of Paul Cullen* (Irish Manuscripts Commission), a project that received a major grant from the Irish Research Council for the Humanities and Social Sciences. His current research project is a history of the Irish Catholic Church in the British Empire between 1830 and 1922.

HILARY M. CAREY is professor of imperial and religious history and head of the School of Humanities at the University of Bristol. Her books include *God's Empire* (2011); *Empires of Religion* (ed. 2008); *Church and State in Old and New Worlds* (ed. with John Gascoigne, 2011); and *Methodism in Australia* (ed. with Glen O'Brien, 2015). She is currently writing a history of religion and the campaign to end convict transportation in the British World.

LEIGH-ANN COFFEY received her doctorate from the Department of History, Queen's University, Ontario, in 2014. Her current research focuses on the experiences of protestants and loyalists in the Irish Free State. She is the author of *The Planters of Luggacurran, Co. Laois: A Protestant Community, 1879–1927* (2006).

RICHARD VINCENT COMERFORD is professor emeritus of modern history at the National University of Ireland, Maynooth. His publications include *Ireland* (2003); *The Fenians in Context: Irish Politics and Society, 1848–82* (1985 [2nd ed., 1998]); and *C.J. Kickham: a Study in Irish Nationalism and Literature* (1979).

MIMI COWAN is a PhD candidate in the History Department at Boston College, where she has recently submitted her thesis entitled: "Immigrants, Nativists, and the Making of Nineteenth-Century Chicago." Her research and publications examine Irish and German immigrant interactions and their contributions to the creation of modern Chicago.

BARRY CROSBIE is assistant professor of history at the Hong Kong Institute of Education. His research focuses on the cultural and political interconnections between nineteenth- and twentieth-century Ireland and the British World. He has published work on various aspects of Ireland's historical relationship with the British Empire for the *Historical Journal*, *Historical Studies*, and *History Compass*. He is the author of *Irish Imperial Networks: Migration, Social Communication and Exchange in Nineteenth-Century India* (Cambridge University Press, 2012) and co-editor of *The Cultural Construction of the British World* (Manchester University Press, 2015).

MICHAEL GLADWIN is lecturer in history at St Mark's National Theological Centre, Charles Sturt University, Canberra. His research focuses on the religious, cultural, and military history of Australia in the context of the British World. He is the author of *Captains of the Soul: A History of Australian Army Chaplains* (2013) and *Anglican Clergy in Australia, 1788–1850: Building a British World* (2015).

DIANNE HALL is lecturer in history at Victoria University, Melbourne. She is author of *Women and the Church in Medieval Ireland c. 1140–1540* (2nd ed. 2008); and co-author with Lindsay Proudfoot of *Imperial Spaces: Placing the Irish and Scots in colonial Australia* (2011). She is currently working on Irishness in nineteenth-century Australia.

MYRTLE HILL is a research associate in history and women's studies at Queen's University Belfast. She is the author of *The Time of the End: Millenarian Beliefs in Ulster* (2001); and *Women in Ireland: A Century of Change* (2003). Recently, she has been working on female Protestant missionaries from the North of Ireland in the late nineteenth century, on the northern Irish suffrage campaign, and on the "second wave" of Irish feminism.

JEFF KILDEA is an adjunct professor in Irish Studies at the University of New South Wales. In 2014 he held the Keith Cameron Chair of Australian History at University College Dublin. He is the author of *Tearing the Fabric: Sectarianism in Australia 1910–1925* (2002); *Anzacs and Ireland* (2007); and *Wartime Australians: Billy Hughes* (2008). He is currently researching a biography of Hugh Mahon, the Irish-Australian politician expelled from the Australian Parliament in 1920 for his criticism of British rule in Ireland.

CAROLYN LAMBERT received her doctorate from Memorial University of Newfoundland in 2010. Her thesis is entitled "Far from the Homes of Their Fathers: Irish Catholics in St John's, Newfoundland, 1840–86." Her research and publications examine Irish Catholic identity and migration.

MARK G. MCGOWAN is professor of history at the University of Toronto. He is the author of the award-winning books *Catholics at the Gathering Place: Historical Essays on the Archdiocese of Toronto* (ed. 1992 with Brian Clarke); *The Waning of the Green: Catholics, the Irish and Identity in Toronto, 1887–1922* (1999); and *Michael Power: The Struggle to Build the Catholic Church on the Canadian Frontier* (2005). He has written *Creating Canadian Historical Memory: The Case of the Famine Migration* (for the CHA Canadian Ethnic Groups Series, 2006); and *Death or Canada: The Irish Famine Migration to Toronto, 1847*, (2009) which has been made into a docudrama featured on RTE and History Television. He is currently writing a book on Canada's Irish Catholics and the Great War and researching a new book on the engagement of religion and the media in Canada.

MIKE MCLAUGHLIN is a PhD candidate at Carleton University (Ottawa). He is currently working on his dissertation, "From Temperance to Home Rule," which explores the middle-class culture of Irish Catholics in nineteenth-century Canada.

KEVIN MOLLOY is manager manuscripts collection at the State Library of Victoria in Melbourne. He completed his PhD at Trinity College

Dublin on the subject of nineteenth-century Irish historiography and has written and published on international Irish print networks, book history, cultural memory, and the Irish-American novel in Australia. He is currently researching postwar Irish migration to Australia.

ERIC RICHARDS is emeritus professor of history at Flinders University in Adelaide, South Australia, and also Carnegie Trust centenary professor at the University of the Highlands and Islands. He is a specialist in the history of Australian, British, and international migration. He is the author of numerous award-winning studies of British emigration, including *Britannia's Children* (2004); *Debating the Highland Clearances* (2007); and *Destination Australia* (2008). With Margrette Kleinig, he edited *On the Wing: Mobility Before and After Emigration to Australia* (2013).

RANKIN SHERLING has taught history at Queen's University, Ontario, and Atlanta Metropolitan State College. He is currently a tenure-track instructor at the Marion Military Institute, the Military College of Alabama. His first book, *The Invisible Irish: Finding Protestants in the Nineteenth-Century Migrations to America*, is set to be published by McGill-Queen's University Press in the Fall of 2015.

JOHN STENHOUSE is associate professor of history at the University of Otago. He has written prolifically on the history of religion in New Zealand, and his publications include: J. Stenhouse and B. Knowles, eds., *Christianity in the Post-Secular West* (2007); John Stenhouse and Jane Thomson, eds., *Building God's Own Country: Historical Essays on Religions in New Zealand* (Dunedin: University of Otago Press, 2004); and Ronald L. Numbers and John Stenhouse, eds., *Disseminating Darwinism: The Roles of Place, Race, Religion, and Gender* (1999).

Index